U.S. NAVY

A COMPLETE HISTORY

U.S. NAVY

A COMPLETE HISTORY

M. HILL GOODSPEED

NAVAL HISTORICAL FOUNDATION

BEAUX ARTS EDITIONS

NAVAL HISTORICAL FOUNDATION

Page 2: *Hundreds of thousands of young Americans emerged from the Great Depression of the 1930s to serve in the Navy in World War II. (U.S. Naval Institute)*

In 1926, Commodore Dudley Knox wrote in the U.S. Naval Institute *Proceedings* about the "glaring deficiencies" in collecting and preserving the Navy's written records. Knox's article on "Our Vanishing History and Traditions" gave birth to the Naval Historical Foundation in 1926 under the sponsorship of the Secretary of the Navy. From its initial focus on safeguarding the material culture of the Navy, the Foundation has developed into a nonprofit organization dedicated to preserving and promoting the full range of naval history.

Today, in addition to providing much-needed support to the Navy's historical programs and its flagship United States Navy Museum in Washington, D.C., the Foundation collects oral histories of Navy veterans from World War II through the Cold War, and publishes articles and sponsors symposiums on important naval history topics. To provide increased access by the public to the Navy's historical collections of art, artifacts, documents, and photographs, the Foundation provides historical research and photo reproduction through its Historical Services Division.

Individuals may learn more about the Naval Historical Foundation and become an NHF member at http://www.navyhistory.org.

Naval Historical Foundation
1306 Dahlgren Avenue, S.E.
Washington Navy Yard, D.C. 20374-5055
Tel: (202) 678-4333
Fax: (202) 889-3565
nhfwny@navyhistory.org
http://www.navyhistory.org

Published by Hugh Lauter Levin Associates, Inc.
© 2003 Naval Historical Foundation
Design: Charles J. Ziga
Project Editor: James O. Muschett
Technical Editor: John C. Reilly, Jr.
Copy Editor: Wendy Leland
Design Production: Chris Berlingo

ISBN 0-88363-618-2
Beaux Arts Editions
Printed in China
http://www.HLLA.com

CONTENTS

PREFACE

This chronology, featuring a collection of essays and pictorials arranged in a sequential fashion, is both a history of our Navy and of our nation; for as the Navy grew in capability and strength, so did the United States of America. While no book can relate the history of every ship and sailor that ever served, the chronology is a clear and succinct summary of the many roles played by a navy tailored to meet the changing needs of the people it is sworn to support and defend.

From shallow-water craft and small men-of-war challenging the dominant Royal Navy in the American Revolution to the giant, nuclear-powered aircraft carriers and their awesome battle groups of the twenty-first century, the Navy has represented and defended the country and its interests in both peace and war. Today, it is a force ranging the globe defending freedom and supporting democracy worldwide.

As the reader goes through the chronology it will soon become apparent that while the Navy grew, it passed through myriad transitions in size, missions, technology, and people. Yet, no matter what the difficulties or the opportunities, a history and heritage evolved and still grows. Even as transitions continue, it will be the history and heritage of our Navy that will remain its core and sustenance into the future.

From the smallest of beginnings, even ceasing to exist for a time after the Revolution, the Navy's size waxed and waned according to the needs of the nation and the monies available to fund it. Until the middle of the twentieth century the rule seemed to be, "In times of peace lay up the ships; as war or crisis approaches, build more ships." The Cold War changed that traditional mindset by underscoring the value and usefulness of a navy. Lest we fall into the old trap, that story can never be told too often. A slogan of the 1950s applies: "Keep the Fleet to Keep the Peace."

Just as the dimensions of the Navy changed over the years, missions have changed too. Whether ridding the seas of pirates in the nineteenth century, exploring the unknown waters of the Pacific and the polar regions, carrying out diplomatic missions on every continent, or fighting small wars or global ones, the men and women of the United States Navy have brought great credit upon themselves and their fellow citizens.

From the beginning the Navy has been a "technical service" and the technologies have been in constant change. Learning the ropes and maintaining a frigate far from home was a technical challenge. So too was changing from sail to steam, from wood to iron and ultimately steel, from smoothbore cannon to rifles to missiles, from wood for fuel to coal to oil to jet fuel and nuclear power, from messenger boats and flags to lights and wireless to radio to the Internet, to space-based communications and beyond. This chronology reflects those changes.

People have also changed. At first, sailors came from merchant service; "landsmen" weren't really wanted. Many, if not most, were foreigners. Some sailors were restricted in the types of duties they could perform. And of course, until recently, seagoing billets were limited to men. Now, our people are a cross-section of America. They are bright, eager, intelligent, educated, and self-starting. They are the pride of the nation and the real strength of the fleet.

All of this is reflected in the pages of this chronology, in words as well as on canvas and film. Today, the Navy's aircraft own the skies over the seas and, when necessary, well inland. Its ships sail far and wide, on the high seas and in shallow waters. Its submarines deter, protect, and strike at great distances. Its sailors are second to none in professionalism, courage, and stamina. The world has never before known such a powerful force.

This book is the story of how your United States Navy got to be that way.

Robert F. Dunn
Vice Admiral, U.S. Navy (Retired)
President
Naval Historical Foundation

A NEW NATION
SETS SAIL

1775-1815

A NEW NATION SETS SAIL

1775-1815

It has always been the destiny of America to be a seagoing nation. The vast waters of two great oceans border her to the east and west, avenues for the exchange of goods between the Old World and the new. The genealogical fabric of her citizens includes the blood of great maritime nations such as England, France, Spain, and Portugal, which sent intrepid explorers to lay claim to the untamed lands of North America over the course of a period of history known as the Age of Exploration. At the birth of the United States of America, the patriots who affixed their signatures to the Declaration of Independence included many with mercantile backgrounds who owed their livelihood to the sea. The success of their endeavor to create a new nation depended on their ability to withstand Great Britain on land and on the sea. Thus, into the flames of revolution was cast a small collection of sailing ships and seafaring men, which the Continental Congress actually created on 13 October 1775, some nine months before it proclaimed the independence of the colonies.

Combating the world's greatest naval power provided a distinct challenge to the fledgling Navy. Joined by privateers, its ships sought out British merchantmen in an effort to disrupt the flow of goods to the British Isles and staged far-flung raids that were oftentimes no more than a nuisance to the Royal Navy. Only on rare occasions did the Continental vessels do battle with British men-of-war, and it was against this backdrop of booming cannons that a tradition was born. "I have not yet begun to fight"— the immortal words of John Paul Jones as his ship, *Bonhomme Richard*, battled the British frigate *Serapis*—expressed a fighting spirit that formed the very foundation upon which the U.S. Navy rests today.

Wrote John Adams during the revolution, "a navy is our natural and only defense."

In the years following the revolution, the traditions of an American navy were all that survived as the high financial cost of independence prompted the Continental Congress to disband the nation's naval establishment. The sale of *Alliance*, the last Continental Navy ship, was completed on 1 August 1785. Ironically, this event came less than a week after marauding corsairs seized two American merchantmen in the Mediterranean Sea, a direct challenge to national honor that over the course of the ensuing decade would trigger debates within the government of the new republic over whether the United States should build a navy. When the "Barbary Corsairs" renewed their attacks against American commerce in 1793, Congress determined that the United States required a naval presence on the world stage, and on 27 March 1794 authorized the construction of six frigates that symbolized the rebirth of American naval power.

The creation of the U.S. Navy added weight to the negotiations of American diplomats with the Barbary States during this crisis, and the reborn seagoing force was not required to fire a single shot. However, over the next two decades the nation would call upon her Navy to respond to numerous crises in home and foreign waters. U.S. Navy ships waged an undeclared war on French men-of-war and privateers that threatened American commerce during the period 1798–1800, hunting enemy sailing vessels in waters stretching from the Caribbean to the Indian Ocean. Renewed activity by the Barbary powers in the Mediterranean prompted the dispatch of U.S. Navy warships to the region, where the courageous actions of Lieutenant Stephen Decatur, Jr., inspired a navy and a nation.

Perhaps the greatest challenge to the United States came during the War of 1812, when the familiar redcoats of the Revolutionary War returned to American shores, and an outgunned U.S. Navy once again battled the world's preeminent naval power. American men-of-war scored stirring victories over their British counterparts, the most notable coming on 19 August 1812, when the American frigate *Constitution* engaged *Guerriere* and defeated her, the cannonballs of the British frigate bouncing off the sides of the American frigate, giving birth to her famous nickname "Old Ironsides." "Long may she ride, our Navy's pride, and spur to resolution," went a Navy song of the early 1800s. "And seaman boast, and landsmen toast, the Frigate *Constitution*."

Taking the war to enemy commerce, Captain David Porter and the crew of the frigate *Essex* completed an epic sixteen-month voyage, becoming the first American warship to round Cape Horn and proving a scourge to British merchantmen. In addition to action on the high seas, naval forces waged battles against the British along the nation's northern frontier in a battle for control of the Great Lakes. "Don't Give Up the Ship," proclaimed the flag unfurled over the flagship of Master Commandant Oliver Hazard Perry as he fought British ships in the Battle of Lake Erie. Yet, despite these victories, the small size of the U.S. Navy made it impossible to counter the British on a widespread scale,

enabling the enemy to put armies ashore. One of them set fire to the nation's capital and forced the Secretary of the Navy to give the dreaded order to burn several of the Navy's own ships at the Washington Navy Yard to prevent their capture.

The signing of a treaty ending the War of 1812 effectively ended the threat of invasion of the United States by a European power, but unlike the previous experience in the wake of a war with Great Britain, the United States retained her Navy. The importance of doing so was no more evident than in the fact that, just days after the treaty was ratified, naval forces were dispatched to the Mediterranean in response to Algerian attacks on American commerce. The words of John Adams never rang more true.

Above: *Naval warfare in the days of sail often meant boarding enemy vessels and engaging in vicious hand-to-hand combat. ("Decatur Boarding the Tripolitan Gunboat," Dennis Malone Carter, Navy Art Collection)*

Pages 8–9: *Cannons boom during the epic engagement between* Bonhomme Richard *and* Serapis *on 23 September 1779, which immortalized Captain John Paul Jones. ("Bonhomme Richard and Serapis," Thomas Mitchell, U.S. Naval Academy Museum)*

A NEW NATION SETS SAIL
1775-1815

1775

18 May
Forces under the command of Colonel Benedict Arnold capture a British supply sloop and christen her *Enterprise*, destined to become one of the famous ship names in the U.S. Navy.

12 June
Manning the sloop *Unity*, patriots in Machias, Massachusetts (now Maine), having the night before captured two British merchant sloops conducting trade in their town, board and capture the British armed schooner *Margaretta*, the first Royal Navy vessel to surrender to an American force. The colonists, armed with weapons ranging from guns to pitchforks, are led by Jeremiah O'Brien and his crew includes his five brothers. The following month O'Brien leads his fellow Massachusetts mariners in the capture of two ships in the Bay of Fundy.

15 June
On the same day Abraham Whipple receives his appointment as commodore of two ships outfitted for defense of the colony of Rhode Island's trade, he captures a small utility ship belonging to the British frigate *Rose*. Whipple's ship *Katy* eventually is taken over by the Continental Congress, and is fitted out as the sloop-of-war *Providence*. The Continental Navy and Army both conduct naval operations during the Revolutionary War, and each of the thirteen colonies raises its own small naval force.

18 July
The Continental Congress passes a resolution stating in part that "each colony, at their own expense, make such provisions by armed vessels or otherwise...for the protection of their harbours and navigation on their coasts."

3 August
A small flotilla of galleys under the command of Lieutenant Colonel Benjamin Tupper in *Washington* attacks the Royal Navy warships *Phoenix* and *Rose* on the Hudson River. A two-hour battle at close range results in substantial damage to *Phoenix* at the cost of four Americans killed and fourteen wounded. This and other actions do not deter the British from capturing Manhattan, New York, weeks later.

24 August
George Washington takes possession of *Hannah*, a small fishing schooner, and arms her with four 4-pounders, making her the first armed vessel to sail under Continental pay and control. Commanded by an Army officer, Nicholson Broughton, she puts to sea on 5 September 1775 with the mission of preventing provisions from reaching besieged British forces in Boston, Massachusetts. Other fishing craft are also acquired for this duty, and histories sometimes refer to these vessels as "Washington's cruisers."

28 August
Ships, including the sloop *Enterprise*, embark more than 1,000 troops and mount an expedition against St. Johns, Montreal, and Quebec, Canada. Despite capturing or besieging all three cities, the arrival of superior British forces compels American forces to withdraw from Canada in 1776.

Right: *Typical of the small sloops fitted out for service in the American Revolution was* Providence, *which participated in two cruises against British forces in the Bahamas and was at one time commanded by Captain John Paul Jones.* ("Providence," W. Nowland Van Powell, Naval Historical Center)

Opposite: *Not uncommon among the officers of the Continental Navy, John Barry was foreign born, having come to the colonies from his native Ireland. He commanded two ships during the American Revolution, suffering serious wounds as skipper of* Alliance *in 1781.* ("John Barry," Naval Historical Center)

3 October

The General Assembly of their colony having fitted out two armed vessels the previous summer, members of the Rhode Island delegation to the Continental Congress introduce a resolution calling for "building and equipping an American fleet."

5 October

John Barry, captain of the merchantman *Black Prince*, delivers to the Continental Congress letters brought from England detailing the departure of a pair of brigantines bound for Quebec, Canada, with arms and ammunition. The news spurs the creation of a committee that within days recommends the creation of a Continental Navy.

10 October

Hannah is run aground near Beverly, Massachusetts, by the British sloop *Nautilus*. The townspeople prevent her capture by removing her cannon and firing upon the enemy ship. *Hannah* is soon decommissioned, ending her service as a combat vessel.

13 October

The Continental Congress, meeting in Philadelphia, Pennsylvania, appoints a Naval Committee—comprised of Silas Deane, Christopher Gadsden, and John Langdon—to prepare an estimate of expense and to contract the fitting out of two sailing vessels as fighting ships. These ships will be used to intercept British vessels transporting munitions and supplies to redcoats fighting on shore. This date is celebrated as the birthday of the U.S. Navy.

30 October

The Continental Congress authorizes the equipping of two additional armed vessels, one to carry twenty guns, the other thirty-six, "to be employed in such manner, for the protection and defence of the united Colonies." When completed the two vessels authorized on this date and the two authorized previously are named *Alfred*, *Andrew Doria*, *Cabot*, and *Columbus*. In other business, the Naval Committee of the Continental Congress is expanded to seven members with the addition of John Adams, Joseph Hewes, Stephen Hopkins, and Richard Henry Lee.

2 November

The Continental Congress appropriates $100,000 for the fitting out of vessels as warships.

5 November

The Continental Congress appoints Esek Hopkins, a brigadier general in the Rhode Island Militia, as Commander in Chief of the Continental Navy. "I suppose you may be more serviceable to your Country, in this very dangerous Crisis of its affairs, by taking upon you this Command than you can in any other Way," writes his brother Stephen Hopkins, a member of the committee that appointed him.

25 November

The Continental Congress authorizes the capture and confiscation of all British armed vessels, transports, and supply ships, and directs the issuing of commissions to captains of cruisers and privateers. In the case of privately owned vessels, "the captures made shall be to the use of the owner or owners." In the case of vessels partially or fully funded by a colony or the United Colonies, captors receive one-third of the prize, which increases to one-half in the case of vessels of war.

28 November

The Continental Congress adopts the first *Rules for the Regulation of the Navy of the United Colonies of North America.* Authored in large part by future President of the United States John Adams, the regulations outline the conduct expected of officers and such provisions as divine services on board ship, punishments for crimes such as blasphemy and drunkenness, and the issuing of rations.

Above: *Page from the "Journal of the Continental Congress" containing the initial part of the resolution authorizing a Continental Navy. (National Archives)*

Right: *The Continental Navy ship* Alfred *raising the Grand Union flag while at anchor at Philadelphia, Pennsylvania, 3 December 1775. ("Alfred," W. Nowland Van Powell, Naval Historical Center)*

29 November

The Continental Army schooner *Lee*, under the command of Captain John Manley, happens upon the British brigantine *Nancy* in the waters off Boston, Massachusetts. Mistaking *Lee* for a pilot boat, the British ship lays her sails aback and runs up signal flags. Manley dispatches a boat, ordering its occupants to conceal their weapons and take the crew of *Nancy* by surprise. They are successful and capture significant stores of ordnance and gunpowder for use by General George Washington's army. Washington writes of the capture, "We must be thankful, as I truly am, for this instance of Divine favour."

3 December

On the day of her commissioning in Philadelphia, Pennsylvania, crewmen on board the Continental sloop *Alfred* raise the Grand Union flag over their ship, the first American flag to fly over an American naval vessel. Serving as First Lieutenant of *Alfred* is a Scottish-born mariner by the name of John Paul Jones, who becomes the most famous Continental Navy captain of the American Revolution.

11 December

Congress appoints a committee to devise ways and means for furnishing the colonies with a naval armament. One member from each colony, with the exception of Georgia, is appointed: Samuel Adams, Josiah Bartlett, Stephen Crane, Silas Deane, Christopher Gadsden, Joseph Hewes, Stephen Hopkins, Richard Henry Lee, Francis Lewis, Robert Morris, William Paca, and George Read.

13 December

At the recommendation of the committee appointed two days earlier, the Continental Congress authorizes the construction of thirteen frigates as the foundation of the Continental Navy. All are eventually captured or destroyed; seven of them never go to sea.

14 December

The Continental Congress appoints a Marine Committee to carry out the resolves regarding naval armament: Josiah Bartlett, John Hancock, Stephen Hopkins, Silas Deane, Francis Lewis, Stephen Crane, Robert Morris, George Read, Samuel Chase, Richard Henry Lee, Joseph Hewes, Christopher Gadsden, and John Houston. After the dissolution of the Naval Committee in 1776, the Marine Committee continues to guide the fledgling Navy until the creation of the Board of Admiralty in 1779.

22 December

The Continental Congress formally commissions its first officers, including Commodore Esek Hopkins as Commander in Chief. The captains include Esek's son, John Hopkins, along with Nicolas Biddle, Dudley Saltonstall, and Abraham Whipple. Only Whipple, a native of Pennsylvania, is not a Rhode Islander.

24 December

The armed schooner *Warren* captures the brig *Sally* north of Cape Ann, Massachusetts. Carrying 153 quarter casks of wine, *Sally* is sailed into nearby Marblehead, an appropriate Christmas present for General George Washington.

1776

6 January
The Continental Congress authorizes the appointment of surgeons and surgeon's mates in the naval service, the beginning of Navy medicine.

25 January
The schooner *Hancock*, part of "George Washington's Navy," captures two British transports and, while prize crews sail them into Plymouth Harbor, Massachusetts, engages an eight-gun British schooner attempting to thwart the capture of the transports.

30 January
The British brig *Hope*, having sailed from Boston, Massachusetts, with the express purpose of capturing the schooner *Hancock*, intercepts her off Plymouth. Captain John Manley, skipper of *Hancock*, runs her aground to prevent the deeper-draft *Hope* from pursuing her. Refloated days later, *Hancock* continues her service in support of General George Washington's forces.

17 February
In the first cruise of a Continental Navy squadron, Commodore Esek Hopkins sails from Philadelphia, Pennsylvania, in command of eight ships with orders to destroy British shipping in the Chesapeake Bay and protect merchant shipping off the Carolinas.

19 February
The Continental schooner *Fly* collides with the sloop *Hornet* off the Atlantic coast, damaging the sloop to such an extent that she returns to port.

23 March
The Continental Congress legalizes privateering, issuing General Letters of Marque and Reprisal. All British vessels, armed or unarmed, are liable to capture by American ships.

3 March
Without informing the Continental Congress, Commodore Esek Hopkins raids the Bahamas. The naval squadron under his command executes the first amphibious landing in the history of the U.S. Navy when sailors and Marines go ashore and capture Fort Montague on New Providence Island. They capture heavy artillery pieces and gunpowder urgently needed by forces at home.

Above: *Continental sailors and Marines land on New Providence Island, Bahamas, on 3 March 1776. Their initial objective, Fort Montagu, is in the left background. Close off shore are the small vessels used to transport the landing force to the vicinity of the beach. Amphibious operations remain an integral part of the Navy's mission today. ("New Providence Invasion, March 1776," V. Zveg, Navy Art Collection)*

13 March

The Marine Committee of the Continental Congress purchases the brigantine *Wild Duck* in Philadelphia, Pennsylvania, and renames her *Lexington* in honor of the opening battle of the American Revolution. She is the first of five American naval vessels to carry the famous name.

28 March

The Marine Committee of the Continental Congress purchases the merchantman *Molly* and renames her *Reprisal*.

4 April

The armed ship *Columbus*, returning from the previous month's Bahamas expedition, captures the British schooner *Hawke*.

6 April

Five ships under the command of Commodore Esek Hopkins, flying his flag in the Continental sloop *Alfred*, engage the British sloop-of-war *Glasgow* off Long Island, New York. The lone vessel eludes capture and inflicts damage on the American ships, which raises questions about the competence of Continental officers when the squadron returns.

7 April

The brigantine *Lexington*, commanded by Captain John Barry, engages the British sloop *Edward* off the Virginia Capes. The British vessel strikes her colors after a fierce hour-long battle in which Barry reports *Lexington* "shattered her in a terrible manner." Later fitted out as a Continental Navy ship under the direction of seventeen-year-old Joshua Barney, who receives a commission as a lieutenant during the process, *Edward* is renamed *Sachem*.

17 April

Bostonian John Manley receives his commission as a captain in the Continental Navy and takes command of the frigate *Hancock*. One of the new Navy's most capable officers, he had served as commodore of the small armed ships fitted out by General George Washington to harass the British and seize supply vessels attempting to enter Boston Harbor, Massachusetts. Manley seizes ten prizes individually and participates in the capture of five others during the Revolutionary War.

8 May
The Continental schooner *Wasp*, in company with a number of galleys, bombards the British ship *Roebuck*, which had run aground in the Delaware River, and also captures the British brig *Betsey*.

10 May
John Paul Jones takes command of the sloop *Providence*, a command which he had previously

declined, and in August embarks on a cruise to the waters off the Grand Banks, capturing sixteen British prizes and destroying local fishing fleets off Nova Scotia, Canada.

21 May
The Continental frigate *Raleigh*, named for the English explorer Sir Walter Raleigh, is launched at Portsmouth, New Hampshire.

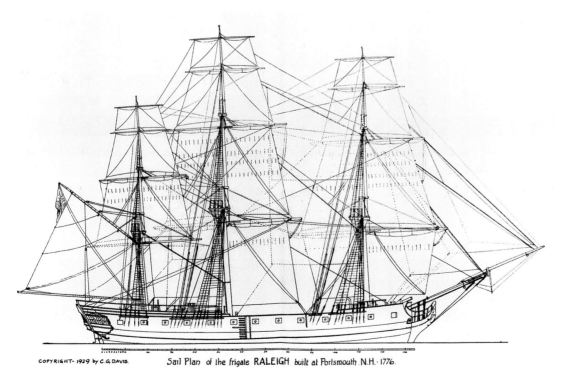

COPYRIGHT- 1929 by C.G. DAVIS.   Sail Plan of the frigate RALEIGH built at Portsmouth N.H.- 1776.

Above: *Naval actions of the American Revolution were not limited to the high seas. In the Battle of Valcour Island in October 1776, a force of Army gunboats under General Benedict Arnold engaged a British force on Lake Champlain. ("British and American Fleets in Battle on Lake Champlain, 11 October 1776," Edward Tufnell, Navy Art Collection)*

Left: *Line drawing of the frigate* Raleigh, *captured in 1778 by the British. (Naval Historical Center)*

Right: *The 14-gun brig* Andrew Doria, *named for the Genoese Renaissance admiral, was one of the first four ships purchased for the Continental Navy. She was sometimes referred to as* Andrea Doria, *the Italian form of Doria's name. (*"Andrew Doria," *W. Nowland Van Powell, Naval Historical Center)*

Page 20, top: *Issued in mid-1777, this recruiting poster advertised service in the sloop* Ranger *under the command of Captain John Paul Jones. It appealed to two elements important to many men during the period by promising a chance for both glory and fortune. (Naval Historical Center)*

Page 20, bottom: *The Continental Navy brig* Reprisal *passes the French fleet at Belle Isle, Quiberon Bay, on the way to Auray, France, with Benjamin Franklin on board, 10 December 1776. She was the first Continental Navy ship to arrive in European waters. (*"Reprisal," *W. Nowland Van Powell, Navy Art Collection)*

29 May

The Continental brig *Andrew Doria* captures the British transports *Crawford* and *Oxford*, placing prize crews on board both ships. British troops seize the latter ship from the prize crew and set course for Virginia, expecting a welcome from the Tory government. Instead, patriots seize *Oxford* upon her arrival.

10 July

The Continental frigate *Randolph* is launched at Philadelphia, Pennsylvania, and Captain Nicholas Biddle assumes command of the vessel the following day.

7 August

John Paul Jones assumes command of the sloop *Alfred*, a ship in which he had once served as first lieutenant.

The Continental frigate *Washington* is launched near Philadelphia, Pennsylvania. The second Revolutionary War ship to bear the name, she never sails, being destroyed by fire near Bordentown, New Jersey, on 7 May 1778.

12 August

The Continental sloop *Sachem* fights the British brigantine *Three Friends* off the Delaware Capes, forcing the brig's surrender after a pitched battle lasting over two hours.

GREAT
ENCOURAGEMENT
FOR
SEAMEN.

ALL GENTLEMEN SEAMEN and able-bodied LANDSMEN who have a Mind to diftinguifh themfelves in the GLORIOUS CAUSE of their Country, and make their Fortunes, an Opportunity now offers on board the Ship RANGER, of Twenty Guns, (for France) now laying in Portsmouth, in the State of New-Hampshire, commanded by JOHN PAUL JONES Efq; let them repair to the Ship's Rendezvous in Portsmouth, or at the Sign of Commodore Manley, in Salem, where they will be kindly entertained, and receive the greateft Encouragement.---The Ship Ranger, in the Opinion of every Perfon who has feen her is looked upon to be one of the beft Cruizers in America.---She will be always able to Fight her Guns under a moft excellent Cover ; and no Veffel yet built was ever calculated for failing fafter, and making good Weather.

Any Gentlemen Volunteers who have a Mind to take an agreable Voyage in this pleafant Seafon of the Year, may, by entering on board the above Ship Ranger, meet with every Civility they can poffibly expect, and for a further Encouragement depend on the firft Opportunity being embraced to reward each one agreable to his Merit.

All reafonable Travelling Expences will be allowed, and the Advance-Money be paid on their Appearance on Board.

In CONGRESS, March 29, 1777.

Resolved,

THAT the Marine Committee be authorifed to advance to every able Seaman, that enters into the Continental Service, any Sum not exceeding FORTY DOLLARS, and to every ordinary Seaman or Landfman, any Sum not exceeding TWENTY DOLLARS, to be deducted from their future Prize-Money.

By Order of Congress,

JOHN-HANCOCK, Prefident.

DANVERS: Printed by E. Russell, at the Houfe late the Bell-Tavern.

26 August
The Continental sloop *Warren*, one of the original ships of "George Washington's Navy," strikes her colors after a one-sided engagement with the British frigate *Liverpool*.

5 September
The Continental Congress issues the first regulations governing uniforms for naval officers, specifying a blue coat with standing collar, red lapels, yellow metal buttons, blue breeches, and a red waistcoat. Captains are permitted to wear gold on parts of their uniform, a small bit of flourish on otherwise plain clothing.

7 September
David Bushnell unsuccessfully attacks *Asia*, a British ship-of-the-line anchored in New York Harbor, in his submersible *Turtle*. Wrote an observer of the innovative craft and its inventor the previous year, "I well know the man and have seen the machine while in embryo, and every addition made to it fills me with fresh astonishment and surprize."

11 October
A makeshift naval squadron under the command of General Benedict Arnold engages British forces on Lake Champlain in the Battle of Valcour Island. He loses eleven of his sixteen ships, most of them beached on the shores of the lake, but delays a British offensive in New

York until the following spring, when they confront a more powerful American army.

27 October

The brig *Hampden* under Captain Hoysted Hacker, and the sloop *Alfred* commanded by Captain John Paul Jones, depart Newport, Rhode Island, on a cruise to the waters off Newfoundland, Canada. Their goal is the disruption of fisheries and the rescue of prisoners of war held on Cape Breton Island. *Hampden* runs aground shortly after the force's departure, and her crew transfers to *Providence* for the voyage.

6 November

The Continental Naval Board, consisting of three members "well skilled in maritime affairs," is formed to conduct the business of the Navy under the direction of the Marine Committee.

12 November

The sloop *Alfred* captures the British transport *Mellish*, whose cargo includes thousands of winter uniforms bound for the forces under General John Burgoyne in Montreal, Canada. They are transferred to the Continental Army.

16 November

The Dutch fort at St. Eustatius, West Indies, salutes the Grand Union flag flying from the Continental Navy brig *Andrew Doria*, the first salute rendered to an American flag.

20 November

The Continental Congress authorizes the construction of three 74-gun ships-of-the-line. Only one, *America*, is ever completed, her prospective commanding officer the famous John Paul Jones. Before she ever puts to sea under the colors of the United States, the Continental Congress presents her to France as a gift to replace the French ship *Magnifique*, which had run aground in Boston Harbor, Massachusetts.

29 November

The Continental brig *Reprisal* arrives in Nantes, France, the first vessel of the Continental Navy to arrive in European waters. On board is Benjamin Franklin, the United Colonies' first Commissioner to France.

20 December

The British frigate *Pearl* captures the brig *Lexington* off the Delaware Capes. The Royal Navy captain removes the officers from the ship, but leaves seventy crewmen on board guarded by a prize crew. Luring the British below decks with a promise of rum, the Continental sailors recapture their ship and sail her to Baltimore, Maryland.

Above: *In a symbolic act, the Continental Navy brig* Andrew Doria *receives a salute from the Dutch fort at St. Eustatius, 16 November 1776. ("First Foreign Salute to the American Flag," Phillips Melville, Navy Art Collection)*

PRIVATEERS AND THE U.S. NAVY

by The Honorable John F. Lehman, Jr.

Privateering as an exercise of naval power is older than navies themselves. Professional navies as we know them today did not emerge in Europe until the seventeenth century. In the battle of the Spanish Armada with England in 1588, the most famous naval battle of the age, most of the ships on both sides were privately owned and taken over by the Crown for temporary service. Kings had long depended on issuing written commissions to ship owners giving them authority to attack, sink, or seize enemy vessels in time of war. Such commissions came to be called "Letters of Marque and Reprisal" and were well recognized in international law. Presidential authority to grant such commissions was later enshrined in the American Constitution.

The early decades of the U.S. Navy are deeply entwined with privateering. American privateers made a much greater contribution to independence than did the fledgling Continental Navy. When the Revolution broke out in 1775, the colonies had no warships and no navy. When the British instituted a blockade of Boston and the New England ports, American mariners, shipowners, and fishermen found themselves in dire financial straits. Privateering sprang up almost at once out of necessity, and by early 1776 British merchantmen were being seized regularly along the New England coast. Such seizures provided General George Washington's struggling army with its principal source of supplies in its first year of operations. According to the records of the Continental Congress, 1,697 vessels were issued Letters of Marque during the Revolution. A total of 58,400 men shipped out in these privateers. In addition, there were at least another 400 privateers commissioned by the states and by colonial agents in Europe. These ships ranged from small sloops armed with a single gun to sizable ships of twenty-four guns.

At the beginning of the war the ranks of privateers consisted primarily of converted merchantmen or fishermen, usually fast packets and schooners hastily armed. Realizing that privateering was a lucrative business, investors soon began commissioning newly constructed ships. The preferred designs were brig, schooner, or hybrid rigs that were essentially fore and aft rigged vessels built for speed and ability to sail close to the wind, but had at least one square rigged sail for fighting qualities.

While the purpose of privateers was to prey on unarmed merchantmen and avoid battle with British men-of-war, there were numerous occasions when they did so, either because they felt superior enough to subdue a smaller man-of-war as a prize, or they simply could not escape from the larger man-of-war and were forced to fight. There were some notable ship-to-ship battles, such as the September 1781 capture of the British sloop-of-war *Savage* by the largest privateer ever built for the purpose, the twenty-four-gun *Congress* sailing out of Philadelphia. The archives of Lloyd's Insurance Exchange in London contain documentary evidence of 3,087 British ships insured by Lloyd's syndicates that were captured by American ships during that war. Only about 400 of these vessels were captured by the Continental Navy. The combined figure represented nearly 15 percent of the entire British merchant fleet of the war years and resulted in a substantial increase in insurance rates; some 30 percent for ships in convoy and at least a 50 percent increase for ships sailing alone. The most significant military impact of the privateers was in forcing the Royal Navy to institute convoying for its merchant ships, a practice that slowed trade and tied up Royal Navy ships that would otherwise be used in blockade. It also prompted the Royal Navy to dispatch ships on cruises to find marauding American privateers.

The greatest impact was economic, a dimension of war that is all too frequently ignored by naval historians. Privateers greatly reduced the profitable British trade with the Caribbean Sugar Islands and damaged the British economy. Moreover, since most of the captured merchant ships were insured by Lloyd's, their capture had ruinous effects on some members of Parliament and of His Majesty's government who were, in fact, the underwriters of the Lloyd's syndicates who had to pay for those catastrophic losses. After the defeat at Yorktown these economic losses became decisive when Parliament made it clear to George III that the war must be brought to an end.

When the fledgling republic next battled Great

Right: *Fortune favors the brave—an American privateer attacks a British convoy escorted by the Royal Navy warship* Tartar *off Boston, 23 November 1775 ("American Privateer Attacking British Convoy Off Boston, November 1775, Warren, Mariner's Museum, Newport News, VA)*

Britain during the War of 1812, American privateers proved valuable, but in a diminished role because the new U.S. Navy had by this time become a stronger fighting force. During the war, 513 registered American privateers took approximately 2,300 British merchant ships compared to 165 taken by the U.S. Navy. Of the combined total, the Royal Navy retook approximately 750. One of the most famous privateer battles of all time took place at the end of the war when the American privateer *General Armstrong*, under Captain Samuel Reid, was trapped in the Azores by the British squadron bringing the invasion force to attack New Orleans. In a furious battle, *General Armstrong* held off three larger British attackers until Captain Reid was forced to abandon ship. Reid had delayed the British expedition against New Orleans for ten days. Thus, General Andrew Jackson was able to arrive and prepare his defenses before the attack, which ended in one of the greatest victories in American military history. Upon meeting Reid after the war, "Old Hickory" told him that, without this action, "There would have been no battle of New Orleans."

The United States issued no Letters of Marque during the Civil War, though Congress passed the Union Privateering Act in support of wealthy New Yorkers like the Vanderbilts, who wanted to outfit privateers against the Confederacy. The U.S. Navy effectively blocked the issuance of Letters of Marque in order to preserve for its officers the prize money that came with the capture of blockade-runners. By contrast, the Confederacy had high hopes for privateering and issued more than 100 Letters of Marque. However, Southern privateer owners soon found it was much more lucrative and less risky to use their ships as blockade-runners.

The traditional contempt for privateering is exemplified in the words of John Paul Jones, who dismissed them as no more than "licensed robbers… actuated by no nobler principle than that of self-interest." Seafaring men were drawn to privateering because the pay was much better, the danger much less, and the discipline not nearly as harsh. There was, moreover, a chance for even the lowliest of crewmen to make himself a fortune in privateers, and many of them did. In contrast, the Continental Navy always had difficulty manning its ships because of the competition of privateers. Navy ships often lay in ports for months unable to go to sea because of insufficient crews, while privateersmen never had any trouble recruiting. The Continental Navy was never large enough to have a significant impact and in the late years of the Revolution had been all but swept from the seas. During the same period the numbers of American privateers increased exponentially, and this provided an opportunity for American naval officers and seamen to continue to participate in the war. Virtually every one of the Continental captains at one time or another during the Revolution took up privateering. At least sixty of the most successful privateers during the war were commanded by men who were captains in the Continental Navy or who later became captains in the U.S. Navy. Increasingly manned with large numbers of experienced officers and seamen from the Continental Navy, as well as by seasoned privateersmen and the pick of the best seamen in every port, it was small wonder that they became such a decisive war-winning force.

The United States has issued no Letters of Marque since the War of 1812, and, while customary international law has moved to outlaw privateering, the authority remains in the U.S. Constitution.

Left: *The Continental brig* Lexington *engages the British cutter* Alert *off France on 19 September 1777. Broadsides from the Royal Navy vessel seriously damaged* Lexington's *rigging, forcing Captain Henry Johnson to strike his colors. All told,* Lexington *was involved in the capture of fifteen enemy ships during her brief career. ("Engagement Between U.S. Brig* Lexington *and HMS* Alert, *1777," Childs Gallery, Boston)*

Above: *An engraving by J. Rodgers commemorating the prominent naval officers of the American Revolution. (Naval Historical Center)*

1777

3 March
The British frigate *Milford* forces the brig *Cabot* aground in Nova Scotia, Canada. Though her crew escapes, *Cabot* becomes the first Continental Navy ship captured by the British.

26 March
The Continental Congress, citing disobedience of orders and complaints of his conduct, suspends Commodore Esek Hopkins from command of the Continental Navy.

1 May
Surprize, a lugger purchased in France by agents of American commissioners in that nation, puts to sea from Dunkirk. She captures two prizes, but upon returning to France the ship is confiscated and her prizes released, a sign of France's unwillingness to break with England during the early stages of the American Revolution.

10 May
The Continental sloop *Ranger* is launched at Portsmouth, New Hampshire, with Captain John Paul Jones in command.

19 May
The schooner *Lynch*, carrying secret documents and arms and clothing for the Continental Army, strikes her colors

after an unsuccessful attempt to escape the British ship-of-the-line *Foudroyant* off the coast of France. Her captain manages to throw the documents overboard.

28 May
The Continental Navy ships *Lexington*, *Reprisal*, and *Dolphin* sail from France. In a foray around Ireland that sends ripples throughout the Royal Navy, the ships capture eighteen prizes.

7 June
The frigates *Hancock* and *Boston* engage the British frigate *Fox* in the North Atlantic, capturing her after knocking out her mainmast and causing other severe damage. British forces recapture *Fox* the following month.

28 June
Pursued by British blockaders, the Continental armed brig *Nancy* runs aground in Delaware. The crews of the Continental Navy ships *Reprisal* and *Lexington* remove 286 barrels of gunpowder from the ship, leaving aboard 100 barrels with a long fuse that explodes just as a group of British sailors board *Nancy*.

4 July
Crewmen on board the sloop *Ranger* in Portsmouth, New Hampshire, hoist the first "Stars and Stripes" flag flown on board a Continental warship.

7 July
British naval forces on Lake Champlain descend upon ships and craft evacuating men and material from Fort Ticonderoga, capturing two ships and prompting the American forces to run three more aground and burn them in order to prevent their capture.

7 July
After a spirited chase and engagement lasting some thirty-nine hours, the Continental frigate *Hancock* strikes her colors under the guns of the British ship *Rainbow*. She is renamed *Iris* and achieves a sterling reputation in the Royal Navy, even turning the tables by capturing the American ship *Trumbull* on 8 August 1781.

17 July
Revenge, under the command of Captain Gustavus Conyngham, known as the "Dunkirk Pirate," departs France under cover of darkness. During the ensuing voyage in the North and Irish seas, the schooner's crew captures or destroys at least twenty ships.

29 August
The Continental schooner *Lee* captures the British merchant brigantine *Industrious Bee*. The Navy Board at Boston, Massachusetts, purchases the prize in December. Fitted with eighteen guns, she is renamed *General Gates*.

Above: *Action between British and American vessels off Cape Sable, Newfoundland, 7 July 1777. Ships involved in the action included the American frigates* Boston *and* Hancock. *British ships included* Rainbow, Flora, *and* Victor. *("British and American Vessels in Action, 7 July 1777," Warren, Mariner's Museum, Neport News, VA)*

4 September

The Continental frigate *Raleigh* disables the sloop *Druid* during an attack against a British convoy, but the approach of the remaining British escorts forces her to break off.

19 September

The Continental brig *Lexington* is forced to strike her colors after her rigging is damaged in an engagement with the British cutter *Alert* off the coast of France.

26 September

In response to the British capture of Philadelphia, Pennsylvania, the Continental frigate *Delaware* and several smaller vessels open fire on enemy fortifications under construction there, unleashing their cannon at a range of 500 yards. The following day *Delaware* runs aground during the ebb tide. Taken under fire by British artillery, she strikes her colors.

1 October

The Continental brig *Reprisal* is lost off the banks of Newfoundland, Canada. Except for the ship's cook, the entire crew goes down with the ship.

6 October

The uncompleted frigate *Montgomery*, having been launched at Poughkeepsie, New York, is burned to prevent her capture by British forces following their capture of New York City.

26 October

The schooner *Lee*, the last of the ships of "George Washington's Navy," returns to Marblehead, Massachusetts, from her final cruise. During her service she played a role in the capture of nineteen prizes.

1 November

The sloop *Ranger* sails for France carrying news of the victory over the British at the Battle of Saratoga to the Continental Commissioners in Paris. The dispatches are delivered personally to Benjamin Franklin by the sloop's skipper, Captain John Paul Jones.

2 November

Her crew having been ordered from their ship by General George Washington, the uncompleted Continental frigate *Effingham* is sunk in the Delaware River to prevent her capture by British forces that had recently captured Philadelphia, Pennsylvania.

Above: *The Continental Navy frigate* Randolph *duels the British ship-of-the-line* Yarmouth *on 7 March 1778. Before the battle ended, an explosion blew the American ship apart. (*"Randolph vs. Yarmouth," *J. O. Davidson, Naval Historical Center)*

Left: *During late 1777, Continental Navy ships engaged in ultimately unsuccessful attempts to hinder British movements on the Delaware River. (*"Conflict on the Delaware River," *Lt. A. Eliot, Naval Historical Center)*

21 November
British naval gunfire and shore batteries force the evacuation of Forts Mifflin and Mercer guarding the entrance to the Delaware River. The defenders burn Continental ships assisting in the defense in order to prevent their capture.

1778

2 January
The Continental Congress dismisses Commodore Esek Hopkins from the naval service. He never again goes to sea.

27 January
The crew of the Continental frigate *Providence*, whose ship participated in the successful raid against the Bahamas in 1776, single-handedly spikes the guns of Fort Nassau, captures 1,600 pounds of powder, and rescues thirty American prisoners during a raid against New Providence Island. During this Bahamas cruise she also seizes one prize and recaptures five other vessels.

14 February
The sloop *Ranger* enters Quiberon Bay, France, flying the new American flag, the "Stars and Stripes," to which the French fleet fires a salute. This occasion marks the first official salute to the new flag received by a Continental ship.

15 February
The Continental frigate *Boston* departs on a transatlantic voyage to France carrying John Adams, a recently appointed commissioner. During the voyage

the frigate is struck by lightning and engages an armed British merchantman before arriving at Bordeaux on 31 March. In addition to Adams, the ship carries as a passenger his son, John Quincy, thus claiming the distinction of hosting two men who later become presidents of the United States.

26 February
A boat party under the command of Captain John Barry captures four transports and the British schooner *Alert* at Fort Penn on the Delaware River.

7 March
The Continental Navy frigate *Randolph* engages the British ship-of-the-line *Yarmouth*. Despite the frigate's inferiority in armament, her crew wages a valiant fight and is on the verge of victory when her magazine ignites and blows *Randolph* to pieces. Out of a crew of 315, only 4 survive, and not until 1944 is another U.S. Navy vessel named *Randolph*.

9 March
The British warships *Ariadne* and *Ceres* capture the Continental sloop *Alfred* as she returns from France.

27 March
Chased ashore on Point Judith, Rhode Island, by a British squadron, the crew of *Columbus* strips her of her sails and most of her rigging and abandons her. She meets a fiery demise at the hands of the British.

Above: *Mural depicting the Continental sloop* Ranger *receiving the salute of the French fleet at Quiberon Bay. ("First Foreign Salute to the Stars and Stripes, 14 February 1778," Howard B. French, U.S. Naval Academy)*

Left: *Engagement off Carrickfergus, Ireland, 24 April 1778. ("USS* Ranger *versus HMS* Drake," *Arthur N. Disney, Sr., Navy Art Collection)*

Below: *John Paul Jones sails from Lorient. His squadron includes (left to right) the cutter* Le Cerf; *the frigate* Pallas; *Jones' flagship* Bonhomme Richard; *and the frigate* Alliance. *(Naval Historical Foundation)*

31 March

The Continental frigate *Virginia* runs aground off Hampton, Virginia, during an attempted night passage into the Atlantic to avoid the British blockade. Battered by winds and high surf, she surrenders to the British the following day. Two years later, in the service of the Royal Navy, *Virginia* participates in the capture of Charleston, South Carolina.

22 April

Captain John Paul Jones takes a landing party from the sloop *Ranger* ashore at Whitehaven, England,

spiking the cannons of the harbor's defenses and burning colliers in port. "Intrepid & bold…a small specimen of that Conflagration & distress, we have so often experienced from our Enemies," a Virginian in the Continental Congress says in reference to Jones's daring raid.

24 April

The Continental sloop *Independence*, returning from a voyage to France in which she delivered diplomatic dispatches, is wrecked on a sandbar while attempting to enter Ocracoke Inlet, North Carolina.

The Continental sloop *Ranger* engages the British sloop-of-war *Drake* off Carrickfergus, Ireland, forcing the enemy to strike her colors after an hour's battle. Two Americans and forty British sailors are killed.

6 July
A French fleet under the command of Vice Admiral Charles Henri Comte d'Estaing arrives off Delaware, joining American forces. The French ships remain in American waters until November, and engage in no combat action.

3 August
General Gates, under the command of Captain John Skimmer, engages the British brigantine *Montague* off Newfoundland, Canada. In a bitter engagement lasting five hours, the British ship exhausts her ammunition, and her crew resorts to firing jackknives, crowbars, and any iron aboard from her cannons. One shot kills Skimmer, but his crew valiantly continues the battle, forcing *Montague* to strike her colors.

28 September
The frigate *Raleigh*—with the British ships *Experiment* and *Unicorn* in pursuit since the previous night, during which *Raleigh* and *Unicorn* engaged in a seven-hour gun battle—runs aground on Wooden Ball Island off Penobscot Bay, Maine, while engaging the enemy a second time. A large portion of the crew

makes it ashore, but a midshipman sent to remove the remainder of the crew and destroy the ship strikes the colors when taken under fire, allowing the capture of *Raleigh*. Under British colors the frigate later takes part in the capture of Charleston, South Carolina.

October
Reverend Benjamin Balch, the first Continental Navy chaplain, reports aboard the frigate *Boston*.

28 October
Under the cover of darkness and steering their small sloop *Hawke* with poles, Major Silas Talbot and his force of sixty soldiers slip past British batteries guarding the eastern channel of Narragansett Bay, Rhode Island, and attack the British ship *Pigot*. The two forces exchange broadsides, which result in no loss of life and the surrender of the British.

8 November
The Continental frigate *Confederacy* is launched at Norwich, Connecticut.

Above: *The Continental Navy frigate* Raleigh *is forced ashore near Penobscot Bay, Maine, by the British ships* Experiment *and* Unicorn *after a sixty-hour chase.* ("British Vessels Drive Continental Navy Vessel Raleigh Ashore, 27 September 1778," Warren, Mariner's Museum, Newport News, VA)

5 January
Stephen Decatur, Jr., destined to become one the U.S. Navy's most acclaimed combat leaders, is born in Sinepuxent, Maryland.

14 January
The frigate *Alliance* departs Boston bound for France carrying as a passenger the Marquis de Lafayette, who becomes one of George Washington's most able lieutenants. At sea, thirty-eight members of her crew, composed largely of Irish and British sailors under French-born Captain Pierre Landais, plot a mutiny, which is uncovered. The guilty sailors spend the remainder of the voyage in irons.

Above: *The Continental Navy sloop* Ranger *and frigates* Warren *and* Queen of France *battle British ships off the New England coast, 7 April 1779. Seven British vessels were captured in the sharp engagement. ("Continental Navy Vessels* Ranger, Warren, *and* Queen of France *Capture Seven British Vessels, 7 April 1779," Warren, Mariner's Museum, Newport News, VA)*

Left: *A sketch of the operations before Charlestown, South Carolina, 1780, and a sketch of Sir Peter Parker's attack on Fort Moultrie, 28 June 1776. ("Attacks on Charleston, South Carolina, 28 June 1776 and April–May 1780," Naval Historical Center)*

Right: *Though the September 1779 battle at Flamborough Head, England, involved multiple British and Continental Navy ships, it was the engagement between* Bonhomme Richard *and* Serapis *that overshadowed other actions. The ships were eventually lashed together, their crews raking each other with cannon and small arms fire. Almost 50 percent of each crew were either killed or wounded. ("The Action Between* Serapis *and* Countess of Scarborough, *and John Paul Jones's Squadron, 23 September 1779," Richard Paton, U.S. Naval Academy Museum)*

4 February

Captain John Paul Jones assumes command of the ship on whose deck he becomes a legend in the annals of the history of the U.S. Navy. He christens the frigate *Bonhomme Richard*, the French equivalent of "Poor Richard," in honor of Benjamin Franklin, author of the popular periodical *Poor Richard's Almanac*.

12 March

Revenge is sold at auction in Philadelphia, Pennsylvania, an end not befitting her glorious service. A scourge of the British Empire, she captured more than sixty vessels over the course of some nineteen months of service.

7 April

An American squadron consisting of the sloop *Ranger* and the frigates *Queen of France* and *Warren* capture seven British vessels including the 20-gun British ship *Jason*. On board the prizes are provisions, dry goods, and equipment for a British dragoon regiment. Despite the success of his squadron, Captain John B. Hopkins is relieved of his command for returning to port too soon and not sending his prizes to the nearest port.

7 May

The Continental Navy sloop *Providence* captures the British brig *Diligent* off Cape Cod, Massachusetts, firing two broadsides and a volley of musketry to damage the enemy ship's masts, rigging, and hull.

July

The sloop *Ranger* and the frigates *Providence* and *Queen of France*, operating in thick fog off Newfoundland, Canada, inadvertently sail into a fleet of some sixty British merchantmen. They capture eleven prizes worth more than one million dollars.

13 August

As part of the Penobscot Expedition against British forces in Maine, ships under Captain Dudley Saltonstall break away from supporting a planned assault against enemy defenses in the face of a powerful British squadron. The Americans suffer heavy losses in ships, resulting in Saltonstall's court-martial and dismissal.

6 September

The Continental frigates *Deane* and *Boston* return to Boston Harbor, Massachusetts, after completing one of the most successful wartime cruises of the Continental Navy, having captured eight prizes and taken some 250 prisoners of war.

23 September

The frigate *Bonhomme Richard* engages the British frigate *Serapis* at Flamborough Head, England, in an epic battle lasting three and one-half hours. *Bonhomme Richard* combats *Serapis* in a deadly duel at point-blank range. At one point the British captain hails the American skipper and asks whether he has struck his colors, to which Captain John Paul Jones replies with the immortal words, "I have not yet begun to fight."

Above: *With colors flying high and her deck shrouded by smoke from cannon fire,* Alliance *turns the tables on the British warships* Atalanta *and* Trepassey, *which earlier in the 29 May 1781 engagement had battered the Continental frigate when she was becalmed. Both British ships eventually surrendered. ("USS* Alliance *captures HMS* Atlanta *and HMS* Trepassy, *29 May 1781," Warren, Mariner's Museum, Newport News, VA)*

Below: *French and British men-of-war engage in battle off the Virginia Capes, 1 September 1781. French naval presence doomed the British army at Yorktown, Virginia, prompting Lord Charles Cornwallis to surrender to General George Washington. ("Battle off the Virginia Capes," V. Zveg, Navy Art Collection)*

Serapis eventually strikes her colors, but the victorious *Bonhomme Richard* stays afloat only until the following day. The victorious crew returns to shore on board the vanquished ship.

28 October
The Continental Congress passes a resolution creating the Board of Admiralty for administration of the Continental Navy.

7 November
Confederacy is almost completely dismasted during her voyage to France. Only the skilled seamanship of her crew prevents the frigate's loss. Among those on board are John Jay, the first American Minister to Spain, and his family. The frigate puts into Martinique for repairs.

23 November
Ships under the command of Captain Abraham Whipple set sail from Boston, Massachusetts, bound for Charleston, South Carolina, to support the defenders of the city in an anticipated attack by British forces.

8 December
The Continental Congress orders the referral of all future marine matters to the Board of Admiralty, thus ending the tenure of the Marine Committee.

Right: *The surrender of the British at Yorktown, Virginia, on 19 October 1781 ended the American Revolution. American General Benjamin Lincoln is at the center on a white horse with French officers on the left and Americans on the right, led by General George Washington on the brown horse. The British were represented by officers, but Lord Cornwallis himself was not present. ("Surrender of Lord Cornwallis," John Trumbull, U.S. Capitol)*

1780

10 April
The Continental sloop *Saratoga*, the first of six ships so named, is launched at Philadelphia, Pennsylvania.

4 May
The Board of Admiralty adopts the first American naval seal.

12 May
The besieged city of Charleston, South Carolina, falls to the British with devastating consequences for the Continental Navy. While crewmen are able to sink the frigate *Queen of France* before British forces reach her, the frigates *Boston* and *Providence* and the sloop *Ranger* are all captured.

1 June
Trumbull, the last surviving frigate of the thirteen authorized by the Continental Congress in 1775, engages the British ship *Watt* in the Atlantic. "Upon the whole there has not been a more close, obstinate and bloody engagement," a participant later writes. The two ships batter one another from ranges between fifty and eighty yards, suffering 21 killed and 110 wounded between them, until *Watt* withdraws.

9 June
Protector, a ship of the Massachusetts state navy, engages the British privateer *Admiral Duff* off the New England coast. For one and one-half hours, the American ship trades broadsides with her British counterpart until the latter is set afire and explodes. *Protector*'s crew pulls survivors from the water, though some continue to fight their would-be rescuers.

1781

9 March
The Continental frigate *Alliance*, under the command of Captain John Barry, anchors in Groix Roads, France, disembarking Colonel John Laurens, the Continental Congress's envoy to France; *Common Sense* author Thomas Paine; Continental Army officer William Jackson; and the Viscount de Noailles, cousin of the Marquis de Lafayette.

18 March
Captain John Young, captain of the sloop *Saratoga*, places a prize crew on board a captured British merchantman off Cape Francois, Haiti, and pursues a second enemy vessel. While the prize crew makes efforts to follow *Saratoga*, their vessel is caught in a fierce wind and almost capsizes. Regaining control, they no longer see *Saratoga* and no trace of her is ever found.

2 April
The frigate *Alliance* engages the British privateer sloops *Mars* and *Minerva*, capturing both vessels after a brief exchange of cannon fire.

7 May
Foreshadowing the shifting fortunes of the Continental Navy, Captain John Paul Jones pens a letter to General

George Washington, stating, "The importance and necessity of a marine establishment does not appear sufficiently impressed on the minds of our Legislature."

29 May

Alliance engages the British sloops of war *Atalanta* and *Trepassey*. The wind dies, rendering the large American frigate powerless to maneuver, and the smaller enemy ships move into firing position. In the bombardment, Captain John Barry suffers a shoulder wound and loses consciousness. His ship is on the verge of striking her colors when Barry awakens and denies the request of his executive officer to surrender. The wind having come up, *Alliance* maneuvers to unleash broadsides against her adversaries, knocking *Trepassey* out and forcing *Atalanta* to strike her colors.

28 August

Her fore-topmast and main topgallantmast damaged in a storm, *Trumbull* fights the British ships *Iris* and *General Monk* in a one hour and thirty-five minute engagement before Captain James Nicholson reluctantly strikes his colors. *Trumbull* is the last of the thirteen frigates originally authorized by Congress in 1775, and, ironically, *Iris* is the former Continental frigate *Hancock*.

1 September

A French fleet under Comte Francois De Grasse traps British forces under Lord Charles Cornwallis at

Yorktown, Virginia, and on 26 September defeats a British fleet off the Virginia coast. Isolated from friendly ships and besieged by French and American forces, Cornwallis surrenders to General George Washington on 19 October 1781.

Opposite, top: *("HMS General Monk Engages the Pennsylvania State Ship Hyder Ally off Cape May, New Jersey, 8 April 1782," L. P. Crepin, U.S. Naval Academy Museum)*

Opposite, bottom: *("Portrait of Robert Morris," Charles Wilson Peale, University of Michigan)*

Right: *The frigate* Alliance, *the Continental Navy's last ship. ("USS* Alliance," *U.S. Naval Academy Museum)*

7 September
Robert Morris of Pennsylvania, elected Superintendent of Finance by the Continental Congress the previous February, is assigned the duties of Agent of Marine and assumes control of naval matters.

1782

8 April
Hyder Ally, purchased by Philadelphia merchants to combat the British ship *General Monk* (the former Rhode Island privateer *General Washington*), engages her at the entrance to Delaware Bay. After a fierce engagement of one half hour, *General Monk* strikes her colors. She is taken into service by the state of Pennsylvania and her original name is restored.

1783

9 March
The frigate *Alliance*, protecting *Duc de Lauzun*, which carries a valuable cargo of gold from Havana for the Continental Congress, engages *Sybil*. Despite his ship being hit by a shot from the British warship, Captain John Barry holds his fire until *Alliance* is at point blank range, then unleashes a broadside. After a forty-minute engagement, *Sybil* retires. This marks the last naval engagement of the American Revolution.

12 March
General Washington, now a Continental Navy vessel, arrives in Philadelphia, Pennsylvania, with a preliminary copy of the treaty ending the Revolution.

24 March
Upon receiving news of agreement on specific articles of peace between British and American officials, the Continental Congress directs Agent of Marine Robert Morris to recall all armed Continental Navy vessels.

1784

8 April
Agent of Marine Robert Morris writes to the President of the Continental Congress regarding the sale of vessels to settle wartime debts of the young nation. "As to a marine we must give up the Idea and whenever the Situation of American Finances will permit we can certainly build better Ships than any we have yet had."

1785

25 July
The American merchant schooner *Maria* is seized by "Barbary Pirates," the name given to marauding corsairs of the North African states of Algiers, Tripoli, Tunis, and Morocco. An Algerian corsair seizes a second merchantman, *Dauphin*, on 30 July. A total of twenty-one American sailors are taken prisoner.

1 August
Alliance, the last ship on the rolls of the Continental Navy, is sold in Philadelphia, Pennsylvania.

LIFE AT SEA

by Commander Tyrone G. Martin, U.S. Navy (Retired)

I t was a hard life in the age of sail. Every day was based on alternating four-hour watches around the clock in a constantly rolling, pitching, and yawing world. In the watch on deck, generally one-half the section was allowed to rest easy during the night, permitted to try and catch a nap somewhere between the guns for an hour before changing status with the other half of the section. Similarly, men in the most exposed positions, e.g., in the tops, regularly were relieved to thaw out or dry out a little. Long hours on deck aside, the labor of making, taking in, and adjusting sail was heavy and dangerous, and required the teamwork of the hands involved.

The workday began at first light and continued until evening twilight. The men first stored their hammocks, then went about sweeping and swabbing down the decks. Breakfast was timed so as to feed the ongoing watch and then the offcoming watch. The men were organized in "messes" of eight to twelve who shared the food from a communal pot and took turns getting the food and cleaning up afterwards. Breakfast consisted of bread and cheese, and perhaps some leftovers from earlier issues. After breakfast, the crew broke up into various work parties to maintain the guns, overhaul sails and rigging, and perform other necessary shipboard tasks. Around 10:00 a.m., if necessary, all hands were called to witness punishment, which, according to regulation, was limited to a dozen lashes of the cat-o'-nine-tails per offense. Brutal it was, but swift and generally more effective than less painful punishments.

Dinner was the one hot meal of the day, served around noon in succession to ongoing and offcoming watches. It was mostly salted meat and a starchy vegetable boiled together in the ship's coppers. Tasty it was not, but well-suited to provide the calories needed to support the heavy work. After dinner, the crew was issued its first ration of grog for the day. In the U.S. Navy, it was a tot of bourbon and water. The officers ate an hour after the crew, and the captain still later.

Afternoons were often taken up with general exercises of the great guns, sail-handling, or small arms practice. Otherwise, ship's work resumed. The evening meal, again leftovers or bread and cheese, occurred around 4:00 PM—another watch change—and was followed by another issue of "spirits." At this point the crew was often allowed to relax, sing or dance, or swap sea stories, and then, as the sun began to disappear, the men began a final sweeping of the decks and hammocks were piped down. By the end of evening twilight, all hands off watch were in their hammocks and the master-at-arms and the ship's corporals began prowling below decks to guard against illicit activity. The officers generally were allowed another hour before "lights out."

Life aboard ship was very close and privacy really existed only for the captain. The men were allotted hammocks eighteen inches wide, which were hung on rows of hooks set twenty-three inches apart. The environment was damp and dank, hot or cold as Mother Nature provided, and odiferous. Baths and washing clothes were a rarity. Contagious illness spread quickly, and although the ship's surgeon held daily sick calls, his treatments generally were no more effective and sometimes more deleterious than doing nothing at all. Germs aside, abrasions, broken bones, and hernias were daily occurrences; operations, such as amputations, were acts of last resort and often proved fatal.

The crew was a heterogeneous mix of men from many parts of the world, particularly in the years after the War of 1812. Indeed, by mid-century a crew consisting of more than half aliens was common. In the earliest days, there were prohibitions against

enlisting blacks or Native Americans, but they were observed mostly in the breach and by 1812 had largely been discarded. Pay in the U.S. Navy was rather better than that received by British sailors, for American sailors were volunteers and had to be enticed away from privateer or merchant service. A sliding scale of pensions was available to those suffering permanent injury or loss of limb.

Why did men choose the life? Many reasons: the money, escape from boredom, avoidance of marriage, "three squares a day," and sometimes even patriotism. In any event, go they did, and for many the awesome immensity of the earth and sky as seen from the ocean's surface and the endless variety of that watery domain drew them back again and again.

Left: *The crypt of John Paul Jones in the Naval Academy Chapel serves as an inspiration to future naval leaders. (National Archives)*

Below: *Act by Congress on 2 December 1793 authorizing the establishment of the U.S. Navy, the aquisition of ships, manning levels, pay, and rations. (National Archives)*

Opposite: *Created by French sculptor Jean Antoine Houdon, this is reputed to be the best likeness of John Paul Jones. (Naval Historical Center)*

1786

11 July
U.S. Minister to France Thomas Jefferson, in a letter to the U.S. Minister to England John Adams, favors war over negotiating with the Barbary States in response to the seizing of American merchant vessels. He writes of the necessity for a naval force "of one hundred and fifty guns, the one half of which shall be in constant cruise."

31 July
Responding to the letter from Thomas Jefferson, John Adams writes, "I agree in opinion of the wisdom and necessity of a navy, but am apprehensive it will make bad worse with the Algerines. I will go all lengths with you in promoting a navy, whether to be applied to the Algerines or not."

1787

18 July
The Senate ratifies a treaty between the United States and Morocco, the terms of which provide protection for American merchantmen at sea and in Moroccan ports.

1788

No events of note occur during this year.

1789

7 August
The first United States Congress, convened under the new Constitution, passes a bill establishing the Department of War and assigning responsibility for the nation's naval affairs to the Secretary of War.

1790

No events of note occur during this year.

1791

6 January
The Senate Committee on Mediterranean Trade issues a report stating "that the trade of the United States to the Mediterranean cannot be protected but by naval force."

1792

18 July
John Paul Jones dies alone in Paris, France, having only the previous month been appointed Consul for the United States at the Port of Algiers. He is only twelve days past his forty-fifth birthday.

1793

8 October
Algerian pirates seize the American merchant ships *Dispatch*, *Hope*, and *Thomas* and enslave members of their crews. "We was all stript of all our Cloaths some Came on shore without even a shirt," writes Samuel Calder, "we was immediately put into Chains and put to hard Labour…its not possible to Live long, in this situation." The trio are among eleven American vessels captured by Algeria between April 1791 and December 1795.

1794

27 March
Congress approves the Naval Act of 1794 providing naval armament for the purpose of protecting American commerce from the Barbary Powers. Among its provisions is authorization for the construction of six frigates, the establishment of manpower levels and rates of pay, and a clause suspending the act upon the signing of a peace treaty with Algiers.

5 June
President George Washington appoints six captains to command the frigates authorized by the Naval Act of 1794. The officers are Joshua Barney, John Barry, Richard Dale, Samuel Nicholson, Silas Talbot, and Thomas Truxtun.

19 November
The United States and England sign a treaty that establishes the former's claim for damages from British seizures of American vessels and gives the United States limited trading rights in the West Indies. Called "Jay's Treaty" after its chief negotiator, John Jay, the agreement averts a commercial war between the two nations, though the United States agrees to a broad definition of contraband.

1795

23 February
The U.S. Office of Purveyor of Supplies is established, the birth of the present-day Supply Corps.

5 September
Representatives of the U.S. and Algiers sign a Treaty of Peace and Amity that results in the release of 65 U.S. sailors held captive by the Algerians. The Senate ratifies the treaty on 2 March 1796, thereby suspending construction of the frigates authorized in 1794.

1796

20 April
Congress authorizes completion of *Constitution*,

16 May
President John Adams appears before both houses of Congress and espouses the need for naval power to defend the nation's sovereignty. He urges Congress to allow American merchantmen to defend themselves on the high seas, complete construction of previously approved frigates, and assign other warships to escort unarmed ships.

1 July
Making provisions for war in response to privateering against American shipping by France, Congress authorizes the president to man and employ the frigates *Constitution*, *Constellation*, and *United States*.

11 July
The frigate *United States* is placed in commission at Philadelphia, under the command of Captain John Barry.

28 August
The United States signs a peace treaty with Tunis. It will not be ratified by the Senate until 10 January 1800.

Constellation, and *United States*, three of the frigates originally authorized in 1794.

4 November
The United States concludes a peace treaty with Tripoli, which includes among its articles payment of money and presents to the Pasha of Tripoli for his consideration.

7 December
In his last annual message to Congress, President George Washington expresses his support for the gradual creation of a navy, which he states is indispensable to protect commerce and secure respect for the nation abroad.

1797

2 March
Renouncing some provisions of the Franco-American Treaty of Amity and Commerce of 1778, France expands the list of items considered contraband and declares that vessels not carrying official documents proclaiming clearances for the ship, crew, and cargo are considered legal prizes subject to search and seizure. The measure is a veritable declaration of war on American commerce and comes after French privateers have seized American merchantmen.

This morning, precisely at 9 o'clock, at the navy-yard of major Stodder, the builder, was launched, the UNITED STATES FRIGATE, CONSTELLATION. The novelty of the scene, (she being the first Frigate ever built at this port) drew forth an immense concourse of citizens, of both sexes, and of all ages; and, notwithstanding the earliness of the hour, appointed for the launch, the number, we are warranted in saying, was never equalled on any occasion, in this place. The surface of the Patapsco was covered with innumerable boats, and the adjacent hills east of Harris's Creek, swarmed with spectators; so admirably too were the situations around, that every one had the pleasure of gratifying his curosity, without risking the least accident.

A number of Volunteers, in uniform, were admitted on board, while others were set to guard the yard and permit no one to enter, unless engaged in the business of the day. The workmen, amounting to 200, being thus unobstructed, carried on their work with such regularity and dispatch, as reflected the greatest credit both on themselves and their able conductors.—Every order was communicated by a ruffle from the drum, and the operations of the men in wedging up the vessel &c. were apparently performed with as much exactness and precision, as the manual exercise by a regiment of veterans.

The anxious moment now arrived—and now description is beggared.—Every thing being in the most complete preparation—all the blocks taken away, every man from under the vessel, and the hull standing on almost nothing but the slippery tallow, orders were given for knocking away the last staunchion. This being done, she moved gracefully and majestically down her ways, amidst the silent amazement of thousands of spectators, to her destined element, into which she plunged with such ease and safety, as to make the hills resound with reiterated bursts of joyful exclamations. Her plunge into the water was attended with so little velocity that she came to anchor within 100 yards of the shore, and we can pronounce, from the authority of able and experienced judges, that no vessel was ever taken from the stocks in a more safe and judicious manner than the CONSTELLATION; and that no man, on a similar

7 September

The frigate *Constellation* is launched at Baltimore, Maryland, and placed under the command of Captain Thomas Truxtun. She is the U.S. Navy's second frigate, and possesses such speed under sail that she receives the nickname "Yankee Race Horse."

21 October

The frigate *Constitution* is launched at Boston, Massachusetts, and placed under the command of Captain Samuel Nicholson.

1798

18 January

France issues a decree stating that any ship, of whatever nationality, carrying British goods is subject to capture.

9 March

Dr. George Balfour of Virginia receives an appointment as the U.S. Navy's first surgeon.

27 April

In response to the notorious XYZ affair in which French officials attempted to bribe American negotiators seeking to end French privateering, Congress authorizes President John Adams to acquire, arm, and man twelve vessels to defend American shipping.

30 April

A bill signed into law by President John Adams establishes the Department of the Navy and provides for a secretary and clerical staff. The salary for the post of Secretary of the Navy is set at $3,000.

1 May

President John Adams nominates George Cabot, a former Massachusetts senator, as the first Secretary of the Navy, a position that he declines.

3 May

Government agents purchase the merchantman *Ganges* at Philadelphia, Pennsylvania, the first warship made ready for sea to conduct operations in the so-called Quasi-War with France. Under the command of Captain Richard Dale, she is one of eight merchantmen purchased by the United States and outfitted with cannon for combat operations.

Opposite, top: *("George Washington," Charles M. Lang, Navy Art Collection)*

Opposite, bottom: *Newspaper report published in* The Time Piece, *New York, recounting the frigate* Constellation's *launching in Baltimore, Maryland, on 7 September 1797. (Naval Historical Center)*

Above: *Launching of the frigate* Constitution *at Boston, Massachusetts, 21 October 1797. ("The Launching of the* Constitution," *Naval Historical Center)*

4 May

Congress authorizes President John Adams to buy or build ten vessels for defense of the United States.

5 May

Government agents purchase the merchant vessel *Hamburgh Packet* for service in the U.S. Navy. Renamed *Delaware*, she is placed under the command of Captain Stephen Decatur, Sr.

23 May

The Navy purchases *Adriana* and renames her *Baltimore*, placing her under the command of Captain Isaac Phillips.

28 May

President John Adams instructs public armed vessels to make reprisals against France by seizing and bringing into port any vessels of that nation engaging in privateering against American commerce off the coast of the United States.

18 June

Benjamin Stoddert, a Continental Army officer and Secretary of the Board of War during the Revolutionary War, takes office as the first Secretary of the Navy. "I cannot believe he will accept," one observer incorrectly surmised upon hearing of President John Adams's appointment of Stoddert. "He appeared to be a man of good sense."

23 June

The frigate *Constellation* puts to sea to patrol a section of the East Coast in search of French privateers. Her commanding officer, Captain Thomas Truxtun, spent many of his years at sea during the American Revolution in command of privateers.

25 June

Congress passes legislation permitting the arming of merchantmen.

30 June

Congress authorizes President John Adams to procure twelve additional ships by gift or loan for service in the U.S. Navy. The same act also authorizes construction of *President*, *Congress*, and *Chesapeake*, the remaining three of the frigates authorized in 1794.

7 July

Maneuvering *Delaware* cautiously in a manner that makes her appear to be a merchantman, Captain Stephen Decatur, Sr., draws the attention of the French privateer *Le Croyable* in the waters off New York. Pursuing the enemy vessel into Egg Harbor, *Delaware* forces her to strike her colors, the first prize captured by the U.S. Navy during the Quasi-War.

9 July

President John Adams signs an act authorizing operations by American warships and privateers against French armed vessels.

16 July

Congress authorizes construction of the remaining three frigates, originally authorized on 27 March 1794, on which work had been halted.

29 July

The British schooner *Mosquito*, mistaking the United States schooner *Unanimity* for a French privateer, gives chase to the American vessel and fires upon her, causing the ship to run aground on a sand bar at Dewee's Inlet, South Carolina. With *Unanimity* suffering only minor damage, the incident does not strain diplomatic relations between the two countries.

30 July

Secretary of the Navy Benjamin Stoddert, in a letter to President John Adams, outlines the strategy for the U.S. Navy in hostilities against France. He advocates offensive operations in the Caribbean, carrying "the war to their own ground." On this date the U.S. Navy has a total of five ships at sea.

22 August

The frigate *United States*, under the command of Captain John Barry, pursues the French schooner *Sans Pareil* for ten hours before capturing her near the passage between the islands of Martinique and Dominica. The prize is the first for an American frigate and the first French ship captured in the Caribbean in the Quasi-War.

8 September

With Captain Samuel Nicholson ordering all sails set, *Constitution* pursues her first quarry off Cape Hatteras, North Carolina. Despite the fact that the ship runs up English colors, she is treated as a suspected pirate vessel until she heaves to. Though captained by a Fenchman, *Niger* is indeed a British vessel, but is nevertheless taken as the new frigate's first prize.

Opposite, top: *Benjamin Stoddert was the first Secretary of the Navy . ("Benjamin Stoddert," E. F. Andrews, Department of the Navy)*

Opposite, bottom: Delaware *captures her first prize, the French privateer* La Croyable, *off New York, 7 July 1798. (Naval Historical Center)*

Above: *("President John Adams (1735–1826)," Asher B. Durand, U.S. Naval Academy Museum)*

19 September

The frigates *Delaware* and *United States* and two prizes return to Philadelphia after a cruise in the Caribbean. "Upon the whole it is better than to have kept ships sleeping on our own shore," Secretary of the Navy Benjamin Stoddert writes of the first extended cruise of American naval vessels during the Quasi-War. "Tho' the result of the enterprise falls very short of my hopes."

30 September

The frigates *Baltimore* and *Constellation* depart Havana, Cuba, escorting forty-seven merchant vessels to Norfolk, Virginia. That night the British schooner *Nancy* infiltrates the convoy and comes alongside *Baltimore*, whose crew boards the English vessel. A number of American citizens serving in *Nancy*'s crew volunteer to transfer to serve in *Baltimore* before the British vessel is ordered away from the convoy.

12 October

The merchant vessel *George Washington* is purchased at Philadelphia and converted to a warship. Her first commanding officer is Captain Patrick Fletcher.

16 November

The frigate *Baltimore*, escorting a convoy to Havana, Cuba, happens upon a squadron of British warships that signals the convoy to stop. Ignoring the fact that the captain of the American ship hands over his sailing orders from the Secretary of the Navy as proof, the British treat *Baltimore* as a private merchantman and impress five members of her crew. The American captain, Isaac Phillips, is dismissed from the service for not resisting the British actions and an order is issued for U.S. Navy ships to "repel such outrage on the honor of the American flag."

Left: *Commodore John Barry as he appeared during the Quasi-War. ("John Barry," Gilbert Stuart, Navy Art Collection)*

Below: *Commodore Thomas Truxtun first went to sea in the merchant service and was a privateersman during the American Revolution, commanding* Independence, Mars, *and* St. James *operating in British waters. Appointed a captain in the new U.S. Navy in 1794, he superintended the construction of* Constellation *and, as her commanding officer, captured* l'Insurgente *and engaged* La Vengeance *in the West Indies. He also was the first Commanding Officer of the frigate* President. *(Naval Historical Center)*

Opposite: *The frigate* United States, *ceremoniously dressed with the flags of European and Mediterranean powers during her overseas service. (Navy Art Collection)*

23 November
The crew of the American schooner *Retaliation*, believing two frigates sailing nearby to be British ships, is surprised when the pair unleash broadsides against them. The French ships, *l'Insurgente* and *Volontaire*, capture *Retaliation*, but fail to pursue nearby vessels of a U.S. Navy squadron after being convinced of their superiority by *Retaliation*'s skipper, Lieutenant William Bainbridge, thus bypassing the chance to inflict a terrible blow on the American war effort.

Secretary of the Navy Benjamin Stoddert proposes the construction of twelve ships-of-the-line, twelve frigates, and twenty lesser ships.

29 December
The first annual report of the Secretary of the Navy is submitted to Congress, a practice that continues until December 1948.

1799

16 January
Constitution pursues two French ships in the waters near Bermuda, but a sudden storm thwarts her attempt to overtake them. The weather clears, allowing the frigate to capture one of the vessels, a British merchantman taken as a prize by the French. *Constitution*'s captain, Samuel Nicholson, decides to return the vessel to the prize crew over fears that he has no authority to recapture English merchant vessels. This action contributes to Nicholson eventually being moved to a shore command.

17 January
An American squadron under the command of Captain Thomas Truxtun arrives at St. Kitts in the Lesser Antilles, which becomes the U.S. Navy's primary operating base in the Caribbean during the Quasi-War.

THE WASHINGTON NAVY YARD

by Dr. Edward J. Marolda

Throughout much of the nineteenth and twentieth centuries, when one thought of the U.S. Navy in the nation's capital, the Washington Navy Yard, the country's oldest naval installation, came naturally to mind. Many of the Navy's early warships, including the storied frigate *Constitution*, put in at the Washington shipyard for repairs, refits, and provisions. During the early years of the republic, shipbuilding was the main activity at the Washington Navy Yard. There, the Navy built the seventy-four-gun ship-of- the-line *Columbus*, frigate *Potomac*, and vessels of President Thomas Jefferson's coastal defense fleet. Later in the eighteenth century, yard shops manufactured small arms, anchor, chain, and other equipment.

Before the Civil War the Washington Navy Yard took on another important function—the design, testing, and manufacture of naval guns. Commander John H. Dahlgren, "the father of American naval ordnance," operated an experimental gun battery on the navy yard shore of the Potomac's Eastern Branch, later called the Anacostia River. Established in 1886, the Naval Gun Factory gave birth over the next seventy-five years to many of the Navy's weapons, including the huge 14-inch and 16-inch rifles that armed naval railway batteries in World War I and *Iowa*-class battleships in World War II and the Cold War.

The Washington Navy Yard was also home to the Experimental Model Basin, the nation's first facility for scientifically testing prototype ship hulls. Under pioneering naval engineer Rear Admiral David W. Taylor, the EMB's staff evaluated the seagoing properties of many new hull designs. Much of the early work on seaplanes, shipboard catapults, and other naval aviation equipment was directed by navy yard activities. Appropriately, in 1922 *Langley* (CV 1), the Navy's first aircraft carrier, moored at the yard.

The history of the Washington Navy Yard is intertwined with that of the nation. When British troops invaded the capital in 1814, the attackers burned not only the White House but also structures in the navy yard. (The U.S. Navy burned other structures and vessels to deny them to the British.) Spared by the enemy, however, were several buildings constructed during the first years of the nineteenth century. Latrobe Gate, created by Benjamin Latrobe, one of the original architects of Washington, D.C., graces the northern perimeter of the yard. Quarters A, more commonly known as Tingey House after Captain Thomas Tingey, first Commandant of the Washington Navy Yard, has since 1978 served as the official residence of the Chief of Naval Operations. Quarters B, occupied in 1814 by subordinate naval officers, currently is the home of the Commandant, Naval District Washington.

Names that resonate with the history of America are also connected to the Washington Navy Yard. President John Quincy Adams bid farewell there to the Marquis de Lafayette when the French fighter for liberty sailed for his home country in 1824. In 1860, the first delegation sent to the United States by the emperor of Japan following Commodore Matthew C. Perry's path-breaking call at Tokyo six years earlier arrived at the navy yard.

The Navy's Washington base played a prominent role during the Civil War. Union naval and land forces deployed from there to battle the Confederates on the rivers of Virginia and North Carolina and along the East Coast. During this period the yard was host to important figures in American history, including President Abraham Lincoln, who frequently visited the commandant, his friend John Dahlgren. Lincoln's assassin, John Wilkes Booth, also is connected with the yard. Union officials autopsied his body on board a Union monitor anchored in the Anacostia. Rafael Semmes, commander of the famous Confederate raider *Alabama*, was imprisoned at the yard for several months after the war.

In 1907, President Theodore Roosevelt traveled from the Washington Navy Yard to Norfolk, Virginia, in his yacht *Mayflower* to launch the "Great White Fleet" on its historic round-the-world cruise. Since *Sequoia*, *Williamsburg*, and other yachts were based at the navy yard for use by the Commander in Chief and the Secretary of the Navy for much of the twentieth century, presidents and first ladies were frequent

visitors to the site. Other notable figures in American history who passed through Latrobe Gate included Charles A. Lindbergh, who returned by ship from France after his epic flight across the Atlantic in 1927. Franklin and Eleanor Roosevelt welcomed King George VI and Queen Elizabeth to the United States in 1939. Emperor Hirohito joined President Gerald R. Ford on board *Sequoia* for a cruise from the navy yard to Mount Vernon and back in 1975.

With a decline in the Navy's need for guns in the 1960s, the Naval Weapons Plant, formerly the Naval Gun Factory, was disestablished and the Washington Navy Yard increasingly took on administrative and ceremonial functions. In the last half of the twentieth century it became home to the Military Sealift Command, Naval Sea Systems Command, Naval Historical Center, Marine Corps Historical Center, and other Navy Department organizations. Ceremonies to welcome foreign dignitaries, present awards, mark retirements from the service, and commemorate the epic World War II victory at Midway occur frequently in the yard's Leutze Park, known as the "Quarterdeck of the Navy." In that regard, President George W. Bush visited the navy yard for an official function honoring the Australian prime minister one day before the fateful events of 11 September 2001.

Tens of thousands of American men and women toiled within the walls of the Washington Navy Yard. Throughout its history, skilled workmen, laborers, naval officers, bluejackets, and Marines built naval vessels in the ship houses, stoked fires in the massive furnaces of the gun factory, or hosted official visitors in Leutze Park. Indeed, the Washington Navy Yard has made important contributions to the success of the United States and the U.S. Navy in most of America's nineteenth- and twentieth-century military endeavors.

Above: *A view of the Washington Navy Yard during the Civil War showing ship repair facilities and smokestacks signaling that war production is in full gear. (Naval Historical Center)*

Below : *Leutze Park is at the center of this aerial view of the Washington Navy Yard taken during the 1990s. The bow of the destroyer* Barry *(DD 933), named for the famed Revolutionary War hero Commodore John Barry, is visible in the upper right corner. (Naval Historical Center)*

Left: *In 1794, Captain Thomas Truxtun asked naval architect Josiah Fox for a drawing of his design for spars and rigging for a 44-gun frigate. He later commissioned two Chinese porcelain punchbowls featuring Fox's drawing inside the bowl. Truxtun used one, and presented the other to President George Washington. (Naval Historical Center)*

Opposite: *The frigate* Boston *captured eight prizes in the Caribbean during the Quasi-War with France. ("Frigate* Boston," *James A. Flood, U.S. Naval Institute)*

21 January
The frigate *General Greene* is launched at Warren, Rhode Island, and placed under the command of Captain Christopher R. Parry.

3 February
The frigate *United States*, after chasing the French privateer *L'Amour de la Patrie* for five hours, pulls within range of the enemy ship and opens fire. The third round passes through the French ship, leaving her close to foundering. She sinks, but the crew of the American frigate manages to pull fifty-eight prisoners from the water. They are later exchanged for American prisoners held on Guadaloupe.

8 February
The British ship *Solebay* fires shots at a convoy escorted by American warships in the waters near Cuba. In

Right: *The frigate* Constellation *battles the French frigate* l'Insurgente *on 9 February 1799. Writes Captain Thomas Truxtun to the Secretary of the Navy following his victory, "[she] is esteemed one of the fastest sailing Ships in the French Navy. I have been much shattered in my Rigging and Sails, and my fore top Mast rendered from Wounds useless; you may depend the Enemy is not less so." ("High Seas Diplomacy," Tom W. Freeman)*

response to the request of the British captain to search the ships of the convoy, Captain Stephen Decatur, Sr., of *Delaware* refuses to stop, later writing that he was "hurt at seeing the flag over my head insulted."

9 February
Constellation engages the French frigate *l'Insurgente* in the Caribbean, the two ships unleashing their first broadsides at a range of only fifty yards. The ensuing close-range battle lasts almost an hour until Captain Michel Pierre Barreaut orders the French flag hauled down from its position atop his battered ship. "I must confess the most gratifying sight my eyes ever beheld was seventy French pirates…wallowing in their gore, twenty-nine of whom were killed and forty-one wounded," writes Lieutenant John Rodgers of boarding the captured vessel.

21 February
Officers from the British ship *Surprize* board *Ganges* off Cape Nichola Mole, Hispaniola, demanding the surrender of all Englishmen on board. Captain Thomas Tingey replies with the words, "A public ship carries no protection but her flag. I do not expect to succeed in a contest with you; but I will die at my quarters before a man shall be taken from the ship." His resoluteness avoids an incident. Ironically, the American skipper is a native of Great Britain.

5 March
Escorting a convoy off Havana, a squadron consisting of the frigates *Baltimore* and *General Greene* under the command of Captain Stephen Decatur, Sr., captures the French vessel *le Marsouin*, an armed privateer masquerading as a merchantman.

12 March
The U.S. Navy receives orders to search suspicious French ships and retake any armed prizes captured by France.

12 May
Montezuma, under the command of Captain Alexander Murray, returns to Philadelphia, Pennsylvania, after completing an extended cruise in which she participated in the capture of two French vessels, convoyed over 100

ships, and served on all four of the U.S. Navy's operating stations in the West Indies theater. Her cruise is one of the longest of the Quasi-War.

20 May
The frigate *Boston* is launched at Boston, Massachusetts, and commissioned soon afterwards under the command of Captain George Little.

28 May
Captain Silas Talbot is appointed to command of *Constitution*, relieving Captain Samuel Nicholson. A privateer captain who was captured by the British during the American revolution, Talbot gains an illustrious reputation for the frigate.

5 June
The frigate *John Adams* is launched near Charleston, South Carolina, and eventually placed under the command of Captain George Cross.

8 June
The frigate *Adams* is launched at New York. Her first skipper, Captain R. V. Morris, assumes command upon her completion later in the year.

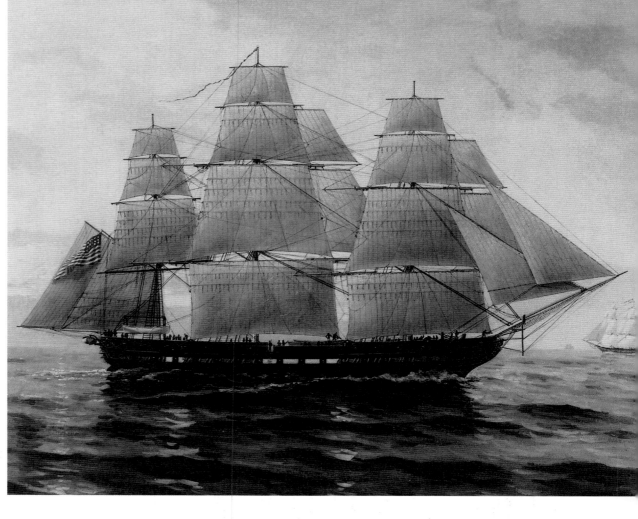

Opposite, top: *A veteran of service in two wars, Commodore Isaac Chauncey served in the U.S. Navy for forty years.* ("Commodore Isaac Chauncey, USN," Gilbert Stuart, U.S. Naval Academy Museum)

Opposite, bottom: *Plan of the frigate* Congress's *spars and sails, circa 1819.* ("USS Congress," C. Ware, National Archives)

Right: *Sails unfurled, the frigate* Chesapeake *plows through open seas.* ("USS Chesapeake," F. Muller, Navy Art Collection)

26 June

President John Adams decides to lift the U.S. embargo on St. Domingo on Hispaniola, creating the need for U.S. Navy warships to protect American commerce in the waters surrounding the port. Trade resumes on 1 August.

28 June

With one broadside, the brig *Merrimack* captures the French schooner *Magicienne*, which before her capture seven months earlier had carried the name *Retaliation* and sailed with the U.S. Navy.

27 July

The frigate *General Greene* returns to Newport, Rhode Island, after a brief cruise to Cuban waters to protect American commerce against Matanzas pirates. Her hasty return is the result of a yellow fever epidemic that sweeps the ship, killing twenty members of the crew and afflicting thirty-seven others.

1 August

Upset over a presidential decision making Captain Silas Talbot senior to him in rank, Captain Thomas Truxtun resigns his commission in the U.S. Navy. "This avarice of rank in the infancy of our service is the devil," writes Secretary of the Navy Benjamin Stoddert.

13 August

The sloop *George Washington*, the first ship of a force that eventually encompasses ten U.S. Navy vessels, arrives in the waters off Hispaniola to protect American commerce. Between August 1799 and July 1800, the squadron captures twenty French privateers.

14 August

Insurgent, the former French frigate *l'Insurgente* captured by the frigate *Constellation* on 9 February, 1799, sets sail for Gibraltar under the command of Captain Alexander Murray. "I feel an ambition to hoist our flag in the European seas," he writes before his departure. *Insurgent* arrives at Gibraltar on 21 September.

15 August

The frigate *Congress* is launched at Portsmouth, New Hampshire, some five years after construction of the ship begins. Her first commanding officer is Captain James Sever.

30 September

The frigate *Essex*, built at Salem, Massachusetts, and paid for by the people of Essex county, is launched. She is presented to the U.S. Navy on 17 December 1799, and accepted by her first commanding officer, Captain Edward Preble.

2 October

The Washington Navy Yard is established. Still active today as a headquarters and administrative center, it is the U.S. Navy's oldest shore establishment.

3 November
The frigate *United States* departs Newport, Rhode Island, bound for France carrying envoys Chief Justice Oliver Ellsworth and North Carolina Governor William Richardson seeking to negotiate peace.

10 November
Delaware and the revenue cutter *Scammel* arrive at Curacao, a base for pirates attacking American merchant ships. The ships remain in port as a show of force.

18 November
The French corsair *l'Egypte Conquise* descends upon the brig *Pickering* in the waters off Guadeloupe. Undaunted by the fact that his ship is outgunned and undermanned, *Pickering*'s skipper, Lieutenant Benjamin Hillar, engages in a running gun battle and forces the French ship to strike her colors after she proves unable to get into position to fire a broadside.

Above: *Pirates attack the schooner* Experiment *in the Caribbean, 1 January 1800. (Naval Historical Center)*

Left: *A party from the frigate* Constitution, *embarked in the sloop* Sally, *boards the French privateer* Sandwich *in the harbor of Puerto Plata, Dominican Republic, 11 May 1800. A party is landing to spike the guns of the fort. (*"Capture of a French-Ship by the* Constitution," *R. Salmon, Boston Athanaeum)*

2 December

The frigate *Chesapeake* is launched at the Gosport Navy Yard in Virginia. Commissioned in early 1800, she is placed under the command of Captain Samuel Barron.

25 December

Persuaded to return to the service of his country with word that peace with France is near at hand and time is short for gathering "laurels," Captain Thomas Truxtun takes the frigate *Constellation* to sea bound for St. Kitts.

1800

1 January

In the early morning hours boats carrying some 500 pirates approach a convoy escorted by the schooner *Experiment* anchored south of St. Marc. When the boats close to musket range, *Experiment*'s crew unleashes a hail of fire that sinks two of them and forces the intruders to retire. *Experiment* beats back a second attack and over the course of the day expends all her grapeshot. Though no U.S. Navy men are killed, two merchantmen are captured.

1 February

The frigate *Constellation* and the French frigate *la Vengeance*, after a chase that had consumed much of the day, engage in night action in the waters west of Guadeloupe. For five hours the two frigates exchange broadsides under the light of battle lanterns and the flame of their cannon. His first attempt at surrender having gone unnoticed, the French captain strikes his colors in the early morning of 2 February. However, a fallen mainmast prevents *Constellation*'s crew from pursuing their prize, which drifts away into the darkness.

27 February

The frigate *General Greene*, under the command of Captain Christopher Raymond Perry, lends support to an assault on Jacmel during an uprising in Hispaniola, as forces under General François-Dominique Toussaint L'Ouverture seize forts in the city from forces under the command of André Rigaud.

Above: *On 1 February 1800 the frigate* Constellation *engaged the French frigate* la Vengeance *in a five-hour battle. The latter ship struck her colors several times, but this was not observed on board* Constellation. *With* Constellation's *mast shot away,* la Vengeance *eluded capture. ("USS* Constellation *Engages the French Frigate* Vengeance *1 February 1800," Warren, Mariner's Museum, Newport News, VA)*

5 April

The frigate *Philadelphia* is commissioned in her name city under the command of Captain Stephen Decatur, Sr. During her first cruise between May 1800 and March 1801, she captures five French armed vessels and recaptures six merchant ships previously captured by French privateers.

10 April

The frigate *President* is launched at New York, and placed under the command of Commodore Thomas Truxtun.

11 May

Employing a subterfuge in an attempt to capture the French privateer *Sandwich*, sailors and Marines under the command of Lieutenant Isaac Hull with two Marine officers hide in the hold of the merchant ship *Sally* as she enters Puerto Plata harbor. Coming alongside *Sandwich*, the men spring from the hold and go "aboard like devils," capturing the enemy vessel. Marines also spike the guns of a nearby Spanish fort.

13 June

The crew of the frigate *John Adams* captures the French schooner *Decade*, the ninth ship seized during the frigate's cruise to the West Indies.

3 August

The sloop-of-war *Trumbull* captures the French schooner *Vengeance*, whose passengers include officers of one of the rival factions in the civil war on Hispaniola and their wives and children.

8 August

Under the command of Captain William Bainbridge, the sloop *George Washington* departs Philadelphia, Pennsylvania, carrying a load of stores and timber as tribute to the Dey of Algiers. Arriving at her destination in September, she is the first American warship to enter the Mediterranean, though she will not be the last as the American policy of attempting to buy protection from the Barbary pirates through tribute soon gives way to war.

ed States Frigate *President* 44 guns, Flagship of the American Squadron, Captain Stephen Decatur

The frigate *Insurgent* departs Hampton Roads, Virginia, for her station in the West Indies. She is never heard from again and is presumed lost in a storm that strikes the area on 20 September.

20 August
The brig *Pickering* sails from Newcastle, Delaware, bound for Guadeloupe in the West Indies. She is never seen again, presumed lost at sea with all hands in a gale.

23 September
The sloop *Patapsco* enters St. Ana Bay at Curacao in support of an effort to break a French siege. Braving fire from French batteries on shore for two hours as her sailors and Marines return fire, *Patapsco* successfully reaches a position from which she lands her leathernecks the following morning. Two days later the brig *Merrimack*, patrolling the coast, discovers that French forces have withdrawn from the island.

1 October
The schooner *Experiment*, after being pursued by a French brig and schooner off St. Barts, turns on the latter ship and forces her to strike after one broadside. The ship is *la Diana* and among those captured is General André Rigaud.

12 October
The frigate *Boston* and the French corvette *le Berceau* engage in a night battle, fighting to a draw despite the American ship's superior firepower. Preparing to resume the engagement the following morning after separating during the night, the French ship's foremast and mainmast collapse and her captain strikes his colors. She is one of eight prizes captured by *Boston* during the ship's fall 1800 cruise on the Guadeloupe station in the West Indies.

16 October
In a meeting with American consul James L. Cathcart, Yusuf Caramanli, the Pasha of Tripoli, demands payment of either an annuity or sum of cash as a price for keeping the peace in the Mediterranean.

28 November
The frigate *Essex* arrives in New York after a cruise of nearly eleven months to the Indian Ocean, during which she becomes the first U.S. warship to twice round the Cape of Good Hope.

Opposite: *The frigate* President *showed the American flag in the Mediterranean Sea during the first Barbary War and cruised during the War of 1812 until her capture by the British in 1815. (Naval Historical Center)*

Above: *The schooner* Experiment *captures the French brig* la Diana *in the Caribbean on 1 October 1800. ("USS* Experiment *vs.* Diana," *Captain William Bainbridge Hoff, Navy Art Collection)*

1801

3 February
The Senate approves the Treaty of Mortefontaine, signed the previous September, ending the Quasi-War with France. During two years of war a U.S. Navy averaging just sixteen ships had captured eighty-six French privateers.

18 February
Benjamin Stoddert tenders his resignation as Secretary of the Navy. He executes the duties of his office until 31 March.

3 March
President John Adams signs the Peace Establishment Act, which stipulates that the Navy maintain a force of thirteen frigates, six of which are to be kept in active service. The bill also includes cuts in the officer corps, directing the retention of only 9 captains, 36 lieutenants, and 150 midshipmen.

10 May
The Pasha of Tripoli declares war on the United States, beginning a naval war that will last for five years.

20 May
Captain Richard Dale receives instructions from the Navy Department to prepare a squadron consisting of the frigates *Essex, Philadelphia*, and *President* and the schooner *Enterprise* for a cruise to the Mediterranean.

The squadron is intended as a show of force, protecting American commerce and discouraging the demands for presents and favorable treaties on the part of the Barbary States. If a state of war exists upon his arrival, Dale is instructed to wage war on enemy shipping and, in the case of Tripoli, blockade the port.

Right: *Crewmen from* Enterprise *man a boat from which they soon board the shattered Tripolitan corsair* Tripoli, *faintly visible through the smoke that marks the fierce battle between the two ships on 1 August 1801. ("Lieutenant Sterrett Leaving USS* Enterprise *to Board the* Tripoli, *1 August 1801," Rodolfo Claudus, U.S. Naval Academy Museum)*

22 May

Captain Thomas Truxtun turns over command of the frigate *President* to Captain Richard Dale at Hampton Roads, Virginia, writing that she is "the finest frigate that ever floated on the waters of this globe." Truxtun, a hero of the Revolutionary War and the Quasi-War, never commands a ship at sea again and tenders his resignation from the U.S. Navy on 3 March 1802.

29 May

Captain Richard Dale's squadron departs Hampton Roads, Virginia, and sets sail for the Mediterranean.

1 June

Captain William Bainbridge, reflecting the discipline in the U.S. Navy at the time, issues orders regarding relieving watches on board the frigate *Essex*. Punishment for anyone falling asleep at his station or leaving his station before being properly relieved includes riding the "spanker boom," restriction of grog, and placement in irons.

10 June

Ganges, the first armed ship to put to sea for service in the Quasi-War, is ordered sold under the provisions of the Peace Establishment Act. All told, she had played a role in the capture of eleven French vessels.

1 July

The squadron under the command of Captain Richard Dale arrives at Gibraltar. "I am Very sorry to say our Barbary affairs look very gloomy," Dale writes the

Acting Secretary of the Navy the following day, having learned that the Pasha of Tripoli had declared war on the United States in May.

5 July

Civil War naval hero and future admiral David Glasgow Farragut is born in Knoxville, Tennessee.

19 July

Captain Richard Dale writes to the Acting Secretary of the Navy of the deteriorating situation in the Mediterranean, saying that "there is nothing that will keep their avericious minds in any degree of order, and prevent them from commiting depredations on our commerce whenever they May think Proper, but for the United States to keep constantly four or six Frigates in the Mediterranean."

23 July

A circular letter from the American Consulate in Tunis informs European powers in friendship with the United States of the blockade of Tripoli. The following day the frigate *President* takes station in the waters off Tripoli and, aside from one brief absence, remains there until 3 September.

27 July

Robert Smith, a Baltimore lawyer and former Maryland state legislator, assumes office as the second Secretary of the Navy. Smith assumes the duties of Attorney General in 1805, and though Jacob Crowinshield is nominated as his replacement, he never takes office and Smith is never

reconfirmed. Thus, though Smith continues to carry out the duties of the office, officially there is no Secretary of the Navy between 1805 and 1809.

1 August

The schooner *Enterprise* defeats the Tripolitan corsair *Tripoli* after a fierce engagement in the waters west of Malta. According to a report by her skipper, Lieutenant Andrew Sterrett, the "action immediately commenced within pistol shot, which continued three hours incessantly. She then struck her colors…the carnage on board was dreadful; she having 30 men killed and 30 wounded. Her sails, masts and rigging were cut to pieces with 18 shots between wind and water."

3 September

The frigate *President*, low on provisions and with over one hundred members of her crew on the sick list, ceases her blockade of Tripoli and sets course for Gibraltar.

29 September

The frigates *Essex* and *Philadelphia* open fire on Tripolitan gunboats that approach and fire on the American ships as they blockade the coast of Tripoli.

1802

6 February

Congress approves "An Act for the Protection of the Commerce and Seamen of the United States against Tripolitan Cruisers," the terms of which authorize the President of the United States to equip, man, and employ the number of armed vessels that "may be judged requisite" for the protection of American commerce. The measure removes restrictions of the previously passed Peace Establishment Act.

27 April

Commodore Richard Morris, flying his flag in the frigate *Chesapeake*, departs Hampton Roads, Virginia, where he assumes command of a squadron blockading Tripoli and escorting American merchantmen. In addition to *Chesapeake*, the ships under Morris eventually include the frigates *Adams*, *Constellation*, *John Adams*, and *New York* and the schooner *Enterprise*.

22 June

James Simpson, the U.S. consul at Tangiers, receives word of the Sultan of Morocco's declaration of war against the United States. However, the presence of

28 February
In an effort to enforce trading rights on the Mississippi River, the president approves an act of Congress authorizing the construction of gunboats for the U.S. Navy.

12 May
The frigate *John Adams*, under the command of Captain John Rodgers, captures *Meshuda*, the Tripolitan ship blockaded at Gibraltar since 1801 and recently allowed to sail under the flag of Morocco, as she attempts to enter the harbor of Tripoli.

20 May
Commodore Edward Preble assumes command of the frigate *Constitution* at Boston, Massachusetts.

22 May
Having sailed from Malta, the frigates *John Adams* and *New York* and the schooner *Enterprise* arrive on station off Tripoli. Just hours after their arrival, *Enterprise* pursues a ship approaching Tripoli and is taken under

Commodore Richard Morris's Mediterranean Squadron prompts a reversal of the Sultan's decision and Simpson announces the conclusion of a peace on 16 August.

16 May
The frigate *Boston* battles between six and seven Tripolitan gunboats during action in the Mediterranean, forcing one ashore.

23 October
The Secretary of the Navy orders the frigates *Chesapeake* and *Constellation* home from the Mediterranean, leaving just three frigates and one schooner there.

15 December
In a message to Congress, President Thomas Jefferson calls for the construction of a dry dock in Washington, D.C., as an economy measure for the preservation of inactive U.S. Navy ships. The measure is never passed by the legislative branch.

Opposite: *("The fight between the Schooner USS* Enterprise *and Barbary Corsair* Tripoli, *August 1801," Warren, Mariner's Museum, Newport News, VA)*

Above: *("President Thomas Jefferson (1743–1826)," Asher B. Durand, U.S. Naval Academy Museum)*

Right: *("Commodore Richard Dale, USN," John Ford, U.S. Naval Academy Museum)*

fire by shore batteries. She returns fire but fails to capture the vessel, which runs ashore and is unloaded.

23 May

A landing party from the frigate *New York* under the command of Lieutenant David Porter goes ashore west of Tripoli, setting fire to a dozen beached feluccas. The crews engage the Americans in a brief

action before Porter orders his men to retire, having suffered fifteen casualties.

27 May

The frigates *Adams, John Adams,* and *New York* engage nine Tripolitan gunboats escorting a 14-gun xebec into port. *John Adams* fires 108 rounds at the enemy, but the other two ships play a negligible role in the battle and darkness eventually thwarts American efforts.

31 May

The frigate *Adams* and the schooner *Enterprise* corner ten small Tripolitan merchantmen and, throughout the following day, keep them under steady fire to prevent their unloading. Joined by the frigate *New York,* the American force orders the merchantmen alongside, and when the demand is refused dispatch seven boats on 2 June in an attempt to burn them. Two are destroyed, but the cargoes of the others are saved.

7 June

A delegation including Commodore Richard Morris and six officers lands in Tripoli to deliver the American proposal for a peace treaty with Tripoli. The Tripolitans find the terms unacceptable.

21 June

The frigate *John Adams* and the schooner *Enterprise* capture a 22-gun Tripolitan vessel, a blow that greatly weakens the state of Tripoli and allows the U.S. Navy to focus efforts against Tunis, Algiers, and Morocco, which support operations of the Barbary Corsairs.

Angered by Commodore Richard Morris's inactivity and negligence in relaying information about his movements and intentions, the Secretary of the Navy issues orders suspending him from command of the Mediterranean Squadron. He is eventually censured and dismissed from the naval service.

25 June
All U.S. Navy ships depart Tripoli, thus breaking the blockade of that city.

13 July
Commodore Edward Preble, appointed in May to command a new squadron for service in the Mediterranean, receives orders directing him to maintain a blockade of Tripoli. In addition, should any other Barbary States declare war, Preble is to protect American commerce.

26 August
The frigate *Philadelphia*, under the command of Captain William Bainbridge, recaptures the American brig *Celia* from the Moroccan warship *Mirboka*. A search by an armed boarding party led by Lieutenant John S. H. Cox finds the captain of *Celia* and most of his crew held below decks on board *Mirboka*. *Philadelphia* returns to Gibraltar with both ships.

12 September
The frigate *Constitution* arrives at Gibraltar, joining the frigate *Philadelphia*. The following day Commodore Edward Preble writes to U.S. consul to Morocco James Simpson, informing him that he will capture and bring into port any vessel belonging to the Emperor of Morocco.

14 September
Arrivals of American warships result in the presence of the frigates *Constitution*, *John Adams*, *New York*, and *Philadelphia* and the schooners *Nautilus* and *Vixen* in Gibraltar. Between them the ships mount 168 guns.

Opposite, top: *Commodore Edward Preble's courage and inspirational leadership in the first Barbary War influenced a generation of naval officers, who were known collectively as "Preble's Boys." ("Commodore Edward Preble, USN," Rembrandt Peale, U.S. Naval Academy Museum)*

Opposite, bottom: *Operating near Tetuan, Morocco, under Captain William Bainbridge on 26 August 1803, the frigate* Philadelphia *captured the* Mirboka *and her prize, the American brig* Cecilia. *("USS Philadelphia," Naval Historical Center)*

Above: *The schooner* Enterprise *pictured with flags and sails out to dry. (Naval Historical Center)*

Left: *Both the Navy's first destroyer and first nuclear-powered frigate were named after Commodore William Bainbridge. (Naval Historical Center)*

Below: *While blockading Tripoli, the frigate* Philadelphia *chased a small ship close to shore, ran aground on uncharted rocks, and was subsequently captured on 31 October 1803. (Naval Historical Center)*

Opposite: *Naval engagement at Tripoli, 3 August 1804. Commodore Preble's squadron includes (left to right):* Enterprise; Nautilus; Argus; Siren; Vixen; Mortar Boat No. 1; Gunboat No. 1; Constitution; Mortar Boat No. 2; *and* Gunboat No. 3. *Preble's flagship,* Constitution, *successfully bombarded Tripolitan defenses at close range. In the center background are Stephen Decatur's three gunboats, and a gunboat commanded by James Decatur. ("Battle of Tripoli," Michel F. Corne, U.S. Naval Academy Museum)*

17 September

The frigates *Constitution* and *John Adams* arrive at Tangier Bay, Morocco, receiving by boat letters from U.S. consul James Simpson informing of the seizure of an American brig at Mogador, and the intention of the Moroccans to seize other American vessels in port and perhaps at sea.

20 September

The schooner *Enterprise*, under the command of Lieutenant Isaac Hull, arrives at Gibraltar.

1 October

The brig *Syren*, under the command of Lieutenant Charles Stewart, arrives at Gibraltar.

4 October

The frigate *Constitution* and the schooner *Nautilus* drop anchor in the harbor at Tangier, to be joined two days later by the frigates *John Adams* and *New York*. The ships remain there until 14 October, with Commodores Edward Preble and John Rodgers participating in negotiations that result in peace with Morocco.

31 October

The frigate *Philadelphia* runs aground on an uncharted reef off Tripoli Harbor while pursuing a Tripolitan vessel. Her crew makes repeated attempts to refloat her while under fire from shore batteries and gunboats, but Captain William Bainbridge has little choice but to surrender his command. He and his men become prisoners of war, and despite their efforts to destroy their ship, *Philadelphia* falls into enemy hands.

1804

2 February

The brig *Syren*, under the command of Lieutenant Charles Stewart, and the ketch *Intrepid*, under the command of Lieutenant Stephen Decatur, Jr., and manned almost entirely by volunteers from the schooner *Enterprise*, depart Syracuse harbor in the Mediterranean Sea on what is termed a secret expedition.

COMMODORE STEPHEN DECATUR, JR.

by Dr. Michael J. Crawford

Among the officers of the U.S. Navy's formative years, none personified the traditions of courage, honor, and commitment more than Stephen Decatur, Jr. In an era in which personal bravery in battle was the hallmark of a successful naval officer, his daring deeds were unparalleled, while his charismatic leadership won the loyalty of his men.

Decatur's destiny lay with the sea. His father, Stephen Decatur, Sr., a Philadelphia sea captain, merchant, and manufacturer, served as a privateersman during the American Revolution and as a captain in the U.S. Navy during the Quasi-War with France. Stephen, Jr., received his midshipman's warrant in 1798, and his lieutenant's commission the following year while serving in the West Indies during the Quasi-War.

Decatur's extraordinary exploits during the war with Tripoli in 1801–1805 earned him a permanent berth among America's foremost naval heroes. The first of these exploits was the burning of the frigate *Philadelphia.* After the American ship grounded on a reef and was captured by the Tripolitans, Commodore Edward Preble sent a captured ketch into Tripoli Harbor, manned by eighty-five volunteers and disguised as an innocent Mediterranean trader, under Decatur's command. The ketch entered the harbor on the night of 16 February 1804, and its pretended master asked permission to tie up to *Philadelphia* until daybreak. The deceit succeeded until the ketch was nearly alongside, when aboard the frigate the alarm was sounded. Led by Decatur, the boarding party, until then carefully concealed, climbed aboard, dispatched the Tripolitans or forced them overboard, placed combustibles throughout the vessel, and ignited them. Decatur, the last to leave, leapt into the ketch's shrouds as it sought to escape the indraft created by the inferno aboard *Philadelphia* in the final moments before the frigate blew up. No American was killed, and only one wounded. Congress awarded the leader

of the intrepid band with a promotion, and Decatur, twenty-five years old at the time, remains to this day the youngest American naval officer to attain the rank of captain.

The second of Decatur's most notable exploits took place in August of the same year, when Preble's squadron bombarded Tripoli. As the American squadron approached the city at midday on 3 August, Decatur's division of three gunboats went straight for a Tripolitan detachment of nine gunboats guarding an opening in the reef that formed the harbor. Decatur, with nineteen men, boarded the largest of the enemy boats and drove the thirty-six defenders back toward the stern until they surrendered. Taking the gunboat as a prize, he and his men boarded the next enemy vessel, manned by a crew of twenty-four. Decatur engaged the enemy commander, a giant of a man, in hand-to-hand combat. When the two men grappled and fell to the deck, another Tripolitan raised his scimitar to kill the American captain. One of Decatur's men, wounded in both arms, interposed his own head, receiving a dangerous scalp wound. The Tripolitan commander then pinned Decatur under him and drew a knife. Decatur pulled a pistol from his coat and, with the enemy in the crook of his elbow, fired it into his opponent's back. The ball passed up through the Tripolitan's body and struck Decatur, without penetrating. The American tars soon had the enemy gunboat in their possession.

Decatur reached the apex of his career when, in command of the frigate *United States* during the first months of the War of 1812, he captured and brought into port a frigate of the highly vaunted Royal Navy. Encountering *Macedonian* at sea, he maneuvered to take advantage of his ship's superiority in long guns and thereby forced his opponent to strike his flag after the British frigate had suffered a disproportionate share of casualties and damage.

When the War of 1812 ended, Decatur returned to the Mediterranean with a squadron of three

frigates and seven smaller vessels to address a situation with Algiers, which had renewed attacks on American merchantmen. Before the harbor of Algiers, Decatur dictated the terms of peace from the mouths of his ships' cannon, forcing the dey to give up all claims to future tribute. This occurred just forty-one days after the American squadron had set sail from the United States.

When Captain James Barron shot Decatur to death in a duel on 22 March 1820, the commodore stood at the pinnacle of his profession as a member of the Board of Navy Commissioners. Maintenance of honor, pursuit of glory, and promotion of country were the ideals that inspired him. In turn, his personification of those ideals inspired the esteem of his peers and the devotion of his men.

16 February

Under the cover of darkness and disguised as a neutral merchantman, the ketch *Intrepid* slips into Tripoli Harbor. Pretending to have lost her anchor, the ship is permitted to make fast to the captured the frigate *Philadelphia*. Once she is close enough, Lieutenant Stephen Decatur, Jr., leads his men in boarding the American frigate. Overpowering the Tripolitan guards, the Americans set fire to *Philadelphia* before escaping on board *Intrepid* while under fire from enemy gunboats and shore batteries. Decatur is the second man to board and last to leave *Philadelphia*, which, ironically, is a ship once commanded by his father. For his heroic leadership in what Lord Horatio Nelson calls "the most bold and daring act of the age," Decatur is promoted to the rank of captain. At twenty-five years of age, he is the youngest captain in the history of the U.S. Navy.

26 March

Congress enacts a bill that levies an additional import duty, the revenue from which is for use in equipping and operating more frigates for employment in the Mediterranean, the building or purchase of two vessels mounting sixteen guns or less, and the purchase of gunboats in the Mediterranean.

13 May

The King of Naples agrees to lend Commodore

Edward Preble six gunboats and two mortar vessels for use in operations against Tripoli.

7 July

The brigs *Argus*, *Scourge*, and *Syren*, and the schooner *Vixen* pursue a ship attempting to break the American blockade and enter Tripoli Harbor. The vessel runs aground and, with the wind calm, sailors from *Syren* attempt to approach her in boats while other boats tow *Vixen* to within range of the Tripolitan ship. The running gun battle that ensues ends in stalemate.

3 August

The frigate *Constitution*, six gunboats, and two bomb ketches attack Tripoli. The engagement includes spirited and bloody battles with Tripolitan gunboats that include hand-to-hand combat. Lieutenant Stephen Decatur, Jr., personally leads the capture of two Tripolitan gunboats, and suffers minor wounds. His boarding parties kill thirty-three of the enemy and wound nineteen. However, one of the Americans lost in the day's battle is Decatur's brother James, shot in the head while boarding a Tripolitan boat that had tricked the Americans by striking her colors.

7 August

Nine American gunboats, supported by six ships, bombard Tripoli. The force scores some hits against shore batteries, but loses one gunboat whose magazine explodes, killing or wounding most of her crew. Three other gunboats are damaged.

23–24 August

After a reconnaissance of enemy defenses and many aborted attempts, American gunboats bombard Tripoli with relatively little effect.

28 August

In the early morning hours American ships and gunboats attack Tripoli. During a bombardment that lasts some two hours, the gunboats fire an average of forty-two rounds before retiring. After sunrise, *Constitution* fires nine broadsides at Tripolitan gunboats and fortifications on shore.

1 September

Converting the ketch *Intrepid* into a "fire ship," a small crew attempts to sail her into a group of Tripolitan gunboats. However, just a few hundred yards from the target, a sudden change in the wind direction carries her away from the harbor at Tripoli. Two nights later, another attempt is made, and *Intrepid* explodes prematurely after successfully entering the harbor. All thirteen men aboard are lost.

3 September

American gunboats again bombard Tripoli, and when taken under fire by enemy shore batteries, the frigate *Constitution* sails to within 600 yards of Tripoli's fortifications and fires eleven broadsides in forty minutes.

9 September

Commodore Samuel Barron relieves Commodore Edward Preble in command of the Mediterranean Squadron.

Opposite, top: *Page from the log of Midshipman William Lewis kept during his service in the ketch* Intrepid *in 1803. ("USS* Intrepid," *William Lewis, Naval Historical Center)*

Opposite, bottom: *Commodore John Rodgers passed down the tradition of naval service to his son, who rose to the rank of rear admiral, and his great-grandson, who became the U.S. Navy's second aviator. ("Commodore John Rodgers," Unknown Artist, Navy Art Collection)*

Above: *Secretary of the Navy Robert Smith. ("Robert Smith," Freeman Thorpe, Department of the Navy)*

1805

2 March

President Thomas Jefferson signs a bill authorizing the construction of as many as twenty-five additional gunboats to protect harbors and ports in the United States. In reality, gunboats also serve to protect vessels in U.S. territorial waters, patrol the Mississippi River, and monitor smuggling on offshore islands and inlets. The emphasis on gunboat construction is viewed by some as a threat to the seagoing Navy and a political measure given the Federalist Party's support of a large standing Navy. It also reflects Jefferson's desire to reduce naval expenditures. All told, Congress authorizes the construction of 272 gunboats between 1803 and 1806, 176 of which are eventually built.

28 April

The brig *Argus*, the sloop *Hornet*, and the schooner *Nautilus* support ground forces led by Hamet Karamanli, brother of the Pasha of Tripoli, and American diplomat William Eaton in a successful attack against the fortified town of Derna.

22 May

Commodore John Rodgers relieves Commodore Samuel Barron in command of the Mediterranean Squadron, a force that now includes four frigates, three brigs, one sloop-of-war, three schooners, two bomb vessels, and nine gunboats. Four days later this imposing force stands off Tripoli and influences the Pasha of Tripoli's decision for peace.

3 June

The U.S. Agent in Tripoli, William Eaton, concludes a peace treaty ending the first Barbary War. However, the U.S. Navy maintains a presence in the Mediterranean.

31 July

Ships of the Mediterranean Squadron under the command of Commodore John Rodgers assemble off the entrance to the Bay of Tunis. Under threat of bombardment, the Bey of Tunis decides to seek peace with the United States.

1806

25 March

Congress votes to appropriate money for the building of shore fortifications and gunboats, but rejects a request for $660,000 for the construction of six 74-gun ships-of-the-line. "I believe that the Navy is fast going to destruction," writes a dejected Commodore Edward Preble.

17 April

The Senate ratifies the peace treaty ending the war with Tripoli. It includes a provision paying $60,000 for the release of American prisoners, including those from the frigate *Philadelphia*.

18 April

Congress passes the Nonimportation Act, which forbids the importing of certain British goods into the United States. The measure is an attempt to force

Great Britain to relax its policy of impressments.

21 April
Congress passes a law authorizing the U.S. Navy just 13 captains, 9 masters commandant, 72 lieutenants, and 925 seamen and boys. The measure creates crew shortages that affect the sailing of warships.

26 April
While stationed off New York Harbor to monitor ships bound for French ports, the British frigate *Leander* fires upon the American merchantman *Richard* after she refuses to submit to a search. The errant shot across the bow kills an American sailor.

Opposite: *("USS* Chesapeake *vs. HMS* Leopard," *Fred S. Cozzens, Naval Historical Center)*

Right: *Captain Salusbury P. Humphreys commanded the British frigate* Leopard *in her encounter with the frigate* Chesapeake. *("Salusbury Pryce Humphreys, British Navy Captain," Naval Historical Center)*

Above: *Sailors on board the frigate* Chesapeake *signal the British frigate* Leopard *to stop firing, 22 June 1807. ("Leopard vs. Chesapeake," William Gilkerson, U.S. Naval Institute)*

Responding to public outrage, President Thomas Jefferson orders all British ships out of New York Harbor.

1807

22 June

After *Chesapeake*'s captain refuses to allow a search for British seamen on board his ship, the British *Leopard* fires on the American frigate off the eastern seaboard. The cannon fire kills three U.S. Navy sailors and wounds eighteen others, including the captain. The British impress four Americans from the damaged *Chesapeake*, which puts into Norfolk for repairs. The unlawful act by the Royal Navy aggravates an already tense relationship between the United States and Great Britain, which eventually leads to the War of 1812.

27 August

In response to a British squadron anchoring in Hampton Roads, Virginia, Captain Stephen Decatur, Jr., mobilizes fourteen gunboats and gets the frigate *Chesapeake* ready for action. However, the shortage of personnel in the U.S. Navy allows the operation of only eight of the gunboats, and only an emergency transfer of men from Baltimore, Maryland, makes *Chesapeake* capable of going to sea if needed.

11 November

One of a series of British orders in council issued during the Napoleonic Wars decrees that neutral nations are forbidden from trading with France and her allies unless they first pay tribute to Great Britain.

11 December

French emperor Napoleon Bonaparte issues the Milan Decree making neutral vessels which pay tribute to Great Britain, and allow a search by the Royal Navy, subject to confiscation by France. Combined with the earlier British orders in council, the measure spurs the United States to enact economic sanctions.

22 December
Congress passes the Embargo Act, which forbids all international trade to and from U.S. ports, in response to commercial restrictions decreed by Great Britain and France.

1808

17 April
Napoleon Bonaparte issues the Bayonne Decree ordering the seizure of American ships entering French ports in violation of the Embargo Act.

1809

1 March
The Non-Intercourse Act replaces the Embargo Act of 1807 and allows for the resumption of U.S. trade with all nations except Great Britain and France.

15 May
Paul Hamilton, a Revolutionary War veteran who served under the famed Francis Marion and a former Governor of South Carolina, takes office as the third Secretary of the Navy.

1810

22 February
Secretary of the Navy Paul Hamilton recommends to Congress the creation of a separate fund to establish

naval hospitals in the United States. Four days later, Congress responds favorably, passing an act to do so.

1811

9 January
The schooner *Revenge* runs aground in heavy fog, striking the rocks off Newport, Rhode Island, and breaking up. Her young captain, twenty-five-year-old Oliver Hazard Perry, avoids disciplinary action when it is determined that the pilot is to blame for the mishap.

22 January
The Secretary of the Navy directs Captain Hugh C. Campbell, commandant of the naval station at Charleston, South Carolina, to patrol the coastal areas of South Carolina and Georgia, intercepting vessels of any flag suspected of engaging in slave trading in violation of the law enacted in 1808 making the practice illegal. Interestingly, Paul Hamilton, the man issuing the order, is a wealthy planter in South Carolina.

16 May
The frigate *President*, having put to sea on 12 May in search of the British frigate *Guerriere*, which had seized an American seaman from the brig *Spitfire*, attacks the British sloop-of-war *Little Belt*. After an exchange of broadsides in the night, the two ships draw apart and the next morning the crew of *President* offers to help with the wounded on board *Little Belt*. The incident draws outrage from Great Britain.

Opposite, top:
Engagement between frigate President *and British sloop-of-war* Little Belt, *16 May 1811. (U.S. Naval Institute)*

Opposite, bottom: *Third Secretary of the Navy Paul Hamilton. ("Paul Hamilton," G. B. Matthews, Department of the Navy)*

Right: Constitution *escapes from a British squadron off New Jersey after a sixty-six-hour chase, July 1812. ("USS Constitution," Francis Muller, Navy Art Collection)*

7 August–11 September

Reflecting the mission of U.S. Navy vessels operating in the Gulf of Mexico, Gunboat Number 162 under the command of Lieutenant F. H. Gregory engages five pirate vessels, crippling one, capturing two, and forcing their crews to burn two others to prevent capture.

1812

18 June

In response to a request by President James Madison, Congress declares war on Great Britain. Across the Atlantic, on the previous day, the British cabinet had revoked the objectionable orders in council in an effort to prevent war.

23 June

The frigate *President*, sailing in a four-ship squadron in the North Atlantic, stages a running battle with the British frigate *Belvidera*. The effort is for naught as *Belvidera* escapes to fight another day. The action foreshadows a disappointing cruise for the squadron and its commander, Commodore John Rodgers. In a cruise lasting more than two months, the American ships capture only four merchantmen. It proves to be the last deployment of a squadron of American ships during the War of 1812.

17 July

Nautilus, a brig under the command of Lieutenant William Crane, is captured by the British ship-of-the-line *Africa* and the frigates *Aeolus* and *Shannon* in the waters off New York. Outgunned by 122 guns, *Nautilus* is the first U.S. Navy warship captured during the War of 1812.

17–20 July

In a testament to the seamanship of her captain, Isaac Hull, and her crew, the frigate *Constitution* escapes a squadron of British ships off the coast of New Jersey. His ship becalmed in close vicinity of the enemy, Hull orders two anchors carried out and has the crew warp the ship to them. In the ensuing days the captain uses light wind to his fullest advantage in distancing his ship from the enemy. One of the pursuers is the British frigate *Guerriere*, which meets *Constitution* in an epic sea battle a few weeks later.

13 August

The frigate *Essex*, under the command of Master Commander David Porter, captures the British sloop *Alert* after an engagement lasting only eight minutes. This marks the end of a most successful cruise in the Atlantic in which the crew of *Essex* captures nine British ships in just thirty-four days. In addition, *Alert* is the first British warship captured by the U.S. Navy during the War of 1812.

19 August

The frigate *Constitution*, under the command of Captain Isaac Hull, engages the British frigate *Guerriere* in the waters off the Gulf of St. Lawrence, Canada. The British vessel opens fire first and many of her shots bounce off the side of the American frigate, whose crew bestows upon her the famous name "Old Ironsides." Drawing abreast of one another, the two ships exchange broadsides. Within one-half hour *Guerriere* is a dismasted hulk. Her captain strikes her colors, giving *Constitution* and the young nation of the United States a stirring victory. Less than two years later, a U.S. frigate is christened *Guerriere* in honor of this historic engagement.

3 September

Commodore Isaac Chauncey receives orders to assume command of American naval forces on Lake Erie and Lake Ontario, the control of which will determine the result of the war in the west.

25 September

The Secretary of the Navy orders Captain John Shaw to bolster the defense of New Orleans, Louisiana, by stationing two blockships and twenty gunboats there.

28 September

Lieutenant Thomas Macdonough receives orders to report to Lake Champlain to assume command of naval forces there, which at the time consisted of not one floating vessel.

Above: *("Commodore Isaac Hull, USN (1773–1843),"* *Samuel L. Waldo, U.S. Naval Academy Museum)*

Opposite: *The frigate* Essex *batters the British sloop* Alert, *which after defeat in the 13 August 1812 battle becomes the U.S. Navy's first prize of the War of 1812. ("USS* Essex *Capturing HMS* Alert, *13 August 1812," William Bainbridge Hoff, Navy Art Collection)*

Below: *("USS* Constitution *and HMS* Guerriere: 'In Action,' 19 August 1812," Michel Felice Corne, U.S. Naval Academy Museum)*

OLD IRONSIDES

by Commander Tyrone G. Martin, U.S. Navy (Retired)

Early in 1794, innovative Philadelphia shipbuilder Joshua Humphreys suggested that the United States, whose Congress then was considering building a navy, ought to construct oversize frigates capable of beating anything roughly their size and fast enough to escape a superior force. A few months later, Humphreys found himself selected to design the authorized frigates. One was launched in Boston on 21 October 1797, receiving the name *Constitution*.

The big frigate first went to sea in July 1798, and quickly was involved in the Quasi-War with France. For three years in that conflict and then four more in the Barbary Wars (1804–1807), she served well, but

without particular distinction. This was to change with the coming of the War of 1812, which brought the ship to the pinnacle of naval prominence. War was declared on 18 June 1812, and early the following month *Constitution* sailed from Annapolis under orders to join Commodore John Rodgers's squadron operating from New York. Off the New Jersey shore, she met a squadron of British men-of-war, and in two days of great effort proved that she indeed possessed Humphreys's designed capability to evade a stronger enemy. Captain Isaac Hull next called at Boston to check for orders, as he couldn't get into New York. Sailing early in August, he first raided British shipping off the entrance to the Gulf of St. Lawrence, then turned southeastward, toward Bermuda.

About mid-afternoon on 19 August, another British frigate was sighted. She was *Guerriere*. The two ships jockeyed for position for about two hours. Finally, they closed to very short range on parallel courses, and commenced a heavy exchange of fire. Hull, firing double-shotted guns, quickly gained an upper hand and shot away his foe's mizzen mast. He continued to press his advantage, and by sunset *Guerriere* lay a mastless hulk. The U. S. Navy had won its first victory over the vaunted Royal Navy, and *Constitution* had both proved the validity of Joshua Humphreys's ideas and gained the nickname "Old Ironsides" (from her men seeing British shot bounce off her stout oaken hull).

On 29 December 1812, then commanded by Commodore William Bainbridge, *Constitution* did battle with the faster British frigate *Java* in the waters off Brazil. *Java* proved to be a much tougher foe. Bainbridge himself was wounded twice, and his ship's wheel was shot away. Nonetheless, the inherent strength and maneuverability of Old Ironsides eventually carried the day, and a mastless *Java* became the big frigate's second victory.

Constitution began her last war cruise in mid-December 1814, even as peace negotiations were

going forward. Charles Stewart was her captain, and he took her on a wide swing to the southeast from Boston before heading to the waters off Gibraltar. He and his crew were hungry for some of the "glory" the ship had achieved earlier, and were beginning to get desperate as news from merchant ships they met seemed to bring peace ever closer. Then, on 20 February, two British men-of-war came into view and the Americans gave chase.

The pair had joined up and were preparing to fight together by the time Stewart got in range. The battle opened in the late afternoon with the sloop *Levant* off the American's larboard bow and the frigate *Cyane* off her larboard quarter. The shoot-out stopped after twenty minutes because the gunsmoke was so thick. As it cleared from astern, Stewart thought he saw *Cyane* trying to cut under his stern. He backed his sails to the masts, quickly closed the range on his foe, and sent her staggering off in a welter of almost unbearable damage. As he was finishing with *Cyane*, Stewart saw *Levant* trying to cross his bow. Filling his sails ahead again, he swung *Constitution* sharply to larboard and poured at least two broadsides into the Briton's vulnerable stern. It was all over. After taking possession of *Cyane*,

Stewart then ran *Levant* down and captured her as well. The Americans had gained their glory, ironically three days after U.S. Senate ratification of the Treaty of Ghent that ended the war.

Americans entered the War of 1812 more commonly identifying themselves with their home states than with their country. As a result of *Constitution*'s wartime efforts, there was great pride generated in the infant navy, and citizens more readily called themselves "Americans." The big frigate went on to serve actively for more than sixty-five years, even making a voyage around the world. Since 1931, she has been maintained at Boston as the symbol of a proud nation ready and able to defend her liberties.

Above: *Having dressed ship, the crewmen on board the frigate* Constitution *position themselves on her masts as her cannons fire a Washington's Birthday salute in Malta, 1837.*

Opposite: *Twenty-four-pounder guns, their muzzles closed by plugs called tompions, protrude from* Constitution's *gun-deck ports. The frigate remains the world's oldest commissioned warship afloat. (U.S. Navy/ PH1 Alexander C. Hicks, Jr.)*

8 October

Before daybreak two boat parties under the command of Lieutenant Jesse D. Elliott approach the British brigs *Detroit* and *Caledonia* at anchor in the waters of Lake Erie, capturing the two British vessels.

In one of the earliest naval actions on Lake Erie, and one of Commodore Isaac Chauncey's few aggressive measures, the brig *Oneida* and four schooners give

chase to British sloop *Royal George*, forcing her aground in Kingston Harbor under the cover of shore batteries.

18 October

Having sighted a British convoy the previous evening off the Atlantic coast, Commandant Jacob Jones takes his sloop-of-war *Wasp* into action against the convoy's escort, the sloop *Frolic*. Exchanging fire at a range of

Above: *("USS* United States *Capturing HMS* Macedonian, *25 October 1812," Edward Tuffnell, Naval Historical Foundation)*

Left: *("USS* Constitution *Sighting HMS* Java, *December 1812," Edward Tuffnell, Naval Historical Foundation)*

Opposite: *Boats from the sloop* Hornet *carry boarding parties to the heavily damaged British brig* Peacock, *24 February 1813. ("*Hornet *Sinking the* Peacock," *A. Bowen, Anne S.K. Brown Collection)*

between fifty and sixty yards, the two ships engage in a brief but bloody skirmish that ends with an American boarding party under Lieutenant James Biddle forcing the British ship's surrender. The battle takes a toll on both ships and is destined to be *Wasp*'s first and last under the American flag, for she is captured along with her new prize a few hours later by the 74-gun British ship-of-the-line *Poictiers*.

25 October

United States, under the command of Captain Stephen Decatur, Jr., a midshipman on the frigate's first cruise, engages the British frigate *Macedonian* near the Azores Islands. The American vessel, her crew taking advantage of the greater power of her 24-pounders, fires the first shots of the battle at 0920 and with her second broadside knocks out the British ship's mizzen-topmast, which in turn hinders her maneuverability by letting the driver gaff fall. Taking advantage of his opponent's position, Decatur maneuvers *United States* off *Macedonian*'s quarter, raking the ship until she strikes her colors. Her decks are bloodied with 104 casualties as compared to 12 suffered by the Americans. *Macedonian* is repaired and subsequently operates as a U.S. warship.

27 November

The frigate *Essex*, under the command of Captain David Porter, departs the Delaware Capes bound for the Pacific. Capturing two British ships en route, she rounds Cape Horn, completing her passage through this treacherous body of water on 14 February 1813.

26 December

The British declare a limited blockade of the Chesapeake and Delaware bays, leaving the less "hawkish" New England states and New York free to trade. Royal Navy ships begin the blockade on 13 January 1813, and the following March enter Chesapeake Bay and begin sending forces into the tidewater areas of Virginia and Maryland to destroy supplies that might benefit the American war effort.

29 December

The frigate *Constitution*, under Commodore William Bainbridge, engages the British frigate *Java* in the waters off Brazil. In the first exchange of broadsides, shot from *Java* destroys *Constitution*'s wheel, leaving the ship to be steered by tackle attached to the rudder. Despite this arrangement, the American frigate maneuvers closer to the enemy vessel and systematically dismasts her. The nearly three-and-one-half-hour battle costs the Americans nine killed and twenty-six wounded, including Bainbridge. British casualties total fifty-six killed and eighty-four wounded. The British captain, mortally wounded, dies soon afterward. *Java*, too badly damaged to be taken as a prize, is blown up on New Year's Day, 1813, after her wheel is installed in *Constitution*.

31 December

Paul Hamilton resigns as Secretary of the Navy in the face of the unpopular War of 1812 and criticism of the administration of President James Madison.

1813

2 January
A bill passed by Congress authorizing the construction of four 74-gun ships and six 44-gun frigates is signed into law.

6 January
Having suffered damage in her engagement with the British frigate *Java* on 29 December 1812, the frigate *Constitution* heads for the United States for repairs.

19 January
William Jones, who in 1801 declined the offer of the post, takes office as the fourth Secretary of the Navy.

4 February
The brig *Hornet*, under the command of Captain James Lawrence, having evaded capture by the British ship *Montague* eleven days earlier, captures the English brig *Resolution*. Among her cargo of foodstuffs is an estimated $23,000 in specie. Unable to spare men to sail her as a prize, Lawrence orders *Resolution* burned.

8 February
Master Commandant Oliver Hazard Perry, in command of gunboats at Newport, Rhode Island, since the previous June, receives orders to the Great Lakes where he is directed to construct a naval squadron to combat the British and win control of Lake Erie.

24 February
The brig *Hornet* engages the British brig *Peacock* in the Caribbean Sea. The two ships exchange their first broadsides passing one another "within half pistol shot."

Within fifteen minutes, after receiving concentrated and accurate fire from the American ship, *Peacock* strikes her colors with her skipper, Captain William Peake, among the dead lying on deck.

3 March
In a response to a request from the Secretary of the Navy for the construction of fast sailing ships that can be completed quickly and put to sea for the purpose of commerce raiding, Congress authorizes the building of six sloops of war. *Wasp*, one of the ships authorized, eventually carries the war to British waters in 1814.

25 March
The frigate *Essex* captures the Peruvian privateer *Nereyda*, the first prize taken by the U.S. Navy in the Pacific. Discovering the crews of two American merchantmen held as prisoners, Porter orders *Nereyda's* cannon thrown overboard and sends the ship to Lima, Peru, so that her captain may face punishment.

27 April
Commodore Isaac Chauncey leads a squadron of twelve ships in landing some 1,700 men under the command of Major General Henry Dearborn at York, Upper Canada. Confronted by a heavy wind and "galling fire" from the enemy, the vessels carry out the amphibious operation in just two hours and provide important

gunfire support for the forces ashore. In addition, one British ship is captured and another destroyed. At 2000 hours Chauncey pens a message to the Secretary of the Navy from his flagship *Madison*. "I have the satisfaction to inform you that the American Flag is flying upon the Fort at York." American forces eventually withdraw from York, only to return on 30 July on board ships of Commodore Chauncey's squadron.

29 April
Captain David Porter employs boat parties from the frigate *Essex* in the capture of the British man-of-war

Oppsite, top: *Commodore Oliver Hazard Perry, the hero of Lake Erie, first went to sea at age fourteen and was one of four brothers to serve as naval officers.* ("Commodore Oliver Hazard Perry, USN," Orlando S. Lagman, Navy Art Collection)

Opposite, bottom: *("USS* Essex *and Her Prizes Leaving Tumbey Bay, 1813," William Bainbridge Hoff, Navy Art Collection)*

Above: *On 1 June 1813, the British frigate* Shannon *captures the frigate* Chesapeake, *already notorious because of the affair with the British frigate* Leopard *in 1807.* ("Chesapeake-Shannon," J. C. Schetky, Esquire, U.S. Naval Academy Museum)

Montezuma and the British privateers *Policy* and *Georgiana*. In one of the boats is twelve-year-old midshipman David G. Farragut, who in the Civil War will serve as an admiral in the Union Navy alongside another admiral named David Dixon Porter, son of his captain in the frigate *Essex*.

27 May
Naval vessels under the command of Master Commandant Oliver Hazard Perry bombard British forces at Fort George on Lake Ontario at the northern end of the Niagara River. Perry personally leads the landing party that consists of Army forces under the command of Colonel Winfield Scott. The joint expedition succeeds in capturing the fort and prompts the British to evacuate Fort Erie on the opposite end of the Niagara River. With these enemy bulwarks captured, American small craft at Black Rock on the Niagara River are able to join the fleet of ships under construction by Perry on Lake Erie.

28 May
The frigate *Essex*, in company with her prize vessel *Georgiana*, captures four British whalers in what will become a landmark voyage that disrupts the activities of the British whaling fleet in the Pacific.

Above: *Her sails holed by British cannon,* Niagara *charges forward to engage British warships during the Battle of Lake Erie. This mural is in Memorial Hall at the U.S. Naval Academy. ("Battle of Lake Erie," Charles R. Patterson and Howard B. French, U.S. Naval Academy)*

Left: *Commodore Oliver Hazard Perry transfers his flag from flagship* Lawrence *to* Niagara *at the height of the Battle of Lake Erie. ("Battle of Lake Erie, 10 September 1813," William H. Powell, U.S. Capitol)*

1 June

The frigate *Chesapeake*, under the command of Captain James Lawrence and manned by an inexperienced crew, engages *Shannon*. The British ship scores hits that cut away the American frigate's rigging and render her unable to maneuver. With Lawrence mortally wounded, *Chesapeake* eventually surrenders after a valiant defense.

The brig *Hornet* and the frigates *Macedonian* and *Unitd States* arrive at New London, Connecticut, having been driven into port by a British squadron. Though *Hornet* slips out in late 1814, the other two vessels remain blockaded in port until the end of the War of 1812.

3 June

On Lake Champlain the sloops *Growler* and *Eagle* are captured by British gunboats.

13 June

His father away at sea on board the frigate *Essex*, future Civil War admiral David Dixon Porter is born in Chester, Pennsylvania.

2 July

In a letter to the Secretary of the Navy, Captain David Porter, in command of *Essex*, writes, "I have suffered greatly for the want of officers and you must be well persuaded of my deficiency when you are informed that I am under the necessity of appointing my Marine Officer & Chaplain to the command of prizes." First Lieutenant John M. Gamble, in command of the captured British warship *Greenwich*, becomes the first and only Marine officer to command a ship.

20 July

After landing U.S. Minister to France William H. Crawford at the French port L'Orient, the brig *Argus* under the command of Lieutenant William H. Allen embarks on a cruise against British merchant shipping in the English Channel and off the coast of southern Ireland. She takes nineteen prizes in twenty-two days. On 14 August *Argus* meets her end, striking her colors after a forty-five-minute battle with the British ship *Pelican*. Her skipper is among the fallen.

10 August

A three-day engagement with British forces on Lake Ontario by a squadron under the command of Commodore Isaac Chauncey ends with the capture of the American gunboats *Growler* and *Julia*. Coupled with the loss of the schooners *Scourge* and *Hamilton* in a storm on 8 August, the action is a blow to American forces on the lake.

5 September

Refitted as a brig the previous year, *Enterprise* engages the Royal Navy brig *Boxer* in the waters off Maine. The ensuing engagement takes the lives of the commanding officers of both ships. After *Boxer* strikes her colors, the two ships put in to Portland, Maine, where Lieutenant William Burrows of *Enterprise* and Captain Samuel Blyth of *Boxer* are laid to rest.

10 September

An American force under the command of Master Commandant Oliver Hazard Perry engages a British force led by Captain Robert Heriot Barclay on Lake Erie. As the two fleets approach one another, a fortuitous shift in wind direction allows Perry's force to maneuver into a more favorable position. Approaching the enemy force, Perry orders a flag run up on his

Above: *Commodore Oliver Hazard Perry's flagship at the Battle of Lake Erie wore a banner bearing Captain James Lawrence's immortal words. This flag is now in Memorial Hall at the U.S. Naval Academy. (U.S. Naval Academy)*

THE BATTLE OF LAKE ERIE

by Vice Admiral George Emery, U.S. Navy (Retired)

"I see Perry has cleared the way for Land operations near Lake Erie."

So wrote retired Navy captain and Quasi-War hero Thomas Truxtun to a friend on 29 September 1813. Oliver Hazard Perry, Master Commandant, U.S. Navy, had done just that.

The first year of the War of 1812 pummeled the American public with discouraging reports from their army. Early successes anticipated in the land campaign to wrest control of Canada from Britain had not been realized. American troops had been humiliated at Mackinac Island, Detroit, Fort Dearborn, and the River Raisin. These failures, combined with the inability of the Navy to gain supremacy on Lakes Ontario and Erie, caused politicians and public alike to question the ability of their military to achieve victory. Perry's victory over the British fleet on Lake Erie on 10 September 1813 not only bolstered public faith and spirit, but also changed the strategic balance of the war effort overnight.

As stirring and dramatic as the story of the battle may be—Perry, near defeat, rowing from his mauled flagship, *Lawrence*, to the frigate *Niagara*, and snatching victory from defeat—the more remarkable story is that of the building and manning of the nine ships that Perry led into battle that day. A year earlier there had been no American naval presence on Lake Erie.

Fate found American merchant ship captain Daniel Dobbins at Mackinac Island in Lake Huron when the garrison on that island fell to British forces in July 1812. Escaping his captors, he made his way first to Detroit where he barely escaped the surrender of General William Hull's army to an inferior British force, then on to the protected Lake Erie harbor of Presque Isle (present-day Erie). There he reported the disasters at Mackinac and Detroit to General David Meade of the Pennsylvania Militia, who hurriedly dispatched him to Washington to brief President James Madison. Stunned by Dobbins's news and impressed with his initiative, Madison commissioned him a sailing master on 16 September 1812 and, authorizing the expenditure of $2,000, tasked him to return to Presque Isle "without delay,"

there to construct an American naval presence on Lake Erie.

A number of factors made Dobbins's task a difficult one, not the least of which was the inhospitable winter of 1812–1813. In addition, there was the remoteness of Lake Erie from industrial centers where shipbuilding materials could be found and the inadequate road system over which to transport those materials. Finally, the lack of local skilled artisans and the ever-present danger of marauding Indians and British land- and lake-borne raiding forces, added to Dobbins's trials. Yet, he persevered. Reaching Presque Isle in October 1812, he and the shipwrights and sailors he imported from the eastern seaboard found a way to build and outfit six of the nine vessels that would see action on the 10th of September: two 20-gun brigs, *Lawrence* and *Niagara*, and four schooners. Augmenting these vessels during the action would be three converted trading vessels, the largest of which was the former British North West Company's 3-gun brig *Caledonia* previously captured by the naval officer who would be Perry's second in command during the battle, Lieutenant Jesse Elliott.

Arriving to assume command on Lake Erie in March 1813, Perry found construction far ahead of his expectations, but that progress was made nearly irrelevant by the lack of sailors to man the vessels. Despite repeated pleas to his immediate superior, Commodore Isaac Chauncey, on Lake Ontario, and directly to the Secretary of the Navy, too few sailors found their way through the wilderness trails or along the contested shores of Lake Erie to the building ways at Presque Isle. Finally Perry begged for assistance from the Army and got it. When he sailed to meet the enemy on 10 September, approximately 200 of the 530 Americans manning his ships were Army regulars or militia volunteers.

Three hours after the first gun was fired, the British flotilla struck its colors. Every British naval ship on Lake Erie was now in American hands. With control of the lake and a well-established working relationship with General William Henry Harrison,

the Army commander in the Northwest, American soldiers and sailors wasted not a moment joining forces to retake Detroit and soundly defeat the British Army and its Indian allies at the Battle of the Thames. The latter action proved momentous; with defeat, British and allied Indian forces abandoned resistance and unceremoniously deserted region.

With victory both on the lake and ashore, Perry and Harrison had at once restored the public's confidence in their military leadership, forever freed the Old Northwest Territory of foreign occupation, and established an American presence in Canada that directly influenced the eventual favorable outcome of the War of 1812.

flagship, the brig *Lawrence*, named for Captain James Lawrence, killed the previous June on board the frigate *Chesapeake*. Flying high over the ship, the banner carries the hero's final words, "Don't Give Up The Ship." Struck repeatedly by long-range cannon that eventually leave her dead in the water with only nineteen of her crew fit for duty, *Lawrence* continues to pound away at the British flagship *Detroit*. Perry shifts his flag to the brig *Niagara* and turns her in the direction of the enemy line, raking it with broadsides from both port and starboard. The British squadron soon surrenders, prompting Perry to proclaim in his after-action report, "We have met the enemy and they are ours." The victory solidifies American control of Lake Erie and the waterways into Canada, thus removing the threat of future British invasions from Canada into the region.

20 September
Naval forces transport troops under the command of General William Henry Harrison across Lake Erie. Once landed, they pursue retreating British forces and their Native American allies, defeating them at the Battle of the Thames on 5 October.

26 September
The frigate *President*, under the command of Commodore John Rodgers, returns to Newport, Rhode Island, after a five-month cruise in the North Atlantic. Her capture of twelve prizes makes her cruise the third most successful of the U.S. Navy during the year.

25 October
The frigate *Essex*—her hull, sails, and rigging battered by nearly a year at sea and with rats infesting the ship—arrives in the Marquesas Islands. Captain David Porter establishes an anchorage off the island of Nuku

Opposite, top: *The scourge of the Pacific during the War of 1812, the frigate* Essex *finally succumbs to the Royal Navy off Valparaiso, Chile, 28 March 1814. ("USS* Essex vs. HMS Phoebe *and HMS* Cherub," *Captain David Porter, Navy Art Collection)*

Opposite, bottom: *("Commodore David Porter," Navy Art Collection)*

Right: *("USS* Peacock *Captures British Ship* Epervier, *29 April 1814," Tomiro, Department of the Navy)*

Hiva and the crew begins immediate repairs on their ship. Over the ensuing days, crewmen from *Essex* engage hostile tribesmen in combat and construct a fort ashore for their protection and that of tribes friendly to them. On 19 November Porter claims the island of Nuku Hiva for the United States, though his country never acknowledges the annexation.

At his own request, Oliver Hazard Perry turns over command of naval forces in Lake Erie to his second-in-command, Jesse D. Elliott.

16 November
Admiral Sir John B. Warren issues a proclamation declaring a blockade of the eastern seaboard of the United States stretching from New York to "all the Entrances from the Sea, into the said River of Mississippi." The measure, bolstered by the arrival of more warships from Great Britain, extends an existing blockade that before only included the Chesapeake and Delaware bays.

1814

25 February
The brigs *Enterprise* and *Rattlesnake*, having effectively operated in concert during a cruise in the Caribbean by capturing three prizes, are forced to separate by a British warship. The crew of the veteran *Enterprise* jettisons most of her cannon in order to evade her would-be captor.

28 March
Having sailed into the harbor of Valparaiso, Chile, and subsequently been blockaded there by the British frigates *Phoebe* and *Cherub*, the frigate *Essex* attempts to sail into open waters. Strong winds topple her main-topmast and she is rendered helpless in the face of intense bombardment by the British ships. After suffering repeated hits which kill some 155 of his crew, Captain David Porter strikes his colors, ending one of the most successful wartime cruises ever made by an American warship.

14 April
The frigate *John Adams*, sailing under a flag of truce, arrives at Wargo Island, Norway, and disembarks American peace commissioners Henry Clay and Jonathan Russell.

20 April
The sloop-of-war *Frolic*, while sailing the waters of the Florida Straits, happens upon the British frigate *Orpheus* and schooner *Shelbourne*. The crew lightens their ship by cutting away the starboard anchor and casting ordnance overboard, and *Frolic* evades her pursuers for six hours until captured.

29 April

The sloop *Peacock,* under the command of Master Commandant Lewis Warrington, duels the British brig *Epervier* off Cape Canaveral, Florida. In a battle lasting just forty-five minutes, the American ship inflicts ten times her own losses on her adversary, earning Warrington a gold medal from Congress.

1 May

Wasp, a ship-rigged sloop-of-war launched earlier in the year at Newburyport, Massachusetts, puts to sea for a cruise in the western approaches to the English Channel to carry the war to the enemy.

10 June

The Chesapeake Bay flotilla under the command of Captain Joshua Barney and consisting of the cutter *Scorpion*, thirteen barges, two gunboats, one galley, and one lookout boat engages British forces in the shallow waters of St. Leonard's Creek in Maryland. The Americans twice repulse attacks by enemy barges firing Congreve rockets and pursue a British schooner until she runs aground, raking her with fire.

22 June

Independence, the first ship-of-the-line commissioned in the U.S. Navy, is launched at Boston, Massachusetts. Her first commanding officer is Captain William Crane. On the same day, the brig *Rattlesnake* is captured by the British frigate *Leander* off Nova Scotia.

26 June

The Chesapeake Bay Flotilla attacks the British frigates *Loire* and *Narcissus*, hitting the former ship fifteen times and also causing damage to the latter. Both ships retire down the Patuxent River despite their superiority in firepower over the American attackers.

28 June

Having taken five prizes in English waters, the sloop-of-war *Wasp* engages the British sloop-of-war *Reindeer* in the waters west of Plymouth, England. Though the battle lasts but nineteen minutes, a murderous fire of grape and solid shot and repeated efforts by the British to board *Wasp* produce relatively high casualties of eleven dead and fifteen wounded among the Americans and thirty-three dead and thirty-four wounded from *Reindeer*. *Wasp* suffers six hits in her hull and damage to some of her rigging, but a boarding party finally forces *Reindeer*'s surrender.

20 July

Expanding Great Lakes operations into Lake Huron, an amphibious force of five ships and 750 troops under

the command of Captain Arthur Sinclair begins an expedition aimed at disrupting the British fur trade and capturing Fort Mackinac. The force burns trading posts, but fails in its 4 August assault against the fort. Sinclair leaves the schooners *Scorpion* and *Tigress* to blockade the mouth of the Nautawassaga River, its main supply line, but the ships are captured by the British in September.

12 August

A daring raid by a British force under Captain Alexander Dobbs, which carries boats overland a distance of twenty-eight miles, surprises and captures the schooners *Somers* and *Ohio* on Lake Erie.

22 August

In response to British ships landing forces near Benedict, Maryland, in an effort to surround the Chesapeake Bay Flotilla of Captain Joshua Barney, the Americans burn fifteen of the sixteen barges of the flotilla to prevent their capture.

24 August

On the order of the Secretary of the Navy, Captain Thomas Tingey sets fire to the Washington Navy Yard, in the process destroying the frigates *Boston*, *General Greene*, and *New York*, in addition to *Argus* and *Columbia*, two ships under construction, to prevent their capture. The following day, British troops burn buildings at the Navy Yard and set fire to the Navy Department. Fortunately, all official papers, books, and records are gone, having been moved to safety before the arrival of the British in the capital.

Naval personnel, formerly of the Chesapeake Bay Flotilla, under the command of Captain Joshua Barney take part in a battle against British regulars at Bladensburg, Maryland. The force repeatedly beats

Opposite: *The victory of the American fleet under Commodore Thomas MacDonough in the Battle of Plattsburg. ("Battle of Plattsburg, Lake Champlain, 11 September 1814," Edward Tufnell, Navy Art Collection)*

Right: *British troops burn the nation's capital, including the Washington Navy Yard. ("Burning of the City of Washington, August 1814, by the British Army," G. Thompson Publishers, London, U.S. Naval Institute)*

back determined assaults by redcoats before being forced to retreat, abandoning their cannon. Barney is wounded in the thigh by a sharpshooter.

11 September

In support of an assault by British ground forces against Plattsburg, New York, a British squadron under the command of Captain George Downie attacks a force under the command of Commodore Thomas Macdonough in Plattsburg Bay on Lake Champlain. Positioning his ships—rigged with spring lines to their anchors enabling them to turn in such a manner that the British would have to break their line to enter the bay of Plattsburg—Macdonough strikes the first blow against the enemy flagship *Confiance*. However, she responds with a withering fire on Macdonough's flagship, the corvette *Saratoga*, leaving forty killed or wounded. Within forty minutes the squadrons are fully engaged, with small groups of vessels fighting pitched battles. The schooner *Ticonderoga* drives the British ship *Finch* from the battle and then her crew beats off a determined attack

Left: *("Launch of the Steam Frigate Fulton at New York, 29 October 1814," B. Tanner, Naval Historical Center)*

by five enemy gunboats. In the climax of the action, Macdonough skillfully maneuvers *Saratoga* into position to rake *Confiance* with repeated broadsides. Unable to maneuver to counter, the British ship strikes her colors, as does the British brig *Linnet* shortly thereafter. The remaining British ships retire.

12 September

Sixty men formerly of Captain Joshua Barney's Chesapeake Bay Flotilla man a battery in Fort McHenry during a bombardment by British ships as part of the attack on Baltimore, Maryland. The giant flag that flies over them and their fellow defenders inspires Francis Scott Key to pen the words that in 1931 become the national anthem.

16 September

Confronted by a flotilla that includes the schooner *Carolina*, a smaller schooner, and six gunboats, pirates under Jean Lafitte at Grand Terre on Barataria Bay, Louisiana, set fire to their vessels and retreat into the surrounding swamp. American forces seize ships, ordnance, and contraband merchandise before setting fire to the pirate stronghold.

21 September

The sloop-of-war *Wasp* captures the 8-gun British brig *Atalanta* and sends her to the United States with a prize crew. The American ship, which captures or sinks fifteen British ships during a cruise to English

waters, is last seen on 9 October and is presumed lost in a storm in the Caribbean.

29 October

The first American steam-powered warship, the harbor-defense ship *Fulton*—also called *Demologos* by her designer, Robert Fulton—is launched in New York. Advanced for her time, the ship is a catamaran with a paddle wheel located in the center of the vessel between the hulls, and carries only auxiliary sails. Much of her machinery is below the water line for protection from enemy shot. She is not delivered to the U.S. Navy until 1816.

15 November

Secretary of the Navy William Jones submits plans for a reorganization of the U.S. Navy to Congress. Among his suggestions are the building of a number of ships-of-the-line capable of breaking a naval blockade of the United States, the standardization of ordnance and equipment, a draft system for seamen, the establishment of a naval academy, and the creation of a board of inspectors.

1 December

Having tendered his resignation the previous September, William Jones leaves the office of Secretary of the Navy, citing exhaustion as the reason for his departure. During part of his term, Jones also served as acting Secretary of the Treasury (May 1813–February 1814).

Opposite: *("The Gallant Attack and Capture of the American Flotilla near New Orleans, December 1814," T. L. Hornbrook, U.S. Naval Academy Museum)*

Right: *Battle between the British frigate* Endymion *and frigate* President *("President vs. Endymion," Naval Historical Center)*

14 December

With two of his ships already lost, a flotilla of five gunboats under the command of Lieutenant Thomas ap Catesby Jones is defeated by a superior British force numbering forty-two armed ships' boats on the waters of Lake Borgne near New Orleans, Louisiana. On board Jones's flagship, Gunboat Number 156, the crew beats back two attempts by the British to board her, with a wounded Jones calling out orders while lying on the deck during the second attempt. The gunboat is eventually captured along with the remainder of the flotilla, which opens the way for the British to attack New Orleans.

19 December

Benjamin W. Crowninshield becomes the fifth Secretary of the Navy. A veteran sea captain whose family business owns one of the most successful privateers of the War of 1812, Crowninshield does not take office officially until 16 January 1815.

23 December

In an effort to delay the advance of British forces toward New Orleans, Louisiana, the schooner *Carolina* travels down the Mississippi River and bombards an enemy encampment. Four days later heated shot from a British artillery battery destroy her.

Left: *On 20 February 1815 the frigate* Constitution *engaged the British frigate* Cyane *and sloop* Levant *off Madeira. After receiving much damage from "Old Ironsides," both British warships surrendered. ("Capture of the British Ships of War* Cyane *and* Levant *by USS* Constitution, *February 1815," Unknown Artist, Navy Art Collection)*

8 January

In an engagement that becomes known as the Battle of New Orleans, British forces launch an attack against American positions at New Orleans, Louisiana. Attacking the forces of General Andrew Jackson on both sides of the Mississippi River, the British suffer a staggering number of casualties with over 2,000 men killed or wounded in comparison to only 71 American troops. A naval battery established on the west bank of the river provides support to Jackson's defenses before it is overrun by British forces.

15 January

Damaged during a grounding the previous evening, the frigate *President*, under the command of Captain Stephen Decatur, Jr., encounters a squadron of four British frigates off New York and attempts to outrun them. *President's* gunners damage one enemy ship, the frigate *Endymion*, and force her to retire. However, two other British ships draw within bombardment range of the American ship. With twenty-four members of his crew killed and fifty-five others wounded, and little hope for evading capture, Decatur strikes his colors. *President* is taken into the service of the Royal Navy and broken up in 1817.

19–21 January

Following the British defeat at the Battle of New Orleans, war continues on Lake Borgne in Louisiana with six boats under the command of Purser Thomas Shields capturing two British schooners, a launch, and six boats.

7 February

Congress passes a bill establishing the Board of Commissioners consisting of three officers, appointed by the president and confirmed by the Senate, to direct the building, equipping, and repair of Navy ships under the Secretary of the Navy, who retains control and direction of naval forces. The first members of the board are Commodores Isaac Hull, David Porter, and John Rodgers.

15 February

The Secretary of the Navy orders construction suspended on a second steam-powered warship.

17 February

The Senate ratifies the Treaty of Ghent, ending the War of 1812.

20 February

Unaware of the war's end, the frigate *Constitution*, under the command of Commodore William Bainbridge, pursues the British frigate *Cyane* and sloop *Levant*. After firing the first broadside, the American frigate maneuvers between the two Royal Navy ships and engages both simultaneously, her gunners to port and starboard scoring repeated hits on the enemy and forcing both vessels to strike their colors. Levant is later recaptured.

2 March

Just days after the ratification of the treaty ending the War of 1812, the United States declares war on Algiers. The measure is in response to the renewal of attacks against American merchantmen by the Dey of Algiers, who is unhappy with the amount of tribute received from the United States.

Left: *The sloop* Hornet *engages the British sloop* Penguin *near the island of Tristan da Cunha in the South Atlantic on 23 March 1815. ("USS* Hornet *Captures HMS* Penguin *off Tristan D'Acunha, March 1815," S. Walters, U.S. Naval Academy Museum)*

Opposite, top: *USS* Constellation *with* Mashuda, *the Algerian flagship, near Cape de Gat, 17 June 1815. ("USS* Constellation *with* Mashuda," *Arthur N. Disney, Sr., Navy Art Collection)*

Opposite, bottom: *("Stephen Decatur," John Wesley Jarvis, Navy Art Collection)*

23 March
The sloop *Hornet* captures the British sloop *Penguin* off the island of Tristan da Cunha in the South Atlantic, the crews of the ships not having heard that the war between the United States and Great Britain has ended.

15 April
The Secretary of the Navy orders a naval squadron to the Mediterranean Sea, stating in a letter to the squadron commander, Captain Stephen Decatur, Jr., his desire that the U.S. Navy ships blockade the port of Algiers and intercept and capture ships sailing under the Algerian flag.

20 May
Flying his flag in the frigate *Guerriere*, Commodore Stephen Decatur, Jr., departs New York City in command of a squadron of nine warships, including the frigates *Constellation* and *Macedonian*, bound for the Mediterranean Sea in response to the recently declared war with Algiers.

17 June
Ships of the squadron commanded by Commodore Stephen Decatur, Jr., engage and capture the Algerian frigate *Mashuda*, killing thirty of her crew, including Algerian Admiral Rais Hamida, and capturing over 406 Algerian sailors.

19 June

The American brig *Epervier* and other ships run the Algerian ship *Estedio* aground, capturing her. Twenty-three Algerians are killed and eight taken prisoner.

28 June

Arriving with his squadron at Algiers, Commodore Stephen Decatur, Jr., joins American Consul-General William Shaler in opening negotiations with the Dey of Algiers. Among the pair's treaty demands is an end to any payment of tribute, and they do not accept a temporary truce during the negotiations. To this end and as a sign of his seriousness, Decatur sends his ships in pursuit of an Algerian cruiser approaching Algiers.

30 June

A peace treaty is signed between the United States and the Dey of Algiers. Under the terms of the treaty, Algiers releases crewmen of the American brig *Edwin* being held prisoner and pays an indemnity of $10,000 for her capture, and also surrenders claim to tribute from the United States. In writing to the Secretary of the Navy, Commodore Stephen Decatur, Jr., informs him that the treaty was "dictated at the mouth of the cannon" and urges that the United States maintain a naval presence in the Mediterranean Sea.

The sloop *Peacock* under the command of Master Commandant Lewis Warrington captures the British East India Company brig *Nautilus*. Though the British ship's skipper, Lieutenant Charles Boyce, hails the

American ship and informs her of the Treaty of Ghent, Warrington does not believe him and opens fire. The brief action results in six British sailors killed and eight wounded, and marks the last naval engagement of the War of 1812.

3 July

In his flagship, the ship-of-the-line *Independence*, Commodore William Bainbridge departs Boston, Massachuetts, with a squadron of ships for service in the Mediterranean Sea. Relieving a force under the command of Commodore Stephen Decatur, Jr., the squadron represents a powerful presence in the theater and serves as a deterrent force in preserving the recent peace with Algiers.

14 July

The brig *Epervier* passes Gibraltar en route back to the United States carrying dispatches from Commodore Stephen Decatur, Jr., but disappears in the Atlantic.

26 July

Commodore Stephen Decatur, Jr., arrives in Tunis with ships of his squadron. Four days later he concludes a treaty with the Bey of Tunis, a provision of which is payment to the United States of $46,000 in compensation for prizes sent into port by an American privateer during the War of 1812, and returned to the British by Tunis in violation of their treaty with the United States.

5 August

Commodore Stephen Decatur, Jr., concludes his summer of diplomacy in the Mediterranean Sea, collecting $25,000 from the Pasha of Tripoli as payment for damages resulting from the returning of American prizes to the British during the War of 1812. Four days later he concludes a peace treaty with Tripoli on behalf of the United States.

12 November

Commodore Stephen Decatur, Jr., and his squadron return to New York City in triumph after their successful cruise to the Mediterranean Sea. Decatur is feted as a hero and in his next duty assignment joins the Board of Navy Commissioners as a replacement for Commodore Isaac Hull. He and his wife build a house across from the White House in Washington, D.C., which still stands today as a memorial to the great naval hero.

20 November

The Board of Navy Commissioners issues a report detailing its desire for a reorganization of the Navy. Among the recommendations is a reduction in the number of navy yards, the construction of dry docks, naval hospitals, and a national foundry, the creation of an ordnance department within the Navy, and an annual shipbuilding program. Recommended reforms include the creation of the rank of admiral and a better system of promotion. The Secretary of the Navy acts on few of the board's proposals.

Above: *("Triumphant Return of the American Squadron under Commodore Bainbridge from the Mediterranean, 1815," Michael F. Corne, Naval Historical Center)*

Left: *Fifth Secretary of the Navy Benjamin W. Crowninshield. ("Benjamin W. Crowninshield," U. D. Tenney, Department of the Navy)*

DISTANT STATIONS

1816-1860

DISTANT STATIONS

1816-1860

They were years of Manifest Destiny for the young nation, as trains of covered wagons ventured forth across wide expanses of open prairie with "westward ho" their universal cry. The era provided the U.S. Navy an opportunity to fulfill its own manifest destiny, representing the nation in distant waters. The concept of "forward presence" so familiar to naval personnel of the modern era traces its roots to the decades before the Civil War, when the Navy created six squadrons for the purpose of protecting American interests in vital regions of the world. The Mediterranean Sea was familiar territory for United States men-of-war, but the establishment of other squadrons addressed emerging crises of the times. Sailors assigned to the West India Squadron found themselves in pursuit of roving bands of pirates that preyed on American commerce, and the protection of merchantmen was also the primary duty of the Brazil and Pacific Squadrons. Perhaps no issue divided America more during this period than slavery, and with a congressional declaration in April 1818 making the slave trade illegal, U.S. Navy warships found themselves positioned off the west coast of Africa, intercepting vessels smuggling illicit human cargo out of that continent. Yet, it was the East India Squadron that carried the flag to the most distant lands, crossing the blue waters of the Pacific to the Far East. The presence of naval forces in the region facilitated the opening of formal diplomatic relations with China. In addition, it was while in command of the East India Squadron that Commodore Matthew C. Perry led his famous expedition to Japan, during which his flagship *Susquehanna* and three other warships anchored in what is now Tokyo Bay, opening a vital trade route for the United States.

"Knowledge of naval matters is an art as well as any other and not to be attended to at idle times and on the by . . ." wrote Pericles around 460 B.C. The naval officers who fought the War of 1812 learned the art of naval warfare at sea, their classrooms the decks of sailing vessels. Yet, there were elements within the Navy that sought to formalize the education of naval officers through the establishment of a naval school, and by the mid-1800s the changing face of the Navy's ships buttressed their argument. The appearance of the first truly seaworthy steam warships foreshadowed a future in which naval officers would require a high degree of technical knowledge, a fact also supported by Commander John Dahlgren's advances in naval ordnance and the work of naval scientist Lieutenant Matthew Fontaine Maury. The result was the establishment in 1845 of a naval school at Annapolis, Maryland, which five years later was renamed the U.S. Naval Academy.

In a similar vein, traditionally iron-willed men who had proven themselves in battle occupied the Navy's leadership ranks, their very personalities shaping the direction of the entire service. During the period of 1816–1842 this direction could be characterized as reactionary, particularly with respect to the technological advancement of the sea service. Thus, in 1842 Secretary of the Navy Abel P. Upshur instituted a far-reaching administrative reform of the Navy Department, establishing five bureaus, their specialties ranging from the development of ordnance to the outfitting of sailors with uniforms. Though not without its inefficiencies and conflict, the bureau system modernized naval administration, recognizing the importance of non-line officers to the sea service, and lasted for more than a century.

In contrast to the thrilling sea battles on which the Navy had built its tradition, the conflicts of the pre-Civil War era called sailors to arms in much different arenas that called for innovation. The personnel of the so-called Mosquito Fleet waged a long struggle against the Seminole Indians in the swamps and marshes of Florida, a riverine war against an elusive enemy in which capital ships consisted of canoes and flat-bottom boats. The Mexican War also presented few opportunities for classic sea engagements, with the ships of the Navy's Gulf Squadron initially tasked with blockading the Mexican coast and launching offensive attacks in an effort to seize Mexican ports. In addition, the Navy staged the largest amphibious landing in history up to that time, putting troops under the command of General Winfield Scott ashore at Veracruz on 9 March 1847. Recognized as a proving ground for the generation of Army officers that fought on the bloody battlefields of the Civil War, the Mexican War had a similar, if less wide-ranging effect on the Navy. David Dixon Porter and Raphael Semmes were among the seafaring men who experienced combat in Mexican waters.

A period of transition, the years 1816–1860 witnessed a shift from the Navy of John Paul Jones and Stephen Decatur to one poised on the threshold of change with respect to technology and the shaping of the men who waged war upon the sea. Ironically, an era marked by ships flying the Stars and Stripes venturing to all corners of the globe preceded a trying time in which all efforts focused on a titanic struggle at home that threatened to tear apart the very fabric of the republic.

Above: *Portrayed pounding through heavy seas in the Gulf of Mexico off Veracruz during the Mexican War, the steam frigate* Mississippi *represented a Navy in transition from sail to steam. (Naval Historical Center)*

Pages 94–95: *The ships of the Mediterranean Squadron— the ship-of-the-line* North Carolina, *the frigates* Brandywine *and* Constitution, *and the sloops* Erie *and* Ontario—*depart Port Mahon in 1825. ("U.S. Squadron Departing from Port Mahon," A. Carlotta, Naval Historical Center)*

DISTANT STATIONS
1816-1860

1816

29 April
Congress appropriates $1 million for a period of eight years for the construction of nine ships to rate not less than seventy-four guns and twelve ships of not less than forty-four guns. Among the vessels constructed under the provisions of this act is the ship-of-the-line *Ohio*, about which an English officer once comments "A more splendid ship I never beheld." She serves until 1883.

8 June
The ship-of-the-line *Washington* departs the United States for the Mediterranean Sea, where she serves as flagship of Commodore Isaac Chauncey's Mediterranean Squadron for nearly two years, a show of force to discourage the Barbary states from interfering with American commerce.

22 December
A peace treaty is signed between the United States and Algiers ending the Barbary Wars.

1817

16 November
The Secretary of the Navy, with the authorization of President James Monroe, orders Captain John D. Henley in command of the frigate *John Adams* to use armed force against pirates operating in the waters around Amelia Island off the east coast of Spanish Florida. Two days later he directs Henley to carry out similar operations against a pirate stronghold at Galveston on the Gulf Coast.

22 December
Captain John Henley, having put ashore a landing party from the frigate *John Adams*, forces the surrender of Amelia Island, thus neutralizing a base of operations for marauding pirates.

1818

19 August
Captain James Biddle, in command of the sloop *Ontario*, lands at Cape Disappointment on the Columbia River and claims the Oregon Territory for the United States.

2 September
The Secretary of the Navy issues sailing orders to Captain John Downes, commanding the frigate *Macedonian*, to sail to the Pacific Ocean to afford protection to United States persons and property, particularly the whaling fleet and merchant shipping. Downes is a veteran of Pacific service, having served as Captain David Porter's first lieutenant on board the frigate *Essex* during the War of 1812.

Opposite: *One of two brothers to rise to command in the post-Revolutionary War Navy, John D. Henley stormed enemy gunboats at Tripoli in 1803, participated in the Battle of New Orleans, and led U.S. Navy efforts against pirates in the West Indies during the years after the War of 1812. ("Commodore John D. Henley, USN (1781–1835)," Unknown Artist, Navy Art Collection)*

Right: *A 74-gun ship-of-the-line authorized during the War of 1812, Washington served as flagship of the Mediterranean Squadron during 1816–1818. ("USS Washington (1814–1843)," Francois Roux, Naval Historical Center)*

1819

1 January

Smith Thompson, a future justice of the United States Supreme Court, takes office as the sixth Secretary of the Navy.

3 March

President James Monroe signs an act passed by Congress on 26 February 1819 authorizing the protection of United States commerce and the punishment of those participating in acts of piracy. U.S. Navy warships begin convoying merchant ships and engage in an active campaign against pirates operating in the Caribbean.

Congress authorizes the U.S. Navy's participation in the suppression of American ships participating in the slave trade in West Africa, which leads to the formal establishment of the African Squadron the following year. In addition to capturing slave ships, the warships support the establishment of a colony in Liberia by American blacks.

15 March

The frigate *Macedonian*, having rounded Cape Horn and entered the Pacific the previous January, puts to sea from Valparaiso, Chile, becoming the first ship to operate on what will come to be called the Pacific Station.

23 August

Following the conclusion of a successful mission to the newly created nation of Venezuela in an effort to negotiate a treaty to prevent the harassment of American merchantmen, Commodore Oliver Hazard Perry dies of yellow fever on board the schooner *Nonsuch*. The hero of Lake Erie is just three days shy of his thirty-fourth birthday.

1820

22 March

Commodore Stephen Decatur, Jr., engages in a duel with Commodore James Barron at Bladensburg, Maryland, following the latter's challenge. Barron, who believes Decatur dishonored him by openly opposing his reinstatement in the U.S. Navy after being court-martialed for his role in the *Chesapeake-Leopard* affair of 22 June 1807, is wounded in the hip. Decatur is mortally wounded by a shot that hits his hip and ricochets into his groin, and he dies later in the evening at the age of forty-one.

5–12 April
The frigate *Cyane*, under the command of Captain Edward Trenchard, captures five slave ships in the waters off present-day Liberia, marking the first major success of the African Squadron.

6 November
The Scot Lord Cochrane, in command of a Chilean naval force, leads a boat assault against the Spanish frigate *Esmeralda* at Callao, Peru. Anchored nearby, the U.S. frigate *Macedonian* is hit by gunfire and her crew is suspected of assisting Cochrane in his attack. When a boat from the American frigate is sent ashore later in the day flying the national flag, Spanish soldiers fire into it, killing two sailors and wounding five others.

20 November
With American and British citizens evacuated from Lima, Peru, on board, the frigate *Macedonian* sets sail from Callao, Peru, escorting a group of seven U.S. and British merchantmen.

1821

16 March
In the aftermath of General Andrew Jackson's successful invasion of Spanish Florida, the brig *Hornet* is ordered to carry dispatches from the Secretary of State to Havana, Cuba, and then proceed to Pensacola, Florida, and convoy surrendered Spanish authorities and troops to Cuba. The following month the brig *Porpoise* is directed to carry out the same mission for Spaniards captured at St. Augustine, Florida.

19 March
Relieved by the frigate *Constellation*, the frigate *Macedonian* departs Valparaiso, Chile, bound for the United States. During her cruise of two years and nine months, the ship logs 58,878 miles and loses twenty-six members of her crew.

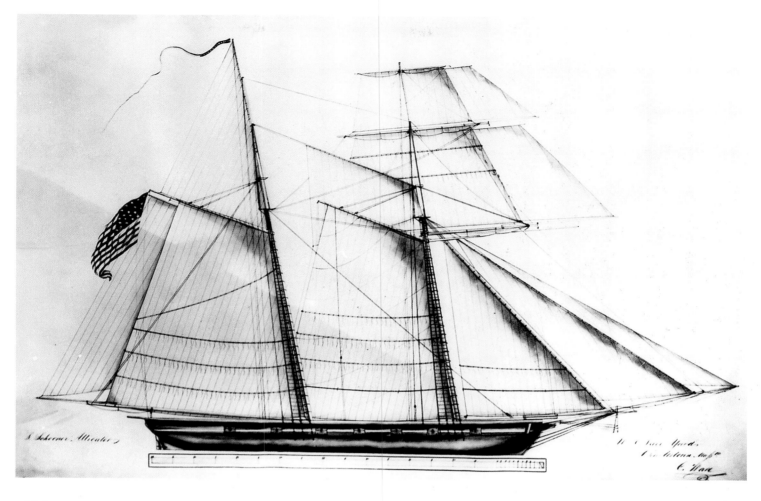

16 May

Under the command of Captain John D. Henley—one of two brothers to serve in the U.S. Navy during the early nineteenth century and a hero in action at Tripoli in August 1804—the frigate *Congress* departs Hampton Roads, Virginia, for a cruise to the Indian Ocean. During the voyage she puts in to China, becoming the first U.S. Navy vessel to visit that country.

17–25 May

The topsail schooner *Alligator*, under the command of Lieutenant Robert F. Stockton, captures four French slave ships off the mouth of the Gallinas River in Africa. During the cruise Stockton also supports the efforts of the American Colonization Society by persuading tribal leaders to cede land that eventually becomes the Republic of Liberia.

11 October

The ship-of-the-line *Franklin* departs New York for the Pacific, arriving at Valparaiso, Chile, on 6 February 1822. Along with the schooner *Dolphin*, she forms the Pacific Squadron, protecting American commercial and whaling interests in the face of revolution in Latin America.

16 October

The brig *Enterprise* under the command of Lieutenant Lawrence Kearny sights a quartet of pirate ships in the process of robbing two American ships and one British vessel off Cape Antonio, Cuba. Many of the pirates escape by running their vessels ashore. They set one ship afire and Kearny orders a second one put to the torch. The remaining ships are taken as prizes.

29 October

Cruising the waters of the West Indies under the command of Captain Robert Henley, the brig *Hornet* captures the pirate ship *Moscow* off Santo Domingo.

5 November

While operating in the Atlantic Ocean, the topsail schooner *Alligator* is taken under fire by the Portuguese naval ship *Marianno Flora*. Each mounting twelve guns, the two ships engage in a battle lasting one hour and twenty minutes before the Portuguese ship strikes her colors. Combined with *Alligator*'s seizure of French ships the previous month, the action with *Marianno Flora* prompts a letter from the Secretary of the Navy to *Alligator*'s skipper, Lieutenant Robert F. Stockton, directing him to restrict offensive action to slavers flying the American flag.

7 January

The schooner *Porpoise* puts ashore a landing party in Cuba that destroys a pirate base of operations and six of their vessels.

The brig *Spark*, under the command of Lieutenant John H. Elton, captures a Dutch sloop that had been seized by pirates. Elton takes the ship and seven captured pirates to Charleston, South Carolina, where the outlaws are put on trial.

8 March

The brig *Enterprise* captures seven pirate vessels off Cape San Antonio, Cuba, destroying all of them. It is the last significant combat action for the veteran ship, which on 9 July 1823 is stranded and breaks up on Little Curacao Island in the West Indies.

25 March

Arriving at present day Key West, Florida, on board the schooner *Shark*, Lieutenant Matthew C. Perry claims the territory for the United States, naming it Thompson's Island in honor of the Secretary of the Navy.

26 March

U.S. Navy warships hunting pirates in the West Indies are placed under the overall command of Commodore James Biddle. This force will become the West India Squadron.

8 November

The schooner *Porpoise*, under the command of Lieutenant James Ramage, captures a pirate boat while operating off Cape San Antonio, Cuba.

21 December

Continuing her successful campaign against West Indies pirates, *Enterprise* captures and burns a corsair near Cape San Antonio, Cuba. Lieutenant Lawrence Kearny orders a landing party ashore that destroys the pirate base and burns five prizes.

30 April–1 May

The U.S. Navy schooners *Alligator* and *Grampus*, along with the chartered ship *Jane*, participate in the capture of four pirate vessels in the Caribbean and rescue one pirate prize.

16 August

The pirate schooner *Palmyra* surrenders to the schooner *Grampus* under the command of Lieutenant Francis H. Gregory after a brief engagement off Puerto Rico. Gregory, held as a prisoner of war by the British during the War of 1812, eventually achieves the rank of rear admiral supervising the construction of gunboats during the Civil War.

28–30 September

Reflecting the cooperative effort between the U.S. Navy and Revenue Cutter Service (now U.S. Coast Guard) that still exists today, the sloop-of-war *Peacock* and revenue cutter *Louisiana* mount an expedition that destroys a pirate stronghold at Bahia Honda, Cuba, yields five prizes, and frees a captured merchant ship.

9 November

Lieutenant William Allen, in command of the topsail schooner *Alligator*, leads boat parties from his ship to recapture five American ships from pirates off Mantanzas, Cuba. American sailors kill fourteen pirates and capture one pirate schooner. However, the success comes at the price of Lieutenant Allen, who is mortally wounded in the engagement.

20 December

Congress formally authorizes the creation of the West India Squadron to suppress pirate activities in the Caribbean. The following day Commodore David Porter is appointed the squadron's commander.

1823

14 February

Sea Gull, the U.S. Navy's second steamer, sails from Norfolk, Virginia, bound for the waters of the West Indies. A former river steamer purchased for operations in shallow inshore waters, *Sea Gull* becomes the first steam-powered vessel to see active service in the U.S. Navy.

6 March

While on a mission to San Juan, Puerto Rico, to inquire about another ship of the West India Squadron sent to explain to the Spanish governor the squadron's mission, the schooner *Fox* is fired upon. Her commanding officer, Lieutenant William H. Cocke, is mortally wounded. While the Spanish issue a formal apology, the reason for the hostile action remains a mystery.

8 April
Supported by the eighteen guns of the sloop *Peacock*, the barges *Mosquito* and *Gallinipper* capture the pirate schooner *Pilot* near Havana, Cuba. The three vessels then land Marines to pursue fleeing pirates ashore.

July
The barges *Mosquito* and *Gallinipper* capture the pirate schooner *Catalina* and a boat at Sigaunba, Cuba. Among those captured is the pirate leader Diaboleto.

21 July
Lieutenant Lawrence Kearny, in command of the schooner *Greyhound*, joins the schooner *Beagle* under Lieutenant J. T. Newton in an attack against a pirate stronghold at Cape Cruz, Cuba. While cannon fire from the ship draws the attention of the pirate defenders, a force of sailors and Marines under Lieutenant David G. Farragut lands and attacks the rear of the enemy positions.

16 September
Samuel Lewis Southard, a former U.S. Senator from New Jersey, takes office as the seventh Secretary of the Navy, replacing Smith Thompson, who resigns to become a Supreme Court justice.

5 October
The schooner *Shark* departs New York carrying Commodore John Rodgers and three Navy surgeons for passage to Thompson's Island to evaluate it as a potential site for a naval base.

18 November
The schooner *Alligator* runs aground on Carysfort Reef in the West Indies and is wrecked. Her crew, all of whom survive, set fire to their ship. The remains of *Alligator* still lie on the appropriately named Alligator Reef off Islamorada, Florida.

2 December
In his seventh annual message to Congress, President James Monroe proclaims that henceforth the Americas are "not to be considered as subjects for future colonization by any European powers," and signals European nations that efforts to the contrary will be viewed as "dangerous to our peace and safety." The foreign policy proclamation is called the "Monroe Doctrine."

1824

17–26 August
The schooner *Terrier*, under the command of Lieutenant Thomas Paine, Jr., captures a pirate launch and a schooner in Cuban waters.

20 October

The schooner *Porpoise*, under the command of Lieutenant Charles W. Skinner, and five boats under the command of Lieutenant William M. Hunter, capture a pirate schooner and three boats near Matanzas, Cuba.

27 October

Upon receiving word that property stolen by pirates from an American warehouse at St. Thomas in the Danish West Indies is at Fajardo, Lieutenant Charles Platt sails the schooner *Beagle* to the small Puerto Rican port. Venturing ashore in the company of Midshipman Robert Ritchie to confer with Spanish authorities regarding the stolen goods, Platt and Ritchie are placed under arrest.

28 October

The schooner *Wild Cat*, her crew having just endured a bout with yellow fever the previous summer, is lost with all hands in the waters between Cuba and Thompson's Island.

14 November

Enraged by the treatment of Lieutenant Charles Platt and Midshipman Robert Ritchie at the hands of the Spanish in Puerto Rico, Commodore David Porter lands a force of 200 sailors and Marines from the frigate *John Adams* at Fajardo. Demanding an apology in a letter to the town, he threatens destruction of "Foxhardo" if one is not forthcoming. The Spanish issue a formal apology to Platt. Coming on the heels of the seizure of Florida from the Spanish, Porter's actions result in his court-martial and six-month suspension from duty, which prompts

him to resign on 1 July 1826 and accept the post of commander in chief of the Mexican Navy.

27 December

Captain Lewis Warrington assumes command of the West India Squadron, relieving Commodore David Porter.

1825

4 February

The schooner *Ferret* capsizes in a storm off the coast of Cuba. While their fellow crewmen lash themselves to the wreck, an officer and three men take the ship's small boat in search of assistance. When the small schooner *Jackal* arrives the following morning, the survivors have been clinging to the wreck for some twenty-one hours. Five men are lost.

3 March

Congress authorizes the construction of ten sloops-of-war.

Joining the Senate, the House of Representatives passes a bill authorizing the construction of a navy yard and depot at Pensacola, Florida. The measure is enacted despite the fact that the results of a study to determine if it is the most suitable site for a naval installation have not been received.

25 March

In a joint attack, an Anglo-American force—consisting of the barge *Gallinipper*, under the command of Lieutenant Isaac McKeever, and boat parties from the Royal Navy vessels *Dartmouth*, *Lion*, and *Union*—destroys a pirate base at Rio Sagua la Grande near Matanzas, Cuba.

8 September

The frigate *Brandywine* sets sail from the Washington Navy Yard, D.C., carrying Revolutionary War hero the Marquis de Lafayette for a return passage to France following a tour of the United States. Fittingly, the ship is named after a famous battle of the American Revolution.

1826

9 January

While engaging in the pursuit of mutineers from the American whaling ship *Globe*, the schooner *Dolphin* under the command of Lieutenant John Percival arrives at Honolulu. She becomes the first American warship to visit the Sandwich Islands (Hawaii).

6 August

The sloop *Peacock* commanded by Master Commandant Thomas ap Catesby Jones enters Matavia Bay at Otaheiti (Tahiti) in the Society Islands. During the following week Jones negotiates a

treaty outlining trading parameters and the protection of American ships in Tahitian waters that, though never ratified by the Senate, serves as a "binding" agreement into the 1840s.

16 August

In response to a mutiny on board the whaling ship *Fortune* in Tahiti, Marines from the sloop *Peacock* board the vessel and apprehend six sailors responsible

for the event. After a trial on board the U.S. Navy vessel, two mutineers are flogged.

3 September
The sloop-of-war *Vincennes* sails from New York under the command of Master Commandant William B. Finch. She returns on 8 June 1830, having become the first American naval vessel to circumnavigate the globe.

22 December
Master Commandant Thomas ap Catesby Jones concludes a treaty with the people of Hawaii, which provides most favored nation status to the United States, protects American commerce, and stipulates that the Hawaiians assist in the salvage of American ships and the suppression of desertion.

1827

3 March
Congress authorizes the construction of two drydocks at Boston, Massachusetts, and Norfolk, Virginia.

2 April
Construction begins on the first U.S. Naval Hospital at Portsmouth, Virginia, which is completed in 1833.

4 October
In response to pirate activity by Greek-flagged vessels against American merchant ships during the Greek war of independence from Turkey, the sloop-of-war *Warren* captures her first pirate vessel. *Warren*'s commanding officer is Master Commandant Lawrence Kearny, a veteran of pitched battles with pirates in the West Indies.

16 October
While convoying merchantmen from Smyrna, Turkey, to Port Mahon, Minorca, the schooner *Porpoise* under the command of Lieutenant Benjamin Cooper encounters pirates, who capture one of the merchantmen after nightfall. Cooper dispatches four boats carrying forty men under the command of Lieutenants Louis M. Goldsborough, John A. Carr, and Thomas J. Manning, and Midshipman Alexander W. Wilson. The boat crews recapture the captured ship and inflict some forty casualties on the pirates, forcing them to retreat. There are no American casualties.

25 October
The sloop-of-war *Warren*, in response to recent attacks on the American merchant ships *Cherub* and *Rob Roy*, chases a pirate brig ashore on the island of Argenteiro in the Mediterranean Sea. Though her crew escapes, the brig is rendered inoperable by *Warren*'s crew, who cut away the masts and strip the sails.

29 October–2 November
Learning of pirates in the vicinity from the crew of the Austrian brig *Silence*, the sloop-of-war *Warren* cruises the waters surrounding the island of Mykonos, Greece, capturing a pirate galley of forty oars. Putting into Mykonos Harbor, crewmen from the Navy ship recover stolen goods and rigging from American and Austrian ships, and take into custody five pirates.

7 November
Lieutenant William L. Hudson leads a boat party from the sloop-of-war *Warren* in search of pirates operating around Andros Island, Greece. Mistakenly fired upon by a brig in the darkness, Hudson and his men eventually reach the town of Andros, capturing two pirate boats and burning another. One of the captured boats had been intentionally sunk by pirates to avoid detection by the Americans.

1828

The Secretary of the Navy authorizes establishment of a headquarters for the recruitment of sailors at Carlisle, Pennsylvania. This marks the first effort of the Navy to enlist seamen from cities not located on the coast.

1829

3 March
Samuel Southard leaves the post of Secretary of the Navy. Under his administration the Navy increases from thirty-five to fifty-two ships and the number of personnel jumps from 3,400 to 5,600 men.

9 March
John Branch, a former governor of North Carolina and U.S. Senator from that state, takes office as the eighth Secretary of the Navy.

4 June
While serving as a receiving ship in the Brooklyn Navy Yard, New York, the U.S. Navy's first steamer *Fulton* explodes, killing twenty-four people and injuring nineteen others.

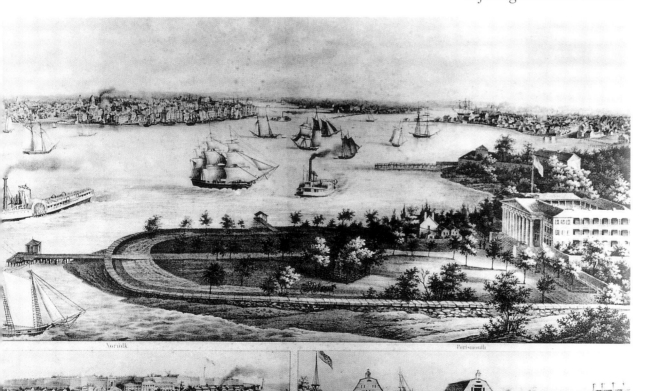

VIEWS OF NORFOLK AND PORTSMOUTH
FROM THE MARINE HOSPITAL.

Left: *The upper frame shows the naval hospital in the right foreground with the city of Portsmouth, Virginia, beyond and Norfolk at left. The lower frames show the Navy Yard at Portsmouth and Old Point Comfort. ("Views of Norfolk and Portsmouth from the Marine Hospital," Norfolk Naval Shipyard)*

Opposite, bottom: *USS* Hornet *foundering off Tampico, Mexico, on 29 September 1829. Engraving from "The Sailor's Magazine," March 1830. ("USS* Hornet *(1805–1829)," Naval Historical Center)*

Right: Fulton, *called* Demologos *by her designer, was a catamaran coast defense ship designed by Robert Fulton. Built in New York by Adam and Noah Brown and displacing 2,475 tons,* Fulton *was the first steam war vessel ever built. With no occasion for active service, she was never commissioned but was used at the New York Navy Yard as a receiving ship. She was totally destroyed by an accidental explosion on 4 June 1829. ("USS* Fulton *(The First)," Samuel Ward Stanton, Department of the Navy)*

September

Caught in a gale off Tampico, Mexico, the brig *Hornet* is lost at sea with all 140 members of her crew.

1830

6 December

Following the recommendation of Lieutenant Louis M. Goldsborough, the Navy establishes the Depot of Charts and Instruments at Washington, D.C., and places it under his command. Later renamed the U.S. Naval Observatory, it relocated from the original site in the Foggy Bottom section of the nation's capital to an area above Georgetown, where it still operates today. A home built at the observatory for the Superintendant of Charts and Instruments later became the official home of the Chief of Naval Operations, and since 1974 has been the official residence of the Vice President of the United States.

FROM SAIL TO STEAM

by Dr. Wade G. Dudley

For centuries, muscle and wind moved the fleets of the world. Then the Industrial Revolution, with its transition from natural to artificial sources of power, offered navies a new paradigm. A young United States, hard-pressed by military necessity, became the first nation to tentatively embrace the concept of a steam warship.

Robert Fulton's *Clermont*, the first American steamship, opened operations on the Hudson River in 1807. With the outbreak of war with Great Britain in 1812, the talented inventor turned his attention to protecting his nation's coast. His ideas included naval mines, often called "Fultons" in recognition of his deadly efforts, a semisubmersible torpedo boat, and a steam warship. Fulton began building his warship, the *Demologos* (Voice of the People), in New York Harbor in 1814. Featuring thirty 32-pounders and wooden sides five feet thick, the builder solved the problem of a vulnerable paddlewheel by placing it between two catamaran-style hulls. Early steam plants being very uncertain in their operation, lateen-rigged masts supplemented its engine. Completed shortly after the War of 1812 and named *Fulton* by the Navy in honor of its inventor, peace found the vessel relegated to service as a receiving ship until a powder explosion destroyed her in 1829.

As the first captain of *Fulton*, veteran commander David Porter quickly realized the usefulness of steam power. In 1822, while leading an antipiracy squadron in the shallow coastal waters of the Caribbean, he purchased the 100-ton Hudson River steamer *Sea Gull*. With three guns mounted on its shallow-draft hull, its dual paddlewheels allowed the vessel to capture or destroy pirate craft with ease, and made it the first steamer used in combat by a navy. Unfortunately, Porter left the service shortly after his success against piracy, leaving steam warships without a champion in the American naval hierarchy.

That hierarchy, especially the aged men of the Board of Naval Commissioners, both resented and distrusted steam power—and not without some sound reasons. Coupled with complaints that smoke from the

"teakettles" covered ships and men with filth were legitimate fears that sparks from the boilers did not mix well with wood, canvas, and tar. Alongside cries that the lack of sail-drill would make the men lazy stood the knowledge that the poor performance of early, coal-hungry engines limited the range of any steamship to a few paltry miles. The plume of smoke floating from the funnel made it difficult to take an enemy unawares, and the vulnerable paddlewheels put a warship at risk in action. As a result of a negative mindset supported by reasonable arguments, the navy that had pioneered steam warships languished in its canvas shroud for over a decade.

Then, in the mid-1830s, two champions of steam power arose in the United States. Secretary of the Navy Mahlon Dickerson, appalled at the disparity in modernization between the leading European navies and his fleet, used an 1816 law allowing the building of "steam batteries" to fund the first American steam frigate, also named *Fulton*. With her four funnels and three masts, the vessel could achieve 10 knots of speed under coal alone. Dickerson found a kindred spirit in the ship's first captain, Matthew Calbraith Perry. In 1838, Perry steamed up the Potomac River to Washington, D.C., impressing President Martin Van Buren and Congress with *Fulton*'s abilities. The following year, Congress authorized two side-wheel frigates, *Missouri* and *Mississippi*. Though *Missouri* burned in 1843, her sister ship proved the equal of any wooden-hulled steam warship in Europe.

The 1840s saw several innovations revolutionize naval design. The use of anthracite coal, steam-powered blowers, and more efficient engines improved cruising range and reduced smoke signature. In 1842, the U.S. Navy launched its first iron-hulled steam warship, *Michigan*, which served on the Great Lakes until 1923. Captain Robert F. Stockton invited Swedish engineer John Ericsson to the United States where they designed a screw propeller, first used in the sloop-of-war *Princeton* in 1846.

For three decades following the reintroduction of steam, the U.S. Navy tested its vessels in war and peace. The conflict with Mexico showed both the need for additional coaling stations and the value of steam power in shallow waters. In 1853–1854, Commodore Matthew C. Perry used his "burning ships" in Tokyo Bay to open trade with Japan. These events so impressed Secretary of the Navy James Dobbin that he authorized the building of six steam frigates during 1855–1856, followed by seven steam sloops in 1858. The fiery civil war of 1861–1865 tested those vessels, and such famed warships as *Alabama*, *Kearsarge*, *Monitor* and *Virginia* proved, time and again, the value of steam power.

By the end of the Civil War, there could be no denying that the days of wood and canvas naval vessels had ended. Though steam-sail hybrids would continue to be built through 1890, the shift to steel hulls coupled with more efficient engines and the acquisition of coaling stations abroad numbered their days.

Opposite: *Robert Fulton not only was the father of the steam navy, he also developed a prototype submarine and amphibious boats during his lifetime. He died before he could see the Navy commission its first steam-powered ship, which was named in his honor. (Corbis)*

Below: *Early steam warships like the side-wheel steamer* Susquehanna, *depicted with the frigate* Congress *at Naples, Italy, in 1857, retained sails to complement their steam engines. However, the future pointed to a Navy less reliant on Mother Nature to propel its warships. (Thomas De Simone, Navy Art Collection)*

23 May

After his predecessor resigns, Levi Woodbury takes office as the ninth Secretary of the Navy. A New Hampshire native, he is a former member of the Senate Naval Affairs Committee.

15 June

In an effort to end the issuance of the traditional grog ration on board Navy ships, the Secretary of the Navy authorizes the payment to sailors of six cents in lieu of each ration. The general order is unpopular and rarely obeyed.

24 September

The Secretary of the Navy decrees that the flogging of a man can occur only in the presence of a ship's captain and under his orders.

1832

1 January

Sailors and Marines from the sloop *Lexington* under the command of Master Commandant Silas Duncan land in the Falkland Islands in response to the seizure of two American whaling vessels.

6 February

Inhabitants of Quallah Battoo, Sumatra, had boarded the American merchantman *Friendship* in February 1831, killing three members of her crew and plundering her. Master Charles Endicott escapes and later recaptures his

1831

3 February

An act of Congress authorizes the construction of three schooners, which upon completion are christened *Experiment*, *Enterprise*, and *Boxer*.

Oppsosite, top: *The practice of flogging was one means of enforcing discipline aboard ship. Sketch by Captain's Clerk Charles F. Sands from his journal kept on board the brig* Porpoise *in 1848. ("USS Porpoise," Charles F. Sands, Naval Historical Center)*

Opposite, bottom: *("The Action at Quallah Battoo, Sumatra, 6 February 1832," Naval Historical Center)*

Right: *The ship-of-the-line* Delaware *pictured in dry dock at Norfolk, Virginia. The establishment of repair facilities was vital to the maintenance of the burgeoning fleet during the mid-1800s. ("USS* Delaware," *R.G. Bruff, Naval Historical Center)*

ship. When word of the attack reaches Washington, the frigate *Potomac* is dispatched to the East Indies to protect American commerce. She sails on 28 August 1831. On this day, disguised as a merchantman, she anchors off Quallah Battoo at dawn and lands 282 sailors and Marines, who capture four forts defending the town and burn Quallah Battoo. Sumatran casualties include Rajah Po Mahomet, their leader.

8 March
The sloop *Peacock* under the command of Captain David Geisinger departs Boston, Massachusetts, bound for the Pacific. Carrying Edmund Roberts, a merchant accredited by the State Department, the ship travels to the Far East to conclude treaties with nations bordering the Indian Ocean.

1833

20 March
Edmund Roberts and Captain David Geisinger of the sloop *Peacock* conclude a commercial treaty with the King of Siam, marking the first treaty between the United States and a nation in the Orient. Later in the cruise Roberts negotiates a treaty with the Sultan of Muscat in Arabia.

17 June
The ship-of-the-line *Delaware* enters drydock at Norfolk, Virginia, marking the opening of the U.S. Navy's first drydock. Despite the fact that it is not fully completed, Commodore Lewis Warrington orders the action in a successful effort to become operational before another federal drydock in Boston, Massachusetts.

24 June
Vice President Martin Van Buren and the Secretaries of War and the Navy join other onlookers in watching the venerable frigate *Constitution* enter Dry Dock Number 1 at the navy yard in Boston. Both ship and drydock still exist today.

31 October
The sloop *Lexington* lands a party of forty-three sailors and Marines at Buenos Aires, Argentina, to protect foreign interests in the city.

1834

30 June
Congress appropriates the sum of $5,000 for use in conducting experiments with shipboard steam

engines, which will eventually revolutionize the ships of the U.S. Navy.

1 July

Mahlon Dickerson, former New Jersey governor and U.S. Senator from that state, assumes duties as the tenth Secretary of the Navy.

1835

29 October

The Secretary of the Navy issues orders to Commodore Alexander J. Dallas, commander of the West India Squadron, directing him to send a ship to cruise along the west coast of Florida to assist in the removal of the Seminole Indians.

1836

1 January

Responding to the request of Florida Governor John Eaton, Lieutenant Edward T. Doughty departs Pensacola with a force of twenty-nine sailors and Marines to patrol the coast between Pensacola and Tampa Bay in search of Seminole Indians.

28 January

The sloop-of-war *Vandalia* under the command of Master Commandant Thomas T. Webb departs Pensacola, Florida, and sets course for Tampa Bay to help protect Fort Brooke. During March and April, Lieutenant Levin M. Powell mounts two boat expeditions from the ship reconnoitering the area around Tampa Bay.

1 April

A detachment from the boat expedition of Lieutenant Levin M. Powell surprises a group of Seminole Indians in their encampment. Under the command of Lieutenant Stephen C. Rowan, the attackers kill two Indians and wound two others in a brief skirmish.

19 June–17 July

The steamboats *American*, *Major Dade*, and *Lieutenant Izard*, purchased by the War Department but manned by U.S. Navy crews, operate on the Chattahoochee River in support of General Winfield Scott's campaign against the Creek Indians in Alabama and Georgia. All three eventually shift their operations to Florida for use against the Seminoles, during which time *Lieutenant Izard* sinks. Her commander is Lieutenant Raphael Semmes, who gains fame in the Civil War as skipper of the Confederate raider *Alabama*.

12 July

Charles H. Haswell becomes the first engineer commissioned in the U.S. Navy. He remains in the service until 1852 and during his time in uniform writes the standard engineering reference book *Mechanic's and Engineer's Pocket Book.*

2 October

The sloop-of-war *Vandalia* and the revenue cutter *Washington* depart Pensacola, Florida, bound for Key West. On board is Lieutenant Levin M. Powell, who upon arrival in Key West leads an expedition searching for Seminole Indians. Though the sailors and Marines do not engage any significant number of the enemy, the force enters the Everglades and represents the first efforts at riverine warfare during the Seminole War. A member of Powell's expedition is Stephen R. Mallory, a future U.S. senator from Florida and Confederate Secretary of the Navy during the Civil War.

1837

24 September

Lieutenant Levin M. Powell, writing to the Secretary of War, offers his service to lead another expedition against the Seminole Indians in the Everglades in which he proposes to take the war to the enemy by searching out villages. The following month he presents his proposal, "Project of an Expedition to the Everglades of South Florida," to War Department officials in Washington, D.C., which forms the basis for joint Army and Navy operations commencing in December 1837.

13 December

Fulton, the first seagoing steamship to see operational service in the Navy, is commissioned in New York.

1838

15 January

Employing a captured Indian woman as a guide, Lieutenant Levin M. Powell leads a force of some eighty soldiers, sailors, and Marines down a trail along the Jupiter River, Florida. Coming upon a Seminole encampment about five miles inland, the force engages in a firefight with the well-concealed enemy, suffering four killed and twenty-two wounded, including Powell and three fellow officers, which prompts a withdrawal before nightfall.

22 March

Using a trail discovered by Lieutenant Levin M. Powell, Lieutenant Colonel James Bankhead leads an attack against a Seminole band on an island in the Florida Everglades. The Native Americans are driven from the island, though not before exchanging fire with Powell's boats. The event marks the first deep penetration into the swamp hideaway of the Seminoles by United States military forces.

SCIENCE, EXPLORATION, AND THE U.S. NAVY

by Mark Jan K. Herman

Science, exploration, and the U.S. Navy have been intertwined since the first half of the nineteenth century. When American vessels began plying the world's trade routes, Navy warships were soon on station protecting their interests. Charting those seas and getting the lay of the land bordering them was why the Navy got into the exploration business. Even before the Civil War, Navy personnel had conducted expeditions to Antarctica, the Amazon River, and the Middle East.

The Wilkes Exploring Expedition (1838–1842) was the most ambitious. During the first circumnavigation by Navy ships, Lieutenant Charles Wilkes made surveys that formed the basis for many American charts used before the Civil War. The expedition's civilian scientists also collected flora and fauna as well as cultural artifacts, and these were a part of the Smithsonian Institution's original collections.

Other Navy-led expeditions to Panama between 1870 and 1875 presaged the construction of a ship canal across the isthmus almost a half century later. Following Wilkes's success, the Navy explored other oceans. Navy surgeon Elisha Kent Kane charted northern Greenland and reached the highest latitude yet attained (80 degrees 35 minutes N.) in 1854. More dramatic still was the ill-fated Jeannette Expedition, whose goal in 1879 was the North Pole. The voyage ended almost before it began when *Jeannette* became icebound. The vessel remained trapped for nearly two years before finally succumbing to the polar ice.

Because Navy vessels required up-to-date charts and accurate chronometers for determining longitude, Congress established the Depot of Charts and Instruments in 1830. Eight years later, Lieutenant James Gilliss became superintendent. Gilliss's hard work and persistence resulted in the eventual construction of new quarters for the depot on a hilltop in Washington, D.C.'s, Foggy Bottom neighborhood. When completed in 1844, the depot, soon to be renamed the U.S. Naval Observatory, began operations under Lieutenant Matthew Fontaine Maury. Using data obtained from logbooks of naval and merchant ships, Maury began publishing his famous wind and current charts and sailing directions. By the time he resigned from the Navy at the outbreak of the Civil War and joined the Confederate cause, Maury had helped establish a scientific reputation for the service.

Although he was leader of one of the world's leading astronomical laboratories, Maury's main interest was not in astronomy, but in subjects associated with the science of oceanography—marine meteorology, winds and currents, tides, the salinity of seawater, the makeup and depth of the ocean bottom, and habits of marine mammals. *The Physical Geography of the Sea*, published in 1855, is considered to be the first

oceanographic textbook, and Maury has come to be called the father of modern oceanography.

James Gilliss was appointed superintendent of the Naval Observatory following Maury's hasty departure in 1861. During his four-year tenure, Gilliss steered the scientific program back toward astronomy by revising star charts and updating the Observatory's scientific instruments. In 1877, Asaph Hall discovered the two moons of Mars while peering through that institution's "Great Equatorial," the world's largest refracting telescope.

Navy oceanography did not end with Maury's departure. Hydrographic research has continued into the present era. Using a newly invented depthfinder, Navy oceanographers began a systematic program of mapping the ocean bottom and developing a series of bathymetric charts in 1922.

The high point of that research, coincidentally, became the "low point" in 1960 when Lieutenant Don Walsh and Jacques Piccard squeezed into *Trieste* and descended 7,000 fathoms to the bottom of the Marianas Trench, the deepest part of the Pacific Ocean. The Navy has continued to focus attention on oceanographic research using other submersibles to explore beneath the sea. *Alvin*, a deep submergence vessel, has had its share of successes, including the discovery of deep-sea hydrothermal vents. The unmanned and remotely-operated submersibles *Jason*

and *Medea* are capable of dives to 20,000 feet.

The other frontier—space—also drew the Navy's attention. In 1951 the Naval Research Laboratory designed the *Viking*, a long, slim high-altitude research rocket that touched the very edge of the atmosphere. Throughout the 1950s and into the early 1960s, the Navy conducted many unmanned and manned balloon ascents. These platforms performed upper-atmosphere research and evaluated man's ability to survive in a near-space environment.

The launch of *Sputnik* in 1957 ignited the space race between the United States and the Soviet Union and spurred the initiation of Project Mercury, which resulted in the Navy's Commander Alan B. Shepard becoming the first American in space. Navy personnel have participated in every space program since then as scientists and/or flight crews, and are contributing to the construction and manning of the International Space Station.

Opposite: *("Doctor Elisha Kent Kane in Cabin of USS* Advance," *Thomas Hicks, U.S. Naval Academy)*

Above: *The deep-diving research bathyscaphe* Trieste *is hoisted out of the water, circa 1958–1959. The pressure sphere can be seen on the underside of the vessel. (Naval Historical Center)*

31 May

Responding to a request by the Secretary of War about how to more efficiently blockade Florida in order to prevent gunpowder from Havana, Cuba, from reaching the Seminole Indians, Lieutenant John McLaughlin outlines specifications for a shallow-draft schooner. The former yacht *Wave*, outfitted as a schooner, is placed under the command of Lieutenant McLaughlin and sent to Florida.

1 July

James Kirk Paulding, a former secretary to the Board of Navy Commissioners and Naval Agent at New York, takes office as the eleventh Secretary of the Navy.

19 August

Under the command of Lieutenant Charles Wilkes, the ships of the United States Exploring Expedition—the sloops-of-war *Vincennes* and *Peacock*, the brig *Porpoise*, the pilot schooners *Flying Fish* and *Sea Gull*, and the storeship *Relief*—depart Hampton Roads, Virginia, to conduct a geographical survey of the uncharted territories of the Pacific.

18 September

Lieutenant John McLaughlin leads boat parties to investigate the wrecks of ships blown ashore during a recent storm off Florida's east coast, the crews of which were attacked by Seminole Indians. McLaughlin and his men engage in a brief skirmish near the wreck of the brig *Alna*, killing three Seminoles and wounding three others.

1839

5 April

The Secretary of the Navy directs Commander Isaac Mayo to assume command of the steamer *Poinsett*, the schooner *Wave*, and barges assigned to the U.S. Army's blockading force in southern Florida. Mayo's orders are to cooperate with land forces in hostilities with the Seminole Indians.

26 April

The schooner *Sea Gull* is lost at sea off the coast of South America. No trace of her crew of sixteen under the command of Midshipman J.W.E. Reid is ever found.

30 July

Learning of the 23 July killing of twelve men at a U.S. Army trading post on the Caloosahatchee River, Florida, boat parties from the steamer *Poinsett* capture a party of Indians under the leadership of Catsha

Left: *Naval landing parties battled stifling heat and the harsh Florida landscape in the campaigns against the Seminole Indians. ("U.S. Navy Lieutenant, Midshipman, and Armed Seamen, 1830," Warner, Curator for the Department of the Navy)*

Opposite, top: *The brig* Porpoise *and the schooner* Sea Gull *operating in heavy seas, probably off Antarctica in March 1839. ("United States Exploring Expedition under Lt. Charles Wilkes, USN (1838–42)," Jordan and Halpin, Naval Historical Center)*

Opposite, bottom: *("Captain Charles Wilkes, circa 1826," Sully, Department of the Navy)*

ER & SCHOONER SEPAR

Tustenuggee (Mad Tiger) that had just departed from a visit to the vessel. The massacre is in direct violation of the treaty concluded with the Seminole Indians by General Alexander Macomb on 18 May 1839.

26 August

The revenue cutter *Washington* discovers the Spanish slave ship *Amistad* lying at anchor near Montauk Point, New York. The ship, which had been seized by her black captives and sailed around the North Atlantic for two months, was captured and the slaves sent to New Haven, Connecticut, to stand trial for piracy and the murder of two members of *Amistad*'s crew. The ensuing trial galvanizes the swelling abolitionist movement in the United States and the case eventually reaches the Supreme Court, where former President John Quincy Adams argues it. The slaves are eventually acquitted and most return to Africa as free men and women.

2 December

Lieutenant John McLaughlin, mirroring Lieutenant Levin Powell's ideas for operating in the Everglades with flat-bottom boats and canoes in an effort to take the war to the Seminole Indians, assumes command of what becomes known as the Mosquito Fleet.

1840

19 January
Sailing on board the sloop-of-war *Vincennes*, Lieutenant Charles Wilkes discovers the continent of Antarctica one day ahead of a French expedition's sighting of the icy land. Wilkes later writes that he "saw the land gradually rising beyond the ice to the height of three thousand feet. . . . It could be seen extending to the east and west of our position fully sixty miles . . . and now that all were convinced of its existence I gave the land the name of the Antarctic Continent."

10 April
A scouting party of twenty-four sailors and Marines from the schooner *Otsego* is attacked by Seminole Indians at Cape Sable, Florida. The men form a defensive perimeter and engage the enemy for some two and one half hours until the sight of boats coming ashore from the schooners *Wave* and *Flirt* prompt the attackers to withdraw.

10 July
Lieutenant John McLaughlin writes to the Secretary of the Navy expressing his concern over the reduction in manpower in the Florida Expedition due to the arrest of black sailors ashore under a territorial act preventing the migration of free blacks into Florida. The Secretary of the Navy responds that he approves of the actions and offers no solution to the problem.

26 July
Exacting retribution for the murder of two officers of his expedition, Lieutenant Charles Wilkes leads a landing party ashore at Malolo in the Fiji Islands, destroying the towns of Sualib and Arro.

6–7 August
A band of some 140 Seminoles under Chief Chakaika

launches a night attack against the settlement at Indian Key, Florida. Though many settlers flee to safety on board the nearby schooner *Medium*, the marauders kill thirteen people and torch many buildings. At a naval hospital one mile away, Midshipman Francis K. Murray receives news of the attack and musters a force of five able-bodied sailors and seven volunteers from the hospital ward in mounting an attack against Chakaika's beached canoes using barges armed with four-pounder cannon. The Seminoles gather to repel the attack and shots are exchanged until the four-pounders recoil overboard. The Indians depart the scene with their booty.

27 September
Naval theorist Alfred Thayer Mahan, whose landmark writings strongly influence today's U.S. Navy, is born in West Point, New York. He is the son of Dennis Hart Mahan, a noted professor at the U.S. Military Academy.

31 December
A joint force consisting of ninety sailors and sixty Marines accompanying ninety soldiers of the U.S. Army's Third Artillery board canoes and enter the Florida Everglades for an extended operation against surviving Seminole Indians. Over the course of the next nineteen days, the force captures the Indian leader Chia and, when the soldiers return to the coast, the sailors cross the Everglades to the west coast of Florida, becoming the first non-Native Americans to accomplish this feat.

1841

7 January
Missouri, a sidewheel frigate, is launched at the New York Navy Yard. One of the U.S. Navy's first true steam warships, she is soon joined by the side-wheel steamers *Mississippi* and *Union*, the latter equipped with the Hunter Wheel, a paddle wheel placed horizontally within the hull below the waterline. Reflecting the period of transition, all three ships retained masts and rigging for sails.

25 February
A landing party from the sloop-of-war *Peacock*, consisting of seventy sailors and Marines, sets fire to three native villages on Upolu in the Samoan Islands. The action on the part of the ship, which is operating as part of the Wilkes Expedition, is in retaliation for the killing of an American merchant seaman.

6 March
North Carolina lawyer George E. Badger becomes the twelfth Secretary of the Navy.

9 April
In a second military action launched by the sloop-of-war *Peacock* against Pacific islanders, an eighty-man detachment lands on Drummond Island in the Gilberts chain in an effort to rescue a seaman kidnapped from a party

Sam Jones. Operating in concert with Army forces, the expedition is unsuccessful and yields only an abandoned camp that the force destroys.

11 October
Abel P. Upshur, a former General Court Judge in Virginia, takes office as the thirteenth Secretary of the Navy.

3 November–23 December
Personnel of the Mosquito Fleet endure hardships during two unsuccessful forays into the Florida Everglades. On one march it takes sailors under the command of Lieutenant John Rodgers five days to cover a distance of twenty-five miles wading through waist-deep mud. By 23 December nearly one quarter of the Mosquito Fleet's sailors and Marines are incapacitated by illness.

19 December
The crew of the sloop-of-war *Vincennes*, sailing as part of the United States Exploring Expedition, sights Wake Island, actually an atoll consisting of three islets. One is named after expedition commander Lieutenant Charles Wilkes and another honors the expedition's chief scientist, Titian Ramsay Peale. Exactly a century later, American naval forces and civilian contractors occupy defenses on Wake in an ultimately unsuccessful attempt to prevent its capture by the Japanese.

1842

previously sent ashore. Though the detachment disperses a force of warriors that outnumbers it by a margin of ten to one and burns two villages, the rescue is unsuccessful.

7 July
The House Naval Affairs Committee approves a bill creating a Home Squadron to patrol the waters off American cities and the Newfoundland Fishing Banks, a measure strongly advocated by the President and Secretary of the Navy in response to a war scare with Great Britain that swept the nation. The Home Squadron is officially created on 1 August.

18 July
The sloop-of-war *Peacock* wrecks on a bar off the Columbia River in Oregon. Fortunately, no members of her crew are lost.

10 October
Two hundred sailors and Marines of the Mosquito Fleet enter the Florida Everglades and engage in a seventeen-day hunt for the Seminole Indian leader

In the Annual Report of the Secretary of the Navy for 1842, Abel Upshur recommends that a law set the number of officers in each rank and proposes that a school be established on shore for the instruction of midshipmen.

11 February
With an estimated 140 Seminole Indians still living in the Florida Everglades, Lieutenant John McLaughlin sends elements of his Mosquito Fleet in a two-pronged sweep of the area. One column under Lieutenant John Rodgers comprises the eastern pincer while the forces covering the west are under the command of Lieutenant John B. Marchand. Nature is the greatest enemy for the men, who endure two months of hardships living in dugout canoes. They spot few Seminole Indians, and offensive action consists mainly of destroying camps and fields of crops.

March

Two ships under the command of Commodore Lawrence Kearny arrive in China under orders to prevent the smuggling of opium into China "by Americans or by other nations under cover of the American flag." While in Chinese waters, Kearny negotiates an agreement granting the United States favored status in trade with China, setting the stage for the Treaty of Wanghia in 1844 that regularizes Sino-American relations.

10 June

The ships of the United States Exploring Expedition arrive at New York, concluding their mission. During nearly four years the officers and men of the command cross the Pacific Ocean three times, surveying more than 200 islands and countless miles of coastline ranging from Antarctica to the Pacific Northwest.

20 June

Offensive operations against the Seminole Indians having ceased on 10 May, the Florida Expedition is formally disestablished.

LITERATURE OF THE SEA

by Dr. C. Herbert Gilliland

Literary tradition in the U.S. Navy may be said to go as far back as John Paul Jones, who composed sonnets to his lady friends and staged Shakespeare aboard his ship. More importantly, Jones's career (eventually the subject of many books, plays and films) inspired the first true sea novel in English, James Fenimore Cooper's *The Pilot* (1824). Cooper, himself a former midshipman, thus initiated the rich modern tradition of literature of the sea. Besides several other nautical novels, he also wrote the first important history of the U.S. Navy. His younger contemporary, Herman Melville, based his novel *White-Jacket* upon his enlisted service in the frigate *United States* in 1844–1845.

Some of the better naval writing in the nineteenth century appeared in reports and memoirs. David Porter's *Journal of a Cruise* (1815) recounts his raids on the British whaling fleet and his visits to various Pacific islands while in command of the frigate *Essex* during the War of 1812. Nathaniel Hawthorne edited Horatio Bridge's *Journal of an African Cruise* (1845). Alexander Slidell Mackenzie was well regarded in literary circles for his travel books and naval biographies. He is now better known as the captain who in 1842 executed for mutiny the son of the Secretary of War on board the brig *Somers*, an act that inspired Melville's short novel *Billy Budd*.

Scant work of literary note emerged from the Civil War Navy experience except some poems by Melville, though Charles E. Clark's memoir *My Fifty Years in the Navy* describes the author's colorful career beginning with the Civil War, and Edward Shippen's autobiographical novel *Thirty Years at Sea* is of some interest. Beginning in the 1890s, many novels aimed at juvenile readers have featured the Navy. Some of the better of these were by Naval Academy graduates Edward L. Beach, Sr., Fitzhugh Green, and Yates Stirling.

The period from just before World War II through the present has produced the greatest wealth of significant literature connected with the American Navy. Marcus Goodrich's novel *Delilah* (1941) draws upon the author's experience in a destroyer in the Philippines just prior to World War I. Retired Chief Machinist Mate Richard McKenna's *The Sand Pebbles* (1962) takes place aboard a fictitious Yangtze River gunboat between the wars.

World War II itself inspired a number of excellent novels. Herman Wouk (who joined the Navy partly because of Goodrich's *Delilah*) created one of fiction's most unforgettable characters,

Captain Queeg of *The Caine Mutiny* (1946). Edward L. Beach, Jr.'s, classic of submarine warfare, *Run Silent, Run Deep* (1955) reflects his own experience in the Pacific. John Claggett's *The Slot* (1957) fictionalizes the author's PT boat service. Edward Ellsberg, already a novelist, wrote a fine nonfiction account of his important salvage work in Massawa, Ethiopia, in *Under the Red Sea Sun* (1946). William Mack's early novels dramatize actions in the Pacific in which he participated. Thomas Heggens' *Mister Roberts* (1946) made the likable title character a household name, and like many Navy-related works of literature, this novel made its way to stage and screen. Dan Gallery began writing at the end of the war, though his humorous "Fatso" and other stories are Cold War tales.

Naval aviation has developed a literature of its own. Samuel Hynes' memoir *Flight of Passage* (1988) describes his coming of age as a Marine Corps pilot during World War II, and James Michener's novel *The Bridges at Toko-Ri* (1953) humanizes carrier aviation during the Korean War. The brown-shoe navy has recently produced such popular techno-thrillers as Stephen Coonts' *Flight of the Intruder* (1986) and Ward Carroll's *Punk's War* (2001).

For the surface navy, there are novels by the likes of David Poyer and P. T. Deutermann. The best known submarine thriller is Tom Clancy's *The Hunt for Red October* (1985). At the same time Poyer and others have turned back to the age of sail and the Civil War as settings for historical novels.

With some notable exceptions, like Clancy, successful authors of American naval literature have seen naval service themselves. Ironically, Navy culture long tended to view writing for publication with suspicion. In the late nineteenth century a senior commodore voiced the common opinion that "it is not the business of a naval officer to write books," and even decades later Edward L. Beach, Jr., felt obliged to explain that he had time to write because, after all, he didn't play golf. Clearly, though, an occupation that combines the romance of seafaring and the fascination of technology with the hazards of combat invites the creative voice. Today's naval authors might say, "we have just begun to write."

Opposite: *Author James Michener pictured while serving as an officer in the U.S. Navy during World War II. His Pulitzer Prize-winning novel,* Tales of the South Pacific, *was based on his wartime experiences and a subsequent work,* The Bridges at Toko-Ri, *is perhaps the finest book to come out of the Korean War. (Corbis)*

Above: *The author of the famous novels* Moby Dick *and* Billy Budd, *Herman Melville learned the ways of the sea as a sailor in the U.S. Navy. (Corbis)*

29 June

Lieutenant Matthew Fontaine Maury, his days at sea ended by a leg injury suffered in a stagecoach accident, is assigned to the post of Superintendent of the Depot of Charts and Instruments. In this capacity he becomes a world-renowned expert on oceanography, publishing *The Physical Geography of the Sea* in 1855. He has gone down in history as the "Pathfinder of the Seas."

9 August

A clause in the Webster-Ashburton Treaty between the United States and Great Britain includes a provision for each nation to operate a naval squadron off the west coast of Africa in an effort to suppress slave traders operating under each nation's respective flag.

31 August

In landmark legislation that changes the face of naval administration, Congress abolishes the Board of Navy Commissioners and replaces it with five bureaus: Yards and Docks, Construction and Repair, Provisions and Clothing, Ordnance and Hydrography, and Medicine and Surgery. Those appointed to the posts of bureau chief wield enormous power within the hierarchy of the Navy.

Congress passes a bill authorizing an engineer-in-chief and directing the assignment of one chief engineer to every steamship in the U.S. Navy.

21 October

Responding to erroneous reports of war between the United States and Mexico and the imminent cession of California to Great Britain, a landing party from the frigate *United States*—flagship of Pacific Squadron commander Thomas ap Catesby Jones—and the sloop-of-war *Cyane* goes ashore at Monterey, California, to accept the surrender of the small Mexican garrison there. The landing party raises the American flag over a dilapidated castle, which they nickname Fort Catesby. The following day Thomas Larkin, an American merchant in Monterey, produces papers from August that reveal no mention of war between the two nations. Realizing his mistake, Jones hauls down the flag, returns Monterey to Mexico, and withdraws his forces.

1 December

By order of Commander Alexander Slidell Mackenzie, skipper of the brig *Somers*, three mutineers are hanged after officers on board the ship uncover a plot to throw officers and loyal crewmen overboard and take over the ship. Those sentenced to death are Boatswain's Mate Samuel Cromwell, Seaman Elisha Small, and Midshipman Philip Spencer, the son of the Secretary of War. Following the ship's return to New York on 14 December, Mackenzie faces a court of inquiry and court-martial proceedings, both of which exonerate him of any wrongdoing in squelching the only attempted mutiny to ever occur on a U.S. Navy vessel.

1843

24 July
David Henshaw, former Collector of the Port of Boston, Massachusetts, becomes the fourteenth Secretary of the Navy.

25 August
The side-wheel frigate *Missouri* arrives in Gibraltar after a nineteen-day crossing, thus becoming the first steam-powered Navy ship to cross the Atlantic Ocean. The following evening her life ends ignominiously when the engineer's yeoman working in a storeroom breaks a jug of turpentine that ignites, engulfing the ship in flames.

9 September
Princeton, the first screw steam warship in the U.S. Navy, is commissioned at the Philadelphia Navy Yard, Pennsylvania, under the command of Captain Robert F. Stockton. Her power plant consists of three coal-burning tubular iron boilers and two vibrating-lever engines driving a six-bladed propeller measuring fourteen feet in diameter.

5 December
In launching ceremonies at Erie, Pennsylvania, the side-wheel steamer *Michigan* slides partly down the ways before becoming stuck. Darkness ends efforts to push her into the water, but the next morning shipwrights awaken to find her floating in Lake Erie, having launched herself during the night. It is an awkward beginning for *Michigan*, the U.S. Navy's first iron-hulled warship.

15 December
A landing party of two hundred sailors and Marines under Commodore Matthew Perry engage in a conference with King Ben Krako near the village of Little Berebee on Africa's Ivory Coast. The subject of discussion is the 1841 seizure of the American schooner *Mary Carver* and the murder of her crew. A melee erupts during the conference, during which Krako and several natives are killed. In the wake of the violence, local tribal leaders sign an agreement not to plunder traders or interfere with missionaries.

1844

19 February
Thomas Walker Gilmer, a former governor of Virginia and a U.S. Representative from that commonwealth, takes office as the fifteenth Secretary of the Navy.

25 February
President John Tyler signs into law a Naval Appropriation Act for Fiscal Year 1845 that establishes a limit of 7,500 enlisted men, prompting the Secretary of the Navy to eventually withdraw remaining ships-of-the-line from active service.

29 February
Tragedy befalls members of an official party on board the screw steam warship *Princeton* during a cruise on the Potomac River near Washington, D.C., when a 12-inch "Peacemaker" cannon bursts during a demonstration firing. The blast kills Secretary of the Navy Thomas Gilmer, Secretary of State Abel Upshur; Chief of the Bureau of Construction, Equipment, and Repair Captain Beverly Kennon; and four others. Among the wounded are *Princeton*'s skipper Captain Robert F. Stockton and Senator Thomas Hart Benton. Gilmer's death after nine days in office marks the shortest tenure in history for a Secretary of the Navy.

Opposite, top: *The screw steamer* Princeton. *Among the designers of her unique power plant was John Ericsson, who would become famous in the Civil War as the designer of the ironclad* Monitor. *(Naval Historical Center)*

Opposite, bottom: *("Matthew Fontaine Maury," E. Sophonisba Hergesheimer, U.S. Naval Academy)*

Above: *Commodore Thomas ap Catesby Jones depicted while in command of the Pacific Squadron. ("Commodore Thomas Catesby Jones," Naval Historical Center)*

26 March
John Young Mason, experienced in naval affairs from a stint as head of the House Naval Affairs Committee, takes office as the sixteenth Secretary of the Navy.

29 March
In a largely Protestant officer corps, Uriah Levy becomes the first Jewish officer appointed to the rank of captain.

29 January
The Secretary of the Navy requests that the bureau chiefs form a board for the purpose of examining plans for diving bells, submarines, and mines produced by Captain George W. Taylor.

26 February
In an effort to clearly define the relationship between engineering officers and officers of the line, the Secretary of the Navy issues a General Order specifying the duties of engineers on board ship and outlining the measures to be taken in the care of machinery and the training of firemen.

11 March
George Bancroft, a prominent historian, becomes the seventeenth Secretary of the Navy.

20 March
In response to the joint resolution of Congress

Opposite, top: *The bodies of two of the three alleged mutineers hanged on board the brig* Somers *swing from the yardarm as the ship returns home from the African coast on 1 December 1842. ("USS* Somers," *Naval Historical Center)*

Opposite, bottom: *("USS* Michigan," *Charles Patterson, Dossin Marine Museum, Belle Isle, Michigan)*

Right: *Survivors row clear of the side-wheel frigate* Missouri, *which accidentally was set on fire at Gibraltar in 1843. ("Burning of the United States Steam Frigate* Missouri," *E. Duncan, Naval Historical Center)*

annexing Texas, ships of the Home Squadron under the command of Commodore David Conner receive orders to sail to Mexican waters. The following month a squadron under the command of Commodore Robert F. Stockton is diverted from a planned voyage to the Mediterranean to support operations off Mexico. Together, the two forces number eight ships.

25–29 March
Lieutenant S. F. Blunt commands a joint boat expedition from the brig *Truxtun* and HBMS *Ardent* to capture the American slaver *Spitfire* in the Rio Pongas, West Africa.

31 March
Mexico breaks diplomatic relations with the United States.

2 June
The annual board for the examination of midshipmen convenes at the Naval Asylum in Philadelphia, Pennsylvania, a school conducted by Professor William Chauvenet. By the direction of Secretary of the Navy George Bancroft, the board considers the suitability of Fort Severn in Annapolis, Maryland, as the site for a naval academy, the contents of a suitable course of instruction, and the selection of three officers to assist in planning for the establishment of an academy.

4 June
Under the command of Commodore James Biddle, the ship-of-the-line *Columbus* and the sloop-of-war *Vincennes* depart New York under orders to carry Alexander H. Everett to China where he will deliver the ratified copy of the Treaty of Wanghia, giving the United States rights to trade in Chinese ports. During the passage, Everett's poor health prompts him to go ashore in Rio de Janiero, Brazil, leaving Biddle to continue to China on board *Columbus* to complete the mission.

25 July
An army under the command of General Zachary Taylor lands near Corpus Christi, Texas, after Texas approves a resolution agreeing to annexation by the United States. The convoy which carried them from New Orleans was escorted by the sloop-of-war *St. Mary's*.

15 August
The Secretary of War authorizes the transfer of Fort Severn in Annapolis, Maryland, to the Navy. On this day, the Secretary of the Navy appoints Commander Franklin Buchanan, an officer with a reputation as a strict disciplinarian, as the first superintendent of the U.S. Naval School scheduled to open in Annapolis in October.

U.S. NAVAL ACADEMY:
"HEARTBEAT OF A GREAT NATION"

by Lieutenant Commander Thomas J. Cutler, U.S. Navy (Retired)

After viewing a parade at the U.S. Naval Academy, a retiring officer once wrote: "As I feel the thunder of drums on Worden Field, I sense that I am feeling the heartbeat of a great nation. As I hear the echoes of bugles reverberating against the monuments that proliferate this campus we call 'The Yard,' I am reminded of the greatness that has gone before us and will continue to emerge from within these walls." His musings in many ways sum up the essence of an institution that has been preparing young Americans for service to their country as officers in the naval service for more than a century-and-a-half.

The idea of a naval academy went back to the earliest days of the Republic, when John Adams called for the establishment of a naval school. Eventually created through the determination and clever maneuvering of Secretary of the Navy George Bancroft, the "Naval School," as it was then called, opened its doors at the site of an old Army fort on the Severn River on 10 October 1845 with Commander Franklin Buchanan as its first Superintendent.

In the years following its establishment, the Academy underwent many changes. "Midshipmen" were renamed "cadets" and then became "midshipmen" again. The course of instruction went through many iterations, both in length (ranging from two years to six) and content (naval engineering intruding upon the traditional "learning the ropes" of the sailing navy, for example). During the Civil War, the Academy was moved from its rather vulnerable southern location to Newport, Rhode Island, where it remained for the duration of the war.

In 1873, two seminal events occurred. The first was the graduation of Albert Michelson, who would later be awarded the Nobel Prize for Physics when he obtained the most precise terrestrial measurement of the speed of light ever made. The second occurred when a group of officers met to commiserate over the stagnant conditions then prevalent in the Navy; that group became the founders of the unofficial but beneficial U.S. Naval Institute, a unique organization that has remained on the grounds of the Academy and—through its books and magazines—has preserved an open forum that has often led the way in innovation and philosophical evolution.

Although the original purpose of providing the Navy with properly trained officers still remained paramount, the mission and method evolved with time. Until 1917, when the first of two world wars

demanded a much larger navy, the Academy was the Navy's sole source of officers. Today's Naval Academy continues to provide a nucleus of officers to both the Navy and the Marine Corps.

The Academy's mission of developing "midshipmen morally, mentally, and physically" has emphasized ethical behavior and physical readiness while striving for the proper balance between professional and academic development. Professional learning takes place not only in the classroom but also in the summer cruise program that sends midshipmen out to the fleet for "real-world" experience. Academics have long flourished "where Severn meets the tide." The Paris Exposition of 1878 awarded the Academy a certificate for "having the best system of education in the United States." The Trident Scholar program was initiated in 1964, and five years later a majors program greatly enhanced academic depth and variety; today midshipmen may choose from among eighteen different majors.

Naval Academy graduates have used the knowledge, skills, and personal development acquired on the banks of the Severn to achieve victory in two world wars and ultimately transform the nation into a superpower. They have faced the rigors of life at sea, met the challenges of battle, suffered the loneliness and deprivations of ocean patrols, and left their remains in the deep and on distant shores. But Academy graduates have also contributed to the nation in ways other than military. They have been elected to both houses of the U.S. Congress and the presidency. They have been captains of industry, diplomats, judges, scientists, doctors, lawyers, astronauts, authors, and professional athletes. They have earned Medals of Honor, Nobel and Pulitzer prizes, Medals of Freedom, Olympic Medals, and Super Bowl rings. Since the days of Bancroft and Buchanan, the U.S. Naval Academy has met and most likely exceeded the expectations of its founders, and serves as what some have described as "the heart and soul of the Navy."

Opposite: *John Grimes Walker pictured in the standard uniform worn by U.S. Naval Academy midshipmen during the pre-Civil War era. Walker, who attended the academy during the period 1853–1856, served with distinction during the war, and eventually attained the rank of rear admiral. (Naval Historical Center)*

Above: *With swords drawn, midshipmen pass in review during a parade commemorating the 150th anniversary of the U.S. Naval Academy in 1995. (Paul A. Souders/Corbis)*

29 August–2 September

The Cabinet makes two decisions regarding the employment of naval forces in the event of war with Mexico: a blockade of all but two Mexican ports on the Gulf coast, and the treatment as pirates of any foreigners operating under Mexican Letters of Marque.

31 August

The Secretary of the Navy issues a General Order granting assimilated rank to surgeons in the U.S. Navy. However, the order denies them command authority.

10 October

At 11:00 a.m. Commander Franklin Buchanan addresses fifty-six midshipmen prior to the commencement of classes at the U.S. Naval School. He reads regulations that include obeying the commands of professors, not lounging or promenading about the school grounds, and avoiding bringing intoxicating spirits to school. The school's faculty includes three civilian professors and four officers, including brothers Henry H. Lockwood and Surgeon John A. Lockwood. Thus, after repeated failed attempts to create a formal school for the education of naval officers, the institution that will become the U.S. Naval Academy is born.

31 October

Commodore David Conner withdraws his ships from Veracruz, Mexico, as a condition for that nation receiving a new United States minister to Mexico, former Louisiana congressman John Slidell. The sloop-of-war *St. Mary's* transports the minister to his new post, disembarking him at Veracruz on the last day of November.

30 November

The sloop *Yorktown* captures the American slaver *Pons* off Kabenda, Africa, the first of three slave ships captured by the ship during her service in the Africa squadron.

24 December

The ship-of-the-line *Columbus* reaches Macao, China, where Commodore James Biddle disembarks with a group of officers and two missionaries and proceeds to Canton to deliver the ratified copy of the Treaty of Wanghia. The ceremony takes places in Canton on New Year's Eve and Biddle subsequently establishes the first U.S. legation in China.

1846

17 January

The Secretary of the Navy orders Commodore David Conner to once again take the ships of his Home Squadron to Veracruz, Mexico, and directs him to send a sailing vessel to support the movement of General Zachary Taylor's force to the Rio Grande. Eventually the revenue cutter *Woodbury* and brigs *Lawrence* and *Porpoise* support Taylor's force.

1 April

Commodore John D. Sloat, commander of the Pacific Squadron, orders the sloop-of-war *Portsmouth* to proceed to Monterey, California, to protect Americans there in the wake of unrest between the Mexican authorities and Army Captain John C. Frémont, leader of an expedition to find a railroad route to the Pacific.

17 April

Carrying out General Zachary Taylor's order blockading the Rio Grande to prevent supplies from reaching Mexican forces opposite his army, the brig *Lawrence* and the revenue cutter *Woodbury* stop the schooners *Equity* and *Floridian*, bound from New Orleans to Matamoros, and turn them away.

Marine Lieutenant Archibald H. Gillespie, on a secret mission to assist California in overthrowing Mexican rule, arrives at Monterey on board the sloop-of-war *Cyane*.

4 May
Having received a copy of a document dated 23 April in which Mexican President Mariano Paredes y

Arrillaga declares war against the United States, Commodore David Conner sails with ships of the Home Squadron from Veracruz, Mexico, to take station off the Rio Grande. The ships arrive at their destination on 8 May, the same day General Zachary Taylor defeats a Mexican army that has crossed the Rio Grande into Texas in the Battle of Palo Alto.

13 May
The United States declares war on Mexico. The Secretary of the Navy directs Commodore David Conner to blockade Mexican ports and seize any enemy vessels attempting to enter the waters of the Gulf of Mexico. The blockade commences the following day and becomes the main focus of U.S. Navy operations during the Mexican War. Secretary of the Navy George Bancroft also orders Commodore John D. Sloat to blockade California and detaches ships from Chinese and Brazilian waters to strengthen Sloat's Pacific Squadron.

15 May
The Secretary of the Navy orders Commodore John D. Sloat to seize San Francisco, Monterey, and other ports in California.

19–25 May
Indicative of the requirement for light-draft vessels for service in Mexican War, the Navy authorizes the

Above: *Secretary of the Navy George Bancroft ably directed naval operations during the Mexican War and left as his legacy the U.S. Naval Academy. ("Seventeenth Secretary of the Navy, George Bancroft," Arthur S. Conrad, Department of the Navy)*

Left: *The frigate* Raritan *served as Commodore David Conner's flagship and participated in the landings at Veracruz. ("USS* Raritan," *Franklin D. Roosevelt Collection)*

Opposite: *Commodore John D. Sloat led the first American naval forces landing in California, July 1846. (Naval Historical Center)*

purchase of two steamers (*Vixen* and *Spitfire*) and three schooners (*Bonita*, *Petrel*, and *Reefer*) from the New York shipbuilding firm of Brown and Bell. Ironically, all of the ships were under construction for the Mexican navy.

14 June

Six days after causing negligible damage to Mexican forts at the mouth of the Pánuco River, the sloop-of-war *St. Mary's* launches a boat expedition against the forts under the cover of darkness. The boats are recalled after one runs aground on a sandbar, alerting the defenders. The following morning, *St. Mary's* bombards the forts and Mexican gunboats under construction in their vicinity.

7 July

Commander Alexander Slidell Mackenzie meets with Mexican General Antonio Santa Anna in Havana, Cuba, presenting U.S. peace terms. The meeting is the result of President James K. Polk's opinion that, if he returns to Mexico, Santa Anna might bring about a negotiated peace settlement.

A landing party consisting of over 225 sailors and Marines from the frigate *Savannah* and the sloop-of-war *Cyane* goes ashore at Monterey, California, and occupies the town. On this day Commodore John D. Sloat sends a message to the inhabitants of California, stating in part "that although I come in arms with a powerful force, I do not come among them as an enemy to California; on the contrary, I come as their best friend—as henceforward California will be a portion of the United States."

9 July

A landing party from the sloop-of-war *Portsmouth* occupies San Francisco, California.

20 July

Ships of the East India Squadron under the command of Commodore James Biddle put into Edo (Tokyo) Bay, Japan, marking the first attempt by the U.S. Navy to open communications with the Japanese government. When Japanese officials respond negatively to his inquiries about formulating a treaty between the two countries, Biddle departs.

21 July

A board is appointed by the Secretary of the Navy to consider the merit promotion of three commanders, three lieutenants, and six passed midshipmen. The Senate refuses to confirm any of the nominees and thus perpetuates a system of promotion based on length of service.

29 July

Commodore Robert F. Stockton relieves Commodore John D. Sloat in command of the Pacific Squadron. Stockton assumes his duties having already set in motion plans for a land campaign against Los Angeles, California, in concert with Army Captain John C. Frémont's forces. On this day the sloop-of-war *Cyane* anchors off San Diego, capturing the Mexican brig *Juanita* and landing Frémont's men ashore.

4 August

The frigate *Congress* puts into Santa Barbara, California, landing a small party that receives the surrender of the town.

6 August

The frigate *Congress* arrives at San Pedro, California, and puts a landing party ashore that takes possession of the town.

7 August

U.S. steamers and gunboats commence a bombardment of a fort guarding the mouth of the Alvarado River, Mexico, operating in such close proximity to the enemy that musket fire is exchanged with Mexican infantrymen. Before a boat expedition can be mounted to attack the fort and pursue Mexican gunboats in the river, indications that a storm is approaching prompt a cancellation of operations and a withdrawal of all but one vessel.

Left: *As boats ferry men ashore, the Stars and Stripes fly high over Yerba Buena (San Francisco), 9 July 1846. (Naval Historical Center)*

Below: *With ships of the Pacific Squadron anchored off Monterey, California, the flag is raised over the city. (W. A. Coulter, Naval Historical Center)*

Opposite: *The first U.S. warships visit Japan in 1846. (Naval Historical Center)*

10 August

President James K. Polk signs a bill increasing the authorized strength of the Navy from 7,500 to 10,000 men for the duration of the Mexican War.

11 August

In a most unlikely scenario, a 360-man force of naval personnel under the command of Commodore Robert F. Stockton departs San Pedro, California, to conduct a land campaign against Los Angeles. The force reaches the town two days later and on 14 August the remaining Mexicans surrender Los Angeles.

14 August

En route to her blockading station off Tampico, Mexico, the brig *Truxtun* grounds on Tuxpan Reef in a gale. The ship's commanding officer, Commander Edward W. Carpender, sends one of *Truxtun*'s cutters

to attempt to reach American ships at Antón Lizardo on 16 August. That same day another of the ship's cutters, under the command of Lieutenant Bushrod W. Hunter, seizes a small Mexican vessel. The Americans successfully sail their prize to Antón Lizardo, capturing a Mexican schooner in route. In the meantime, Carpender hoists a white flag over *Truxtun*, surrendering to Mexican forces. He and his remaining crew are eventually exchanged for Mexican prisoners. A landing party from the screw steam warship *Princeton* burns *Truxtun* on 22 August.

19 August
Commodore Robert F. Stockton proclaims a blockade of the entire west coast of Mexico.

29 August
Secretary of the Navy George Bancroft informs Commodore David Conner of rumored operations of Mexican privateers off Key West, Florida, and directs him to obtain information about the roads and geography in Tampico and Veracruz, Mexico, for possible landings by American forces.

2 September
The sloop-of-war *Cyane*, under the command of Commander Samuel F. Du Pont, anchors at San Blas at the southern tip of Baja California. Over the course

of the next two days she captures a Mexican sloop and brig and puts a landing party ashore that spikes twenty-four Mexican cannon.

6 September
The sloop *Warren* arrives at Mazatlán, and the following day launches a boat party that captures the Mexican brig *Malek Adhel*. On 8 September *Warren* captures another Mexican brig, *Carmelita*.

9 September
George Bancroft resigns as Secretary of the Navy to accept an appointment as U.S. Minister to London. John Young Mason takes office as the eighteenth Secretary of the Navy the following day, having preceded Bancroft in the office.

14 September
The sloop-of-war *Cyane* arrives at La Paz, Baja California, proclaiming the blockade and seizing nine Mexican ships.

17 September
Seaman Samuel Jackson is hanged on board the sloop-of-war *St. Mary's* for the offenses of striking and threatening an officer and using mutinous and seditious language.

1 October

The sloop-of-war *Cyane* arrives at Loreto on the west coast of the Gulf of California, seizing two schooners. Over the next few days, the U.S. Navy warship operates in the waters surrounding Guayamas on the west coast of Mexico, capturing three additional Mexican ships and destroying three while engaged in a bombardment of the town.

8 October

A force consisting in part of crewmen from the frigate *Savannah* under the command of Captain William Mervine are repulsed in their attempt to regain control of Los Angeles, which had been surrendered by Mexican forces in the wake of a rebellion by Californians the previous month.

Above: *Captain John C. Frémont's troops going ashore from the sloop-of-war* Cyane *to relieve the naval landing force that had captured San Diego that morning, 29 July 1846.* ("USS Cyane," Carlton T. Chapman, San Diego Maritime Museum)

Opposite, top: *Reform-minded with respect to naval discipline and an advocate of steam powered warships, Commodore Robert F. Stockton was also a leading Navy commander during the Mexican War.* ("Robert F. Stockton," Franklin D. Roosevelt Collection)

Opposite, bottom: ("President James K. Polk (1795–1849)," Thomas C. Cole, U.S. Naval Academy)

15 October

U.S. naval forces make a second attempt to capture Alvarado, Mexico, with the side-wheel steamer *Mississippi* bombarding the outer fort guarding the entrance to the Alvarado River while the steamer *Vixen* leads small vessels in a column past the fort, firing their guns at the enemy fortifications. In the second phase of the attack, two columns of warships attempt to cross the sandbar at the mouth of the river and pursue Mexican gunboats. The lead ship of the second column, the steamer *McLane*, runs aground and, by the time she is freed, Commodore David Conner has canceled the attack.

23 October

Six vessels under the command of Commodore Matthew C. Perry cross a sandbar leading into the Tabasco River, Mexico, and make their way upstream to the port of Frontera, where they capture a schooner and two steamers. Perry lands a small force under the command of Lieutenant Joseph C. Walsh to hold the town.

25 October

A landing party goes ashore near the town of Tabasco, Mexico, capturing Fort Acachapan, which was abandoned by Mexican forces upon sighting Commodore Matthew C. Perry's approaching ships in the Tabasco River. When the town refuses to surrender, the steamer *Vixen* fires shots over the town and Perry lands a force under the command of Marine Captain French Forrest, which takes sporadic enemy fire as they go ashore. In the meantime, Perry's ships capture five Mexican warships.

26 October
Despite the desire of the townspeople to surrender, Mexican Lieutenant Colonel Don Juan Traconis persists in his desire to defend Tabasco, Mexico, directing his troops to fire at American vessels. Not wanting to risk killing innocent civilians, Commodore Matthew C. Perry holds his fire, but when Lieutenant Charles W. Morris is mortally wounded while assisting a prize vessel that runs aground in front of the town, American ships open fire. Mexican fire eventually subsides and Perry, not having enough men to hold the town, returns to the American base at Antón Lizardo with most of the prizes, two of which are taken into American service.

27 October
Sailors and Marines from the frigates *Savannah* and *Congress* receive a few shots from Californians ashore, but manage to make a successful landing and seize control of San Pedro.

14 November
A force consisting of two steamers and four schooners under the command of Commodore David Conner lands a force of 300 men in seizing the port town of

Tampico, Mexico, the only shot fired being the one to signal the beginning of the assault. Three Mexican military schooners and two commercial schooners are also captured.

15 November
The sloop-of-war *Boston*, en route to join the Home Squadron off Mexico, encounters a squall off the Bahamas, and is wrecked when high winds sweep her onto Eleuthra Island.

18 November
Commander Josiah Tatnall leads a boat expedition up the Pánuco River to seize Pánuco, Mexico. Accepting the town's surrender on 19 November, Tatnall's men seize a 24-pounder cannon and other equipment and destroy nine 18-pounder cannon to prevent their use by the Mexicans.

26 November
Under the cover of darkness, a boat party from the brig *Somers* seizes the Mexican schooner *Criolla*, which had previously evaded the blockading U.S. Navy vessel and put into Veracruz, Mexico. Without enough wind to sail her out of Veracruz, the men set the schooner ablaze. Later, it is revealed that she was a spy ship authorized passage through the blockade by Commodore David Conner.

JOHN DAHLGREN AND THE EVOLUTION OF NAVAL ORDNANCE

by Dr. Robert J. Schneller, Jr.

Dahlgren guns were the most powerful and reliable naval cannon in the world when they were first introduced to the fleet in the mid-1850s. They remained the Navy's standard armament until replaced by steel rifled cannon, beginning in the late 1870s.

The guns sprang from the fertile mind of John Adolphus Bernard Dahlgren (1809–1870), known to history as the "Father of American Naval Ordnance." In 1847, Dahlgren was assigned to ordnance duty at the Washington Navy Yard and soon received the task of constructing range tables for a system of 32-pounders and 8-inch shell guns that the Navy had adopted in 1845. Dahlgren determined their ranges by firing them and plotting the fall of their projectiles with equipment and techniques borrowed from the U.S. Coast Survey. He found that the lighter models were accurate but not powerful, and that the heavier models were powerful but inaccurate. Worse, one of the 32-pounders he was testing exploded and nearly killed him. He concluded that the design of each gun was unsafe and that the performance of the system as a whole was dangerously inconsistent.

Dahlgren solved these problems by inventing a new system of ordnance based on 9- and 11-inch shell guns. The salient features of these heavy smoothbores were their peculiar "soda-water bottle" shape and their weight. Dahlgren based his design on previous work done by European and U.S. Army ordnance experts and his own scientific research in ballistics and metallurgy. The design fit strength to strain, corresponding to the curve of pressure generated on a gun barrel between the ignition of the gunpowder and the exit of the projectile from the barrel. To ensure their reliability, Dahlgren had the new guns manufactured under the most comprehensive quality control program seen in the Navy

Left: *Rear Admiral John A. Dahlgren pictured next to one of his creations on board the screw sloop* Pawnee. *(Corbis)*

Right: *The trademark bottle shape of the Dahlgren gun is visible in this illustration depicting the interior arrangement of the turret of the ironclad monitor* Passaic. *Note the tracks on the deck to facilitate the movement of round shot. (Naval Historical Center)*

to that time. The program included detailed specifications, production monitoring, and a rigorous system of proof testing. Dahlgren also instituted a gunnery-training program to teach naval officers and enlisted men how to use the new weapons.

When the Dahlgren guns first appeared on board the *Merrimack*-class steam frigates, they were the heaviest naval cannon in the world and they fired the world's heaviest naval projectiles. The 9-inch gun barrel weighed 9,000 pounds and fired a 72.5-pound shell with ten pounds of powder. The 11-inch gun barrel weighed 16,000 pounds and fired a 136-pound shell with fifteen pounds of powder. Many foreign powers, including Great Britain, Russia, and Egypt, tried unsuccessfully to obtain Dahlgren guns for use in their own navies.

After the 11-inch guns on the Union ironclad *Monitor* failed to penetrate the armor of the Confederate ironclad *Virginia* during the battle of Hampton Roads, Virginia, on 9 March 1862, Dahlgren began experiments with ordnance against armor. In one series of tests, he fired the 11-incher with increasing increments of powder against a target plated with four inches of iron, similar to *Virginia*'s armor. He found that with a 30-pound powder charge, twice the standard 15-pound service charge, the 11-incher could penetrate the four inches of armor, and concluded that had *Monitor*'s 11-inchers been fired with 30-pound charges at Hampton Roads, *Virginia* would have been destroyed. This claim gave rise to the famous myth that *Monitor*'s guns were limited to half charges during the battle.

Dahlgren also invented light bronze boat guns, heavy rifled cannon, and a 15-inch smoothbore, as well as various experimental pieces that never saw service. The boat guns were revered throughout the Navy and admired around the world. The heavy rifled cannon tended to burst prematurely and was withdrawn from service in 1862. The 15-inch guns were developed to arm *Passaic*-class and subsequent classes of monitors. The 15-incher weighed 42,000 pounds and fired a 350-pound shell with 35 pounds of powder.

During the Civil War Dahlgren's guns were mounted on board almost every Union warship and many Confederate naval vessels. Not a single 9- or 11-inch gun failed prematurely in combat. One veteran of Mobile Bay and Fort Fisher said of Dahlgren's guns, "the men stand around them and fight them with as much confidence as they drink their grog." Admiral David Dixon Porter considered the Dahlgren gun "the best of its kind in the world."

Because of their stellar performance during the Civil War, the large quantity manufactured during the war, and the lack of money available to develop ordnance after the war, Dahlgren guns remained in service well past the point of obsolescence. In the 1870s a number of 11-inch Dahlgren guns were bored out and fitted with steel sleeves to create stopgap 8-inch rifled cannon. Many Dahlgren guns remained in service on board Civil War era wooden vessels until nearly the end of the nineteenth century.

5–6 December
Midshipman R. Clay Rogers and Surgeon John N. Wright from the brig *Somers* go ashore near Veracruz, Mexico, to investigate reports of a Mexican powder magazine near the beach. Happening upon an enemy patrol, Wright escapes but Rogers is captured and held prisoner by Mexico for a number of months until he, too, escapes.

8 December
The brig *Somers*, while in pursuit of a blockade-runner, is caught in a squall and sinks. Thirty-two members of her crew drown and seven are captured by the Mexicans. The remaining thirty-seven officers and men, including skipper Lieutenant Raphael Semmes, are rescued by ships from Great Britain, France, and Spain cruising nearby.

Lieutenant Washington A. Bartlett, of the sloop-of-war *Warren*, is seized by Californians while on a foraging expedition near San Francisco. His captors hope to exchange him for a member of John C. Frémont's expedition who was wanted for his harsh treatment of natives in the area.

21 December
Under the command of Commodore Matthew C. Perry, the schooners *Bonita* and *Petrel* and the steamer *Vixen* capture the town of Carmen on the Yucatan Peninsula, seizing gunpowder and destroying Mexican munitions.

27 December
The side-wheel steamer *Mississippi*, flagship of Commodore Matthew C. Perry, captures the Spanish schooner *Isabel* and the Mexican schooner *Amelia* attempting to break the blockade of Mexico and sail for Havana, Cuba.

1847

8 January
In the Battle of San Gabriel naval and Army forces under the overall command of Commodore Robert F. Stockton defeat a Californian force after crossing the San Gabriel River, California, and staging a flank assault and turning back enemy counterattacks. The battle lasts ninety minutes and results in two Americans killed and nine wounded.

Left: *The attack of the Mexicans from the chaparral on the first division of the naval expedition to Tabasco, Mexico. ("Mexican War 1847," Lieutenant H. Walke, USN, Naval Historical Center)*

Opposite, top: *The sloop-of-war* Boston, *while en route to operations off Mexico, was wrecked in a squall on 15 November 1846. ("USS Boston," Naval Historical Center)*

Opposite, bottom: *Lieutenant Charles W. Morris was mortally wounded while attempting to assist a prize vessel that had run aground at Tabasco, Mexico, on 26 October 1846. ("Lieutenant Charles W. Morris, USN," M. P. Rice, Naval Historical Center)*

9 January

Commodore Robert F. Stockton's forces again engage Californians defending the approach to Los Angeles, driving them back with concentrated fire. The following day he accepts the surrender of Los Angeles.

12 January

Lieutenant John A. Dahlgren reports for duty at the Bureau of Ordnance and Hydrography. During his subsequent tour he founds the Ordnance Establishment and begins work on the revolutionary gun designs that will lead many to call him the "Father of American Naval Ordnance."

14 January

The sloop-of-war *St. Mary's* takes station off Brazos Santiago on present-day South Padre Island, Texas, to protect transports assembling to support General Winfield Scott's planned landings at Veracruz, Mexico.

22 January

Commodore William B. Shubrick supersedes Commodore Robert F. Stockton in command of the Pacific Squadron. Shubrick relinquishes command on 2 March with the arrival of Commodore James Biddle in Monterey, California.

5 February

The sloop-of-war *St. Mary's* arrives at the island of Lobos, off Mexico, to protect and assist the force of transports gathering to participate in the landings at Veracruz, Mexico. When *Ondiaka*, one of the transports carrying an Army regiment, runs aground. Commander John L. Saunders, commanding officer of *St. Mary's*, orders her burned to prevent capture by the enemy.

3 March

The Naval Appropriation Act in part provides the sum of $250,000 for the construction of a drydock at the Pensacola Navy Yard, Florida, to enable the adequate repair of ships of the Home Squadron operating in Mexican waters.

6 March

Commodore David Conner joins General Winfield Scott and his staff on board the small steamer *Petrita* to scout potential landing sites at Veracruz, Mexico. Among those on board are future Civil War generals Pierre G. T. Beauregard, Joseph Johnston, Robert E. Lee, and George G. Meade.

9 March

Supported by fourteen warships of the Home Squadron, forces under the command of General Winfield Scott land at Veracruz, Mexico. "The tall ships of war sailing leisurely along under their topsails, their decks thronged in every part with dense masses of troops whose bright muskets and bayonets were

flashing in the sunbeams," were words used by one participant to describe the scene. All told, more than 8,600 men are put ashore in the amphibious operation.

10 March

The steamer *Spitfire* under the command of Commander Josiah Tatnall, in an effort to draw attention from General Winfield Scott's encirclement of Veracruz, Mexico, fires upon the fort of San Juan de Ulloa located on an island opposite the city.

21 March

Commodore Matthew C. Perry relieves Commodore David Conner in command of the Home Squadron.

22 March

Six ships of the Home Squadron—the steamers *Spitfire* and *Vixen*, and the schooners *Bonita*, *Falcon Reefer*, and *Tampico*—support Army artillery ashore by bombarding Veracruz, Mexico. The flotilla is fired upon, but suffers no damage.

23 March

Ships of the Home Squadron bombard Veracruz, Mexico, and positions surrounding it for a second day, taking position between the fort of San Juan de Ulloa and Fort Santiago and suffering minor damage from intense Mexican gunfire.

24 March

Having been put ashore two days earlier to augment Army artillery, a naval battery consisting of two 32-

Left: *The brig* Somers *founders off Veracruz, Mexico, December 1846. ("Wreck of the American Brig* Somers," *Naval Historical Center)*

pounders and three 8-inch guns exchanges fire with Mexican batteries at Fort Santa Barbara, Veracruz. Four Americans are killed and six wounded in the battery, the construction of which is supervised by future Confederate general Robert E. Lee. The naval battery is back in action the next day, firing until ammunition is exhausted and suffering two men killed and three wounded. All told, the naval battery accounts for some 45 percent of all shells fired by American artillery during the siege of Veracruz.

30 March
The sloop-of-war *Portsmouth* lands a force of some 140 men at San José del Cabo at the tip of Baja California, taking control of the town. Three days later the ship puts a landing force ashore at nearby San Lucas, raising the American flag over the town. On 13 August a party from *Portsmouth* accepts the surrender of La Paz, the capital of Baja California.

31 March
The steamer *Scourge* under the command of Lieutenant Charles G. Hunter captures the town of

Alvarado, Mexico, and pursues fleeing Mexican vessels up the Alvarado River, burning one schooner and capturing three other ships. His forces also capture the town of Tlacotalpán on 1 April. This disrupts the timetable of a joint Army and Navy effort to capture horses in the town, leading to Hunter's court-martial.

18 April
Commodore Matthew C. Perry leads a force consisting of the steamers *Scourge, Spitfire,* and *Vixen* and the schooners *Bonita, Petrel,* and *Reefer* escorting some thirty barges that land forces to capture the port of Tuxpan, Mexico. Two ships suffer minor damage from enemy fire.

17 May
A landing party from a flotilla consisting of the brigs *Porpoise, Vesuvius,* and *Washington* seize the Mexican town of Carmen. The ships are part of a sizeable force under the command of Commodore Matthew C. Perry that over the course of the next two days seizes a number of villages along the Coatzacoalcos River.

14 June
A twelve-ship flotilla under the command of Commodore Matthew C. Perry braves Mexican ambushes along the Tabasco River to land a force of 1,173 men that marches overland to seize the town of Tabasco. Overcoming Mexican fortifications en route, the force arrives at the town only to discover that it has already been captured by ships of the flotilla that steamed up the river after putting the men ashore. Tabasco is the last significant Mexican port to fall into American hands.

30 June
Responding to repeated attacks by Mexicans against the American garrison at Tabasco, the steamers *Scourge* and *Vixen* land a force of some two hundred men to capture the town of Tamulté located four miles upriver from Tabasco. Despite this effort, Tabasco is eventually evacuated in July, primarily due to the onset of yellow fever.

19 July
Deeming his presence in California no longer necessary, Commodore James Biddle departs, turning over command of the Pacific Squadron once again to Commodore W. Branford Shubrick.

1 October
After capturing the Mexican schooner *Magdalen,* which is damaged to such an extent that she is burned, a party from the sloop-of-war *Dale* attacks the town of Mulejé, Mexico.

20 October

After Mexican authorities refuse to surrender the town, the frigate *Congress* and the sloop-of-war *Portsmouth* bombard Guaymas, forcing its surrender. The Americans choose not to garrison the town, but instead station a ship in the harbor as a deterrent.

11 November

A landing party from the frigates *Congress* and *Independence* and the sloop-of-war *Cyane* goes ashore at Mazatlán, Mexico, seizing control of the town and capturing Mexican arms. Skirmishes between Mexican forces and naval personnel continue into February 1848, but there is no serious effort on the part of the Mexicans to retake the town.

17 November

With the sloop-of-war *Dale* on station at Guaymas, Mexican troops attempt to reoccupy the town, prompting *Dale*'s skipper Lieutenant Thomas O.

Selfridge to lead a landing party ashore. During an exchange of gunfire, Selfridge is seriously wounded. Pinned down by a superior force, the landing party is saved by fire from their ship, which drives the Mexicans away.

1848

2 February

A treaty between the United States and Mexico is signed at Guadalupe Hidalgo, Mexico. The Senate ratifies it on 10 March, ending the Mexican War.

13 February

A landing party consisting of sixty sailors and Marines from the sloop-of-war *Dale* under the command of Lieutenant Fabius Stanly attacks a Mexican force at Bocachicacampo, Mexico.

15 February

A landing party from the sloop-of-war *Cyane* goes ashore in an attempt to relieve beleaguered American forces at San José del Cabo, Mexico. The sight of the American warship contributes to the withdrawal of the Mexican forces.

8 April–10 May

A party under the command of Lieutenant William Lynch surveys the Sea of Galilee and travels the River Jordan until it reaches the Dead Sea.

9 April

After spiking three Mexican guns located near Guaymas, Mexico, a landing party from the sloop-of-war *Dale* under the command of Lieutenant Fabius Stanly engages

in a brief skirmish with Mexican forces, the last shots fired by U.S. Navy personnel in the Mexican War.

6 May

Commodore Thomas ap Catesby Jones relieves Commodore W. Branford Shubrick as commander of the Pacific Squadron.

1849

8 March

William Ballard Preston, a former U.S representative from Virginia, takes office as the nineteenth Secretary of the Navy.

16 August

Lieutenant James M. Gillis sails from New York on a voyage of scientific discovery in which he will conduct astronomical observations in an effort to improve navigation at sea. He completes his work, most of which is done at an observatory in Santiago, Chile, in 1852.

1850

26 May

Navy volunteers under the command of Lieutenant Edward J. De Haven sail the brigs *Advance* and *Rescue*, lent to the government by philanthropist Henry Grinnell, out of New York. Outfitted for service in the bitter cold and ice of the Arctic, the ships and their crews head north in search of the expedition of British Royal Navy Captain Sir John Franklin, missing in the Arctic since 1847. Dubbed the First Grinnell

Expedition, it locates Franklin's first winter quarters, but the onset of winter prevents further discovery and forces the expedition to winter over into 1851.

1 July
The U.S. Naval School at Annapolis, Maryland, is officially renamed the U.S. Naval Academy.

2 August
A former U.S. senator from North Carolina, William Alexander Graham takes office as the twentieth Secretary of the Navy.

6 September
The sloop *Yorktown* wrecks on Isla de Mayo in the Cape Verde Islands. Fortunately, no member of the crew is lost.

28 September
President Millard Fillmore signs an appropriations bill containing a rider abolishing the practice of flogging as a method of punishment for U.S. Navy personnel.

1851

21 May
The Navy continues its efforts in the field of navigation with the launching of the Herndon Expedition in which Lieutenant William L. Herndon, Passed Midshipman Lardner Gibbon, and Master's

Mate Henry J. Richards explore the Amazon basin to determine the navigability of the river. Departing Lima, Peru, Herndon travels 4,366 miles before he reaches Para, Brazil, on 11 April 1852. Gibbon and Richards take a different route and arrive the following November.

6 August
The sloop-of-war *Dale*, under the command of Commander William C. Pearson, anchors off Johanna Island in the Indian Ocean to demand indemnity from the local king, who has imprisoned a New England merchant ship captain. When Pearson receives a negative response, he unleashes a bombardment on the town. The indemnity is paid the following day.

15 November
The U.S. Naval Academy introduces a continuous four-year curriculum that replaces the previous system, in which a midshipman's time at Annapolis was interrupted halfway through by three years of sea duty. Henceforth, midshipman cruises occur during the summer months.

1852

26 July
In the wake of William Alexander Graham's resignation to run for the office of vice president, former Maryland congressman John Pendleton Kennedy takes office as the twenty-first Secretary of the Navy.

30 September
Under the command of Lieutenant S. P. Lee, the brig *Dolphin* sets sail from New York for a scientific voyage to test the theories of Lieutenant Matthew Fontaine Maury regarding winds and currents in the Atlantic Ocean. The journey concludes on 12 November 1853.

1853

19 January
The side-wheel steamer *Water Witch* under the command of Lieutenant Thomas J. Page departs Baltimore, Maryland, to begin a three-year exploration and survey of the Plate River in South America.

15 February
President Millard Fillmore issues an executive order making official a forty-six-chapter "System of Orders and Instructions" governing punishment in the U.S. Navy.

8 March
North Carolinian James C. Dobbin enters office as the twenty-second Secretary of the Navy.

30 May

The brig *Advance* departs New York as part of the Second Grinnell Expedition under Doctor Elisha Kent Kane, a U.S. Navy surgeon. The following year the ship becomes trapped in the Arctic, eventually prompting Kane to lead an eighty-three day journey overland to Greenland, which is reached in July 1855.

11 June

Extending its operations westward toward the waters of the Far East, an expedition led initially by Commander Cadwallader Ringgold, and later by Lieutenant John Rodgers, charts Pacific coasts and islands in Hawaii, the Aleutians, and Japan. The expedition concludes on 19 October 1855.

21 June

In a show of force to protect an American citizen, the sloop *St. Louis* under the command of Commander Duncan N. Ingraham prepares for action at Smyrna, Turkey, after Austrian officials refuse to release an American citizen named Martin Kostza, arrested for participating in the Hungarian Revolution in 1848. Though Austrian ships clear their decks for action, a battle is avoided when an agreement is reached, setting Kostza free.

8 July

Commodore Matthew C. Perry, in command of a squadron consisting of the side-wheel steamers *Mississippi* and *Susquehanna* and sloops *Plymouth* and *Saratoga*, enters Edo (Tokyo) Bay, to establish formal relations between the United States and Japan. Cautious of the West, the Japanese nevertheless accept a formal letter from President Millard Fillmore.

31 August

The Franklin board, established to design a new class of war steamers, recommends the inclusion of new 9-inch Dahlgren shell guns as part of their armament. This marks the first adoption of a series of innovative gun designs by pioneering ordananceman John A. Dahlgren that will eventually become standard on board U.S. Navy warships.

1854

19 January

In one of the earliest efforts on the part of the United States to explore the possibility of a canal connecting the Atlantic and Pacific oceans, Lieutenant Isaac G. Strain leads a detachment of twenty-five officers and enlisted

Opposite, top:
Lieutenant James M. Gillis, a foremost authority on astronomical navigation, was instrumental in establishing the Naval Observatory and published the book Astronomical Observations. *(Naval Historical Center)*

Opposite, bottom:
Nineteenth Secretary of the Navy William A. Graham. ("William A. Graham," Jacques Busbee, Department of the Navy)

Right: *A chart illustrating the cruise of the American Acrtic Expedition (Grinnell Expedition) in search of a previous expedition, 1850–1851. (P. Welsh, USN, Department of the Navy)*

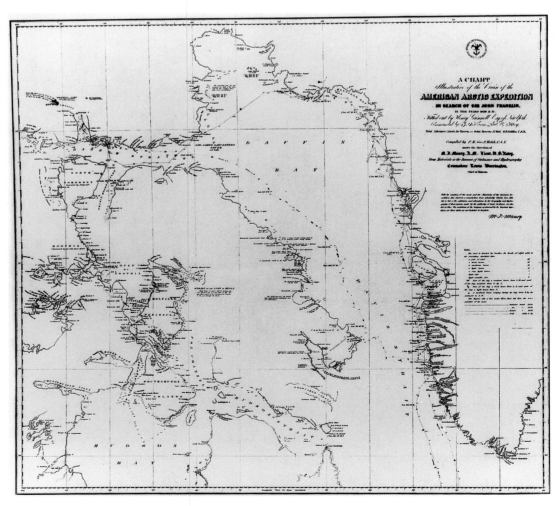

THE U.S. NAVY AND JAPAN

by Dr. Roger Dingman

For the past 150 years, the U.S. Navy has had a closer relationship with Japan than any other nation, save perhaps Great Britain. The Navy has functioned as agent of change, enemy, and protector-partner and, in so doing, has transformed itself and America's relations with the island nation.

During the first fifty years of the relationship, from Commodore Matthew C. Perry's visit in 1853 to 1899, when the so-called unequal treaty regime that he helped initiate ended, the Navy was present in Japan to promote commerce and protect American businessmen, missionaries, and educators from samurai, who opposed opening the country to Western ways. Only once in that period, in 1863, when the screw sloop *Wyoming* joined British and French ships in bombarding Shimonoseki, was American naval force used against Japan. No longer

a threat after 1868, Japan became a haven for the ships and men of the Asiatic fleet. Their presence there helped Americans and Japanese learn more about one another, but it also provided the most enduring stereotype of their relationship. The real Lieutenant Pinkerton, who loved then left Cho Cho San in Puccinni's *Madame Butterfly*, was a member of the Naval Academy class of 1888 who visited Nagasaki in the screw sloop *Lancaster*.

From the turn of the twentieth century through 1945, first hypothetical, then real, war defined the Navy's relationship with Japan. The acquisition of Hawaii, Guam, and the Philippines in the last years of the nineteenth century gave the Navy defensive responsibilities and bases, which demanded that its leaders think about the possibility of war against Japan. For the first two decades of the century,

Right: *The aircraft carrier* Kitty Hawk *(CV 63) returns to her homeport of Yokosuka, Japan, in 2002, following months of launching sustained bombing missions into Afghanistan in support of Operation Enduring Freedom. The U.S. Navy's ability to forward-deploy naval assets in Japan is essential to maintaining stability in the Far East. (U.S. Navy/PH2 David A. Levy)*

Right: *A Japanese naval delegation led by Vice Admiral Osami Nagano lays a wreath at the Tomb of the Unknown Soldier in Arlington National Cemetery, circa 1927. The Japanese officer pictured at the far right is Captain Isoroku Yamamoto, mastermind of the attack on Pearl Harbor that drew the United States into war with Japan in December 1941. (Naval Historical Center)*

American and Japanese admirals competitively expanded their fleets with an eye to war against one another. Although the Washington naval treaties of the early 1920s set limits on Pacific island fortifications and battleship strength, they did not halt development, refinement, and rehearsal of War Plan Orange, the Navy-Marine Corps scheme for war against Japan. When Japan ended the naval arms limitation regime and lunged into war against China in the mid-1930s, it provided the rationale for the Navy's building an increased number of aircraft carriers and long-range submarines. The Navy also expanded its intelligence capabilities by sending more language students to Japan and intensifying its radio monitoring and code-breaking efforts.

War against Japan from 1941 to 1945 prompted the greatest transformation of the Navy in its history. Fighting the Japanese in every sector of the Pacific demanded a larger, more complex fleet manned by a greater diversity of men, with a wider array of skills. In order to speed the enemy's defeat, the Navy trained over a thousand Japanese language officers. As combat interpreters, translators, cryptographers, and prisoner of war interrogators they provided intelligence that helped the Navy destroy the Japanese Empire and secure command of the Pacific.

Japan's surrender on the deck of the battleship *Missouri* (BB 63) in Tokyo Bay on 2 September 1945 marked the beginning of the third era of American naval relations with that country. For the first twenty postwar years, the U.S. Navy contributed mightily to reconciliation by sending tens of thousands of ordinary sailors and Marines who demilitarized Japan, demonstrated democracy to its people, and demanded the consumer goods whose sale fueled its economic recovery. For a quarter century after 1950, bases at Yokosuka, Sasebo, and Okinawa provided logistic and personnel support which enabled the Navy to fight wars in Korea and Vietnam, protect Taiwan, and keep open the sea lines of commerce throughout the Western Pacific. In the 1970s the Navy metamorphosed from a visible, and at times highly controversial, symbol of the security treaty that linked America and Japan into an innovative Cold War partner. By providing Japan with advanced underwater submarine detection and AEGIS weapons control systems, the Navy nudged Japan's Maritime Self-Defense Force into the active cooperative relationship that continues to this day. In homeporting a series of carrier task groups in Japan, beginning with *Midway* (CVA 41) in 1973, the Navy enhanced the power projection capabilities of its Seventh Fleet and revived the tradition, begun by Commodore Perry, of internationalizing Japanese and Americans alike. Its continued presence in Japan makes both more aware of the cultural, as well as the economic and strategic ties that bind their nations together in peace and friendship.

men from the sloop-of-war *Cyane* on an expedition across the isthmus of Panama. Nine members of the expedition perish in the harsh jungle, but Lieutenant Strain nevertheless pushes on to reach the Pacific Ocean.

February

In response to the seizure of a pilot boat under American colors by the Chinese imperial warship *Sir*

Herbert Compton, Lieutenant John Gueat leads an armed boat crew from the sloop *Plymouth* to free the prisoners without firing a shot.

8 March

With his squadron anchored off Yokohama, Japan, on 13 February, Commodore Matthew C. Perry goes ashore to open treaty negotiations with the Japanese. On 31 March he signs the Treaty of Kanagawa, which leads to the opening of commerce between the United States and Japan.

4–5 April

In response to Chinese imperial troops camping near the international settlement in Shanghai and committing acts of aggression against British and American citizens, a landing party of ninety men from the sloop-of-war *Plymouth* under the command of Commander John Kelly operates with British naval detachments to drive the imperial troops from their encampment. The *Plymouth* sailors shell the Chinese with field pieces and exchange small arms fire, losing one man killed and three wounded.

11 July

Commodore Matthew C. Perry concludes the Treaty of Naha with the regency of the Loo Choo Islands (the modern Ryukyus), which promises peace and amity between the regency and the United States.

Opposite, top: *Though outnumbered by Japanese boats in Tokyo Bay, armed sailors from the frigate* Mississippi *display the resolve to open negotiations with Japan, 11 July 1853. ("Perry Expedition to Japan," W. H. Brown, Naval Historical Center)*

Opposite, bottom: *("Matthew C. Perry," William S. Mount, U.S. Naval Academy Museum)*

Right: *The black smoke from Perry's ships intimidated the Japanese and helped facilitate a landing without incident. ("Landing of Perry at Yokohama," W. Heine Brown, Navy Art Collection)*

13 July

The sloop-of-war *Cyane* arrives at Greytown, Nicaragua, to respond to the arrest of the American ambassador to that country. When city officials refuse to apologize and pay an indemnity for this act, *Cyane's* skipper Commander George N. Hollins orders the town bombarded, which results in its nearly total destruction by fire.

16 September

Commander David G. Farragut takes possession of Mare Island, California, which becomes an important shipyard on the West Coast.

21 September

The brig *Porpoise* is last seen on this date in the Formosa Straits. She later disappears with all hands.

29 September

The sloop-of-war *Albany* departs Aspinwall, Panama, bound for New York City. She is never seen again.

17 November

A landing party consisting of sailors and Marines from the sloop-of-war *Vincennes* goes ashore at Okinawa, Japan, to enforce the provisions of the Treaty of Naha signed in July.

1855

1 February

The side-wheel steamer *Water Witch* is fired upon during a survey expedition in the Paraguay River.

19 May

Powhatan, a side-wheel steamer operating in Chinese waters, lands her Marine detachment at Shanghai, China, to protect American lives and property.

4 August

The side-wheel steamer *Powhatan* joins the British screw-sloop *Rattler* in suppressing Chinese pirates in the anchorage at Khulan, China. The American vessel dispatches an armed boat party of one hundred sailors and Marines in three boats under the command of Lieutenant Robert Pegram. The joint expedition nets seventeen pirate junks, and costs the U.S. Navy five dead and eight wounded, most of the casualties suffered when the powder magazine on one of the junks explodes as *Powhatan* crewmen board her.

28 August

The sloop-of-war *Germantown* lands Marines to safeguard United States interests in Montevideo, Uruguay.

12 September

A landing party from the sloop-of-war *John Adams* goes ashore at Nukulau, Fij Islands, to redress grievances against American citizens. Ten days later, the native king of Viti Levu in the Fijis is seized by crewmen from *John Adams* and taken to the ship, where he is compelled to sign a treaty compensating American citizens for damage and destruction to their property.

28–31 October

The sloop-of-war *John Adams* puts a landing party ashore at Viti Levu, Fiji Islands. In response to the king's failure to comply with the provisions of the treaty he signed on board the ship the previous month, the sailors and Marines of the landing party burn three villages, losing one man killed and three wounded.

27 November

The sloop-of-war *Germantown* puts sailors and Marines ashore at Montevideo, Uruguay, for a second time, joining naval landing parties of three other nations to protect foreign consulates and customs houses during an insurrection in that city.

1856

26 January

The sloop-of-war *Decatur* lands a small force and provides fire support to assist settlers in Seattle, Washington, in repelling an attack by some 1,000 Native Americans.

20 September

With continuing unrest in Central America, 160 sailors and Marines from the frigate *Independence* and the sloop-of-war *St. Mary's* land at Panama City to protect American interests in the wake of disturbances there.

23 October

A landing party of 150 men from the sloops-of-war *Levant* and *Portsmouth* go ashore to protect American lives and interests in Canton, China.

Above: *The steam frigate* Niagara's *most noteworthy mission was assisting in laying cable for the first transatlantic telegraph. Commissioned in 1857, she served until 1865. (G. H. Andrews, Naval Historical Center)*

Left: *The side-wheel steamer* Water Witch *is fired on by Fort Itapiru, Paraguay, while steaming on the Parana River between Argentina and Paraguay, 1 February 1855. The ship's helmsman was killed by the shot. (*"USS Water Witch," *Thomas J. Page, USN, Navy Department Library)*

Below: *(*"The U.S. Brig Porpoise *in a Squall,*" *W. J. Bennett, Navy Art Collection)*

20–22 November

In response to Chinese Barrier Forts firing on U.S. naval vessels attempting to proceed up the Pearl River, China, to retrieve the landing party that went ashore at Canton the previous October, a force of 287 men led by Commander Andrew Foote storms the Barrier Forts. Supported in their endeavor by fire from the sloops-of-war *Levant* and *Portsmouth*, the force marches across rice fields and fords a creek in attacking the first fort, and captures the remaining three forts over the course of two days. The Americans lose forty-two men killed and wounded, and *Portsmouth* and *Levant* suffer over twenty hits. However, the Chinese suffer some 400 casualties and, more importantly, lose four modern forts containing some 176 cannon.

1857

7 March
Isaac Toucey, former U.S. Attorney General and U.S. Senator, takes office as the twenty-third Secretary of the Navy.

1858

2 January
The frigate *St. Lawrence* lands her Marine detachment at Montevideo, Uruguay, to safeguard American interests threatened by disturbances in the city.

29 July
Following a failed attempt the previous year, the steam frigate *Niagara*, operating in concert with the British warship *Agamemnon*, succeeds in laying a telegraph cable across the Atlantic Ocean. The work of the two ships is completed on 5 August and, eleven days later, Britain's Queen Victoria sends a message to President James Buchanan. The cable fails a week later, but the feasibility of a transatlantic cable has been demonstrated. A permanent cable will be laid in 1866.

Above: *The landing of sailors and Marines from the screw frigate* San Jacinto *and the sloops-of-war* Levant *and* Portsmouth *to attack the barrier forts at Canton, China, on 21 November 1856. Two of the ships are supporting the operation with gunfire. ("The Attack on the Barrier Forts near Canton, China," Naval Historical Center)*

6 October
A landing party of forty-four men under Lieutenant C.H.B. Caldwell lands from the ship-sloop *Vandalia* on the island of Waya in the Fijis. The men destroy a village in retribution for the murder of two American traders.

17 October
In a delayed response to the firing upon the side-wheel steamer *Water Witch* on 1 February 1855, nineteen ships under Flag Officer William B. Shubrick put to sea bound for Paraguay. Arriving the following January, Shubrick wins indemnity for the attack and concludes a commercial treaty with Paraguay. This is the largest force of U.S. Navy warships assembled up to this time.

1859

25 June
British gunboats, during an attempt to remove obstructions placed at the mouth of the Peiho River by the Chinese during the so-called Opium War, come under fire from the Chinese Taku Forts. Observing the operation from the deck of the chartered steamer *Toey-Wan*, Commodore Josiah Tatnall, commander of the East India Squadron, takes a boat party to assist the British, saying that "blood is thicker than water." He later employs *Toey-Wan* to tow British reinforcements into the fray.

31 July
A landing party from the sidewheel steamer *Mississippi* goes ashore at Shanghai, China, to protect American interests in the city.

1860

1–4 March
Fifty sailors and Marines from the sloop-of-war *Marion* go ashore at Kissembo on the west coast of Africa to protect American property.

25 September
The sloop-of-war *Levant* sails from Hilo, Hawaii, and disappears on passage to Aspinwall, Colombia.

27 September
A landing party from the sloop-of-war *St. Mary's*, soon followed by a force from the British warship *Clio*, goes ashore at Panama City to assist in putting down unrest.

10 October
The screw steamer *San Jacinto* captures the slave ship *Bonito* in the South Atlantic. The capture of the vessel, which carries 622 slaves, marks the end of a nineteen-month period in which the U.S. Navy captures eighteen slave ships.

1 November
Signaling the continuing evolution from sail to steam, the Navy Department announces plans to convert

seven sailing vessels to steam power. Total projected cost for the endeavor is $3,064,000.

20 December
In the aftermath of the election of President Abraham Lincoln, South Carolina is the first state to secede from the Union. In response to this development, six days later Major Robert Anderson, commander of United States forces in Charleston, South Carolina, moves his command from Fort Moultrie to Fort Sumter, located on an island in Charleston Harbor.

Above: *Enemy fire splashes around the sloop-of-war* Portsmouth *as it is taken in tow by the American steamer* Williametta *during the bombardment of the Barrier Forts at Canton, China, November 1856. (*"USS Portsmouth," *R.G. Skerrett, Naval Historical Center)*

Right: *Bombardment of the forts at the entrance of the Peiho River, 25 June 1859, as seen from the junks, in which were two battalions of Marines. This plate depicts the U.S. chartered steamship* Toey-Wan, *which rendered conspicuous service to the English and French gunboats. (*"The Chinese Expedition," *T. G. Dutton, U.S. Naval Academy)*

A NAVY DIVIDED

1861-1865

A NAVY DIVIDED

1861-1865

It was a struggle that divided a nation and a navy. On 12 April 1861, batteries in Charleston, South Carolina, roared a defiant note with their bombardment of Fort Sumter in the city's harbor. Within days it became readily apparent how important the role of the U.S. Navy was to be in the Civil War. On 19 April President Abraham Lincoln issued orders for Union vessels to begin blockading ports from Texas to South Carolina. This blockade became a central element of the so-called Anaconda Plan, a strategy for the defeat of the Confederacy. In addition to blockading the South's coastline, naval forces were called upon to play a major role in seizing control of the Mississippi River, the nation's most vital artery, which in Union hands would effectively divide the Confederacy in two.

The U.S. Navy was ill prepared to wage the kind of war it was being tasked to fight. During the previous decades ships had rarely been concentrated for extensive operations, their cruises instead posting them to squadrons located throughout the globe. In 1860 the naval inventory included just twenty-four vessels that could be categorized as warships, and with the secession of southern states the officer corps shrank by 24 percent as men resigned their commissions and cast their lot with the Confederacy. Among them was Virginian Matthew Fontaine Maury and Franklin Buchanan of Maryland, the latter officer the first superintendent of the U.S. Naval Academy, whose graduates would to a large degree fill junior officer rolls of the opposing navies. Thus, a wartime buildup was required, and the result was a U.S. Navy constructed around the new technologies of the day that in the end transformed it into a truly modern force.

That naval warfare had changed forever was displayed in dramatic fashion at Hampton Roads, Virginia, on 9 March 1862. The antagonists in the battle that occurred on that day did not bear the classic lines of the great wooden sailing ships, and were rather ugly in appearance, with one likened to a "cheese box on a raft." They also maneuvered clumsily. However, steam rather than wind filling canvas sails propelled them through the water, and their hulls were protected by iron. And when the Confederate ironclad *Virginia* met the Union Navy's *Monitor* on that historic day, though the results of the battle were inconclusive, there was no doubt that it marked a watershed event in the technological development of warships. And not only did the Civil War witness the coming of age of the ironclad, it also proved a harbinger of change with respect to ordnance, with the introduction of the capable Dahlgren guns to combat, including those contained in the revolving turrets of monitors, and the extensive use of underwater mines (then called torpedoes) and rifled guns. Finally, the sinking of a Union warship by the Confederate submarine *H.L. Hunley* foreshadowed a distant, but inevitable future in which warships would attack from beneath the waves.

Yet it would be officers reared in the age of sail that led the Union to victory at sea during the Civil War. Some of the stirring actions pitted ships against land fortifications, Admiral David G. Farragut leading heroic dashes through gauntlets of fire and underwater minefields to capture the strategically vital ports of New Orleans, Louisiana, and Mobile, Alabama. In addition, in the western theater, General Ulysses S. Grant's string of victories could not have happened without the support of the Union Navy's riverine

Right: *Ship's officers gather on the sidewheel steamer* Philadelphia *during the Civil War. A trading vessel taken into service by the Union, she participated in action along the North Carolina coast and at Charleston, South Carolina. (Naval Historical Center)*

Pages 160–161: *With the frigate* Cumberland *already sinking in the background, the Confederate ironclad* Virginia *steams away from her next victim, the frigate* Congress, *at Hampton Roads, Virginia, 8 March 1862. ("Congress Burning," Tom Freeman)*

forces in the Mississippi River, a motley assortment of shallow-draft steamers converted to warships and ironclad monitors. At Forts Henry and Donelson and in the campaign against the river fortress of Vicksburg, Mississippi, naval firepower was decisive in achieving ultimate victory. These operations on the Mississippi, along with the campaigns against Charleston, South Carolina, and Wilmington, North Carolina, involved joint operations, with naval ships providing fire support and transporting troops to shore.

Though most of the significant actions during the Civil War occurred within sight of land, nothing captured the public imagination more than the daring exploits of Confederate commerce raiders, which prowled the seven seas in epic voyages and captured some 255 Union merchantmen. The most famous of the raiders was *Alabama,* under the command of the dashing Captain Raphael Semmes, which over the course of twenty-three consecutive months at sea took sixty-eight prizes before meeting her end in a battle with the Union warship *Kearsarge* in the waters off Cherbourg, France. Fittingly, the last Confederate flag lowered following General Robert E. Lee's surrender at

Appomattox was that flown over the raider *Shenandoah,* which hauled down her colors in November 1865.

During the Civil War the U.S. Navy grew by staggering proportions, the number of ships increasing to nearly 700 and the number of personnel on active duty growing from 9,942 men in 1860 to 58,296 in 1865. Though casualties were not as heavy as those suffered by Army troops on bloody fields at Antietam, Gettysburg, and elsewhere, 2,112 bluejackets were killed and 1,710 more were wounded during the war. Largely overshadowed by the events on shore, the Navy's contributions to final victory are undisputed. It was the Navy that provided the squeeze of the Anaconda Plan by blockading the Confederacy's coastline and capturing ports whose defenses were thought to be impregnable and played a significant role in securing the nation's river highways and denying their use to the enemy. As President Abraham Lincoln wrote of the Union Navy's sailors in 1863, "At all the watery margins they have been present. Not only on the deep sea, the broad bay, the rapid river, but also up the narrow muddy bayou, and wherever the ground was a little damp, they have made their tracks."

A NAVY DIVIDED
1861-1865

9 January
The U.S. steamer *Star of the West,* carrying reinforcements destined for Fort Sumter, arrives off Charleston Harbor, South Carolina, and takes fire from Confederate forces at Fort Moultrie and Morris Island. This marks the first shots fired at a vessel flying the American flag during the Civil War.

23 January
With Virginia seceded from the Union, Commander John A. Dahlgren takes measures to protect the Washington Navy Yard, D.C., in the event of an attack, relocating the cannon and ammunition from the yard's magazine to the main building.

29 January
The screw sloop *Brooklyn,* under Captain William S. Walker, is ordered not to land reinforcements at Fort Pickens near Pensacola, Florida, unless Union forces there are attacked by Confederate forces. The following month the screw sloop *Brooklyn* joins the frigates *Macedonian* and *Sabine* and the sloop-of-war *St. Louis* off the harbor at Pensacola.

15 February
Commodore Raphael Semmes, later captain of the famed Confederate raiders *Sumter* and *Alabama,* joins numerous other Southern-born U.S. Navy officers in resigning his commission.

20 February
The Confederate States Congress formally establishes a Navy Department. On the following day President Jefferson Davis names former Florida Senator Stephen R. Mallory as the first and only Confederate Secretary of the Navy.

27 February
Congress authorizes the construction of seven steam sloops to augment the existing strength of the U.S. Navy, which stands at forty-two vessels.

7 March
Gideon Welles, a newspaper publisher from Connecticut, takes office as the twenty-fourth Secretary of the Navy.

20 March
The sloop *Isabella* is seized at Mobile during an attempt to carry supplies to the Union garrison at Fort Pickens, at Pensacola Bay, Florida. Such efforts had been forbidden by an order of Confederate Brigadier General Braxton Bragg issued two days earlier.

21 March
Gustavus Fox, a former naval officer, reconnoiters Charleston Harbor, South Carolina, under orders of President Abraham Lincoln to determine the best method for relieving Fort Sumter. Fox proposes to relieve the garrison from the sea, filling two steamers with troops under the escort of the screw sloop *Pawnee* and the revenue cutter *Harriet Lane.* If opposed the escorts would engage Confederate naval vessels with assistance from guns at Fort Sumter. Lincoln approves Fox's plan on 4 April.

5 April
The Secretary of the Navy issues orders directing the sidewheel steamer *Powhatan,* the screw sloop *Pawnee,* the screw steamer *Pocahontas,* and the revenue cutter *Harriet Lane* to sail under the command of Captain Samuel Mercer for Charleston, South Carolina, to provision Fort Sumter. The following day, *Powhatan,* under Lieutenant David

Dixon Porter, is diverted to reinforce Fort Pickens and is joined by the frigate *Sabine*.

10 April

The Secretary of the Navy directs Captain Charles S. McCauley, Commandant of the Norfolk Navy Yard, Virginia, to make the steam frigate *Merrimack* ready for movement to a northern port in the event of a Confederate effort to seize the Yard. Over the course of the next two days, *Merrimack* receives a commanding officer, Commander James Alden, and Chief Engineer Benjamin Isherwood is sent to Norfolk to make ready the ship's engines.

12 April

His demand for the evacuation of Fort Sumter refused, Confederate General Pierre G. T. Beauregard fires upon the fort, which, ironically, is commanded by his former artillery instructor at West Point. The fort surrenders the following day and its garrison is evacuated by ships of the aborted Fox relief expedition on 14 April.

A squadron consisting of the frigate *Sabine*, sloops-of-war *Brooklyn* and *St. Louis*, and screw steamer *Wyandotte* lands Army troops and Marines to reinforce Fort Pickens. Five days later the steamer *Atlantic*, under the escort of the side-wheel steamer *Powhatan*, lands an additional 600 troops, thus fulfilling President Abraham Lincoln's desire that the fort be "saved at all hazards." Confederate forces eventually abandon

Pensacola, and the city's navy yard serves as a valuable base for the Union Navy in the Gulf of Mexico.

19 April

As a centerpiece of Union strategy for defeating the Confederacy, President Abraham Lincoln declares a blockade of Southern ports from South Carolina to Texas.

The steamer *Boston* and ferry boat *Maryland* depart Philadelphia and Perryville, Pennsylvania, respectively, with troops bound for Washington, D.C., which is cut off by rail from the North.

20 April

Union forces partially destroy the Norfolk Navy Yard to prevent its facilities from falling into Confederate hands, and then abandon it. In addition to the yard itself, the departing Union forces burn or sink nine ships, and abandon the old frigate *United States*. One of the ships sunk is *Merrimack*, which is raised by the Confederates and later becomes the ironclad *Virginia*.

21 April

The Secretary of the Navy directs commandants of the navy yards at Philadelphia, New York, and Boston to procure shallow-draft steamers of sufficient strength and speed for coastal operations. This same day, four steamers are seized near Washington, D.C., and ordered to be outfitted at the Washington Navy Yard to protect the capital.

DESTRUCTION OF THE UNITED STATES NAVY-YARD AT NORFOLK, VIRGINIA, BY FIRE, BY THE UNITED STATES TROOPS, ON APRIL 20, 1861.

Left: *Virginia's secession from the Union prompted the burning of facilities and ships at the Norfolk Navy Yard to prevent their use by the Confederates. One of the ships sunk was the steam frigate* Merrimack, *which was later raised and transformed into the Confederate ironclad* Virginia. *(Naval Historical Center)*

Below: *Secretary of the Navy Gideon Welles. ("Gideon Welles," Matthew Wilson, Department of the Navy)*

22 April

The steamer *Boston*, carrying troops of the Seventh New York Regiment, arrives at Annapolis, Maryland, and assists in helping refloat the ferry boat *Maryland*, which had run aground in the Chesapeake Bay. Both ships land their embarked troops, which help defend Washington, D.C., and assist in keeping Maryland in the Union. In time, a "flying flotilla" of Union ships operates in the Chesapeake Bay and its tributaries.

24 April

The venerable frigate *Constitution* departs Annapolis, Maryland, under tow by the steamer *R.R. Cuyler*, carrying officers and midshipmen from the U.S. Naval Academy. On 9 May she arrives at Newport, Rhode Island, in company with the steamer *Baltic*. Newport serves as the temporary home of the academy for the duration of the war.

27 April

President Abraham Lincoln extends the Union blockade to cover ports in North Carolina and Virginia, while the Secretary of the Navy orders Union ships to seize Confederate privateers they encounter.

2-3 May

General Winfield Scott, in letters to President Abraham Lincoln and General George B. McClellan, outlines a strategy for the defeat of the South that includes a blockade of the Confederacy and a "powerful movement down the Mississippi to the ocean…the object being to clear out and keep this great line of communication in connection with the strict blockade of the seaboard, so as to envelop the insurgent States and bring them to terms with less bloodshed than by any other plan." Control of the sea and inland waters forms the essence of Scott's celebrated "Anaconda Plan" that will eventually win the Civil War for the Union.

3 May

President Abraham Lincoln issues a call for the enlistment of an additional 18,000 seamen for service

in the U.S. Navy. Enlistment terms are for not less than one or more than three years.

6 May
The Confederate Congress passes an act recognizing the existence of a state of war with the United States. Included in the provision is the authority to issue Letters of Marque to private vessels.

9 May
Confederate Secretary of the Navy Stephen R. Mallory dispatches Commander James D. Bulloch to England to purchase ships, guns, and ammunition for the Confederacy. Mallory instructs Bulloch to request ships "enabled to keep the sea, and to make extended cruises, propellers fast under both steam and canvas suggest themselves to us with special favor." On 10 May the farsighted Mallory writes the Confederate Congress, saying that procurement of armored ships is "a matter of the first necessity....Naval engagements between wooden frigates, as they are now built and armed, will prove to be the forlorn hopes of the sea, simply contests in which the question, not of victory, but of who shall go to the bottom first, is to be solved." That day the Congress authorizes the sending of a naval agent abroad to purchase six propeller steamers, rifled cannon, small arms, and other war material and appropriates $1 million for the purpose.

13 May
Britain's Queen Victoria proclaims British neutrality and forbids the nation's vessels from attempting to break the Union blockade. The proclamation comes one day after the steam frigate *Niagara* captures the blockade runner *General Parkhill*, bound from Liverpool, England, to Charleston, South Carolina.

15 May
Lieutenant Thomas M. Brasher is appointed commanding officer of the brig *Bainbridge* and directed to take his ship to Aspinwall, New Granada (present day Panama) to protect gold-laden California steamers traveling from Aspinwall to New York City.

16 May
Commander John Rodgers receives orders directing him to report to the War Department to work on establishing naval forces for service on the western rivers. He soon obtains the necessary arms and personnel and purchases three steamers that are converted to the gunboats *Conestoga*, *Lexington*, and *Tyler*.

24 May
Supported by the gunboats the screw steamer *Anacostia*, the screw tug *Resolute*, and the gunboat *Thomas Freeborn*, Union troops make an amphibious landing at Alexandria, Virginia, and the town surrenders upon the demand of Commander S. C. Rowan of the screw sloop *Pawnee*. The following day *Pawnee* captures the Confederate steamer *Thomas Colyer*.

26-28 May
Union ships set the blockade off the Southern port cities of New Orleans, Louisiana, Mobile, Alabama, and Savannah, Georgia, as well as the mouth of the Mississippi River.

29 May–1 June
Fresh from the capture of Alexandria, vessels of the Potomac Flotilla engage Confederate shore batteries at Aquia Creek, Virginia. The flotilla ships include the screw steamer *Anacostia*, the screw sloop *Pawnee*, the screw tug *Resolute*, and the gunboat *Thomas Freeborn*.

Above: *General Winfield Scott's blueprint for defeating the Confederacy included a naval blockade and stressed the importance of controlling the Mississippi River. (Naval Historical Center)*

NAVAL BLOCKADES: THEORY AND PRACTICE

by Dr. Wade G. Dudley

The concept of blockade—the interdiction of an enemy's maritime traffic by naval forces—is as old as history, while its principles have transcended changes in technology. From an Athenian captain standing off the harbor of Syracuse in 413 B.C. to an American admiral sailing into the Persian Gulf in 1990, the central tenets have remained the same: confine enemy warships to port, protect your own nation's coasts and shipping from attack; capture, destroy, or turn away merchant shipping succoring the enemy; and launch rapid raids against the enemy's coast, damaging infrastructure and weakening the enemy's will to resist.

The U.S. Navy learned blockade theory from British interdictions of our own coasts during the American Revolution and the War of 1812. Time and again, however, captains such as John Paul Jones, Isaac Hull, and David Porter slipped through the British cordon to hound merchantmen around the globe and

even to raid the very shores of the British Isles. Though the relatively brief Mexican-American War of 1846–1848 tested the blockading skills of the U.S. Navy, the true trial of its capabilities came during the American Civil War of 1861–1865.

In April 1861, Secretary of the Navy Gideon Welles faced a daunting challenge. As part of the Anaconda Plan, designed to squeeze the rebellious states into submission, Welles had to blockade some 3,500 miles of coastline featuring countless bays, sheltered waterways, and river mouths (all potential havens for rebel shipping), while protecting the far-reaching American merchant marine. With only forty-two ships, some antiquated and others scattered on distant stations, and less than 8,000 men, the task seemed impossible, but three months later Welles could report to President Abraham Lincoln that at least one vessel blockaded each of the nine major Confederate ports with rail connections to the interior. From these

meager beginnings, the U.S. Navy, thanks to an aggressive building and conversion program complemented by numerous volunteers, including former slaves and foreigners seeking citizenship, increased to over 670 vessels crewed by more than 58,000 officers and men by the end of the conflict.

The under-industrialized Confederacy suffered mightily at the hands of the U.S. Navy. As the blockade developed strength, not only did the influx of European war materials slow to a trickle, but the rebellious South lost its coastal shipping capacity. Without a strong system of railways and roads, the loss of estuarial waters linking regional rivers crippled the Confederacy's domestic trade. The inability to shift both food and locally manufactured goods within the region led to shortages, hunger, and the gradual erosion of morale. Still, the U.S. Navy quickly discovered that a blockade alone could not isolate the Confederacy from international support. Amphibious campaigns were required to establish local bases for the blockaders and to completely close southern ports.

The capture of Hatteras Inlet on the coast of North Carolina in August 1861, and the subsequent campaign which firmly established a Union presence in the sounds of that state, provided Abraham Lincoln with his first major victory of the war and initiated a series of amphibious actions. The result was the closure all but two of the South's major ports; Charleston, South Carolina, finally fell to General William T. Sherman's army in 1865, while Galveston, Texas, though briefly held by the Union in 1862, resisted through the final surrender.

The remainder of the nineteenth and the twentieth centuries featured continued use of blockades by the U.S. Navy. During the Spanish-American War of 1898, the Navy destroyed a Spanish squadron as it attempted to escape the blockade off Santiago, Cuba. American warships participated in the British blockade of the North Sea in World War I

and isolated both Germany and Japan from international trade in World War II. The Cold War found the U.S. Navy operating blockades along the coasts of Korea and Vietnam, as well as prosecuting a brief but vigorous "quarantine" of Cuba during the Cuban Missile Crisis of October 1962.

As the Cold War ended, the U.S. Navy and its allies enforced an effective blockade of Iraq during the Gulf war of 1990–1991. Coalition forces intercepted some 7,500 merchant vessels, stopped the shipment of oil from that nation (thus crippling Iraq financially), and isolated Saddam Hussein from the bulk of his international arms suppliers. In keeping with the principles of the blockade, naval forces raided ashore, thus diverting numerous Iraqi troops to coastal defense, and supported offensive action with naval air, cruise missiles, and accurate 16-inch gunfire from the battleship *Wisconsin* (BB 64).

After the end of the conflict, naval forces never left the Arabian Gulf, continuing to effectively blockade Iraq in enforcing a United Nations embargo for over a decade. Increased to support Operation Iraqi Freedom in 2003, they helped ensure ultimate victory.

Opposite: *The screw gunboat* Kanawha *cuts out a blockade runner in Mobile Bay, Alabama, under the guns of Fort Morgan. Whether in the Gulf of Mexico or the Atlantic, the Union blockade served to strangle the Confederacy by denying the import of vital war materiel. (Naval Historical Center)*

Above: *A boarding party from the destroyer* Joseph P. Kennedy *(DD 850) approaches the Lebanese freighter* Marucia *in the waters off Cuba during the early days of the naval quarantine of the island. The decision to implement a blockade contributed to the defusing of the Cuban Missile Crisis in October 1962. (Naval Historical Center)*

27 June
The gunboat *Thomas Freeborn* and screw steamer *Reliance*, in concert with boats from the screw sloop *Pawnee*, attack Confederate forces at Mathias Point, Virginia. *Thomas Freeborn*'s commanding officer, Commander James Harmon Ward, is killed.

30 June
The Confederate raider *Sumter* runs the blockade at the mouth of the Mississippi River, evading the sloop-of-war *Brooklyn*. This begins the first voyage of Commander Raphael Semmes, destined to become the most famous skipper of Confederate raiders during the Civil War.

30 May
Confederate forces raise the steam frigate *Merrimack,* previously scuttled and burned by Union forces as they abandoned the Norfolk Navy Yard. On 10 June, Lieutenant John Mercer Brooke receives orders to design an ironclad using the machinery and underwater hull of *Merrimack*. Work begins on the new vessel on 23 June.

3 July
The Confederate raider *Sumter* captures her first Union ship, *Golden Rocket*, off the coast of Cuba, and burns her. Commander Raphael Semmes and his crew capture seven additional prizes over the course of the following three days. The success of *Sumter* and *Jefferson Davis*, during the month of July prompts the Navy Department to increasingly worry about Confederate raiders on the high seas.

25 June
The Secretary of the Navy receives reports detailing the construction of "an infernal submarine vessel" by Confederates in New Orleans. The design features a pointed prow designed to hole the hull of a wooden ship and explode, sinking her.

24 July
Congress passes acts authorizing the creation of the post of Assistant Secretary of the Navy and giving the president the power to take vessels into the naval service and appoint officers to man them. On 1 August

Above: *With Washington, D.C., bordered by the Confederate state of Virginia, naval vessels maintained a presence on the Potomac River. In this illustration the steamer* Mount Vernon *reconnoiters Confederate batteries on Mathias Point in mid-1861. (Naval Historical Center)*

Left: *The steam frigate* Niagara *at sea during 1861–1862. At the time she supported the blockade of the Confederacy, a duty that occupied many a Union warship during the Civil War. ("USS* Niagara," *Clara Ray, Naval Historical Center)*

Right: *Foreshadowing operations that would be executed on a much broader scale by the Union Navy on the nation's rivers, warships engage Confederate batteries at Aquia Creek, Virginia, on 29 May–1 June 1861. (Naval Historical Center)*

former naval officer Gustavus Fox, leader of the unsuccessful effort to relieve Fort Sumter, South Carolina, receives the appointment as the nation's first Assistant Secretary of the Navy.

3 August
Following successful balloon reconnaissance missions from Fort Monroe, Virginia, during the previous month, John LaMountain makes his first ascent in a balloon from the steamer *Fanny* at Hampton Roads, Virginia. The subsequent observation of Confederate batteries on Sewell's Point, Virginia, marks the first launching of an aircraft from a U.S. naval vessel.

Congress appoints a board of naval officers to investigate "plans and specifications…of iron or steel-clad steamships or steam batteries." A sum of $1,500,000 is appropriated for the project.

8 August
A Union squadron consisting of six warships and two transports under the command of Flag Officer Silas H. Stringham successfully lands soldiers and Marines above Forts Hatteras and Clark in North Carolina. This event marks the first joint amphibious operation of the war and, with the surrender of the forts the following day, seals off Pamlico Sound from commerce raiding and blockade running.

9 August
The Confederate privateer *York* captures the schooner *George G. Baker*, which is then pursued by the gunboat *Union* later in the day. *York* is set fire on by her crew off Cape Hatteras, North Carolina, to avoid capture by the pursuing Union Navy ship.

12 August
The gunboats *Conestoga*, *Lexington*, and *Tyler* arrive at Cairo, Illinois, to protect the vital strategic junction of the Ohio and Mississippi rivers. On 15 August, two of the vessels reconnoiter the Mississippi River into Missouri and later in the month Confederate troops occupying Commerce, Missouri, withdraw from their positions after observing the approach of the gunboats.

30 August
The Confederate tug *Harmony* attacks the frigate *Savannah* at Newport News, Virginia, damaging the Union vessel before withdrawing.

5 September
Captain Andrew H. Foote relieves Commander John Rodgers in command of Union forces operating on the western rivers.

6 September
The gunboats *Lexington* and *Tyler* spearhead the capture of Paducah and Smithland, Kentucky, by forces under General Ulysses S Grant. The effort secures the mouths of the Tennessee and Cumberland rivers and helps hold the state of Kentucky in the Union. It also foreshadows the widespread use of riverine forces in Grant's future campaigns on the Mississippi River.

10 September
The gunboats *Conestoga* and *Lexington* cover advancing troops by silencing a Confederate gun battery and damaging the rebel gunboat *Yankee* at Lucas Bend, Missouri.

16 September
A board appointed by Secretary of the Navy Gideon Welles recommends the construction of three ironclads—*Galena, Monitor*, and *New Ironsides*—vessels that revolutionize naval operations in the riverine warfare in the west and other engagements.

16–17 September
A landing party from the screw sloop *Pawnee* destroys Confederate guns and fortifications on Beacon Island, effectively closing Ocracoke Inlet in North Carolina to operations of rebel blockade runners.

17 September
Following the Confederate evacuation of Ship Island, Mississippi, a landing party from the screw steamer *Massachusetts* goes ashore, securing the island, which serves as the staging point for the forthcoming Union assault on New Orleans, Louisiana.

18 September
Flag Officer Samuel F. Du Pont is appointed Commander, South Atlantic Blockading Squadron.

22 September
Flag Officer William W. McKean assumes command of the Gulf Blockading Squadron.

23 September
Flag Officer Louis M. Goldsborough receives command of the North Atlantic Blockading squadron. In an earlier letter to Goldsborough, Secretary of the Navy Gideon Welles writes, "It is essentially necessary that the Navy should at this time put forth all its strength and demonstrate to the country and to foreign powers its usefulness and capability in protecting and supporting the Government and the Union."

As part of the effort to contain Confederate advances in the border states, the gunboat *Lexington* proceeds to Owensboro, Kentucky, keeping the Ohio River open and protecting Union interests in the area.

25 September
In addressing the presence of persons of color subsisted at navy yards and on board Union warships, the Secretary of the Navy instructs Flag Officer Samuel F. Du Pont to enlist them into the naval service "under the same forms and regulations as apply to other enlistments." Limited to service in the rating of ship's boy, African-Americans enlisted under this directive receive ten dollars per month and one daily ration.

1 October
A Confederate naval force that includes the sidewheel steamer *Curlew,* the screw tug *Junaluska,* and the gunboat *Raleigh* under Flag Officer William F. Lynch, captures the steamer *Fanny,* which carries Union troops, in Pamlico Sound. This victory stems the tide of Union success along the coast of North Carolina, and brings other benefits in the form of two rifled guns and a large quantity of army supplies carried by *Fanny.*

12 October
A Confederate naval force led by the ironclad ram *Manassas,* described by one observer as being shaped like "a cigar cut lengthwise," attacks the steam sloop *Richmond,* sloops-of-war *Preble* and *Vincennes,* side-wheel steamer *Water Witch,* and ship *Nightingale* near Head of Passes, Mississippi River. *Manassas* rams *Richmond,* holing her side, and forcing her and *Vincennes* aground under heavy fire before retiring.

Opposite, top: *The new post of Assistant Secretary of the Navy was ably filled by Gustavus Fox, a former naval officer. (Naval Historical Center)*

Opposite, bottom: *The Confederacy's naval forces on the high seas consisted primarily of commerce raiders, such as* Sumter, *portrayed here capturing two merchantmen. (W. H. Moody, Naval Historical Center)*

Above: *Union ships bombarded Forts Hatteras and Clark in North Carolina on 28–29 August 1861. (Francis Garland, Naval Historical Center)*

"She must be covered with railroad iron as all the shells which struck her glanced off, some directly at right angles," writes Acting Master Edward F. Devens of *Vincennes*.

The Confederate side-wheel steamer *Theodora* successfully runs the blockade from Charleston, South Carolina. On board are James Mason and John Slidell, Confederate Commissioners to England and France, respectively. Arriving in Cuba, the commissioners board the British mail steamer *Trent* bound for England.

25 October

John Ericcson begins construction of the single-turret, 2-gun ironclad *Monitor* at Greenpoint, New York.

29 October

A Union expedition consisting of seventy-seven ships, under Flag Officer Samuel Du Pont, sails from Fort Monroe, Virginia. The largest U.S. fleet assembled to date, its vessels carry some 16,000 Union troops for an assault against Port Royal, South Carolina, which Du Pont considers "the most important point to strike, and the most desirable to have first and hold" because of its ability to admit large ships and its value as a coaling station.

5 November

In preparation for the assault against Port Royal, South Carolina, the gunboats *Ottawa*, *Pembina*, and *Seneca*, and the screw sloop *Pawnee* engage and disperse a small Confederate naval squadron in Port Royal Sound and fire upon Forts Beauregard and Walker guarding the sound.

7 November

Naval forces under the command of Flag Officer Samuel Du Pont steam into Port Royal Sound, South Carolina, pouring withering fire into Forts Beauregard and Walker and forcing the Confederates to abandon the positions. With only minor resistance from a Confederate squadron, the Union ships put ashore landing parties that occupy the forts until relieved by Army troops under General William T. Sherman. The capture of Port Royal yields forty-three Confederate cannon, and the victorious Du Pont writes, "It is not my temper to rejoice over fallen foes, but this must be a gloomy night in Charleston."

The gunboats *Lexington* and *Tyler* support troops under the command of General Ulysses S. Grant during the Battle of Belmont in Missouri by engaging Confederate batteries along the Mississippi River and covering Grant's withdrawal upon the arrival of Confederate reinforcements.

8 November

In a controversial action, the screw frigate *San Jacinto*, under Captain Charles Wilkes, stops the British mail steamer *Trent* in Old Bahama Channel. Crewmen from the Union ship remove Confederate Commissioners James Mason and John Slidell, and *San Jacinto* proceeds to Fort Monroe, Virginia, arriving on 15 November. The international uproar caused by the seizure of the men from a ship of a neutral nation prompts the release of the Confederate officials, who on 1 January 1862 depart Boston, Massachusetts, for England on board the British ship *Rinaldo*.

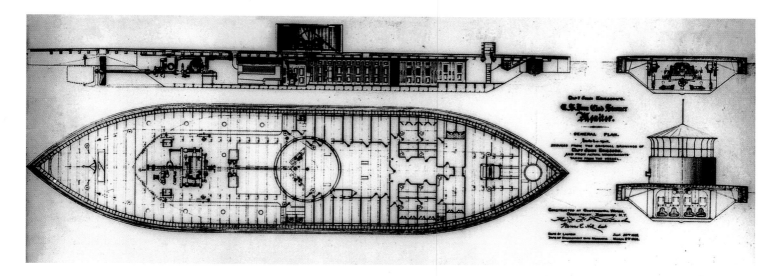

9 November

Union gunboats take possession of Beaufort, South Carolina, blockading the mouth of the Broad River and cutting off water communications between Charleston, South Carolina, and Savannah, Georgia.

11 November

Operating from the balloon-boat *G.W. Parke Custis*, procured for $150 and readied for service at the Washington Navy Yard, D.C., Thaddeus Lowe makes balloon observations of Confederate forces in Virginia, spotting enemy encampments and the construction of batteries at Freestone Point.

12 November

Fingal, a ship purchased in England by the Confederacy, becomes the first ship to successfully run the blockade under the sponsorship of the Confederate government. Reaching Savannah, with a cargo of military supplies, she is later put into naval service and renamed *Atlanta*.

22 November

Union batteries at Fort Pickens near Pensacola, Florida, join the steam frigate *Niagara* and the steam sloop *Richmond* in bombarding Confederate defenses at Fort McRee, the Pensacola Navy Yard, and the town of Warrington. The bombardment lasts two days.

24 November

A landing party from a squadron of five Union ships led by Commander John Rodgers, in the screw steamer *Flag*, captures Tybee Island in Savannah Harbor, Georgia.

Opposite: *The Confederate ram* Manassas *scored a victory near Head of Passes, on the Mississippi River, on 12 October 1861. She is depicted here ramming the steam sloop* Richmond *during the action. (Naval Historical Center)*

Above: *General plan of the ironclad* Monitor, *1862. (Naval Historical Center)*

Left: *A former coal barge converted to handle observation balloons,* George Washington Parke Custis *pioneered this early form of aerial reconnaissance during the Civil War, observing Confederate activities along the Potomac. (Naval Historical Center)*

2 December
In his Annual Report of the Secretary of the Navy, Gideon Welles reports the capture of 153 vessels attempting to run the blockade and indicates that, upon completion of vessels already purchased, the Union Navy will encompass 264 vessels of 218,016 tons mounting 2,557 guns.

The Confederate side-wheel steamer *Patrick Henry* attacks four Union steamers above Newport News, Virginia, suffering damage in the two-hour action.

10 December
The screw steamer *Isaac Smith* puts a landing party ashore on Otter Island in the Ashepoo River in South Carolina, taking possession of an abandoned Confederate fort.

17 December
Seven ships of the so-called Stone Fleet, old vessels filled with stone to be used as underwater obstacles, are sunk at the entrance to Savannah Harbor, Georgia. Three days later additional "Stone Fleet" ships are sunk at Charleston, South Carolina.

21 December
President Abraham Lincoln signs an Act of Congress creating the Medal of Honor for enlisted members of the Navy and Marine Corps, and an act of 3 March 1915 extends the Navy medal to officers. The medal is the nation's oldest continuously awarded decoration.

26 December
A Confederate squadron consisting of five ships under Commodore Josiah Tattnall attacks ships of

blockade at the mouth of the Savannah River, Georgia, temporarily driving them seaward.

31 December
A landing party covered by the side-wheel steamer *Water Witch*, screw steamer *New London*, and *Henry Lewis* captures Biloxi, Mississippi. A Confederate battery is destroyed in the action, which also results in the capture of an enemy schooner.

31 December–2 January 1862
A naval squadron consisting of the gunboats *Ottawa*, *Pembina*, and *Seneca* and four armed boats mounting howitzers supports a successful amphibious assault at Port Royal Ferry and other positions on the Coosaw River, South Carolina. Sailors and landing force guns are put ashore as artillery support during the action, which prevents a Confederate attempt to isolate Federal troops on Port Royal Island.

1862

7 January
As Flag Officer Andrew H. Foote labors to outfit gunboats for service on the western rivers, Lieutenant Samuel L. Phelps, in command of the gunboat *Conestoga*, leads an expedition up the Tennessee and Cumberland rivers during which he reconnoiters the area around Forts Henry and Donelson. Ten days later the gunboat *Lexington* joins *Conestoga* in an expedition to gather further intelligence, which serves Union forces in their assault against the Confederate stronghold five weeks later.

9 January
The Navy Department issues orders appointing Flag Officer David G. Farragut as Commander of the West Gulf Blockading Squadron. Thus, the veteran of the War of 1812 is placed in a position to command one of the most important naval efforts thus far in the war—the capture of New Orleans, Louisiana.

Opposite, top: *Captain Louis M. Goldsborough, USN. (Naval Historical Center)*

Opposite, bottom: *Fort Walker, Port Royal Sound, South Carolina, under bombardment by ships of the Union Navy, 7 November 1861. (Naval Historical Center)*

Above: *The Trent Affair, involving the screw frigate* San Jacinto, *8 November 1861. (U.S. Naval Academy)*

11 January

The gunboats *Essex* and *St. Louis* engage Confederate gunboats in a running battle in the waters of the Mississippi River near Lucas Bend, Missouri, forcing the Confederate ships to withdraw.

12 January

A Union amphibious expedition under the command of Flag Officer Louis M. Goldsborough and carrying troops led by General Ambrose E. Burnside departs Fort Monroe, Virginia, bound for Roanoke Island, North Carolina. The key strategic point guards the narrow connection between Pamlico and Albemarle Sounds, the latter used extensively for blockade running.

13 January

Lieutenant John L. Worden receives orders to take command of the ironclad *Monitor*, the ship in which he and his crew will change the face of naval history at Hampton Roads, Virginia.

16 January

The screw sloop *Hartford* employs her guns and a landing party of sailors and Marines in destroying a Confederate battery, seven small vessels, and the railroad depot and telegraph office at Cedar Keys, Florida. The attack at the relatively remote site is indicative of the Federal Navy's ability to strike points along the extended coastline of the Confederacy.

Flag Officer Andrew H. Foote reports the commissioning of seven Eads gunboats. These shallow-draft armored vessels, built or converted by James B. Eads for service on the Mississippi, will help provide significant victories for Union forces.

26–29 January

A Union squadron—the gunboats *Ottawa* and *Seneca*, and other vessels—carrying 2,400 Army troops under the command of General Horatio G. Wright conducts a strategic reconnaissance of Wassaw Sound, Georgia. The effort results in an engagement with Confederate gunboats attempting to resupply nearby Fort Pulaski, and perhaps more importantly strikes a blow against the morale of Confederates in the area.

30 January

Monitor, the Union's first ironclad vessel, is launched at Greenpoint, New York. It is a timely appearance for the revolutionary ship, as the Confederate ironclad *Virginia* (ex-*Merrimack*) is nearing completion at Norfolk, Virginia, and in the words of Captain John Marston of the blockading squadron off Virginia, holding "as a rod over us."

6 February

With heavy rains hindering the movement of soldiers, naval forces consisting of the gunboats *Carondelet, Cincinnati, Conestoga, Essex, Lexington, St. Louis*, and *Tyler* carry the burden of capturing Fort Henry on the Tennessee River. Sailors unleash accurate fire from the river, knocking out all but four of the fort's batteries and prompting the Confederate commander to strike

his colors. "The labor you have performed and the services you have rendered in creating the armed flotilla of gunboats on the Western waters…can never be overestimated," the Secretary of the Navy writes to Flag Officer Andrew H. Foote, the commander of naval forces in the assault against Fort Henry, which is soon renamed Fort Foote.

7 February

The gunboat *Conestoga* engages Confederate forces on the Tennessee River, forcing the enemy to abandon and burn three steamers in order to prevent them from falling into Union hands.

Opposite, top: *Ironclads on both sides represented a new era in naval warfare. ("CSS* Atlanta," *R.G. Skerrett, Naval Historical Center)*

Opposite, bottom: *Captain Andrew H. Foote commanded the Union's initial efforts to seize Confederate strongholds on western rivers. (Naval Historical Center)*

Below: *Loaded with Union Army troops, ships gather at Fort Monroe, Virginia, the night before departing for an amphibious assault against Roanoke Island, North Carolina. (Naval Historical Center)*

7–8 February

In a joint expedition led by Flag Officer Louis M. Goldsborough and General Ambrose E. Burnside, Union vessels bombard Confederate defenses on Roanoke Island, and employ their guns in covering the landing of Federal troops. On 10 February a naval flotilla pursues Confederate naval forces up the Pasquotank River, capturing, sinking, or forcing the destruction of four gunboats and destroying rebel batteries at Elizabeth City, North Carolina. During the engagement shot passes through the powder magazine of the screw steamer *Valley City* and explodes in a locker containing fireworks. A quarter gunner named John Davis calmly sits atop an open barrel of powder in order to keep the fire away from it and continues to pass powder required by the ship's gunners. He becomes the first Navy man recommended for the Medal of Honor. The capture of Roanoke Island and the defeat of Confederate forces near Elizabeth City, combined with follow-up operation in the area, effectively cut off Norfolk, Virginia, from its main supply lines and secures the coast of North Carolina.

10 February

Secretary of the Navy Gideon Welles directs Commander David Dixon Porter to assign twenty-two sailing vessels and seven steamers to outfit the Mortar Squadron for use in suppressing fire from Forts Jackson and St. Philip at the entrance to New Orleans.

14 February

Six gunboats under Flag Officer Andrew H. Foote support General Ulysses S. Grant's assault against Fort Donelson on the Cumberland River in Tennessee. Located on high ground, the fort's batteries are able to unleash withering fire on the gunboats below, hitting Foote's flagship *St. Louis* fifty-nine times and wounding him. Yet the support of naval forces contributes to the surrender of the fort the next day.

Galena, an experimental seagoing ironclad, is launched.

17 February

The Confederate ironclad *Virginia* is commissioned under Captain Franklin Buchanan, a former U.S. Navy officer and first superintendent of the U.S. Naval Academy.

19 February

The ironclad *Monitor* engages in sea trials in New York Harbor, with Chief Engineer Alban C. Stimers reporting his belief that her maximum speed would be approximately six knots.

The side-wheel steamers *Commodore Perry* and *Delaware* engage Confederate forces at Winton, North Carolina, while engaged in a reconnaissance of the Chowan River. The following day, the vessels cover the landing of Union troops in their capture of the town.

20 February

Secretary of the Navy Gideon Welles addresses orders directing the ironclad *Monitor* to proceed from New York to Hampton Roads, Virginia. This comes on the same day General John E. Wool at Fort Monroe, receiving word of the Confederate ironclad *Virginia*'s impending attack on Newport News, requests a larger naval force in the region.

Below: Harper's Weekly *illustration of the Union gunboats (left to right)* Tyler, Conestoga, Carondelet, Pittsburg, Louisville, *and* St. Louis *bombarding Fort Donelson, Tennessee, 14 February 1862. (Naval Historical Center)*

21 February

Flag Officer David G. Farragut assumes command of the West Gulf Blockading Squadron on board the screw sloop *Hartford*, which he will lead to glory at New Orleans, Louisiana, and Mobile Bay, Alabama.

24 February

Captain Franklin Buchanan is ordered to assume command of Confederate naval forces defending the James River. He flies his flag in the ironclad *Virginia*. "The condition of our country, and the painful reverses we have just suffered, demand our utmost exertions," writes Confederate Secretary of the Navy Stephen Mallory in his orders to Buchanan.

25 February

The Union ironclad *Monitor*, which one observer likens to a "cheese box on a raft" and another calls "a mere speck, like a hat on the surface," is commissioned. She departs the New York Navy Yard two days later, but is forced to turn back because of a steering failure.

2 March

The gunboats *Cincinnati* and *Louisville* engage in a reconnaissance of Confederate positions at Columbus, Kentucky, foreshadowing for the defenders the imminent arrival of Union troops. Two days later Union forces land to discover that Columbus has been abandoned, the Confederates having left a large amount of ordnance and powder behind.

3 March

Forces under the command of Flag Officer Samuel F. Du Pont support an amphibious operation that succeeds in capturing Cumberland Island and Sound,

Fernandina and Amelia Island, and the town of St. Mary's. This action, combined with landings at St. Simon's and Jekyl islands and Brunswick six days later, places the entire coast of Georgia under Union control.

8 March
The Confederate ironclad *Virginia*, her crew having never trained in their ship while underway, engages ships of the Union blockade at Hampton Roads, Virginia. In her first attack she rams the frigate *Cumberland* below the waterline, causing the vessel to sink rapidly. Turning their attention to the frigate *Congress*, run hard aground, *Virginia*'s gunners fill her with hot shot and incendiary shells, setting her ablaze. The battle is not without cost for the ironclad, however. Franklin Buchanan is wounded; part of *Virginia*'s ram is missing from striking *Cumberland*; two of her guns are damaged and she is leaking forward. Yet, as Confederate Secretary of the Navy Stephen Mallory states in a letter to President Jefferson Davis, the performance of *Virginia* is "the most remarkable victory which naval annals record." That night the ironclad *Monitor* arrives at Hampton Roads.

9 March
The Union ironclad *Monitor* and the Confederate ironclad *Virginia* engage in an epic four-hour engagement at Hampton Roads, Virginia, the first clash between ironclad warships. With their crews fighting in the extreme heat and poor ventilation of their iron encasements, the two ships exchange fire and at one point draw close enough for *Virginia* to attempt ramming her Union counterpart. In addition, a direct hit on the pilothouse of *Monitor* blinds her skipper, Lieutenant John L. Worden, as he peers through one of the viewing slits. Yet, the Union vessel continues to pound away at *Virginia*, which runs aground. The battle ends in a draw, the only casualty on both sides being Worden.

14 March
A joint amphibious operation lands some 12,000 Marines and Union Army troops at New Bern, North Carolina, resulting in the capture of the town, which contains a Confederate arms depot, two steamers, and four forts.

16 March
Flag Officer Andrew H. Foote, having departed Cairo, Illinois, two days earlier in command of seven gunboats and ten mortar boats, orders his gunners to begin bombarding Confederate positions on Island Number 10, the first shots in what becomes an intense campaign to capture that bulwark against further Union advances down the Mississippi River.

17 March
Naval forces begin transporting elements of the Army of the Potomac from Alexandria, Virginia, to Fort Monroe for the commencement of what will become known as the Peninsular Campaign.

The Confederate side-wheel steamer *Nashville* successfully runs the Union blockade, steaming through the gunfire of the screw steamer *Cambridge* out into the open sea. Assistant Secretary of the Navy Gustavus Fox calls the escape the "Bull Run of the Navy."

In an effort to engage Confederate batteries along the Tennessee shore and at Island Number 10, Flag Officer Andrew H. Foote's flagship, the gunboat *Benton*, is lashed between the gunboats *Cincinnati* and *St. Louis*. The three vessels close to within 2,000 yards of the enemy batteries, knocking out one enemy gun at the price of hits on all of the Union gunboats.

Opposite, top: *The Confederate ironclad* Virginia *rams the Union frigate* Cumberland *through a broadside from the wooden warship. ("Iron Versus Wood—Sinking of the* Cumberland *by the* Merrimac *in Hampton Roads, 8 March 1862," Edward Moran, U.S. Naval Academy)*

Opposite, bottom: *Captain Franklin Buchanan, who commanded the Confederate ironclad* Virginia *in her first action. (Naval Historical Center)*

Above: *("Monitor v. Virginia, 9 March 1862," Lebreton, Naval Historical Center)*

CLASH OF IRON:
MONITOR AND VIRGINIA

by Dana M. Wegner

The battle between the ironclads USS *Monitor* and CSS *Virginia* remains one of the most popular and symbolic sea fights in history. The idea of cladding ships in armor to protect them from projectiles was not new, and when the Civil War began in 1861, several European navies were already building major ironclad warships. By April 1861, a Union naval blockade of the southern coastline from Virginia to Texas had been declared, soon crippling the Confederacy's ability to move goods by water and preventing other nations from directly supplying the South.

Southern leaders envisioned ironclad warships driving off oppressive blockaders and supporting army campaigns. Lieutenant John Brooke, constructor John Porter, and chief engineer William Williamson planned to raise and convert the hulk of the steam and sail-powered screw frigate *Merrimack*, which had been fired and sunk when Federal forces evacuated the navy yard at Norfolk, Virginia. Reusing part of the 275-foot wooden hull and the engines of the frigate, Confederates built a casemate of sloping, thick timber walls covered with four inches of iron plate to shield ten broadside-mounted guns.

Through spies and southern newspapers, the North was aware of the enemy's plans. In August 1861 the U.S. Navy solicited proposals from contractors to build ironclad warships. Three different builders were

Opposite: *Wooden sailing ships are spectators to a battle marking a revolution in technology that will one day render them obsolete as the ironclads* Monitor *and* Virginia *duel at Hampton Roads, Virginia, on 9 March 1862. (U.S. Naval Institute)*

Right: *The turret of* Monitor *shows battle damage from its engagement with* Virginia. *The canvas roof over the turret was erected only when the ship was quietly at anchor in order to provide shade for the crew. (Naval Historical Center)*

chosen. Because the New York City–based engineer and his syndicate promised a ship within 100 days, the smallest, most radical, and least predictable of the three ships would be the Union's counter-challenge. The innovative designer was John Ericsson, a Swedish-born engineer with an established, though controversial, international reputation. His 172-foot ship featured an ironclad raft with a wooden hull below. Rising less than a foot above the water, the raft mounted a revolving turret of 8-inch iron plates, enclosing two 11-inch Dahlgren shell guns. The ship was greatly underpowered, but it was, nonetheless, a marvel of nineteenth-century American ingenuity and industrial technology.

On 8 March 1862, the former *Merrimack*, renamed *Virginia*, left the Norfolk Navy Yard and ventured into Hampton Roads, a large anchorage near Norfolk where several rivers flow into Chesapeake Bay, to attack the anchored Federal blockade fleet. As shot from the Federal ships and land batteries bounced off her armored casemate, *Virginia* sank the outmatched wooden sailing warships *Cumberland* and *Congress*. When *Virginia* withdrew at the end of that bloody day, the carnage foretold that, against iron, wooden warships were but eggshells and tinderboxes.

Monitor had departed New York harbor under tow on 6 March 1862, almost foundered in frighteningly heavy seas during her passage to Hampton Roads, and arrived during the evening of 8 March. She was ordered to protect the blockaders, specifically the powerful steam frigate *Minnesota*, which had run aground and would be an easy kill for *Virginia*.

At sunrise on Sunday, 9 March, *Virginia*, under the command of Lieutenant Catesby Jones, reappeared and spied the unimpressive little *Monitor* squatting, almost invisible, in front of *Minnesota*. The Confederate ship began shelling *Minnesota*. *Monitor*, commanded by Lieutenant John Worden, advanced. Federal, Confederate, and international dignitaries lined the shoreline to witness the contest, the first battle in history between ironclad warships.

The ironclads circled each other probing for weak spots and frequently fired at close range. With a wide turning radius and troublesome engines, *Virginia* proved slow and unwieldy. *Monitor* had trouble training her turret, compounding her handicap of mounting only two guns. After four hours, *Virginia* began to show signs of her pounding. *Monitor* temporarily hauled off when her pilot house was struck, injuring Lieutenant Worden. *Virginia* mistook the timeout as a welcome sign that the tenacious *Monitor* was retiring for the day and the Confederates returned to port. *Minnesota* was safe, the blockade remained intact, and the famous ironclads never again fought each other. In May 1862, *Virginia* was blown up to prevent capture by Union troops. Seven months later, in an eerie replay of her maiden voyage, *Monitor* foundered under tow in a storm off North Carolina, unfitting ends to two warships that transformed naval warfare.

22 March

Florida, the first ship built in England for the Confederacy, clears Liverpool disguised as a British steamer and sets course for Nassau, Bahamas. She becomes one of the Confederacy's most successful raiders.

25 March

The Confederate side-wheel steamer *Pamlico* and the gunboat *Oregon* test the strength of Flag Officer David G. Farragut's forces assembling for the assault against New Orleans, Louisiana, engaging the Union screw steamer *New London* at Pass Christian, Mississippi. In the two-hour engagement, neither side suffers any damage.

1 April

As part of the campaign against Island Number 10, a combined Army-Navy boat expedition led by Master John V. Johnston, from the gunboat *St. Louis,* lands and spikes the guns of Fort Number 1 located on the Tennessee shore above Island Number 10.

4 April

The gunboat *Carondelet*, under Commander Henry Walke, makes a successful run past the formidable Confederate batteries on Island Number 10. Her passage shrouded by a heavy evening storm and her defensive armor buttressed by piled cord-wood, extra deck planking, and anchor chain, *Carondelet* completes a vital link-up with Union troops at New Madrid,

Missouri. The side-wheel gunboat *Pittsburgh* joins her on 7 April, and the two gunboats cover the crossing of forces under the command of General John Pope to the Tennessee side of the Mississippi River.

6 April

During the bloody battle of Shiloh in Tennessee, the Union gunboats *Tyler* and *Lexington* bombard advancing Confederate lines and help stave off defeat and, the following day, contribute to driving the graycoats to retreat.

7 April

Island Number 10 surrenders to Union naval forces under the command of Flag Officer Andrew H. Foote, thus completing the conquest of the upper Mississippi River. The surrender of the island yields heavy cannon and munitions, four steamers, and the Confederate ship *Red Rover*. Damaged by mortar fire, the vessel is taken to Cairo, Illinois, and converted into the U.S. Navy's first hospital ship. Among those who serve in her are the Sisters of the Holy Cross, volunteer nurses who are the predecessors of the modern day Navy Nurse Corps.

Commander Raphael Semmes receives orders to lay up the Confederate raider *Sumter* because of a major breakdown of her boilers at the Mediterranean island of Gibraltar. She finishes her career having captured eighteen vessels and wreaked havoc on the Union Navy.

14 April

In preparing for further advances down the Mississippi River, Union mortar boats begin shelling Fort Pillow in Tennessee.

18 April

In dire straits in the face of the blockade and the steady advance of the Union Navy in inland waterways, the Confederate Congress authorizes the

Above: *The casemate ironclad* Carondelet *served with distinction on the western rivers from 1862 to 1865, taking part in the capture of Forts Henry and Donelson, the siege of Vicksburg, and the Red River expedition. (Naval Historical Center)*

Right: *Inboard and outboard profile drawings of the ironclad gunboat* Benton, *which participated in action at Island Number 10 and Vicksburg and served on expeditions on the Yazoo and Red Rivers. She served first in the Army's Western Gunboat Flotilla before her transfer to the Navy in October 1862. (Naval Historical Center)*

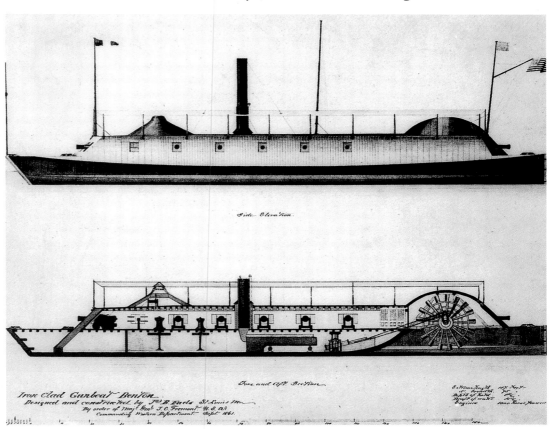

GUNBOATS ON THE MISSISSIPPI: ISLAND NUMBER 10

by Dr. Craig L. Symonds

In addition to prosecuting the coastal blockade and pursuing Confederate commerce raiders, the U.S. Navy's other main role in the Civil War, and arguably its most important one, was seizing and controlling the Mississippi River and its tributaries. In this effort, the main obstacle was not the tiny Confederate navy, but the formidable shore fortifications erected by the Confederates along the banks of the Tennessee, Cumberland, and Mississippi rivers. The war on the western rivers, therefore, was less often a matter of ship vs. ship than it was Union ships vs. Confederate forts. And in that confrontation, the most important key to eventual Union victory was effective interservice cooperation between the Union Army and Navy. Against a creative and determined foe, neither service, by itself, could have achieved the kind of dramatic success that Union forces did while working together as a combat team. Moreover, that success is all the more remarkable because there was no such thing as combined operational command in the Civil War— when Army generals and Nnavy flag officers worked together, it was because they each decided to do so. Neither could give orders to the other.

The first important triumph of Union forces against Confederate river forts came at Fort Henry on the Tennessee River on 6 February 1862. In this action a Union squadron of armored warships under Flag Officer Andrew H. Foote out-dueled the rebel gunners ashore and compelled the fort's surrender before U.S. Army troops under General Ulysses S. Grant arrived. Ten days later it was the Army's turn to win the laurels as Grant surrounded Fort Donelson on the Cumberland River and dictated terms of "unconditional surrender." But at Island Number 10 on the Mississippi, it was a different story. Here Foote's gunboats could not take on the heavy shore batteries unassisted, and the Army troops—this time under General John Pope—were cut off from the enemy by the river itself. Unless these forces could

find a way to work together, the Union advance down the Mississippi would be halted before it fairly began.

What made Island Number 10 so daunting an obstacle was its peculiar geography. Just where the Mississippi River flowed southward from Kentucky into Tennessee, it took a 180-degree turn, swinging northward again back into Tennessee, before looping south once more. In the first bend of that S turn, on the tenth island counting southward from where the Ohio flowed into the Mississippi, the Confederates had erected a series of shore fortifications bolstered by a substantial floating battery. From there, the Confederate gunners could shoot upstream along the length of the river from the moment Union gunboats came into range. Unlike the circumstances at Fort Henry, Foote's gunboats could not simply pull up alongside and slug it out with the enemy.

But neither could U.S. Army forces under Pope assail the rebel fortifications from the landward side as Grant had at Fort Donelson, because a tributary on the Mississippi's eastern side widened into a swampy marsh called Reelfoot Lake that made an approach from that direction impossible. A better line of attack was from the south, but that was feasible only if Pope's men, positioned on the western bank, could somehow get across the river behind the fort. Only if Foote's gunboats could get past the island was this possible. Neither the Navy's gunboats, nor the Army's soldiers could subdue the enemy, or even approach him menacingly, without support and assistance from the other.

Recognizing the situation, Foote tried to see if he could cut a canal through the marshy swampland in the bend of that S curve in the river in order to bypass Island Number 10 and link up with Pope's soldiers at New Madrid, Missouri. That gambit, however, proved fruitless. There was no other way but for some brave soul to try to run past the Island Number 10 batteries. The man who volunteered to try was Commander Henry Walke of the gunboat *Carondelet*. On the night

of 4 April 1862, Walke attempted to slip past the enemy batteries in the darkness. A spark from his stack, however, alerted the sentries, and the Rebels opened fire. Despite the gauntlet of fire from shore, and the danger of navigating the winding river at night, Walke and *Carondelet* made it safely past the island. Now that Walke had proved it possible, the next night the side-wheel gunboat *Pittsburg*, under Lieutenant Egbert Thompson, made the same run, and on 7 April those two ships successfully transferred Pope's soldiers across the Mississippi so they could approach the rebel defenses from their unprotected southern flank.

The geography of the Confederate position at Island Number 10, once its great strength, now proved to be a trap. Once Pope cut off its communication southward, and with Foote's gunboats holding the river itself above and below the island, the Confederate defenders could do little but accept the inevitable. Pope captured both the fort and its 6,000-man

garrison, making him a hero in the North and winning him the command of a field army in Virginia. As for Foote, his deteriorating heath soon compelled him to relinquish command of the Mississippi squadron. Nevertheless, he had shown the way. At Vicksburg almost exactly one year later, Rear Admiral David Dixon Porter and Major General Ulysses S. Grant would use a strategy nearly identical to Foote's in another effective Army-Navy partnership. This one sealed the fate of the Confederate citadel on the Mississippi, thus fulfilling one element of Winfield Scott's Anaconda Plan.

Above: *Mortar boats unleash a barrage against Island Number 10 as Union gunboats advance on the Confederate fortress with their guns blazing, 7 April 1862. (Currier and Ives Lithograph, Naval Historical Center)*

issuance of contracts for the purchase of not more than six ironclads. Payment is to be made in cotton.

In preparation for the attack against New Orleans, Louisiana, mortar boats under the command of Commander David Dixon Porter begin a five-day bombardment of Fort Jackson, one of the forts guarding the approaches to the city. One mortar boat is sunk by Confederate fire from the fort during the action.

20 April

The gunboats *Itasca* and *Pinola* breach an obstruction consisting of chains supported by hulks stretching across the Mississippi River, thus clearing the way for Union ships under Flag Officer David G. Farragut to move against New Orleans, Louisiana.

24 April

At 2:00 a.m., upon receiving a signal from the flagship, the screw sloop *Hartford*, Union ships and gunboats get underway to commence the assault against New Orleans, Louisiana. Answering withering fire from Forts Jackson and St. Philip with broadsides, the Union vessels successfully pass the forts and engage a Confederate flotilla. In the ensuing battle, eight rebel ships are destroyed, one sunk, and two surrendered. Two other ships are destroyed to prevent their capture. Union losses include the screw sloop *Varuna*, which slips beneath the waters of the Mississippi after being rammed. *Hartford*, though run aground and set afire, survives to fight another day. On 25 April the Union squadron anchors off New Orleans and Flag Officer David G. Farragut accepts the surrender of the city. Before the battle he had written, "As to being prepared for defeat, I certainly am not."

5 May

President Abraham Lincoln, in company with Secretary of War Edwin Stanton and Secretary of the Treasury Salmon P. Chase, boards the steamer *Miami* for transport to Hampton Roads, Virginia. Over the course of the ensuing five days Lincoln personally directs gunboat operations in the James River in support of the stalled Peninsular campaign.

Opposite, top: *Illustration from* Harper's Weekly *showing the Union flotilla descending the Mississippi River to attack Fort Pillow, April 1862. (Naval Historical Center)*

Opposite, bottom: *Rear Admiral David Glasgow Farragut photographed in New Orleans in 1863. Having seen his first combat at the age of twelve during the War of 1812, Farragut was the foremost naval commander of the Civil War. (Naval Historical Center)*

Right: *Flag Officer David G. Farragut in the screw sloop* Hartford *faced tough resistance during an attempt to capture New Orleans, Louisiana, on 24 April 1862, as Confederate artillerymen at Fort Jackson blasted away at his ship. (Tom Freeman)*

6–7 May

The screw sloop *Wachusett* and gunboats *Chocura* and *Sebago*, under Commander William Smith, escort Army transports up the York River and support the landings of Union troops at West Point, Virginia.

8 May

The ironclad *Monitor*, the steam sloop *Dacotah*, the screw steamer *Naugatuck*, the screw sloop *Seminole*, and the side-wheel steamer *Susquehanna* shell Confederate batteries at Sewell's Point, Virginia. Two enemy ships, the gunboat *Jamestown* and the side-wheel steamer *Patrick Henry*, are forced to return up the James River.

9 May

Flag Officer Andrew H. Foote relinquishes command of the Western Flotilla because of the lingering effects of wounds received during the assault against Fort Donelson.

10 May

Duplicating the actions of Union forces in 1861, retreating Confederates in Virginia set fire to the Norfolk Navy Yard, as they withdraw up the peninsula toward Richmond, Virginia. Further south, Union forces reoccupy Pensacola, Florida, though the city's navy yard, along with Forts Barrancas and McRee, are destroyed by departing Confederates. Thus, two strategic ports once again fly the flag of the United States.

Eight vessels of the Confederate River Defense Fleet attack Union gunboats and boats of the mortar flotilla at Plum Point Bend, Tennessee. The gunboat *Cincinnati* is rammed by *Bragg* and sinks, while the Confederate ram *General Earl Van Dorn* runs the gunboat *Mound City* aground. Shallow waters prevent further attacks by the Confederates and they withdraw. Both Union vessels are repaired and return to service.

The ironclad steamer *New Ironsides* is launched.

Left: *The collection of steamers, ironclads, and other vessels assembled to operate against the Confederacy on the nation's rivers was a varied lot. This is clearly visible in this depiction of the ironclads* Monitor, Galena *and* Naugatuck, *and the gunboats* Aroostook *and* Port Royal *bombarding Fort Darling at Drewry's Bluff, Virginia, 15 May 1862. ("Fort Darling Bombardment," Naval Historical Center)*

11 May

With the fall of Norfolk, Virginia, removing her base of operations and her draft preventing movement up the James River, the Confederate ironclad *Virginia* is blown up by her crew off Craney Island to prevent capture. *Virginia*'s demise allows for passage further up the James River to support Union forces fighting their way toward Richmond.

13 May

With the captain of the tug *Planter* ashore in Charleston, South Carolina, an entirely African-American crew led by Robert Smalls seizes her, steams past Confederate batteries and forts saluting with her whistle, and then turns her over to *Onward*, a Union ship operating as part of the blockade off the city.

15 May

The James River Flotilla, consisting of five vessels including the celebrated ironclad *Monitor*, under Commander John Rodgers engages Confederate sharpshooters and batteries at Drewry's Bluff along the James River in Virginia. The ironclad *Galena* is heavily damaged, but this does not prevent Rodgers from advancing along the river to within eight miles of Richmond before being forced to turn back.

20 May

Union gunboats occupy the Stono River above Cole's Island, South Carolina, bombarding Confederate positions there and securing a base of operations for future operations against Charleston.

6 June

With Confederate forces having abandoned Fort Pillow, allowing Union naval forces to approach Memphis, Tennessee, the Confederate River Defense Fleet has little choice but to engage the invaders. In a pitched battle, seven of eight rebel vessels are captured, sunk, or grounded to avoid sinking after a pitched battle on the Mississippi River. The city of Memphis surrenders.

17 June

As part of an expedition to open Army communications down the White River, a flotilla of ironclads, gunboats, and transports under Commander Augustus H. Kilty engages Confederate batteries at St. Charles, Arkansas. Though Union troops successfully capture the enemy positions, the effort comes at a high cost when a projectile penetrates the casemate of the gunboat *Mound City*, puncturing the boiler and steam chest, and filling the vessel with steam. Of the crew of 175, some 150 are killed or wounded. The number killed accounts for seven percent of all Union Navy casualties during the Civil War.

Flag Officer Charles H. Davis relieves Flag Officer Andrew H. Foote in command of U.S. Navy forces on the Mississippi River.

Right: *The destruction of the Confederate flotilla off Memphis, Tennessee, as depicted in* The Illustrated London News, *July 1862. (Naval Historical Center)*

Below: *Photo of the ironclad* Galena *taken after action at Drewry's Bluff, Virginia, in May 1862, during which the Union vessel was hit numerous times. A plugged hole from enemy shot is visible near the waterline. (Naval Historical Center)*

19 June
The Confederate States Navy employs the war's first minelayer, *Teaser*, in the James River. Commander Matthew F. Maury commands the operation, in which electric torpedoes (the Civil War term for underwater mines), made of boilerplate encased in watertight wooden casks, are planted.

28 June
Flag Officer David G. Farragut, the victor at New Orleans, Louisiana, leads ships of his squadron past the Confederate stronghold at Vicksburg, Mississippi. Supported by mortar boats under the command of Commander David Dixon Porter, Farragut's ships exchange heavy fire with enemy batteries. Three days

Above: Harper's Weekly *illustration of Union vessels gathered at Harrison's Landing on the James River, base of General George B. McClellan's Army of the Potomac during the Peninsular Campaign, 1862. (Naval Historical Center)*

Left: *Crewmen break for a meal on board the* Monitor. *(Naval Historical Center)*

Opposite: *On 15 July 1862 the Confederate ironclad* Arkansas *disabled two Union gunboats on the Yazoo River. ("The Confederate Ram Arkansas," J. O. Davidson, Naval Historical Center)*

later, Farragut's ships join the gunboats of the Western Flotilla and begin preparing for the arduous campaign against Vicksburg, Mississippi.

1–2 July
Ships under Flag Officer Louis M. Goldsborough cover the withdrawal of General George B. McClellan's Army of the Potomac following its pitched battle at Malvern Hill with Confederate forces under the command of General Robert E. Lee. During the battle, gunboats protect McClellan's flanks, firing on the Confederate rear as well as Lee's army's advancing columns. The Navy also safeguards the Army of the Potomac's supply line, escorting transports up and down the James River. Of the naval support, Lee later writes: "As far as I can now see there is no way to attack him (McClellan) to advantage nor do I wish to expose the men to the destructive missiles of his gunboats."

4 July
The side-wheel steamer *Maratanza* engages the Confederate minelaying vessel *Teaser* in the James River. When a shell from a Union cannon explodes in the boiler of their ship, the crew of *Teaser* abandons ship and the unique vessel falls into Union hands.

5 July
Congress passes an act reorganizing the Navy Department, specifically increasing the number of bureaus to eight. Thus, the Navy now includes the Bureaus of Yards and Docks, Equipment and Recruiting, Navigation, Ordnance, Construction and Repair, Steam Engineering, Provisions and Clothing, and Medicine and Surgery.

7 July
President Abraham Lincoln and his military party board the schooner *Ariel* for transport to Harrison's Landing, Virginia, to confer with General George B. McClellan.

14 July
Congress passes an act eliminating the dispensing of a daily ration of spirits to the crews of U.S. Navy ships and forbidding the presence of "spiritous liquors" not part of medical stores aboard ship. In lieu of the ration, Union sailors are paid an additional five cents per day.

15 July

In action on the Yazoo River in Mississippi, the Union gunboats *Carondelet* and *Tyler* and the ram *Queen of the West* engage the Confederate ironclad *Arkansas*. *Arkansas* partially disables *Carondelet* and *Tyler* as the Union forces attempt to withdraw. Forced to run past the guns of Farragut's fleet when she enters the Mississippi River to return to Vicksburg, Mississippi, *Arkansas* suffers severe damage and numerous casualties before she is able to gain refuge under the guns of Confederate batteries surrounding the city. For his daring foray against the overwhelming force of Union ships, *Arkansas*'s skipper, Lieutenant Isaac N. Brown, receives a promotion to the rank of commander.

16 July

Congress passes a measure reorganizing the rank structure in the U.S. Navy and establishing the number of officers in respective grades. In addition to creating the ranks of rear admiral, commodore, and lieutenant commander, the act sets a force of nine rear admirals, eighteen commodores, thirty-six captains, seventy-two commanders, and 144 officers each in the remaining ranks through ensign. In recognition of his victory at New Orleans, David G. Farragut is the first officer to be promoted to rear admiral.

17–18 July

The screw steamer *New London* and vessel *Grey Cloud* support a force of forty Marines and sailors in an expedition up the Pascagoula River in Mississippi that results in the capture or destruction of a steamer and two schooners and disrupts telegraph communications between Pascagoula and Mobile, Alabama.

21 July

Demonstrating the value of naval control of the Ohio River in thwarting Confederate attempts to make inroads in the border states, the steamers *Clara Dolsen* and *Rob Roy* join the tug *Restless* in retaking Henderson, Kentucky, from Confederate guerillas and protecting Evansville, Indiana.

22 July

The gunboat *Essex* and the ram *Queen of the West* boldly advance into the waters near Vicksburg, Mississippi, to engage the damaged Confederate ironclad *Arkansas*. Despite the fact that most of the crew is absent from the ship, *Arkansas* fights off the two vessels, and the following day steams up and down the Mississippi River under the protection of the guns of Vicksburg. "*Essex* ranged up alongside us, and at the distance of 20 feet poured in a broads[ide], which crashed against our sides like—nothing that I ever heard before," writes Confederate Midshipman Dabney

Scales of the attack. "We were so close that our men were burnt by the powder of the enemy's guns."

24 July

The falling water level in the Mississippi River and illness among the crews of many ships prompts Rear Admiral David G. Farragut's fleet to depart the waters below Vicksburg, Mississippi, and return to Baton Rouge and New Orleans, Louisiana. This demonstrates the importance of the Confederate hold on Vicksburg, which allows for the continuing reinforcement of the men in gray operating in the west.

28 July

The bark *Agrippina* receives orders to rendezvous in the Azores Islands with *Enrica* steaming out of Liverpool, England for the purpose of transferring guns, ammunition, coal, and other cargo. *Enrica* soon receives the name *Alabama* and becomes the Confederacy's most renowned commerce raider.

6 August

For the second time in less than two months, the ironclad *Arkansas* meets the gunboat *Essex* in an engagement on the Mississippi River. Ordered into action in support of a Confederate offensive to take Baton Rouge, Louisiana, *Arkansas* becomes unmanageable due to engine failure and is destroyed be her crew in order to prevent capture. With its naval support eradicated, the Confederate offensive fails.

7 August

Confederate raider *Florida* departs Nassau, Bahamas, beginning her storied career as a thorn in Union's side.

16 August

The gunboats *Benton* and *Mound City* and *the* side-wheel steamer *General Bragg* join the rams *Monarch, Lioness, Samson,* and *Switzerland* in an expedition up the Mississippi River from Helena, Arkansas, to the Yazoo River. The vessels land Army troops at various points along the route, resulting in the capture of the Confederate steamer *Fairplay*, the dispersing of rebel troops, and destruction of a battery located some twenty miles up the Yazoo River.

16–18 August

A Union naval force consisting of four vessels under Acting Lieutenant John W. Kittredge bombards Corpus Christi, Texas, and puts a landing party ashore to capture a Confederate battery protecting the town. The force is driven back by Confederate cavalry.

22 August

Secretary of the Navy Gideon Welles orders Rear Admiral Louis M. Goldsborough to employ ships of his North Atlantic Blockading Squadron to assist in transporting the Army of the Potomac northward after the failed Peninsular Campaign.

Opposite: *Typical of the gunboat designs of the Civil War,* Essex *featured an angular hull to deflect enemy cannonballs. (*"USS Essex," *R.G. Skerrett, Naval Historical Center)*

Above: *The most feared Confederate warship was the raider* Alabama. *(Naval Historical Center)*

Right: *Captain Raphael Semmes pictured on the deck of* Alabama. *Under his command she captured sixty-eight vessels. (Naval Historical Center)*

24 August
Captain Raphael Semmes assumes command of the Confederate raider *Alabama* at sea off the Azores Islands. To the playing of "Dixie" and the cheering of the crew, the Confederate ensign is hoisted to the gaff.

26 August
Captain Franklin Buchanan, in recognition of his successful engagement of Union ships at Hampton Roads, Virginia, while in command of the ironclad *Virginia*, is promoted to the rank of admiral in the Confederate States Navy.

1 September
Rear Admiral Samuel P. Lee relieves Rear Admiral Louis M. Goldsborough in command of the North Atlantic Blockading Squadron.

4 September
The Confederate raider *Florida*, a great number of her crew suffering from yellow fever, runs the blockade and enters Mobile Bay, Alabama, despite suffering damage from three pursuing Union ships.

5 September
The Confederate raider *Alabama* begins her reign of terror against Union shipping, seizing and burning the ship *Ocmulgee* near the Azores Islands.

8 September
The presence of the Confederate raiders *Florida* and *Alabama* prompts the creation of a "Flying Squadron" of seven U.S. Navy ships formed specifically to capture the two feared ships. The squadron is ultimately unsuccessful in its mission. The Navy Department eventually announces that it will issue a reward of $500,000 for the capture of *Alabama*.

25 September
The screw steamer *Kensington* and schooners *Henry James* and *Rachel Seaman* bombard Confederate batteries at Sabine Pass, Texas, forcing their evacuation. A landing party subsequently destroys a railroad bridge, but no troops are available to hold the town.

Opposite, top: *David Dixon Porter first went to sea at the age of ten, in the frigate* John Adams, *commanded by his father. A lieutenant when the Civil War began, by 1865 he had risen to the rank of rear admiral. (Naval Historical Center)*

Opposite, bottom: *The Confederate raider* Florida *runs the blockade at Mobile Bay, 4 September 1862. ("CSS* Florida," *R.S. Floyd, Naval Historical Center)*

Right: *Sailors conduct a loading drill on a Dahlgren rifled howitzer, mounted on an iron field carriage, on the gunboat* Hunchback. *Note the different uniforms worn by the sailors. (Naval Historical Center)*

26 September

Rear Admiral Samuel F. Du Pont requests a coal hulk capable of holding a thousand tons of coal to be loaded aboard men-of-war. This method of advanced-base refueling foreshadows the system of underway replenishment that still is a hallmark of the U.S. Navy.

1 October

The Western Gunboat Flotilla transfers from the jurisdiction of the War Department to that of the Navy Department. The flotilla is renamed the Mississippi Squadron and placed under the command of David Dixon Porter, who is promoted from the rank of commander to that of acting rear admiral.

3 October

A five-ship naval force bombards and captures the Confederate defenses at Galveston, Texas, and forces the surrender of the city six days later.

15 October

Continuing attacks at strategic points along the extended coastline of Texas, boat crews from the schooner *Rachel Seaman* and the screw steamer *Kensington* destroy a railroad bridge at Taylor's Bayou, and also burn the Confederate schooners *Lone Star* and *Stonewall*.

24 October

A landing party from the gunboat *Baron De Kalb* goes ashore at Hopefield, Arkansas. In the process of engaging a small Confederate scouting party, the sailors impress horses and pursue the rebels on horseback for a distance of nine miles before capturing them.

31 October

A naval expedition consisting of the steamers *Commodore Perry*, *Hetzel*, *Hunchback*, and *Valley City* and the Army gunboat *Vidette* bombards a Confederate encampment at Plymouth, North Carolina. This marks the beginning of an eight-day campaign that supports Army forces in the capture of Hamilton, North Carolina.

3 November

Operating in concert with Confederate shore batteries, the steamer *Cotton* engages four Union ships in Berwick Bay, Louisiana. With firing so intense that crewmen in *Cotton* cut off the legs of their trousers for use as improvised cartridge bags, the Confederate ship causes significant damage to the Union ships before being forced to retire.

18 November

The screw frigate *San Jacinto* briefly blockades *Alabama* at Martinique in the Caribbean. However, benefiting from foul weather the following day, the Confederate raider manages to put to sea and evade the U.S. Navy warship.

19 November

Demonstrating the versatility of Union naval forces operating on the rivers of the Confederacy, the gunboat *Wissahickon* and screw steamer *Dawn* divert from their blockade of the Confederate side-wheel steamer *Nashville* in Ossabaw Sound, Georgia, to bombard Fort McAllister on the Ogeechee River. *Wissahickon* is temporarily disabled in the duel with the fort's batteries.

23 November

A landing party from the side-wheel steamer *Ellis* under the command of Lieutenant William B. Cushing captures arms and two schooners at Jacksonville, North Carolina. The following day *Ellis* grounds while under attack from Confederate batteries, and Cushing orders her burned to prevent capture by the enemy. The young officer, who finds his way into the ranks of the wartime Navy despite his previous dismissal from the U.S. Naval Academy, trains *Ellis's* loaded gun on the enemy so that she "might fight herself after we had left her."

1 December

The Secretary of the Navy's annual report notes that the Navy consists of 427 vessels afloat or nearing completion with a total displacement of 240,028 tons and armed with 1,577 guns. Naval personnel aboard ship amount to some 28,000 officers and enlisted men.

Above: *Off Cape Hatteras, North Carolina, 6 July 2002. Photographer's Mate First Class Chadwick Vann shoots video of the inside of* Monitor's *turret after a section of the armor belt was removed to facilitate its lifting during the raising of the ship. Since being designated our nation's first marine sanctuary in 1975,* Monitor *has been under intense investigation. The turret was the first revolving gun of its kind and will eventually be displayed in the Mariners' Museum in Newport News, Virginia. The famed warship sank 240 feet during a heavy storm off Cape Hatteras on 31 December 1862. Four officers and twelve men were lost. (U.S. Navy, Chief Photographer's Mate Eric J. Tilford)*

2 December

Pursued by boats from the gunboat *Sachem*, the Confederate steamer *Queen of the Bay* runs aground on Padre Island, Texas, her crew deploying and taking the Union boats under fire. With their commander, Acting Ensign Alfred H. Reynolds, wounded by enemy fire, the boats return to their ship.

7 December

Among the passengers on board the California steamer *Ariel* when the Confederate raider *Alabama* captures her are 150 Marines and U.S. Navy Commander Louis C. Sartori.

9 December

Rear Admiral Theodorus Bailey assumes command of the East Gulf Blockading Squadron.

12 December

The gunboat *Cairo*, while engaged in an expedition on Mississippi's Yazoo River in search of Confederate mines, hits one of the underwater weapons. Twelve minutes after the explosion she sinks, the first of some forty Union vessels sent to the bottom by Confederate "torpedoes," as mines were then called, during the Civil War.

20 December

Rear Admiral David Dixon Porter joins General William T. Sherman at Helena, Arkansas, and prepares for the joint assault against Vicksburg, Mississippi. The ships under Porter's command form the largest fleet ever placed under one officer up to that time, the number of vessels equaling the entire ship complement of the U.S. Navy at the outbreak of the Civil War.

27 December

Union naval forces continue the clearing of Confederate mines on the Yazoo River, Mississippi, engaging in a heated gun battle with batteries at Drumgould's Bluff. The forces eventually clear mines to within one and one-half miles of the bluff.

31 December

The Union ironclad *Monitor* founders in heavy seas off Cape Hatteras, North Carolina, and sinks while under tow by the side-wheel steamer *Rhode Island*. Designated the nation's first maritime sanctuary in 1975, the wreck of the pioneering warship has been the scene of recent recovery expeditions that have brought the ironclad's engine and turret to the surface for conservation and eventual display.

TORPEDOES

by Dr. Norman Friedman

"Damn the torpedoes. Full speed ahead." The immortal words of Rear Admiral David G. Farragut are at the core of our naval tradition, and though the meaning of the word *torpedo* has changed since Farragut's time, the underwater weapons have been an important part of the U.S. Navy's arsenal for over a century.

The most efficient way to sink a ship is to blow a hole in its bottom, and since the Revolution, when several men produced mines intended to sink British warships, Americans have sought to perfect underwater weapons. Although none succeeded during the war for independence, the idea of mining as the natural defense of a weaker naval power became widely accepted. The Russians employed mines in the Crimean War, and during the Civil War, the Confederates used mines, which were then called torpedoes, in several cases sinking major Union warships. The most famous was the monitor *Tecumseh*, which sank with heavy loss of life during the Battle of Mobile Bay in August 1864. Shortly after the Civil War, a British engineer working in Austria, Robert Whitehead, built a successful self-propelled mine, which he called an automobile torpedo. It was the basis of modern torpedoes, which are defined as self-propelled underwater weapons. A few years later the U.S. Navy established a naval torpedo station at Newport, Rhode Island. It and its successors were responsible for the development of U.S. torpedoes until World War II.

Whitehead's torpedo and its immediate successors were fired directly at their targets; these weapons were, in effect, slow-running shells. By 1910 there were two major improvements to Whitehead's 1866 prototype. Improved propulsion enabled higher speed (up to about 45 knots) and greater range (to about 10,000 yards). In addition, the ability to set the torpedo to make a turn after it was fired increased tactical flexibility greatly. Torpedoes were fired by both surface ships and submarines, but only at surface targets. During World War I the Royal Navy added torpedo attack aircraft to its arsenal, as did the U.S. Navy during the postwar era. The major U.S. development between the wars was the magnetic exploder, intended to ignite the torpedo warhead as it passed under a ship. It turned out that exploding some feet under a target's keel was far more effective than actually hitting a ship. The torpedo creates a rising, pulsing gas

Right: *The Union ironclad* Cairo *strikes a torpedo in the Yazoo River in Mississippi, the first of more that forty U.S. Navy vessels destroyed or damaged by the weapons during the Civil War. At the time the term torpedo referred to underwater mines. (Rear Admiral Henry Walke, Naval Historical Center)*

Right: *A T4M aircraft of Torpedo Squadron 9S drops an aerial torpedo during the late 1920s. In World War II, carrier-based aircraft and patrol planes launched torpedoes against enemy warships, though it was dive-bombing that proved the most effective weapon against the Japanese. (National Museum of*

bubble, which actually lifts the ship and then, as it contracts, often breaks the ship's back. By contrast, damage from a contact hit could be contained by compartmentation.

Unfortunately, as the U.S. Navy discovered, magnetic fusing was, at best, tricky, and problems with new magnetically fused torpedoes crippled the U.S. submarine offensive against Japan for the first year and a half of World War II. It is only fair to observe that the Germans and the British separately developed similar fuses that suffered similar problems, discarding the defective exploders earlier than the U.S. Navy did. U.S. submariners blamed the failure of their new torpedo (which also did not maintain its set depth, and which sometimes circled back on the firing submarine) on the bureaucracy of the Bureau of Ordnance and its Newport torpedo factory. Private contractors developed later torpedoes.

Despite this setback, World War II brought a new generation of underwater ordnance, namely homing torpedoes intended to attack both surface ships and submarines. They generally detected noise made by the target, although some other forms of homing were devised. After the war, homing torpedoes of various types replaced the earlier straight-runners. Once the Cold War began, the U.S. Navy concentrated much of its energy on countering a huge Soviet submarine fleet. Homing torpedoes were the main weapons. At about the same time, the shift from emphasis on enemy warships to emphasis on sea-based strike airpower led to a concentration on antiaircraft weaponry in destroyers. Their large-caliber torpedo tubes, which had been intended to deal with enemy surface warships, were largely eliminated. Thus, the weapon became the province almost exclusively of submarines.

At the same time a new class of lightweight antisubmarine torpedoes, initially built as replacements for depth charges, appeared. They could be carried on board surface ships more easily and on board aircraft. During the 1960s, the U.S. Navy added standoff missiles (Asroc and Subroc) carrying either lightweight torpedoes or nuclear depth bombs. Later, the Navy fielded Captor, an antisubmarine mine whose warhead consisted of a lightweight homing torpedo. The mine was triggered by the sound of a passing submarine.

Torpedo developers encountered a serious problem when nuclear submarines appeared. Torpedo homing speed is limited by the flow noise over the nose of the torpedo, since that same nose houses the transducer the torpedo uses to hear either the target or a returning sonar ping from the target. As an interim step, the Navy fielded a nuclear-armed torpedo, Astor (Mk 45), the theory being that even if it could not quite hit a submarine, its explosion would be fatal. By the late 1960s, however, a very fast, heavy homing torpedo, the Mk 48, was entering service. Its companion was the lightweight Mk 46. Both are still in service, albeit in much modified form, almost four decades later. The current version of the Mk 48 is ADCAP, for Advanced Capability. There are also Mk 50 and Mk 54 lightweight homers. All of these torpedoes are designed mainly to hit submarines, although they have considerable capability against surface ships—which is increasingly important in the post-Cold War era.

As for mines, there are now submarine-launched mobile mines, in effect torpedoes that fall to the ocean floor at the end of their run to become static mines of the classic type. Having entered service in the 1950s, they allow a submarine to lay a minefield from a safe standoff distance, adding further lethality to the Navy's stealthy submarines lurking beneath the seas.

1863

1 January

In a surprise attack against Galveston, Texas, the Confederate gunboats *Bayou City* and *Neptune*, part of their protection consisting of bales of cotton, engage a six-ship Union squadron. In a wild and heated action, the steamer *Harriet Lane*, under Commander Jonathan M. Wainwright, rams *Bayou City* and then is rammed by *Neptune*. The collision, coupled with damage incurred from gunfire from *Harriet Lane*, sends *Neptune* to the bottom. *Bayou City* then rams *Harriet Lane* with such force that the two vessels cannot separate from one another. In the ensuing hand-to-hand combat, Commander Wainwright is killed. The Union Navy loses another ship's skipper during the action when Commander William B. Renshaw dies in the premature explosion of the side-wheel steamer *Westfield*, which he had ordered destroyed to prevent her capture after she ran aground in Bolivar Channel prior to the Confederate attack. The subsequent withdrawal of the remaining ships of the squadron coupled with the capture of Army occupation forces in Galveston by Confederate troops spells defeat for the Union at Galveston.

9 January

Boat crews from the bark *Ethan Allen* destroy a salt manufacturing factory near St. Joseph's, Florida, continuing an effort begun in Florida the previous year to deny the Confederacy the ability to produce this staple.

9–11 January

Vessels of the Mississippi Squadron join troops under the command of General William T. Sherman in forcing the surrender of Fort Hindman on the Arkansas River. At one point, gunboats position themselves a scant sixty yards from the fort, unleashing withering fire in support of the attacking Army forces, prompting some of the fort's defenders to reportedly comment, "You can't expect men to stand up against the fire of those gunboats." The loss of Fort Hindman forces the Confederates to abandon other positions on the White and St. Charles rivers, and during the campaign the Union captures some 6,500 prisoners.

11 January

In an attempt to reestablish the blockade at Galveston, Texas, Union ships bombard the city, but do not attempt to force an entrance into the channel leading to it for fear of grounding. U.S. Navy forces in the Gulf of Mexico have more important worries as demonstrated the following evening when the Confederate raider *Alabama* sinks the side-wheel steamer *Hatteras* in a night engagement just thirty miles off Galveston. The action lasts just thirteen minutes, with Confederate Captain Raphael Semmes reporting minimal damage to his ship.

Opposite: *("The Bombardment and Capture of Fort Hindman, Arkansas, 11 January 1863," Currier & Ives, Naval Historical Center)*

Right: *The monitor* Montauk's *armament consisted of an 11-inch and a 15-inch Dahlgren shell gun. (Naval Historical Center)*

Below: *The Confederate raider* Alabama *battles the side-wheel steamer* Hatteras *off Galveston, Texas, on 11 January 1863. (Naval Historical Center)*

13–14 January
In three separate actions, Army and Navy forces operate jointly to destroy buildings at Mound City, Arkansas, in retaliation for Confederate guerilla attacks on river steamers, attacking Confederate positions near Franklin, Louisiana, and advancing up the White River in Arkansas. The rivers of the western theater provide numerous opportunities for joint warfare.

14 January
The screw steamer *Columbia* runs aground on the coast of North Carolina and is captured by the Confederates three days later, her captain and crew made prisoners of war.

16 January
The Confederate raider *Florida*, having remained in Mobile, Alabama, for some four months undergoing

repairs, successfully runs the Union blockade and enters the Gulf of Mexico. During her escape she passes within 300 yards of the Union steamer *R.R. Cuyler*.

16–17 January
Vessels of the Mississippi Squadron clear out Confederate forces located along the White River in Arkansas, before the squadron focuses its attention on forthcoming operations against Vicksburg. "The Department may rest assured that the navy here is never idle," Rear Admiral David Dixon Porter writes the Secretary of the Navy. "My opinion is that Vicksburg is the main point. When that falls all subordinate posts will fall with it."

21 January
Turning the tables on the Union blockade at Sabine Pass, Texas, the Confederate side-wheel steamer *Josiah Bell* and gunboat *Uncle Ben* capture the blockaders *Morning Light* and *Velocity*.

27 January
In an evaluation of the usefulness of ironclads in a planned assault against Charleston, South Carolina, *Montauk* engages Fort McAllister in Georgia. She is struck repeatedly without damage, but the inaccuracy and slow rate of fire of her guns diminishes her offensive effectiveness. Further evaluations occur on 1 February.

31 January
Two Confederate rams attack the Union blockading fleet off Charleston, South Carolina. *Palmetto State*

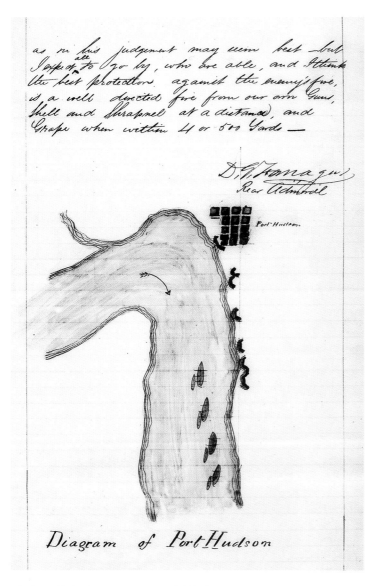

as in his judgment may seem best — but I expect all to go by, who are able, and I think the best protection against the enemy's fire, is a well directed fire from our own Guns, Shell and Shrapnel at a distance, and Grape when within 4 or 500 Yards —

D. G. Farragut
Rear Admiral

Port Hudson

Diagram of Port Hudson

plows into the Union gunboat *Mercedita*, forcing her to strike her colors, while *Chicora* cripples the Union side-wheel steamer *Keystone State*. Two other Union ships are struck by fire from the rams before they withdraw to the defenses of Charleston.

2–3 February
In a daring foray that disrupts Confederate naval operations on the Mississippi River, the ram *Queen of the West* attacks the steamer *City of Vicksburg*. In an exchange of fire, both vessels are briefly set ablaze, *Queen of the West*'s fires are partially the result of the cotton bulwarks serving as protection around her sides. After the inconclusive engagement, the Union ram continues down the Mississippi and captures three steamers, two loaded with provisions for the Confederate army in the region.

3 February
Union forces open the levee at Yazoo Pass in order to gain access to the Yazoo River, on which a joint Army-Navy force will descend to attack Fort Pemberton, capture Yazoo City, and assault Vicksburg from the rear. Three days later Rear Admiral David Dixon Porter orders the first ships of the Mississippi Squadron through the pass.

14 February
The ram *Queen of the West*, which, along with the side-wheel screw steamer *Indianola*, blockades the Red River, heads up the Black River to investigate the

Above: *The second page of Rear Admiral David G. Farragut's "General Order for Passing Port Hudson," issued prior to the March 1863 battle. This page includes Farragut's famous quote, "the best protection against the enemy's fire, is a well directed fire from our own guns." (National Archives)*

Left: *The ram* Queen of the West *engages the Confederate steamer* City of Vicksburg *off Vicksburg, Mississippi, 2 February 1863. (Naval Historical Center)*

reported presence of Confederate vessels at Gordon's Landing, Louisiana. Taken under heavy fire by shore batteries, the ram runs aground attempting to back down the river and has to be abandoned.

24 February

A Confederate squadron consisting of three vessels, including the recently captured *Queen of the West*, engages the side-wheel screw steamer *Indianola* below Warrenton, Mississippi. The Confederates overtake the slower Union ship, and stage a night attack during which *Indianola* is rammed twice. Filling with water, she is run aground on the west bank of the Red River. The Confederates begin a feverish attempt to raise her until a Union gunboat is sighted coming down the Mississippi River. The Confederates decide to destroy *Indianola* on 25 February to prevent her being retaken by the Union, only to discover that what they believe is a gunboat is actually a barge disguised as a gunboat.

28 February

The ironclad *Montauk*, supported by other vessels of the Union Navy, succeeds in destroying the blockade-runner *Rattlesnake*, formerly the side-wheel steamer *Nashville*, on the Ogeechee River in Georgia. During the engagement *Montauk* hits a mine, the explosion forcing her crew to run the ironclad onto the mud bottom to effect repairs.

3 March

Continuing preparations for an assault against Charleston, South Carolina, the Union ironclads *Nahant*, *Passaic*, and *Patapsco* join mortar boats and gunboats in engaging the guns of Fort McAllister at Savannah for six hours.

11 March

Having completed an arduous journey through the Yazoo Pass, vessels of the Mississippi Squadron stage their first attack against Fort Pemberton on the Tallahatchie River. Engaging the cotton and earthwork fort at a range of 800 yards, the steamer *Chillicothe* is damaged by two shots from Confederate cannon. During subsequent attacks alongside the gunboat *Baron de Kalb*, *Chillicothe* suffers extensive damage, with a direct hit knocking out one entire gun crew, killing four men and seriously wounding ten others.

13 March

The steamer *Chillicothe*, the gunboat *Baron de Kalb*, and a mortar schooner engage Fort Pemberton for a second time. *Chillicothe* suffers thirty-eight hits in one

Below: *Confederate batteries at Port Hudson, Louisiana, batter Rear Admiral David G. Farragut's fleet on the river below, 14–15 March 1863. The sidewheel steamer* Mississippi *is burning at the rear of battle. She does not survive the passage. (Naval Historical Center)*

and one-half hours of action and *Baron de Kalb* exchanges fire with the fort for three hours.

14 March

Rear Admiral David G. Farragut leads a squadron of seven ships in an attempted passage of Port Hudson, Louisiana. With Army forces staging a diversionary attack, Farragut's force proceeds up the Mississippi River with smaller ships lashed to heavier ones. They endure withering fire that hits the steam sloop *Richmond*'s steam plant, disabling the ship, and batters the screw sloop *Monongahela* and side-wheel steamer *Mississippi* after both run aground. *Mississippi* later blows up, though fortunately her crew, including future Spanish-American war hero George Dewey, have already abandoned ship. Thus, only two ships—Farragut's flagship, the screw sloop *Hartford,* and the screw steamer *Albatross*—make it past Port Hudson.

Rear Admiral David Dixon Porter launches an expedition consisting of ironclads, mortar boats, and tugs aimed at crossing Steele's Bayou, Mississippi, and entering the Yazoo River to launch an attack against the rear defenses at Vicksburg. The force encounters difficult natural barriers in the form of a dense forest, made worse by obstructions placed by Confederate troops, that eventually prompt Porter to cancel the expedition lest it become surrounded.

Above: *As she sat grounded on a shoal,* Mississippi *succumbed to Confederate guns firing from high bluffs on a hairpin curve in the Mississippi River at Port Hudson, Louisiana, 14 March 1863. (Tom Freeman)*

Below: *(*"Rear Admiral Samuel Francis DuPont, USN," *Alonzo Chappel, Naval Historical Center)*

Right: *Though images are compressed in order to allow for detailed depictions of Fort Sumter and the ships involved, the depiction of* New Ironsides *and her April 1863 attack on Charleston Harbor captures the fury of the engagement. In the two-hour battle, the ship took some fifty hits but suffered no significant damage. (Tom Freeman)*

16 March

The steamer *Chillicothe* stages her final attempt at knocking out the guns of Fort Pemberton, on the Tallahatchie River, suffering eight hits that render her guns inoperable. All told, she loses twenty-two members of her crew and the following day the Yazoo Pass expedition against the fort is abandoned.

25 March

In attempting a run past the batteries at Vicksburg in order to join Rear Admiral David G. Farragut's ships in blockading the Red River, the rams *Switzerland* and *Lancaster* are battered by enemy fire. "Shot after shot struck my boat," writes the skipper of *Switzerland*, which takes a hit in her boiler that stops her engines. She drifts downstream under heavy fire. *Lancaster's* steam drum is holed and a high trajectory shot passes through her deck and pierces the hull, sinking her.

7 April

Rear Admiral Samuel F. Du Pont leads nine ironclads in the long-anticipated attack against Confederate defenses at Charleston, South Carolina. The force encounters obstructions placed by the Confederates in the channels leading to Charleston, which were also marked with ranges to assist gunners in Forts Moultrie and Sumter. The monitor *Weehawken*, the lead ship, strikes a "torpedo" (mine) and takes some fifty-three hits, foreshadowing what is to come for the vessels trailing behind her. All told, Confederate gunners score 346 hits on the assaulting ironclads, nearly one-quarter of them impacting the ironclad steamer *Keokuk*, which sinks the following day. Du Pont calls the assault "a failure instead of a disaster" and concludes that Charleston cannot be taken by a naval attack alone.

16–17 April

Gunboats of the Mississippi Squadron under the command of Rear Admiral David Dixon Porter endure two and one-half hours of enemy fire as they escort Army transports and tow coal barges past Vicksburg. The successful passage reinforces Union positions at New Carthage, Mississippi.

29 April

Gunboats of the Mississippi Squadron attack the Confederate works at Grand Gulf, Mississippi, silencing the lower batteries during an engagement that lasts five and one-half hours. The attack by naval forces opens the way for a landing by forces under General Ulysses S. Grant, who proceeds to the area to the rear of the Confederate stronghold only to find that it has been evacuated. Rear Admiral David Dixon Porter writes Secretary of the Navy Gideon Welles, saying "…it is with great pleasure that I report that the Navy holds the door to Vicksburg."

2–9 May

When Confederate guerillas attack Union ships operating on the White River near Greenville, Mississippi, firing upon *Era* and destroying the steam frigate *Minnesota*, Union gunboats are called to action. The side-wheel steamer *Cricket* engages a Confederate battery on 3 May, and a week later the gunboat *General Bragg* destroys houses affording protection to the enemy guerillas.

5–7 May

Gunboats under the command of Rear Admiral David Dixon Porter push past obstructions in the Mississippi River below the abandoned Fort De Russy, Lousiana,

and capture Alexandria, Louisiana, without any resistance from the enemy. Turning over the town to Army control, Porter's force returns to Fort De Russy, destroying it to prevent further use by the Confederates.

6 May

As a sign of wavering support for the Confederacy abroad, Commander James H. North of the Confederate Navy writes Confederate Secretary of the Navy Stephen Mallory of his fear that vessels being built in England "stand in much danger of being seized by this Government." Efforts to gain support from the French in warship construction prove difficult because of a shortage of currency in the Confederacy.

12 May

Union gunboats operating along the Tennessee River support an Army assault against Confederate forces at Linden, Tennessee. Demonstrating the versatility of riverine forces in support of ground forces, the gunboats ferry Union cavalry across the river, and cover different points so the horsemen can stage a retreat if necessary. The surprise attack against Confederate cavalry at Linden proves successful.

18 May

In a joint operation with Union forces under the command of Generals Ulysses S. Grant and William T. Sherman, naval riverine forces support an assault against the rear defenses at Vicksburg. Gunboats bombard Confederate troops cut off by Union ground forces at Snyder's Bluff, and carry provisions to the bluecoats that capture the position. With Confederate forces evacuating Haynes' Bluff, Rear Admiral David Dixon Porter orders gunboats into position to bombard the hill batteries at Vicksburg, which commences on 19 May, and support further assaults by Grant and Sherman.

21 May

In support of a planned assault against Vicksburg, mortars on board Union gunboats unleash a bombardment against positions in the city that lasts throughout the night. On 22 May the gunboats proceed to engage the hill and water batteries guarding the city, closing to within a quarter mile of the latter. Despite this support of naval forces, which exhaust their ammunition, an assault against Vicksburg fails.

Opposite, top: *The Confederacy's first and only Secretary of the Navy was Stephen R. Mallory. (Naval Historical Center)*

Opposite, bottom: *Rear Admiral David Dixon Porter and General Ulysses S. Grant meet to discuss strategy. The pair's mutual respect for one another translated into successful joint operations that brought victory in the western theater. (Naval Historical Center)*

Right: *Rear Admiral David Dixon Porter's fleet runs past rebel guns on the heights at Vicksburg, Mississippi, 16 April 1863. (U.S. Naval Academy)*

Five gunboats proceed up the Yazoo River, prompting Confederate Navy Commander Isaac N. Brown to destroy three steamer rams under construction and a navy yard at Yazoo City, Mississippi to prevent capture.

24–30 May
In an ascent up the Yazoo River, a force of five gunboats burns four Confederate steamers sunk on a bar in the river and seizes materials from the abandoned enemy navy yard at Yazoo City. Entering the Sunflower River, the squadron travels a distance of 10 miles, destroying enemy foodstuffs and shipping. The expedition destroys nine Confederate steamers in all.

27 May
The Union gunboat *Cincinnati* attacks Confederate rifle pits hindering the Union siege of Vicksburg. Though she is packed with logs and hay for protection, a shot enters *Cincinnati*'s magazine, causing her to fill rapidly with water. Fire from the defenses of Vicksburg score repeated hits on the gunboat, and she sinks with her colors nailed to the mast. Twenty-five members of her crew are killed or wounded, and some fifteen drown.

Despite the support of Union naval forces, an attack by ground troops on Port Hudson, Louisiana, is turned back by the Confederates.

30 May
The Confederate blockade runner *A.D. Vance* sails from Great Britain to Wilmington, North Carolina. During the course of the war, this ship breaks the Union blockade eleven times.

31 May
Receiving word of Union forces cut off by attacking Confederates at Perkins Landing, Louisiana, the gunboat *Carondelet* proceeds to that point and shells enemy forces advancing against the bluecoats. When a transport arrives to take aboard the retreating ground troops, *Carondelet* lays down heavy fire, forcing the Confederates to break off the assault.

7 June
The gunboats *Choctaw* and *Lexington* defend Union troops under assault by a superior Confederate force at Milliken's Bend, Mississippi, firing shell, grape, and canister into enemy lines as the soldiers withdraw.

9–11 June
Union mortar boats continue the bombardment of Vicksburg, lobbing 443 shells into the beleaguered city. Writes Rear Admiral David Dixon Porter to Secretary of the Navy Gideon Welles, "Vicksburg must fall without anything more being done to it. I only wonder [how] it has held out so long."

17 June

The Confederate ironclad ram *Atlanta*, in company with the wooden steamers *Isondiga* and *Resolute*, engage the Union monitors *Weehawken* and *Nahant* in Wassaw Sound, Georgia. With a spar torpedo fitted to her bow, *Atlanta* heads toward *Weehawken*, but runs aground. Her crew manages to refloat her but have difficulty steering her. Struck repeatedly by fire from *Weehawken*, which knocks two gun crews out of action, *Atlanta* strikes her colors.

18 June

The ram *General Sterling Price* and the gunboat *Mound City* return from a three-day reconnaissance down the Mississippi River in which the pair destroys between sixty and seventy barges, skiffs, and boats.

23–30 June

In an example of the continuous support provided by the Union Navy to operations along the waterways of Virginia, four naval gunboats join two from the Army in escorting and covering landings at White House on the Pamunkey River. The landing party destroys a Confederate earthwork intended to house a railroad car mounting a heavy gun.

26 June

Rear Admiral Andrew Hull Foote, the hero of Forts Henry and Donelson, dies in New York City from wounds received in action.

Left: The Union monitor Weehawken *captures the Confederate ram* Atlanta *in Wassaw Sound, Georgia, 17 June 1863. ("US Monitor "Weehawken" and Confederate Ram* Atlanta," *F. Gutekunst, Naval Historical Center)*

Opposite: *Flying the first national flag of the Confederacy, the steamer* Advance *lies at anchor at Nassau, Bahamas. Note the feathering paddle wheel that enhanced her speed, which was so important to a blockade runner. (Naval Historical Center)*

Right: *Rear Admiral John A. Dahlgren pictured with his staff on* Pawnee. *As commander of the South Atlantic Blockading Squadron, the ordnance inventor led efforts to capture Charleston, South Carolina. (Library of Congress)*

26–27 June

Archer, a Confederate commerce raider commanded by Lieutenant Charles Read, enters the harbor at Portland, Maine, under the cover of darkness and captures the U.S. revenue cutter *Caleb Cushing*. Only twenty miles off the harbor at daybreak, the newly acquired Confederate prize is pursued by two large steamers and three tugs. His shells expended after firing at his pursuers, Read orders *Caleb Cushing* burned and his crew into lifeboats. The capture of Read and his crew ends a reign of terror against U.S. commerce that stretches as far north as New England waters and results in the taking of twenty-two prizes.

28–30 June

With General Robert E. Lee's Army of Northern Virginia invading the North, ships are immediately ordered to Washington, D.C., for defense of the capital.

4 July

Confederate forces surrender Vicksburg, prompting President Lincoln to write, "The Father of Waters again goes unvexed to the sea." The Navy plays a decisive role in the victory, which coinciding with the Confederate defeat at the Battle of Gettysburg in Pennsylvania and the fall of Chattanooga marks a turning point in the war. "Without its [the Navy's] assistance," writes General Ulysses S. Grant, "the campaign could not have been successfully made with twice the number of men engaged."

The gunboat *Tyler* repels a Confederate attack against Helena, Arkansas, preventing defeat of the outnumbered Union Army force there. The accurate fire of *Tyler*'s guns halts the enemy advance and force a retreat.

6 July

Rear Admiral John A. Dahlgren relieves Rear Admiral Samuel F. Du Pont in command of the South Atlantic Blockading Squadron.

9–10 July

Following an advance into Ohio and Kentucky on the waters of the Ohio River and the capture of two steamers, Union gunboats begin pursuit of Confederate forces under the command of General John H. Morgan. On 19 July they engage Morgan's command as it attempts to cross the river at Buffington Island, firing at his front while Union ground troops attack his rear. Some 3,000 Confederate soldiers are taken prisoner and the audacious northward thrust ends.

9 July

Long subjected to heavy bombardment by Union naval forces, Port Hudson, Louisiana, surrenders, thus removing the final barrier to Union control of the Mississippi River.

10 July

Wasting no time in taking his new command into action, Rear Admiral John A. Dahlgren leads four ironclads in a bombardment of Morris Island in Charleston Harbor. The effort is in support of a landing by Army troops and includes close-in support by naval boats mounting howitzers. During the

engagement, which continues into the following day, the Union ironclads suffer some damage, with *Catskill* alone taking sixty hits.

The screw sloop *Shenandoah* and bark *Ethan Allen* put to sea from the Boston Navy Yard to pursue the Confederate commerce raider *Florida*, which is active in the waters of the northeast.

13 July
A squadron consisting of five Union gunboats convoys transports carrying some 5,000 troops for a landing at Yazoo City, Mississippi. Though the gunboat *Baron de Kalb* strikes a mine and sinks within fifteen minutes, the troops successfully go ashore and capture the city. The evacuating Confederates destroy nineteen vessels to prevent their capture.

Above: *The ironclad gunboat* St. Louis, *renamed* Baron De Kalb *when transferred from the Army to the Navy in 1862, succumbed to a Confederate mine in 1863. (Oscar Parkes, Naval Historical Center)*

Left: *The sidewheel steamer* Commodore Barney *is damaged by the explosion of a Confederate electrically-fired mine close aboard, above Dutch Gap on the James River in Virginia, 5 August 1863. (Naval Historical Center)*

14 July

Naval forces capture Fort Powhatan on the James River in Virginia, marking a further encroachment on the Confederate capital of Richmond.

16 July

Despite being struck some forty times by enemy fire and forced to retreat down the Stono River in South Carolina, the screw sloop *Pawnee* joins the gunboat *Marblehead* in successfully engaging Confederate forces attacking Union batteries at Grimball's Landing, forcing their retreat.

18 July

Union ironclads and gunboats renew their assault against Fort Wagner in Charleston Harbor, the ironclads closing to within three hundred yards of the enemy position during the engagement. The naval forces silence the fort, but a ground assault is repelled despite the supporting naval fire. A similar effort is made on 24 July with more advances ashore by Union ground forces.

22 July

A four-gun naval battery is placed ashore on Morris Island to assist in the bombardment of Fort Sumter in Charleston Harbor.

5 August

The sidewheel steamer *Commodore Barney* is severely damaged during operations in the James River in Virginia when a 1,000-pound electric mine detonates near her, blowing twenty men overboard. As the expedition up the James River continues, on one occasion *Commodore Barney* is disabled by a shot through one of her boilers and on another Confederate gunners hit her more than thirty times.

7 August

The renewed Union naval attacks against Charleston prompt Confederate General Pierre G.T. Beauregard to request that a "submarine boat" under construction in Mobile, Alabama, be transferred north. The vessel is the famed *H.L. Hunley*, which the following year makes naval history off Charleston Harbor.

Above: *("The Disabling and Capture of the Federal Gunboats* Sachem *and* Clifton *in the Attack on Sabine Pass, Texas, 8 September 1863," Naval Historical Center)*

16 August

While operating in the Stono River in South Carolina, the screw sloop *Pawnee* endures the explosions of four mines in close proximity to the ship. Though one detonates under her stern and another explodes just thirty yards away, *Pawnee* escapes undamaged.

17 August

Rear Admiral John A. Dahlgren leads Union ironclads and gunboats in a five-day engagement against Confederate defenses in Charleston Harbor. In addition to directing fire against Fort Sumter, the naval forces cover an advance by Union ground troops against Fort Wagner.

21 August

The Confederate torpedo boat *Torch* makes a night attempt to sink the Union ironclad *New Ironsides* in the channel near Morris Island in Charleston Harbor. *Torch* approaches close to her quarry, but steering problems prevent her spar torpedo from striking the ironclad.

22 August

Having sighted the Confederate blockade runner *Alexander Cooper* in New Topsail Inlet, North Carolina, during a reconnaissance ten days earlier, Lieutenant William B. Cushing orders a boat expedition to destroy the schooner. Under the command of Acting Ensign Joseph C. Cony, two boat crews assault from behind the Confederate works, burning *Alexander Cooper* and destroying salt works there.

Above: *The steam torpedo boat* David *employed a powder charge mounted on a spar at her bow, and resembled a submarine. (Naval Historical Center)*

Below: *Captain Oscar Badger was wounded by gunfire from Fort Moultrie, South Carolina, in September 1863. (Naval Historical Center)*

Opposite: *The rescue of survivors of the monitor* Weehawken, *6 December 1863. (Naval Historical Center)*

23 August

A Confederate boat expedition under the command of Lieutenant John Taylor Wood captures the Union steamers *Reliance* and *Satellite* off Windmill Point on the Rappahannock River in Virginia. Two days later Wood employs his prizes in seizing three more schooners. A shortage of coal prevents further operations, and Wood orders all prizes burned.

29 August

The Confederate submarine *H.L. Hunley* sinks in Charleston Harbor when the steamer to which she is fastened moves away from the dock unexpectedly, swamping the submarine. Five seamen die in the unfortunate accident, but she is raised and refitted.

1–2 September

Union ironclads complete a five-hour bombardment of Fort Sumter, that destroys much of its eastern scarp. In return Confederate gunners at Fort Moultrie score more than seventy hits on the attackers, one of them hitting Rear Admiral John A. Dahlgren's flagship and wounding Captain Oscar C. Badger. He is the third flag captain lost by Dahlgren in a period of just two months.

6 September

Confederate forces evacuate Morris Island at night, the measure in large part due to the accurate and wide-ranging bombardment of Union naval forces. The following day Rear Admiral John A. Dahlgren asks for the surrender of Fort Sumter. When his request is refused, Union ironclads renew their bombardment.

8 September

The gunboat *Clifton* leads the Union assault against Sabine Pass, Texas. Confederate gunners hold their fire until the attackers are at close range, then unleash a cannonade that hits the boiler of the gunboat *Sachem*, disabling her, and forces the grounding of *Clifton*. The two vessels are captured and the attempt to take Sabine Pass ends in failure.

8–9 September

An assault force consisting of some 400 sailors and Marines on board thirty boats attempts a night assault against Fort Sumter. Using a captured signal codebook, the Confederate defenders are ready and drive the attackers back. Some 100 Union naval personnel are captured.

19–23 September

A Confederate small boat expedition enters the Chesapeake Bay, capturing four schooners and once again proving the ability of the Confederate navy to penetrate northern waters.

5 October

The Confederate steam torpedo boat *David* successfully attacks the Union ironclad *New Ironsides*, exploding a spar torpedo against her hull. The ironclad does not sink, but the explosion damages her to such an extent that she is forced to depart for repairs.

15 October

Under the command of one of her designers, the Confederate submarine *H.L. Hunley* sinks while making practice dives under the receiving ship *Indian Chief* in Charleston Harbor. Horace Hunley and his

seven-member crew perish in the accident. Raised and refitted, *H.L. Hunley* is needed more than ever as Union gunboats and ironclads begin a two-week bombardment of Fort Sumter on 26 October, which results in 9,306 shots being unleashed on the fort.

15–16 November
The Union tug *Lehigh* runs aground while patrolling the waters off Cumming's Point on Morris Island, South Carolina, which is under bombardment by Confederate gunners in Fort Moultrie. She is taken under heavy fire and the following morning five members of her crew carry a line to *Nahant*, which pulls her to safety. All five of the men receive the Medal of Honor for their action.

6 December
The Union monitor *Weehawken*, the flagship of Rear Admiral John A. Dahlgren, accidentally sinks in Charleston Harbor with the loss of some twenty-four members of her crew.

7 December
The third annual report of the Secretary of the Navy notes the success of the blockade covering 3,549 miles of coastline and details a naval strength of 34,000 seamen and 588 ships displacing 467,967 tons and mounting 4,443 guns.

10 December
Union vessels destroy the Confederate salt works at St. Andrew's Bay, Florida, destroying the town in the process. A second attack on 19 December finishes the work begun on this date.

31 December–1 January 1864
In action at Pass Cavallo, Texas, naval forces make a reconnaissance of the area and cover the landing of Union troops. The intervention of the Confederate gunboat *John F. Carr* is ended prematurely when a severe gale runs her aground and she is destroyed by fire. Following the attack, naval vessels safely withdraw the Union forces.

1864

18 January
Rear Admiral David G. Farragut arrives off Mobile Bay to inspect Confederate defenses and the ships under his command for the forthcoming assault against the Alabama coastal city.

Secretary of the Navy Gideon Welles directs the screw sloop *Sacramento* to seek out Confederate raiders, writing, "You will bear in mind that the principal object of your pursuit is the *Alabama*." By this time, Captain Raphael Semmes and his crew on board *Alabama* are the captors of over sixty prizes.

Left: *Rear Admiral David G. Farragut and Captain Percival Drayton stand by the wheels of a Dahlgren Howitzer on the sloop* Hartford's *quarterdeck, circa 1864. Note the all-iron carriage for the gun, belaying pins at right, and rigging details. Farragut's famed flagship was not decommissioned for good until 1926. (Naval Historical Center)*

Above: *The Confederate submarine* H.L. Hunley *at Charleston, South Carolina, 6 December 1863. (Conrad Chapman, The Museum of the Confederacy, Richmond)*

Below: *("Lieutenant William B. Cushing, USN (1842–1874)," Robert Hinckley, U.S. Naval Academy)*

2 February

A Confederate boat party led by Commander John Taylor Wood silently makes its way toward the steamer *Underwriter* anchored in the Neuse River near New Bern, North Carolina, approaching to within one hundred yards of the vessel before being sighted. Capturing her in hand-to-hand combat with her crew, Wood and his men burn *Underwriter* while under fire from nearby Union batteries.

10 February

The commerce raider *Florida*, after receiving repairs in France, puts to sea from the port of Brest, using a rainy night to mask her departure from blockading Union ships.

16 February

Union naval forces begin bombarding Fort Powell, Alabama, the beginning of Rear Admiral David G. Farragut's campaign to capture Mobile.

17 February

The Confederate submarine *H.L. Hunley* becomes the first underwater vessel in the history of naval warfare to sink an enemy ship when she rams a torpedo-tipped spar into the side of the sloop-of-war *Housatonic* off Charleston. The Union ship quickly sinks. *H.L. Hunley* also sinks, taking Army Lieutenant George E. Dixon and his entire crew to the bottom with her. In 2000 the long-lost submarine is raised from the depths for conservation and eventual display.

THE CONFEDERATE SUBMARINE
H. L. HUNLEY

by Mark K. Ragan

ithout question the Confederate submarine *H.L. Hunley* was cutting-edge technology for the mid-nineteenth century. Although several vessels capable of venturing beneath the surface had been fabricated in Europe and the United States before the American Civil War, these craft, in most cases, were crude, clumsy affairs that often proved fatal to their operators. One reason that *H.L. Hunley* was so advanced for her time was that construction of the vessel was preceded by two earlier Confederate submarines, *Pioneer* and *American Diver*.

Pioneer was designed and fabricated in early 1862 in New Orleans by partners Horace Hunley, James McClintock, and Baxter Watson. "This boat demonstrated to us the fact that we could construct a boat that would move at will in any direction desired, and at any distance from the surface," McClintock wrote of *Pioneer* in a postwar letter. So impressive was she that her inventors requested a Letter of Marque from the Confederate government, which was granted, thus opening the way for the first underwater privateer. However, with the capture of New Orleans by Union forces in April 1862, Hunley, Watson and McClintock followed the example set by the retreating army, scuttling their underwater invention in a canal, and fleeing to Mobile, Alabama, with hopes of building a second, more formidable underwater vessel.

After several months of trial and error, *American Diver* was launched in Mobile Bay. Unfortunately for the Confederates, she was accidentally sunk at an unknown location off Fort Morgan in February 1863, where she rests to this day. Within weeks after the loss of their second submarine, a unit of Confederate engineers that included Hunley, McClintock, and Watson was formed at Mobile. From lessons learned through the construction of both *Pioneer* and *American Diver*, the three inventors designed a third vessel, and obtained funding to construct it. Named for the vessel's leading financier, Horace Hunley, it was launched and tested in mid-July 1863. "Whilst lying at Mobile in company with my officers and

others of the C. S. Navy, I witnessed the experiments of the Submarine Boat which appeared to be a perfect success," remembered one Confederate naval officer who observed the submarine's harbor trials. Just days after this demonstration, *H.L Hunley* was loaded aboard two flat cars and sent by rail to the blockaded harbor city of Charleston, South Carolina.

Arriving in early August, she was soon seized from her owners by military authorities and turned over to the Confederate navy. With sailors unfamiliar with her controls, the vessel was accidentally sunk through carelessness near Fort Johnson in late August, killing five of her nine-man crew. Some weeks later the submarine was raised, cleaned, and once again moored at a Charleston pier. It was during this time that Horace Hunley himself requested command of the vessel that bore his name. With a volunteer crew, including Confederate Army Lieutenant George E. Dixon, who had participated in the submarine's trials in Mobile, Hunley hoped for better luck. However, just days after Hunley took command of the vessel, she was lost a second time with all hands. Only the life of Dixon, who was absent that day, was spared.

By early November the submarine was again raised, and Dixon, with another volunteer crew, awaited orders. After repairing *H.L. Hunley* and drilling his new crew night and day for weeks, the new skipper received the much-anticipated order directing him to "proceed to-night to the mouth of the harbor, or as far as capacity of the vessel will allow, and…sink and destroy any vessel of the enemy with which [you] can come in conflict." Dixon's first officer, William Alexander, who was soon transferred to Mobile, later described the submarine's initial forays into Charleston Harbor. "We were ordered to moor the boat off Battery Marshall, on Sullivan's Island. The nearest vessel which we understood to be the United States Frigate Wabash, was about twelve miles off, and she was our objective point from this time on. On several occasions we came to the surface for air, opened the cover and heard the men in the Federal picket boats talking and singing. During this time we went out on an average of four nights a week."

H.L. Hunley's operations brought a reward during the evening of 17 February 1864. Mounting a spar torpedo, the submarine approached the Federal sloop-of-war *Housatonic*. Lookouts on board the warship initially thought the spar was a floating log or some other debris, and, by the time they realized their mistake, *H.L. Hunley* was so close that *Housatonic*'s guns could not be depressed enough to hit her. Planting the spar torpedo against the ship's side, the submarine's crew triggered it with a line. The resulting explosion sent the Union warship to the bottom with the loss of five crewmen. Tempering this landmark event, the first time in the history of naval warfare that a ship had been sunk by a submarine, was the loss of *H.L. Hunley*, which sank with all hands. She remained lost until her final resting place was discovered in 1995 by a team led by adventure novelist Clive Cussler. Five years later she was brought to the surface and returned to Charleston, 136 years after departing on her last voyage.

Opposite: *The recovery of* H.L Hunley *and subsequent excavation of her interior has yielded a wealth of artifacts, including the pocket watch that belonged to the skipper on her last cruise, Confederate Army Lieutenant George Dixon. Archaeologists hope it will reveal the exact time that the submarine sank. (U.S. Navy)*

Above: H.L Hunley's *target on the night of 17 February 1864, the sloop-of-war* Housatonic *fell victim to the submarine's spar torpedo and went to the bottom off Charleston, South Carolina. (R.G. Skerrett, Naval Historical Center)*

29 February

Two boats carrying crewmen from the gunboat *Monticello* under the command of Lieutenant William B. Cushing land at Smithville, North Carolina, under the cover of darkness in an attempt to capture Confederate General Louis Hebert. Finding that the flag officer is away, Cushing and his men capture a captain instead.

29 February–5 March

A reconnaissance expedition consisting of the paddle-wheel monitor *Osage* and five gunboats travel up the Black and Ouachita rivers, battling Confederate sharpshooters on shore and suffering damage to the gunboat *Fort Hindman* below Harrisonburg, Louisiana. In addition, landing parties from the expedition's vessels go ashore at various points along the rivers, engaging Confederate troops and capturing field pieces and cotton.

5 March

Commander John Taylor Wood leads a force of fifteen men across the Chesapeake Bay and seizes the Union telegraph station at Cherrystone Point, Virginia. The two Union steamers *Aeolus* and *Titan* put into shore not knowing that the station is in Confederate hands. Wood's small force disables *Aeolus* and boards *Titan* to steam up the Piankatank River. Pursued by Union gunboats, Wood eventually destroys *Titan* and successfully evades capture.

6 March

A Confederate *David*-type torpedo boat attacks the screw steamer *Memphis* in the North Edisto River near Charleston, South Carolina. Sighted by the Union ship's crew while fifty yards away, the torpedo boat rams her explosive-laden spar into *Memphis* without effect and her second attempt manages to strike only a glancing blow. The torpedo boat then retreats under enemy fire.

8 March

The gunboat *Conestoga* is inadvertently rammed by the ram *General Sterling Price* below Grand Gulf, Mississippi, and sinks in four minutes with the loss of two crewmen.

12 March

Union gunboats under Rear Admiral David Dixon Porter head up the Red River in Louisiana as part of an effort to advance into Texas. By 14 March the naval forces have supported the capture of Fort De Russy, a key Confederate position thwarting the Union advance.

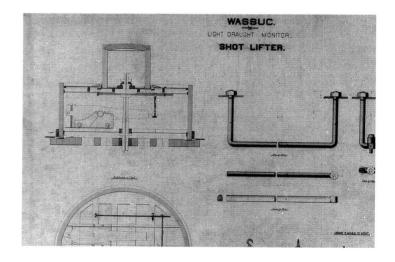

16 March

Union naval forces capture Alexandria, Louisiana, sending a landing party into the city to maintain control until the arrival of Army forces.

9 April

The Confederate torpedo boat *Squib* successfully explodes a spar torpedo against the Union steam frigate *Minnesota* off Newport News, Virginia. Attacking in the early morning hours, the crew of the torpedo boat is sucked under the port quarter of her quarry by the blast. Her second in command climbs back on deck and pushes her clear from *Minnesota*. *Squib* escapes under heavy enemy fire.

12 April

In action on the Red River, Union gunboats and transports steaming toward Shreveport, Louisiana, come under Confederate gunfire from high bluffs overlooking the river. At Blair's Landing shots fired from the gunboat *Lexington* knock out rebel batteries, but Confederate cavalry troopers throw heavy rifle fire at the naval forces for over an hour until silenced by the superior firepower of the gunboats.

The small gunboat *New Era* supports Union forces defending Fort Pillow, Tennessee, against an attack by Confederate cavalry under the command of General Nathan Bedford Forrest. The action is to no avail for Forrest's force eventually takes the fort, turning captured artillery on the gunboat and forcing her to withdraw. They later commit one of the war's worst atrocities by murdering African-American soldiers taken as prisoners of war.

15 April

The Union gunboat *Eastport* strikes a Confederate torpedo in the Red River, in Louisiana, forcing her commanding officer to run her aground. Assisted by the crews of other gunboats in pumping out water, she gets underway on 21 April, only to ground eight times as she travels further down the river. She is scuttled by a gunpowder explosion on 26 April.

19 April

The Confederate ram *Albemarle* attacks Union warships off Plymouth, North Carolina, in the wake of an attack by ground forces. The wooden gunboats *Miami* and *Southfield*, lashed together for mutual support, attack the ram, which strikes *Southfield* and sends her to the bottom. *Albemarle* controls the approaches to Plymouth, which falls to Confederate forces on 20 April.

Above: *Having left the gunboat* Southfield *sinking, the Confederate ram* Albemarle *turns her attention to the gunboat* Miami *during action off Plymouth, North Carolina, on 19 April 1864. This drawing appeared in* Harper's Weekly. *(Naval Historical Center)*

21 April

The gunboat *Petrel*, operating with naval forces in supporting an attack by Union troops against Yazoo City, is disabled by Confederate rifle and artillery fire. Attempts to destroy her to prevent capture fail and she falls into enemy hands.

26–27 April

Union gunboats under the command of Rear Admiral David Dixon Porter continue to face opposition from Confederate troops and artillery along the banks of the Red River. On 26 April, Confederate ground forces stage an unsuccessful attempt to forcefully board Porter's flagship *Cricket*, and later in the day intense

fire hits her repeatedly and disables two other gunboats, one of which is captured. The following day, another gunboat is grounded because of excessive damage. The Union forces push forward past the Confederate batteries, but Porter later describes the action as the "heaviest fire I ever witnessed."

30 April

Indicating the deteriorating state of Confederate naval forces in the east, the South's Secretary of the Navy Stephen Mallory reports a strength of only thirteen ships and a floating battery mounting a total of thirty-three guns.

5 May

The Confederate ram *Albemarle*, in company with the steamers *Bombshell* and *Cotton Plant*, engage Union forces in a pitched battle off the mouth of the Roanoke River in North Carolina. *Bombshell* is captured early in the battle and *Cotton Plant* withdraws up the Roanoke River. The side-wheel steamer *Sassacus* unsuccessfully attempts to ram *Albemarle*, and is knocked out of action after taking a direct hit in her starboard boiler. The Union side-wheel gunboat *Mattabesett* and the side-wheel steamer *Wyalusing* continue to battle the Southern ram for three hours during which shot and shell are likened to hail filling the air. Only darkness forces the end of the battle.

While much of Rear Admiral David Dixon Porter's gunboat force stalls because of low water levels above the rapids at Alexandria, Louisiana, Union vessels below the city suffer heavy losses at the hands of

Above: *The ironclads* Osage *and* Neosho *run through a break in the Red River Dam to reach safety over the rapids, 9 May 1864. ("Red River Dam, Alexandria, Louisiana," George M. Bache, Naval Historical Center)*

Left: *The side-wheel steamer* Sassacus *battles the Confederate ram* Albemarle, *May 1864. (Naval Historical Center)*

Opposite: *A Navy poster presents an alternative to conscription into the Army. (Naval Historical Center)*

Confederate forces. On this date two wooden steamers and a transport are destroyed or captured after engagements with infantry and artillery.

6 May
The side-wheel steamer *Commodore Jones*, while engaged in dragging for mines in Virginia's James River, strikes a 2,000-pound electric mine that destroys her and takes the lives of forty of her crew. A landing party of sailors and Marines captures the Confederates who triggered the mine, one of whom is placed on the bow of a lead ship engaged in sweeping the James River as an incentive to tell the location of more of the deadly underwater ordnance.

Confederate forces capture the side-wheel steamers *Granite City* and *Wave* in the Calcasieu River in Louisiana.

6–7 May
In an effort to assist a blockade runner, the Confederate ram *Raleigh* engages Union vessels off New Inlet, North Carolina. She runs aground on 7 May, suffering severe damage that prompts her commanding officer to order her destroyed in order to prevent capture.

10 May
In the first test of a difficult plan to dam the Red River and release the water so that Union vessels can ride the crest and pass the rapids above Alexandria, Louisiana, two ironclads and two wooden steamers successfully make it through, prompting construction of a new dam. The following day three ironclads are hauled across the upper falls by soldiers of the Union Army, and on 13 May the last ships of Rear Admiral David Dixon Porter's squadron successfully pass the rapids.

12 May
Rear Admiral Samuel P. Lee establishes a "torpedo and picket division" consisting of three side-wheel steamers to drag the James River for mines and to reconnoiter the shore.

23 May
Confederate forces capture the tug *Columbine* after a heated engagement with the crew of the Union vessel after she had run aground at Horse Landing near Palatka, Florida. Shortly after taking their prize, the Confederates burn her in order to prevent her from being recaptured by an approaching Union ship.

25 May
Five sailors from the side-wheel gunboat *Mattabesett* stage an unsuccessful attempt to destroy the powerful

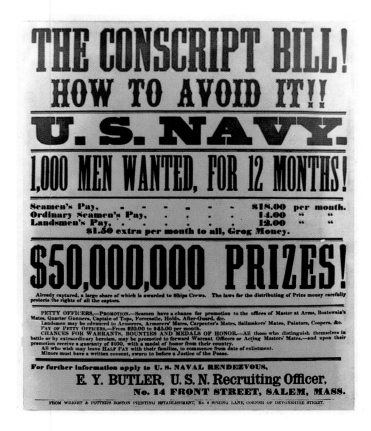

Confederate ram *Albemarle*, swimming across the Roanoke River towing two torpedoes and attempting to position them on either side of her hull. Though a sharp-eyed sentry foils the plan, which results in the capture of one Union sailor, all five bluejackets ultimately receive the Medal of Honor for their daring effort.

26 May
Rear Admiral David Dixon Porter reports the end of the trying Red River campaign in Louisiana from his headquarters at Cairo, Illinois.

3 June
A 130-man Confederate boat expedition approaches the side-wheel steamer *Water Witch* in Ossabaw Sound, Georgia, during the early morning hours, and despite being sighted fifty yards from the vessel succeeds in boarding her. In the ensuing hand-to-hand combat, the Confederates overwhelm the Union crew despite losing their commanding officer.

11 June
The Confederate commerce raider *Alabama*, badly in need of repairs after a prolonged period at sea, puts in to Cherbourg, France. The American Vice-Consul in the city relays the news to the commanding officer of the Union screw sloop *Kearsarge*, which arrives off Cherbourg on 14 June and awaits *Alabama*'s departure.

19 June

With spectators gathered on the heights above the town of Cherbourg to witness the spectacle, the Confederate commerce raider *Alabama* puts to sea to engage the screw sloop *Kearsarge*. Though virtually evenly matched in the number of guns on board, the Union ship boasts a heavier broadside and fresher ammunition and sports heavy chains hanging over the side for extra protection. Closing to a range of one and one-half miles, Captain Raphael Semmes opens the battle with an order to fire *Alabama*'s guns. For more than an hour the two antagonists duel, with the Confederate raider suffering severe damage and heavy casualties. Protected by the chain and benefiting from the fact that some of *Alabama*'s shots fail to explode on contact, *Kearsarge* suffers only minimal damage. His ship sinking, Semmes strikes his colors. Only 41 of *Alabama*'s 149-man crew survive the battle.

23–24 June

Lieutenant William B. Cushing leads a reconnaissance party that provides valuable intelligence concerning the defense of Wilmington, North Carolina, and Confederate shipping located there.

24 June

Supported by artillery, Confederate cavalry attacks and captures the side-wheel steamer *Queen City* lying at anchor off Clarendon, Arkansas.

Above: *A Marine and sailors man a Dahlgren 11-inch pivot gun in a Union warship. (National Archives)*

Below: *Section of the screw sloop* Kearsarge's *sternpost, with a defective shell imbedded in it that had been fired by the Confederate raider* Alabama *during their battle on 19 June 1864. (Naval Historical Center)*

Opposite: *Disposition of ships and overview of the Battle of Mobile Bay on 5 August 1864. (Naval Historical Center)*

5 July

Union monitors, operating in support of Army operations along the Stono River in South Carolina, employ their guns in driving Confederates from rifle pits and preventing the construction of earthworks along the shore.

10 July

The South's foremost commerce raider in the wake of the loss of *Alabama*, *Florida* captures and burns the bark *General Berry* a scant thirty-five miles off the Maryland shore. This marks the continuation of a daring campaign against Union coastal shipping. This day also brings orders to the Union screw steamer *Mount Vernon* and the gunboat *Monticello* to put to sea for the specific purpose of capturing *Florida*.

25 July

Acting Master's Mate John Woodman leads three men in the first of three daring reconnaissance patrols up the Roanoke River to Plymouth, North Carolina. A later expedition provides intelligence that contributes to the destruction of the feared Confederate ram *Albemarle*.

Boats from Union ships assembled off Mobile Bay conduct a reconnaissance of the underwater defenses guarding the entrance to the bay, cutting loose many of the torpedoes. More of these expeditions occur over the course of the next few days, the last taking place on the night of 3 August.

1–4 August

A landing party from the sloop-of-war *Saratoga* raids a meeting of civilians forming a coastal guard at McIntosh Court House, Georgia, taking all those present prisoner.

5 August

In one of the epic battles in naval history, Rear Admiral David G. Farragut leads his squadron of eighteen ships into the teeth of Confederate defenses guarding Mobile Bay. Farragut positions a column of armored monitors to the starboard of the squadron's wooden ships to take most of the fire from the powerful guns of Fort Morgan. However, the first blow against the Union force is struck by a mine that explodes against the hull of the monitor *Tecumseh*, sending her to the bottom in a matter of seconds. Seeing his ships veering away from their course in the wake of the explosion, Farragut, who is lashed to the rigging of his flagship so that he can better observe the action, utters his immortal words, "Damn the torpedoes, full speed ahead." Passing through the underwater defenses, the Union ships confront a Confederate squadron composed of the

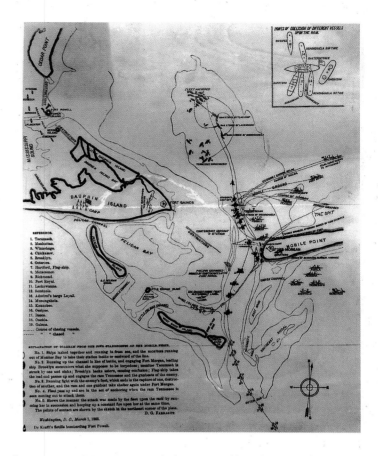

heavy ram *Tennessee* and three smaller ships under the command of Admiral Franklin Buchanan. The latter are quickly defeated or run aground, allowing Farragut to concentrate on *Tennessee*, pouring shot into her. The ensuing battle rages for more than an hour and ends with the surrender of the badly damaged ram. The victory results in the closing of the last major port in the South.

9 August

In an ironic twist, the former Confederate ram *Tennessee*, which was captured by Rear Admiral David G. Farragut's squadron, bombards Fort Morgan at the entrance to Mobile Bay. The fort surrenders on 23 August.

10–12 August

Operating off the coast of New York, the Confederate commerce raider *Tallahassee* takes sixteen prizes, prompting an uproar among civilians and the dispatching of Union ships to capture her. *Tallahassee* takes fifteen more prizes and escapes blockaders' gunfire to put into Wilmington, North Carolina, on 25 August.

9 September

In response to the withdrawal of Union troops from the city, the screw gunboat *Kanawha* reinstitutes the blockade of Brownsville, Texas, which had been lifted by President Abraham Lincoln the previous February.

KEARSARGE vs. ALABAMA
THE CLASSIC SHIP-TO-SHIP DUEL

by Dr. Craig L. Symonds

O f all the Confederacy's commerce raiders, the one that cost the Union the most ships, the most money, and provoked the most aggravation was *Alabama,* commanded by Captain (later Rear Admiral) Raphael Semmes. Built in the Birkenhead shipyards in Liverpool, England (ostensibly for the Turkish navy), and identified simply as Hull No. 290, she went to sea on what was advertised as her trial run on 29 July 1862, and never returned. Instead, she made her way to the Portuguese Azores where she took on a battery of guns, an international crew, and a handful of Confederate naval officers led by Semmes. Rechristened *Alabama*, the ship then began a two-year odyssey during which she ravaged Union shipping and raised both alarm and maritime insurance rates all along the Atlantic coast of the United States.

It was not Semmes' purpose to take prizes; he was no privateer looking for booty. His goal was to do so much damage to American merchant commercial shipping that it would encourage antiwar sentiment in the North. Besides, taking prizes would compel him to put prize crews on board his captures, thus weakening

his own crew and depleting his small officer complement. What he did instead, therefore, was burn his prizes at sea. Only when the cargo from one of them could replenish his own larder or ordnance locker did he bother with booty. Altogether, Semmes made sixty-eight captures on his two-year cruise. He used four of those vessels as "cartels" to rid himself of the prisoners he had accumulated (less the handful who volunteered to stay on board *Alabama* as crewmen), and burned the rest.

The U.S. Navy repeatedly sent warships to track him down (at one point as many as two dozen warships were searching for him), but Semmes was a naval will-o'-the-wisp. Never staying long in one area, he took *Alabama* across the Atlantic, ranged along the American east coast down to the Gulf of Mexico, then continued south along the Brazilian coast. In the summer of 1863, as Generals Robert E. Lee and George Meade fought at Gettysburg, and General Ulysses S. Grant assailed Vicksburg, Semmes recrossed the Atlantic to Capetown, South Africa, and entered the Indian Ocean. Sailing eastward below the 30th parallel, he seemed to have disappeared from the face of the earth until he

Right: *With their battered quarry in the distance, members of a gun crew on board the screw sloop* Kearsarge *wave their hats in triumph after scoring a hit with one of the ship's 11-inch guns. Recalled the Confederate raider* Alabama's *executive officer, "The enemy's 11-inch shells [did] severe execution upon our quarterdeck." ("Kearsarge vs. Alabama," J.O. Davidson, Naval Historical Center)*

Right: *The Confederate raider* Alabama *begins to settle by the stern, the final moments of her legendary career, following a battle with the Union screw sloop* Kearsarge *off Cherbourg, France, on 19 June 1864. ("USS Kearsarge vs. CSS Alabama," Xanthus Smith, Naval Historical Center)*

reemerged in the Sunda Strait between Java and Sumatra and carried the Confederate flag into the South China Sea. Then he cruised back through the Straits of Malacca to India, Madagascar, and into the Atlantic once again. In the spring of 1864, with Union forces on the march in Virginia and Georgia, Semmes made his way northward to Cherbourg, France, where he put in for a much needed refit. If *Alabama* was to leave, she would have to fight her way out, for arriving off France a short time later was the Union screw sloop *Kearsarge,* commanded by Captain John A. Winslow.

To this point, Semmes had fought only one other warship during his amazing odyssey. In January 1863, he had deliberately lured a U.S. blockading vessel, *Hatteras,* away from her station off Galveston, Texas, and then turned on her and sank her. But with that exception, he had devoted himself to commerce raiding, knowing that it was sure to have a greater impact on Union sentiment than individual victories over warships. Now in Cherbourg he had to decide whether to fight his way out, or allow his vessel to be interned by the French. Back in 1862 when he had commanded the much smaller raider *Sumter,* he had abandoned that vessel in Gibraltar when he found himself trapped there by superior Union vessels. But Winslow's *Kearsarge* was not demonstrably more powerful than his *Alabama,* and a victory off the coast of France might have a beneficial impact on the French attitude toward the Confederacy. Whatever his motives, Semmes decided to sortie to meet *Kearsarge.*

Winslow and Semmes both made careful preparations for the fight, but Winslow possessed two advantages that would prove decisive. First, he draped heavy chains over the side of his wooden ship, then

planked over the chains so they were not visible. This gave his ship and his gun crews greater protection from *Alabama*'s heavy shot. (Later, Semmes would argue that this was a dirty Yankee trick since Winslow had effectively turned his vessel into an "ironclad" and had disguised that fact.) Another advantage Winslow had was that while his powder and shells were relatively fresh, *Alabama*'s ammunition was at least two years old and its reliability was uncertain.

The duel took place on 19 June 1864 in international waters off the coast of France, but close enough so that the vessels were visible from shore. The two warships circled one another, firing as fast as the crews could load. Even more important than *Kearsarge*'s chain mail armor was the fact that some of *Alabama*'s shells failed to explode. One shell lodged in the sternpost of *Kearsarge* and almost certainly would have been fatal had it detonated. Instead it was *Alabama* that took several hits and began taking on water. Semmes fought her until she sank, and—defiant to the last—he threw his sword into the sea and swam to the safety of a nearby British yacht that had come out to watch the excitement.

Winslow returned to the U.S. a hero and was promoted to commodore; Semmes made his way back to the Confederacy and was promoted to rear admiral. During the Confederate evacuation of Richmond, Semmes led a brigade of infantry, and after the war took to identifying himself as "Raphael Semmes, Admiral and General." The famed raider influenced world events even after her sinking. Once the war was over, the U.S. filed claims against Great Britain for allowing the construction of *Alabama* in her yards, and an international court awarded the U.S. government $15 million in damages.

19 September

Confederates under Acting Master John Yates Beall capture and burn two steamers on Lake Erie. The action is part of a larger abortive plan to capture the iron side-wheel steamer *Michigan*, which is guarding prisoners at Sandusky, Ohio.

28 September

Rear Admiral David Dixon Porter is detached from command of the Mississippi Squadron in order to assume command of the North Atlantic Blockading Squadron. Rear Admiral Samuel P. Lee replaces him.

7 October

The screw sloop *Wachusett*, after scouring the sea lanes for months in search of the Confederate commerce raider *Florida*, anchors near the enemy ship after she puts in to Bahia Harbor, Brazil. Fearing she might escape, *Wachusett*'s skipper Commander Napoleon Collins hatches a plan in which in the early morning hours of this day he rams the famous raider. A brief exchange of gunfire occurs before the Confederate ship surrenders. The action occurs despite a wartime agreement between the U.S. and Brazil that no attacks would be made in the nation's territorial waters. Thus, *Wachusett* is fired upon as she tows *Florida* out to sea. Collins is court-martialed for his role in the incident, but is restored to his command by Secretary of the Navy Gideon Welles.

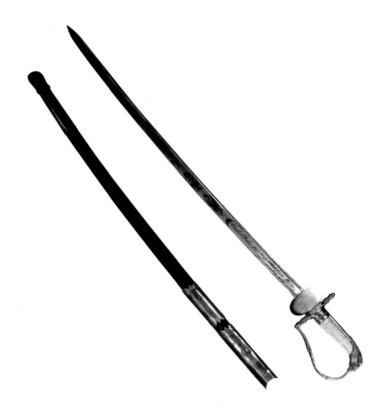

Above: *Sword of David Glasgow Farragut, the first naval officer appointed to the rank of admiral. (Alex Weyers)*

Below: *The side-wheel gunboat* Agawam *in the James River, Virginia, July 1864. (Naval Historical Center)*

Opposite: Wachusett *ends* Florida's *days of commerce raiding, Brazil, 7 October 1864. (Naval Historical Center)*

12 October

Rear Admiral David Dixon Porter assumes command of the North Atlantic Blockading Squadron, while Rear Admiral Cornelius K. Stribling takes command of the East Gulf Blockading Squadron.

19 October

The steamers *Laurel* and *Sea King* rendezvous near the island of Las Desertas in the Madeiras. Both ships carry Confederate officers and, after *Laurel* transfers her cargo of guns, ammunition, and supplies, *Sea King* is renamed *Shenandoah* and commissioned as a commerce raider in the Confederate Navy.

25 October

Rear Admiral George F. Pearson relieves Rear Admiral Charles H. Bell in command of the Pacific Squadron.

27 October

Lieutenant William B. Cushing leads a boat expedition consisting of fourteen men in a steam picket launch to attack the Confederate ram *Albemarle* at Plymouth on the Roanoke River in North Carolina. With its passage masked by darkness and an intense rain, the expedition passes Confederate defense undetected until spotted by a sentry on board *Albemarle*. Taken under fire, Cushing turns his boat for a full-speed run at the ram, which

is protected by a mass of floating logs. Lurching over the log barrier, Cushing pushes a boom mounting a torpedo into *Albemarle*'s side, the resulting explosion producing a gaping hole and causing the ram to sink. The blast also sinks the steam picket launch, forcing the Union sailors to swim away and attempt to avoid capture. Cushing makes it to shore, seizes a skiff, and rows eight miles until rescued by the screw steamer *Valley City*.

29 October–1 November

With the threat of *Albemarle* removed, Union naval forces move against Plymouth, North Carolina. Failing in their attempt to approach via the Roanoke River, the gunboats attack down the Middle River and engage the defending Confederate batteries at close range, putting a landing party ashore after a Union shell ignites a powder magazine on land. The result is the capture of thirty-seven defenders, twenty-two cannon, and a large quantity of stores.

30 October

The Confederate commerce raider *Shenandoah* captures her first prize, the bark *Alina*, south of the Azores.

Union riverine forces in the Western theater still face threats from Confederate shore batteries as rebel gunners along the Tennessee River near Johnsonville,

ADMIRAL DAVID G. FARRAGUT AND THE BATTLE OF MOBILE BAY

by Dr. Robert J. Schneller, Jr.

Admiral David Glasgow Farragut (1801–1870) was the greatest naval officer of the Civil War, Union or Confederate, and among the greatest American naval officers of the nineteenth century. Farragut entered the Navy in 1810 and spent much of the next half century at sea. This vast experience served him well when he became a flag officer in January 1862, appointed to command the West Gulf Blockading Squadron. With the appointment came orders to capture New Orleans, push up the Mississippi River, blockade the Gulf coast, and reduce the forts defending Mobile Bay, all vital to the North's successful prosecution of the war. By 1864, he had captured New Orleans and Union naval forces had seized control of the Mississippi. That left Mobile the Confederacy's sole remaining Gulf port for blockade running.

The approaches to the city were heavily defended. Two forts lay astride the entrance to Mobile Bay, Fort Morgan to the east and Fort Gaines to the west. A line of submerged pilings driven into the seabed extended two miles out from Fort Gaines, and a field of torpedoes, as mines were then called, lengthened the barrier to within a quarter mile of Fort Morgan. Inside Mobile Bay, the Rebels deployed a naval squadron including three small gunboats and *Tennessee*, the Confederacy's most formidable ironclad.

Farragut envisioned a joint operation in which the fleet would run past the forts and cut their communications by sea. The Navy would then support Army siege and assault operations and prevent the Confederate vessels from harassing the troops. The main Union attack force included 1,500 soldiers, four ironclad monitors, seven large warships, and seven small gunboats.

Farragut intended to employ similar tactics to those he had used at Port Hudson on the Mississippi in March 1863. Each large ship would have a small gunboat lashed to her disengaged side, so that if

Left: *Ships and monitors under the command of Rear Admiral David G. Farragut steam past the Confederate gun batteries at Fort Morgan as Confederate forces hasten to meet them in the Battle of Mobile Bay, 5 August 1864. A mine has just detonated under the lead Union monitor* Tecumseh *at the center of the painting. ("Battle of Mobile Bay," J.O. Davidson, Library of Congress)*

Right: *The screw sloop* Hartford, *flagship of Rear Admiral David G. Farragut, engages in close combat with the ironclad ram* Tennessee, *flagship of Confederate Admiral Franklin Buchanan, during the Battle of Mobile Bay on 5 August 1864. Farragut is seen standing in the mizzen shrouds. (William H. Overend, Wadsworth Atheneum)*

enemy fire disabled one, the other could pull her through. The monitors would steam into the bay in a column east of the main column of paired ships. Once past the forts, the monitors would attack *Tennessee* while the gunboats went after their Rebel counterparts.

Well before dawn on 5 August 1864, the ships got up steam and formed columns. Lashed in the rigging of the flagship *Hartford*'s mainmast high above the deck, Farragut had a bird's-eye view as his fleet fought past the booming guns of Fort Morgan. Suddenly, the monitor *Tecumseh* rolled to starboard, her bow knifing into the water and stern rearing up with the propeller still spinning, then plunged out of sight like an arrow shot from a bow. Farragut knew instantly that she had struck a torpedo. As the gunfire from Fort Morgan intensified, the screw sloop *Brooklyn*, the lead ship in the main column just ahead of *Hartford*, started backing down, her skipper reporting a line of torpedoes across the channel.

Farragut realized that the decisive moment had arrived. The column was bunching up under the enemy guns. To try to maneuver around the torpedoes would lengthen the ships' exposure to the cannonade. To go forward would hazard the fleet against the torpedoes. To retreat was out of the question. "Damn the torpedoes!" Farragut shouted. "Full speed ahead!" *Hartford* plowed through the torpedo field unscathed and the rest of the ships followed her into Mobile Bay.

Tennessee engaged the Union warships shortly thereafter. At the height of the battle, *Hartford* tried ramming the Rebel ironclad. As the two ships closed

head on at full steam, Farragut scrambled into the port mizzenmast rigging for a better view. At the last moment *Tennessee* put her helm over to avoid a head-on collision. The two ships scraped against each another, the muzzles of their guns nearly touching. Meanwhile, the monitor *Chickasaw* worked behind *Tennessee* and pumped round after round from the 11-inch Dahlgren guns in her forward turret into the ram's stern. *Tennessee* struck her colors after a furious hour-long fight. Meanwhile, Union gunboats had destroyed two of the Rebel gunboats. Thus ended the Civil War's bloodiest naval battle.

With the Confederate naval squadron gone, the forts fell several days later. Although Mobile remained in Confederate hands until April 1865, blockade running into the port ended once and for all. With General William T. Sherman entrenched before Atlanta and no end to General Ulysses S. Grant's siege of Petersburg in sight, Farragut's victory—his most spectacular of the war—gave Union morale a badly needed boost.

Farragut possessed all the attributes of a great commander: intelligence, confidence, determination, boldness, and, above all, courage. He remained aware of the overall tactical situation even as the battle raged around him and his ability to divine the decisive moment for action was almost uncanny. As a reward for his contributions, in 1866 he was appointed America's first four-star admiral.

Left: *A Union torpedo launch, under Lieutenant William B. Cushing, torpedoes the Confederate ram* Albemarle *at Plymouth, North Carolina, 27 October 1864. (Naval Historical Center)*

Below: *The side-wheel steamer* Commodore Hull *engages the Confederate batteries at Plymouth, North Carolina, 29 October 1864. Rebel gunners got their revenge, damaging her two days later. (F. Gutekunst, Naval Historical Center)*

Tennessee, capture the gunboat *Undine* and two Army transports under her escort. *Undine's* crew puts up a gallant defense, engaging the Confederate batteries for some three hours until forced to strike her colors for lack of ammunition.

1 November
Rear Admiral Samuel P. Lee assumes command of the Mississippi Squadron.

2–4 November
On 2 November the paddle-wheel steamers *Key West* and *Tawah* engage the Confederate gunboats *Undine* and *Venus*, both former Union Navy vessels captured by the South in action on the Tennessee River. After a heated battle, the Union force recaptures *Venus*. Two days later *Key West* and *Tawah*, along with the small steamer *Elfin*, engage Confederate batteries while protecting the Union depot at Johnsonville, Tennessee. For nearly an hour the gunboats and batteries

exchange cannon fire, which one observer describes as "the most terrific I have ever witnessed." Though the Union force is compelled to surrender, the heroic stand prevents Confederate General Nathan Bedford Forrest from moving to capture Johnsonville.

27 November

An explosion, probably triggered by a Confederate "coal torpedo" (an explosive charge disguised as a lump of coal) planted in her boiler, destroys *Greyhound*, the headquarters steamer of General Benjamin Butler, on the James River. In addition to Butler, Rear Admiral David Dixon Porter, on board for a conference, narrowly escapes harm.

29 November

In action below Richmond, the monitors *Onondaga* and *Mahopac* engage Howlett's Battery on the James River, exchanging fire for three hours.

30 November

A naval brigade, consisting of some 500 sailors and Marines from ships of the South Atlantic Blockading Squadron under Commander George H. Preble, join Union army forces in fighting the Battle of Honey Hill in South Carolina. The landing party's role is to cut the Charleston-Savannah Railroad, thus assisting the efforts of General William T. Sherman in his march toward Savannah. The naval brigade is not withdrawn until 28 December, after nearly one month of action.

3–4 December

Union gunboats operating on the Cumberland River engage Confederate field batteries near Bell's Mills, Tennessee, recapturing three transports in the process and gaining valuable intelligence on enemy forces opposing the Union Army as it advances on Nashville.

5 December

Secretary of the Navy Gideon Welles issues his annual report, commenting on the effectiveness of the blockade, which is responsible for the capture of some 1,400 prizes. Welles also notes the tremendous expansion of the Union Navy from a force that numbered 42 ships in March 1861 to one of 671 vessels mounting more than 4,600 guns.

6 December

A Union force consisting of the ironclad *Neosho*, three steamers, and several transports moves down the Cumberland River to engage Confederate batteries near Bell's Mills, Tennessee. *Neosho* battles the enemy alone, battering the rebel defenses and suffering over 100 hits in the process. After two and one-half hours, *Neosho* withdraws after Lieutenant Commander LeRoy Fitch determines that the smaller ships cannot make it past the batteries.

Above: *Whether black or white, sailors serving on board the gunboat* Hunchback *shared the same hardships that were part of shipboard life, including combat with the enemy. During the Civil War the Navy was very much an integrated force. (Naval Historical Center)*

run aground and come under fire from Union shore batteries. The Union monitor *Onondaga* bombards the grounded enemy ironclads, forcing them to withdraw. This action marks the final battle between ironclad warships during the Civil War.

27 January

After nightfall, a Union boat party under the command of Acting Ensign Thomas Morgan proceeds up the James River and captures the Confederate spar torpedo boat *Scorpion*, which had run aground during the battle of 23–24 January. The men refloat her and return to Union lines.

9 February

The screw sloop *Pawnee*, gunboat *Sonoma*, and side-wheel steamer *Daffodil* engage Confederate batteries near the North Edisto River in South Carolina. In an example of the naval support of General William T. Sherman's march through South Carolina, *Pawnee* suffers ten hits and the other vessels two each before silencing the enemy guns.

10 February

Raphael Semmes, former skipper of the raider *Alabama*, is appointed a rear admiral in the Confederate Navy and soon assumes command of the James River Squadron.

15 February

The sidewheel steamer *Merrimac*, her boilers given out and pumps not able to keep pace with rising water levels in the ship, is abandoned at sea off Florida.

16–17 February

Ships under the command of Rear Admiral David Dixon Porter ferry two Army divisions to the west bank of the Cape Fear River, and bombard Fort Anderson in support of an assault by Union troops. So successful is that naval bombardment that all of the fort's twelve guns are silenced. The attack against Fort Anderson is the first step of the Union attempt to capture Wilmington, North Carolina.

17–18 February

After enduring a 567-day siege, Confederate forces evacuate Charleston, South Carolina. The movement comes a day after ships of the South Atlantic Blockading Squadron support a diversionary attack against Bull's Bay, South Carolina, to draw Confederate troops away from General William T. Sherman's approaching army.

19–22 February

With Fort Anderson neutralized, Union forces head up the Cape Fear River. Gunboats under the command of Rear Admiral David Dixon Porter engage Confederate guns in Fort Strong, supporting a ground assault that results in the evacuation of the position by its Confederate defenders. The path to Wilmington open, the Union ships steam to the city, which is already occupied by Union troops.

12 March

The tug *Althea*, while engaged in dragging the channel of the Blakely River in Alabama, sinks after hitting a mine.

24 March

Escorted by the side-wheel steamer *Bat*, the steamer *River Queen* carrying President Abraham Lincoln arrives at City Point, Virginia, for a meeting with Generals Ulysses S. Grant and William T. Sherman, and Rear Admiral David Dixon Porter.

27 March

Secretary of the Navy Gideon Welles dispatches the screw sloop *Wyoming* to join the screw sloop *Wachusett* and steam sloop *Iroquois* in searching for the Confederate raider *Shenandoah*.

28 March

The monitor *Milwaukee* strikes a mine in the Blakely River during the Union effort to capture Mobile, Alabama. She sinks in an hour, one of three Union warships sunk by underwater ordnance in the Blakely River during the final days of the Civil War.

One of the forts guarding the entrance to Lisbon Harbor in Portugal fires upon the steam frigate *Niagara*.

Secretary of the Navy Gideon Welles advises Sylvanus W. Gordon of his appointment as an acting rear admiral in command of the Brazil Squadron.

Opposite: *The Union fleet departs Hampton Roads, for Fort Fisher, December 1864. (Naval Historical Center)*

Above: *On 23-24 January 1865,* Onondaga *fought the last engagement between ironclad warships of the Civil War. (Naval Historical Center)*

Right: *("Bombardment of Fort Anderson on the Cape Fear River, 11 February 1865," T. L. Jeffers, Naval Historical Center)*

Left: *Officials examine the body of John Wilkes Booth on board the monitor* Montauk *off the Washington Navy Yard, District of Columbia, 27 April 1865. Booth had shot President Abraham Lincoln on 14 April. (Naval Historical Center)*

2–3 April
Rear Admiral Raphael Semmes, carrying out the orders of Confederate Secretary of the Navy Stephen Mallory, puts the ships of the James River Squadron to the torch, their crews joining the forces under the command of General Robert E. Lee in the evacuation of Richmond, Virginia. On 4 April Semmes and his naval personnel assume defensive positions around Danville, Virginia.

4 April
President Abraham Lincoln joins Rear Admiral David Dixon Porter on board the latter's flagship, the steamer *Malvern* for a trip up the James River to inspect the former Confederate capital of Richmond, Virginia.

8 April
After repeated bombardment by naval forces, Spanish Fort and Fort Alexis surrender, thus opening the way for the capture of Mobile, Alabama, which surrenders on 12 April.

9 April
General Robert E. Lee surrenders the Army of Northern Virginia to General Ulysses S. Grant at Appamattox Court House, Virginia.

14 April
The gunboat *Sciota* strikes a mine and sinks off Mobile, Alabama.

17–25 April
As authorities round up accomplices in the plot to assassinate President Abraham Lincoln, the suspects are held on board the monitors *Montauk* and *Saugus* anchored off the Washington Navy Yard D.C.

23–24 April
The Confederate tug *Webb*, under Lieutenant Charles W. Read, enters the Mississippi River and attempts to make a run for the open ocean. Successfully passing New Orleans on the night of 24 April, *Webb* encounters the steam sloop *Richmond*, which in concert with pursuing Union gunboats runs the Confederate vessel aground. She is burned by her crew, which despite fleeing into the swamps are apprehended.

27 April
The body of John Wilkes Booth, assassin of President Abraham Lincoln, arrives in the nation's capital and is examined on board the monitor *Montauk* anchored off the Washington Navy Yard, D.C.

20 May
A board convened by Secretary of the Navy Gideon Welles begins deliberations on the future of the U.S. Naval Academy, reviewing all aspects of the institution.

9 June
In a reorganization of the U.S. Navy, the East and West Gulf squadrons are combined and redesignated the Gulf Squadron with headquarters at Pensacola, Florida. Similarly, the North and South Atlantic squadrons are combined to form the Atlantic Squadron. The following month the strength of these squadrons is set at twelve and ten vessels, respectively.

31 July
Secretary of the Navy Gideon Welles orders Commodore Henry H. Bell to command the reconstituted East India Squadron.

12 August
Rear Admiral Sylvanus Godon arrives in Bahia, Brazil, to assume command of the reconstituted Brazil Squadron, which consists of seven ships.

28 August
Rear Admiral David Dixon Porter is appointed the first postwar superintendent of the U.S. Naval Academy, which returns to Annapolis, Maryland from Newport, Rhode Island.

6 November
The Confederate raider *Shenandoah* arrives at Liverpool, England. Upon being informed by the British Foreign Ministry that the Civil War has ended, skipper Lieutenant James I. Waddell lowers the last official Confederate flag.

4 December
Secretary of the Navy Gideon Welles announces the reestablishment of the West India Squadron under the command of Commodore James S. Palmer. The squadron consists of nine ships.

Above: *Confederate raider* Shenandoah *out of the water at Williamstown Dockyard, Melbourne, Australia, February 1865. Nine months later, her Confederate flag would be hauled down for the final time. (Naval Historical Center)*

RETRENCHMENT AND REBIRTH

1866-1899

RETRENCHMENT AND REBIRTH

1866-1899

With the surrender of the Confederacy in April 1865, the navy that had braved troubled waters from Mobile Bay to Fort Fisher and helped conquer the Mississippi River disappeared almost overnight. In his last years in office, Secretary of the Navy Gideon Welles, who had presided over the tremendous expansion of the fleet, returned it to peacetime levels. A force that, at its wartime peak numbered nearly 700 ships, was transformed to a fleet of 120 vessels of all types by the end of 1865. This drastic reduction foreshadowed a dark age for the U.S. Navy, marked by neglect by administrations of the era. Through it all, the nation, as it always had, called upon Navy to patrol distant waters, defending the flag and serving as a symbol of America thousands of miles from her shores.

The Civil War proved a watershed event in the advance of naval technology, the urgent demands of combat inspiring the invention and introduction of new weapons of war. This was certainly apparent in ship design, with the introduction of ironclads and a growing reliance on steam power for propulsion. However, the postwar years witnessed a renewed debate between traditionalists reared in the age of sail and disciples of the new technology. Thus, while the smoke from railroad locomotives filled the air as the United States pushed westward with a transcontinental railroad, most U.S. Navy warships still plied the oceans under sail and American naval power fell behind that of other nations. An outward demonstration of this diminished strength came on 31 October 1873, when a Spanish gunboat seized the steamer *Virginius* as she attempted to smuggle supplies to revolutionaries in Cuba, and executed fifty-three of her passengers and crew, including the American-born captain, Joshua Fry, a former naval officer. It took three months for the U.S. fleet to assemble in Key West, Florida, in response; fortunately, diplomacy defused a tense international incident.

Yet, signs on the horizon pointed to an increased emphasis on the Navy. In the Pacific the United States expanded its territorial holdings with the purchase of Alaska, establishment of a naval base in Pago Pago, Samoa, and annexation of Midway Atoll, far-flung territories that demanded a naval presence. What form this should take in the Pacific and throughout the world was a topic much debated by naval officers and civilians of the era, particularly at the Naval War College, which began classes at Newport, Rhode Island, in 1885. Among the faculty members of the new institution was Captain Alfred Thayer Mahan, who in 1890 assembled some of his lectures into an influential book titled *The Influence of Sea Power Upon History, 1660–1783.* "It is not the taking of individual ships or convoys, be they few or many, that strikes down the money power of a nation; it is the possession of that overbearing power on the sea which drives the enemy's flag from it. This overbearing power can only be exercised by great navies," Mahan wrote. This concept of command of the sea served as a voice for a rebirth of American naval power already underway.

Even before Mahan penned his influential words, the Navy took steps to modernize its antiquated fleet, actively seeking legislation for the construction of

more capable ships. The result was the commissioning of the steel-hulled "ABCD" ships—*Atlanta*, *Boston*, *Chicago*, and *Dolphin*. More reflective of technological advancement than these ships, which incorporated the traditional sail rig, was the commissioning of the Navy's first battleships, *Maine* and *Texas*, in 1895. Entirely coal powered, they included main batteries housed in rotating turrets that turned hydraulically, thus allowing for firing at multiple angles. These ships were followed by three *Indiana*-class battleships featuring centerline main batteries of 13-inch guns, and by *Iowa*, commissioned in 1897.

That the new American Navy was poised to assume an important role on the world stage was demonstrated in dramatic fashion during the Spanish-American War in 1898. A strong supporter of Cuban independence, the United States sent *Maine* into Havana Harbor as a show of force. On 15 February 1898, an explosion rocked the ship, sending her to the bottom. At the time attributed to a Spanish mine, the tragedy galvanized support for a war against Spain, with "Remember the *Maine!*" becoming a battle cry for the nation. On 25 April the United States declared war, and within days a fleet under Commodore George Dewey scored a stunning victory over a Spanish squadron at the Battle of

Manila Bay in the Philippines. In Cuba, with troops led by former Assistant Secretary of the Navy Theodore Roosevelt, who left his official duties to command a regiment of volunteers, capturing San Juan Hill ashore, the U.S. Navy scored another lopsided victory over the Spanish at the Battle of Santiago on 3 July 1898.

The stunning victory in the Spanish-American War resulted in Spain ceding Puerto Rico and Guam to the United States, which, combined with the annexation of Hawaii and the Philippines, represented an emerging world power, one whose primary guardian would be a resurgent U.S. Navy.

Above: *Members of the crew gather for Sunday services on board the second-class battleship* Texas *at anchor off Key West, Florida, 1898. (Naval Historical Center)*

Pages 242–243: *The North Atlantic Squadron at Hampton Roads, Virginia. Ships present include (l–r):* New York, Indiana, Texas, Massachusetts, Columbia, *and* Iowa. *("Before the War," Carlton T. Chapman, Navy Art Collection)*

RETRENCHMENT AND REBIRTH
1866-1899

1866

4 January
The armed tug *Narcissus* wrecks on Egmont Key, Florida, taking the lives of all thirty-two members of her crew.

6 May
The ironclad *Miantonomoh,* in company with the sidewheel gunboat *Ashuelot* and the sidewheel steamer *Augusta,* departs New York on a transatlantic crossing, the first by a monitor-type ironclad. *Miantonomoh* and *Augusta* (*Ashuelot* had been detached for service in the Far East) return to the United States on 22 July 1867, having traveled a distance of more than 17,700 miles and visited ten European nations, including Russia. Among the passengers on board the ironclad during the cruise is Assistant Secretary of the Navy Gustavus Fox, who is engaged in a technical mission to Europe.

20 June
A landing party consisting of 100 sailors and Marines under Lieutenant John W. Philip departs the screw sloop *Wachusett* and lands at New Chwang, China, to capture the leader of a band that had assaulted the American consul.

21 June
Congress passes a law establishing the Hydrographic Office to assume the responsibilities of the pre-Civil War Hydrographical Office.

25 June
A law enacted by Congress creates the rank of admiral and, as was the case with the ranks of rear admiral and vice admiral, David G. Farragut is selected as the first officer promoted to the new rank.

1867

2 March
Congress passes a law creating the Civil Engineering Corps. On 3 March 1871, legislation is passed directing that, at the president's discretion, civil engineers may receive relative rank to line officers.

13 June
Crewmen from the screw sloops *Hartford* and *Wyoming* land on Formosa and skirmish with inhabitants in retaliation for the massacre of the crew of the American merchantman *Rover*. Of the 181 men who go ashore under the command of Commander George C. Belknap, the only casualty is Lieutenant Commander Alexander S. MacKenzie.

Left: *The ironclad* Miantonomoh *(1865–1875) at Malaga, Spain, in 1867, during her European cruise. The side-wheel steamer* Augusta, *her companion on the voyage, is in the left background. (Naval Historical Center)*

19 June
The screw sloop *Sacramento* runs aground on a shallow bar off Madras, India. the ship is wrecked, but no members of her crew are lost.

28 August
Captain William Reynolds of the screw sloop *Lackawanna* raises the American flag over Brooks' Islands (later renamed Midway Atoll). It is formally annexed on 28 December. "It is exceedingly gratifying to me to have been thus concerned in taking possession of the first island ever added to the dominion of the United States, beyond our own shores," Reynolds later writes of Midway, which is destined to play a significant role in the Navy's history.

1868

4 February
In a year marked by U.S. Navy intervention in Japan, a landing party from the screw sloop *Oneida* goes ashore at Hiogo, Japan, to protect Americans under attack during the Meiji Restoration that restores imperial rule to Japan. One sailor is wounded in the action. Between February and November 1868 naval forces go ashore at Nagasaki, Yokohama, and again at Hiogo.

7 February
A squadron consisting of the screw sloops *Guerriere* and *Quinnebaug*, the side-wheel steamer *Shamokin*, and the gunboats *Kansas* and *Wasp* arrives at Montevideo, Uruguay, to protect foreign interests and the customs house during an insurrection. Squadron commander Rear Admiral C. H. Davis orders a landing party ashore on 19 February, and it remains in place until order is restored seven days later.

11 February
During a trial run the commerce-destroying cruiser *Wampanoag* achieves a speed of 17.75 knots, the highest speed any Navy ship would achieve until 1889.

9 July
The gunboat *Suwanee*, while steaming to Vancouver, British Columbia, wrecks in Queen Charlotte Sound.

13 August
The bark *Fredonia* and the gunboat *Wateree*, while operating near Arica, Peru, are caught in a tidal wave. Carried 1,500 feet inland, *Fredonia* breaks up while *Wateree* is badly damaged. Twenty-seven Navy men are lost.

8 December
Jiunzo Matsumura enrolls at the U.S. Naval Academy in accordance with an act passed the previous July that allows for the instruction of Japanese nationals at Annapolis. He graduates in 1873.

1869

9 March
Philadelphian Adolf E. Borie takes office as the twenty-fifth Secretary of the Navy. His term is destined to last less than four months.

26 April
Congress authorizes the Good Conduct Medal for issuance to U.S. Navy enlisted personnel. Originally a Maltese cross made of nickel, the design is changed to a bronze medal in 1892.

9 June
The Secretary of the Navy issues orders for the construction of the sea service's first torpedo station on Goat Island at Newport, Rhode Island.

18 June
The Navy Department issues General Order Number 131 limiting the use of steam engines on board Navy ships equipped with full sail rig to the "most urgent circumstances." The order reflects a Navy in transition.

Above: *Lieutenant Commander Alexander S. MacKenzie survived the Civil War only to lose his life on Formosa on 13 June 1867, during a retaliatory attack against some of the island's inhabitants for the murder of the crew of an American merchantman. (Naval Historical Center)*

Left: *Constructed during the Civil War as part of a program to equip the Navy with large and fast steam cruisers, Wampanoag could reach a speed of seventeen knots. Commissioned in 1867, her days as a warship ended the following year. ("USS Wampanoag, John Charles Roach, Navy Art Collection)*

Below: *Coxwain William Halford captures an albatross to feed the crew of the launch sent from Ocean Island to Hawaii to rescue the crew of the wrecked side-wheel steamer Saginaw in 1870. Halford, the sole survivor of this 1,500-mile boat voyage, received the Medal of Honor. (Naval Historical Center)*

26 June

George M. Robeson, a former Attorney General of New Jersey, takes office as the twenty-sixth Secretary of the Navy. His tenure is marked by charges of corrupt administration of the Navy Department and the physical deterioration of the fleet.

28 June

William M. Wood is appointed Surgeon General, the first man to hold the newly created Navy post.

21 September

Idaho, one of the fastest sailing ships of her day, cannot outrun a typhoon near Yokohama, Japan. The storm's high winds and raging seas carry away her masts and severely damage her hull, but she remains afloat and returns to Yokohama. Her hulk remains there until she is decommissioned on 31 December 1873, and sold in 1874.

1870

22 January

Under the command of Commander Thomas O. Selfridge, Jr., the gunboat *Nipsic* sails on a surveying expedition investigating locations for an interoceanic canal on the Isthmus of Darien (now the Isthmus of

LIEUT.-COMMANDER W. L. STEWART.—[See Page 181.]   COMMANDER E. H. WILLIAMS.—[See Page 181.]   LIEUT.-COMMANDER A. W. MULDAUR.—[See Page 181.]

Panama). Selfridge's ensuing report, which is issued in 1874, details four potential routes.

24 January

The steamer *Oneida*, a veteran of runs past the guns of Vicksburg and the Battle of Mobile Bay, is struck by the British steamer *City of Bombay* off Yokohama, Japan. The screw sloop sinks with the loss of 117 of her crew.

17 June

Lieutenant Willard H. Brownson leads six boats from the screw sloop *Mohican* in search of a band of pirates operating in the Teacapan River in western Mexico. The boat party finds the pirate ship, the former British gunboat *Forward*, and burns her.

11–13 August

The gunboat *Palos* becomes the first U.S. Navy vessel to transit the Suez Canal.

14 August

Civil War hero Admiral David G. Farragut dies in Portsmouth, New Hampshire at the age of sixty-nine.

29 October

The side-wheel steamer *Saginaw* breaks up on a reef off Ocean Island in the middle of the Pacific Ocean. The remote location offers little hope of rescue, prompting five volunteers under the command of Lieutenant John G. Talbot to man a ship's gig and attempt to reach Hawaii. After sailing some 1,500 miles, the men reach Kauai on 20 December after thirty-one days at sea. Tragically, Talbot and four sailors are drowned in heavy surf as they come ashore. Only Coxswain William Halford survives to bring help to his shipmates. He receives the Medal of Honor and a promotion to the rate of Acting Gunner.

1871

3 March

Congress establishes the Pay Corps, which is renamed the Supply Corps in 1919.

30 May

Rear Admiral John Rodgers leads a squadron consisting of the screw frigate *Colorado*, the gunboats *Alaska*, *Monocacy*, and *Palos*, and the screw sloop

Benicia into the mouth of the Han River in Korea. Carrying Frederick Low, the U.S. minister to China, to attempt to negotiate a treaty with Korean leaders, the squadron instead takes fire the following day from one of five forts guarding the river. Silencing the enemy guns, Rodgers demands an apology and, when one is not forthcoming, he orders his command into action. On 10 June, under covering fire from *Monocacy* and *Palos*, a landing party consisting of 575 bluejackets and 109 Marines goes ashore with seven guns. The force easily captures two forts and the following day attacks the principal Korean position, known as The Citadel. A bitter struggle for the position results in the loss of three men killed and seven wounded, including Navy Lieutenant Hugh W. McKee, who is speared as he leads attackers into The Citadel. Its capture costs the Koreans 243 men killed and 481 captured cannon. Fifteen bluejackets and Marines receive the Medal of Honor for their actions in Korea. Rodgers's squadron sails on 3 July.

29 June
Commanded by Captain Charles F. Hall, the screw tug *Polaris* departs New York City on an expedition to the Arctic. She eventually arrives at the position 82°11' north latitude, then the furthest point north reached by a vessel. Subsequently, tragedy befalls her. Captain Hall dies while the crew winters over in Greenland, and, while returning home in October 1872, *Polaris* is caught in the ice and crushed, her crew eventually rescued.

1872

11 September
Nearly a decade after the issuance of the Emancipation Proclamation, James Henry Conyers becomes the first African-American to enroll at the U.S. Naval Academy. He leaves the following year.

1873

7 May
Operating in the waters off the Colombian province of Panama, the screw sloop *Tuscarora* puts ashore a landing party consisting of 200 men to protect Americans threatened by revolutionary activity in the region. The force is fully withdrawn on 22 May.

24 September
Revolutionary activity in Panama again draws the attention of Navy warships when the screw steamer

Pensacola and the screw sloop *Benicia* put ashore a landing party of 190 men to guard American interests.

9 October
A group of fifteen officers assigned to the U.S. Naval Academy meet in Annapolis, Maryland, to form a professional society that eventually becomes the U.S. Naval Institute. The first issue of the *United States Naval Institute Proceedings* is published in 1875.

31 October
The Spanish warship *Tornado* captures the American steamer *Virginius* attempting to carry arms to

Opposite: *Studying charts, senior officers gather in the frigate* Colorado *to plan the 1871 expedition to Korea. (Naval Historical Center)*

Above: *The monitor* Terror, *pictured at the Philadelphia Navy Yard, circa 1873. (Naval Historical Center)*

Right: *The gunboat* Monocacy *and the screw tug* Palos *in the Han River in Korea after U.S. Navy warships responded in force after being taken under fire by forts guarding the river. (Naval Historical Center)*

insurrectos in Cuba. The Spanish execute fifty-three of *Virginius*'s passengers and crew, including former naval officer Joshua Fry. An American cruiser under the command of Commander William B. Cushing joins the British warship *Niobe* in responding to the incident, which is resolved peacefully with the payment of an indemnity by the Spanish government.

1874

12 February
The coronation of King Kalakaua creates disturbances that prompt the landing of a force of 150 men from the sloop *Portsmouth* and the screw sloop *Tuscarora* at Honolulu, Hawaii.

31 July
The Navy commissions the first warship armed with torpedoes, the experimental "steam torpedo ram" *Intrepid*. She does not enjoy a successful career.

1875

6 May
William D. Leahy, future fleet admiral and adviser to President Franklin D. Roosevelt during World War II, is born in Hampton, Iowa.

18 June
The side-wheel steam sloop-of-war *Saranac* goes to the bottom in the Seymour Narrows off Vancouver Island after striking a rock. No members of her crew are lost.

Opposite, top: *Waves smash the sloop-rigged steamer* Huron, *sinking near Nags Head, North Carolina, 24 November 1877. (Naval Historical Center)*

Opposite, bottom: *The steam torpedo ram* Intrepid *in drydock during the 1870s. Note her hull plating and the torpedo projection device at her forefoot. (Naval Historical Center)*

Right: Jeanette *enters Arctic ice in September 1879 carrying a North Pole expedition. Soon iced in, she and many of her men are destined not to return from their voyage. (Naval Historical Center)*

1876

No significant events occur during this year.

1877

13 March
Richard W. Thompson, a former member of Congress from Indiana, takes office as the twenty-seventh Secretary of the Navy.

24 November
The iron sloop-rigged steamer *Huron* is caught in a storm off Nags Head, North Carolina and wrecked. Ninety-eight members of her 132-man crew are lost in the storm.

1878

23 November
Ernest J. King, a future fleet admiral and World War II-era Chief of Naval Operations and Commander in Chief, U.S. Fleet, is born in Lorain, Ohio.

7 December
Under the command of Commodore Robert W. Shufeldt, the screw sloop *Ticonderoga* departs Hampton Roads, Virginia, on a voyage that will last nearly two years.

1879

7 August
The ill-fated Jeannette Expedition departs San Francisco, California, to explore the North Pole. Under the command of Lieutenant George Washington DeLong, the expedition consists of the former private yacht *Jeannette* manned by twenty-eight officers and men accompanied by three civilians. The vessel arrives in the Arctic in September, and is immediately iced in for the next twenty-one months. On 13 June 1881 the pressure of the ice proves too great even for the reinforced hull of *Jeannette*, forcing the members of the expedition to make their way overland to Siberia. Dragging three boats from the vessel, the men reach the edge of the ice cap and enter the water for the voyage to the mainland. One boat sinks with the loss of all aboard, while that commanded by DeLong lands in an uninhabited area. Only the boat commanded by Chief Engineer George W. Melville arrives in the inhabited part of the Lena Delta. DeLong, his men weakened by an attempt to reach help by traveling overland, eventually sends two of his strongest men ahead to find help. They eventually reach Melville's party, but are too late to save those they left behind. Melville finds their frozen corpses on 23 March 1882. Preserved in the ice are the expedition's records, which eventually prove valuable to others exploring the Arctic region.

1880

---

9 November
The screw sloop *Ticonderoga* returns to Hampton Roads, Virginia, after having completed the first around-the-world cruise by a U.S. Navy steam-powered vessel.

1881

---

7 January
Nathan Goff, Jr., a federal attorney from West Virginia, becomes the twenty-eighth Secretary of the Navy. Filling the balance of his predecessor's term, his term is the second shortest in history, lasting less than two months.

7 March
William H. Hunt, the father of a naval officer and longtime Louisiana attorney, takes office as the twenty-ninth Secretary of the Navy. He inherits a Navy in deplorable physical condition, with only 52 of a total of 140 ships in commission considered effective.

28 June
The Secretary of the Navy forms a Naval Advisory Board under Rear Admiral John Rodgers that, later in the year, recommends a cruiser construction program with the majority of the vessels featuring steel hulls. Congress replies with a bill approving a less ambitious building program.

30 November
The steamer *Rodgers* is destroyed by fire in St. Lawrence Bay, Canda, after completing a search for the missing members of the Jeanette Expedition. Fortunately, only one member of her crew is lost.

1882

---

23 March
The Office of Naval Intelligence is established.

17 April
William E. Chandler of New Hampshire, a former Assistant Secretary of the Treasury and secretary of the Republican National Committee, takes office as the thirtieth Secretary of the Navy. Under his leadership the U.S. Navy begin to gain a renewed stature in the world.

19 May
Commodore Robert W. Shufeldt, in command of the screw sloop *Swatara*, lands in Korea and commences negotiations that, three days later, result in a commercial treaty between that nation and the United States.

14 July
A landing party of 133 sailors and Marines from the screw sloops *Lancaster* and *Quinnebaug*, and the gunboat *Nipsic* go ashore at Alexandria, Egypt, to assist in protecting American people and property and quelling disturbances in the wake of a bombardment of the city by British warships.

15 November
Lieutenant Commander French E. Chadwick becomes the first naval attaché sent overseas when he receives a posting to London, England.

30 November
The U.S. Naval Academy plays its first football game, losing to the Clifton Football Club by a score of 8 to 0.

Opposite: *Cartoon referring to aid rendered by the U.S. Navy during the British bombardment of Alexandria, Egypt, in July 1882. Parties from the screw sloops* Lancaster *and* Quinnebaug *and the gunboat* Nipsic *landed after the 14 July bombardment. The cartoon also makes note of the poor condition of the U.S. Navy at that time. (Naval Historical Center)*

Right: *Flying the flag of Rear Admiral John G. Walker, the protected cruiser* Chicago *lies at anchor with other ships of the "Squadron of Evolution," including the gunboat* Yorktown *and the protected cruisers* Boston *and* Atlanta, *1889. (Naval Historical Center)*

Squadron of Evolution.
U.S. Navy.
Rear Admiral John G. Walker, Com. in Chief.
1889.

Copyright by

1883

18 February
The side-wheel gunboat *Ashuelot* runs aground on rocks near the mouth of the Swatow River in China. Eleven crewmen drown as a result of the accident.

3 March
Under the Naval Appropriations Act of 1883, Congress funds the construction of four warships known collectively as the "ABCDs." The first warships constructed of American-made steel, the three cruisers *Atlanta*, *Boston*, and *Chicago*, and the dispatch vessel *Dolphin* represent the first step in the transformation of the U.S. Navy into a modern force.

7 June–21 August
While berthed at the New York Navy Yard, the screw steamer *Trenton* receives the first electric lights ever installed in a U.S. Navy warship. At a cost of $5,500, the Edison Company for Isolated Lighting installs machinery capable of illuminating 238 lamps of various powers on board the ship.

Above: *Ship's captains often served as de facto diplomats in their voyages abroad. Commodore Robert W. Shufeldt successfully negotiated a commercial treaty with Korea in May 1882. (Naval Historical Center)*

THE FOUNDING OF THE NAVAL WAR COLLEGE

by Dr. John B. Hattendorf

On 6 October 1884, Secretary of the Navy William E. Chandler signed the Navy Department General Order that created the Naval War College on Coaster's Harbor Island in Narragansett Bay at Newport, Rhode Island. At the same time, Chandler appointed Commodore Stephen B. Luce, commanding the North Atlantic Station, to be the first president of the institution devoted to the "higher branches of professional study."

The new institution was the product of many years of work on Luce's part. A leading figure in the U.S. Navy, he was a widely experienced naval officer who had played key roles in establishing the Naval Institute, writing the leading textbook for practical seamanship at the Naval Academy as well as establishing training institutions for merchant seamen and for naval apprentices. As early as 1877, Luce had first formally recommended that the U.S. Navy create a place for advanced study in naval affairs, underscoring the fact that, "With the recent revolution in naval warfare comes a demand for a higher order of talent in the conduct of naval operations." While Luce saw that most navies of the world shared this deficiency, he found a precedent in some aspects of the advanced-level work being done at the German navy's

Kreigsakademie and at the British Royal Navy College in Greenwich. More important to his thinking, however, was the example of Brigadier General Emery Upton. Inspired by the successes of the German General Staff during the recent Franco-Prussian War, Upton tried to implement ideas along these same lines at the U.S. Army's Artillery School at Fort Monroe, Virginia. Yet, none of these earlier approaches did what Luce envisaged for creating a distinct theory of naval science.

As Luce later reflected on the purpose of the institution, it was to be "a place of original research on all questions relating to war and to statesmanship connected with war, or the prevention of war." Luce thought carefully in naming it. "That particular name has been given to the college in order that its special mission may be kept steadily in view…that it may never be lost sight of," he wrote. "War and its cognate branches constitute the college curriculum. It is only by a close study of the science and art of war that we can be prepared for war, and thus go very far toward securing peace." From the outset, he stressed that the college was not a place of ordinary instruction, "not teaching war," but giving its students the opportunity to understand it.

In gathering the faculty for the college for the first course, which opened in September 1885, Luce clearly identified the focus of the college on the broadest political and military aspects of naval affairs as the means by which naval officers could control more adequately the purpose and direction of the burgeoning technology within the Navy.

Among the early figures in the college's institutional history, Lieutenant Tasker Bliss, who later rose to be the first president of the Army War College and then Army Chief of Staff, was the college's first instructor in military theory, providing a comparative basis for creating naval science. Captain Alfred Thayer Mahan came as the first instructor in naval history and tactics and then succeeded Luce by serving two terms as the college's president in 1886–1889 and 1892–1893. During these periods, Mahan wrote the basis for the first two volumes of his *Influence of Sea Power* series as lectures for Naval War College students. Mahan's innovative historical analysis provided the first intellectual foundation for understanding the role of navies in international affairs and had worldwide influence on a range of contemporary national naval policies as well as scholarly interpretations. Professor James Soley, a future undersecretary of the Navy, became the first lecturer in international law, and one of his successors, Captain Charles Stockton, wrote the world's first *Code of Naval*

Warfare at the college in 1900. Adapted to international law in the Declaration of London in 1909, it established the first codified legal restraints on the conduct of war at sea, which have remained largely in force since that time. Working in the same period at the college, Lieutenant William McCarty Little became the most important figure in refining the technique of war-gaming, so that it could be used as an effective tool to assess the capabilities of rapidly changing naval technology in modern warfare in the light of broad war objectives and restraints on the conduct of war. These early figures in the history of the Naval War College used the study of naval history, tactics, law, and politics to provide the foundations for future contributions, which by the end of the twentieth century would be classified as policy, strategy, command, operational doctrine, management, and logistics.

Opposite: *The first administrative building at the Naval War College, within whose walls naval strategists were born. (Naval Historical Center)*

Below: *The strategy and tactics that formed the blueprint for victory in World War II were played out on the wargaming board at the Naval War College during the 1920s and 1930s.*

1884

24 April
The steamers *Alert*, *Bear*, and *Thetis*, under
Commander Winfield Scott Schley, depart New York
to search for members of an expedition under the
command of Army Lieutenant Adolphus W. Greely.
Greely's twenty-five man party departed in 1881, bound
for the North Pole. When Schley's expedition rescues
the survivors at Cape Sabine, Grinnell Land, on 22
June, there are only seven men left, including Greely.

6 October
By order of the Secretary of the Navy, the Naval War
College is established at Newport, Rhode Island.
Commodore Stephen B. Luce, who during the Civil
War envisioned a professional curriculum for the
training of naval officers in the art of war, is appointed

the institution's first president. Among the officers he
brings to the college is Commander Alfred Thayer
Mahan. Instruction begins on 3 September of the
following year.

1885

18 January
The gunboat *Alliance* puts ashore a detachment of
Marines at Aspinwall in the Colombian province of
Panama to guard a railroad connecting the east and
west coasts of the province in the wake of
revolutionary activity.

24 February
Chester W. Nimitz, a future fleet admiral and
commander in chief of naval forces in the Pacific
during World War II, is born in Fredricksburg, Texas.

Opposite: *A bearded Army Lieutenant Adolphus W. Greely is surrounded by fellow survivors of his expedition to the North Pole and some of the U.S. Navy officers who rescued them after they spent nearly three years on the ice. (Naval Historical Center)*

Right: *"Spinning a Yarn" on board the sloop-of-war* Enterprise, *circa 1880. (Naval Historical Center)*

Below: *During the late nineteenth century the U.S. Navy became increasingly involved in Central American affairs, particularly in the Colombian province of Panama. In 1885, the extended service away from their ships to maintain order in country prompted these sailors to occupy quarters at Aspinwall. (Naval Historical Center)*

Left: *Secretary of the Navy Benjamin F. Tracy. (Naval Historical Center)*

Below: *Cushing (TB 1), the Navy's first modern torpedo boat, pictured during sea trials in 1890. She foreshadowed an era in which small combatants became increasingly important in naval operations. (Naval Historical Center)*

Opposite: *Unpopular among his fellow officers and prone to seasickness, Rear Admiral Alfred Thayer Mahan advanced the importance of establishing command of the seas through his writings and shaped naval strategy. (Naval War College)*

7 March
Massachusetts-born corporate lawyer William C. Whitney takes office as the thirty-first Secretary of the Navy.

16 March–25 May
In response to the revolution in the Columbian province of Panama, the steamer *Galena*, the steam sloop-of-war *Iroquois*, the screw sloops *Shenandoah* and *Swatara*, and the transport vessel *City of Para* land Marines at Aspinwall in Panama in an effort to protect

railroad transit of the isthmus. The forces withdraw on 2 May.

1886

3 July
Raymond A. Spruance, a future admiral who leads U.S. naval forces to victory at the Battle of Midway in June 1942 and commands the wartime Fifth Fleet, is born in Baltimore, Maryland.

6 August
Congress authorizes the building of the armored cruiser *Maine,* reclassified during construction as a "second-class" battleship, and the battleship *Texas.* The two vessels, each displacing over 6,000 tons with *Maine* mounting 10-inch guns and *Texas* 12-inch guns, mark the birth of the battleship in the U.S. Navy.

1887

No significant events occur during this year.

1888

17 May
The Commonwealth of Massachusetts establishes a naval militia, a measure enacted by many states in future years. This marks the first step toward the creation of a naval reserve.

19 June
A twenty-five man landing party from the screw steamer *Essex* under Marine First Lieutenant Robert D. Wainwright lands at Chemulpo, Korea, and

proceeds to Seoul in order to protect American citizens in the city. Ironically, Chemulpo eventually receives a new name that, during the Korean War, goes down in the annals of naval history because of another successful landing by Marines there—Inchon.

7 September
Congress authorizes the construction of the armored cruiser *New York* (ACR 2) and six smaller cruisers. One of them is *Olympia,* which will play an important role in the future war with Spain.

14 November
In response to a civil war in Samoa, Marines from the gunboat *Nipsic* land at Apia, Samoa, to protect American interests there.

20 December
The arrival of the steamer *Galena* and gunboat *Yantic* at Port-au-Prince, Haiti, inspires the Haitian authorities to release a recently captured American steamer.

1889

6 March
Benjamin F. Tracy, a brevet Union general in the Civil War and veteran of the Wilderness campaign, takes office as the thirty-second Secretary of the Navy.

15–16 March
When a typhoon ravages the island of Samoa, warships of the United States, Great Britain, and Germany at Apia suffer extreme damage. The U.S. Navy gunboat *Nipsic* is intentionally beached, while the screw steamer *Trenton* and screw sloop *Vandalia* are sunk. Approximately 150 seamen of all nationalities are lost; 49 are Americans.

30 July
The gunboat *Adams* lands a party of Marines at Honolulu, Hawaii, to protect members of the American legation during a period of unrest.

1890

23 April
The Navy commissions *Cushing* (TB 1), its first steam torpedo boat, a forerunner of the destroyer.

May
With the publication of his landmark book *The Influence of Sea Power Upon History, 1660–1783,* Captain Alfred Thayer Mahan advances the doctrine of

BATTLESHIPS

by Paul Stillwell and John C. Reilly, Jr.

Since the days of sail the essence of naval warfare was ships maneuvering at sea in an effort to bring their guns to bear on the enemy. The commissioning of *Texas* and *Maine* in 1895 marked a dramatic evolution in this most important dimension of naval warfare and was the beginning of the reign of the battleship as the U.S. Navy's capital ship.

A battleship played a prominent role in the emergence of the United States as a world power, though it was in a most unexpected manner. The sinking of *Maine* at Havana, Cuba, in February 1898 provided the spark that led to that year's Spanish-American War. During that conflict the battleship *Oregon* (BB 3) displayed the capabilities of the great warships, completing a voyage from California through the Straits of Magellan to Florida. She then joined other battleships off Cuba for the Battle of Santiago on 3 July 1898, during which the American warships defeated a force of Spanish cruisers. *Oregon*'s long trip demonstrated the need for a Central American canal, and work on the Panama Canal began soon afterward.

In the next decade, under the leadership of President Theodore Roosevelt, the battleship force increased steadily in size, and in 1907–1909 the president sent a force of sixteen U.S. battleships nicknamed the "Great White Fleet" around the world, dramatically demonstrating the vitality of American sea power. These early battleships had been armed with a combination of heavy (12–13-inch) and medium (5–8-inch) caliber guns, the faster firing of the smaller guns supplementing the more powerful, but slower, fire of the big guns. This was reasonably effective as long as gunfire control was rudimentary and battle ranges were short. By the early 1900s, however, fire control was rapidly improving and effective firing ranges were steadily increasing.

Middleweight guns were losing their effectiveness at the new, longer ranges and improved breech mechanisms speeded up the rate of heavy gunfire. At this time a new type of "all big gun" battleship emerged. The first of these was Great Britain's *Dreadnought*. Armed with a homogeneous main battery of heavy guns, she gave her name to this new breed of battleships, which would henceforward be known as

"dreadnoughts." Two ships of the *South Carolina* (BB 26) class, mounting eight 12-inch guns, went into commission in 1910 as the first American dreadnoughts. In the years that followed, a succession of new battleship classes increased in size and firepower. The *New York* (BB 34) class was armed with 14-inch guns. Oil fuel replaced coal in the *Nevada* (BB 36) class. The three-ship *Colorado* (BB 45) class introduced the 16-inch gun to the fleet.

World War I erupted in Europe in 1914, and in April 1917, the United States joined the conflict, dispatching a squadron of older, coal-burning battleships to the British Isles to beef up the Royal Navy in its blockade of the German High Seas Fleet. Because they burned oil, which was scarce in Britain, the newer oil-fired battleships remained on America's east coast, where they served as training ships. In 1919, the year after the war ended, the newest U.S. battleships were dispatched to California to form the backbone of a new Pacific Fleet. During the next twenty peacetime years, the ships operated primarily in the eastern Pacific.

The major exception to the pattern was a fleet voyage to Australia and New Zealand in 1925. By that time, the United States had agreed to an international arms-limitation treaty that called for a moratorium on the construction of capital ships. As a result, no new U.S. battleships went into commission between 1923 and 1941. The international naval arms limitation scheme began to break down during the 1930s as the world moved toward war, and the major navies began to build a new generation of fast, modern capital ships. In 1941 the U.S. Navy commissioned *North Carolina* (BB 55) and *Washington* (BB 56), capable of over 27 knots where their predecessors had been designed to make 21 knots, and with modern fire control systems for their 16-inch batteries.

On 7 December 1941 the Pacific Fleet battleships, based at Pearl Harbor, were principal targets for the Japanese surprise attack that drew the United States into World War II. *Arizona* (BB 39) and *Oklahoma* (BB 37) were destroyed beyond repair; three others sank in shallow water and were salvaged; and another three were damaged. The fiery destruction of *Arizona*, with the loss of most of her crew, became a national symbol and helped rally the nation to avenge the attack.

After Pearl Harbor, aircraft carriers and submarines emerged as embodying the fleet's offensive capability. Throughout World War II the newer battleships provided essential heavy antiaircraft protection to the fast carrier task force, while the older ships became shore bombardment specialists and lent powerful support to amphibious landings. During the war, four ships of the 27-knot *South Dakota* (BB 57) class and four of the 33-knot *Iowa* (BB 61) class joined the fleet and had a prominent role in operations in the southern and western Pacific.

On two occasions during the war, American battleships fulfilled their intended mission—surface action against enemy battleships. On the night of 14–15 November 1942, off Guadalcanal, Rear Admiral Willis A. Lee, Jr., commanded a task force that sank the Japanese battleship *Kirishima*, helping end the Japanese effort to recapture Guadalcanal. Nearly two years later, on the night of 24–25 October 1944, Rear Admiral Jesse Oldendorf's force of six old battleships defeated the Japanese in the Battle of Surigao Strait in the Philippines. The Americans' superior gunnery sank the battleships *Yamashiro* and *Fuso*.

That battle was essentially the last gasp for the Japanese surface fleet. Hostilities finally ended in August 1945, and the Japanese officially surrendered on 2 September. The formal ceremony took place on the deck of the battleship *Missouri* (BB 63), named for the home state of President Harry S. Truman. The U.S. Navy ended the war with twenty-three battleships in commission. Within a few years, all but *Missouri* had been decommissioned, either to be scrapped or preserved for possible future use.

Soon after the beginning of the Korean War in June 1950, calls came for *Missouri*'s three sisters to rejoin the active fleet. One by one, *New Jersey* (BB 62), *Iowa* (BB 61), and *Wisconsin* (BB 64) shook off the cobwebs and began hurling their 16-inch projectiles at shore targets in Korea, supporting friendly ground troops by bombarding enemy positions. By the late 1950s, with the emergence of missile-armed ships and planning for missile-armed nuclear submarines, the battleships were no longer affordable, and all returned to the reserve fleet.

Yet, when the United States became embroiled in the Vietnam War, the need for the big guns arose again. Losses of manned aircraft mounted as they were shot down while attacking North Vietnam. In order to provide a source of bombardment not vulnerable to enemy fire, the Navy pulled *New Jersey* from mothballs, modernized her, and sent her to Southeast Asia in September 1968. There she fired hundreds of rounds in a

short-lived operational period that ended the following year when she was decommisioned to save money.

A decade later, the nation was humiliated by the seizure of U.S. hostages in Iran, an event that helped Ronald Reagan win the presidency. His administration set out to rebuild the nation's defense forces, which had eroded since the end of the Vietnam War, and no ship symbolized the tradition of the U.S. Navy more than the battleship. All four ships of the *Iowa* class were recommissioned and modernized with the addition of long-range missiles, giving battleships an offensive role for the first time since before World War II. They rejoined the fleet at two-year intervals, beginning in 1982, and performed a variety of missions, including firing in anger in support of U.S. peacekeeping forces in Lebanon during 1983–1984.

In 1990, following its victory in the Cold War against the Soviet Union, the United States drew down its defense forces, as it had after Vietnam. However, when Iraqi forces invaded Kuwait, *Wisconsin* and *Missouri* received a brief reprieve. Their planned decommissioning was delayed, and they fired hundreds of rounds at enemy targets from the Persian Gulf. In February 1991 the short Gulf war ended in a victory for the United States and its Coalition allies. The event marked the final combat use of U.S. battleships. In March 1992, nearly a century after the nation commissioned its first battleships, it decommissioned its last, the venerable *Missouri*. Now, she and other old dreadnoughts serve as floating museums and symbols of a bygone era in naval warfare.

Above: *Flame billows from the 16-inch guns on board the battleship* Wisconsin *(BB 64), the concussion sending ripples through the water. The same guns that pounded Pacific islands during World War II also struck targets in Iraq during the 1991 Gulf war. (Naval Historical Center)*

command of the seas, arguing that naval preeminence is achieved by concentrating a fleet to defeat that of an opponent. Mahan's influential treatise comes at a time of heated debate on the expansion of the U.S. Navy and the strategy for its employment.

30 June
Though Secretary of the Navy Benjamin F. Tracy's first annual report calls for the construction of twenty armored battleships to provide the Navy adequate strength to defend the nation, Congress authorizes only three. Christened *Indiana* (BB 1), *Massachusetts* (BB 2), and *Oregon* (BB 3) and commissioned in 1895–1896, the ships displace some 10,000 tons each and boast an armament of four 13-inch guns.

30 July
Responding to unrest in Buenos Aires, Argentina, the side-wheel steamer *Tallapoosa* lands a detachment of Marines to guard the American legation in the city.

29 November
The first game of the epic gridiron rivalry between the U.S. Naval Academy and the U.S. Military Academy is played at West Point, New York, with the Navy team achieving a shutout victory by the score of 24 to 0.

1891

3 March
Vacant since shortly after the end of the Civil War, the post of Assistant Secretary of the Navy is reinstituted. James Russell Soley, a former U.S. Naval Academy professor, is selected for the office, which over the course of the next three decades is occupied by future presidents Theodore and Franklin Roosevelt.

2 June
The screw sloop *Kearsarge* lands Marines in response to civil disorder on Navassa Island in the Caribbean.

28 August
A landing party from the cruisers *Baltimore* (C 3) and *San Francisco* (C 5) goes ashore at Valparaiso, Chile, to protect the U.S. Consulate during the Chilean Civil War.

Opposite: *Army squares off against Navy in the first game of perhaps the most storied rivalry in college football. (U.S. Naval Academy)*

Right: *The landing party from the protected cruiser* Boston *during inspection in front of their station at the Arlington Hotel in Honolulu, Hawaii, at the time of the overthrow of the monarchy, January 1893. (Naval Historical Center)*

Below: *The forward compartment of the berth deck in* Boston, *1888. The mess tables suspended from the overhead are triced up when not in use. (Naval Historical Center)*

16 October

A liberty party from the cruiser *Baltimore* quarrels with a mob of Chileans at the True Blue Saloon in Valparaiso, Chile, resulting in the death of two American bluejackets and injury to sixteen others. The Chilean foreign minister's negative remarks made in the wake of the incident deepen the crisis.

1892

21 January

President Benjamin Harrison demands an apology for the Chilean foreign minister's remarks in connection with the 16 October 1891 incident at the True Blue Saloon. Six days later, with the United States having threatened to break diplomatic negotiations, Chile issues a formal apology and pays an indemnity of $75,000 to the families of the dead sailors.

19 July

Congress authorizes construction of the battleship *Iowa* (BB 4).

1893

16 January

American settlers in Hawaii, their efforts aided by the presence of Marines landed from the protected cruiser

Boston, overthrow the monarchy of Queen Liliuokalani in Honolulu, Hawaii, and establish a provisional government. The Americans, consisting primarily of pineapple growers, establish the Republic of Hawaii the following year.

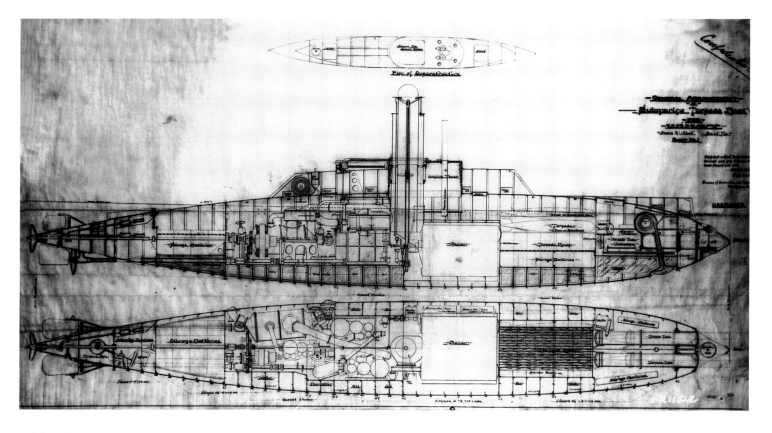

7 March
Hilary A. Herbert, a former officer in the Confederate Army and a one-time chairman of the House Naval Affairs Committee, takes office as the thirty-third Secretary of the Navy.

1 August
The Navy commissions its first armored cruiser, *New York*. During her builder's trials the previous May, the ship reaches a speed of 21.09 knots.

2 February
The screw sloop *Kearsarge*, victor over the Confederate raider *Alabama* during the Civil War, wrecks on Roncador Reef in the West Indies. All members of the vessel's crew are rescued eight days later. The venerable name *Kearsarge* is quickly assigned to one of the new fleet of battleships under construction, the only one not named after a state.

Above: *Plans for* Plunger, *which included a steam power plant. Her cancellation in 1900 made* Holland *the Navy's first submarine. (National Archives)*

Left: *Battleship* Texas *at sea in 1898. Note her decorative bow ornament, common on warships of the era. (Naval Historical Center)*

Opposite: *The ill-fated battleship* Maine *steams into Havana Harbor, Cuba, on 25 January 1898. (Naval Historical Center)*

A World War II aircraft carrier and a modern amphibious landing ship will also carry on the name.

6 July
Unrest in Nicaragua prompts the landing of sailors and Marines from the cruiser *Columbia* (C 12) to protect American lives and property at Bluefields.

24 July
A landing party of fifty sailors and Marines from the cruiser *Baltimore* goes ashore at Seoul, Korea, to protect the American legation in that city after Japanese forces land in Korea during the Sino-Japanese War.

1895

2 March
Continuing the expansion of the Navy, Congress authorizes the construction of two battleships, *Kearsarge* (BB 5) and *Kentucky* (BB 6).

8 March
Demonstrating the importance of maintaining a wide-ranging naval presence in the world, on the same day half a world apart landing parties from the cruisers *Baltimore* and *Atlanta* go ashore at Chefoo, China, and Boca del Toro, Colombia, respectively to protect American interests in a time of unrest.

13 March
The Navy awards a contract for a submarine to the John P. Holland Torpedo Boat Company of New York. This is the first *Plunger*, canceled in 1900 with the funds credited toward a new *Plunger* (SS 2).

15 August
The battleship *Texas* is commissioned, thus becoming the first battleship to serve in the U.S. Navy. With her main battery located off-center, *Texas* is eventually classified as a second-class battleship in the wake of the commissioning of more advanced designs featuring centerline main battery turrets.

17 September
Maine, originally classified an armored cruiser but redesignated a second-class battleship while under construction, is commissioned. Her career is destined to last less than three years, ending in one of the most momentous events in the history of the U.S. Navy.

20 November
Indiana, the first battleship to bear a hull number and the first of the so-called first-class battleships featuring centerline turrets, is commissioned. She is the first of a class of three battleships that includes *Massachusetts* and *Oregon*. All are in commission by July 1896.

FATEFUL SERVICE:
THE BATTLESHIP *MAINE*

by Dana M. Wegner

By the late 1890s the people of Cuba had a long history of violent rebellion against their often-oppressive Spanish colonial rulers. Fueled by the popular press, the United States government was concerned about the human rights of Cubans, the safety of American citizens, and U.S commercial interests on the island. In 1897 the U.S. Navy designated the second-class battleship *Maine* to protect American interests in the region. She cruised off Florida and in the Gulf of Mexico in a high state of combat readiness, on call to be sent to Cuba to rescue American citizens, show the flag, or fight. Commissioned in 1895, *Maine* was the largest and most heavily armed ship in the fleet that could operate within the confines of the harbor at Havana.

Spanish authorities were caught by surprise when President William McKinley turned up the heat and *Maine* entered Havana Harbor on 25 January 1898 to pay an extended "friendly" visit. Secretly, the ship was ready for combat and was heavily guarded by its seasoned crew. Local authorities coolly, but cordially, welcomed Captain Charles D. Sigsbee and his officers. After remaining anchored in the harbor for three uneventful weeks, at 9:40 P.M. on the night of 15 February 1898, *Maine* blew up, the devastating explosion ultimately killing 266 of her crew. It would be the largest single loss of American sailors until the Japanese attack on Pearl Harbor, Hawaii, in 1941.

With the tangled wreck of *Maine* protruding above the surface of Havana Harbor, a U.S. Navy Court of Inquiry, composed of three line officers, was convened on 21 February to determine the cause of the explosion. While the court was in session the United States mobilized for war with Spain. A month later the Court of Inquiry announced that the forward magazines of the ship had exploded and the cause of the explosion had been a mine planted under the ship by unknown saboteurs. A month later, precipitated by the court's finding, and spurred

by the newspapers proclaiming, "Remember the *Maine*!" the U.S. declared war on Spain. When the ninety-day-long Spanish-American War ended, Spain ceded to the U.S. Puerto Rico, Guam, the Virgin Islands, and temporary control of the Philippine Islands and Cuba, making the United States a nascent global power.

The total number of American combat deaths during the Spanish-American War was about 100 more than the number killed on board *Maine*. No attempt was made to determine or apprehend those who allegedly destroyed the ship and, to this day, no

one has come forward to claim credit for the deed or to accuse others of the act.

The wreck of the battleship remained in Havana Harbor until the U.S. Army Corps of Engineers refloated her in 1912. During that Herculean effort the Navy's Board of Inspection and Survey briefly reexamined the wreck and affirmed that a mine had sunk *Maine*. The hulk of the battleship was towed to deep water off Cuba and, with great and solemn ceremony, on 16 March 1912 the battleship was committed to her azure sepulchre.

Since 1898 naval officers, engineers, and historians had questioned the official pronouncement that a mine had sunk *Maine*. In 1975 the matter was reinvestigated by an interdisciplinary team of scientists, engineers, and historians under the direction of Admiral Hyman G. Rickover, the powerful head of the U.S Navy's nuclear propulsion program. The team reviewed plans, models, and dozens of photographs taken of *Maine*'s wreck and applied modern expertise regarding the effects of explosives on ships. The Rickover team determined that there was no evidence that the explosion that destroyed *Maine* originated from outside the ship. The most likely cause of the explosion was spontaneous combustion of coal in a bunker adjacent to one of her forward magazines. Thus, the loss of *Maine* in 1898 was a tragic, coincidental, and convenient accident.

Opposite: *Both a reminder to midshipmen of the Navy's heritage and a testament to the dangers of service at sea, the foremast of* Maine *sits on the waterfront at the U.S. Naval Academy. The power of the blast that sank the battleship is evident in the damage to the mast's platform. The ship's main mast is in Arlington National Cemetery.*

Above: *Divers conduct salvage operations on the wreckage of the battleship* Maine *in the aftermath of an explosion that caused her to sink in Havana Harbor, Cuba. This view shows the forward section of the ship. (Naval Historical Center)*

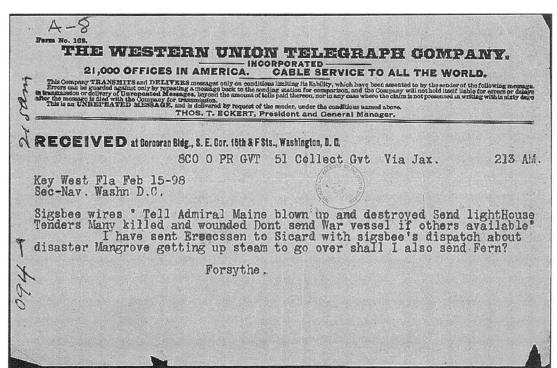

1896	1897

2–4 May

A landing party from the gunboat *Alert* goes ashore at Corinto, Nicaragua, to protect American lives and property during a period of unrest.

10 June

Congress authorizes construction of an experimental ship-model testing tank at the Washington Navy Yard, D.C.

6 March

Former Governor of Massachusetts John Davis Long takes office as the thirty-fourth Secretary of the Navy. He assumes the helm of a Navy that ranks sixth in the world in terms of size.

16 June

The battleship *Iowa*, the only ship of her class, is commissioned.

A-8

Form No. 108.

THE WESTERN UNION TELEGRAPH COMPANY.
——— INCORPORATED ———
21,000 OFFICES IN AMERICA.   CABLE SERVICE TO ALL THE WORLD.

This Company TRANSMITS and DELIVERS messages only on conditions limiting its liability, which have been assented to by the sender of the following message. Errors can be guarded against only by repeating a message back to the sending station for comparison, and the Company will not hold itself liable for errors or delays in transmission or delivery of Unrepeated Messages, beyond the amount of tolls paid thereon, nor in any case where the claim is not presented in writing within sixty days after the message is filed with the Company for transmission.

This is an UNREPEATED MESSAGE, and is delivered by request of the sender, under the conditions named above.

THOS. T. ECKERT, President and General Manager.

RECEIVED at Corcoran Bldg., S. E. Cor. 15th & F Sts., Washington, D. C.

8CO O PR GVT   51 Collect Gvt   Via Jax.   213 AM.

Key West Fla Feb 15-98
Sec-Nav. Washn D.C.

Sigsbee wires " Tell Admiral Maine blown up and destroyed Send lightHouse Tenders Many killed and wounded Dont send War vessel if others available"
      I have sent Ereecssen to Sicard with sigsbee's dispatch about disaster Mangrove getting up steam to go over shall I also send Fern?

                        Forsythe.

Above: *The U.S. Navy was born amidst a war with Great Britain, a far cry from these American and British sailors who served in a joint landing force that went ashore in Bluefields, Nicaragua, in 1898 to protect lives and property during turmoil in the nation. (Naval Historical Center)*

Left: *A Western Union telegram delivered to the Secretary of the Navy announcing the news of the sinking of the battleship* Maine. *(National Archives)*

1898

25 January

The battleship *Maine* arrives in Havana Harbor, Cuba, her dispatch "an act of friendly courtesy" on the part of the United States after Spain's agreement to change its policy with respect to Cuban independence. It proves to be a fateful decision.

7 February

The gunboat *Alert* puts a landing party ashore at San Juan del Sur, Nicaragua, to protect American lives and property during political turmoil in that nation.

15 February

An explosion sinks the battleship *Maine* anchored in Havana Harbor, Cuba, killing 266 members of her 358-man crew. A subsequent court of inquiry headed by Captain William T. Sampson concludes that the battleship's sinking is the result of an underwater mine, igniting a wave of anger on the part of Americans against Spain. "Remember the Maine" becomes a rallying cry for an entire nation. Subsequent research points to an internal cause of the explosion, heat from a fire in one of the ship's coal bunkers igniting the ammunition in an adjacent magazine. Ironically, a report delivered to the Secretary of the Navy less than a month before *Maine*'s sinking pointed to the danger of this occurring.

9 March

In the wake of the *Maine* disaster and deteriorating relations with Spain over its handling of the insurrection in Cuba, Congress passes the so-called Fifty Million Bill, appropriating the sum of $50 million dollars for national defense. More than half of this total is earmarked for the U.S. Navy.

Above: *The battleship* Kentucky *(BB 6) ready for launching at the Newport News Ship Building Company, Virginia, 24 March 1898. Note the hull fittings chalked onto plates. (Naval Historical Center)*

THE BATTLE OF MANILA BAY

by Dr. Brian M. Linn

For many Americans the vision of Commodore George Dewey standing on the bridge of the cruiser *Olympia* (C 6) at the Battle of Manila Bay, Philippines, embodies the rise of the United States to world power. As tensions with Spain escalated over Cuba in the 1890s, strategists advocated using the U.S. Navy's Pacific forces to launch a secondary attack on Spanish possessions in the Philippines. Believing war was imminent, Assistant Secretary of the Navy Theodore Roosevelt helped secure the appointment of his friend Commodore George Dewey—a Civil War veteran and a tough, no-nonsense sailor—to command the Asiatic Squadron. Assuming his duties on 1 January 1898, Dewey labored to bring the squadron into fighting condition. By 26 April, the day he received notice that war had broken out, Dewey had six warships under his command—the flagship *Olympia*, the armored cruisers *Boston, Baltimore* (C 3), and *Raleigh* (C 8), and the gunboats *Concord* (PG 3) and *Petrel* (PG 2). Leaving port immediately, he reached the entrance to Manila Bay late on the evening of 30 April.

Although they had accurate information on the American plans, the Spanish naval and military officials had done little to prepare. Admiral Patricio

Montojo's squadron—consisting of two old and unarmored cruisers, the *Reina Cristina* and the *Castilla*, and the gunboats *Don Juan de Austria, Don Antonio de Ulloa, Isla de Cuba, Marques del Duero*, and *Isla de Luzon*—was inferior to Dewey's ships in every way. Not only were the four major American warships armored, they also possessed more powerful guns, greater speed, and better trained crews. In contrast, the best Spanish warship, the *Reina Cristina*, was so vulnerable to shellfire that cargo vessels, loaded with sand, were anchored around her.

Dewey had received word that the Spanish had placed coastal artillery on the islands at the entrance to Manila Bay and had mined its waters. He calculated that a night passage would nullify the Spanish artillery and that the strong currents and the deterioration caused by tropical waters would render the mines ineffective. At midnight, Dewey and *Olympia* led the squadron into Manila Bay. His courageous gamble paid off. Save for four shots that fell harmlessly, the Spanish batteries did not contest his passage, and none of his ships struck a mine. Once past the entrance, Dewey steamed toward Manila, where he expected the Spanish squadron to have anchored under the protection of the city's shore-based artillery. However, Montojo feared that this might result in the bombardment of Manila, and had instead anchored his ships in a crescent formation across Cañacao Bay, near the naval base of Cavite, some three miles to the southeast. When early morning revealed the absence of the enemy ships in front of Manila, Dewey turned south toward the waiting enemy.

Dewey's six warships formed a column of attack, roughly two hundred yards apart from each other, with *Olympia* in the lead. At 5:15 A.M. the shore batteries at Manila opened up. Unfazed by this ineffective fire, Dewey's squadron turned west and began running parallel to Cañacao Bay. When they had approached to within 5,000 yards, Dewey calmly told the *Olympia's* captain, "You may fire when you are ready, Gridley." One of *Olympia's* massive 8-inch

guns thundered, immediately followed by the rest of the squadron's guns. The American warships steamed across the Spanish line, turned, and steamed past again, making a total of five passes, the last one at less than 2,000 yards, sending a torrent of fire—almost 6,000 shells—at their opponents, who fought bravely, but ineffectively.

Two hours into the fight, Dewey received a garbled message revealing that *Olympia* had almost exhausted her ammunition. He broke off the fight and conferred with his captains, who explained that they had more than enough ammunition. The pause allowed the smoke from the guns to clear, and it was soon obvious that the Spanish squadron had been severely damaged. *Castilla* was on fire; *Reina Cristina* and one of the gunboats were so damaged that they would soon sink. Montojo pulled his battered remnants back further into Cañacao Bay, but when Dewey's squadron returned to the fight shortly before noon, the Spanish soon raised the white flag.

They had lost 161 killed and another 210 wounded and their ships were in ruin. The Americans had nine sailors wounded.

Coming less than a week after the declaration of war, the victory created great public enthusiasm for the U.S. Navy and made Dewey a national hero. His leadership prompted a grateful Congress to award him in 1903 the rank of Admiral of the Navy, the only officer ever to receive this honor.

Above: *Led by Commodore George Dewey's flagship,* Olympia, *ships of the Asiatic Fleet blast the Spanish fleet defending the Philippines in the Battle of Manila Bay. The first victory of the Spanish-American War also put the United States on the path to acquiring the Philippines as part of a burgeoning empire. (Naval Historical Center)*

Opposite: Olympia *leads a column of cruisers, circa 1900. ("USS* Olympia," *Francis Muller, Navy Art Collection)*

18 March
Under the command of Acting Commodore Winfield Scott Schley, a "Flying Squadron"—composed of the armored cruiser *Brooklyn* (ACR 3), the battleships *Texas* and *Massachusetts*, and the cruisers *Columbia* and *Minneapolis* (C 13)—begins operating in the Atlantic Ocean to protect the East Coast of the United States.

19 March
The battleship *Oregon*, demonstrating the mobility of the modern warship, sails from San Francisco, California, for Jupiter Inlet, Florida, traveling over 14,000 miles in sixty-seven days. During the voyage she averages a speed of nearly 12 knots.

24 March
Captain William T. Sampson, head of the investigation into the sinking of the battleship *Maine*, relieves Rear Admiral Montgomery B. Sicard in command of the North Atlantic Squadron. Sampson is soon promoted to the rank of rear admiral.

25 March
Assistant Secretary of the Navy Theodore Roosevelt recommends the appointment of officers to evaluate a flying machine under development by Professor Samuel P. Langley and determine its applicability as a weapon of war. Though Langley's machine is ultimately unsuccessful, when the Navy commissions its first aircraft carrier in 1922, she carries the name *Langley*.

11 April
After the Spanish government ignores an ultimatum issued by President William McKinley demanding independence for Cuba, the chief executive asks Congress for the authority to intervene militarily.

19 April
Congress gives President William McKinley the authorization to use force in expelling the Spanish from Cuba, attaching to the bill an amendment promising that the United States will not annex the island nation. Six days later Congress makes a formal declaration of war. Over the course of the Spanish-American War, the Navy adds 128 ships, increases enlisted personnel from 12,500 to 24,123, and adds 1,038 officers.

22 April
In one of his first measures after the act of 19 April, President William McKinley orders a blockade of Cuba by the North Atlantic Squadron, which puts to sea on this day. Shortly after departing, the gunboat *Nashville* (PG 7) encounters the Spanish freighter *Buenaventura*, firing two shots across her bow before capturing her. These are the first shots of the Spanish-American War. The following day, the North Atlantic Squadron arrives off Cuba and sets a blockade of four ports.

25 April
Secretary of the Navy John D. Long orders ships of the Asiatic Squadron under the command of Commodore George Dewey to proceed from Hong Kong to the Philippine Islands and commence offensive operations against the Spanish fleet. Dewey's ships depart two days later, and arrive off Luzon on 30 April.

27 April
Fire from the armored cruiser *New York*, the cruiser *Cincinnati* (C 7), and the monitor *Puritan* (BM 1) silence Spanish batteries at Matanzas, Cuba, that had previously fired on the U.S. torpedo boat *Foote* (TB 3).

1 May

Ships of the Asiatic Squadron, having been ordered to employ "utmost endeavors" in capturing or destroying vessels of the Spanish fleet in the Philippines, enter Manila Bay. Commodore George Dewey arranges his fleet in column formation with his flagship, the cruiser *Olympia*, in the lead, followed by the cruisers *Baltimore* and *Raleigh* (C 8), the gunboats *Petrel* (PG 2) and *Concord* (PG 3), and the cruiser *Boston*. The Spanish commander, Rear Admiral Don Patricio Montojo, chooses to keep his ships at anchor off Sangley Point, thus creating a stationary battle line. "You may fire when you are ready, Gridley," Dewey tells the commanding officer of *Olympia*, Captain Charles V. Gridley, at 5:40 a.m., after which the American ships begin blasting the Spanish fleet at a range of 3,000 yards. Over the course of the next two hours, Dewey's gunners fire 5,859 shots, and although less than three percent of them hit their target, every one of the Spanish vessels is hit at least once. After breaking for breakfast, the American fleet renews the bombardment at 11:00 a.m., eventually sinking or burning Montojo's entire fleet. No U.S. ship is hit by enemy fire.

2–3 May

A landing party from the gunboat *Petrel* occupies the Spanish naval arsenal at Cavite in the Philippines, while Marines from the cruisers *Baltimore* and *Raleigh* capture the island of Corregidor in Manila Bay.

4 May

Congress passes a naval act providing for the construction of three battleships, sixteen torpedo boat destroyers, twelve torpedo boats, and one gunboat, the largest building program since the Civil War.

Opposite: *The armored cruiser* New York *signals ships maintaining the Spanish blockade in Cuba. ("Keeping the Blockade," Henry Reuterdahl, Navy Art Collection)*

Above: *George Dewey, shown on board* Olympia, *was appointed a rear admiral after the Battle of Manila Bay, and was promoted to Admiral of the Navy in 1903. (Naval Historical Center)*

Below: Oregon *made an epic 14,000 mile voyage from San Francisco to join the fleet off Cuba. Her voyage was later cited as evidence of the need for the Panama Canal. (Naval Historical Center)*

11 May

Boat parties consisting of volunteers from the cruiser *Marblehead* (C 11) and the gunboat *Nashville*, commanded by Lieutenants C. M. Winslow and E. A. Anderson, respectively engage in a daring expedition to disable Spanish communications between Cuba and Madrid. Approaching to within 100 yards of the shore at Cienfuegos, Cuba, the men dredge up two cables and cut them, conducting their work for a period of two and one-half hours while under enemy fire. All told, four men are killed or mortally wounded and seven others are wounded.

The torpedo boat *Winslow* (TB 5), under Lieutenant John B. Bernadou, makes a run into the harbor at Cárdenas, Cuba, to attack a Spanish gunboat. She is hit three times by Spanish shore batteries, with one

shot disabling her steering. Towed to safety by the revenue cutter *Hudson*, *Winslow* suffers four men killed and three wounded, the latter including Bernadou. Among the dead is Ensign Worth Bagley, the only naval officer killed in action during the Spanish-American War.

In a most unusual circumstance during time of war, Theodore Roosevelt resigns the post of Assistant Secretary of the Navy to join the Army in the hope of seeing combat in Cuba. Charles Herbert Allen replaces him on this day.

12–19 May

Ships of the North Atlantic Squadron under Rear Admiral William T. Sampson search for a Spanish squadron under Rear Admiral Pascual Cervera y Topete. During the search Sampson's squadron bombards San Juan, Puerto Rico, but never meets the enemy fleet. On 19 May Sampson directs the "Flying Squadron" under Commodore Winfield Scott Schley to blockade the Cuban port of Cienfuegos. On that same day Cervera's ships arrive at Santiago, Cuba.

24–28 May

Upon learning from signal communications with Cuban insurgents that the Spanish squadron they seek is not at Cienfuegos, Commodore Winfield Scott Schley, whose fleet has operated off the city since 21 May, sets course for Santiago. En route he determines that the difficulty of coaling his ships at sea necessitates a return to Key West, Florida. However, on 27 May, with calm seas having enabled the battleship *Texas* to take on coal, Schley reverses course and heads for Santiago. On 28 May a scouting of Santiago by the cruiser *Marblehead* confirms the presence of the Spanish fleet, and a blockade is established. Rear Admiral William T. Sampson later criticizes Schley's conduct of

the search, one element of a bitter dispute between the two men that affects the upper echelons of the Navy.

31 May
The battleships *Massachusetts* and *Iowa*, in concert with the cruiser *New Orleans*, bombard fortifications at Santiago, Cuba.

1 June
Rear Admiral William T. Sampson, with the armored cruiser *New York*, the battleship *Oregon*, and the torpedo boat *Porter* (TB 6), and the auxiliary cruiser *Mayflower*, arrives off Santiago. He assumes command of all U.S. naval forces off Santiago.

3 June
Congress authorizes a medal to be awarded to the participants in the Battle of Manila Bay, Philippines, the U.S. Navy's first official campaign medal.

As part of a daring plan to block the narrow channel leading into Santiago Harbor, thus bottling up the Spanish squadron, seven sailors under Lieutenant Richmond P. Hobson attempt to scuttle the collier *Merrimac* in the channel. Fire from Spanish shore batteries thwarts the attempt, and the vessel sinks at the edge of the channel. Hobson and his men are pulled from the water by a Spanish launch. All eventually receive the Medal of Honor, Hobson by a special Act of Congress in 1933 given the fact that officers were not eligible for the decoration at the time of his actions.

6 June
U.S. naval forces operating off Santiago bombard Spanish fortifications guarding the channel leading into the harbor, and engage the enemy cruiser *Reina Mercedes*.

7–15 June
A testing of the defenses at Guantanamo Bay, Cuba, by the cruiser *Marblehead* and auxiliary cruiser *Yankee* on 7 June is followed three days later by the landing of Marines at the location, the first American forces to set foot on the island. Over the course of the next four days, the dispatch boat *Dolphin* supports the leathernecks in operations against Spanish forces nearby. On 15 June gunfire from *Marblehead*, the battleship *Texas*, and the auxiliary cruiser *Suwanee*

Opposite, top: *A dramatic depiction of the death of Ensign Worth Bagley as the torpedo boat* Winslow *(TB 5) is fired upon by Spanish shore batteries off Cárenas, Cuba, 11 May 1898. ("Engagement Off Cardenas," Henry Reuterdahl, Navy Art Collection)*

Opposite, bottom: *Boats from* Nashville *and* Marblehead *cut telegraph cables off Cienfuegos, Cuba, on 11 May 1898, while under fire. Their ships are returning fire from the background. (Naval Historical Center)*

Above: *Ships on station off Cuba not only blockaded the Spanish fleet, but also supported Marines like these pictured at Guantanamo. (Naval Historical Center)*

THE NAVAL BATTLE OF SANTIAGO DE CUBA

by Mark L. Hayes

The American tactical victories at San Juan Hill and El Caney, Cuba, on 1 July 1898 forced Spanish admiral Pascual Cervera to make a decision—either attempt an escape from Santiago or remain and face certain capture. He had dreaded having to make this decision since the day he brought his squadron into the Cuban port. His ships were in no condition to challenge the most powerful elements of the U.S. fleet, having been forced by the Spanish government to sail for Cuba before they were ready. Two 10-inch guns had not yet been installed in the new armored cruiser *Cristóbal Colón*. Two of the 5.5-inch guns in *Vizcaya* and one in *Almirante Oquendo* were useless, and only one out of seven shells available for these guns actually fit into the breech. Cervera's crewmen had little gunnery practice, and almost all the shore batteries at the mouth of the harbor were obsolete, some dating back to the eighteenth century. Although they were designed to make 20 knots, foul bottoms and the availability of only low-grade coal

at Santiago slowed the speed of the modern armored cruisers to no more than 14 knots. In short, Spain had sent a naval squadron unprepared to fight, to operate from a base incapable of supporting its needs.

Arrayed outside the entrance to Santiago de Cuba were the armored cruiser *Brooklyn* (ACR 3) along with the battleships *Texas*, *Oregon* (BB 3), *Iowa* (BB 4), and *Indiana* (BB 1) and the armed yachts *Gloucester* and *Vixen*. Yet, it was a fleet without its commander, for Rear Admiral William T. Sampson and his flagship *New York* (ACR 2) had left the formation at 4:00 A.M. to meet farther up the coast with Major General William R. Shafter regarding the next stage of operations. It was at this time that Cervera's fleet attempted its breakout. Just before 9:30 A.M. on 3 July 1898, lookouts spotted a column of smoke moving toward the entrance. Alarms were sounded and, three minutes later, the American warships were underway with guns ready to shoot, ammunition on hand, fire hoses laid out, and watertight hatches shut.

Cervera's flagship, the armored cruiser *Infanta Maria Teresa*, emerged from the narrow channel and steamed straight for *Brooklyn*. The Spanish admiral hoped that by ramming and disabling the fastest of the American blockaders, the rest of his squadron would have a better chance to escape. The U.S. armored cruiser turned sharply to starboard and avoided the oncoming Spanish flagship, but in doing so, it nearly collided with *Texas*. *Infanta Maria Teresa* took a terrible beating as the battleships concentrated their fire on their adversary. Although the Spanish constructed their steel cruisers from modern designs, old traditions of gracing their warships with large amounts of ornate woodwork remained, with deadly results for her crew. The wood on *Infanta Maria Teresa* easily caught fire from the explosions of American shells. In addition, one hit severed the ship's fire main (the pipe carrying water for fighting shipboard fires), leaving her crew with no means to extinguish the blaze. Now a raging inferno, the ship turned to starboard to avoid being rammed and at 10:15 A.M. Cervera was grounded on shore.

Almirante Oquendo received similar treatment from the American battleships, and at 10:35 a.m., only minutes after coming under concentrated fire, the second Spanish cruiser grounded, a blazing wreck. Taking advantage of the attention given to their cohorts, the cruisers *Cristóbal Colón* and *Vizcaya* cleared the destruction near the mouth of the channel and headed west along the coast. The last Spanish vessels to enter the open sea were the destroyers *Pluton* and *Furor*. Medium caliber shells from the battleships rained down from long range, but ironically the unprotected armed yacht *Gloucester* delivered the coup de grace. Lieutenant Commander Richard Wainwright, who had survived the explosion on board the battleship *Maine* four and a half months earlier, commanded the outmanned and outgunned yacht, and directed his crewmen to "get at them quickly." Rapidly closing the range, *Gloucester*'s gun crews pummeled the Spanish destroyers with their rapid-firing three-pounder and six-pounder guns. Within twenty minutes both of Cervera's destroyers were in flames, and *Furor* surrendered to Wainwright after an American shell smashed the doomed vessel's steering gear.

The rest of the battle was a running fight as the blockading vessels attempted to get up enough steam to pursue the fleeing *Cristóbal Colón* and *Vizcaya*. Ranges between the combatants were often greater than the American crews had trained for and longer than their range finders could handle. Eventually, the steady course maintained by the combatants simplified the gunnery problem. *Vizcaya* ran on shore at 11:15 a.m., after fires started by American shells spread out of control. The chase for the remaining cruiser ended over two hours later when shells fired from *Oregon* bracketed *Cristóbal Colón* and the Spanish captain turned his ship toward shore, grounding her at 1:30 P.M. Cervera had lost his entire squadron, with 474 casualties, including 323 killed, while the American fleet suffered little damage to its ships with one killed and ten wounded.

Although one-sided, the naval battle of Santiago de Cuba had a strong influence on subsequent developments in the U.S. Navy. Many officers pushed for rapid improvements in gunnery techniques and technology when they discovered that only 1.29 percent of American shots fired in the battle actually hit their targets. The ease with which the Spanish ships went up in flames validated past decisions to break free from traditional ship designs and placed a high priority on damage control. The victory also confirmed noted naval strategist and educator Alfred Thayer Mahan's emphasis on control of the seas in time of war, and set the U.S. Navy on a course of continual growth and improvement.

Opposite: *Rear Admiral Winfield Scott Schley commanded the "Flying Squadron" off Cuba and, in the absence of Rear Admiral William T. Sampson on 3 July 1898, commanded the North Atlantic Squadron in the Battle of Santiago. (Naval Historical Center)*

Above: *Having waited for months for the Spanish fleet to sortie from Santiago, Cuba, and attempt to break the blockade, the ships of the North Atlantic Squadron were ready on 3 July 1898. When the smoke cleared after the Battle of Santiago, every Spanish ship had either been destroyed or surrendered. (Alfonso Sanz, Navy Art Collection)*

Left: *Wrecks of Spanish ships on the beach near Santiago, Cuba, testify to the U.S. Navy's victory in the 3 July 1898 battle. (Naval Historical Center)*

Opposite, top: *Flags flying from the armored cruiser* New York *(ACR 2) mark the end of the Battle of Santiago, 3 July 1898. (Naval Historical Center)*

Opposite, bottom: *Rear Admiral William T. Sampson commanded the North Atlantic Squadron off Cuba during the Spanish–American War. (William C. Loring, Navy Art Collection)*

destroys a Spanish fort at Guantanamo Bay. These actions combine to enable the Marines to consolidate their hold on the bay, which becomes a vital coaling station for Rear Admiral William T. Sampson's forces operating off Santiago.

21 June
The cruiser *Charleston* (C 2) captures the island of Guam, its Spanish colonial government unaware that their country is at war with the United States.

22 June
In action off San Juan, Puerto Rico, the auxiliary cruiser *St. Paul* disables the Spanish destroyer *Terror* as she attempts an attack.

28 June
The auxiliary cruiser *Yosemite*, operating as part of the blockade of San Juan, Puerto Rico, drives the Spanish supply ship *Antonio Lopez* onto a reef and destroys her with gunfire. *Yosemite* is successful in the face of support from two Spanish cruisers and a torpedo boat covering the supply ship's passage into San Juan.

1 July
The first American troops arrive in Manila Bay, Philippines, their transports having been escorted by the cruiser *Charleston*.

3 July
The Spanish fleet at Santiago, Cuba, attempts to break out into the open sea, led by the cruiser *Infanta Maria Teresa*. The cruiser *Brooklyn* (ACR 3), flagship of Commodore Winfield Scott Schley, initially turns away

before joining other ships in attacking the enemy. The battleships *Indiana*, *Iowa*, *Oregon*, and *Texas*, along with *Brooklyn*, open a devastating barrage against the four Spanish cruisers, driving *Infanta Maria Teresa* and *Almirante Oquendo* aground. *Oregon*, *Brooklyn*, *Texas*, and *Iowa* then pursue the remaining cruisers west along the coast of Cuba, pummeling *Vizcaya*, which in turn beaches. *Cristóbal Colón* proves more dogged in her attempt to outrun the pursuing American ships, but a long-range shot from one of *Oregon*'s 13-inch guns scores a damaging near miss that forces her to run aground. In addition to the four cruisers, the Spanish lose two destroyers. All told, the U.S. Navy loses one man killed and ten wounded, while the Spanish force suffers 474 casualties, including 323 killed in action. The overwhelming victory perpetuates the controversy between Schley and Rear Admiral William T. Sampson. The latter officer takes credit for the victory even though absent for much of the battle, as he was traveling on board the armored cruiser *New York* to confer with the commander of U.S. ground forces in Cuba. In addition, Schley receives criticism for the maneuvering of his flagship in the early part of the battle, which almost results in a collision with *Texas*.

4 July
A Spanish attempt to block the entrance to Cuba's Santiago harbor by scuttling the cruiser *Reina Mercedes* across the channel leading into it is thwarted by gunfire from the battleships *Massachusetts* and *Texas*. The cruiser is sunk, but is eventually raised by the U.S. Navy and becomes a station ship at the U.S. Naval Academy. Many a midshipman from the early part of the twentieth century recalls being sentenced

to confinement on board *Reina Mercedes* as punishment for some transgression.

17 July
Spanish forces at Santiago, Cuba, surrender the city to troops under the command of Major General William T. Shafter. The surrender comes seven days after a bombardment of the city by U.S. Navy warships, and results in the capture of eight Spanish vessels.

18–21 July
U.S. Navy gunboats, auxiliary cruisers and armed tugs conduct attacks along the Cuban coast. On 18 July a squadron enters Manzanillo harbor, destroying seven Spanish gunboats and one blockade runner, while three days later U.S. Navy warships bombard enemy fortifications at Nipe, and sink the Spanish light cruiser *Jorge Juan*.

21 July
U.S. Navy ships, including the battleship *Massachusetts*, the cruiser *Columbia*, and the auxiliary cruisers *Dixie*, *Gloucester*, and *Yale*, escort transports carrying troops under the command of Major General Nelson A. Miles to Puerto Rico. A naval landing party from *Gloucester* secures the landing site at Guánica on 25 July, and Miles's troops go ashore the following day.

28 July

The auxiliary cruiser *Dixie* accepts the surrender of the city of Ponce on the southern coast of Puerto Rico.

12 August

Officials of the governments of the United States and Spain agree to an armistice ending the Spanish-American War following negotiations in Washington, D.C. Though a formal peace treaty is not signed until 10 December, the armistice cedes Puerto Rico and Guam to the United States and grants independence to Cuba.

12–13 August

Unaware of the signing of the armistice in Washington, D.C., U.S. Navy warships shell the port of Manzanillo, Cuba, and capture it.

13 August

Under the terms of a secret agreement reached between Spanish authorities and Commodore George Dewey, the city of Manila, Philippines, surrenders after a token bombardment of Fort San Antonio by the cruiser *Olympia* and gunboat *Petrel*. Troops from the transport *Zafiro* occupy the city in the afternoon after Dewey's flag lieutenant raises the Stars and Stripes over Manila.

14 August

The armed lighthouse supply ship *Mangrove* fires upon two Spanish gunboats off Caibarién, Cuba, learning of the armistice when the enemy vessels raise

a flag of truce. These are the last shots fired during the Spanish-American War.

4 November
A Marine detachment from the cruisers *Baltimore*, *Raleigh*, and *Boston* goes ashore in Peking, China, to establish a U.S. Legation Guard in the city.

23 November
Paymaster W. B. Wilcox and Naval Cadet Leonard R. Sargent submit a report to Commodore George Dewey detailing their findings during a visit to the interior of Luzon. There the pair finds resistance to American control of the Philippines and preparations underway for insurrection against colonial rule. The report is too late to affect the annexation of the Philippines by the United States, but its contents prove accurate.

10 December
A formal peace treaty is signed between Spain and the United States in Paris, France. Under the terms of the agreement, the United States pays Spain the sum of $20 million for Puerto Rico, Guam, and the Philippines which, combined with the 7 July 1898 annexation of Hawaii, creates a far-flung empire that requires a strong Navy.

1899

17 January
The gunboat *Bennington* (PG 4) arrives at Wake Island. Her commanding officer, Commander E. D. Taussig, claims the island for the United States.

4 February
Filipino forces under General Emilio Aguinaldo attack American occupation troops in Manila, marking the beginning of the Philippine Insurrection. The following day the cruiser *Charleston*, the monitor *Monadnock* (BM 3), and the gunboats *Callao* and *Concord* provide gunfire support for a counterattack by U.S. troops outside Manila.

Opposite, top: *West Indies Naval Campaign Medal (Sampson Medal), 1898 . (Naval Historical Center)*

Opposite, bottom: *The gunboat* Bennington *in San Francisco Bay, circa 1894–1898. (Naval Historical Center)*

Above: *The first U.S. flag is hoisted over Fort Malate, San Antonio, Philippine Islands, during the Manila Campaign, 13 August 1898. (Naval Historical Center)*

11 February

The gunboat *Petrel* shells Filipino insurgents occupying a fort on Panay, which is then seized by a landing party. Eleven days later the gunboat captures the island of Cebu.

24 February

A landing party from the gunboat *Marietta* (PG 15) goes ashore at Bluefields, Nicaragua, to protect American interests.

2 March

Admiral George Dewey is promoted to the rank of Admiral of the Navy, the only man in the history of the U.S. Navy to ever hold that rank.

3 March

The signing of the Naval Personnel Act of 1899 merges engineering officers with line officers, the division of which is a long-standing source of conflict in the Navy's officer corps. The act also changes the U.S. Naval Academy curriculum to include more emphasis on engineering.

1 April

Put ashore in response to an outbreak of tribal warfare that threatens American and European consulates that

Above: A U.S. floating battery, pictured during an expedition up the Orani River near Manila, attempting to recover the small ex-Spanish gunboat Urdaneta, *which had grounded on 17 September 1899 and was captured by Filipino insurgents. (Naval Historical Center)*

Below: His predecessors had to master lines and canvas, but the new technology mandated new skills. This sailor on board the battleship Oregon *(BB 3) had to be proficient in operating an electric generator. (U.S. Naval Institute)*

administer the islands of Samoa, a landing party of American and British naval personnel is ambushed in the interior of Upolu Island. Seven men are killed and seven others wounded. Among the dead is the landing party commander, U.S. Navy Lieutenant Philip Van Horn Lansdale. The uprising is put down by 25 April.

10–13 June
U.S. Navy monitors and gunboats support offensives against Filipino insurgents in Cavite Province south of Manila.

18–23 September
The cruisers *Charleston* and *Baltimore* join the monitor *Monterey* (BM 6) and gunboat *Concord* in bombarding Filipino insurgent positions at Olongapo. Troops from the transport *Zafiro* seize the location, which controls Subic Bay.

25 September
The armed patrol boat *Urdaneta,* under Naval Cadet Welborn C. Wood of the U.S. Naval Academy Class of 1899, is ambushed while aground near Manila. Wood and four of his crew are killed while four other crewmen are captured in the firefight with Filipino

insurgents. *Urdaneta* is the only naval vessel lost to enemy action during the Philippine Insurrection.

8 October
The gunboats *Callao* and *Petrel* support Marine forces in their capture of an enemy stronghold at Novaleta, Philippines.

2 November
The cruiser *Charleston* wrecks on an uncharted reef near Camiguin Island in the Philippines. Fortunately, no crewmembers are lost.

26 November–10 December
Landing parties from the battleship *Oregon* and the cruiser *Baltimore* occupy Vigan and the navy yard at Olongapo on Subic Bay, Philippines. The latter is a vital strategic harbor for U.S. Navy warships for much of the twentieth century.

Above: *The gunboat* Petrel *employs both sail and steam while underway, though the former's days were drawing to a close. ("USS* Petrel,*" Francis Muller, Navy Art Collection)*

A NAVY FOR A
NEW CENTURY

1900-1918

A NAVY FOR A NEW CENTURY

1900-1918

Victory in the Spanish-American War thrust the United States increasingly into world affairs and sparked a naval renaissance. Embodying this transformation of the Navy and the nation was the dynamic figure of Theodore Roosevelt, who assumed the presidency upon the assassination of President William McKinley in September 1901. The most naval-minded chief executive to enter the Oval Office up until that time, Roosevelt had long been a student of the history of sea power and had served as Assistant Secretary of the Navy. "The Navy of the United States," he once said, "is the right arm of the United States and is emphatically the peacemaker." During his first term, he sought to strengthen the nation's right arm. The fleet increased by thirty-one ships during his first term alone, including ten battleships that in 1907–1909 would form the centerpiece of the "Great White Fleet" in an epic round-the-world voyage that symbolized the resurgent might of the Navy.

The strengthening of the Navy correlated with dramatic events. In June 1902 Congress approved an expenditure of millions of dollars for the construction of what would become the Panama Canal, increasing American presence in Latin America and building an avenue between the Atlantic and Pacific for merchant vessels and warships. During the first decade of the twentieth century, Navy ships were dispatched south to respond to crises in Panama and Venezuela, and in Roosevelt's famous speech regarding the Monroe Doctrine, in which he uttered the words, "Speak softly and carry a big stick," the big stick was the Navy. Another event occurred halfway around the world on 27 May 1905 when a Japanese fleet overwhelmingly defeated a Russian fleet in the Battle of Tsushima. Roosevelt would receive the Nobel Peace Prize for brokering a peace that ended the Russo-Japanese War, but clearly a new balance of power existed in the Pacific. The Navy responded with the creation of the Pacific and Asiatic Fleets and the development of a forward base at Pearl Harbor, Hawaii.

The Navy's emergence also coincided with a European arms race, with the chief contenders being Great Britain and Germany. In an effort to maintain its traditional place as the world's dominant naval power, the British turned to new technology, in 1906 commissioning *Dreadnought*. Boasting ten 12-inch guns, the behemoth displaced some 18,000 tons and possessed a top speed of 21 knots. She foreshadowed the future, and lent her name to the new type of modern battleships. The United States joined other nations in constructing its own dreadnoughts, commissioning *Michigan* (BB 27) in January 1910, the first of four American dreadnoughts completed during that year.

One of the young officers who served in *Michigan* was Lieutenant (junior grade) John Henry Towers, who applied for aviation duty after witnessing French pilots conducting aerial maneuvers during one of the battleship's port calls in Cherbourg, France. After dramatic demonstrations by civilian pilot Eugene Ely, during which he landed and took off from wooden platforms erected on board the cruisers *Birmingham* (CL 2) and *Pennsylvania* (ACR 4), the Navy ordered its first airplanes in 1911. Towers joined the cadre of adventurous men at the controls of the wood and fabric biplanes of the day, pioneering aviation in fleet exercises and actual operations, including America's first combat flights during the Veracruz intervention in

Veracruz intervention in Mexico in 1914. Among the experiments they conducted were aerial searches for submerged submarines, another weapon that appeared during the first years of the new century. The Navy took delivery of its first submarine, *Holland* (SS 1), in 1900, and in 1912 established a submarine flotilla under the command of Lieutenant Chester W. Nimitz as part of the Atlantic Fleet. Contrasting with the big-gunned battleships, fast destroyers joined the fleet beginning with the commissioning of *Bainbridge* (DD 1) in 1902, adding a new dimension to naval warfare that would be put to the test when the United States entered World War I in April 1917.

The American experience during the Great War lasted only nineteen months, and the actions of American doughboys on the ground and fighter aces jousting in the skies over the trenches largely overshadowed actions upon the sea. Yet the war proved a watershed event in the shaping of modern warfare, especially with respect to the Navy. Germany's unrestricted submarine warfare contributed greatly to American entry into the war. "We are ready now, sir," announced Commander Joseph K. Taussig on 4 May 1917, when his destroyer squadron became the first American warships to arrive in European waters. Indeed, U.S. destroyers were ready, contributing greatly to the war effort by shepherding convoys across the Atlantic, helping dramatically reduce the tonnage

sunk by enemy U-boats. The first American military forces to set foot in France were the members of the Navy's First Aeronautical Detachment, which arrived in June 1917. Naval aviation's greatest contribution to the war effort involved long-distance antisubmarine patrols from coastal air stations, but by war's end wearers of the wings of gold had flown fighter and ground attack missions with Allied squadrons and staged long-range bombing missions. Perhaps most importantly, they had witnessed British shipboard airplane operations, planting fertile seeds in the minds of air power advocates that eventually resulted in the aircraft carriers of the U.S. fleet.

When the guns fell silent in November 1918, the Navy numbered 774 ships, more than twice the number in service when America entered World War I, and 530,338 men and women wore the uniform of the sea service. Never before had the Navy marshaled such resources to fight such wide-ranging battles. In the course of service, whether plowing through the swells of the North Atlantic or soaring in the cockpit of a flying boat, important lessons were learned that would prove valuable when the Navy once again waged a world war.

A NAVY FOR A NEW CENTURY
1900-1918

1900

January
U.S. Navy gunboats capture the Batan Islands and support Army troops engaging insurgent forces in the Philippine Islands.

February
U.S. Navy gunboats operating in the Philippines support the capture of Biniktigan Village near Olangapo, cover landings at Perez in the Gulf of Ragay, and destroy an insurgent base camp at Pasacao.

10 February
Commodore Seaton Schroeder assumes duties as first naval governor of American Samoa. Nine days later President William McKinley places the administration of the island under the Navy Department.

20 February
The battleship *Kearsarge* (BB 5) is placed in commission, the only battleship not named for a state in the Union. She is the lead ship of a class of battleships that also includes *Kentucky* (BB 6).

5 March
During the Philippine Insurrection, the gunboat *Nashville* (PG 7) lands a detachment of Marines that supports Army forces in the capture of Calapacuan.

13 March
Avoiding the movement to create a general staff to control naval planning, the Secretary of the Navy instead establishes the General Board consisting of senior naval officers vested only with advisory powers. First headed by Admiral of the Navy George Dewey, the General Board conducts studies on war plans, shipbuilding, and personnel matters.

April
Gunboat operations in the Philippine Islands include the capture of the Filipino insurgent vessel *San Jose* by the gunboat *Paragua*, and support of the capture of the towns of Bailer and Calaguaquin on Luzon.

May
The gunboats *Pampanga* (PG 39) and *Paragua* participate in the capture of Masing and Santa Margarita on the island of Leyte in the Philippines, and combine to destroy four insurgent vessels in Philippine waters.

18 May
In response to the increasing wave of violence perpetrated by the Boxers, a secret society centered in North China opposing the presence of Western nations in the country, U.S. Minister to China Edwin Conger sends word of the seriousness of the situation in Peking and asks the Asiatic Fleet to send a landing force to help guard the American legation.

31 May
Fifty-six sailors and Marines from the cruiser *Newark* (C 1) and battleship *Oregon* (BB 3) land as part of an international force of 337 men from eight nations sent to guard the legations in Peking, China. The landing comes just nine days before the Boxers cut the telegraph line between Peking and Tientsin, thus isolating the legations.

June

Gunboats operating in the Philippines capture nine insurgent small craft and support the operations of ground forces on the island of Samar.

13 June

The Boxers attack an international force of 2,129 men under the command of Vice Admiral Sir Edward Seymour, KCB, en route by train from Tientsin, China, to reopen communications with Peking. The force, which includes 112 sailors and Marines from the cruiser *Newark*, is forced to retire on 17 June under heavy attack. Boxers, supported by troops of China's imperial government, are cutting the rail line faster than it can be repaired. Seymour and his men reach Hsiku Arsenal six miles from Tientsin on 22 June, and after beating back enemy attacks are rescued by a column from the city three days later.

16 June

The gunboat *Villalobos* captures her twenty-second insurgent vessel over the course of two months operating in Philippine waters.

17 June

The gunboat *Monocacy* takes fire from the Taku forts during a bombardment of the Chinese batteries there by an international force of warships. *Monocacy*, the only U.S. ship facing the forts, is ordered not to participate in the bombardment for fear of precipitating a war with China.

18 June

The gunboat *Nashville*, having made a high-speed run from Manila, Phillipines, disembarks a detachment of 140 Marines at Taku, China, to join Russian troops in the defense of Tientsin, which was captured from the Boxers by allied troops, including U.S. soldiers and Marines.

July

In the most intense month in support of offensive operations during the Philippine Insurrection, U.S. Navy gunboats capture and destroy twelve insurgent vessels and provide gunfire support for Army troops on Samar and Mindanao.

2–25 August

The gunboat *Pampanga* destroys nine insurgent bancas during operations in Philippine waters.

8–26 September

The gunboat *Panay* burns four insurgent small craft during operations in Philippine waters.

October

The gunboat *Paragua* captures two insurgent vessels and joins the gunboat *Callao* in the support of Army troops engaged at Carles, Balasen, Estancia, and Malabung in the Philippine Islands.

12 October

Holland (SS 1), the U.S. Navy's first submarine, is placed in commission. She is built as a private venture

by Irish-American John P. Holland, who writes in the December 1900 issue of the *North American Review*, "When the first submarine torpedo-boat goes into action, she will bring us face to face with the most puzzling problem ever met in warfare. She will present the unique spectacle, when used in attack, of a weapon against which there is no defense."

12 November

The gunboat *Bennington* supports the assault of Army forces against the town of Borongon on the island of Samar, Philippines. The town is captured after gunfire from *Bennington* prevents insurgents from setting fire to its buildings.

13 December

A typhoon hits Guam, wrecking the station ship *Yosemite* at Apra Harbor. Five members of her crew are lost.

1901

January

U.S. Navy gunboats score several successes during the Philippine Insurrection. Boat parties capture eighteen insurgent boats on the Imus River near Cavite on 2–3 January, and the unprotected cruiser *Don Juan of Austria* supports attacks against Donsol and Maringondon on the island of Luzon. During the latter part of January and into early February, *Don Juan of Austria* also lands parties that capture three villages on Luzon.

24 February–3 March

The gunboat *Villalobos* supports the operations of Army troops at Loorg Bay and Lubang Island, Philippines.

23 March

During a campaign on Luzon supported by the gunboat *Vicksburg* (PG 11), the insurgent leader General Emiliano Aguinaldo is captured by U.S. forces. Except for minor operations, this effectively ends the Philippine Insurrection, though another revolt by the Moslem Moros breaks out in the southern Philippine islands of Samar, Mindanao, and Jolo.

1 July

On this date, a total of sixty ships destined for service in the U.S. Navy are under construction. In the fall, Congress appropriates over $78 million for naval construction, to date the largest in history.

3–17 July

The armed vessel *Basco* engages insurgent forces in a series of actions on the Gandara River on the island of Samar, Philippines. Her commanding officer is naval cadet James H. Comfort, just thirteen months after his graduation from the U.S. Naval Academy.

16 September

The battleship *Illinois* (BB 7) is placed in commission. The lead ship of a class of three battleships that includes *Alabama* (BB 8) and *Wisconsin* (BB 9), she is the last ship of the class to be placed in commission. However, she serves much longer than her two sisters. Redesignated as a pierside training hulk in 1924 and renamed *Prairie State* in 1941, she is not stricken until 1956.

2–16 November

The gunboat *Vicksburg* shells insurgent trenches near Nipanipa on the island of Samar, Philippines. Two weeks later she lands a boat party to support Marine operations against insurgents operating along the Basey River on Samar.

18 November

The signing of the Hay-Pauncefote Treaty between the United States and Great Britain allows for the construction of a canal across Central America by the United States. The site eventually chosen is Panama.

24 November–4 December

The gunboats *Concord* (PG 3), *Machias* (PG 5), and *Marietta* (PG 15) join the battleship *Iowa* (BB 4) in landing Marines in Panama to protect American property during a period of unrest.

13 December

The final report of a court of inquiry headed by Admiral of the Navy George Dewey concludes the long-festering controversy between Rear Admirals William T. Sampson and Winfield Scott Schley. Convened at the request of Schley after questions about his conduct in the Spanish-American War are raised in a new edition of Edgar S. Maclay's book *History of the Navy*, the court is divided in its final decision. While the majority report criticizes Schley for his actions in the search for the Spanish Fleet in Cuba, a minority report, prepared by

Dewey, credits Schley with the victory at the Battle of Santiago. President Theodore Roosevelt upholds the verdict, but narrows the criticism of Schley in hopes of ending the divisive controversy. By the time of the verdict, Schley is already retired and Sampson is in ill health. He dies in May 1902.

1902

16–19 April
A landing party from the gunboat *Machias* goes ashore in Panama to protect American interests during unrest. This landing is followed by another from the survey ship *Ranger* in May and the putting ashore of Marines from the cruiser *Cincinnati* (C 7) and the transport *Panther* in September. The presence of the sizeable force allows Rear Admiral Silas Casey, commander of U.S. naval forces off the coast of Panama, to arrange a peace between Colombian troops and rebels in Panama in November.

1 May
William H. Moody, a Massachusetts congressman, takes office as the thirty-fifth Secretary of the Navy.

24 November
More than a century of tradition begins with the commissioning of the U.S. Navy's first destroyer, *Bainbridge* (DD 1).

29 December
Maine (BB 10), named for the battleship sunk in Havana Harbor, Cuba, in 1898, is commissioned. She is the lead ship of a class of three battleships that includes *Missouri* (BB 11) and *Ohio* (BB 13).

December–January 1903
Naval forces of Germany, Great Britain, and Italy blockade Venezuela in an effort to force the South American nation to pay debts. In response, President Theodore Roosevelt sends ships to the Caribbean under Admiral of the Navy George Dewey and takes a prominent role in negotiations. A peaceful settlement is reached, ending the potential crisis and heightening the reputation of the young American president.

Below: *William H. Moody, 35th Secretary of the Navy, 1 May 1902–30 June 1904. ("William H. Moody," Frank W. Benson, Naval Historical Center)*

23 February

In an effort to establish a presence in the Caribbean, the United States leases Guantanamo Bay, Cuba, which becomes the site of a strategic naval base. This land acquisition becomes increasingly important with the signing of a treaty between the United States and Cuba on 22 May 1903 granting America the right to intervene in the island nation to maintain order or preserve its independence.

21 March–16 April

The wave of revolution and unrest in Central America reaches Honduras, prompting the dispatch of the cruisers *Olympia* (C 6), *San Francisco* (C 5) and *Raleigh* (C 8), the gunboat *Marietta*, and the transport *Panther* to the waters off the nation. Upon arrival, the force lands Marines to protect the U.S. Embassy at Puerto Cortez.

1–19 April

The cruiser *Atlanta* puts ashore a landing party of Marines in the Dominican Republic to protect the U.S. Consulate at Santo Domingo during an insurrection.

2 April

During a speech in Chicago, Illinois, President Theodore Roosevelt tells the audience, "There is a homely old adage which runs, 'Speak softly and carry a big stick: you will go far.' If the American nation will speak softly, and yet build, and keep at a pitch of the highest training, a thoroughly efficient navy, the Monroe Doctrine will go far."

7–13 September

The armored cruiser *Brooklyn* (ACR 3) puts ashore a landing party of sailors and Marines at Beirut, Syria, to protect U.S. citizens and the American University during a period of unrest. The following month a landing party from the cruiser *San Francisco* spends a week in the city protecting American interests in the face of renewed unrest. It is the U.S. Navy's first extended exposure to a city that eighty years later is the backdrop for a tragic event in naval history.

17 October

The General Board issues a secret document calling for the construction of forty-eight battleships and auxiliaries by 1920. The report is not made public for a decade, but its conclusions influence Congress as the Navy expands during the first two decades of the twentieth century.

U.S. T.B.D. BAINBR
13-24-7.

4–6 November

A renewed rebellion in Panama in the wake of the failed Hay–Herrán Treaty providing the United States the right to construct and control a canal across the Isthmus of Panama prompts the gunboat *Nashville* to take action against Colombian forces on 4 November. Arriving at Colón on the Atlantic coast, *Nashville*'s skipper, Commander John Hubbard, puts ashore a landing party and takes control of the Panama Railroad, thus denying rail transport to a sizeable Colombian military force preparing to travel to Panama City in order to crush the rebellion. The following day, two companies of Marines go ashore at Colón from the transport *Dixie* and, on 6 November, the United States recognizes the independence of Panama.

18 November

American Secretary of State John Hay concludes a treaty with Philippe Bunau-Varilla, Panamanian ambassador to the United States, the provisions of which include the construction of a canal across the Isthmus of Panama and control of a canal zone. In return, the United States pays a sum of $10 million and an annuity of $250,000 and agrees to maintain the independence of Panama.

PRESIDENTS AND THE U.S. NAVY

by M. Hill Goodspeed

Even before he became the nation's first president, George Washington espoused the merits of naval forces, writing in 1780 that "a decisive naval superiority is to be considered a fundamental principle and the basis upon which all hope of success must ultimately depend." Washington and the men who have succeeded him as the nation's chief executive constitutionally hold the title of Commander in Chief of the armed forces, a responsibility that has connected them to the U.S. Navy. Yet, throughout our nation's history some presidents have possessed a special relationship to the naval service through a personal interest in matters of the sea or as onetime wearers of its uniform.

Of the early presidents, it was Massachusetts-born John Adams who more than any other championed a strong navy. His understanding of the importance of sea power dated to his days in the Continental Congress, where he led the fight to permit the outfitting of privateers and urged the creation of the Continental Navy, for which he drafted the first regulations. While Adams was president, he oversaw the creation of the Navy Department, naming its first secretary, and presided over a mobilization of American naval forces for the Quasi-War with France.

John Tyler is believed to have been the first Chief Executive to visit a Navy ship when, on 28 February 1844, he boarded the steam sloop *Princeton* for a demonstration of the vessel's capabilities. Fortunately, he was below decks when one of the warship's guns exploded upon firing, killing congressmen and cabinet members nearby. Over the course of the ensuing fifty-four years, only two presidents, Franklin Pierce and William McKinley, would visit naval vessels.

Though his military service consisted only of command of volunteers during the Black Hawk War, President Abraham Lincoln proved to be one of the most able wartime commanders in chief in our nation's history. In Gideon Welles, he appointed perhaps one of the most capable Secretaries of the Navy to ever hold the office. In addition, he recognized the importance of sea power to the ultimate defeat of the

Confederacy through the employment of a blockade, seizure of key Southern ports, and control of the Mississippi River. Among the frequent visitors to the Lincoln White House was naval ordnance expert Rear Admiral John A. Dahlgren. Though the presidents of the post-Civil War era are noted for their mediocrity and were no friends of the Navy, President Rutherford B. Hayes holds the distinction of being the first to employ a Presidential yacht, *Despatch*.

The turn of the century brought to the presidency Theodore Roosevelt, perhaps the most naval-minded Chief Executive. The nephew of James Bulloch, a Confederate agent responsible for securing the construction of the famed raider *Alabama* during the Civil War, Roosevelt was also a student of naval history, having published a study of the Navy's operations during the War of 1812. And if these naval credentials were not enough, he had served as Assistant Secretary of the Navy during the period 1897–1898. That the U.S. Navy emerged as a world power at the turn of the century was to a great extent the result of Theodore Roosevelt's championing of sea power, embodied in his dispatching of the "Great White Fleet" on its famous cruise around the world in 1907.

If Theodore Roosevelt was not the president most supportive of the Navy, the title would certainly be claimed by his relative, Franklin D. Roosevelt, whose path to the White House also led through the office of the Assistant Secretary of the Navy. Roosevelt made no secret of his preference for the sea service; Army General George C. Marshall once proclaimed during a meeting with the commander in chief, "Mr. President. Could you please stop referring to the Army as them and the Navy as us." Roosevelt loved the sea and in the prewar years oftentimes took a break from his official duties with cruises on board Navy warships. In 1941 it was the cruiser *Augusta* (CA 31) that carried him to his first meeting with British Prime Minister Winston Churchill, which resulted in the Atlantic Charter, and throughout World War II Navy warships carried him at least part of the way to his major conferences with

other Allied leaders. During the war, Roosevelt commanded a Navy that at its height numbered over 3 million men, among them six who in the ensuing years would follow him into the Oval Office.

In January 1961, John F. Kennedy took the oath of office as President of the United States, the first Navy veteran to become the nation's Chief Executive. A decorated. PT-boat skipper whose boat was sliced in half by a Japanese destroyer during a night mission in the Solomon Islands in August 1943, Kennedy appreciated his service in uniform, writing in 1963, "Any man who may be asked in this century what he did to make his life worthwhile, I think can respond with a good deal of pride and satisfaction, 'I served in the United States Navy.'" Kennedy selected as his Vice President Lyndon B. Johnson (Kennedy's successor following his assassination), who was a congressman at the time of the attack on Pearl Harbor, Hawaii, and went on active duty on 9 December 1941. He served as an observer in the South Pacific, receiving the Silver Star from the Army under questionable circumstances, before returning to Washington, D.C., in 1942. In January 1969 Richard Nixon became the third consecutive president to have served in the Navy during World War II. Achieving the wartime rank of lieutenant commander, he served in various aviation commands in the states and abroad. His successor, President Gerald R. Ford, trained aviation cadets and was a plank owner in the light carrier *Monterey* (CVL

26), serving in combat operations during 1943–1944. James E. Carter, wartime Naval Academy midshipman and eventually a submariner, followed Ford into office, the fifth consecutive Navy veteran to achieve the presidency.

The sixth president to have served in the Navy, George H.W. Bush was a torpedo pilot flying from the light carrier *San Jacinto* (CVL 30) during World War II. A recipient of the Distinguished Flying Cross, the Torpedo Squadron (VT) 51 pilot was shot down near Chichi Jima on 2 September 1944. The only man able to bail out of his crippled aircraft, he was rescued from certain captivity by a nearby submarine.

Whether they wore the uniform or not, presidents have traditionally relied on naval forces to protect American interests abroad. Whether it be John Adams rebuilding the fleet, called "the wooden walls of America," or presidents of the latter part of the twentieth century in a time of crisis asking the location of the nearest aircraft carrier, the Commander in Chief will always be able to call upon those who fight on, above, and under the sea.

Above: *With a sea of sailors as a backdrop, President George W. Bush addresses naval personnel at Naval Air Station Mayport, Florida, 13 February 2003. (U.S. Navy/Photographer's Mate Third Class Monica Nelson)*

Left: *With Mount Surmin rising in the background, the cruiser* Brooklyn *(ACR 3) shows the flag off Beirut, November 1903. (Naval Historical Center)*

Opposite, top: *John Hay, U.S. Secretary of State, in 1904. (Naval Historical Center)*

Opposite, bottom: Nashville *(PG 7) represented the "gunboat diplomacy" of the early twentieth century, serving in the Philippines, China, and the waters off Central America. (Naval Historical Foundation)*

18 December–15 January 1904
Nineteen Marines under the command of Captain George C. Thorpe and Navy Lieutenant Charles L. Hussey escort a U.S. diplomatic mission across the difficult terrain of Ethiopia to the capital city of Addis Ababa.

1904

3 January
The Marine detachment from the cruiser *Detroit* (C 10) goes ashore at Puerto Plata, Dominican Republic, in response to an insurrection in the island nation. Four days later, the cruiser puts Marines ashore at Sosúa.

5 January–23 April
In response to the requirement for guards at the U.S. legation in Seoul, Korea, the transport *Zafiro* lands 103 sailors and Marines. Though most are withdrawn in April, twenty-five remain until November 1905.

17 January
The cruiser *Detroit* is joined by the screw sloop *Hartford*, Admiral David G. Farragut's Civil War flagship, in putting ashore a landing party at Puerto Plata, Dominican Republic, to protect American citizens there during a period of unrest.

11 February
The escalating violence in the Dominican Republic shifts to the city of Santo Domingo as insurgent forces open fire on the steamer *New York*. In response, the cruisers *Columbia* (C 12) and *Newark* land a force of 300 sailors and Marines under

covering fire from the latter ship. The force expels the insurgents from the city by nightfall.

25–27 February
The Marine detachment from the training ship *Yankee* goes ashore at Santo Domingo, Dominican Republic, to protect the U.S. Consulate located in that city.

12 March
With the Russo-Japanese War raging in the Far East, the Marine detachment from the cruiser *Cincinnati* lands and evacuates U.S. citizens from Seoul and Chemulpo, Korea.

13 April
While the battleship *Missouri* conducts gunnery training in the Gulf of Mexico, a flareback from the port gun in her after turret ignites a powder charge and sets off two others. No explosion occurs, but the rapid burning of the powder suffocates thirty-six members of her crew. Three crewmen—Chief Gunner Robert Edward Cox, Chief Gunner's Mate Mons Monssen, and Gunner's Mate First Class Charles S. Schepke—receive the Medal of Honor for heroically braving flames to extinguish the fire.

30 May
The Marine detachment from the cruiser *Brooklyn* lands at Tangier in Morocco in response to the unlawful kidnapping of a naturalized American citizen by bandits. He is returned unharmed.

1 July
Railroader Paul Morton takes office as the thirty-sixth Secretary of the Navy. A letter of instruction from

President Theodore Roosevelt reads, "It is [the] military efficiency of the fleet which needs to receive most attention and as regards which there should be systematic development of policy."

6 December

In a message to Congress, President Theodore Roosevelt issues the so-called Roosevelt Corollary to the Monroe Doctrine, stating, "As a mere matter of self-defense we must exercise a close watch over the approaches to [the Panama] canal, and this means that we must be thoroughly alive to our interests in the Caribbean. The Monroe Doctrine may force the United States . . . to the exercise of an international police force." The most vital element in supporting this policy aimed at European nations attempting to make inroads in the Western Hemisphere is naval forces, which in coming years are instruments for increased American intervention in Central America and the Caribbean.

1905

20 January

With the cruiser *Detroit* patrolling the waters off the Dominican Republic, U.S. Navy and Marine Corps officers take control of that nation's customs service, improving its operations in an effort to reduce public debt.

3 March

The approval of Congress to construct the 16,000-ton battleships *South Carolina* (BB 26) and *Michigan* (BB 27) ends the first stage of President Theodore Roosevelt's building program in which the legislative branch authorizes ten battleships, four armored cruisers, and seventeen other ships displacing some 250,000 tons.

16 December

Seeking to demonstrate the ability to dispatch U.S sea power around the globe and mindful of the sheer pageantry of the undertaking, President Theodore Roosevelt orders the Atlantic Fleet's battleship divisions to begin what will turn into a round-the-world cruise. Sixteen battleships—*Alabama, Connecticut, Georgia, Illinois, Kansas, Kearsarge, Kentucky, Louisiana, Maine, Minnesota, Missouri, New Jersey, Ohio, Rhode Island, Vermont,* and *Virginia*—and their supporting vessels under the command of Rear Admiral Robley D.

"Fighting Bob" Evans, depart Hampton Roads, Virginia, on this date. Called the "Great White Fleet" by the press because of the gleaming white paint that adorns the hulls of its ships (the standard peacetime color scheme for U.S. Navy ships at that time), the force passes through the Strait of Magellan and proceeds up the west coast of South and Central America to San Francisco, California. Here *Alabama* and *Maine* are replaced by *Nebraska* and *Wisconsin*. After refitting, the Great White Fleet then heads west across the Pacific, stopping in Australia, New Zealand,

the Philippines, and Japan before entering the Indian Ocean. Passing though the Suez Canal, the ships enter the Mediterranean Sea and then cross the Atlantic Ocean, returning to Hampton Roads on 22 February 1909. The voyage encompasses some 46,000 miles and demonstrates the technological capabilities of modern warships and the true global reach of the U.S. Navy. "That is the answer to my critics," President Theodore Roosevelt proclaims while witnessing the return of the Great White Fleet. "Another chapter is complete, and I could not ask a finer concluding scene for my administration."

1908

1 February

The battleship *Mississippi* (BB 23) is placed in commission, lead ship of a class of battleships that also includes *Idaho* (BB 24). During her service *Mississippi* becomes the first ship in the history of the U.S. Navy to operate with airplanes.

1 April

The battleship *Idaho* is placed in commission. She is the last pre-dreadnought battleship built for the U.S. Navy. In the wake of the ship's commissioning, President Theodore Roosevelt sends a special message to Congress requesting construction of four more battleships.

13 May

The U.S. Navy Nurse Corps is established. Called the "Sacred Twenty," the initial nurses are the first women to formally serve in the Navy.

7 July

The destroyer *Decatur* (DD 5) runs aground in Batangas Harbor south of Manila Bay, Phillipines. The ship's commanding officer, Ensign Chester W. Nimitz, faces a court-martial, but is found guilty of only "neglect of duty," thus preserving the career of the man who will go on to command the U.S. Pacific Fleet during World War II.

Below: *U.S. warships in Havana Harbor, Cuba, 22 September 1906, (l–r):* Virginia *(BB 13),* Louisiana *(BB 19),* Newark *(C 1), and* Des Moines *(C 15). Visible beyond* Louisiana's *third funnel is the wreck of the battleship* Maine. *(Naval Historical Center)*

THE GREAT WHITE FLEET

by Commander John D. Alden, U.S. Navy (Retired)

Their guns blasting a departing salute to President Theodore Roosevelt, sixteen gleaming white-hulled battleships set forth from Hampton Roads, Virginia, on 16 December 1907, on what would become a 434-day, 42,227-mile odyssey circumnavigating the globe. Although their announced itinerary extended only to Magdalena Bay on the Pacific coast of Mexico, rumors abounded that the fleet might then continue on to Hawaii, the Philippines, or beyond. Many Americans were sure that the voyage was intended to give the world a sobering glimpse of United States might. While this was undoubtedly one of Roosevelt's objectives, it was not the overriding one. Although he stressed in his autobiography that his "prime purpose was to impress the American people," his motives were more complex—political, diplomatic, military, and personal.

In the latter half of his second term, Roosevelt was politically a "lame duck," but he was not about to admit it. Agitators were demonstrating against Japanese immigration and extremists in Japan were countering by demanding preparations for war. Wall Street was in financial panic and conservatives in the Republican Party were trying to undermine Roosevelt's plan to make William H. Taft his successor. As a final "grand gesture," what could be more impressive than to send the battle fleet on an unprecedented cruise around the world? It would distract the people's attention from domestic concerns, reassure residents of the West Coast, stimulate popular support for the continued expansion of the Navy, send peaceful messages to foreign friends and subtle warnings to potential enemies, and show opponents in Congress that the Commander in Chief was not to be thwarted. Most important of all, it would bring the Navy a long way toward readiness for war.

The battleships, from the seven-year-old *Kearsarge* (BB 5) of 11,540 tons to the new 16,000-ton *Kansas* (BB 21), indeed appeared warlike to the casual observer. So rapid was the pace of warship development, however, that all were recognized by

naval experts as obsolete in design. The British *Dreadnought*, exemplifying a radical new type of all-big-gun battleship, had been in service for over a year and the Navy's first two dreadnoughts were already taking shape in the building yards. Flaunting a fleet of obsolescent ships in anachronistic peacetime white would not impress knowledgeable military leaders as a symbol of American power, but it would impress them and their political superiors as evidence of the nation's determination and technological competence.

Little noticed by press and public, the battleships were accompanied by six of the Navy's first destroyers and their tender, a repair ship, and two refrigerated storeships. The hospital ship *Relief* joined the fleet on the West Coast. Although not intended to accompany the battleships around the world, the auxiliaries were the harbingers of the great logistic force that would ultimately enable the Navy to support itself for months away from homeports. Coal supplies presented a problem; U.S. stockpiles were few and far apart, so over forty colliers, mainly British, were hired to rendezvous with the fleet in foreign ports. The very audacity of trusting a fleet of coal-burning, reciprocating-engine ships to complete so long a cruise without embarrassing breakdowns would impress the naval architects and shipbuilders of any maritime nation. The great benefit to the Navy was to make its ships and men better prepared for war. None of its officers were experienced in handling large fleets, so what better way to provide such training than a serious cruise? Month-long gunnery exercises in Magdalena Bay and the Philippines would ensure major improvements in accuracy and fire control. Finally, giving the new ships a complete workout would reveal weaknesses in material, personnel, and organization.

The Great White Fleet's voyage took it through the Straits of Magellan and up to the West Coast of the United States, where its first stop was San Francisco, California. There, illness forced the fleet's commander, Rear Admiral Robley "Fighting Bob" Evans, to relinquish command to Rear Admiral

Charles S. Sperry. The fleet departed the West Coast on 7 July 1908, and would not return to the continental United States until the following year. During the intervening months the battlewagons made port calls in New Zealand, Australia, the Philippines, China, and Japan, before transiting the Suez Canal en route to a passage home via the Mediterranean and Atlantic. Though it on one occasion encountered a typhoon at sea, it was the swelling crowds at ports of call, not seas, that proved most prevalent.

When the outgoing president reviewed the returned fleet on George Washington's Birthday, 1909, all of his objectives had been accomplished. Political support for the expanding Navy had been assured, the fleet had left an aura of goodwill and respect around the world, new officers had risen to command, and serious lessons had been learned. When the salutes died down and the crowds dispersed, the battleships were quickly stripped of their gilded peacetime ornaments and their white paint was covered by a sober coat of gray. America had come of age as a naval power.

Above: *Using a gun turret as a pulpit, President Theodore Roosevelt, the father of the "Great White Fleet," addresses the crew of the battleship* Connecticut *(BB 18) upon her return to Hampton Roads, Virginia, February 1909. (Naval Historical Center)*

15 August
The first shipboard Navy post offices are established on board the transport *Prairie*, and the battleships *Illinois* and *Rhode Island*.

3–17 September
The Navy dispatches two official observers, Lieutenant George C. Sweet and Naval Constructor William McEntee, to the first military trials of the aircraft designed by Wilbur and Orville Wright held by the U.S. Army at Fort Myer, Virginia. The following November, Sweet becomes the first naval officer to ever fly in an aircraft.

1 December
Truman H. Newberry, former officer in the Michigan naval militia, is promoted from the post of Assistant Secretary of the Navy to become the thirty-ninth Secretary of the Navy.

1909

27 January
President Theodore Roosevelt forms the Commission on Naval Reorganization, also known as the Moody-Mahan Commission, which recommends an organization in the Navy Department consisting of five divisions, the heads of three of which form a military council to advise the Secretary of the Navy.

Opposite, top: (*"Great White Fleet," John Charles Roach, Naval Historical Center*)

Opposite, bottom: *Victor H. Metcalf, 37th Secretary of the Navy. ("Victor H. Metcalf," R. L. Partington, Naval Historical Center)*

Right: *The crew of the destroyer* Decatur *(DD 5), including her skipper, Ensign Chester W. Nimitz (seated fifth from right), pictured in 1907. (Naval Historical Center)*

The commission's plans do not make it out of committee in the Senate, but reflect the growing sentiment for reform in administration of the Navy.

3 March
Thwarting a November 1908 effort by President Theodore Roosevelt to remove Marine detachments from naval vessels and place them ashore as a standby force, Congress passes a measure requiring that at least 8 percent of the personnel complement on board U.S. Navy ships consist of leathernecks.

6 March
George von Lengerke Meyer, a Massachusetts native and former U.S. ambassador to Italy and Russia, takes office as the fortieth Secretary of the Navy.

6 April
On his seventh expedition to the Arctic, having lost all but two of his toes to frostbite, Commander Robert E. Peary, a Civil Engineer Corps officer on leave from the Navy, reaches the North Pole in company with his African-American assistant Matthew Henson and four Inuit. "My life work is accomplished," he records in his diary. "The thing which it was intended from the beginning that I should do, the thing which I believed could be done, and that I could do, I have done. I have got the North Pole out of my system."

1 December
Administrative reform within the Department of the Navy results in the creation of four divisions within the department, dealing with fleet operations, materiel, inspections, and personnel. Each is headed by an "aide," who reports directly to the Secretary of the Navy and advises him on matters pertaining to his specific division. Admiral of the Navy George Dewey endorses the plan, and Congress grants it a trial period of one year. As part of the reorganization, Secretary of the Navy George von Lengerke Meyer also restricts the terms for bureau chiefs to eight years. In 1915 the post of aide for operations develops into that of Chief of Naval Operations.

18 December
In response to a revolution in Nicaragua against the dictatorship of President José S. Zelaya, during which two American citizens fighting with the rebel forces are captured and executed, Marines are dispatched to the Central American nation on board the transport *Buffalo*. Remaining embarked off Corinto, they are joined by other leathernecks stationed in Panama. They are never sent ashore, for Zelaya resigns after the United States severs diplomatic ties with his government.

Left: *"The Sacred Twenty" of the Navy Nurse Corps. (l–r): Mary R. DuBose, Adah M. Pendleton, Elizabeth M. Hewitt, Della V. Knight, J. Beatrice Bowman, Lenah S. Higbee, First Superintendent of Nurses, Martha E. Pringle, Esther V. Hasson, Elizabeth J. Wells, Sara B. Myer, Clare L. DeCeu. Back row: Elizabeth Leonhardt, Estelle Hine, Ethel R. Parsons, Florence T. Milburn, Bonigace T. Small, Victoria White, Isabel Rose Ray, Margaret D. Murray, Sara M. Cox. (Naval Historical Center)*

1910

4 January

The battleship *Michigan* (BB 27) is placed in commission. Displacing 16,000 guns and boasting a main battery of eight 12-inch guns complemented by twenty-two 3-inch guns, she is the U.S. Navy's first dreadnought, the term applied to all "big-gun" battleships after the commissioning of *Dreadnought* by the Royal Navy in 1906. *Michigan*'s sister ship, *South Carolina* (BB 26), is commissioned less than two months later.

4 April

The battleship *Delaware* (BB 28) is commissioned. She displaces 20,380 tons with a main battery of ten 12-inch guns complemented by fourteen 5-inch guns.

11 April

The battleship *North Dakota* (BB 29) is commissioned.

19 May

When government forces employ an armed steamship to blockade rebel forces at Bluefields, Nicaragua, the United States lands bluejackets and Marines from the gunboats *Dubuque* (PG 17) and *Paducah*. Once ashore the men establish so-called neutral zones to protect American lives and property. The gunboats alternate duty, one shuttling Marines from Panama to Bluefields while the other prevents the armed steamship from blockading and bombarding Bluefields. The leathernecks remain at Bluefields until 4 September.

22–30 October

Captain Washington Irving Chambers serves as an official observer at the International Air Meet at Belmont Park, New York, an event that impresses upon him the potential of aviation as an element of naval operations. A former battleship skipper who is assigned the then-unenviable task of handling Department of the Navy correspondence related to aviation, Chambers becomes one of naval aviation's earliest advocates and eventually serves as the first Director of Naval Aviation.

14 November

Eugene Ely, a civilian stunt pilot, successfully nurses a Curtiss pusher aircraft into the air from a wooden platform erected on board the cruiser *Birmingham* (CL 2) anchored at Hampton Roads, Virginia. Thus, the twenty-four-year-old pilot becomes the first to ever take off from a ship.

23 December

Responding to the offer of aircraft manufacturer Glenn Curtiss to provide flight training to a naval officer, the Navy Department orders Lieutenant Theodore G. Ellyson to San Diego, California, Curtiss's winter training site. "Spuds" Ellyson is eventually designated the first naval aviator.

31 December

At the end of the year, the U.S. Navy boasts a total tonnage of 717,202 with an additional 824,162 tons under construction, ranking second in the world only to Great Britain.

Right: *Commander Robert E. Peary on board the steamer* Roosevelt *with some of his sled dogs at about the time of his expedition to the North Pole in 1909. Note the explorer's fur garment to ward off the cold. (National Archives)*

Below: *Navy recruiting poster, circa 1909. (Naval Historical Center)*

1911

18 January
Further demonstrating the possibility of aircraft operating from ships, Eugene Ely successfully lands a Curtiss pusher aircraft on a wooden platform built on board the armored cruiser *Pennsylvania* (ACR 4) anchored in San Francisco Bay, California. Hooks on his aircraft engage a series of ropes weighted down by sandbags, bringing the aircraft to a stop. After a brief time aboard, Ely takes off from the ship and returns to shore. Tragically, the young pilot dies a few months later, the victim of a crash during an aerial exhibition in Macon, Georgia.

26 January
Airplane manufacturer Glenn Curtiss conducts the first successful "hydroaeroplane" flight at North Island, San Diego, California.

1 February
The cruiser *Tacoma* puts ashore a landing party to protect American citizens at Puerto Cortez, Honduras, during a revolution in that nation. Later in the month a peace treaty ending the revolution is concluded on board the ship.

8 May
With Congress having appropriated the sum of $25,000 for naval aviation, Captain Washington Irving Chambers draws up contract specifications for the first naval aircraft. Although no approval for expenditures is granted on this date, it is considered the birthday of U.S. naval aviation.

YOUNG MEN WANTED FOR U.S. NAVY.

PAY $17⁶⁰ TO $77⁰⁰ PER MONTH AND ALLOWANCES. BOARD, LODGING, MEDICAL-ATTENDANCE AND FIRST OUTFIT OF UNIFORM FREE.

AN OPPORTUNITY FOR PROMOTION LIBERAL PAY TO THOSE WHO PROVE EFFICIENT

1 July

The Navy's first aircraft, the Curtiss A-1 Triad, makes its first flight from Lake Keuka at Hammondsport, New York. During the five-minute flight, the airplane reaches an altitude of twenty-five feet.

31 August

The battleship *Utah* (BB 31) is placed in commission. Her first skipper is Captain William S. Benson, who later in his career serves as the first Chief of Naval Operations. Her sister ship, *Florida* (BB 30), is commissioned fifteen days later. *Utah* eventually becomes a training and target ship and is sunk during the Japanese attack on Pearl Harbor, Hawaii, on 7 December 1941.

September

With most naval aviators having been trained by aircraft manufacturers up until this time, the Navy establishes an aviation camp at Annapolis, Maryland. Located at Greenbury Point at the Navy Engineering Experiment Station across the Severn River from the U.S. Naval Academy, the camp is a makeshift establishment. Such is the respect accorded naval aviation at this time that the camp is located at the end of the midshipmen's rifle range, forcing personnel to vacate the camp on some days lest errant rounds fly into the tent hangars.

24 September

A landing party from the gunboat *Pampanga* captures Mundang on the island of Basilan, Philippines, after a fiercely fought engagement in which the bluejackets brave intense fire to root out the defenders from concealed positions in huts. Five sailors receive the Medal of Honor for their actions in the close quarters engagement.

4–14 November

The outbreak of the Chinese Revolution, which had prompted a reinforcement of the legation guard at Peking in October, also necessitates the landing of twenty-four Marines from the cruiser *Albany* (CL 23) and the transport *Rainbow* to guard the cable station at Shanghai.

24 November

The armored cruiser *Saratoga* (ACR 2) is dispatched from Shanghai to Taku, China, where she lands Marines to protect American missionaries.

14 December

The armored cruiser *California* (ACR 6) steams through the channel entrance to Pearl Harbor, Hawaii, marking the opening of the Navy's new fleet base. Just over thirty years later, on another December day, Pearl Harbor is attacked by Japanese carrier aircraft and among the ships sunk is the battleship *California* (BB 44).

1912

February

Off San Diego, California, Airplane manufacturer Glenn Curtiss demonstrates the capability of the hydroaeroplane with a flight to the armored cruiser *Pennsylvania*, where he is hoisted aboard by crane. After spending time on board, Curtiss and his aircraft are lowered onto the water for the return flight to shore. The hydroaeroplane is essential to the demonstration of aviation's adaptability to naval purposes.

19 May

The month after the sinking of the giant luxury liner *Titanic*, which hits an iceberg in the North Atlantic, the cruiser *Birmingham* embarks on the first American ice patrol, a task that is assumed by the U.S. Coast Guard when an International Ice Patrol is established in 1914.

28 May

Revolution in Cuba forces the hurried dispatch of Marines to the island nation on board the transport *Prairie*. Between this date and 5 June, two regiments go ashore, eventually garrisoning twenty-six towns and guarding railways.

16 July

Rear Admiral Bradley Fiske receives the first patent for a design of an air-launched torpedo. This is but one of the noted naval officer's inventions, which include an electrically powered gun turret, telescopic sight, electromagnetic system for detonating torpedoes under ships, and electric range finder.

27 July

In a successful test of airborne wireless communication, Lieutenant John Rodgers, the Navy's second aviator, and Midshipman Charles Maddox successfully transmit the letter D in Morse code to the torpedo boat *Bailey* (TB 21) from the cockpit of the Wright B-1 hydroaeroplane flying over the Chesapeake Bay. The message is picked up at a distance of one mile.

4 August

A revolutionary uprising in Nicaragua against the government of President Adolfo Diáz prompts the landing of 100 sailors and Marines at Corinto from the gunboat *Annapolis* (PG 10). The force proceeds to Managua to guard the American legation in the capital city, and on 15 August is joined by Marines of the Panama Battalion.

Opposite, top: Michigan's *(BB 27) crew mans the rails during the New York Naval Review, 3 October 1911. (National Archives)*

Opposite, bottom: *Pennsylvania (ACR 4) fitted with a temporary wooden deck for Eugene Ely's flight in January 1911. Note the canvas positioned at the end of the deck in case of an errant landing. (Naval Historical Center)*

Right: *The A-1 Triad, upon whose wings U.S. naval aviation took flight, pictured at Hammondsport, New York, 1911. (Naval Historical Center)*

17 August

A landing party of bluejackets and Marines from the cruiser *Tacoma* goes ashore at Bluefields, Nicaragua, to maintain order in the coastal town.

24 August

With their fellow leathernecks responding to crises in Central America, a company of Marines begins going ashore from the transport *Rainbow* at Shanghai, China, in order to protect American citizens and their property. The landings are completed two days later.

28 and 30 August

Continuing the buildup of American forces in Nicaragua, the armored cruiser *California* lands a battalion consisting of 364 sailors and Marines at Corinto on 28 August. Two days later a landing party goes ashore at San Juan del Sur from the cruiser *Denver* (C 14).

4 September

The transport *Buffalo* reaches Corinto, Nicaragua, after passage from Philadelphia, Pennsylvania, and puts ashore 790 men of the First Provisional Marine Regiment under the command of Colonel Joseph H. Pendleton. The following day they are joined by 323 bluejackets and leathernecks from the armored cruiser *Colorado* (ACR 7).

17 September

The battleship *Arkansas* (BB 33) is placed in commission, followed twelve days later by her sister ship *Wyoming* (BB 32).

4 October

With ground forces in Nicaragua attempting to seize control of rail transportation in the country, Marines and the landing battalion from the armored cruiser *California* storm rebel positions on Coyotope Hill overlooking the railway near the town of Masaya. The

hill is captured and among the dead found is rebel leader General Benjamin Zeledón, apparently shot by his own men.

6 October
Some 1,200 sailors and Marines capture the town of León located between Corinto and Managua. The force suffers six casualties, but the capture of this stronghold effectively ends organized resistance in Nicaragua. Pendleton's regiment begins embarking on the transport *Buffalo* the following month, though Marines are left behind to guard León and the legation at Managua.

12 November
His previous attempt having ended with his aircraft crashing into the Severn River in Maryland, Lieutenant Theodore G. Ellyson makes a successful catapult launch in the A-1 hydroaeroplane from a barge anchored in the Anacostia River off the Washington Navy Yard, D.C. The development of a successful catapult is vital if aircraft are to be operated from ships at sea.

30 November
With Lieutenant Theodore G. Ellyson at the controls, the Navy's first flying boat, the Curtiss C-1, undergoes flight testing at Lake Keuka in Hammondsport, New York. Flying boats play an essential role in naval aviation operations for the next half-century.

1913

1 February
Operating in the former Marine Barracks at the U.S. Naval Academy in Annapolis, Maryland, the Naval Postgraduate School begins classes.

5 March
Josephus Daniels, a North Carolina newspaper editor whose term in office will greatly impact the naval service, becomes the forty-first Secretary of the Navy. He soon names young Franklin D. Roosevelt to the post of assistant secretary.

6 March
Flying the C-1 flying boat, naval aviators Lieutenant John H. Towers and Ensign Godfrey DeC. Chevalier participate in tactical maneuvers at Guantanamo Bay, Cuba, successfully spotting approaching battleships and enabling an attack by destroyers. This successful demonstration of naval aviation's potential to influence sea battles is a high point of aviation's first participation in the fleet's annual winter maneuvers in the Caribbean.

10 April
The Secretary of the Navy approves performance standards for qualification as a Navy Air Pilot. On 22 March 1915 the designation is changed to Naval Aviator, which it remains to this day.

RECRUIT TRAINING:
THE MAKING OF A SAILOR

by M. Hill Goodspeed

Traditionally, the education of a sailor came at sea, with lessons learned from older and more experienced mariners. Yet, as the Navy transitioned from sail to steam and weapon systems became increasingly complex, there arose a need for specialized training common to all who entered the naval service. For the better part of a century, young people aspiring to serve in the U.S. Navy have boarded trains and buses to take them to training stations established all over the country. Whether it be wartime facilities constructed to meet the needs of global conflict, or at such familiar places as Great Lakes, Illinois, San Diego, California, and Norfolk, Virginia, the mission has remained the same. It is during recruit training that civilians are instilled with order and discipline and learn the value of teamwork, so important at sea where the effectiveness of a ship depends upon shipmates working toward a common goal. They learn the traditions of the sea service and its unique vernacular. Floors become decks and walls

become bulkheads as recruits become men and women of the sea. And at the end of the grueling process, they can proudly wear the uniform that around the world will identify them by the proudest of titles—sailor.

As the 1940 edition of *The Bluejackets' Manual* stated to new recruits on the eve of world war, "You are now beginning a naval career. You enlisted for various reasons, such as to learn a trade, to see the world, to go to sea, to improve your station in life. . . . You are young and your future is before you. . . . The training that starts here at the training station will continue on board ship. In every case this training is for the sole purpose of making you a useful man, a trained man, and a leader of men." It is a quote that still applies to today's recruits who, like their predecessors, are driven by the desire to serve their country above, under, and upon the sea.

Above: *A ship model serves to indoctrinate recruits at Naval Training Station Newport, Rhode Island, with some of the duties they will be called upon to carry out in the fleet, 1940. (Hulton-Deutsch Collection/CORBIS)*

Left: *During "Battle Stations," the final segment of their basic training at Naval Training Center Great Lakes, Illinois, recruits practice procedures for abandoning ship, which may one day save their lives on the high seas.(U.S. Navy/Photographer's Mate First Class Michael Worner)*

Above: *Sailors assemble for their first formation with rifles on the parade ground at Naval Training Station San Diego, California, circa 1930s. (National Museum of Naval Aviation)*

Left: *Since it was first published in 1902,* The Bluejackets' Manual *has served as a cornerstone in the education of every sailor, imparting valuable lessons on generations of recruits including this one at Naval Training Center Great Lakes, Illinois, in 2002. The Navy decided to build the training station at Great Lakes in 1903, and it welcomed its first recruits in 1911. Today, it is the Navy's sole location for recruit training. (U.S. Navy/Journalist 1st Class Preston Keres)*

20 June

While making a test flight in the Wright B-2 hydroaeroplane, Ensign William D. Billingsley and Lieutenant John H. Towers encounter a gust of wind over the Chesapeake Bay. The gust lifts the tail of the aircraft severely, putting it into a steep dive that catapults Billingsley out of the aircraft. He falls some 1,500 feet to his death, while Towers manages to hang onto the aircraft and somehow survives when it hits the water. The accident marks naval aviation's first fatality and makes safety belts standard on all Navy aircraft.

7 July

The cruiser *Albany*, in response to unrest in Shanghai, China, lands her Marine detachment to protect American interests in the city.

5–7 September

Marines put ashore from the transport *Buffalo* evacuate American citizens from Ciaris Estero, Mexico, a nation in the throes of a revolution that the following year will actively involve the U.S. Navy.

7 October

A board headed by Captain Washington Irving Chambers, consisting of both flying and non-flying officers, is appointed to consider the future requirements for naval aviation. When the Chambers Board releases its report, it includes recommendations for the establishment of an Office of Naval Aeronautics within the Navy Department and the selection of Pensacola, Florida, as the site for an aeronautic station. The panhandle town becomes famous as the "Cradle of Naval Aviation."

1 January

In an effort to reform education in the Navy, Secretary of the Navy Josephus Daniels mandates off-duty academic and practical instruction for enlisted men, a policy that takes effect on this date. In a similar vein he later initiates a policy in which 100 enlisted men with at least one year of service are made eligible to compete for entry into the U.S. Naval Academy.

20 January

The Navy's modest aviation force, which consists of nine officers, twenty-three enlisted men, and seven aircraft, arrives at Pensacola, Florida, to establish the first aeronautic station. Facilities at the recently closed navy yard are in a state of disrepair, and tent hangars are erected on shore to protect the flying machines against the Florida sun.

28 January–9 February

Operating as part of a multinational force including British, French, and German troops, Marines from the battleship *South Carolina* go ashore to maintain order in Port-au-Prince, Haiti, during a revolution in that nation.

16 February

Congress authorizes the creation of a naval militia to supplement active duty forces in times of war.

12 March

The battleship *Texas* (BB 35) is placed in commission, joined the following month by her sister ship, *New York* (BB 34). *Texas* will unleash salvoes on beaches at Normandy and Iwo Jima during World War II and survives as a war memorial at San Jacinto, Texas.

9 April

A U.S. Navy boat party consisting of an officer and eight bluejackets is detained for one-half hour while taking on a supply of gasoline at Tampico, Mexico. The following day, Rear Admiral Henry T. Mayo, the commander of the Atlantic Fleet's Fourth Division operating in the waters off Mexico, demands the firing of a 21-gun salute and a formal apology for the unlawful seizure. On 11 April Mexican President Victoriano Huerta issues a formal apology, but refuses to fire the salute, which enrages U.S. President Woodrow Wilson.

14 April

President Woodrow Wilson orders the Atlantic Fleet to Mexican waters after rejecting a request by the Mexican government that any 21-gun salute to the

Opposite, top: California *(ACR 6), pictured before she was renamed* San Diego *in 1914. She was sunk by mines from U-156 on 19 July 1918. (Naval Historical Center)*

Opposite, bottom: *Heavily armed Nicaraguan rebels pictured on an armored train during the period of U.S. intervention, circa 1912–1913. (Naval Historical Center)*

Right: *Loaded down with gear, sailors of a landing force from* Denver *(C 14) board a train for transport back to their ship after action in Nicaragua, 1912. Note the "Homeward Bound" pennant flying from the locomotive. (Naval Historical Center)*

Left: *The Curtiss C-2 flying boat. (National Museum of Naval Aviation)*

Below: *Secretary of the Navy Josephus Daniels pictured with Rear Admiral Edward W. Eberle, Superintendent of the U.S. Naval Academy, circa 1915. (U.S. Naval Academy)*

Opposite: *Albany (CL 23) at anchor at Shanghai, China, circa 1910. Then and now, U.S. Navy warships serve to show the flag in distant regions of the world. (Naval Historical Center)*

American flag in apology for the 9 April Tampico incident be returned by the United States. Wilson sets 18 April as a deadline for Mexico to fire the salute.

18 April

News reaches Washington from the U.S. consul at Veracruz, Mexico, informing officials of the impending arrival of the German steamer *Ypiranga* carrying a cargo of arms for delivery to the Mexican government. Determined that the arms should not reach the military dictatorship of President Victoriano Huerta and angered by the delay in firing the 21-gun salute after the 9 April Tampico incident, President Woodrow Wilson asks Congress for the authority to employ armed force on 20 April.

21 April

Though the Senate has yet to approve the use of force in Mexico (it does not do so until 23 April), President Woodrow Wilson orders the Navy and Marine Corps into action. With the German steamer *Ypiranga* scheduled to arrive on this date, Rear Admiral Frank Friday Fletcher is directed to seize the customs house at Veracruz in order to prevent the steamer's cargo of arms from being loaded onto trains and transported to Mexican authorities. At 1030 a force of 502 Marines from the transport *Prairie* and 285 leathernecks and bluejackets from the battleship *Florida* goes ashore. Despite the fact that Fletcher sends word to the Mexicans of the impending landing and offers one last chance for a peaceful settlement, an armed force consisting of cadets from the Mexican Naval Academy,

members of the home guard, private citizens, and even prisoners released from the city jail stands by to repel the invasion. Nevertheless, the landing parties successfully seize the customs house and control the waterfront after some four and one-half hours of fighting.

22 April

Reinforced by landing parties put ashore during the night by the cruisers *Chester* and *San Francisco* and battleships *Arkansas*, *New Hampshire*, *New Jersey*, *South Carolina*, and *Vermont*, naval forces commence the final assault against Veracruz, Mexico. Overcoming strong resistance from Mexican Naval Academy cadets with the support of gunfire from *Chester*, Marines and bluejackets complete the occupation of Veracruz by noon. All told, the two-day action costs the United States 17 dead and 63 wounded, while Mexico suffers over 300 casualties. With the current stringent requirements for the awarding of the Medal of Honor not yet in place, a total of 55 officers and enlisted men receive the decoration, the largest number ever awarded for a single engagement. The recipients include Lieutenant Frank Jack Fletcher, future commander of carrier forces at the battles of Coral Sea and Midway, and Commander William A. Moffett, who becomes the first Chief of the Bureau of Aeronautics.

24 April

Four Navy airplanes arrive in Mexico on board the cruiser *Birmingham* and the battleship *Mississippi*. The following day, Lieutenant Patrick N.L. Bellinger makes a reconnaissance flight over the harbor at Veracruz in the AB-3 flying boat, the first combat flight by a U.S. military aircraft.

6 May

While on a reconnaissance flight over Mexican lines, the AH-3 hydroaeroplane flown by Lieutenant Patrick N.L. Bellinger and his observer, Lieutenant (junior grade) Richard C. Saufley, is hit by rifle fire, the first damage sustained by a U.S. Navy aircraft in combat. On a later flight Bellinger retaliates in a most unorthodox fashion. Forbidden to carry a firearm aloft, he unleashes a bar of yellow soap at the enemy.

1 July

The teetotaling Secretary of the Navy Josephus Daniels orders the elimination of the traditional flag and wardroom wine messes on board U.S. Navy ships to take effect on this date, sparking a festive atmosphere in the fleet on the evening of 30 June.

The Office of Naval Aeronautics is established, its first officer-in-charge being Captain Mark L. Bristol, whose office space consists of one drawer in the desk of Rear Admiral Bradley A. Fiske, Aide for Operations to the Secretary of the Navy. Bristol receives the official title of Director of Naval Aeronautics on 23 November.

28 July

In response to the assassination of Archduke Franz Ferdinand in Sarajevo, Austria declares war on Serbia, igniting a chain of events that results in World War I.

10–12 October
The collier *Jupiter* (AC 3) becomes the first U.S. Navy ship to transit the Panama Canal following its formal opening on 1 October.

23 November
With President Victoriano Huerta having resigned the previous July, American forces withdraw from their occupation of Veracruz, Mexico.

7 December
Amid rumors that the revolutionary government in Haiti plans to seize the gold reserves of the country's national bank, which is backed by the City Bank of New York, the gunboat *Machias* lands her Marine detachment to seize $500,000 in gold. Once the precious cargo is aboard, the vessel departs for New York.

1915

21 January
In the aftermath of a boiler explosion on board the cruiser *San Diego* (ACR 6), Ensign Robert W. Cary calmly directs evacuation and damage control efforts, while Fireman Second Class Telesforo Trinidad rescues two men from fire rooms. For their actions both men receive the Medal of Honor.

Opposite, bottom: *In this obviously staged view for the benefit of the camera, bluejackets from* Michigan *(BB 27) crouch with their weapons ready during the assault on Veracruz, Mexico, 1914. (Naval Historical Center)*

Right: *Their battalion flag flying proudly alongside the Stars and Stripes, members of the naval landing party that seized Vera Cruz march along a wharf to boats that will return them to their ships. The dirt on their white uniforms is testament to their struggles to capture the Mexican port city. (Naval Historical Center)*

3 March

Congress passes the Naval Act of 1915, which includes provisions for establishing a naval reserve and the post of Chief of Naval Operations. The new post is one long advocated by proponents of a naval general staff to give senior officers more control over the administration of the Navy. The CNO is charged with "the operations of the fleet, and with the preparation and readiness of plans for use in war."

25 March

The submarine *F-4* (SS 23) goes down off Honolulu, Hawaii, with the loss of all twenty-one members of her crew. On 17 April, during salvage operations on the submarine, the lifeline and air hose of diver Chief Gunner's Mate William F. Loughman become entangled. Chief Gunner's Mate Frank W. Crilley dons a diving suit and enters the water, untangling the snarled lines and allowing his comrade to reach the surface. Crilley received the Medal of Honor for his heroism. *F-4* is raised on 29 August 1915.

1 May

The commencement of unrestricted submarine warfare by the German navy in the waters around the British Isles places U.S. shipping increasingly at risk. On this date the American tanker *Gulflight* is torpedoed without warning by a German U-boat off the southwestern coast of England.

7 May

Some fourteen miles off Old Head of Kinsale on the Irish coast, the British liner *Lusitania* is attacked without warning by the German submarine *U-20*. One torpedo hits the ship, igniting what are believed to be munitions in the cargo hold, though this explosion is also attributed to coal dust in the liner's bunkers. *Lusitania* goes down in just eighteen minutes with the loss of 1,201 passengers and crew. Among the dead are 124 Americans, prompting President Woodrow Wilson to send a note of protest to the German government on 13 May.

11 May

Rear Admiral William S. Benson is appointed the first Chief of Naval Operations (CNO).

1 June

The Navy contracts for its first lighter-than-air aircraft, the non-rigid airship DN-1. Its first flight on 20 April 1917 marks the beginning of airship operations in the U.S. Navy.

1 July

The armored cruiser *Washington* (ACR 11) arrives at Cap-Haitien, Haiti, carrying Rear Admiral William B. Caperton, who orders the landing of a detachment of Marines to establish radio communication between the ship and the U.S. consulate there. The dispatch of *Washington* is an effort to stem violence in the wake of a recent revolution elevating General Vilbrun Guillaume Sam to power.

Left: *Typical of naval aviation's pre–World War I aircraft was the AH-3, a seaplane that had no enclosed cockpit and was powered by a pusher engine in which the propeller faced backwards. (Naval Historical Center)*

Below: *A Navy diver descends into the depths during salvage operations after the sinking of the submarine F-4 on 25 March 1915. Note the telephone connections on the back of his helmet, allowing for communication with the surface as he descends to a depth of 300 feet. (Naval Historical Center)*

28 July

The day after a massacre at Port-au-Prince, Haiti, in which the government executes 167 political prisoners and the Haitian president is murdered along with the city's military governor, Marines and bluejackets from the armored cruiser *Washington* go ashore and establish order in the capital city. The same day, the gunboat *Eagle* puts ashore a landing party to protect the French consulate at Cap-Haitien.

29 July–4 August

Marines from the collier *Jason* (AC 12), the gunboat *Nashville*, and the battleship *Connecticut* land in Haiti. The leathernecks reinforce their fellow Marines on station in Port-au-Prince and take control of Cap-Haitien. By 12 August order has been restored in the Haitian capital, a new president elected, and a military government put in place in Cap-Haitien.

15 August

The armored cruiser *Tennessee* (ACR 10) arrives in Haiti carrying a force of over 2,000 Marines under the command of Colonel L. W. T. Waller. The force soon begins a determined campaign against the so-called cacos, bandit groups that have thwarted the establishment of a stable government in Haiti.

Right: *Vital to keeping the fleet in operation were support ships like* Jupiter *(AC 3), a collier that eventually traded coal for aircraft when she was converted to the Navy's first aircraft carrier following World War I. The series of booms rising from the deck could swing downward to transfer coal to a ship alongside. (Naval Historical Center).*

1 September
In the wake of the sinking of the British liner *Arabic* off Ireland on 19 August with the loss of two American lives, the German government pledges to President Woodrow Wilson that U-boats will cease attacking passenger ships without warning. This becomes known as the Arabic pledge.

9 September
An explosion rocks the destroyer *Decatur* (DD 5). Chief Watertender Eugene P. Smith repeatedly ventures below to locate and rescue injured shipmates, actions for which he receives the Medal of Honor.

19 October
The Navy establishes a submarine base at New London, Connecticut.

5 November
In the waters of Pensacola Bay, Florida, Lieutenant Commander Henry C. Mustin makes a successful catapult launch in the AB-2 flying boat from the armored cruiser *North Carolina* (ACR 12). This marks the first successful catapult launching of an aircraft from a ship underway.

11 November
At the urging of Rear Admiral William B. Caperton, Haiti ratifies a peace treaty with the United States.

The agreement gives United States officials charge of the Haitian customs house and public works and stipulates the establishment of a constabulary that is led by Marine commissioned and noncommissioned officers.

17 November
Marines and bluejackets from the battleship *Connecticut* join forces under Marine Major Smedley D. Butler in assaulting Fort Rivière in Haiti, the last caco stronghold. The *Connecticut* leathernecks and sailors provide covering fire as Butler leads a small group up the slope leading to the fort, capturing it and killing more than fifty bandits.

1916

6 January
The first class of enlisted men begins flight training at Naval Air Station Pensacola, Florida.

24 January
On board the battleship *New York*, Gunner's Mate First Class Wilhelm Smith enters a compartment filled with gas and rescues a shipmate, an action for which he receives the Medal of Honor.

24 March

A German U-boat torpedoes the French cross-channel steamer *Sussex* without warning in the English Channel, injuring two American citizens and violating the so-called Arabic pledge of the previous year. Again President Woodrow Wilson makes an official protest to the German government, which on 4 May promises to not sink merchant vessels without warning and consideration for noncombatants on board them.

5 May

A revolt against President Juan Isidro Jiménez by minister of war General Desiderio Arias prompts the landing of two companies of Marines in the Dominican Republic. The leathernecks, who disembark from the transport *Prairie*, are later joined by a landing party from the gunboat *Castine* (PG 6).

12 May

Three companies of Marines land in the Dominican Republic from the store ship *Culgoa*. In addition, the gunboat *Dolphin* (PG 24), carrying Rear Admiral William B. Caperton, arrives at Santo Domingo. In negotiations with General Desiderio Arias two days later, Admiral Caperton secures a withdrawal of forces from the capital.

11 March

The battleship *Nevada* (BB 36) is placed in commission, the first of a class of two battleships that includes *Oklahoma* (BB 37).

1 June

With the suppression of rebel forces in the Dominican Republic left to Marines and bluejackets, a landing party from the repair ship *Panther* (AD 6) and the

Above: *William S. Benson served as the Navy's first Chief of Naval Operations during the period 1915–1919. ("Admiral William S. Benson," Eleanor Beckham, Naval Historical Center)*

Left: *Haitian Army troops and U.S. Marines (center rear) assemble in Port-au-Prince, Haiti, during a U.S. intervention, circa July 1915. (Naval Historical Center)*

Opposite: *Aviation officers pictured at NAS Pensacola, circa 1915. Two men shown, William Corry and Edward McDonnell, were recipients of the Medal of Honor. (Naval Historical Center)*

① SCOFIELD ② CORRY ③ BRONSON ④ HAAS ⑤ PAUNACH ⑥ EVANS ⑦ JOHNSON ⑧ READ ⑨ MUSTIN ⑩ BELINGER ⑪ CUNNINGHAM ⑫ SAUFLEY ⑬ NORFLEET ⑭ EDWARDS ⑮ BARTLETT ⑯ SPENCER ⑰ McDONNELL

destroyer *Lamson* (DD 18) occupies the port of Monte Cristi. In addition, Marines and sailors from the gunboat *Sacramento* (PG 19) seize Puerto Plata, but not before a skirmish with rebels that results in the death of one Marine officer.

12 June
The battleship *Pennsylvania* (BB 38) is placed in commission.

21 June
The transport *Hancock* (AP 3) lands the Fourth Marine Regiment at Monte Cristi, Dominican Republic. Under the command of Colonel Joseph H. Pendleton, it joins the forces already in country in the pursuit of rebel forces. After a series of engagements with the Marines, General Desiderio Arias disbands his forces on 5 July.

19 August
The U.S. Naval Reserve Force is formally established. The Naval Militia is federalized as the National Naval Volunteers.

29 August
Congress passes the Naval Preparedness Act of 1916, the central component of which is a three-year construction program that includes 10 battleships, 6 battle cruisers, 10 scout cruisers, 50 destroyers, 67 submarines, and 16 auxiliary ships. The goal of the program is a fleet of 60 capital ships by 1925, placing the U.S. Navy in a leading position with respect to the other naval powers of the world.

The cruiser *Memphis* (ACR 10) is struck by a tidal wave off Santo Domingo, Dominican Republic, wrecking the ship and killing 40 members of her crew and injuring 204 others. Among those killed is Chief Machinist's Mate George William Rud, who is seriously burned as he remains at his post in the engine room. He is awarded the Medal of Honor posthumously. During the storm Lieutenant Claud Ashton Jones, the ship's senior engineering officer, makes repeated attempts to get the engines and boilers working, and when the boilers explode, he rescues men from steam-filled fire rooms. Machinist Charles H. Willey remains at his post in the engine room and evacuates men from a fire room. For their actions both men are awarded the Medal of Honor.

7 September
The U.S. Shipping Board is established by an act of Congress. The body is given the authority to procure merchant ships for naval purposes, and proves instrumental in assembling the convoys that cross the Atlantic and supply American doughboys fighting in the trenches of Europe.

17 October
The battleship *Arizona* (BB 39) is commissioned, beginning a fateful career that culminates with her sinking at Pearl Harbor, Hawaii, on 7 December 1941. The site of a memorial, today she rests on the bottom of the harbor, her hull the tomb for over a thousand sailors.

29 November
With the administration of the Dominican Republic placed under control of the United States, Captain Harry S. Knapp is appointed military governor of the Caribbean nation.

Left: *Bedecked with cartridge belts and canteens and carrying M1903 rifles, members of the landing party from* New Jersey *(BB 16) prepare to go ashore, 1915. (Naval Historical Center)*

Below: *Personnel of twenty-six ships were eligible for the Dominican Campaign Medal for their services in 1916. (Naval Historical Center)*

1917

13 January
While attempting to refloat the submarine *H-3* (SS 30), which ran aground on the northern California coast, the cruiser *Milwaukee* (C 21) strands off Eureka, California, and is eventually wrecked. There is no loss of life among the members of the crew.

3 February
Two days after Germany announces a policy of unrestricted submarine warfare around the British Isles, the United States severs diplomatic relations with the German government.

25 February
In response to revolution in eastern Cuba, ships of the Atlantic Fleet put Marines ashore to protect American lives and property, particularly sugar plantations in the region.

1 March
At the request of President Woodrow Wilson, Congress approves the arming of merchant vessels to defend against German U-boat attacks. Without authority from Congress, Wilson orders Navy gun crews assigned to these ships.

Right: *Stripped of her guns and equipment following her beaching at Santo Domingo by a tidal wave on 29 August 1916, the hulk of* Memphis *(ACR 10) is left to the mercy of the sea. (Naval Historical Center)*

4 March
President Woodrow Wilson signs the Naval Appropriations Bill, the largest in history up to that time, which provides the Navy $517 million.

17 March
The Navy receives authorization to enlist women for temporary service in the yeoman rate, with the addition of an F for "female" distinguishing them from their male counterparts. Some 11,275 Yeomen (F) don Navy blue during the Great War.

6 April
Congress approves a declaration of war against Germany at the request of President Woodrow Wilson. Two days later diplomatic relations are broken with Austria-Hungary.

4 May
With Rear Admiral William S. Sims, posted to Great Britain as a liaison with the Admiralty, advocating the quick dispatch of antisubmarine vessels to European waters to combat the U-boat menace, the first U.S. warships arrive in European waters on this date. Under the command of Commander Joseph K. Taussig, Destroyer Squadron Eight consists of *Conyngham* (DD 58), *Davis* (DD 65), *McDougal* (DD 54), *Porter* (DD 59), *Wainwright* (DD 62), and *Wadsworth* (DD 60). "We are ready now, sir," Taussig replies when queried by the British commander about his readiness for action upon arriving at Queenstown, Ireland.

29 May
The Cruiser and Transport Force is established under the command of Rear Admiral Albert Gleaves. During the Great War the force transports 911,047 troops across the Atlantic without losing a single man to enemy fire.

5–6 June
Under the command of Lieutenant Kenneth Whiting, the First Aeronautical Detachment lands in France, becoming the first American military force of any service to arrive on the continent of Europe during World War I.

9 June
Six armed yachts depart New York for Brest, France. They become the U.S. Patrol Squadron, a force that escorts convoys when they enter French waters and conducts patrol and minesweeping operations.

July
Responding to the urgent need to combat German U-boats, the United States suspends its capital

ADMIRAL WILLIAM S. SIMS

by Dr. James C. Bradford

Ironically, the man destined to command all United States naval forces in Europe entered the world in a foreign land. William Sowden Sims spent the first thirteen years of his life in his birthplace, Port Hope, Ontario, Canada. His father was an American civil engineer, making Sims an American by birth, but his mother was the daughter of an immigrant to Canada from Leeds, England, and in later life his detractors implied that these factors made Sims overly sympathetic to Britain during the First World War.

Sims moved to Pennsylvania in 1872 and was appointed to the U.S. Naval Academy four years later. Graduating from Annapolis in the middle of his class of 1880, Sims served in the Atlantic and Caribbean before taking a leave of absence to study French in Paris during 1888–1889. While at sea Sims read widely, including works of Charles Darwin and Henry George, their words convincing him of the value of constant competition, the efficacy of the survival of the fittest, and the need for one to continually work for reform in all spheres.

The young officer's service abroad continued with assignment to the Pacific, where he studied lessons of the Sino-Japanese War. As a naval attaché to France and Russia in 1897–1900, Sims learned of the relative backwardness of the U.S. fleet compared to the leading navies of Europe and organized a network of agents to gather intelligence concerning the Spanish navy during the Spanish-American War. While posted to the battleship *Kentucky* (BB 6) in Asian waters, Sims met Sir Percy Scott, the leading gunnery officer in the Royal Navy. Comparing *Kentucky* to European ships, and reviewing the dismal record of U.S. gunnery during the Battle of Manila Bay, Sims became convinced that reforms were necessary. With his commanding officer's support he dispatched numerous reports to Navy Department officials concerning needed improvements in ship design and gunnery.

When these were ignored he audaciously wrote directly to President Theodore Roosevelt. His work earned him the post of Inspector of Target Practice in 1902 and, five years later, he became naval aide to Roosevelt. By the time Roosevelt left office and Sims returned to sea in 1909, great strides had been made in American naval gunnery, though attempts to reform naval administration were less successful.

Ordered to command the battleship *Minnesota* (BB 22), Sims took his ship to Britain for a port call, where he did nothing to diminish his reputation as an outspoken officer. He delivered a speech at the Guildhall in London, declaring that "if ever [their] Empire should be seriously threatened [the British] might count upon the assistance of every man, every ship, and every dollar from their kinsmen across the seas." Many naval officers agreed with Sims' sentiments, but the speech so strained U.S.-German relations that President William Howard Taft publicly reprimanded him for his words. However, his favorable reputation with the British served the nation well as war clouds spread over Europe.

After Germany announced that it would prosecute unrestricted submarine warfare in early 1917, Sims was dispatched to London to discuss cooperation between British and U.S. naval forces. After Congress declared war in April, he became U.S. naval attaché in London, beginning a meteoric rise that saw his promotion to vice admiral in May and assignment as Commander, U.S. Naval Forces Operating in European Waters in June. His impact was immediate. Sims demanded that more ships be sent to England, rejected the belief that German U-boats posed a threat in American waters, and opposed President Woodrow Wilson's suggestion for attacks on German U-boat bases, causing friction with officials in Washington. The result was the dispatching of Admiral Henry T. Mayo, Commander

of the Atlantic Fleet, to London to make an independent assessment of the naval war in European waters. Though Sims was promoted to admiral in December 1918, he was disappointed when Wilson took Mayo to Versailles as his naval advisor.

At war's end Sims returned to America to become president of the Naval War College for a second time. (He was the college's president from February to March 1917, his tenure cut short by the U.S. entry into World War I.) His criticism of the Navy as having been slow to adapt to the rigors of war and poorly led during the war prompted a congressional investigation in 1920. That same year he published *The Victory at Sea*, which won a Pulitzer Prize at the price of further embittered relations between Sims and Secretary of the Navy Josephus Daniels and other naval leaders. After retiring from the Navy in 1922 Sims continued to

write articles for the popular press arguing that the sea service was unprepared to fight a major opponent. In what members of the Navy's "Gun Club" considered virtual treason, Sims sided with air power advocates such as General William Mitchell who claimed that aircraft had rendered battleships obsolete.

The admiral died in Boston on 28 September 1936, a combative advocate of reform to the end. Though he tried the patience of superiors, Sims made important contributions to naval reform and proved that very able officers with well-reasoned agendas could survive competition with senior naval leaders.

Above: *Vice Admiral William S. Sims, left, confers with Rear Admiral Hugh Rodman (Commander Battleship Division Nine) in Atlantic waters during World War I. (National Museum of Naval Aviation)*

shipbuilding program in favor of constructing vessels for employment in antisubmarine warfare.

23 July
While en route to Buenos Aires, Argentina, the cruiser *Pittsburgh* (ACR 4) suffers an ammunition explosion in a casemate. Lieutenant Willis Winter Bradley, Jr., though rendered momentarily unconscious by the explosion, crawls into the casemate to extinguish burning materials, thus preventing further explosions. Seaman Ora Graves, after being blown to the deck, extinguishes burning waste and prevents flames from reaching powder in the casemate. Both men receive the Medal of Honor for their efforts to save their ship.

27 July
Congress authorizes the Army and Navy to take over North Island in San Diego, California, the birth of what will become one of the Navy's most important West Coast air stations.

14 August
Flying a seaplane, Lieutenant Edward O. McDonnell, a Medal of Honor recipient for action at Veracruz, Mexico, conducts the first experiments involving launching a torpedo from an aircraft. The flight tests, carried out in the waters off Huntington, Long Island,

New York, come five years after Rear Admiral Bradley Fiske patented a torpedo-carrying airplane.

17 September
While escorting a convoy to France, the cruiser *Huntington* (ACR 5) releases an observation balloon that is forced down by a squall. The pilot becomes entangled in the balloon's rigging and is dragged underwater. Ship's Fitter First Class Patrick McGunigal climbs down the side of the ship, jumps to the ropes leading to the basket, and frees the pilot, allowing him to be pulled to safety. For his heroic actions, McGunigal receives the Medal of Honor.

15 October
U-61 launches a torpedo at the destroyer *Cassin* (DD 43) off Ireland. Realizing that the torpedo may strike near the destroyer's depth charge racks, Gunner's Mate First Class Osmond K. Ingram attempts to release the charges but is not successful. The torpedo's impact triggers depth charges and badly damages the destroyer. Ingram is killed, the first of 431 Navy men lost in action during World War I. For his heroic effort Ingram receives a posthumous Medal of Honor.

5 November
The motor patrol boat *Alcedo* (SP 166), a converted yacht assigned patrol duty off the coast of France, is sunk by a torpedo fired from *UC-71*. Twenty-two members of her crew are lost. *Alcedo* is the first U.S. Navy vessel lost in World War I.

While serving in the steam yacht *May*, Seaman Tedford H. Cann discovers a leak in a flooded compartment and risks his own life to close it, thereby saving his ship. For his actions he is awarded the Medal of Honor.

17 November
A lookout on board the destroyer *Fanning* (DD 37) operating off Ireland spots the periscope of the German U-boat *U-58*, prompting Lieutenant Arthur S. Carpender to commence a depth charge attack. *Fanning* is joined by the destroyer *Nicholson* (DD 52) just as the submarine comes to the surface, her crew flooding out of the hatches to surrender. The men are rescued before *U-58* goes under, the only U-boat sunk by U.S. Navy destroyers during World War I. Ironically, *Fanning*'s first wartime action was the October 1916 rescue of seamen from a ship sunk in the waters off Nantucket, Massachusetts, by *U-58*.

18 November
U.S. Navy personnel take flying boats aloft from Naval Air Station Le Croisic on the French coast, naval aviation's first aerial patrols during the Great War. The first armed patrol occurs four days later.

19 November
In the early morning darkness 110 miles west of Gibraltar, the British merchant ship *Rose* accidentally rams and sinks the destroyer *Chauncey* (DD 3). Lost are twenty-one members of her crew, including her skipper, Lieutenant Commander Walter E. Reno.

Opposite, top: *Recruiting posters often featured a woman encouraging men to enlist. By war's end many women served on active duty. (Naval Historical Center)*

Opposite, bottom: Arizona *(BB 39) in the East River, New York, circa 1916. (Naval Historical Center)*

Right: *Members of the Naval Reserve Flying Corps during WW I, pictured 2 November 1917. Standing fourth from right is Ensign Stephen Potter, the first naval aviator to shoot down an enemy aircraft. (National Museum of Naval Aviation)*

Left: *The officer in front of the helmsman on the bridge of* Wadsworth *(DD 60) is Commander Joseph Taussig, commander of the first U.S. Navy warships to arrive in European waters in 1917. Note the padding in front of him to prevent injury while operating in heavy seas. (National Museum of Naval Aviation)*

Below: *Recruiting poster painted by James Flagg. (Naval Historical Center)*

Opposite: *Huntington (ACR 5) operates an observation balloon. Note the catapult track above her deck for launching seaplanes. (National Museum of Naval Aviation)*

6 December

Operating independently in the vicinity of the Isles of Scilly, the destroyer *Jacob Jones* (DD 61) takes a torpedo in her starboard side. With her fuel oil tank ruptured and depth charges exploding as her stern settles, Lieutenant Commander David W. Bagley gives the order to abandon ship. Only 38 of 102 crewmen make it off the ship, which sinks in just eight minutes. The attacking *U-53* surfaces, takes two prisoners and humanely radios the Allied naval base at Queenstown, Ireland, the position of the survivors.

7 December

Battleship Division Nine consisting of the dreadnoughts *Delaware*, *Florida*, *New York*, *Texas*, and *Wyoming* under the command of Rear Admiral Hugh Rodman arrive at Scapa Flow off northern Scotland. There they join the British Grand Fleet, though they are destined not to see combat during the war.

17 December

Following a collision between the submarines *F-1* (SS 20) and *F-3* (S 22) off San Pedro, California, the former boat sinks with the loss of nineteen members of her crew.

While operating between France and Spain in the Bay of Biscay, the motor patrol boat *Remlik* (SP 157) encounters a heavy gale that causes a depth charge to break loose. Chief Boatswain's Mate John Mackenzie

sits on the depth charge, holding it in place until the ship heads up into the sea, at which time the explosive is carried to safety. For preventing probable damage to his ship and loss of life, he receives the Medal of Honor.

27 December
The converted yacht *Santee* is hit by a torpedo from a German U-boat while operating off Queenstown, Ireland. She returns to port with no casualties.

1918

7 January
In the Navy's continuing effort to facilitate the shipment of materiel overseas, the Naval Overseas Transportation Service is established at Hampton Roads, Virginia. Under the command of Commander Charles Belknap, the service eventually operates some 450 vessels.

4 March
In what remains a mystery, the collier *Cyclops* departs Barbados in the British West Indies, the ship and her crew of 280 officers and enlisted men never to be heard from again.

19 March
While engaged in escorting a convoy off the coast of

Ireland, the destroyer *Manley* (DD 74) rolls against the side of the British auxiliary cruiser *Motagua*, accidentally triggering the detonation of eighteen of the destroyer's depth charges. The explosions kill fifty-six members of her crew and ignite fuel and alcohol storage drums. *Manley* limps into port two days later with seventy feet of her hull awash or underwater.

In a milestone event in the history of U.S. naval aviation, Ensign Stephen Potter shoots down a German seaplane near the island of Heligoland in the North Sea, the first kill recorded by a U.S. Navy pilot. Potter is flying with a Royal Air Force squadron at the time of the aerial engagement.

25 March
Ensign John F. McNamara records the first attack by a U.S. naval aviator against a submarine, attacking a U-boat off the coast of England.

11 April
The cargo ship *Lake Moor* is torpedoed by *UB-73* off the coast of Scotland, the first of eight Naval Overseas Transportation Service vessels lost to enemy action during World War I.

ANTISUBMARINE WARFARE IN WORLD WAR I

by Dr. William N. Still, Jr.

Antisubmarine warfare (ASW), as a distinct form of naval warfare, was born in the First World War when the Royal Navy initially employed destroyers and other small craft to patrol the waters around the British Isles. They also developed new technology to combat the menace of German U-boats, the most effective being the depth charge. In addition, mines, nets, armed merchant ships, aircraft, and decoy ships (Q-ships) were all employed as weapons in the battle against the underwater enemy.

The U.S. Navy had no experience in ASW when it declared war on Germany in April 1917. The service's first manual dealing with the subject appeared that same month, but was quickly replaced by the one that guided the British. The Navy possessed approximately seventy-five destroyers, including nine that were considered obsolete. In time forty-five of them, including the obsolete ones, were deployed to European waters, their crews lacking any ASW training. Up to that time, emphasis had been on destroyers acting in concert in conventional surface actions.

The Navy soon discovered that ASW would be its primary responsibility during the war. As a result the capital ship construction begun in 1915 was set aside and emphasis was placed on building new destroyers and other antisubmarine craft. These included "Eagle boats" that began reaching the fleet during the last months of the war, and 100-foot wooden subchasers, more than a hundred of which were deployed to the war zone.

As a stopgap measure until the mew construction could be commissioned, the Navy sent armed former private yachts, obsolete Spanish-American War gunboats and cruisers, Coast Guard cutters, and even submarines overseas. Destroyers and other small craft also patrolled the American coastline. Initially, American naval units employed British tactics of patrolling areas where German U-boats operated. Although this would continue to the Armistice, in the summer of 1917 the Allies adopted convoying, which quickly proved to be the most effective measure against the submarine. With the development of underwater detection devices such as the hydrophone, the Navy became more offensive-minded in its tactics, generally using a destroyer along with several subchasers to hunt submarines in the Irish Sea, English Channel, and Adriatic. These efforts met with little success, primarily because acoustic equipment was ineffective. Few submarines were targeted, and even fewer were destroyed or even damaged.

The depth charge was the most effective weapon against the submarine. As with other antisubmarine weapons, the Navy showed little interest in depth charges until a few months before the United States entered the war. A fifty-pound depth charge had been developed, but was worthless against undersea craft. In addition, there existed no mechanisms for dropping the charges; instead they were tossed overboard by hand. American ASW ships in the war zone quickly discarded the existing depth charges in favor of those employed by the British, which contained 300 pounds of explosives. The Navy also developed a similar charge of its own, the Mark II, and equipped its ships with British-developed racks on the stern where charges were housed and rolled into the water. Later the "Thornycroft Thrower" and Y guns, similar to mortars, were added to the arsenals of ASW ships, permitting a spread of four or more charges to be dropped at a time on target.

Having practiced spotting submarines from the air during the prewar years, naval aviators also assumed a prominent place in the Allied ASW effort. Operating from coastal air stations in France, England, Ireland, and Italy, flying boats ranged far and wide in combating German submarines. Though material deficiencies in weaponry made aircraft a minimal threat for German U-boat captains, the mere presence of aircraft over convoys certainly deterred attacks.

The Navy experimented with mine warfare before World War I, and during the war designed and manufactured a new type of contact mine, which was employed in the North Sea Mine Barrage which was created to keep submarines out of the Atlantic. The

Mine Barrage, and the postwar seeping of this huge minefield, marked the beginning of systematic mine warfare development in the fleet.

World War I's antisubmarine efforts may look antiquated over three-quarters of a century later, but they laid the groundwork for victory in the Battle of the Atlantic during World War II. That vital campaign would be largely fought with modern versions of weapons, sensors, and tactics pioneered during the Great War.

Above: Ward *(DD 139) goes down the ways at Mare Island, Naval Shipyard, California. Commissioned on 24 July 1918, she would fire the first American shots of World War II off Pearl Harbor, Hawaii, on 7 December 1941, and be sunk by air attack in the Philippines on 7 December 1944. (Naval Historical Center)*

Opposite: *A destroyer's "main battery" in the war against German U-boats, pictured here on the stern of* Tucker *(DD 67), included depth charges and 4-inch guns. Visible are racks from which the charges were rolled into the ocean and side-throwing depth-charge projectors. (National Museum of Naval Aviation)*

Left: *Crewmen from U-58 stand on deck as* Fanning *(DD 37) comes alongside after having forced the enemy submarine to the surface, 17 November 1917. (Naval Historical Center)*

Below: *Survivors of* Jacob Jones *(DD 61), sunk by a German U-boat on 6 December 1917, photographed after their rescue. (Naval Historical Center)*

17 April

The munitions ship *Florence H.* suffers an internal explosion in Quiberon Bay, France. While serving in the destroyer *Stewart* (DD 13), which is operating nearby, Ship's Cook Third Class Jesse Whitfield Covington and Quartermaster Frank Monroe Upton jump overboard to rescue a survivor surrounded by

powder boxes and too exhausted to help himself. For their heroism both men receive the Medal of Honor.

23 April

While serving with the Fifth Marine Regiment on the Western Front, Lieutenant Commander Alexander Gordon Lyle, Dental Corps, rushes to the side of

Right: *Wearing a leather jacket that became a trademark of aviators, Ensign Fred Beck poses with a mechanic next to a Tellier flying boat at Naval Air Station Le Croisic, France. The majority of naval aviation activity during World War I consisted of antisubmarine missions flying foreign-built aircraft from coastal air stations. (National Museum of Naval Aviation)*

Corporal Thomas Regan, USMC, administering surgical aid under heavy shellfire and saving the man's life. Lyle is awarded the Medal of Honor.

12 May
The first six of what will eventually become 121 subchasers arrives in Great Britain. With steel output devoted to larger warships, the 110-foot-long subchasers are constructed of wood, which gives them the wartime nickname of the "Splinter Fleet." A total of two subchasers are lost to enemy action during the war, both striking mines. Other subchasers serve in the Adriatic.

20 May
The battleship *New Mexico* (BB 40), lead ship of a class of battleships that includes *Mississippi* (BB 41) and *Idaho* (BB 42), is placed in commission.

21 May
The Naval Overseas Transportation Service tanker *William Rockefeller* sinks with the loss of three men after being torpedoed by *UC-58* while en route to Scotland.

During pursuit of a submarine contact off the coast of France by the converted yacht *Christabel*, the explosion of a depth charge dropped into the water causes other depth charges set for firing to scatter about the deck. Ensign Daniel Augustus Joseph Sullivan risks his life

to secure the depth charges despite the fact that they might explode at any moment. Saving his ship from disaster, he receives the Medal of Honor.

24 May
The cruiser *Olympia* puts ashore a landing party in Russia to participate in the Anglo-American occupation of Murmansk and the seizure of Archangel. The latter is the location of stockpiles of war materiel sent to the Russians before the start of the Russian Revolution, which the Allies fear will fall into the hands of the Bolsheviks if left unguarded.

31 May
The transport *President Lincoln* is attacked by *U-90*, and sinks with the loss of twenty-six members of her crew. Of the 689 survivors, one is taken prisoner by the German submarine. Lieutenant Edouard V. Izak gains valuable insight into German undersea warfare and later orchestrates a successful escape for which he receives the Medal of Honor.

6 June
While serving with the Fifth Marine Regiment during action at Belleau Wood, France, Lieutenant (junior grade) Weedon E. Osborne, Dental Corps, repeatedly rescues the wounded from the field of battle and is killed while carrying a wounded officer to safety. He is posthumously awarded the Medal of Honor.

MANLEY IN WET BASIN, HAULBO

8 June

U.S. Navy ships under the command of Rear Admiral Joseph Strauss, in a combined effort with the British, begin the daunting task of laying a minefield covering some 240 miles between Scotland and Norway. The American ships account for some four-fifths of the 70,263 mines laid in just over three months in an attempt to contain German U-boats to the North Sea.

11 June

While serving with the Fifth Marine Regiment at Belleau Wood, France, Lieutenant Orlando Henderson Petty, MC, works at a dressing station under the fire of enemy explosives and gas shells. Knocked to the ground by an exploding shell that tears away his gas mask, Petty continues his efforts to save the lives of wounded Marines until the dressing station is demolished by enemy fire. He then carries a wounded officer to safety. For his devotion to the men under his care, he receives the Medal of Honor.

22 June

The Naval Overseas Transportation Service cargo vessel *Californian* sinks after striking a mine in the Bay of Biscay.

29 June

Reflecting the U.S. government's concern over the fast-moving events of the Russian Revolution, the armored cruiser *Brooklyn* lands her Marine detachment to protect the American consulate in Vladivostok. The leathernecks remain on guard until 28 August.

1 July

The transport *Covington* sinks after being torpedoed by the German submarine *U-86* off Brest, France. Six of her 776 passengers and crew are lost.

11 July

Westover, a cargo ship steaming off the coast of France, is sunk by *U-92* with the loss of eleven of her crew.

19 July

The armored cruiser *San Diego* (ACR 6) strikes a mine laid by *U-156* in the waters off Fire Island, New York, and sinks. Six members of her crew are lost.

The Sixth Marine Regiment engages in combat with German forces in the vicinity of Vierzy, France. During the action, Pharmacist's Mate First Class John Henry Balch repeatedly leaves the relative safety of a dressing station, braving enemy fire to treat the wounded on the battlefield. Meanwhile, Lieutenant Joel Thompson Boone, MC, despite machine gun fire and a heavy mist of gas, renders aid and makes two trips through enemy fire to obtain much-needed medical supplies. Both men receive the Medal of Honor for their heroism.

15 August

Naval aviators commence independent operations of the Northern Bombing Group, a unit consisting entirely of U.S. naval personnel, with a raid against German submarine pens at Ostend, Germany.

21 August

During an air raid against Austrian positions at Pola, Ensign George Ludlow, flying a Macchi M.5 flying boat for the Italian navy, is shot down by enemy fighters. Landsman for Quartermaster Charles H. Hammann, despite the hull of his own flying boat having suffered battle damage, lands next to his fellow aviator and rescues him. For his actions he receives the Medal of Honor. Ironically, Hammann is killed in the crash of a Macchi M.5 in June 1919.

23 August

A second division of U.S. battleships consisting of *Nevada*, *Oklahoma*, and *Utah*, under the command of Rear Admiral Thomas S. Rodgers, arrives at Bantry Bay, Ireland, to thwart possible German battlecruiser attacks against North Atlantic convoys.

27 August

In a tragic incident of friendly fire, SS *Felix Taussig* opens fire on what is thought to be a German vessel off Long Island, New York. The quarry is in fact the submarine chaser *SC 209*, which loses eighteen members of her crew.

Above: *An aerial gunner trains his Lewis gun on a target. His gun is mounted on a Scarff ring, allowing it to quickly train and elevate. (National Museum of Naval Aviation)*

THE NAVY CROSS

by Thomas Daniel Clifton

Since its establishment, the Navy Cross has played a great role in the history of the U.S. Navy, forged into a solid symbol of heroism from the trenches of World War I to the sands of Iwo Jima and Kuwait. It is an award unique to the naval service, its blue ribbon a reminder of the sea.

Until World War I the Navy could bestow only one award for heroism—the Medal of Honor—and until 1915 officers could not receive it. The experience of the Great War spurred the creation of a hierarchy of medals, among them the Distinguished Service Medal and Silver Star. In addition, the Army created the Distinguished Service Cross, a medal unique to that service, a measure mirrored by the Navy with the creation of its own award, the Navy Cross, on 4 February 1919. The medal's creator, James Earle Fraser, experimented with several designs, one of which placed the image of a destroyer on the obverse of the medal. However, Fraser finally settled on the classic image of a sailing vessel to the front of the medal, and "USN" with a pair of crossed anchors on the reverse. The design of the Navy Cross medal has remained constant since its inception, experiencing only variations in color, most notably in the so-called Black Widow. Manufactured during 1941–1942, this version bears a dark, almost black patina. Many awards of this variation were posthumous because of heavy casualties suffered by the naval service during the early months of World War II.

Though not approved until after the end of World War I, receipt of the decoration was made retroactive to April 1917 and not limited to members of the United States naval service. Of the 1,658 Navy Crosses awarded in World War I, foreign military personnel received 95 and 12 were awarded to members of the U.S Army. In addition, Lenah Higbee, Superintendent of the Navy Nurse Corps, became the first woman to receive the award for her service during the Great War. Originally awarded for both combat and non-combat acts, the focus of those responsible for awarding the Navy Cross was immediately blurred. The most common perception is that the lack of established criteria for receipt of the Navy Cross relegated it to third in precedence behind the Medal of Honor and the Navy Distinguished Service Medal.

The years between World War I and World War II were not ones of peace, as evidenced by the 337 Navy Crosses awarded to men who fought in such forgotten conflicts as Nicaragua and Haiti, and endured the sinking of the gunboat *Panay* (PR 5). The broad criteria for the award also allowed for its presentation to those involved in the daring underwater rescue and salvage operations surrounding the sinking of the submarine *Squalus* (SS 192). When Japanese bombs fell on Pearl Harbor, Hawaii, on 7 December 1941, the United States was plunged into warfare on a scale never before known, with the personnel of the Navy numbering nearly 3.5 million men and women by 1945. With sailors facing enemy fire all across the globe, it became necessary to bring order to the sea service's system of combat decorations. Accordingly, on 7 August 1942 Congress passed Public Law 702, placing the Navy Cross second only to the Medal of Honor in the hierarchy of medals awarded to members of the naval service for combat bravery. The criteria for the Navy Cross, as established by Congress, stated that it shall be presented to "any person while serving in any capacity with the Navy or Marine Corps who distinguishes himself with extraordinary heroism not justifying the award of the Medal of Honor."

There were a staggering 3,645 Navy Crosses awarded for service during World War II, with 3,613 awarded to members of the naval service, 13 to men of the U.S. Army, 17 to foreign servicemen and 2 to civilians. Fifty-two Navy Crosses were awarded for heroism at Pearl Harbor, and during the epic Battle of Midway in June 1942, Navy Crosses abounded among the airmen who attacked the Japanese fleet. Among the fighting destroyer sailors who wore the blue and white ribbon of the Navy Cross on his uniform was future Chief of Naval Operations Arleigh Burke. Submarine skippers and their crews, who overcame the unusual lifestyle of living below vast oceans to launch unrelenting attacks on enemy shipping, received a high

proportion of the Navy Crosses awarded during World War II. Perhaps no three submarine skippers personify the Navy Cross more than Commanders Samuel Dealey and Roy Davenport, and Lieutenant Commander Richard O'Kane, who between them received twelve Navy Crosses. Davenport holds the distinction of being the only person in the U.S. Navy to have received five Navy Crosses.

Since the end of World War II, 737 Navy Crosses have been awarded, including 246 for the Korean War, 485 for the Vietnam War and seven for action in various conflicts including Operation Desert Storm, the recipients ranging from hospital corpsmen, SEALS, and riverine small-craft skippers to the Navy's only fighter ace of the Vietnam War. The Navy Cross, much like the service it represents, knows no earthly boundaries. From the brightest skies to the darkest oceans, the Navy Cross rewards the bravery and heroism of the men and women of the naval service. It has recognized those who conquered great oceans and connected continents. It has distinguished those who fought back at Pearl Harbor, froze at Chosin during the Korean War and roomed at the "Hanoi Hilton" during the Vietnam War. Now as America faces a new struggle and a new type of enemy whose focus is terror en masse, the Navy Cross waits at the ready to reward those who display selfless acts of heroism to defend their country and their comrades in arms.

6 September

Rear Admiral Charles Plunkett, in an unlikely command for a naval officer, takes a battery of five 14-inch railway guns into action. Mounted on rail carriages, the heavy guns bombard German positions near Soissons, France.

15 September

The transport *Mount Vernon* falls victim to a German U-boat 200 miles west of Ushant, France. Despite losing thirty-six of her crew, she manages to reverse course and reach Brest.

While serving with the Sixth Marine Regiment during an advance on German positions at Thiaucourt,

France, Hospital Apprentice First Class David E. Hayden observes a Marine fall wounded. Disregarding his own safety, Hayden dresses the man's wound under fire and carries him to safety. For his actions he is awarded the Medal of Honor.

16 September

Steaming off the coast of Spain, the Navy cargo ship *Buena Ventura* is torpedoed by the German submarine *U-46*. She sinks with the loss of nineteen of her crew.

24 September

Lieutenant David S. Ingalls, a member of the First Yale Unit, shoots down his fifth enemy aircraft while flying a Sopwith Camel of the Royal Air Force's

Below: *Lieutenant David S. Ingalls peels away after sending a German observation balloon down in flames, marking his fifth kill that made him the U.S. Navy's only ace of World War I. ("Lt. David S. Ingalls, USNRF, First U.S. Naval Air Ace," Bruce Ungerland, Naval Historical Center)*

Number 213 Squadron. Thus, Ingalls becomes the U.S. Navy's first and only ace of World War I. He later serves as Assistant Secretary of the Navy for Air.

25 September

During a training flight at Naval Air Station Pensacola, Florida, Chief Machinist's Mate Francis Edward Ormsbee, Jr., notices an aircraft crash into the water. The pilot of the airplane in which Ormsbee is flying lands nearby, and the chief dives overboard and swims to the wreck. Partially extricating the gunner from the plane, he holds his head above water until a rescue boat arrives, and then makes repeated dives in an unsuccessful effort to rescue the pilot. For his actions Ormsbee receives the Medal of Honor.

26 September

The Coast Guard cutter *Tampa* is lost with all hands after being torpedoed by *UB-91* in the waters off Great Britain. Eight U.S. Navy sailors are among the 115 crewmen who perish in the attack.

29 September

The battleship *Minnesota* hits a mine off the Delaware Capes and is slightly damaged. None of her crew is injured.

30 September

Spotting *U-152* on the surface while en route to the United States as part of a convoy, the Naval Overseas Transportation Service Ship *Ticonderoga* attempts to ram the German submarine. Gunfire from *U-152* straddles the transport's bridge, wounding her skipper, Lieutenant Commander James J. Madison, and knocking out her radio so that she cannot call for assistance. These are the opening shots of a two-hour surface engagement that ends when *U-152* submerges and puts a torpedo into *Ticonderoga*, sinking her. Only 24 men of the crew of 237 survive, and two are taken prisoner by the U-boat. Among the survivors is Madison, who receives the Medal of Honor for leading the heroic defense of his ship.

2 October

U.S. Navy subchasers blow up mines and screen against enemy submarines during an attack by Allied ships against the Austrian naval base at Durazzo.

9 October

While serving on board the tanker *Chestnut Hill* in the Atlantic, Chief Gunner's Mate Oscar Schmidt, Jr.,

observes an explosion on board a subchaser operating nearby. Seeing a man, whose legs are partially blown off, hanging on a line from the bow of the stricken vessel, Schmidt dives into the water and retrieves him, pulling him to the stern of the ship so that he can be hoisted on board. He receives the Medal of Honor for his actions.

1 November

While serving in the revenue cutter *Mohawk* during rescue operations aboard the schooner *Hjeltenaes*, Boatswain's Mate Second Class John Otto Siegel ventures onto the burning ship three times, rescuing two crewmen. On the third trip into the burning crew's quarters, a steam pipe over the door falls and bars his escape. Overcome with smoke, he collapses and is eventually rescued by shipmates. For his heroic efforts Siegel is awarded the Medal of Honor.

9 November

The Naval Overseas Transportation Service cargo vessel *Saetia* sinks near Fenwick Island, Delaware, after striking a mine.

11 November

The cease-fire ending World War I goes into effect on the eleventh hour of the eleventh day of the eleventh month. Armistice Day is now known as Veterans Day, honoring all who have served in our nation's defense.

Left: *Illustrating the cost of war, a Navy nurse is pictured between two of her Marine patients who lost limbs in combat. (Naval Historical Center)*

THE TREATY NAVY

1919-1938

THE TREATY NAVY

1919-1938

It was called the "War to End All Wars" and, when the guns fell silent on the Western Front on the eleventh hour, of the eleventh day, of the eleventh month in 1918, the world looked forward to a lasting peace. The U.S. Navy, which had grown in vast numbers in ships, planes, and personnel during the hostilities, predictably shrank to a force level more commensurate with peacetime. In this reduction it was very much assisted by an international effort toward disarmament, which was exemplified by the results of the Washington Naval Conference of 1922. Seeking to avoid the expensive naval building races that had preceded World War I, representatives of the world's five largest naval powers—Great Britain, the United States, Japan, France, and Italy—agreed to limit construction on capital ships and set force levels for certain types of warships. By 1923, when the treaty took effect, the U.S. Navy numbered 365 ships of all types, a reduction of more than 50 percent from its peak wartime level. The "Treaty Navy" was further reduced with the onset of the Great Depression, which forced the decommissioning of vessels and compelled the Navy to make do with fewer than 100,000 officers and enlisted men for much of the 1930s. One outward demonstration of the Navy's financial woes was the experience of the Naval Academy Class of 1933, half of whose members were released from active duty after graduation for lack of billets for them to occupy.

The reduction in capital ships spurred the development of weapons that had proven themselves during World War I—the airplane and the submarine. Following the lead of Great Britain, the U.S. Navy began constructing aircraft carriers. Though originally viewed as auxiliaries to the battle line, flattops demonstrated their offensive capabilities during interwar fleet exercises. Submarines, at first envisioned as coastal defense weapons, developed a true offensive capability. By the eve of World War II, the submarines being commissioned were nearly double the size of their World War I predecessors and carried more torpedoes. Capable of depths of some 300 feet, they also could remain submerged longer and operate at greater ranges. Both carrier and submarine proved vital to final victory in World War II.

Despite force reductions, the traditional missions of the Navy did not diminish. Ships supported the Marines in Nicaragua as they sought to quell civil war in that Central American nation. Landing parties from Navy ships protected U.S. citizens and foreign nationals during unrest in China and Honduras, and provided humanitarian aid in the wake of natural disasters. Continuing the tradition of exploration, Commander Richard E. Byrd led expeditions during which naval aircraft became the first to fly over both the North and South Poles. Yet, as the decade of the 1930s began, the Navy's operations were conducted increasingly with an eye on a changing balance of power in the world.

In 1933 Adolf Hitler became chancellor of Germany, and by 1935 his Nazi government had renounced the Treaty of Versailles and begun to rebuild the nation's military forces. Yet, what most attracted the attention of the U.S. Navy was the Pacific and the burgeoning power of Japan. On 18 September 1931, Japanese troops moved into Manchuria, and in 1934 the Japanese government

renounced the Washington Naval Treaty, opening the way for full-scale naval rearmament. By 1937 China and Japan were engaged in a full-scale war, one that would impact the U.S. Navy directly when Japanese planes attacked the U.S. Navy gunboat *Panay* (PR 5) on the Yangtze River near Nanking, China, sinking her and killing two of her crew.

Certainly aided by the fact that Franklin D. Roosevelt, a former Assistant Secretary of the Navy, occupied the White House, the U.S. Navy was able to respond to the growing power of Germany and Japan and rebuild during the 1930s despite a general mood of isolationism in the United States. In March 1934 Congress passed the Vinson-Trammell Act authorizing the buildup of the Navy to treaty limits, and in May 1938 Roosevelt signed into law a Naval Expansion Act that called for a 20-percent increase in active naval vessels. In addition, Navy planners

looked to construct forward bases in the Pacific. Among those bases were Guam, and two small atolls, Wake and Midway. In the coming years, they would join countless other far-flung places as scenes of epic battles in which a great fleet, its foundation the "Treaty Navy" of the interwar years, would achieve its destiny.

Pages 346–347: *The battleship* Arizona *(BB 39) plows through Pacific swells during the 1930s. She symbolized the backbone of America's naval might in the interwar years and, tragically, on 7 December 1941, would become a symbol of the tragedy of war. (Naval Historical Center)*

Above: *"Four-stackers" led by* Wasmuth *(DD 338) execute a turn to starboard during fleet maneuvers in the Pacific in the late 1930s. Behind the speedy destroyers steam the Pacific Fleet's battleships. (National Museum of Naval Aviation)*

1919

3 February
Symbolizing postwar interest in integrating aviation into fleet operations, Captain George W. Steele, Jr., assumes command of the Fleet Air Detachment, Atlantic Fleet. Included among the detachment's ships is the battleship *Texas* (BB 35), which incorporates a wooden turret-top platform from which flying experiments are carried out using Sopwith Camel aircraft at Guantanamo Bay, Cuba.

4 February
Congress creates two medals for the naval service, the Navy Distinguished Service Medal and the Navy Cross, which rank second and third, respectively, behind the Medal of Honor. The criterion for the decorations allows them to be awarded for both combat actions and distinguished service in the line of duty.

8 May
Seaplane Division One consisting of three NC flying boats—NC-1, NC-3, and NC-4—under the command of Commander John H. Towers launches from Naval Air Station Rockaway, New York, in an attempt to become the first aircraft to fly across the Atlantic

Ocean. All three aircraft complete the first legs of the flight to Trepassey, Newfoundland, but only the NC-4 under the command of Lieutenant Commander A. C. Read successfully negotiates the longest and most demanding part of the flight over the North Atlantic to the Azores Islands. On 27 May, the keel of the NC-4 slices into the waters of Lisbon Harbor in Portugal, thus becoming the first aircraft to fly the Atlantic. She continues on to England, arriving on 31 May.

11 July
With a General Board report issued the previous month calling for a naval air service "capable of accompanying and operating with the fleet in all waters of the globe," Congress passes the Naval Appropriations Act of 1919. Among its important provisions is funding to convert the collier *Jupiter* (AC 3) into the Navy's first aircraft carrier and two merchantmen into seaplane tenders, as well as the procurement of two rigid airships.

The Navy Pay Corps is renamed the Supply Corps.

30 July
The submarine *G-2* (SS 27), while being employed as a target for testing depth charges, sinks at her moorings near New London, Connecticut, during an inspection, drowning three men.

Left: *The NC flying boats were designed to combat German U-boats, but the end of World War I left them without a mission until Commander John H. Towers, the Navy's third aviator, proposed a U.S. Navy attempt to fly the Atlantic. Part of a three-plane effort to complete the aerial crossing, NC-4 overcame mechanical troubles early in the flight to become the only one to conquer the Atlantic. (National Museum of Naval Aviation)*

Right: *Destroyers that months before had prowled the seas in search of German U-boats await decommissioning at the Philadelphia Navy Yard, Pennsylvania. The end of World War I brought dramatic reductions in the size of the U.S. Navy as it shifted to peacetime levels. (Naval Historical Center)*

30 July–1 August
Marines from the protected cruiser *New Orleans*, stationed at Vladivostok, Russia, to support operations in Siberia, go ashore at Tyutuke Bay to protect American interests.

1 November
Admiral Robert E. Coontz, a native of Hannibal, Missouri, and veteran of service in the Philippine Insurrection, becomes the second Chief of Naval Operations.

25 December
The U.S. Navy's gunboats in China are formally organized into the Yangtze Patrol, named after the Chinese river on which they operate.

1920

22 January
Under an official program detailing enlisted men to flight training, Chief Quartermaster Harold H. Karr is the first to receive the designation Naval Aviation Pilot (NAP). The NAP program lasts until 1947.

18 March
The submarine *H-1* (SS 28) runs aground on a rocky shoal off Santa Margarita Island, California. The skipper and three members of the boat's crew drown while attempting to swim ashore. The submarine sinks during an attempted salvage on 24 March.

30 June
The battleship *Tennessee* (BB 43) is commissioned. She is joined in the fleet by her sister ship, *California* (BB 44) on 10 August 1921.

12 July
A reorganization of the U.S. Navy's ship forces divides them into three fleets: Atlantic, Pacific, and Asiatic.

1 September
The submarine *S-5* (SS 110), while running submerged off the Delaware Capes during acceptance trials, begins to take on water and sinks to a depth of 194 feet. Applying air to the after ballast and fuel tanks causes the boat to rise so that some seventeen feet of the stern is out of the water. On 2 September, with the assistance of the crews of two steamships, a hole is cut in the hull, allowing the crew to escape.

10 September
The cruiser *St. Louis* (CA 18) departs Philadelphia, Pennsylvania, for Turkish waters. During the ensuing months she evacuates refugees from Russia and provides other humanitarian assistance in the wake of the Russian Civil War and revolution in Turkey.

2 October
On this date a JN-4 Jenny aircraft, flown by Lieutenant Arthur C. Wagner with Lieutenant Commander William M. Corry as a passenger, crashes near Hartford, Connecticut. Corry is thrown clear of the plane, and, despite being injured, rushes into the flaming wreckage in an unsuccessful effort to rescue Wagner. Corry sustains serious burns and dies four days later, and is awarded the Medal of Honor posthumously.

14 October–1 November

Bombing tests are carried out against the battleship *Indiana* (BB 1) in the Chesapeake Bay in an effort to determine the effectiveness of aerial bombardment against a stationary target and the ability of the ship to withstand damage caused by hits and near-misses.

1921

26 February

While steaming off the coast of Panama near Coiba Island, the destroyer *Woolsey* (DD 77) sinks after a collision with the freighter *Steel Inventor*. Sixteen members of the crew are lost.

5 March

Edwin Denby, a naval militiaman during the Spanish-American War and reserve officer in the Marine Corps, takes office as the forty-second Secretary of the Navy.

25 March

The ocean-going tug *Conestoga* (AT 54) puts to sea from Mare Island, California, bound for Samoa. She never arrives at her destination, and though a

Right: *A solemn occasion against the backdrop of gloomy weather in the nation's capital, the cruiser* Olympia *(CL 15) arrives at the Washington Navy Yard on 9 November 1921, after transporting the remains of the Unknown Soldier from France for burial at Arlington National Cemetery. Ships in the background include the destroyers* Barney *(DD 149) and* Blakeley *(DD 150). (Naval Historical Center)*

subsequent search finds a lifeboat with the letter C marked on the bow, no trace of the tug or her 56-man crew is ever found.

21 June

In bombing tests that capture the imagination of the American public, the former German battleship *Ostfriesland* sinks after being hit repeatedly by aerial bombs dropped from Army Air Service aircraft. In the wake of the sinking, despite the fact that his target was unable to maneuver or defend herself, Army Brigadier General William Mitchell proclaims warships obsolete, further proof of his desire to create an independent air force for the United States.

12 July

Congress passes an act creating the Bureau of Aeronautics to administer the Navy's burgeoning aviation force. The new bureau is organized on 10 August. Selected as its first chief is Rear Admiral William A. Moffett, who serves in the post for the next twelve years and earns the title "Father of Naval Aviation."

21 July

The battleship *Maryland* (BB 46) is placed in commission, the first of three *Colorado*-class battleships to enter service. She is joined later by *Colorado* (BB 45) and *West Virginia* (BB 48). Construction of a fourth ship, *Washington* (BB 47), is canceled.

1 August

The Navy conducts the first successful tests of a gyroscopic high-level bombsight manufactured for the Bureau of Ordnance. The famed Norden Bombsight achieves its greatest acclaim in Army Air Forces bombers over Europe during World War II.

24 August

The British-built airship *R-38* (ZR 2), intended for delivery to the U.S. Navy, breaks up and crashes in flames during a test flight near Hull, England. Twenty-two British and sixteen Americans are killed in the accident, which foreshadows the tragic future of rigid airship operations in the U.S. Navy.

9 November

The cruiser *Olympia* (CL 15) arrives in Washington, D.C., after carrying the remains of the Unknown Soldier from France. She fires a salute as the remains are piped over the side and taken to Arlington National Cemetery, Virginia, for interment.

11 November

The First International Conference on Limitation of Naval Armaments convenes in Washington, D.C., with representatives of Belgium, China, France, Great Britain, Italy, the Netherlands, Portugal, and the United States in attendance. An American initiative, the so-called Washington Naval Conference reflects the economy-minded and isolationist position among many in government.

1 December

Over Norfolk, Virginia, the non-rigid *C-7* completes the first flight of an airship inflated with helium gas, which becomes standard on Navy airships in place of highly flammable hydrogen.

1922

25 January
The cruiser *Galveston* (CL 19), operating as part of the Special Service Squadron patrolling the waters off Central America, lands her Marine detachment at Corinto, Nicaragua, for transport to the capital of Managua to reinforce the legation guard in the city during a period of political unrest.

6 February
After nearly three months of deliberations in Washington, D.C., Great Britain, the United States, Japan, France, and Italy conclude the Five-Power Treaty. Its provisions include establishment of a ratio of 5:5:3:1.75:1.75, with an individual limit of 35,000 tons and 16-inch guns, for capital ships (battleships and battle cruisers); a ten-year moratorium on construction of new capital ships; tonnage limits on aircraft carriers; a limit of 10,000 tons and 8-inch guns on all other warships; and a clause regarding no further fortification of Pacific islands by the United States and Great Britain. Called the Washington Treaty, it goes into effect on 17 August 1923.

20 March
Langley (CV 1), the U.S. Navy's first aircraft carrier, is commissioned at Norfolk, Virginia. Formerly the collier *Jupiter*, *Langley*'s appearance soon earns her the nickname "Covered Wagon," which is also appropriate given the pioneering role she will play in the development of naval aviation.

29 March
The General Board issues its "United States Naval Policy," which states in part the need to "create, maintain, and operate a navy second to none and in conformity with treaty provisions."

22 April
In recognition of naval aviation's importance in increasing the accuracy of naval gunfire, the Secretary of the Navy mandates the assignment of one spotter aircraft to each battleship and cruiser in the fleet.

Above: *Diplomats gather in Washington, D.C., on 21 November 1921, for the opening session of the Washington Naval Conference that resulted in a treaty reducing the forces of the world's greatest naval powers. Seated at the head of the table (l–r): Premier Briand (France), Senator Underwood, Elihu Root, Senator Henry Cabot Lodge, Secretary of State Charles E. Hughes, Lord Balfour (United Kingdom), Lord Lee (United Kingdom). Seated at left (l–r): Prince Tokugawa (Japan), Ambassador Jusserand (France), Albert Sarrault (France), M. Vivian (France). Seated at right (l–r): S. Sastri, Sir John Salmond (United Kingdom), Senator George Pearse, Sir Robert Borden (United Kingdom), Ambassador Geddes (United Kingdom). (National Archives)*

28 April
The Marine detachment from the cruiser *Albany* (CL 23) goes ashore at Peking, China, to reinforce the legation guard in the city during the Chinese civil war. One week later a provisional battalion of Marines from ships of the Asiatic Fleet lands at Taku, China, ready to serve as reinforcement in Peking if necessary.

1 July
Under the provisions of the Five-Power Treaty, each signatory is authorized two aircraft carriers displacing 33,000 tons. On this date, Congress authorizes the conversion of the unfinished battle cruisers *Lexington* and *Saratoga* into aircraft carriers, which during the interwar years serve to demonstrate the offensive capabilities of carrier air power.

16 September
Commander Halsey Powell, skipper of the destroyer *Edsall* (DD 219), assumes command of a three-destroyer force tasked with evacuating Greeks from Smyrna after the Turkish victory in the Greco-Turkish War. All told, an estimated 262,578 people are evacuated by nonflagged Greek vessels attended by the destroyers, which also take refugees aboard. It is one of the largest operations of its kind in history.

27 September
Eighteen type PT aircraft of Torpedo and Bombing Plane Squadron One conduct the first mass torpedo practice, scoring eight "hits" against the battleship *Arkansas* (BB 33) during maneuvers off the Virginia Capes.

17 October
A Vought VE-7SF aircraft flown by Lieutenant Commander Virgil C. Griffin makes the first takeoff from a U.S. Navy aircraft carrier, launching from *Langley* while she lies at anchor in the York River, Virginia.

26 October
Lieutenant Commander Godfrey DeC. Chevalier records the first landing on board a U.S. Navy aircraft carrier, trapping on the flight deck of *Langley* while she is underway off the Virginia Capes. The following month Chevalier is killed in an aircraft crash.

Above: *Admiral Robert E. Coontz served as the second Chief of Naval Operations from October 1919 to July 1923, presiding over a Navy forced to make dramatic postwar cutbacks. (Naval Historical Center)*

Left: *Langley (CV 1), the Navy's first aircraft carrier, was known throughout the fleet as the "Covered Wagon." (National Museum of Naval Aviation)*

THE WASHINGTON NAVAL TREATY

by Dr. Jeffrey G. Barlow

With the carnage of World War I fresh in their minds, world leaders pursued policies of disarmament in the years immediately following the Great War. Wartime expenditures had drained national coffers and no country desired an arms race, particularly one involving expensive naval forces. Thus, representatives of eight governments came together for the landmark Washington Conference, which convened on 12 November 1921, in the Daughters of the American Revolution Building in Washington, D.C. The participating countries were the principal allied and associated powers from World War I—the United States, Great Britain, France, Italy, and Japan—and the European nations of Belgium, the Netherlands, and Portugal. However, only the first five were involved in negotiating a naval disarmament treaty.

Following a series of spirited meetings, in mid-December 1921 the "Big Three" naval powers—the United States, Great Britain, and Japan—agreed to a 5:5:3 ratio of capital ships. Japan's acceptance, however, was specifically linked to the maintenance of a status quo on fortifications and naval bases in the Pacific region. The United States, for example, was prohibited from adding new fortifications or naval bases in island possessions west of Hawaii and, aside from Australian and New Zealand territory, the British Empire could not further fortify its insular holdings (including Hong Kong) east of the meridian of 110 degrees east longitude.

The Washington Naval Treaty, which was signed on 6 February 1922, forced the United States, Great Britain, and Japan to scrap sixty-six capital ships, existing or under construction, of some 1,864,000 tons standard displacement. Neither French nor Italian ships were required to be destroyed under the agreement. The treaty established the overall capital ship ratio for the United States, Great Britain, Japan, France, and Italy as 5:5:3:1.75:1.75. Under its terms, the capital ships remaining in the countries' fleets could be replaced only twenty years after their completion. Total capital ship replacement tonnage of the Contracting Powers was set at 525,000 tons each for the United States and Great Britain, 315,000 tons for Japan, and 175,000 tons each for France and Italy. The maximum size of a new capital ship was set at 35,000 tons standard displacement.

Largely because of French opposition, the Contracting Powers were unable to reach an overall agreement limiting "auxiliary vessels," as the treaty referred to smaller warships. Aircraft carriers, however, were included under the agreement's limitations. Article VII of the treaty stated that the total tonnage for aircraft carriers of the five countries was to be 135,000 tons each for the United States and Great Britain, 81,000 tons for Japan, and 60,000 tons each for France and Italy. Although under the terms of the treaty individual aircraft carriers exceeding 27,000 tons standard displacement were not to be built, at the request of the British an initial exception was allowed. Each of the parties could construct no more than two carriers of up to 33,000 tons standard displacement, so long as this fit within the overall carrier tonnage figures allowed those countries.

During much of the Washington Naval Treaty's life, it had a negative effect on the overall strength of the U.S. Fleet. This was because the administrations of Presidents Warren G. Harding, Calvin Coolidge, and Herbert Hoover and the various U.S. Congresses during those years prevented the Navy from building up to treaty strength. Indeed, in 1922–1924 and again in 1929, the United States did not lay down a single ship. During the eight-year period from 1922 through 1929, U.S. shipyards laid down just eight heavy cruisers and three submarines, while Britain and

Japan between them laid down two battleships, an aircraft carrier, twenty-seven heavy cruisers, four light cruisers, sixty-four destroyers, and fifty-three submarines.

For the U.S. Navy the saving grace of the Washington Naval Treaty proved to be the language relating to aircraft carrier tonnage. Using the exception allowed by Article IX of the treaty, the United States converted two of the battle cruiser hulls slated for scrapping into large 33,000-ton flattops. When commissioned in 1927, *Lexington* (CV 2) and *Saratoga* (CV 3) became the first two fast carriers in the U.S. Fleet. Over the course of the following decade, their large flight decks and sizeable complements of aircraft enabled naval aviators to experiment with and thus work through the complexities of operating combat aircraft successfully at sea.

By allowing the United States a substantial amount of tonnage that could be used to build aircraft carriers, the Washington Naval Treaty helped furnish the Navy with the impetus to advance the operation of a new class of warship. Thus, despite the overall sluggishness in the American naval building program in the 1920s and 1930s, the Navy entered the wartime years with a substantial combat capability inherent in its highly trained force of aircraft carriers.

Above: *Navy and civilian personnel examine models showing the conversion of a planned battle cruiser to an aircraft carrier, a provision permitted under the Washington Naval Treaty. When completed,* Lexington *(CV 2) and her sister* Saratoga *(CV 3) provided naval aviation with a true offensive capability and allowed for a quicker integration of the carrier into fleet operations. The man who would lead this revolution, Chief of the Bureau of Aeronautics Rear Admiral William A. Moffett, is standing second from left. (Naval Historical Center)*

27 October

The Navy League of the United States sponsors the first of what becomes an annual celebration of Navy Day in an effort to focus public attention on the importance of the sea service. This particular day is chosen because it is the birthday of former President Theodore Roosevelt, a champion of the Navy.

18 November

Commander Kenneth Whiting, the executive officer of the aircraft carrier *Langley*, records the first catapult launch from a U.S. Navy aircraft carrier, flying a PT aircraft from *Langley* while she lies at anchor in the York River.

20 November–18 December

The light cruisers *Denver* (CL 16) and *Cleveland* (CL 21) deliver relief supplies to Chile in the wake of an earthquake in the South American nation.

6 December

A reorganization championed by Chief of Naval Operations Admiral Robert E. Coontz combines the former Atlantic and Pacific Fleets into the United States Fleet under Admiral Hilary P. Jones. The new fleet is subdivided into the Battle Fleet, Scouting Fleet (redesignated Battle Force and Scouting Force in 1931), Control Force, and Fleet Base Force.

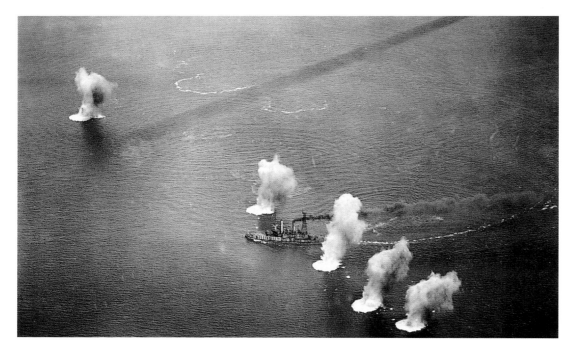

Right: *Crewmen on board the battleship* Mississippi *(BB 41) gather topside to observe the ship's passage through the Panama Canal during the early 1920s. Note the cage masts, a common feature of battleships of the era. (National Museum of Naval Aviation)*

16 December
The crew of the destroyer *Bainbridge* (DD 246) rescues 482 people from the French military transport *Vinh-Long* after she catches fire off Constantinople. Lieutenant Commander Walter A. Edwards, *Bainbridge*'s skipper, receives the Medal of Honor for heroically maintaining position alongside the bow of the transport despite several violent explosions that rock the French ship.

1923

14 February
The gunboat *Asheville* (PG 21) puts ashore a detachment of Marines on Matsu Island, China, to protect American citizens from attacks by bandits.

18–22 February
Ships of the U.S. Fleet participate in Fleet Problem I, involving aviation in evaluating the defense of the Panama Canal against air attack. This is the first of a series of annual fleet exercises that in some respects foreshadow operations during World War II.

26 April
The General Board completes a study on U.S. Navy strategy in the Pacific that anticipates Japan as the only enemy in the foreseeable future; calls for the development of bases at Pearl Harbor, Hawaii, Guam, and in the Philippines; and advocates a fleet capable of sustained operations in the Western Pacific.

2 June
The Naval Research Laboratory is established.

6–7 June
In the skies over San Diego, California, naval aviators establish fifteen world speed, distance, duration, and altitude records for Class C seaplanes.

11 June
Following a boiler explosion on board the destroyer *Bruce* (DD 329) at the Norfolk Navy Yard, Virginia, Machinist's Mate William R. Huber enters the steam-filled fire room and, despite suffering burns on his arms and neck, pulls a shipmate to safety. He is awarded the Medal of Honor for his heroism.

31 July
Admiral Edward W. Eberle, a veteran of service in the battleship *Oregon* (BB 3) during the Battle of Santiago and former Commander in Chief of the Pacific Fleet, assumes his duties as the third Chief of Naval Operations.

1 September
Earthquakes cause heavy damage to Tokyo and Yokohama, Japan. Ensign Thomas J. Ryan rescues a woman from the flames at Yokohama's Grand Hotel and is awarded the Medal of Honor for his actions. On 5 September ships of the Asiatic Fleet anchor off Yokohama to assist in relief efforts.

4 September
Shenandoah (ZR 1), the U.S. Navy's first rigid airship, makes her maiden flight at Naval Air Station Lakehurst, New Jersey.

8 September

Destroyer Squadron 11—including of *Chauncey* (DD 296), *Delphy* (DD 261), *Fuller* (DD 297), *Nicholas* (DD 311), *S. P. Lee* (DD 310), *Woodbury* (DD 309), and *Young* (DD 312)—encounters heavy fog during a high-speed run down the California coast. Due to a navigational error, the flagship *Delphy* turns toward the coast, her captain thinking that she is entering Santa Barbara Channel. Instead, at 2105 she runs into the jagged rocks of Point Pedernales, an unforgiving area known to sailors as the Devil's Jaw. The fog shrouds signals from *Delphy*, and one by one six other destroyers plow into the rocks. The worst fate befalls *Young*, which capsizes in just over a minute, trapping many crewmen below. Chief Boatswain's Mate Arthur Peterson bravely jumps overboard carrying a line to *Chauncey*, allowing many of his shipmates to escape. Twenty of the twenty-two men who die as a result of the disaster are members of *Young*'s crew.

28 October

The submarine *O-5* (SS 66) collides with the United Fruit steamer *Abangarez* in Limon Bay, Panama. Torpedoman Second Class Henry Breault reaches the hatch in time to escape the sinking submarine, but instead returns to his post in the torpedo room to rescue a shipmate trapped there. Closing the torpedo room hatch, Breault and his fellow sailor remain

Above: *Destroyers* Nicholas *(DD 311) and* S. P. Lee *(DD 310) after running aground off California on 8 September 1923. (Naval Historical Center)*

Right: *Members of the Engineer's Mess gather on board* Wyoming *(BB 32). A steward pours coffee, the lifeblood of men working aboard ship. Note the sailor in the foreground sporting a tattoo, a lasting memory for many Navy men. (National Museum of Naval Aviation)*

trapped in the compartment until rescued by a salvage party after thirty-one hours. Breault receives the Medal of Honor for his devotion to his shipmate.

6 December

To protect foreign nationals living in China during the civil war there, destroyers of the Asiatic Fleet are ordered to Canton.

1924

16 January

The light cruiser *Tacoma* (CL 20), while operating in the Gulf of Mexico, is wrecked on Blanquilla Reef off Veracruz, Mexico, with the loss of her captain and three sailors.

23 January

In response to an uprising by the Moros in the Philippines, the gunboat *Sacramento* (PG 19) lands a detachment of Marines on Boca Grande Island. They occupy Socorro and assist in putting down the insurrection.

28 February–19 March

A revolution in the Central American nation of Honduras sparks intervention by U.S. naval forces to protect American lives and property. During this period the light cruiser *Denver* puts ashore landing

parties, twice at La Ceiba and once at Puerto Cortez. On 3 March the destroyer *Billingsley* (DD 293) lands bluejackets and Marines at Tela and between 17–19 March a force of 176 officers and men establishes a neutral zone around the town of Tegucigalpa.

19 March

Curtiss D. Wilbur, U.S. Naval Academy Class of 1888 and former Chief Justice of the California Supreme Court, takes office as the forty-third Secretary of the Navy.

8 August

An important step in the process of employing rigid airships in fleet operations occurs when *Shenandoah* secures to a mooring mast erected on the stern of the oiler *Patoka* (AO 9) while the ship is underway in Narragansett Bay, Rhode Island. One week later *Shenandoah* participates in fleet exercises for the first time, spending forty hours in the air.

10 September

The cruiser *Rochester* (CA 2) lands a force of eleven bluejackets and Marines to protect American lives and property at La Ceiba, Honduras.

7–25 October

The airship *Shenandoah*, in a demonstration of her endurance, completes a long-distance flight from Naval Air Station Lakehurst, New Jersey, to the West

Coast and back. The airship spends 258 hours in the air during the various legs of the transcontinental flight, which covers a distance of 9,317 miles.

20 October
While the light cruiser *Trenton* (CL 11) operates off Norfolk, Virginia, powder charges in her forward gun turret explode, trapping twenty men inside. Observing that the powder charge for the left gun is ignited, Ensign Henry Clay Drexler and Boatswain's Mate First Class George Robert Cholister, without regard to their own safety, attempt to dump the powder charge for the right gun into the immersion tank before it ignites. Their valiant efforts prove unsuccessful and cost both men their lives. Drexler and Cholister are both awarded the Medal of Honor posthumously.

23 October
The Marine detachment from the cruiser *Huron* (CA 9) departs Shanghai, China, and transfers to Peking, ending a period of over two months during which ships of the Asiatic Fleet put ashore landing parties to protect American interests as revolutionary factions fought for control of Shanghai.

25 November
The rigid airship *Los Angeles* (ZR 3), built in Germany and flown across the Atlantic, is christened by First Lady Mrs. Calvin Coolidge and commissioned during ceremonies at Naval Air Station Anacostia, Washington, D.C.

1925

15 January
Renewed violence in Shanghai during the Chinese civil war necessitates the landing of the Marine detachment from the gunboat *Sacramento* to help protect the international settlement in the city. Five subsequent landings by Marines are made throughout the year.

2–11 March
In the first participation by an aircraft carrier in fleet exercises, *Langley* performs scouting missions during Fleet Problem V held off lower California in the waters around Guadalupe Island. Her operations demonstrate the need for more durable and capable aircraft.

4 March
An act of Congress establishes the Naval Reserve Officer Training Corps with units initially established at six universities the following year. To this day, NROTC provides a cadre of capable officers for the naval service.

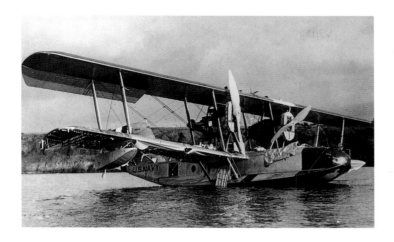

Left: *Battered from spending ten days at sea after being forced down during an attempted flight from San Francisco, California, to Honolulu, the PN-9 rests at anchor in the Hawaiian Islands after rescue in September 1925. Note where the fabric has been torn away on the lower wing by Commander John Rodgers and his crew to use as a makeshift sail. (Naval Historical Center)*

1 April

Lieutenant Commander John Dale Price performs the first night landing on board a U.S. Navy aircraft carrier when he traps on board *Langley* while she steams off the coast of California. Night operations are not routine on board U.S. Navy flattops until after World War II.

20 April

Mirroring actions of the previous year, Marines from the cruiser *Denver* go ashore at La Ceiba, Honduras, to protect American interests there.

1 August

The MacMillan Arctic Expedition reaches Etah, Greenland, and with three Loening OL aircraft begins aerial observation flights that by the end of the month cover some 30,000 square miles. The expedition also performs valuable work in evaluating short-wave and long-range radio transmitting.

1 September

The PN-9 flying boat, having departed California the previous day, runs out of fuel during its attempted flight to the Hawaiian Islands. The aircraft's pilot, Commander John Rodgers (Naval Aviator Number 2), and his crew make a forced landing and employ fabric from the aircraft's wings to rig a makeshift sail. They set course for Kauai Island and after ten days at sea are spotted by the submarine *R-4* (SS 81). They are just ten miles from land. Though they do not achieve their goal, the 1,841 miles covered during the flight establishes a distance record.

3 September

While flying near Ava, Ohio, the rigid airship *Shenandoah* is torn in two and crashes during a severe storm. Fourteen members of her crew, including skipper Lieutenant Commander Zachary Lansdowne, are killed. Following the crash, Army Brigadier General William Mitchell makes bombastic statements regarding the administration of aviation by the War and Navy Departments, which ultimately leads to his court-martial.

Opposite: *Loaded down with helmets, rifles, entrenching tools, and other items for use ashore, a landing party from the cruiser* Pittsburgh *(CA 4) on a boat that will transport them to Shanghai, to protect American interests during a civil war in China, 1927. (Naval Historical Center)*

Right: *Six destroyers undergo repairs in Dry Dock Number 2 at Mare Island Navy Yard, California, during the 1920s. The important base maintained ships operating in the Pacific and constructed new ones for service. (Naval Historical Center)*

AIRSHIPS AND THE NAVY

by Mark L. Evans

The U.S. military's employment of lighter-than-air (LTA) craft in support of operations dates to the Civil War, where Union observers were hoisted aloft in hydrogen-filled balloons tethered to vessels for reconnaissance and artillery spotting. However, the Navy lost interest after 1865 and it was not until Europeans demonstrated LTA efficacy during World War I that Captain Mark L. Bristol, then serving as Director, Naval Aviation, received support for a program. On 1 June 1915, an airship contract was let to the Connecticut Aircraft Company, and on 14 December, the Navy accepted its first free balloon, followed eight days later by delivery of its first kite balloon. In 1915 the Navy also divided LTA into three categories: non-rigid airships, free balloons, and kite balloons. Simultaneously, at Akron, Ohio, Lieutenant Commander Frank R. McCrary and Lieutenant Louis H. Maxfield became the first to complete LTA training.

America's entry into World War I accelerated development, and with McCrary at the controls, the DN-1 (D for dirigible and N for Navy), the Navy's first airship, made its maiden flight on 20 April 1917. When the armistice ending the war was signed in November 1918, the Navy LTA inventory boasted dozens of craft, comprising classes B through E as well as Anglo-French types accepted during the war, an incredible achievement considering wartime shortages and the development of the program from scratch. Just as important was the capable force trained to man them. On 29 May 1917, a contract was let to Goodyear for a training program, which began in June near Akron, Ohio. The experience these trainees gained resulted in the establishment of a formal LTA training syllabus in July 1918, which almost 700 pilots completed without a single fatality by the end of the war.

Wartime operations for these men and machines centered on the hunt for German U-boats. LTA patrol stations were established along the Atlantic coast and in France and Ireland. Patrols could be grueling affairs, punctuated by sheer moments of terror when freezing winds mercilessly buffeted crews or U-boats played a cat and mouse game of survival. B-class dirigibles normally carried three crewmen, who used a bewildering array of equipment: Lewis guns, bombs, radios, flares, Very pistols, signal books, charts, cameras, and even carrier pigeons.

Following the war, kite balloons faded as funds were slashed and interest peaked in rigid airships, which Germany had operated with success in combat. The interwar years marked the heyday of large airship operations, with the Navy procuring five dirigibles including *Shenandoah* (ZR 1), *R-38* (ZR 2), *Los Angeles* (ZR 3), *Akron* (ZRS 4), and *Macon* (ZRS 5). *Shenandoah* became the first airship to cross America,

Left: Macon *(ZRS 4) under construction at Akron, Ohio, 1933. The Navy's rigid airships were administratively treated as ships. They were placed in commission, had an assigned commanding officer and crew, and bore the prefix "USS" (United States Ship).* Macon *crashed into the Pacific during a storm on 12 February 1935. This marked the fourth loss of a U.S. Navy rigid airship in fourteen years and effectively ended their controversial operation in the fleet. (Naval Historical Center)*

Right: *Novelties in their own right, rigid airships also were a part of one of the most unique flight operations in aviation history. F9C-2 Sparrowhawk fighters, housed in a hangar in the dirigible, were launched and recovered by means of a "trapeze." Pilots engaged and disengaged from it by employing a hook located on their aircraft's upper wing. (Naval Historical Center)*

and in 1929 *Los Angeles* was fitted with a trapeze for launching and recovering aircraft. On 3 July, a UO-1 flown by Lieutenant A. W. Gorton hooked on to *Los Angeles* near Lakehurst, New Jersey, and following additional tests, *Akron* and *Macon* were designed to carry five aircraft apiece inside hangars, launching them for scouting as well as on offensive and defensive missions.

Yet, the Navy's experience with rigid airships proved a tragic one, with the operational careers of four of them ending in deadly crashes. *R-38* went down near Hull, England, on 23 August 1921. *Shenandoah* crashed on 3 September 1925 in Ohio. *Akron* was lost on 3–4 April 1933 off New Jersey, and *Macon* plummeted into the Pacific Ocean off California on 11–12 February 1935. These disasters claimed 133 lives, including Rear Admiral William A. Moffett, an airship champion and Chief of the Bureau of Aeronautics, who perished in *Akron*.

Though the expenses of operating the rigid airships were great, the Navy did not ignore the development of its non-rigid fleet, which benefited the service during World War II when the German submarine menace again threatened America's vital convoy routes to Europe. To hold them open, Navy LTA grew into the largest airship fleet in history. Upward of 100 G-, L-, TC-, K-, and M-class craft were accepted into the inventory, forming five fleet airship wings of twenty squadrons, the first of which, Airship Patrol Group One, was established on 2

January 1942. This and other groups were subsequently redesignated Fleet Airship Wings (FASWs). FASW-3 operated in the Pacific and the others in the Atlantic, and all contributed greatly to the war effort. On 11 April 1942, *L-8* secretly rendezvoused with the carrier *Hornet* (CV 8) off California. As the airship delicately hovered over the pitching carrier, she lowered vital spare parts for Army Air Forces Colonel Jimmy Doolittle's B-25 Mitchells, en route to bomb Japan. By 1945 airships were equipped with radar and magnetic anomaly detection gear. Only one airship, Blimp Squadron 21's *K-74*, was lost to enemy action, during a savage night battle with *U-134* off Florida on 18–19 July 1943. During the war, airships proved ideal for convoy operations, their great range enabling them to shadow merchant ships for hours at a time

The advent of the Cold War and the Russian submarine threat forced airships to work closely with antisubmarine warfare groups, and landings and refueling from carriers became commonplace. In addition, Airship Airborne Early Warning Squadron One, established on 3 January 1956, supported the airborne early warning barrier, flying double the average monthly hours of World War II airships. However, defense revisions reduced the squadron's usefulness and it was disestablished on 31 October 1961. Navy LTA officially ended with the last airship flight on 31 August 1962, closing a unique chapter that took the wings of gold from primitive balloons to aircraft carriers in the sky.

25 September
Operating off Rhode Island, the submarine *S-51* (SS 162) collides with the merchant vessel *City of Rome*. Only three of thirty-six crew members survive.

30 November
The President's Aircraft Board (which becomes known as the Morrow Board after its chairman, Dwight Morrow), formed in the wake of the crash of the airship *Shenandoah*, issues its report. After testimony from top civilian and military leaders, the board issues findings on all facets of American aviation. With respect to the Navy, the board recommends against the establishment of an independent air force, favors more aviation representation in the higher levels of the service's administrative structure, and calls for a long-range procurement plan for aircraft. The Morrow Board's report spurs legislative action that has far-reaching impact on the development of naval aviation.

1926

7 May
The light cruiser *Cleveland* lands her Marine detachment at Bluefields, Nicaragua, to protect American and other foreign interests during a civil war. The leathernecks remain ashore until 5 June.

Above: *("U.S. Submarine S-51," William Kolvig, Navy Art Collection)*

Left: *Leading aviation supporters gather at the Mayflower Hotel, 1927, (l–r): Edward P. Warner, Assistant Secretary of Navy for Air, W. T. McCracken, Assistant Secretary of War for Air, Antarctic explorer Lieutenant Commander Richard E. Byrd, Charles A. Lindbergh, Assistant Secretary of War F. T. Davidson, Third Assistant Postmaster W. Irving Glover. (Naval Historical Center)*

Right: *Curtiss F6C-3 of Bombing Squadron 1-B. Formerly Fighting Squadron 5, the famed "Red Rippers," the squadron was redesignated as a bombing squadron in 1928 and served as such on board in* Lexington *(CV 2) until* 1930, *when it reverted to its original fighter mission. The "E" painted prominently on its nose denotes excellence in gunnery. (National Museum of Naval Aviation)*

9 May
Flying a Fokker Tri-motor nicknamed the *Josephine Ford*, Lieutenant Commander Richard E. Byrd and Chief Aviation Pilot Floyd E. Bennett become the first men to fly over the North Pole. The flight from Norway lasts fifteen and one-half hours. Both men receive the Medal of Honor for the daring flight.

6 June
The last elements of the Alaskan Aerial Survey depart Seattle, Washington. Operating from the tender *Gannett* (AM 41) throughout the summer, three Loening OL amphibians complete the first extensive mapping of the territory of Alaska.

2 July
An act of Congress establishes the award of the Distinguished Flying Cross for heroism or extraordinary achievement in aerial flight.

10 July
Edward P. Warner takes office as the first Assistant Secretary of the Navy for Aeronautics, a post created by Congress on the recommendation of the Morrow Board.

27 August
Renewed fighting around Bluefields, Nicaragua, during one of that nation's civil wars prompts the cruiser *Galveston* to put ashore a landing party of 200 men to establish a neutral zone around the town. Ships' parties will land again in October and November to enforce the neutral zone.

10 October
The cruiser *Denver* lands bluejackets and Marines at Corinto, Nicaragua, in an attempt to preserve order during an ultimately unproductive meeting between leaders of the warring Liberals and Conservatives.

22 October
In the first demonstration of the tactic of dive-bombing against ships, F6C-2 Hawks of Fighting Squadron (VF) Two stage a mock attack against battleships as they sortie from San Pedro, California. The attack is deemed a success, and two months later Rear Admiral Joseph Mason Reeves, Commander Aircraft Squadrons, Battle Fleet issues a report that envisions the tactic as a means of knocking out enemy carriers in battle.

24 October
The light cruiser *Milwaukee* (CL 5) and the destroyer *Goff* (DD 247) arrive at the Isle of Pines in the Caribbean Sea to assist in relief efforts following a hurricane. The ships' crews establish a makeshift hospital ashore, deliver fifty tons of supplies, and maintain wireless communication between the devastated island and the rest of the world.

12 November
The auxiliary ship *Gold Star* (AG 12) lands 125 Marines at Chingwangtao, China, to protect American interests in the city.

Left: *Marines board the transport* Henderson *at Quantico, Virginia, en route to Nicaragua, 23 February 1927. The venerable ship was a floating home for Marines beginning in World War I and carried them to battlefields in France, Central America, China, and the Pacific until 1943, when she was converted to the hospital ship* Bountiful. *(Underwood & Underwood/Corbis)*

Below: *Vice Admiral William V. Pratt, photographed in January 1928 as Commander, Battleships, Battle Fleet. He served as Chief of Naval Operations during 1930–1933. (Naval Historical Center)*

1927

6 January

The light cruiser *Galveston* lands her Marine detachment, which reestablishes the legation guard at the Nicaraguan capital of Managua. Additional landings from Navy ships occur throughout the remainder of the year.

18 January

A formal course of instruction in aviation medicine is instituted with the assignment of Lieutenant Commander John R. Poppen to head the Aviation Section of the Naval Medical School in Washington, D.C. This marks the beginning of flight surgeon training in the U.S. Navy.

9 February

Under the orders of Rear Admiral Julian L. Latimer, commander of the Special Service Squadron operating in Central American waters, the light cruisers *Galveston*, *Milwaukee*, and *Raleigh* (CL 7) land their Marine detachments to seize the Corinto-Managua railroad in Nicaragua. This prevents the vital line of communication from being cut by rival forces during the civil war.

21 February

The light cruiser *Trenton*, carrying Marine detachments from the battleships *Arkansas*, *Florida*

Right: *As evidenced by the combat aircraft crowded together behind barriers on her flight deck, the commissioning of the aircraft carrier* Lexington *(CV 2) and her sister ship* Saratoga *(CV 3) added significant striking power to the fleet. Over 800 feet in length, they could each effectively operate some 100 aircraft. (National Museum of Naval Aviation)*

(BB 30), and *Texas*, lands a combined force of 200 leathernecks to guard the railway towns of Chinandega and León, Nicaragua.

4 May
The United States brokers a peace treaty between warring Liberals and Conservatives in Nicaragua, vesting power in the existing Conservative government until elections can be held in 1928. This does not end the violence in the country, as Marines find themselves engaged in a war against bandits.

30 June–4 August
A naval conference is held at Geneva, Switzerland. Delegations from the United States, Great Britain, and Japan fail in their attempt to impose limitations on cruiser construction and the building of warships not outlined in the Five-Power Treaty.

14 November
Rear Admiral Charles Frederick Hughes, having already served in the billets of Commander, Battle Fleet and Commander in Chief, U.S. Fleet, becomes the fourth Chief of Naval Operations.

16 November
The aircraft carrier *Saratoga* (CV 3) is commissioned.

14 December
The aircraft carrier *Lexington* (CV 2) is commissioned.

17 December
While surfacing off Provincetown, Massachusetts, the submarine *S-4* (SS 109) collides with the Coast Guard cutter *Paulding*. *S-4* goes down with the loss of all thirty-nine crewmen despite rescue efforts by Navy divers, including Chief Gunner's Mate Thomas Eadie, who receives the Medal of Honor for rescuing a fellow diver who becomes entangled in an air line. The submarine is later raised and recommissioned, serving until 1933.

1928

12 June
Demonstrating the increased capabilities the Navy's newest carriers bring to the fleet, *Lexington* completes a high-speed run from San Pedro, California, to Honolulu, Hawaii, in a record time of 72 hours and 34 minutes.

1929

23–27 January
In the first participation of the fleet carriers *Lexington* and *Saratoga* in the annual Fleet Problem, Rear Admiral Joseph Mason Reeves formulates a daring plan, separating *Saratoga* and an escort from the main force to engage in a surprise dawn attack against the Panama Canal. The attack is successful and for the

first time demonstrates the potent offensive potential of carrier task forces operating independently. "You can realize how the sentiment as regards aviation has changed," writes one aviator in the days after the operation. "Everybody has been tremendously impressed by what we're doing."

13 February
President Calvin Coolidge signs the so-called Cruiser Bill, which authorizes the construction of fifteen cruisers. Though the legislation specifies light cruisers, it ultimately results in the commissioning of heavy cruisers as well, including the ill-fated *Indianapolis* (CA 35).

5 March
Charles F. Adams, the treasurer of Harvard University, becomes the forty-fourth Secretary of the Navy.

8 May
The first device to provide a means to escape a sunken submarine undergoes its first testing. Developed by Lieutenant Charles B. Momsen, Chief Gunner Clarence L. Tibbals, and civilian engineer Frank Hobson, the so-called Momsen Lung consists of a rubber bag containing a canister of soda lime that removes carbon dioxide from exhaled air and replaces it with oxygen. Inhalation tubes and exhalation tubes attach to a mouthpiece. It will be used successfully in the escape of crewmen from the submarine *Tang* when it sinks to a depth of 180 feet during World War II.

4 June
Lieutenant Apollo Soucek, flying the Wright Apache, reaches an altitude of 38,560 feet, thus establishing a new record for Class C seaplanes.

20 August
In experiments conducted to test the feasibility of operating aircraft from rigid airships, Lieutenant Adolphus W. Gorton pilots a UO-1 in several successful hook-ons to a trapeze lowered from *Los Angeles* operating over Naval Air Station Lakehurst, New Jersey.

Reducing Cruisers to a Minimum

28 November
Commander Richard E. Byrd, flying in a Ford Tri-motor—nicknamed *Floyd Bennett* after the pilot from his 1926 North Pole flight who died in 1928—commands the first flight over the South Pole. In addition to Byrd, who serves as navigator, the nineteen-hour flight includes pilot Bernt Balchen, an officer in the Royal Norwegian Air Force; copilot Harold June, a Navy enlisted pilot on a leave of absence; and Army photographer Captain Ashley McKinley.

1930

16 January
In an unconventional mission for a ship of war, the aircraft carrier *Lexington* completes a period in which she provides electricity to Tacoma, Washington, after a failure of the city's power plant. As one of a small number of Navy ships with turboelectric power plants, the carrier is called to this unlikely duty on 18 December 1929.

22 April
Further efforts to reduce the size of the world's major navies occur at the London Naval Conference in England, at which the United States, Great Britain, and Japan agree to a 10:10:7 ratio in cruiser tonnage, and limits are placed on destroyers and submarines.

15 May
The submarine design appears with the commissioning of *Narwhal* (SC 1) (later SS 167) is commissioned at Portsmouth, New Hampshire. She will later survive the December 1941 attack on Pearl Harbor, Hawaii, and complete fifteen war patrols during World War II.

4 June
Flying a Wright Apache aircraft, Lieutenant Apollo Soucek reaches an altitude of 43,166 feet in the skies over Naval Air Station Anacostia in Washington, D.C.

17 September
Admiral William V. Pratt, a veteran of over forty years of naval service and former Commander in Chief, U.S. Fleet, takes office as the fifth Chief of Naval Operations.

1931

9 January
An agreement reached between Chief of Naval Operations Admiral William V. Pratt and Army Chief of Staff General Douglas A. MacArthur gives the Army Air Corps primacy in coastal defense and concentrates naval aviation on mobile operations with the fleet. The Navy does not operate long-range land-based combat aircraft until World War II.

22 January
The Navy orders its first rotary-wing aircraft, the XOP-1 autogyro, which the following September becomes the first aircraft of its type to land on board an aircraft carrier.

31 March
An earthquake hits Managua, Nicaragua, killing some 2,000 people and prompting the dispatch of the aircraft carrier *Lexington* and the hospital ship *Relief* (AH 1) to provide assistance.

1 April
A reorganization of the U.S. Fleet results in the creation of the Battle, Scouting, Submarine, and Base Forces.

Above: *A newspaper editorial cartoon ridiculing efforts to reduce cruiser tonnage at the London Naval Conference in 1930. (Naval Historical Center)*

FATHERS OF NAVAL AVIATION

by M. Hill Goodspeed

They were men of a different era: nineteenth-century graduates of the U.S. Naval Academy directing a twentieth-century phenomenon; middle-aged men in a distinctly young man's game. They were battleship officers, their entire professional careers having been wedded to the axiom of the big gun as the deciding factor in naval warfare. Yet, they were also opportunists and perceptive students of naval warfare, who envisioned a future in which naval warfare diverged from the conventional wisdom of the day. Thus, William A. Moffett and Joseph Mason Reeves tied their professional fortunes to naval aviation, and in so doing ensured the future of naval air power and laid the foundation for its rise to preeminence in the U.S. Navy.

The year was 1919, and the U.S. Navy had just emerged from the Great War, which greatly expanded its ranks, including aviation. Wartime service also broadened the experience of naval aviators, their British counterparts having imparted valuable lessons. These included the operation of airplanes from ships and the necessity for the Navy to maintain control of sea-based airpower, the latter not accomplished in Great Britain after the consolidation of all military and naval aviation under the Royal Air Force. Interest in shipboard operations was reflected during the winter of 1919, when the Fleet Air Detachment, Atlantic Fleet, the first aviation organization in the fleet, began operating fighter aircraft from wooden decks erected atop the gun turrets of battleships. One of these ships was *Mississippi* (BB 41), commanded by Captain William A. Moffett. A native of South Carolina and a recipient of the Medal of Honor for his actions during the 1914 Veracruz Intervention, Moffett had developed into an aviation-minded officer. As commander of the Great Lakes Naval Training School during World War I, he had been instrumental in establishing an aviation unit there for the training of pilots and mechanics. And now, in the first year of peace, he realized the potential of airplanes to spot the fire of his battleship's main battery. Little did he know what influence aviation would have on his career.

In 1920 Moffett received orders to report to Washington, D.C., as Director Naval Aviation, a staff job that the following year grew in importance with the establishment of the Bureau of Aeronautics to oversee the development of naval aviation. Moffett was named its first chief, a position he held for twelve years. A better steward could not be found for the Navy's air arm. A politically astute officer, Moffett proved quite at home in the halls of Congress, where he courted those who might benefit aviation and, in a Navy bureaucracy slow to embrace the potential of the airplane, he campaigned for a greater role for aviation in fleet operations. While some junior aviators advanced the idea of establishing the Navy's air assets into a corps akin to the Marines, Moffett realized that naval aviation's road to success lay with the integration of the airplane with the fleet. This required a special officer, and in the assignment of Captain Joseph Mason Reeves to command Aircraft Squadrons, Battle Fleet, Moffett found him.

A native of Illinois, Reeves had made a reputation for his gunnery skills during a career that had included participation in the Battle of Santiago during the Spanish-American War. Strategically minded Reeves served on the staff at the Naval War College in Newport, Rhode Island, where he studied the influence aviation might have on future sea battles. This led to his assignment to aviation duty. Reporting aboard *Langley* (CV 1), a converted collier (ironically, once commanded by Reeves) and the U.S. Navy's first aircraft carrier, Reeves wasted little time in shaping his new command. Nicknamed "Bull," he was a hard-driving officer, and within weeks he was pressing his charges to expand their knowledge of the tactical applications of the airplane, issuing his famous "1001 Questions," whose answers formed the basis for the operation of aircraft in the fleet. "The Fleet, and by that I mean the general sentiment and verdict of the officers at sea with the fleet, is bound to have great weight and influence in what aviation is tomorrow and day after tomorrow," he wrote to Moffett in 1926. "Aviation is in a position where she must deliver results

Right: *Rear Admiral William A. Moffett (right) and Captain Joseph Mason Reeves (left) observe flight operations on board* Langley *(CV 1), the Navy's first aircraft carrier. Between them stands Commander Kenneth Whiting, pioneer aviator and the first executive officer of* Langley. *(U.S. Naval Institute)*

right now." To this end, Reeves pushed *Langley* to the limit, expanding the number of aircraft operated by the diminutive flattop, and increasingly sought a greater role for her during fleet exercises. Then came the commissioning of the giant carriers *Lexington* (CV 2) and *Saratoga* (CV 3) in 1927. Carrying some 100 aircraft and capable of thirty knots, these two flattops could keep pace with the battle line and more than provided Reeves with the means to demonstrate the true potential of naval aviation.

That opportunity came in January 1929 with the commencement of Fleet Problem Nine, a tactical exercise carried out in the Pacific off Central America. Reeves hatched a daring plan that involved *Saratoga* and one escort detaching from the main fleet and launching a surprise attack against the Panama Canal.

With the attackers roaring off the flight deck in the predawn darkness, the Navy planes took the defenders by surprise. Reeves's plan was a dramatic success,. This marked the first demonstration of the concept of an independent carrier task force that became a hallmark of Pacific operations during World War II, and there was no doubt who was responsible for the evolution. "You can realize how the sentiment as regards [to] aviation has changed," wrote one pilot. "All the credit is due the Admiral, who said that we could do it, then made us do it. He's a great old man."

Today, carrier battle groups roam the seas, ready to strike quickly and lethally, and aviation has developed into one of the most important arms of the Navy. This is the legacy of William A. Moffett and Joseph Mason Reeves.

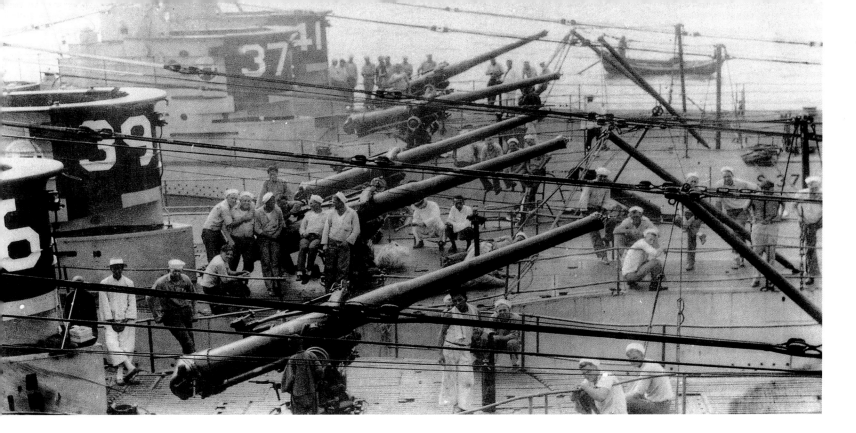

2 April
The Navy contracts Grumman Aircraft Engineering Corporation to build the XFF-1, a carrier-based fighter with a revolutionary design that features metal construction and retractable landing gear.

27 October
The rigid dirigible *Akron* (ZRS 4) is placed in commission at Akron, Ohio. In November she establishes a record by carrying 207 people aloft.

1932

---

3 February
The cruiser *Houston* (CA 30), flagship of the ships operating on the Asiatic Station, lands her Marine detachment at Shanghai, China, to protect American lives and property threatened by hostilities between China and Japan.

1 June
President Franklin D. Roosevelt accepts the resignation of David S. Ingalls as Assistant Secretary of the Navy for Aeronautics. The post is abolished, but will reappear nine years later.

30 June
The rigid airship *Los Angeles* is decommissioned after spending eight years in active service and logging more than 5,000 miles in the air.

Above: *Crewmen relax during their off-duty period on board submarines alongside the tender* Canopus *(AS 9) at Tsingtao, China, circa 1930. (Naval Historical Center)*

Opposite: *("Fleet Maneuvers," James Dietz)*

Left: *Lieutenant Daniel Tomlinson and the members of Fighting Squadron 5 informed friends and families of their travels with the fleet in this 1930 Christmas card. (National Museum of Naval Aviation)*

1933

4 March
Claude A. Swanson, former U.S. Senator and Governor of Virginia, takes office as the forty-fifth Secretary of the Navy.

4 April
During a night flight off the coast of New Jersey, the rigid airship *Akron* crashes into the Atlantic during a storm with the loss of seventy-three men. Among those killed is Rear Admiral William A. Moffett, the long-time Chief of the Bureau of Aeronautics and a champion of lighter-than-air operations.

16 June
A provision of President Franklin D. Roosevelt's landmark New Deal, the National Industrial Recovery Act passes on this date. Roosevelt later allocates $238 million from the legislation to ship construction, bolstering the Navy with the building of thirty-three vessels, including the aircraft carriers *Yorktown* (CV 5) and *Enterprise* (CV 6). Over $7 million is earmarked for aircraft procurement and equipment.

23 June
Destined to be the last rigid airship procured by the Navy, *Macon* (ZRS 5) is commissioned at Akron, Ohio.

1 July
Admiral William H. Standley, veteran of the Spanish-American War and the Philippine Insurrection, becomes the sixth Chief of Naval Operations.

28 October
The Navy contracts with Consolidated Aircraft Corporation for the construction of the XP3Y-1, the prototype for the famous PBY Catalina flying boat that is so successful during World War II.

1934

10–11 January
Six P2Y-1 flying boats of Patrol Squadron (VP) 10F establish time and distance records with a formation flight between San Francisco, California, and Pearl Harbor, Hawaii, that covers 2,399 miles in 24 hours 35 minutes.

27 March
Congress passes the Vinson-Trammel Act, which authorizes "construction of vessels and aircraft to bring the Navy to the prescribed treaty strength." Among the ships that result from the act is the aircraft carrier *Wasp* (CV 7). The passage of the act comes at a time when the U.S. Fleet is just 65 percent of treaty strength whereas the Imperial Japanese Navy is at 95 percent.

Opposite: *The fourteen battleships of the U.S. Fleet in column formation in 1936, led by flagship* Pennsylvania. *The battleships have deployed to fire at an imaginary enemy force to starboard, and three floatplanes are flying out to relieve aircraft already spotting the fire of the ships' big guns. ("Pacific Bulwark," James Flood)*

Right: *A Vought O3U-1 observation floatplane on the turret catapult of* West Virginia *(BB 48), 1930. (National Museum of Naval Aviation)*

4 June
Ranger (CV 4), the first ship in the U.S. Navy built from the keel up as an aircraft carrier, is commissioned.

30 June
The Navy issues a contract to the Douglas Aircraft company for the manufacture of the XTBD-1

Devastator torpedo-bomber, prototype for the first all-metal monoplane to serve in naval aviation.

18 November
A contract is issued to the Northrop Corporation for construction of the XBT-1 dive-bomber, which eventually is developed into the SBD Dauntless employed by Navy and Marine Corps squadrons during World War II.

Left: *Antiaircraft gunners hone their skills during practice on board the heavy cruiser* Houston *(CA 30) off Chatoo, China, 1932–1933. The rise of naval aviation necessitated that gun crews become proficient at hitting targets aloft as well as on the ocean. (Naval Historical Center)*

WEEKEND WARRIORS: THE NAVAL RESERVE

by Commander Peter B. Mersky, United States Naval Reserve (Retired)

Organized military forces have always relied on second-line groups of civilians ready to be called to action when the situation warranted. Whether known as militia or reserves, these units have often meant the difference between staving off enemy advances, final victory, or defeat. While regular service members usually bear the brunt of an enemy's concentrated, sometimes devastating opening attacks, as in World War II and Korea, it is the reserve components that eventually swell defenders' ranks to overwhelming strengths that no enemy can withstand.

In the earliest days of the Continental Navy, sea captains rounded up crews on the waterfront in the great ports along the eastern seaboard, which always had a large pool of willing volunteers eager for adventure on the high seas. These men, mostly sailors on board merchant vessels, provided an informal reserve for the Navy through the Civil War. However, during the late nineteenth century, the rapid advances in technology as the Navy became one of steel and steam required an organization of citizen sailors trained to keep pace with the dramatic changes. Though unsuccessful on the national level, the reserve concept took hold in many states, which began forming naval militias in 1888. Naval militiamen served overseas during the Spanish-American War, and relying upon donations of money and equipment and the earmarking of active naval vessels for training cruises, the states' naval militias were a sizeable presence by the eve of World War I.

The coming of the Great War called many men of the naval militia into active service. The Navy also enlisted women for the duration to fill administrative posts. The Naval Air Reserve developed in 1916 from groups of Yale college students anxious to get into World War I. These so-called "Yale Units" eventually did fight in Europe, mostly flying from coastal air stations on antisubmarine patrols, but occasionally getting into the more glamorous aerial combats that have become part of military lore. The first naval aviator to sink a submarine was Lieutenant H. T. Stanley, one of the members of the Naval Reserve Flying Corps, established in August 1916. The first U.S. Navy ace, Lieutenant (junior grade) David S. Ingalls, was also a reservist.

After the war, the military reserves, along with the other components, diminished and for the next two decades attempts to establish financial allotments for new equipment and programs proved difficult. The reserves continued to grow, and by 1941, with the prospect of American involvement in the fighting in Europe and China, they were nearly ready for recall. After Pearl Harbor, naval reservists soon began having a great impact on the war. The ultimate victories in Europe and Asia were realized in no small measure because of the huge contribution of the reserves, who to a great degree manned the ships, aircraft, and bases of the Navy.

When the war ended in 1945, the reserves again fought postwar deflation schemes, and in 1950, with the Communist invasion of South Korea, America called up its "Weekend Warriors." Hastily rushed to active duty, reserves were among the Marines that landed at Inchon, and in the aviation arena, more than one carrier deployed with air groups that included reserve squadrons. Author James A. Michener wrote a stirring account of a recalled naval air reservist's experience in Korea. In the novel *The Bridges at Toko-ri*, the protagonist, Lieutenant Harry Brubaker, is bitter about having to leave his home and family after seeing action in World War II. It is only at the end of the novel, facing certain death on the ground after bailing out of his plane, that Brubaker understands why he is there.

During the Vietnam War the reserves became something of a refuge for draft-age men who, while not ready to run to Canada and dodge their responsibilities, did not want to serve on active duty and risk being sent to Southeast Asia. A program allowed selected individuals to spend a few months on active duty going through boot camp before returning to their previously selected units as drilling reservists. However, this period also saw experienced, dedicated individuals recently returned from service in Vietnam (and other areas of regular American deployment) join the reserves, anxious to contribute their hard-won knowledge. Many of these were active-duty reservists, called TARs, for Training and Administration of Reserves. Remaining on active duty, the officer and enlisted members did not deploy, but served as regular station keepers and maintainers during the week, assisting the drilling reservists during their monthly meetings and annual training cruises. Some TARs did go overseas during Vietnam, even seeing combat.

The surface reserve and other non-aviation activities made do with traditionally older equipment and ships, and the air reserve also used somewhat older aircraft that had left fleet service. As America gradually pulled its active forces out of Vietnam, the reserves embarked on a long-overdue reorganization. Air and surface reserve forces, split since the end of World War II, were consolidated under one command, the U.S. Naval Reserve Force, commanded by a vice admiral, headquartered in New Orleans, Louisiana.

The Naval Air Reserve soon mirrored the fleet with comparable models of aircraft in front-line service, as well as organizations featuring squadrons included in air wings. Relatively newer ships also made their slow way into the surface reserve, reflecting the Vietnam experience with reserve riverine forces also organized with the smaller combatants. This 1970 revamping is essentially the format for today's reserves, although modern conflicts have greatly refined the overall look and equipment of the Naval Reserve.

By the early 1990s, naval reservists had achieved a greater degree of peacetime use than had ever been seen. The callups that resulted from the Iraqi invasion of Kuwait in August 1990 and the buildup of Operation Desert Shield put reservists in all areas of military activity including filling desk jobs vacated by regular service members now in theater, contributing intelligence expertise to various strategic assessments and daily briefings, participating in the front-line boarding and inspecting of merchant ships, patrolling harbors, and occasionally flying missions over the Gulf.

The successful prosecution of the war dubbed Operation Desert Storm did not see the end of Naval Reserve activities. In fact, the regular Navy found itself relying more and more on its reserve component, especially as American involvement in the building crisis in the Balkans increased in the mid-1990s. Nowhere was the newfound involvement so prominent as the mobilization and ongoing carrier tours of

"GOOD BYE LADIES, WE HATE TO LEAVE YOU NOW"

Electronic Attack Squadron (VAQ) 209, the EA-6B Prowler squadron based at Naval Air Facility (NAF) Washington, D.C., Andrews Air Force Base. From the earliest stages of U.S. operations, VAQ-209 provided electronic countermeasures protection for Allied air groups flying over heavily defended areas in Yugoslavia and Macedonia.

As entry into the twenty-first century has found America facing new and increasingly difficult challenges in all parts of the world, the role of the reserve overall, and the Naval Reserve in particular, has ceased to be the traditional follow-up, backup force. The reserves are now considered part of the regular operation and will likely remain so in the foreseeable future. Gone are the days when, after a war, regular Navy captains might snort and say, "Get these damn reserves out of here!" And James Michener's reluctant hero, Lieutenant Harry Brubaker, might have reached his ultimate understanding of what it means to be a Naval Reservist much sooner.

Above: *Rear Admiral J.L. Jayne bids farewell to yeomanettes who served at his Twelfth Naval District headquarters during World War I. It is appropriate that he does this beneath a Naval Reserve recruiting poster, for over 11,000 women served as reservists during the Great War. (Naval Historical Center)*

Right: Ranger *(CV 4),* the first ship in the U.S. Navy to be built as an aircraft carrier from the keel up, is launched at Newport News, Virginia, 25 February 1933. When completed, she featured a small island superstructure on the starboard side of the flight deck and stacks on both sides of the flight deck that could be rotated down to the horizontal position during flight operations. *(Naval Historical Center)*

1935

12 February

The rigid airship *Macon,* while operating off Point Sur, California, crashes into the Pacific Ocean after encountering a strong gust of wind that causes structural damage. All but two crewmen are rescued at

sea. *Macon* is the fourth U.S. Navy rigid airship lost in an accident, and her demise signals the end of the sea service's dirigible program.

15 April

In an effort to increase the number of aviators in the fleet, Congress passes the Aviation Cadet Act. The measure gives men between the ages of eighteen and

Left: *Bedecked in dress uniforms complete with epaulets and "fore-and-aft" hats, Admiral Joseph M. Reeves, left, and Admiral William D. Leahy shake hands after the ceremony in which Leahy relieved Reeves as Commander, Battle Force, U.S. Fleet, circa June 1936. (Naval Historical Center)*

Right: *With sailors and their personal gear lined up in precise formation, officers conduct an inspection on the deck of the battleship* California *(BB 44) during the 1930s. In the peacetime Navy sailors typically fell in for inspection each Saturday while in port, the reward for enduring the spit and polish routine being the granting of liberty. (National Museum of Naval Aviation)*

twenty-eight the opportunity to receive flight training and serve three years of active duty, at which time they receive $1,000 and commissions in the inactive reserve. The cadet program provides the majority of aviators who man the cockpits during World War II.

30 July
Flying an OJ-2 observation aircraft, Lieutenant Frank Akers performs the first blind carrier landing, employing only instruments in guiding his aircraft to a successful trap on the flight deck of *Langley*.

15 November
Work commencees on the XF2A-1 and XF4F-3 fighter aircraft, the result of a fighter design competition by the Chief of the Bureau of Aeronautics. The latter aircraft, eventually nicknamed the Wildcat, becomes the Navy's first-line carrier fighter during the early part of World War II.

9 December
During a second naval disarmament conference held in London, England, the Japanese naval delegation

Left: *View of gunners on board the gunboat* Panay *(PR 5) firing back at attacking Japanese aircraft on the Yangtze River between Nanking and Wuhu, China, 12 December 1937. The gunner at right is crew member Mahlmann, who went to his battle station minus his pants. Note gun shields for the .30 caliber Lewis guns, and the wooden awning rails at right. (Naval Historical Center)*

CHINA AND THE U.S. NAVY

by Dr. Bernhard D. Cole

The United States has been closely involved in East Asia since 1784, when the *Empress of China* departed New York for Canton on the new nation's first commercial voyage to Asian waters. The venture brought huge profits and launched America's China trade. The rapidly increasing commercial activity soon encountered the piracy endemic to East Asian waters. In 1832, President Andrew Jackson dispatched the frigate *Potomac* to defend U.S. merchant ships. Commodore Lawrence Kearny, in command of the frigate *Constellation* and another warship, sailed to Macao and then Canton in 1842, where he secured for Americans the rights ceded by the Chinese emperor after his recent defeat by Great Britain in the First Opium War. Another warship soon delivered the first American consul to China, and thereafter U.S. Navy ships were regularly assigned to East Asia, and organized as the East India Squadron. The squadron, which was headquartered at Hong Kong, with a depot at Shanghai, usually consisted of three to five warships. U.S. naval officers supported and cooperated with American diplomats in East Asia to protect, endorse, and help expand American business and religious interests, especially in China.

The Yangtze River provided a natural economic and political entryway to the heart of the vast nation for these Americans. When protection was demanded, the Yangtze provided the U.S. Navy with the most effective way of extending that protection into China's interior. In 1854 *Asheulot* became the first American ship to patrol the Yangtze, and in the 1858 Treaty of Tientsin, Peking granted U.S. warships the right to navigate all of China's rivers and visit all its ports. Only one warship was normally assigned during the American Civil War, and the most notable action of that time

occurred in Japan, when the sloop *Jamestown* joined a multinational task force to attack the local ruler of Shimoneseki for firing on foreign merchantmen.

U.S. naval activity in East Asia increased significantly after victory in the Spanish-American War in 1898, which led to the annexation of the Philippine Islands. The Boxer Rebellion followed in 1899, with American naval units serving in the multinational force that attacked Chinese forces besieging the foreign legations in Peking. By 1902, when American naval forces in the Far East were organized into the Asiatic Fleet, gunboats continually patrolled the Yangtze and tributary rivers, as well as the waterways of the Pearl River delta in the south. The ships assigned to the Yangtze were designated as the Yangtze River Patrol in 1921, and the Navy established depots in Tsingtao in northern China, at Hankow in central China, and at Canton in the south. The Asiatic Fleet usually spent the summer operating from Tsingtao, while wintering in Manila, Philippines. The last Chinese dynasty fell in 1912, and a period of near-anarchy ensued; foreign missions were besieged throughout the country, and U.S. naval forces frequently were called upon to protect and rescue American citizens. The most notable incident occurred in March 1927, when the U.S. consulate in Nanking on the Yangtze River was overrun by revolutionary Chinese troops. Two U.S. destroyers rescued the many U.S. and other foreign citizens trapped by the rampaging Chinese.

American naval capabilities improved in 1927–1928 with the advent of six new gunboats built in China and designed especially for duty on the Yangtze River. These ships—*Guam, Luzon, Mindanao, Oahu, Panay,* and *Tutuilla*—faced heightened danger in the face of Japanese aggression in China during the 1930s. This perilous

situation became tragic in December 1937. *Panay* (PR 5) was operating on the Yangtze near Nanking, supporting the U.S. consul in that city, which was under attack by Japanese military forces. Although she was clearly marked by American flags and the visibility was excellent, *Panay* was attacked by Japanese navy aircraft and sunk, with two crewmembers killed. The deliberate sinking of the gunboat drew only brief protests in the United States, and the Tokyo government was quick to apologize and pay compensation for the attack. However, the event foreshadowed worse things to come with respect to relations between the two nations.

Throughout its existence, the Asiatic Fleet had the primary task of preparing to execute War Plan Orange, the blueprint for defeating Japan in a naval war in East Asia. In fact, however, the fleet was neither strong enough nor prepared to carry out this assignment; it was simply too busy patrolling

Chinese waters and protecting American interests. When war with Japan did come in December 1941, it heralded the Asiatic Fleet's demise in February 1942, following defeat by the Japanese Navy at the Battle of the Java Sea. Although the U.S. Navy returned to China in 1945 following Tokyo's defeat, the 1949 Communist victory on the mainland marked the end of an era.

Above: *The gunboat* Tutuila *(PR 4) at anchor below Chungking, China, during 1939. Small in stature, the gunboats patrolled the rivers of one of the largest nations on earth as a symbol of American power.* Tutuila *displaced 395 tons and could make just over 14 knots, her armament consisting of two 3-inch guns and ten .30-caliber machine guns. She was given to the Chinese government early in World War II and renamed* Mei Yuan. *("Far Yangtze Station," Tom Freeman)*

19 August
Experiments in aerial attacks against submarines conducted by a T4M-1 torpedo bomber off the Virginia Capes result in the sinking of the submarine *R-8* (SS *85*) from the cumulative effects of four near misses. This foreshadows naval aviation's pivotal role in fighting German U-boats in the Battle of the Atlantic during World War II.

18 September
With the Spanish Civil War having commenced on 18 July, a squadron under the command of Rear Admiral Arthur P. Fairfield is dispatched to Spain to evacuate U.S. citizens.

2 January
Admiral William D. Leahy, a future five-star admiral and wartime adviser to President Franklin D. Roosevelt, becomes the seventh Chief of Naval Operations.

30 September
The aircraft carrier *Yorktown* is placed in commission.

walks out after the United States refuses to grant the Imperial Japanese Navy parity with the U.S. Navy. The final agreement—rejected by Italy and signed only by the United States, Great Britain, and France on 25 March 1936—is ineffective and represents the end of efforts to curtail a naval arms race.

Above: *The flag that flew over the gunboat* Panay *(PR 5) when she was attacked and sunk by Japanese aircraft while she operated on the Yangtze River, 12 December 1937. (Alex Weyers)*

Right: *The heavy cruiser* Chester *(CA 27) approaches the pier at Rio de Janeiro, Brazil, 27 November 1936. Already moored, at right, is* Indianapolis *(CA 35), which was carrying President Franklin D. Roosevelt, who was making his first stop during the "Good Neighbor" cruise. (Naval Historical Center)*

Right: *F3F-3 fighters, the last biplanes to serve in first-line squadrons in the U.S. Navy, pictured in flight over the East Coast, circa 1939. One in a long line of fighters built for the Navy by the Grumman Aircraft Engineering Corporation, the F3F was the forerunner of the famed F4F Wildcat. The colorful paint schemes of the peacetime Navy would soon be replaced by more subdued tones as the world erupted in war. (Naval Historical Center)*

12 December

In an open act of aggression, Japanese aircraft attack and sink the gunboat *Panay* (PR 5) while she operates on the Yangtze River near Nanking, China. Two crewmen are killed and forty-three others are wounded in an attack the Japanese government terms an error. Although debates in the highest echelons of the U.S. government on how to respond include a possible blockade of Japan, the end result is payment of an indemnity to the United States.

1938

2 February

Participating in naval exercises, two PBY Catalina flying boats collide in the darkness. On board one of the planes, Lieutenant Carlton B. Hutchins remains in the pilot's seat, maintaining control of the aircraft so that four members of his crew can parachute to safety. He is awarded the Medal of Honor posthumously.

12 May

The aircraft carrier *Enterprise*, destined to become the most decorated ship of World War II, is commissioned.

17 May

Congress passes the Naval Expansion Act, which provides for a 20-percent increase in active naval vessels and not less than 3,000 aircraft.

25 June

A naval appropriation act passed by Congress on this date provides for the construction of two battleships, one aircraft carrier, two light cruisers, and a sizeable number of auxiliary vessels.

1 December

The report of the Hepburn Board, established to examine the Navy's requirements for overseas bases, recognizes the need for expanding naval aviation's infrastructure. The board recommends the enlargement of eleven existing air stations and construction of sixteen others, half of which will be built on Pacific islands, including Wake Atoll, Midway Atoll, and Guam.

9 December

A prototype shipboard radar, designed by the Naval Research Laboratory, is installed on board the battleship *New York* (BB 34) for trials. During World War II shipboard radar proves a tremendous advantage in combat between U.S. and Japanese warships.

16 December

The K-2 non-rigid airship, prototype for a successful class of blimps that prove valuable in antisubmarine operations during World War II, arrives at Naval Air Station Lakehurst, New Jersey, for evaluation.

THE TWO OCEAN WAR

1939-1945

S-9

THE TWO OCEAN WAR

1939-1945

On 1 September 1939 Germany introduced *blitzkrieg*—lightning war—to the world as tanks supported by air power rolled into Poland, marking the beginning of World War II. By late 1941, the armies of Adolph Hitler had seized control of continental Europe, joined Italian allies in offensives in North Africa, and launched a campaign against the Soviet Union. Great Britain, her people inspired by the stirring words of Prime Minister Winston S. Churchill and the deeds of her servicemen, resisted the enemy onslaught. However, her position proved precarious, as U-boats prowled the waters of the North Atlantic in an effort to stem the flow of supplies to the island nation.

President Franklin D. Roosevelt understood the grave threat that confronted the world and, despite the fact that the United States was officially neutral in the first years of conflict, he prepared the nation for war. Just four days after the German invasion of Poland, he ordered the establishment of the Neutrality Patrol, tasking U.S. Navy warships with guarding the Western Hemisphere. By 1941 the U.S. Navy was actively involved in escorting convoys to Great Britain, which brought inevitable conflict with German U-boats. In October 1941 German torpedoes struck the destroyers *Kearny* (DD 432) and *Reuben James* (DD 245), sinking the latter ship with tremendous loss of life.

While the blood of American sailors was shed on the high seas in the Atlantic, Roosevelt was mindful of the burgeoning power of Japan, her armies already entrenched in China and threatening to move against strategic points in the Western Pacific. Among the measures taken as a deterrent to Japanese aggression was the reassignment of the U.S. Pacific Fleet from the West Coast to Pearl Harbor, Hawaii, in 1940. The

next year it was there, on a fateful Sunday morning, that Japanese carrier aircraft delivered a devastating surprise attack, drawing the United States into the greatest war the world has ever known.

On 7 December 1941 the U.S. Navy possessed 790 ships of all types manned by some 380,000 sailors. By 1945 America ruled the seas, the Navy having risen from the ashes of Pearl Harbor to achieve victory in a two-ocean war and grown to encompass 3,405,525 men and women and 6,768 ships. It had proven a long, bitter struggle. In the Pacific, left reeling from the initial Japanese onslaught, the Navy was forced to fight defensively during the war's early months, while in the Atlantic U-boats initially ravaged American merchantmen, in many instances within sight of U.S. shores. However, gradually the tide turned in both theaters.

Employing ships ranging in size from small subchasers to escort carriers, combined with revolutionary technology, the Navy helped drive U-boat wolfpacks from the Atlantic, enabling the safe passage of men and materiel to the European Theater. From the sands of North Africa to the beaches of Normandy, Navy ships and landing craft put men ashore to fight the enemy, their efforts supported by the batteries of American warships. "Thank God for the United States Navy," was the enthusiastic message sent by Army V Corps commander Major General Leonard Gerow when he went ashore at Omaha Beach on the afternoon of 6 June 1944, his words on D-Day applicable to all of the Navy's service in the European theater.

While the Allied strategy during World War II aimed at defeating Germany first, the Navy focused its greatest attention on the Pacific. In June 1942

American carrier aircraft sent four Japanese flattops to the bottom during the pivotal Battle of Midway, turning the tide in the Pacific. The battle signaled the rise of the aircraft carrier as the Navy's capital ship, which was to spearhead subsequent campaigns in the Pacific. In August 1942 Marines landed on Guadalcanal in the Solomon Islands, the first Allied offensive in the Pacific. In a bitterly waged contest on land, in the air, and under and upon the sea, the Navy and Marine Corps bested the Japanese and established a foothold in the Solomons, beginning a long march toward the Japanese bastion at Rabaul. This offensive was complemented, beginning in 1943, with a Central Pacific drive through the Gilbert and Marshall islands to the Marianas.

In late 1944 the two-pronged attack converged on the Philippines, where the U.S. Navy and Imperial Japanese Navy waged the Battle of Leyte Gulf in October. The largest naval engagement in history, it proved the death knell for the fleet that in 1941 had so proudly sailed to attack Pearl Harbor. It was also in the Philippines that the Navy felt the first breath of the divine wind, the deadly kamikaze that tormented ships in ensuing campaigns, most notably in the invasion of Okinawa, Japan. Through it all, submarines

had literally strangled Japan, cutting off the vital flow of raw materials to the island nation.

When the mushroom clouds over Hiroshima and Nagasaki brought an end to the war against Japan, the Navy could look with pride on its accomplishments. Supported by a logistical effort unparalleled in history, ships had ranged thousands of miles, conducting amphibious landings on far-flung islands and defeating one of the most powerful navies in the world. Thus, it was a fitting tribute that the deck of the battleship *Missouri* (BB 63) was chosen as the scene for the surrender ceremony, ending a war in which the Navy had played such a pivotal role.

Pages 386–387: *SBD-3 Dauntless dive-bombers of Scouting Squadron 3 from the carrier* Yorktown *(CV 5) fly west of Midway Atoll on the morning of 4 June 1942. ("Dauntless Against a Rising Sun," William S. Phillips)*

Above: *U.S. Navy tank landing ships (LSTs) disembark Australian Army troops at Lae, New Guinea, September 1943. The close proximity of New Guinea to Australia meant that operations in the Southwest Pacific theater were multinational in scope. (Naval Historical Center)*

THE TWO OCEAN WAR
1939-1945

15 May

The Navy issues a contract for the procurement of the XSB2C-1 Helldiver, prototype of the unpopular aircraft that nevertheless forms the backbone of U.S. Navy dive-bombing squadrons in the latter part of World War II.

17 May–18 October

A landing party from the gunboats *Asheville* (PG 21) and *Tulsa* (PG 22) and destroyer *Whipple* (DD 217) protects the U.S. Consulate and a hospital at Kulangsu, China, following the landing of Japanese forces in the area.

23 May

The submarine *Squalus* (SS 192) sinks while executing a practice dive off Portsmouth, New Hampshire. Employing the new McCann Rescue Chamber, rescuers are able to bring 33 of 59 crew members to the surface. The boat is subsequently raised, repaired, and renamed *Sailfish*.

11–13 June

The aircraft carrier *Saratoga* (CV 3) and oiler *Kanawha* (AO 1) participate in underway replenishment trials off the West Coast. The first underway replenishment operations occurred in 1917 when the oiler *Maumee* (AO 2) refueled destroyers steaming across the Atlantic to European waters. Her executive officer at that time was Lieutenant Chester W. Nimitz, whose work on at-sea refueling during World War I led to the perfection of a logistical operation essential to the ships under his command winning the far-flung naval war in the Pacific during World War II.

1 August

Admiral Harold R. Stark becomes the eighth Chief of Naval Operations.

1 September

World War II begins as German air and ground forces invade Poland, prompting France and Germany to declare war two days later.

5 September

President Franklin D. Roosevelt declares American neutrality in the European war, and orders the Navy to inaugurate the so-called Neutrality Patrol off the eastern seaboard to monitor all foreign vessels entering a zone extending 300 miles from the East Coast of the United States. The first ships put to sea to establish the patrol on 6 September.

Left: *At the Portsmouth Navy Yard in New Hampshire, reporters hastily scrawl in their notebooks as they gather around Lieutenant Commander John B. Longstaff to receive news of the sinking of the submarine* Squalus *(SS 192), 23 May 1939. (Naval Historical Center)*

Right: *Marines debark from an experimental landing craft during training in amphibious operations at Quantico, Virginia, during the mid-1930s. Note that the draft of the vessel does not allow it to be driven onto the beach, an important feature of its successors. The development of a doctrine for landing troops on a hostile shore occupied Navy and Marine tacticians during the interwar years. Their work paying dividends in the island-hopping campaign of the Pacific during World War II. (National Archives)*

8 September
President Roosevelt declares a "limited national emergency" and calls for an increase in Navy enlisted strength from 110,813 to 145,000 and the recall of retired officers, enlisted men, and nurses.

5 October
The Hawaiian Detachment, U.S. Fleet—consisting of the aircraft carrier *Enterprise* (CV 6), two heavy cruiser divisions, a light cruiser, two destroyer squadrons, and auxiliary ships—sails for Pearl Harbor, Hawaii. This measure establishes a sizeable naval presence at this Pacific base, deemed important given Japan's continuing aggression against China.

4 November
President Roosevelt signs the Neutrality Act into law. The measure repeals the arms embargo, prohibits U.S. vessels from entering combat zones, and establishes a National Munitions Control Board. Roosevelt immediately declares the waters around the British Isles a combat zone.

1 December
Submarine Division 14 consisting of *Perch* (SS 176), *Permit* (SS 178), *Pickerel* (SS 177), *Pike* (SS 173), *Porpoise* (SS 172), and *Tarpon* (SS 175), arrives on the Asiatic Station to provide the Asiatic Fleet with some degree of offensive firepower in the event of a Pacific war.

14–19 December
U.S. Navy warships trail the German passenger liner *Columbus* and pursuing British destroyers from Mexican waters to a position some 450 miles east of Cape May, New Jersey. On 19 December the crew of *Columbus* scuttles the ship to prevent her capture by the British. The heavy cruiser *Tuscaloosa* (CA 37) rescues 573 passengers and crew and transports them to New York City.

1940

2 January
Charles Edison, son of the famous inventor Thomas Edison, takes office as the forty-sixth Secretary of the Navy.

11 January
Fleet Landing Exercise Number Six begins at Culebra, Puerto Rico. The exercise force includes only one transport, the four-stack destroyer *Manley* (DD 74), recently converted to an amphibious transport and later redesignated APD 1, which performs her role well in an operation repeated time and again in the Pacific War—putting Marines ashore. *Manley* serves throughout World War II, landing her first troops in combat at Guadalcanal in 1942 and her last in the Philippines in 1945.

15–22 January

In a training exercise that foreshadows joint operations in the Mediterranean and European theaters during World War II, Army and Navy forces practice amphibious landings at Monterey, California. A major focus of the training is familiarizing Army troops in boarding and disembarking from landing craft.

15 February

President Franklin D. Roosevelt departs Pensacola, Florida, in the heavy cruiser *Tuscaloosa* on a journey to inspect the Panama Canal and discuss defense of this vital asset.

7–13 April

The destroyer *J. Fred Talbott* (DD 156) makes rendezvous with the Japanese merchantman *Arimasa Maru* off the Panama Canal Zone and provides urgent medical treatment to a member of the steamship's crew.

25 April

The aircraft carrier *Wasp* (CV 7) is commissioned.

7 May

President Franklin D. Roosevelt orders ships of the U.S. Fleet to remain in Hawaiian waters indefinitely as a gesture of American strength aimed at Japan. Admiral James O. Richardson, the fleet's commander, protests that Pearl Harbor's facilities are inadequate to support the fleet and are poorly protected against attack. The manner in which he expresses his opinions to the president results in his removal from command on 1 February 1941.

16 May

President Franklin D. Roosevelt asks Congress for $1.18 billion to strengthen the nation's defense. The funds requested include $250 million for the Navy and Marine Corps, along with a share of $186 million to contract for equipment and other services.

Below: *Secretary of the Navy Frank Knox (second from right) meets with (left to right) Admirals Harry E. Yarnell, Harold S. Stark, and James O. Richardson in Washington, D.C., October 1940. (Naval Historical Center)*

Opposite: *The carrier* Wasp *(CV 7) underway during sea trials prior to her commissioning. She spent the first months of the war operating with the Royal Navy in the Atlantic before transferring to the Pacific to bolster forces for the invasion of Guadalcanal, August 1942. (Naval Historical Center)*

Right: *The submarine* Swordfish *(SS 193) launches at the Mare Island Naval Shipyard in California, April 1939. Her thirteenth war patrol would prove unlucky as the boat was reported missing off Japan in early 1945. (National Archives)*

14 June
The Naval Expansion Act of 1940, authorizing an eleven-percent increase in the fleet, is signed into law. The measure also increases naval aircraft strength to 4,500 planes, which is elevated to 10,000 the next day by order of President Roosevelt. The expansion act is approved on the same day that German troops enter Paris; France asks for an armistice three days later.

17 June
Chief of Naval Operations Admiral Harold R. Stark asks Congress for $4 billion to increase the authorized strength of the Navy by seventy percent. This "Two-Ocean Navy Act" quickly passes the House and Senate and is signed into law on 19 July.

20 June
The Bureau of Construction and Repair is merged with the Bureau of Engineering to form the Bureau of Ships. In addition, the office of Undersecretary of the Navy is established.

The heavy cruiser *Quincy* (CA 39) arrives in Montevideo, Uruguay, to assist in countering German propaganda in the Central American nation. She is later joined by the heavy cruiser *Wichita* (CA 45), and the two ships embark on a tour of South America as a demonstration of U.S. strength.

24 June
Charles Edison leaves the post of Secretary of the Navy.

25 June
Congress abolishes the Naval Construction Corps and gives its officers "engineering duty only" line status.

11 July
Frank Knox, a Chicago newspaper publisher and one of Theodore Roosevelt's famed "Rough Riders," takes office as the forty-seventh Secretary of the Navy.

22 August
James V. Forrestal, a World War I naval aviator, becomes the first to hold the post of Undersecretary of the Navy.

2 September
In what British Prime Minister Winston S. Churchill calls a matter of "life and death," the United States and Great Britain conclude an agreement in which fifty World War I-era destroyers are transferred to Britain in exchange for leases on British bases in the Caribbean. The British also give the United States bases in Bermuda and Newfoundland, Canada. The transfer of ships begins four days later.

12 October
Army Air Corps P-40 fighters and O-47 observation planes launch from *Wasp* during an evaluation of takeoff runs of military and naval aircraft. This marks the first operation of Army aircraft from an aircraft carrier.

Left: *Commissioning ceremonies for Naval Air Station, Trinidad, in the British West Indies, 1 October 1941. British and American Army and Navy officers are present. The U.S. Navy officer at center is Captain Arthur W. Radford, a future Chairman of the Joint Chiefs of Staff. Note the banner hanging from the building. Established as a result of the Lend–Lease Act, Trinidad served as a base for patrol planes searching the Caribbean for U–boats. (Naval Historical Center)*

25 October
During a Japanese bombing raid against Shanghai, China, bombs fall 300 yards from the U.S. Embassy and the river gunboat *Tutuila* (PR 4). Japan attributes the act to equipment malfunction.

1941

1 January
During this year Navy personnel strength reaches 383,150.

6 January
The heavy cruiser *Louisville* (CA 28), after taking aboard over $148 million in British gold, departs Simonstown, South Africa, bound for New York City. She arrives on 22 January, and the gold is deposited in American banks.

9 January
The first group of contractors arrives on Wake Island to begin construction of an air station there.

30 January
The German government announces that its submarines will torpedo any ship attempting to bring supplies to Great Britain, regardless of the vessel's nationality.

1 February
In a reorganization of fleet structure, the Atlantic and Pacific Fleets are reestablished. The following day Admiral Husband E. Kimmel is appointed to command the Pacific Fleet and, also, the U.S. Fleet when both fleets operate together. Admiral Ernest J. King receives command of the Atlantic Fleet, and Admiral Thomas C. Hart commands the Asiatic Fleet.

7 February
The U.S. Naval Academy Class of 1941 graduates four months early because of the national emergency. Forty-one members of the class will be killed in action during World War II.

11 March
The Lend-Lease Act becomes law. This allows the United States to transfer war materials, on loan or on credit, to Allied nations.

27 March
Representatives of the United States, Britain, and Canada sign the ABC-1 Staff Agreement in Washington, outlining a framework for strategic cooperation in the event that the United States enters World War II. The agreement establishes a Combined Chiefs of Staff and stipulates that the U.S. Atlantic Fleet will, as soon as possible, assist the Royal Navy in convoying ships to Britain.

9 April

North Carolina (BB 55), the first battleship to join the fleet since 1923, is commissioned.

11 April

The destroyer *Niblack* (DD 424), while rescuing survivors from a torpedoed Dutch freighter, drops depth charges on a sound contact believed to be a German submarine. It turns out to be a false contact, but the action illuminates the growing involvement of the U.S. Navy in the Battle of the Atlantic.

21 May

En route to Africa, the U.S. freighter *Robin Moor*, with U.S. flags painted prominently on her sides, is torpedoed by the German submarine *U-69* and later sunk by fire from the sub's deck gun. This marks the first sinking of an American merchantman during World War II.

26 May

A British Royal Air Force PBY Catalina flying boat searching for the German battleship *Bismarck* finds her quarry in the Atlantic some 300 miles west of France. The pilot of the Catalina is a U.S. Navy observer, Ensign Leonard B. Smith. British Royal Navy surface and air forces sink the fearsome battleship the following day.

2 June

The aircraft escort vessel *Long Island* (AVG 1) is commissioned at Newport News, Virginia. A

converted merchantman, she is the first of what are later called escort carriers, small flattops that provide yeoman service in the Atlantic campaigns against U-boats, and provide close air support for amphibious assaults in North Africa, Europe, and the Pacific.

15 June

Echoing an amazingly similar incident on 25 October 1940, during an attack against Chungking, China, Japanese planes drop bombs near the river gunboat *Tutuila*, the office of the U.S. military attaché, and a U.S. Navy canteen. The Japanese military terms the attack "wholly unintentional," though the U.S. representatives on the scene doubt the truthfulness of this assessment.

Above: *Admiral Husband E. Kimmel, Commander in Chief, U.S. Fleet and Pacific Fleet (center), confers with his chief of staff, Captain William W. Smith (right) and operations officer, Captain Walter S. Delany. (Naval Historical Center)*

Right: *The battleship* North Carolina's *(BB 55) 16-inch gun torrets and tower foremast rise from the deck in this view taken from her bow during the battleship's maiden voyage in 1941.* North Carolina *was the first U.S. battleship commissioned since 1923. (Naval Historical Center)*

Left: *The escort carrier* Long Island *(AVG 1) moored at Naval Air Station San Diego, California, 1941. She participated in prewar exercises that evaluated the use of escort carriers to support amphibious landings, one of their primary missions during World War II. (National Museum of Naval Aviation)*

Below: *The gunboat* Tutuila *(PR 4) in the Yangtze River, China, while serving with the Yangtze Patrol, circa 1930s. (Naval Historical Center)*

20 June
The submarine *O-9* (SS 70), while engaged in submergence trials off Portsmouth, New Hampshire, sinks during a test dive with the loss of all thirty-three members of her crew.

1 July
Admiral Ernest J. King, Commander in Chief, U.S. Atlantic Fleet, organizes task forces to support the defense of Iceland and escort convoys between the United States and Iceland. The effort is in response to an agreement between the two countries for U.S. troops to occupy and defend the island nation.

26 July
President Franklin D. Roosevelt, in response to Japanese occupation of the northern part of French Indochina, freezes Japanese assets in the United States and stops the export of oil to Japan. Two days later the

Japanese government freezes American assets and the two nations move closer to war.

30 July
During a Japanese air raid against Chunking, China, a bomb splashes eight yards astern of the river gunboat *Tutuila*. Like the two previous close calls, the Japanese term this incident an accident.

5 August
President Franklin D. Roosevelt secretly boards the heavy cruiser *Augusta* (CA 31) in Vineyard Sound, Massachusetts. With the heavy cruiser *Tuscaloosa* and five destroyers, *Augusta* sets course for Argentia, Newfoundland, where the President meets with British Prime Minister Winston S. Churchill.

9–12 August
In a historic meeting, President Roosevelt and Prime Minister Churchill formulate the Atlantic Charter during discussions on board *Augusta* and the British battleship *Prince of Wales*. Though not a formal treaty, the charter serves as a declaration of American intent should the United States be drawn into World War II.

1 September
The U.S Navy assumes responsibility for convoying transatlantic merchant convoys from a point off Argentia, Newfoundland, to a mid-ocean meeting point (MOMP) south of Iceland. The first such escort voyage, in company with Canadian escort ships, begins on 16 September.

Right: *Summit meeting at Placentia Bay, Newfoundland, 10–12 August 1941. Left to right: Ensign Franklin D. Roosevelt, Jr., Sumner Welles (obscured), Prime Minister Winston Churchill, President Franklin D. Roosevelt, and Captain Elliot Roosevelt, aboard the heavy cruiser* Augusta *(CA 31). At this meeting Roosevelt and Churchill proclaimed the Atlantic Charter. (Naval Historical Center)*

4 September

The destroyer *Greer* (DD 145), operating 175 miles southwest of Iceland, maintains sonar contact with *U-652* for several hours. A British patrol plane drops depth bombs and leaves the area. The German submarine fires a torpedo; *Greer* drops depth charges; and *U-652* fires another torpedo, which misses. The destroyer cannot regain contact, and resumes its voyage. In one of his famous fireside chats on 11 September, President Franklin D. Roosevelt calls the attacks against *Greer* "one determined step toward creating a permanent world system based on force, on terror, and on murder." In response, he announces an order to U.S. ships to fire upon any vessel threatening American shipping or ships under American escort, and declares that German and Italian warships enter U.S.-controlled waters "at their own risk."

27 September

Patrick Henry, the first of over 2,700 "Liberty"-type cargo ships that become famous during World War II for their mass production and widespread use, is launched at Baltimore, Maryland.

16–17 October

U.S. Navy warships participate in the defense of convoy SC 48 during a mass U-boat attack, marking the first time an American-escorted convoy engages German U-boats on the high seas. On 16 October the destroyer *Livermore* (DD 429) depth charges *U-553,*

while the destroyer *Kearny* (DD 432) drops depth charges astern of the convoy in an effort to discourage attacks. On 17 October *U-568* puts a torpedo into *Kearny's* starboard side, killing eleven of her crew and wounding twenty-two others. The destroyer regains power in about ten minutes and reaches Iceland under her own steam.

30 October

In the Atlantic Ocean some 700 miles off the coast of Newfoundland, Canada, the German submarine *U-106* torpedoes the oiler *Salinas* (AO 19) as she steams as part of convoy ON 28. Throughout the remainder of the day, escorting U.S. destroyers carry out ten depth charge attacks, and the destroyer *Bernadou* (DD 153) fires on a U-boat, forcing it to submerge.

31 October

While escorting convoy HX 156 west of Iceland, the destroyer *Reuben James* (DD 245) is torpedoed by the German submarine *U-552.* The torpedo detonates in the destroyer's magazine, and she sinks quickly with the loss of 115 men. *Reuben James* is the first U.S. warship lost to hostile action during World War II.

1 November

President Roosevelt issues an executive order placing the Coast Guard under the operational control of the Navy for the duration of the national emergency.

Fighting Squadron (VMF) 211. Based upon a war warning issued the previous day by the Chief of Naval Operations, Vice Admiral William F. Halsey, Jr., issues his famous War Order No. 1 stating that *Enterprise* is operating "under war conditions."

2 December
The first U.S Naval Armed Guard detachment, a gun crew trained to serve in merchant vessels, boards the freighter *Dunboyne*. All told, some 145,000 men serve in the Armed Guard during World War II, manning 6,236 merchantmen. A total of 1,810 men lose their lives, and 5 receive the Navy Cross for extraordinary heroism.

5 December
The aircraft carrier *Lexington* (CV 2) sails from Pearl Harbor, Hawaii, for Midway Atoll to deliver SB2U Vindicators of Marine Scout Bombing Squadron (VMSB) 231.

27 November
Chief of Naval Operations Admiral Harold R. Stark sends "War Warning" messages to the Pacific and Asiatic Fleets. This measure comes a day after a Japanese carrier task force secretly departs the Kurile Islands and sets course for Hawaii to attack the U.S. fleet base at Pearl Harbor in the event negotiations between the United States and Japan break down.

28 November
The aircraft carrier *Enterprise* departs Hawaii for Wake Island to deliver F4F Wildcat fighters of Marine

7 December
In the early morning hours the destroyer *Ward* (DD 139), operating in the channel entrance to Pearl Harbor, Hawaii, attacks a Japanese midget submarine, sinking it with assistance from a PBY Catalina flying boat from Patrol Squadron (VP) 14. Despite this unusual activity, no general warnings are issued, and the ships of the U.S Pacific Fleet continue their Sunday morning routine as two waves of 353 Japanese strike aircraft launched from six carriers wing their way toward Hawaii. At 0755 the first planes launch bombs and torpedoes against the unsuspecting ships.

Above: *Nine of the famed Liberty ships lined up at the California Shipbuilding Yard prior to delivery to the U.S. Maritime Commission, December 1943. The first of some 2,700 Liberty ships was delivered on 27 September 1941. (Corbis)*

Left: *The destroyer* Kearny *(DD 432) pictured alongside* Monssen *(DD 436) at Reykjavik, Iceland, 19 October 1941. The damage from the torpedo fired by U-568 is visible on her starboard side, (Naval Historical Center)*

Right: *A gun crew on board the destroyer* Ward *(DD 139) poses proudly with the 4-inch gun they used to sink a Japanese midget submarine approaching Pearl Harbor, Hawaii, during the early morning hours of 7 December 1941. Two deep diving submersibles operated by the Hawaii Undersea Research Laboratory discovered the wreckage of the submarine on 28 August 2002, the hole in her conning tower testament to the accuracy of* Ward's *gunners. This was the first Japanese naval vessel sunk by the U.S. Navy during World War II. (Naval Historical Center)*

Meanwhile, low-flying A6M Zero fighters attack surrounding airfields, setting parked planes afire. The greatest devastation occurs on Battleship Row, where *Oklahoma* (BB 37), *West Virginia* (BB 48), *California* (BB 44) and *Arizona* (BB 39) are sunk, the latter's final moments coming when a bomb detonates her forward magazine, resulting in a catastrophic explosion that reverberates across the harbor. Despite being hit by both bombs and torpedoes, the battleship *Nevada* (BB 36) manages to get underway, but she is eventually beached. Japanese aircraft also sink the target and training ship *Utah* (AG 16), damage the repair ship *Vestal* (AR 4) to such an extent that she is beached, and damage the battleships *Pennsylvania* (BB 38), *Tennessee* (BB 43), and *Maryland* (BB 46); light cruisers *Honolulu* (CL 48), *Raleigh* (CL 7), and *Helena* (CL 50); heavy cruiser *New Orleans* (CA 32); destroyers *Shaw* (DD 373), *Helm* (DD 388), and *Hull* (DD 350); destroyer tender *Dobbin* (AD 3); repair ship *Rigel* (AR 11); seaplane tenders *Tangier* (AV 8) and *Curtiss* (AV 4); and the garbage lighter *YG 17*. Parked wingtip to wingtip as a precaution against sabotage, most of the island's defending aircraft are destroyed on the ground. In addition, Japanese fighters and "friendly fire" down SBD Dauntless dive-bombers from the aircraft carrier *Enterprise* (CV 6) that unwittingly fly into the middle of the attack. Of the 2,403 servicemen killed in the attack, 2,008 are sailors and Marines, including Rear Admiral Isaac Kidd, Commander Battleship Division One in *Arizona*, the first Navy flag officer killed in action in World War II. In addition, 710 sailors are wounded. It is the most devastating defeat in the Navy's history but, in the face of overwhelming odds, the men of the sea services demonstrate fighting spirit in numerous acts of heroism. Mess Attendant Second Class Doris Miller receives the Navy Cross for assisting in the movement of the mortally wounded captain of *West Virginia* from the bridge and manning a machine gun in defense of the ship. Fifteen men receive the Medal of Honor for their actions, which include numerous acts of devotion by officers and men who sacrifice their lives so that shipmates may escape rapidly sinking battleships. Among them is Chief Watertender Peter Tomich, who remains at his post securing *Utah*'s boilers as she capsizes so that his fellow sailors can abandon ship. His Medal of Honor, awarded posthumously, remains unclaimed by any next of kin.

8 December

Calling 7 December 1941 a "date that will live in infamy," President Franklin D. Roosevelt asks Congress for a declaration of war against Japan. A joint resolution passes the same day.

After unsuccessful efforts to scuttle their ship, the crew of the river gunboat *Wake* (PR 3) surrenders the ship to a Japanese boarding party off Shanghai, China, the only instance in World War II of a U.S. Navy vessel striking her colors.

Above: *The battleship* Nevada *(BB 36) makes a courageous run from her berth in Battleship Row alongside Ford Island, Pearl Harbor, Hawaii, on the morning of 7 December 1941. The only battleship to get underway, she suffered such a heavy attack that her crew finally beached her to prevent her being sunk and blocking the harbor entrance channel. (R. G. Smith)*

Below: *Sailors man a line in an attempt to pull a burning PBY Catalina ashore at Naval Air Station Kaneohe, Hawaii, 7 December 1941. In addition to striking the ships in Pearl Harbor, Japanese carrier planes decimated the surrounding airfields, destroying 169 aircraft and damaging 159 more. (Naval Historical Center)*

Japanese forces seize the International Settlement in Shanghai, China, and conduct landings in the Malay Peninsula and Thailand. In addition, Japanese aircraft bomb Hong Kong, Singapore, the Philippines, Wake Island, and Guam.

9 December

The submarine *Swordfish* (SS 193), foreshadowing a war in which undersea vessels will devastate Japanese shipping, executes the first U.S. Navy submarine attack of the war, claiming the sinking of a Japanese ship 150 miles west of Manila, Philippines. The sinking is not confirmed in postwar records, which indicate that *Swordfish* sinks her initial victim of the war on 16 December, hitting the cargo ship *Atsutasan Maru* with three torpedoes.

10 December

Japanese aircraft bomb the Cavite Navy Yard in the Philippine Islands, destroying shore facilities there, sinking one vessel and damaging six more. During the attack Chief Boatswain Earl D. Payne, a gunner in a PBY Catalina of Patrol Squadron 101, downs a Japanese A6M2 Zero fighter, the Navy's first air-to-air kill of the war.

Captain George J. McMillin, the governor of Guam, surrenders the island to the Japanese.

An SBD Dauntless off the carrier *Enterprise* sinks the Japanese submarine *I-70* off the Hawaiian Islands, the first sinking of a Japanese vessel by U.S. Navy carrier aircraft during World War II.

11 December
Germany and Italy declare war on the United States, acts which are reciprocated by the United States.

12 December
The Naval Air Transportation Service is established.

15 December
The seaplane tender *Tangier*, the oiler *Neches* (AO 5), and four destroyers sail from Pearl Harbor, Hawaii, as part of a force gathered in an effort to relieve the beleaguered garrison on Wake Island.

16 December
Task Force 14—the aircraft carrier *Saratoga*, three heavy cruisers, and nine destroyers—departs Pearl Harbor, Hawaii. Under the command of Rear Admiral Frank Jack Fletcher, the force's objective is the relief of Wake Island.

17 December
Vice Admiral William S. Pye becomes Acting Commander in Chief, U.S. Pacific Fleet, relieving Admiral Husband E. Kimmel.

19 December
The United States Naval Academy Class of 1942 is graduated six months early due to the national emergency. Forty-eight members of the class are killed during World War II service.

22 December
President Franklin D. Roosevelt and British Prime Minister Winston S. Churchill open the so-called Arcadia Conference in Washington, D.C., which results in the commitment to a "Germany-first" strategy, creation of a Combined Chiefs of Staff to direct the war effort, and an agreement that a supreme commander should be appointed for both the Pacific and Atlantic theaters.

Japanese troops make landings on Luzon, Philippines.

23 December
After heroically holding out against repeated aerial bombardment and repulsing the first attempt by the Japanese to land troops on 11 December, the garrison at Wake Island under the command of Commander Winfield Scott Cunningham surrenders. This same day, the ships attempting to relieve the garrison are ordered to turn back.

30 December
Admiral Ernest J. King, a man President Franklin D. Roosevelt says is so tough that he "shaves with a blowtorch," assumes duties as Commander in Chief, United States Fleet. One of his first actions is to change the acronym of his new command from CINCUS, which he thinks sounds like "sink us," to COMINCH.

31 December
Admiral Chester W. Nimitz, a submariner and most recently Chief of the Bureau of Navigation, takes command of the Pacific Fleet on the deck of the submarine *Grayling* (SS 209) at Pearl Harbor, Hawaii.

1 January

Admiral Royal E. Ingersoll assumes the duties of Commander in Chief, U.S. Atlantic Fleet.

5 January

Operating just eight miles from Tokyo Bay, Japan, the submarine *Pollack* (SS 180) torpedoes the Japanese cargo ship *Heijo Maru*. She attacks two more ships off the coast of the Japanese Home Islands on 7 and 9 January.

6 January

Eleven Navy nurses are among the military personnel captured at Manila, Philippines, when it falls to the Japanese. They eventually spend thirty-seven months as prisoners of war.

Left: *Newly appointed Commander in Chief, U.S. Fleet Admiral Ernest J. King shakes hands with his new chief of staff, Rear Admiral Russell Wilson, December 1941. An exacting taskmaster, King was a master strategist who ensured that the Navy received adequate resources for operations in the Pacific. (Naval Historical Center)*

Opposite, bottom: *A wartime Japanese painting depicts the Japanese conquest of Wake Island in December 1941. ("Landing Operation at Wake Island," Matsuzaka Yasu, Naval Historical Center)*

Right: *A submariner, Admiral Chester W. Nimitz chose the deck of the submarine* Grayling *(SS 209) as the scene for his assumption of command of the U.S. Pacific Fleet, 31 December 1941. (Naval Historical Center)*

11 January

The aircraft carrier *Saratoga* is torpedoed by the Japanese submarine *I-6* as she returns to Hawaii after delivering aircraft to Midway Atoll. She is forced to head to the West Coast for repairs, reducing U.S. carrier strength in the Pacific to three.

Five German U-boats commence Operation Drumbeat off the East Coast of the United States, sinking twenty-six Allied ships over the next month.

15 January

The American-British-Dutch-Australian (ABDA) command is established at the island of Java, with British General Sir Archibald Wavell named as supreme commander of forces in the Southwest Pacific. Admiral Thomas C. Hart is named commander of ABDA's naval forces.

16 January

Operating under strict radio silence, a TBD-1 Devastator torpedo bomber flown by Aviation Chief Machinist's Mate Harold F. Dixon and his two-man crew is forced to ditch at sea when it runs out of fuel during a search mission from the aircraft carrier *Enterprise*. The three men scramble into their life raft before the aircraft sinks and spend the next thirty-four days drifting at sea, their sole nourishment consisting of rain water, two birds, and whatever fish they manage to spear with a knife. When they reach the Danger Islands on 19 February, it is estimated that the trio has traveled about 1,200 miles.

23 January

With Japanese forces landing on the Bataan Peninsula in the Philippine Islands, the naval battalion under the command of Commander Francis J. Bridget joins in the initial defense, helping to drive the invaders back on 24 January.

24 January

In the first surface engagement by U.S. Navy forces in the Pacific, Destroyer Division 59 under the command of Commander Paul H. Talbot attacks a Japanese invasion force bound for Borneo in what becomes known as the Battle of Makassar Strait. The flush-deck destroyers *John D. Ford* (DD 228), *Parrott* (DD 218), *Paul Jones* (DD 230), and *Pope* (DD 225) sink three transports and a cargo ship before retiring.

28 January

While flying convoy escort off the coast of Newfoundland, Canada, a PBO Hudson bomber of VP-82 piloted by Aviation Machinist's Mate First Class Donald F. Mason attacks a surfaced U-boat. Mason transmits "Sighted sub, sank same," a memorable radio message that unfortunately turns out to be incorrect, for no U-boat is lost on this date.

1 February

The U.S. Navy strikes back at the Japanese with attacks against Kwajalein and Wotje in the Marshall Islands and Jaluit, Makin, and Mili in the Gilbert Islands. At Kwajalein, aircraft from the carrier *Enterprise* sink a transport and damage nine other vessels while the heavy cruisers *Northampton* (CA 26) and *Salt Lake City*

UNDERWATER SALVAGE IN THE U.S. NAVY

by Commander John D. Alden, U.S. Navy (Retired)

Until the 1920s the Navy had no dedicated salvage organization, but pulled together impromptu teams to refloat stranded vessels or recover material from shallow water. Divers were essential even for such limited work. The traditional diver's outfit of copper helmet and waterproofed canvas suit was developed in the nineteenth century, and, in 1882, the Navy established a school at Newport, Rhode Island, to train these undersea sailors. At the time their normal duties involved untangling fouled propellers, recovering lost anchors or practice torpedoes, and performing other simple tasks at depths less than sixty feet. Going deeper led to poorly understood illnesses and fatalities. Navy divers investigated the sunken battleship *Maine* in Havana Harbor, Cuba, in 1898, but raising the wreck was entrusted to the Army Corps of Engineers. The task of the Navy divers was to investigate the cause of the ship's destruction, not to salvage her.

In 1913 the Navy assigned a team of five divers and a doctor to investigate means of improving diving equipment and procedures. The need for their expertise became critical two years later when the submarine *F-4* disappeared off Oahu, Hawaii. The Navy had to know why the submarine had sunk, so the hulk was salvaged by sweeping cables under both ends and raising it with lifting barges and pontoons. Divers using ordinary compressed air reached the unprecedented depth of 306 feet, staying as long as thirty minutes but suffering exhaustion and decompression sickness. Their accomplishments ensured the Navy's continued support of an experimental diving organization.

Left: *Members of the diving crew emerge from water-filled compartments of the sunken battleship Arizona (BB 39) at Pearl Harbor, Hawaii. They are removing elements of the ship's armament and other items for reuse. It is a testament to the skill of the men of Fleet Salvage Unit at Pearl Harbor that five of the battleships heavily damaged on Battleship Row on 7 December 1941 returned to fight another day. (Naval Historical Center)*

Right: *The bow of* Squalus *(SS 192) broaches the surface during salvage operations to raise the submarine after she sank during a test dive on 23 May 1939. The effort was eventually successful and the boat went on to have a notable wartime career in the Pacific. (Naval Historical Center)*

World War I forced the service to shift emphasis to immediate salvage tasks and harbor clearance. It closed the diving school temporarily and established a hybrid organization using commercial salvage ships manned with naval reservists. A major achievement was refloating the capsized liner *St. Louis* on the New York waterfront, an operation that was repeated on a larger scale during World War II when the former French liner *Normandie* burned and sank alongside Pier 88 in 1942. At war's end the Navy negotiated standing contracts with commercial firms to perform salvage operations when called upon.

Accidents in the expanding submarine force had ensured continued interest in deep diving and submarine salvage, but activity was at a low level until 1925, when *S-51* sank in 132 feet of water off Block Island in Long Island Sound, New York. The Navy raised her with improvised resources, and although great strides were made in developing new tools and procedures, no official follow-up occurred until the tragedy was repeated in 1927. This time six survivors in the torpedo room of the *S-4* tapped out futile messages for two days while storms frustrated all attempts by divers to bring air to them. Congress belatedly provided funds for today's permanent submarine rescue and salvage organization, and experiments were begun using helium and oxygen mixtures to extend diving depths. In 1939 the recently developed McCann rescue chamber was used to save thirty-three survivors from the sunken submarine *Squalus* (SS 192) at a depth of 240 feet.

During World War II the Navy again mobilized commercial resources under the Navy Salvage Service while greatly expanding its own capabilities. The combined forces carried out salvage operations at Pearl Harbor and in combat zones, and massive harbor clearance jobs throughout the world. Such was the success of the Pearl Harbor operation that some battlewagons damaged on the "Day of Infamy" returned to service, the main batteries that had been silent on 7 December bombarding enemy-held beaches to clear the way for landings.

With its postwar resources greatly reduced, the Navy concentrated on diving research and maintaining a nucleus of salvage experts and divers, augmented by industrial assistance as needed. The loss of the submarine *Thresher* (SSN 593) in 1963 stimulated a great spurt in the development of deep-water salvage and rescue capabilities, including manned and remotely operated submersibles and robotic equipment. By 1965 the Navy had demonstrated the effectiveness of saturation diving, enabling divers to work for extended periods at great depths. These improvements were quickly adopted by the offshore petroleum industry, and employed by the Central Intelligence Agency in 1974 to salvage part of a Soviet nuclear submarine from a depth of 17,000 feet.

In recent years the Navy has been called on to recover lost atomic bombs, "black boxes" and wreckage from aircraft disasters, and bodies from sunken ships. Thanks largely to the Navy's pioneering efforts, equipment is widely available today to support salvage operations at almost any depth, anywhere in the world.

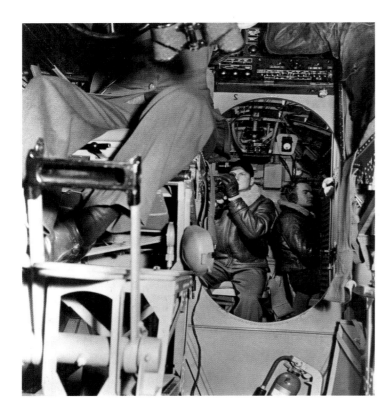

Above: *Bedecked in fur-lined leather flight jackets to ward off the cold, crewmen on board a PBY Catalina pictured in the interior of the flying boat during a patrol over the North Atlantic, November 1941. Framed by the feet of the pilots in the foreground, the navigator can be seen using a sextant to "shoot the sun" in plotting his position. (Bettman/Corbis)*

Right: *Antiaircraft gunners on board the aircraft carrier* Enterprise *(CV 6) fire their .50-caliber machine guns on Japanese planes attacking the "Big E" off the Marshall Islands, 1 February 1942. The enemy attack came in the wake of an air strike against the Marshalls launched from* Enterprise, *one of the hit-and-run carrier raids executed by U.S. Navy flattops during the early months of the Pacific war. (Naval Historical Center)*

(CA 25) sink a gunboat; and the destroyer *Dunlap* (DD 384) sinks an auxiliary submarine chaser at Wotje. In the Gilbert Islands aircraft from the carrier *Yorktown* (CV 5) strafe a gunboat and cargo ship. The raids provide a much-needed morale boost to U.S. Navy forces in the Pacific.

3 February
The submarine *Trout* (SS 202) serves as an undersea transport, delivering ammunition to forces defending the island of Corregidor in Manila Bay, and departing with a cargo that consists in part of 20 tons of gold and silver from Philippine banks.

4 February
Japanese naval land attack planes bomb an Allied naval force under the command of Royal Netherlands Navy Rear Admiral Karel W.F.M. Doorman in the Java Sea. Though two Dutch light cruisers are damaged by near misses, the heavy cruiser *Houston* (CA 30) and light cruiser *Marblehead* (CL 12) bear the brunt of the attack. *Houston*'s after gun turret is put out of action and *Marblehead* is damaged to such an extent that she is forced to return to Java and thence to the United States for repairs.

5 February
The National Naval Medical Center is established at Bethesda, Maryland.

Right: *The stern of the light cruiser* Marblehead *(CL 12) shows the effects of hits from bombs dropped by Japanese aircraft as she steamed in the Java Sea on 4 February 1942. She is pictured undergoing repairs at Tjilatjap, Java. The fact that life goes on is evident in the laundry hanging out to dry atop the gun turret. (Naval Historical Center)*

7 February

President Franklin D. Roosevelt establishes the War Shipping Administration to consolidate operational control of all American merchant vessels. The first director of the new agency is Rear Admiral Emory S. Land.

11 February

The submarine *Shark* (SS 174) is sunk with all hands by the Japanese destroyer *Yamakaze* east of Celebes, Netherlands East Indies.

14 February

Admiral Thomas C. Hart is relieved as Commander in Chief, Allied Naval Forces in the Southwest Pacific by Vice Admiral C.E.L. Helfrich, Royal Netherlands Navy.

17 February

The 1st Naval Construction Battalion, lead unit of the famed Seabees, arrives at Bora Bora in the Society Islands.

19 February

An Allied naval force under the command of Royal Netherlands Navy Rear Admiral Karel W.F.M. Doorman engages Japanese ships retiring from support of the invasion of Bali, Netherlands East Indies. The resulting Battle of Badoeng Strait results in the sinking of the Dutch destroyer *Piet Hein* and damage to the destroyer *Stewart* (DD 224) and the Dutch light cruisers *Java* and *Tromp*. Two Japanese destroyers are

damaged. *Stewart*'s battle damage includes a hit aft below her water line, which floods the steering engine room. However, the steering engine continues to operate under two feet of water, enabling the destroyer to return to Surabaya the following morning. An operational accident in drydock on 22 February, in which she falls off the keel blocks, necessitates her destruction in the face of invading Japanese forces. She is subsequently salvaged and operates as a patrol boat in the Imperial Japanese Navy, and is eventually captured by U.S. forces at Kure, Japan. Recommissioned in the U.S. Navy on 29 October 1945, she is decommissioned the following May, ending a most unusual career.

An attack against Darwin, Australia, by aircraft from the Japanese carriers *Akagi*, *Hiryu*, *Kaga*, and *Soryu* results in the sinking of the destroyer *Peary* (DD 226), which is hit by five bombs and loses eighty men killed; the U.S. Army transport *Meigs*; and the U.S. freighter *Mauna Loa*. The small seaplane tender (destroyer) *William B. Preston* (AVD 7) is damaged along with two freighters. Japanese carrier-based fighters attack a Darwin-based PBY Catalina of VP-22, wounding the pilot, who manages to put his damaged aircraft down on the water. The eight-man crew is rescued by a merchantman that is subsequently sunk by Japanese aircraft. One of the PBY's crewmen is killed in the attack, but the remaining seven are eventually rescued for a second time. The pilot of the PBY is Lieutenant Thomas H. Moorer, who eventually becomes Chief of Naval Operations and Chairman of the Joint Chiefs of Staff.

Left: *The destroyer* Peary *(DD 226) burns in the aftermath of a Japanese air attack at Darwin, Australia, on 19 February 1942. Five bombs hit the destroyer, killing eighty men. She sank in just over two hours. (Naval Historical Center)*

Below: *A recruiting poster aims to attract skilled craftsman, electricians, and machinists into the Navy's newly formed Construction Battalions, more popularly known as the Seabees. (Library of Congress)*

20 February

The aircraft carrier *Lexington* approaches Rabaul for planned attacks against the Pacific stronghold when she is spotted by a Japanese flying boat. Subsequently a squadron of G4M land attack planes attacks the carrier. With the guns of his wingman's F4F Wildcat malfunctioning, forcing his return to the carrier, Lieutenant Edward H. "Butch" O'Hare of Fighting Squadron (VF) 3 is left to defend the ship against the attackers. In a heroic feat of airmanship, the fighter pilot is credited with the destruction of five bombers and the damaging of another in defense of the carrier (postwar records indicate he actually shot down four and damaged two). Antiaircraft gunners and other defending aircraft thwart the other enemy bombers. For his actions, O'Hare receives the Medal of Honor.

The submarine *Swordfish* embarks Filipino President Manuel Quezon and Vice President Sergio Osmena and their families, along with other government officials to prevent their capture by the Japanese. They are brought from Mariveles to San Jose on the Philippine island of Panay.

24 February

The ships of Task Force 16, commanded by Vice Admiral William F. Halsey and centered around the carrier *Enterprise*, strike a blow of revenge by attacking Wake Island. While aircraft bomb and strafe the atoll, the guns of the heavy cruisers *Northampton* and *Salt Lake City* and destroyers *Balch* (DD 363) and *Maury* (DD 401) bombard it from the sea. In addition to damage inflicted on shore installations, the attack sinks two guardboats.

The submarine *Swordfish* continues its evacuation mission in the Philippines, embarking the U.S. High Commissioner to the Philippines, Francis B. Sayre, and his official party for transport from Manila Bay to Java.

Build for your NAVY!

ENLIST! CARPENTERS, MACHINISTS, ELECTRICIANS ETC.
FOR INFORMATION APPLY TO YOUR NEAREST RECRUITING STATION
U.S. NAVY - BUREAU OF YARDS & DOCKS

Right: *Lieutenant Edward H. "Butch" O'Hare (left) and Lieutenant Commander John S. Thach answer the questions of reporters in Hawaii on 27 March 1942. The pair had just returned from a cruise in* Lexington *(CV 2) during which O'Hare had become the Navy's first ace of the war, credited with shooting down five enemy bombers and damaging a sixth in defending the carrier from a Japanese air attack off Rabaul. For his actions he received the Medal of Honor. (National Museum of Naval Aviation)*

27 February

Japanese land attack planes conduct a series of bombing raids against the seaplane tender *Langley* (AV 3) in the waters south of Tjilatjap, Java. The ship, carrying Army Air Forces P-40 fighters for service in Java, suffers such extensive damage that she must be abandoned. Her crew is picked up by the destroyers *Edsall* (DD 219) and *Whipple* (DD 217). *Whipple* delivers the coup de grace to *Langley*, formerly the U.S. Navy's first aircraft carrier.

27–28 February

In the Battle of the Java Sea, an ABDA force consisting of five cruisers and eleven destroyers under the command of Royal Netherlands Navy Rear Admiral Karel W.F.M. Doorman engages a Japanese force covering an invasion convoy bound for Java. In the first day of action, Japanese guns and torpedoes sink two Allied destroyers and another is sunk when she inadvertently hits a mine. The following day the Japanese heavy cruiser *Haguro* sinks the Dutch light cruiser *De Ruyter*, Doorman's flagship, and the Dutch light cruiser *Java* succumbs to fire from the Japanese heavy cruiser *Nachi*. With Admiral Doorman having been killed in action on board his flagship, the remaining Allied ships retire in an effort to reach Australia. The U.S. Navy submarines *S-37* (SS 142) and *S-38* (SS 143) rescue some survivors.

28 February–1 March

The heavy cruiser *Houston* and Australian light cruiser *Perth* engage a force consisting of three Japanese

cruisers and nine destroyers in the Battle of Sunda Strait in the waters off Java. Torpedoes and gunfire from the Japanese heavy cruisers *Mikuma* and *Mogami* ravage the two Allied vessels, sinking *Perth* in one hour and then turning their attention to *Houston*, whose crew fights valiantly, damaging three Japanese destroyers. Eventually, her headway is stopped by torpedo hits and gunfire, a shell burst killing her commanding officer, Captain Albert H. Rooks, who is posthumously awarded the Medal of Honor. *Houston* sinks in the early morning hours of 1 March. Only 368 members of her crew of over 1,000 men survive the action, and are captured by the Japanese.

1 March

The destroyer *Pope* (DD 225), operating as part of a three-ship Allied force that comes under attack by four Japanese heavy cruisers in the waters off Java, manages to avoid being hit by gunfire from the enemy ships. However, a near miss from a Japanese seaplane damages the destroyer and then aircraft from the carrier *Ryujo* bomb her. *Pope* is eventually sunk by the heavy cruisers *Myoko* and *Ashigara*, and her surviving crew members are taken prisoner. One of them, *Pope*'s executive officer Lieutenant Richard N. Antrim, later receives the Medal of Honor for heroic conduct while in captivity.

Just hours after the destroyer *Edsall* finishes transferring survivors from the seaplane tender *Langley* to the oiler *Pecos* (AO 6), *Pecos* is sunk by carrier planes from the Japanese carriers *Akagi*, *Hiryu*, *Kaga*, and *Soryu* in the waters south of Christmas Island.

Left: *SBD-3 Dauntless dive-bombers of Bombing Squadron (VB) 6 prepare to launch from the carrier* Enterprise *(CV 6) for a raid against Wake Atoll, 24 February 1942. (Naval Historical Center)*

Below: *The attack on Pearl Harbor spurred thousands of Americans to enlist. For those who believed they had "something extra," aviators beckoned them to naval aviation. All told, over 61,000 men received their wings as naval aviators during the period 1942–1945. (McClelland Barclay, National Museum of Naval Aviation)*

The destroyer *Edsall* (DD 219) comes under fire from the Japanese battleships *Hie* and *Kirishima* and two heavy cruisers, which together expend 1,141 shells in their effort to sink the resilient tin can. Carrier planes also participate in the attack, which kills all but five of *Edsall*'s crewmen. They are captured and eventually executed.

With the impending fall of Java, the ABDA Command is dissolved.

A PBO Hudson patrol-bomber of VP-82 spots *U-656* on the surface in the waters south of Newfoundland. The subsequent bombing run sinks the German submarine, the first U-boat kill scored by the U.S. Navy during World War II.

2 March
The destroyer *Pillsbury* (DD 227) is sunk by gunfire from Japanese heavy cruisers *Atago* and *Takao* as she attempts to escape Java.

3 March
The submarine *Perch* is scuttled by her crew in the Java Sea after enduring three days of attacks by Japanese surface ships. The first depth charging, which occurs on the evening of 1 March, drives the boat to a depth of 135 feet and causes engine damage and flooding. Her first attempt to surface and make repairs draws another depth charge attack that again forces the boat to submerge, damaging her ballast tanks. Finally, able

to make repairs, *Perch* makes a test dive in the early morning of 3 March, from which she is barely able to make it to the surface. She is then straddled by fire

CADETS for **Naval Aviation** take *that something extra* .... have you got it?
Apply nearest U.S. Navy Recruiting Station

from two enemy cruisers and three enemy destroyers, prompting the decision to scuttle her. All of her fifty-nine-man crew is taken prisoner. Six die in captivity.

The gunboat *Asheville* (PG 21) is sunk by the Japanese destroyers *Arashi* and *Nowaki* south of Java with the loss of all but one crewman, who is captured and eventually dies in captivity.

4 March

In another hit and run raid conducted by U.S. Navy forces against a Japanese-held island, the carrier *Enterprise* launches SBD Dauntless dive-bombers against Marcus Island.

10 March

Task Force 11 and Task Force 17, centered around the aircraft carriers *Lexington* and *Yorktown*, respectively, launch an air strike against Japanese shipping assembled at Lae and Salamaua, New Guinea. The raid, the first of the war to involve more than one flattop, results in the sinking of an armed merchant cruiser, auxiliary minelayer, and transport, as well as damage to ten other vessels. The most successful strike to date by U.S. Navy carriers, the raid prompts the Japanese to send aircraft carriers to the region to support offensive operations in the southwest Pacific.

11–13 March

With the fall of Luzon, Philippines, to the Japanese imminent, Lieutenant General Douglas A. MacArthur and Rear Admiral Francis Rockwell, along with their staffs, board PT boats at Luzon and embark on a 560-mile journey to Mindanao, Philippines. The skipper of the boats, Lieutenant John D. Bulkeley, receives the Medal of Honor for his actions during the evacuation.

15 March

A PBO Hudson patrol bomber of VP-82 sinks the German *U-503* in the waters off Argentia, Newfoundland, Canada, while flying escort over convoy ON 74.

17 March

Vice Admiral Robert L. Ghormley assumes the newly established post of Commander Naval Forces Europe.

Above: *The combined forces of Americans, British, Dutch, and Australians proved no match for the Japanese in the Dutch East Indies (now Indonesia). In the last battle in this area, the cruisers* Houston *(CA 30), HMS* Exeter, *and HMAS* Perth *stumbled onto a Japanese invasion force off Java, 28 February 1942. Both* Houston *and* Perth *were lost in the battle against great odds.* Exeter *escaped, severely damaged, but was sunk the next day. ("Battle of the Sunda Strait," John Hamilton, Navy Art Collection)*

19 March
The motor torpedo boat *PT-41* transports Philippine President Manuel Quezon and thirteen others from Negros to Mindanao, Philippines.

The destroyer *Dickerson* (DD 157) is accidently fired upon by the U.S. freighter *Liberator* while operating off the coast of Virginia. Casualties include three men killed and six wounded. Among the dead is the destroyer's skipper.

26 March
Under the provisions of an executive order combining the duties of Commander in Chief, U.S. Fleet and Chief of Naval Operations, Admiral Ernest J. King relieves Admiral Harold R. Stark and becomes the ninth Chief of Naval Operations.

In an effort to reinforce the British Home Fleet Task Force 39—consisting of the battleship *Washington* (BB 56), aircraft carrier *Wasp*, heavy cruisers *Tuscaloosa* and *Wichita*, and eight destroyers—departs Portland, Maine, for transit to Scapa Flow in the Orkney Islands. The next day, task force commander Rear Admiral John W. Wilcox, Jr., is washed overboard while walking on the deck of the flagship *Washington* and lost at sea. Rear Admiral Robert C. Giffen assumes command of the task force.

After a spirited gun battle in which the antisubmarine vessel *Atik* (AK 101) damages *U-123*, the German submarine sinks the ship with the loss of all 139 on board. *Atik* is the only U.S. "Q-ship," an armed ship disguised as a merchantman, lost in action with the enemy during World War II.

Commissioned on 5 March 1942, her operational career lasts just three weeks.

3 April

Commander in Chief, U.S. Pacific Fleet Admiral Chester W. Nimitz assumes additional duties as Commander in Chief Pacific Ocean Areas (CINCPOA) responsible for operations in the North, Central, and South Pacific. Lieutenant General Douglas A. MacArthur is named Commander, Southwest Pacific Area.

6 April

The river gunboats *Mindanao* (PR 8) and *Oahu* (PR 6) claim the destruction of four Japanese landing barges in a night attack in Manila Bay, Philippines.

8 April

The submarine *Seadragon* (SS 194) delivers food to forces on Corregidor and takes aboard naval radio and communications intelligence personnel, thus completing the evacuation of the last group of these vital specialists from the Philippines.

9 April

The surrender of forces on the Bataan Peninsula, Philippines, prompts the destruction of naval facilities at Mariveles to prevent their use by the Japanese, and the scuttling of the submarine tender *Canopus* (AS 9), minesweeper *Bittern* (AM 36), tug *Napa* (AT 32) and drydock *Dewey*. Small craft, including ferry and motor launches, help transport retreating troops from Bataan to Corregidor.

The motor torpedo boats *PT-34* and *PT-41* engage the Japanese light cruiser *Kuma* and torpedo boat *Kiji* off Cape Tanon on the island of Cebu, Philippines. A torpedo launched against *Kuma* hits the cruiser but fails to explode. *PT-34* is later bombed and strafed by floatplanes and is beached at Cauiut Island. She is destroyed by a second air attack. Of her six-man crew, two are killed and three wounded.

10 April

In a reorganization of the U.S. Pacific Fleet, the following type commands are established:

Battleships: Rear Admiral Walter S. Anderson
Aircraft Carriers: Vice Admiral William F. Halsey, Jr.
Cruisers: Rear Admiral Frank Jack Fletcher

Left: *Shown with the paddles of a landing signal officer, Lieutenant David S. McCampbell, the Navy's top fighter ace and Medal of Honor recipient, began the war serving in the carrier* Wasp *(CV 7). (Naval Historical Center)*

Below: *The destroyer* Roper *(DD 147) pictured during Atlantic convoy duty. In April 1942, she sunk U-85. (Naval Historical Center)*

Opposite, top: *The Doolittle Raiders prepare to launch attacks on Japan from* Hornet *(CV 8) on 18 April 1942. ("Early Launch," James Dietz)*

DDestroyers: Rear Admiral Robert A. Theobald
Service Force: Vice Admiral William L. Calhoun
Amphibious Force: Vice Admiral Wilson Brown, Jr.
Submarine Force: Rear Admiral Thomas Withers
Patrol Wings: Rear Admiral John S. McCain

14 April

The destroyer *Roper* (DD 147), after spotting *U-85* on the surface off North Carolina, pursues the submarine and scores repeated hits on the boat. The destroyer subsequently drops depth charges that help send *U-85* to the bottom. She is the first German submarine sunk off the coast of the United States following the commencement of Operation Drumbeat.

18 April

In a bold stroke, sixteen Army Air Forces B-25 Mitchell medium bombers under Lieutenant Colonel James H. Doolittle, his crews trained in carrier take-offs by Lieutenant (junior grade) Henry L. Miller, launch from the aircraft carrier *Hornet* (CV 8) to strike targets in Tokyo, Yokosuka, Yokohama, Kobe, and Nagoya, Japan. Fifteen of the aircraft land in occupied China, where two crews are captured by the Japanese, and one lands in Vladivostok, U.S.S.R. Launched earlier than planned when a Japanese guardboat spots the ships of Task Force 16, which includes *Hornet* and the carrier *Enterprise*, the attack causes little material damage, but its psychological effect on the enemy and boost to American morale are tremendous. When asked the location from which the U.S. planes launched, President Franklin D. Roosevelt replies, "Shangri-La."

The submarine *Searaven* (SS 196) completes the evacuation of Royal Australian Air Force personnel from Japanese-occupied Timor in the Netherlands East Indies.

20 April

The aircraft carrier *Wasp*, having ferried forty-seven British Royal Air Force Spitfires to the Mediterranean, flies the aircraft off to bolster the defenses of the besieged island of Malta.

26 April
The destroyer *Sturtevant* (DD 240) strikes a mine off Marquesas Key, Florida, and sinks with the loss of fifteen members of her crew.

28 April
A joint Anglo-American force that includes the battleship *Washington*, heavy cruisers *Wichita* and *Tuscaloosa*, and four destroyers sails from Scapa Flow in the Orkney Islands to the waters northeast of Iceland to cover convoy PQ 15, bound for the U.S.S.R.

30 April
Admiral Harold R. Stark takes command of U.S. Naval Forces Europe.

3 May
In the last submarine evacuation of personnel from the island fortress of Corregidor in Manila Bay, Philippines, the submarine *Spearfish* (SS 190) departs carrying personnel that includes nurses.

4 May
Aircraft from the carrier *Yorktown* strike Japanese shipping supporting the landing of ground forces on Tulagi in the Solomon Islands. The raid results in the sinking of four vessels and damage to four others. The action foreshadows the Battle of the Coral Sea.

6 May
Corregidor, the last U.S. stronghold in the Philippines, surrenders to the Japanese. Avoiding captivity, the crew of the minesweeper *Quail* (AM 15) scuttles their ship and sets out from Manila Bay in a motor launch. The eighteen men, including the ship's commanding officer Lieutenant Commander John H. Morrill, reach Darwin, Australia, on 6 June.

7–8 May
The Battle of the Coral Sea opens on 7 May when surface ships under the command of British Royal Navy Rear Admiral John G. Crace attempt to intercept a Japanese invasion force bound for Port Moresby, New Guinea. Bombed first by land-based Japanese bombers and later mistakenly attacked by Army Air Forces aircraft, the foray proves unsuccessful. Meanwhile, on board the aircraft carriers *Lexington* and *Yorktown*, aircraft launch for an attack against the Close Support Force escorting the Port Moresby invasion force. These planes send the Japanese light carrier *Shoho* to the bottom, which prompts Lieutenant Commander Robert Dixon, skipper of Scouting Squadron (VS) 2, to radio the electrifying message "Scratch one flattop!" Meanwhile, Japanese aviators damage the oiler *Neosho* (AO 23) and sink the destroyer *Sims* (DD 409). On board the oiler, Chief Watertender Oscar V. Peterson overcomes his wounds

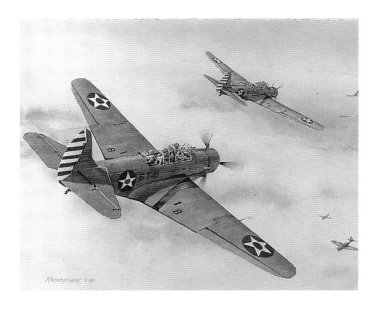

to close bulkhead stop valves, helping save the lives of shipmates. Severely burned, he soon dies, and later is awarded a posthumous Medal of Honor for his actions. The ship he fought so hard to save, fatally damaged, is scuttled on 11 May.

On 8 May aircraft of the two opposing carrier forces spot one another, triggering a launching of strike groups. Naval aviators from *Lexington* and *Yorktown* strike just ahead of the Japanese, heavily damaging the fleet carrier *Shokaku*. One pilot, Lieutenant John J. Powers, dives to within 200 feet. of the enemy carrier's deck before releasing his bomb and is last seen attempting to recover from his dive. He receives a posthumous Medal of

Honor for his actions at Coral Sea. Many miles away, Japanese pilots score hits on *Lexington* and *Yorktown*, despite the heroic defense of pilots like Lieutenant William H. Hall who, while flying an SBD Dauntless dive bomber in antitorpedo defense, is credited with shooting down three aircraft. Hall receives the Medal of Honor for his actions. On board *Lexington*, the damage inflicted by enemy bombs and torpedoes is made worse when gasoline vapors ignite, resulting in explosions that signal the end of the venerable carrier. *Yorktown* suffers severe bomb damage, but the efforts of men like Lieutenant Milton E. Ricketts, who receives a posthumous Medal of Honor for fighting fires despite being mortally wounded, save the ship.

A landmark engagement in naval history—marking the first time a battle is fought without the opposing surface forces coming within sight of each other—the Battle of the Coral Sea is costly, but achieves the strategic goal of blunting Japanese aims on Port Moresby.

9 May
The aircraft carrier *Wasp* (CV 7) once again launches British Royal Air Force Spitfires to help strengthen the defense of Malta, prompting British Prime Minister Winston S. Churchill to comment, "Who said a *Wasp* couldn't sting twice!"

10 May
The aircraft carrier *Ranger* (CV 4), off the Gold Coast of Africa, launches sixty-eight Army Air Forces P-40

Above: *TBD-1 Devastators descend to begin an attack run against Japanese shipping during an early-1942 Pacific raid. Devastators were retired from front-line service after three squadrons were decimated during the Battle of Midway. (Robert L. Rasmussen)*

Left: *Plane handlers await the order to move a Royal Air Force Spitfire to the flight deck of* Wasp *(CV 7), May 1942. The carrier transported British aircraft to the Mediterranean in order to bolster defenses on Malta. (National Museum of Naval Aviation)*

Right: *The Japanese light carrier* Shoho *pictured maneuvering to avoid attacks by U.S. planes from the carrier* Lexington *(CV 2) during the Battle of the Coral Sea, 7 May 1942. Navy pilots found their mark, sending* Shoho *to the bottom, but the Japanese exacted their revenge on "Lady Lex" the next day. (Naval Historical Center)*

fighters for a flight to Accra. She repeats the operation on 19 July, sending seventy-two P-40s off her deck.

13 May
The Bureau of Navigation is renamed the Bureau of Naval Personnel.

20 May
Rear Admiral John S. McCain assumes duties as Commander Air Force, South Pacific, a new command which plays a central role in the upcoming Guadalcanal campaign.

21 May
The North Pacific Force is established under Rear Admiral Robert A. Theobald to cover operations in Alaskan waters.

25 May
While operating off Martinique in the French West Indies, the destroyer *Blakeley* (DD 150) is torpedoed by the German submarine *U-156*. The blast takes away sixty feet of the destroyer's bow, kills six crewmen, and wounds twenty-one others. However, she survives to fight again.

3–6 June
The pivotal Battle of Midway opens on 3 June when a PBY Catalina patrol plane flown by Ensign Jack Reid spots the Japanese Occupation Force carrying troops for the invasion of Midway Atoll. Aircraft from Midway attack the enemy ships, dropping a torpedo that hits a tanker. On the morning of 4 June, a PBY flown by Lieutenant Howard P. Ady radios a message

indicating the sighting of Japanese carriers. Midway-based aircraft immediately launch strikes against the enemy, as do carrier aircraft from *Yorktown*, *Enterprise*, and *Hornet* operating northeast of Midway. They seek out the enemy while aircraft from the Japanese carriers *Akagi*, *Hiryu*, *Kaga*, and *Soryu* attack Midway. The initial attacks against the Japanese carriers meet determined antiaircraft fire and an umbrella of Zero fighters, which cut through the U.S. aircraft. The carrier-based torpedo squadrons are particularly hard hit, with only four of forty-one aircraft managing to land back aboard their carrier. However, attacks against the lumbering TBD Devastator torpedo bombers bring the Japanese fighters down to low altitude just as SBD Dauntless dive-bombers arrive on the scene. Within minutes, the decks of three of the four Japanese carriers are raging infernos and eventually sink. Later in the day, the SBDs knock the surviving carrier, *Hiryu*, out of action, but not before she is able to launch two strikes that severely damage *Yorktown*. On 6 June, Japanese submarine *I-168* torpedoes the damaged *Yorktown* and the destroyer *Hamman* (DD 412), sinking the destroyer. The Japanese heavy cruiser *Mikuma* is also sunk by air attack. *Yorktown* sinks on 7 June, the last casualty of the Battle of Midway. The American victory at Midway turns the tide of the Pacific War.

9 June
Lieutenant Commander Lyndon B. Johnson, future thirty-sixth President of the United States, inspects facilities in the Pacific while on leave from his seat in the House of Representatives. On this day he climbs aboard an Army Air Forces B-26 Marauder for a raid

Above: *The destroyer* Blakeley *(DD 150) in passage from Martinique to St. Lucia, 27 May 1942, after being torpedoed two days previously. Note missing bow and lifeboat being towed astern. (Naval Historical Center)*

Below: *TBD Devastators of Torpedo Squadron 6 unfold their wings aboard* Enterprise *(CV 6) prior to takeoff on 4 June 1942, during the Battle of Midway. Only four planes of this squadron returned from that day's raid on the Japanese carriers. (Naval Historical Center)*

Opposite: *Sailors on board an unidentified ship have grandstand seats for the presentation of medals by Admiral William F. Halsey, Jr., 1943. (National Museum of Naval Aviation)*

against Lae, New Guinea, only to have his plane turn back short of the target because of engine trouble. The future Commander in Chief receives the Silver Star from the Army for the mission.

19 June
South Pacific Area and South Pacific Force is established and placed under the command of Vice Admiral Robert L. Ghormley.

The submarine *S-27* (SS 132) runs aground off St. Makarius Point on Amchitka in the Aleutian Islands. Her crew employs rubber boats to get ashore and all are rescued by PBY Catalina aircraft on 24–25 June.

30 June
A PBM Mariner of VP-74 sinks the German submarine *U-158* with depth charges off Bermuda.

1 July
A tragedy of war occurs when the submarine *Sturgeon* (SS 187) torpedoes and sinks the Japanese transport *Montevideo Maru* off Luzon, Philippines. Among those killed are 1,050 Allied prisoners of war being transported to Hainan Island.

10 July
A PBY Catalina of VP-41 spots the wreckage of a Japanese Zero fighter that crashed in a bog during strikes against the Aleutian Islands on 3 June. The aircraft is subsequently salvaged and restored to

MIDWAY TO VICTORY

by Barrett Tillman

Following six months of uninterrupted victories after the attacks at Pearl Harbor, Hawaii, Japan's warlords sought the decisive battle for which the Imperial Japanese Navy had trained for decades. If a dictated peace were to be obtained, the U.S. Pacific Fleet's aircraft carriers had to be destroyed. Midway Atoll, strategically located 1,100 miles northwest of Oahu, was the obvious venue. U.S. Pacific Fleet commander Admiral Chester Nimitz had to commit his remaining forces to oppose a landing so close to Hawaii. Of necessity, the Battle of Midway turned on naval aviation. With no available fast battleships, and submarines largely ineffective because of material deficiencies in American torpedoes, airpower was the only viable option. It represented a new kind of warfare, for the world's first carrier battle had been fought between American and Japanese flattops only thirty days before in the Coral Sea.

On paper, Japanese Combined Fleet commander Admiral Isoroku Yamamoto held all the advantages: numbers, equipment, experienced personnel, and momentum. He deployed an awesome armada 2,500 miles from home that included eight carriers, eighty-three surface warships, twenty-one submarines, and dozens of auxiliaries. To meet the Japanese onslaught, Nimitz possessed three carriers, forty-three cruisers or destroyers, and eighteen submarines, split between Midway and the Aleutians. Yet therein lay an advantage. With the priceless knowledge of enemy plans via his code breakers, Nimitz knew that the Japanese would first strike Dutch Harbor, Alaska, in a large-scale feint. Consequently, the odds he faced at Midway were reduced. Yamamoto further split his Midway forces, with "only" four heavy carriers, two battleships, and three cruisers at the decisive point. With Midway's ramps jammed with 128 Navy, Army Air Forces, and Marine Corps planes, the aircraft strength wielded by the opposing forces was roughly the same.

The opening act of the pivotal battle occurred on the night of 3 June, when PBY Catalina patrol planes conducted a torpedo attack against the enemy landing force, damaging one ship. At dawn on the following morning, four Japanese carriers under the command of

Vice Admiral Chuichi Nagumo launched 108 planes against Midway, intending to smash the Americans in one blow. The attackers nearly succeeded as Midway's facilities sustained heavy damage. Meanwhile, Catalinas found Nagumo's task force, and Midway's bombers winged northwesterly. It was a staggered, gallant effort with little coordination. Four Army Air Forces B-26 Marauders and six Navy TBF Avengers made heroic, ineffective torpedo attacks, with only three planes returning. Marine dive-bombers attacked, missed, and were bloodied. B-17 Flying Fortresses found the enemy, bombed from altitude, and missed. Meanwhile, Nagumo prepared his second wave to finish off Midway, and then await his opportunity to sink Nimitz's carriers rushing to the atoll's defense.

However, the American carriers *Yorktown* (CV 5), *Enterprise* (CV 6), and *Hornet* (CV 8) were already there, waiting in ambush northeast of Midway. Knowing Nagumo's position, they launched deckload strikes of

Opposite: *Ensign George Gay, the only member of Torpedo Squadron 8 from the carrier Hornet (CV 8) to survive an attack against the Japanese fleet at the Battle of Midway, recuperates in a hospital in Hawaii. The newspaper on his lap announces the American victory in this landmark naval engagement. (Naval Historical Center)*

Right: *View of the flight deck of the aircraft carrier Yorktown (CV 5) after she was hit by Japanese dive-bombers at the Battle of Midway on 4 June 1942. The gallant ship did not survive the battle, but before she sank, her planes helped turn the tide in the Pacific War. (Naval Historical Center)*

SBD Dauntless dive-bombers, TBD Devastator torpedo planes, and F4F Wildcat fighters. Yet the two task forces lacked cohesion; Rear Admiral Raymond A. Spruance, in command of *Enterprise, Hornet,* and their escorts, and Rear Admiral Frank Jack Fletcher, commanding the task force that included *Yorktown,* conducted independent operations, which were splintered by problems in *Hornet.* Other than her TBD "torpeckers," she contributed little to the American effort, her remaining aircraft never finding the target.

Beginning near mid-morning, the three torpedo plane squadrons attacked in succession, largely without the benefit of fighter cover. They were decimated, losing thirty-seven of forty-one airplanes. Meanwhile, Nagumo prepared to launch his second wave against the new threat, switching ordnance from land bombs to ship-killing bombs and torpedoes. In that fatal hour, *Enterprise* and *Yorktown* SBDs found their quarry. Arriving unhampered over the enemy carriers engaged in rearming and refueling aircraft, forty-seven Dauntlesses rolled into 70-degree dives and released their bombs. Three Pearl Harbor veterans—*Akagi, Kaga,* and *Soryu*—were turned into floating infernos. The momentum of six months had been reversed in less than six minutes. Nagumo's remaining flight deck belonged to *Hiryu,* which immediately launched twenty-two dive-bombers and fighters against *Yorktown.* Six survived flak

and attacking F4F Wildcats and hit "Old Yorky," forcing Fletcher to shift his flag and turn over command of American forces to Spruance, who placed a priority on finding the fourth enemy flattop. *Hiryu* wasted no time, launching sixteen more planes to finish the job. They succeeded in putting two torpedoes into *Yorktown.* Listing badly, she was abandoned.

Late that afternoon, *Hiryu* had assembled a tiny strike group consisting of all her remaining aircraft and was preparing to launch her fourth strike of the day when twenty-four SBDs dived from 15,000 feet. Japanese Zero fighters slashed at the formation, downing two, but the others pressed their attack, scoring hits on the flattop. As they winged homeward a prophetic image appeared—the setting sun.

The battle continued for more than two days, ending when a Japanese submarine sank the crippled *Yorktown* on 7 June. More than 300 Americans and 2,000 Japanese had died, and the operational lives of five carriers, an American destroyer, and a Japanese cruiser had ended in the blue waters of the Pacific. The magnitude of the victory was immediately evident, and no one recognized it sooner than Nimitz himself. During the noon hour on the 6 June, before the results were fully known, he told the *Honolulu Star-Bulletin,* "Perhaps we will be forgiven if we claim we are about midway to our objective."

flying condition, proving beneficial in refining fighter designs and tactics.

13 July

The German *U-153*, after being damaged by the submarine chaser *PC 458* and an Army Air Forces aircraft, is sunk off Panama by the destroyer *Lansdowne* (DD 486).

15 July

The U.S. merchantman *Unicoi*, which rams the enemy submarine, and an OS2U Kingfisher observation plane from VS-9 combine to sink *U-576* off the coast of North Carolina.

18 July

Amphibious Force, South Pacific is established under the command of Rear Admiral Richmond Kelly Turner.

20 July

Recalled to active duty, Admiral William D. Leahy becomes Chief of Staff to President Franklin D. Roosevelt.

30 July

The Women Accepted for Volunteer Emergency Service (WAVES) is established, with Lieutenant Commander Mildred H. McAfee assuming duties as

IT'S A WOMAN'S WAR TOO!

JOIN THE WAVES

YOUR COUNTRY NEEDS YOU NOW

JOHN FALTER USNR

Apply to your nearest
NAVY RECRUITING STATION OR OFFICE OF NAVAL OFFICER PROCUREMENT

commanding officer on 2 August. By the end of 1942 total WAVE strength is 3,879 officers and enlisted personnel. By 31 July 1945, that number has grown to 86,291.

4 August

The destroyer *Tucker* (DD 374), her crew uninformed of the presence of a minefield in the waters off Segond Channel, Espiritu Santo, New Hebrides Islands, hits a mine and sinks with the loss of six of her crew.

7 August

Amphibious Force, South Pacific, under the command of Rear Admiral Richmond Kelly Turner, lands the First Marine Division on Florida, Tulagi, Gavutu, Tanambogo, and Guadalcanal in the Solomon Islands, marking the first American offensive of the war. Supported by air and surface forces under the command of Vice Admiral Frank Jack Fletcher, the Marines quickly advance inland and on 8 August capture an airstrip under construction on Guadalcanal, which they christen Henderson Field. During the first two days of operations, Japanese air attacks damage the destroyers *Mugford* (DD 389) and *Jarvis* (DD 393) and transports *Barnett* (AP 11) and *George F. Elliott* (AP 13), the latter to such an extent that she is scuttled.

9 August

A Japanese surface force consisting of four heavy cruisers, three light cruisers, and a destroyer under the command of Vice Admiral Gunichi Mikawa engage in a night action against U.S. and Australian ships protecting the transports unloading off Guadalcanal. In an engagement called the Battle of Savo Island, the Japanese score a stunning victory, sinking the heavy cruisers *Astoria* (CA 34), *Quincy*, and *Vincennes* (CA 44). The Australian cruiser *Canberra* is so badly damaged that she is scuttled, and the heavy cruiser *Chicago* (CA 29) and destroyers *Patterson* (DD 392) and *Ralph Talbot* (DD 390) suffer damage. Though no Japanese surface ships are sunk, American gunners score hits on four enemy ships, including Mikawa's flagship *Chokai*. Despite the overwhelming nature of their victory, the Japanese ships fail to descend upon the defenseless transports, thus enabling the Marines to establish a foothold on Guadalcanal. Nevertheless, the tenacity of Japanese air assaults since 7 August prompts the withdrawal of carrier air support and the transports.

The destroyer *Jarvis* (DD 393), an enemy torpedo having already put a fifty foot gash in her side on 8 August, faces a determined attack by Japanese landbased aircraft as she steams for Australia for

repairs. Her gunners shoot down two of the attackers and damage a third to such an extent that it is forced to ditch. However, the gallant destroyer, which first fired her guns at Japanese aircraft at Pearl Harbor on the morning of 7 December 1941, is sunk with loss of all hands.

12 August

In the first operational testing of antiaircraft projectiles incorporating proximity fuses, gunners on board the light cruiser *Cleveland* (CL 55) shoot down three target drones in the skies over the Chesapeake Bay. The proximity fuse greatly enhances the air defense capability of U.S. Navy ships during World War II.

Above: *Marines storm ashore at Guadalcanal in August 1942. Unlike later Pacific assaults, the leathernecks did not have to endure a firestorm on the beaches, but vicious fighting awaited them in the interior. (Corbis)*

16 August

While flying a patrol off the California coast, the airship *L-8* of Blimp Squadron (ZP) 32 is damaged. She makes it back to the coast under her own power and lands at Dale City, but her control car is empty, the two-man crew having disappeared without a trace.

17 August

The submarines *Nautilus* (SS 168) and *Argonaut* (SS 166) land Marines of the Second Raider Battalion on Makin in the Gilbert Islands. As the Marines destroy Japanese installations on the island, they are supported by fire from the deck gun of *Nautilus*. The two submarines withdraw the Raiders on 18 August.

20 August

The escort carrier *Long Island* (ACV 1) transports the first Marine aircraft to Guadalcanal, launching nineteen F4F Wildcat fighters and twelve SBD Dauntless dive-bombers on their flight to Henderson Field.

22 August

The Japanese destroyer *Kawakaze*, having completed the landing of Japanese troops on Guadalcanal,

encounters the destroyers *Blue* (DD 387) and *Henley* (DD 391) and torpedoes the former ship, killing nine and wounding twenty-one members of her crew. The damaged *Blue* is towed to the island of Tulagi and scuttled off Florida Island the following day.

23 August

A force consisting of the heavy cruiser *Tuscaloosa* escorted by the destroyers *Rodman* (DD 456) and *Emmons* (DD 457) and the British destroyer *Onslaught*

Right: *On board the carrier* Enterprise *(CV 6), a bomb explodes on the flight deck just aft of the island during the Battle of the Eastern Solomons, 24 August 1942. According to the original caption, this explosion killed the photographer, Photographer's Mate Third Class Robert F. Read. However, Read was killed by the bomb that had earlier wiped out the starboard aft 5-inch gun gallery, which can be seen still burning in the upper left. The bomb in this photo inflicted only minor damage. (Naval Historical Center)*

delivers men and equipment of two British Royal Air Force squadrons to Murmansk, Russia.

24 August

In the Battle of the Eastern Solomons, the flattops *Saratoga* and *Enterprise* engage Japanese carriers supporting a major effort to reinforce Japanese troops on Guadalcanal. SBD Dauntless dive-bombers and TBF Avenger torpedo bombers score hits on the Japanese carrier *Ryujo*, but fail to hit the large-deck carriers *Shokaku* and *Zuikaku*, whose planes attack *Enterprise*. The "Big E" is heavily damaged and retires to Pearl Harbor, Hawaii, for repairs. The following day, Marine aircraft from Guadalcanal succeed in damaging four ships in a Japanese convoy en route to reinforce the island, forcing it to turn back.

28 August

Marine and Navy SBD dive-bombers operating from Henderson Field successfully turn back Japanese destroyers attempting to land reinforcements on Guadalcanal, sinking *Asagiri* and damaging *Shirakumo* and *Yugiri*.

The light minelayer *Gamble* (DM 15) employs repeated depth charge attacks to sink the Japanese submarine *I-123* off Florida Island in the Solomons.

A PBY Catalina of VP-92 joins the Canadian corvette HMCS *Oakville* in sinking the German submarine *U-94* in the Caribbean.

30 August

The high-speed transport *Colhoun* (APD 2) is attacked by Japanese land-based bombers off Kukum Point, Guadalcanal, and sinks with fifty-one members of her crew.

31 August

The aircraft carrier *Saratoga* takes a torpedo from the Japanese submarine *I-26* while operating 260 miles southeast of Guadalcanal. The carrier is forced to retire from the combat zone for repairs.

PBY Catalinas of VPs 42 and 43 join the destroyer *Reid* (DD 369) in sinking the Japanese submarine *RO-61* off Atka in the Aleutian Islands.

1 September

Vice Admiral Aubrey W. Fitch becomes the first Commander Air Force, Pacific Fleet.

The first Seabees to serve in a combat zone, the men of the Sixth Naval Construction Battalion land at Lunga Point on Guadalcanal.

5 September

The Japanese destroyer *Yudachi*, assisted by a flare mistakenly dropped from a PBY Catalina patrolling the area, sinks the high-speed transports *Gregory* (APD 3) and *Little* (APD 4) operating off Lunga Point on Guadalcanal.

11 September

In a first for Navy medicine, Pharmacist's Mate First Class Wheeler B. Lipes performs an appendectomy on Seaman First Class Darrell D. Rector on a mess table on board the submarine *Seadragon* (SS 194) while the boat is submerged on patrol in the South China Sea.

15 September

The Japanese submarine *I-19* fires a spread of torpedoes at the ships of Task Force 18 covering a Guadalcanal-bound convoy. The battleship *North Carolina*, the destroyer *O'Brien* (DD 415), and the aircraft carrier *Wasp* are hit. Feeding on aviation gasoline, fires on the carrier also trigger ammunition and force Captain Forrest P. Sherman, a future Chief of Naval Operations, to give the order to abandon ship. The carrier is scuttled by the destroyer *Lansdowne*.

27 September

In an engagement between the U.S. freighter *Stephen Hopkins* and the German auxiliary cruiser *Stier* and supply ship *Tannenfels* in the South Atlantic, gunners of the freighter's Armed Guard and civilian volunteers score hits on *Stier*, sinking her. Unfortunately, *Stephen Hopkins* is also sunk in the engagement. For his actions, Lieutenant (junior grade) Kenneth M. Willett, a naval reservist and commander of the Armed Guard detachment, receives a posthumous Navy Cross.

5 October

The aircraft carrier *Hornet*, in an attempt to hinder resupply of Guadalcanal by the famed "Tokyo Express," launches an air strike against Japanese staging areas in the area of Buin-Tonolei and Faisi on Bougainville in the Solomon Islands. The raid results in damage to two destroyers and near misses on two seaplane carriers.

Right: *The carrier* Wasp *(CV 7) afire and sinking, south of San Cristobal Island, after being torpedoed by a Japanese submarine, 15 September 1942. (Naval Historical Center)*

Pages 428–429: *SBD Dauntless dive-bombers pull out of their dives and head for home during the Battle of Midway on 4 June 1942, leaving the Japanese carrier* Akagi *a blazing inferno. All told, SBDs sank four Japanese flattops during the pivotal battle. ("The Famous Four Minutes," R.G. Smith)*

A PBY Catalina, the personal aircraft of Commander Aircraft South Pacific, sinks the Japanese submarine *I-22* near Indispensable Strait in the Solomon Islands.

A PBY Catalina of Patrol Squadron VP-73 sends *U-582* to the bottom with all hands in the waters off Iceland.

11 October
A powerful Japanese surface force proceeds down the Slot—the body of water running the length of the Solomon Islands chain from Bougainville to Guadalcanal—to reinforce the garrison defending Guadalcanal and bombard Henderson Field. In response, a task group under the command of Rear Admiral Norman Scott maneuvers into a blocking position. In the resulting Battle of Cape Esperance, which begins late in the evening, gunners on board the heavy cruiser *Salt Lake City* and light cruiser *Boise* score numerous hits on the Japanese heavy cruiser *Furutaka*, which cause her to sink the following day. The American task force also sinks the destroyer *Fubuki* and damages the destroyer *Hatsuyuki* and heavy cruiser *Aoba*. The latter is the flagship of the Japanese commander, Rear Admiral Aritomo Goto, who is killed in the engagement. The Japanese damage both *Salt Lake City* and *Boise*, and also score

hits on the destroyers *Duncan* (DD 485) and *Farenholt* (DD 491). *Duncan* sinks the following day.

12 October
During action in the waters off Guadalcanal, Navy aircraft based temporarily at Henderson Field join their Marine counterparts in sinking the Japanese destroyer *Natsugumo* and damaging the destroyer *Murakumo* to such an extent that she is scuttled.

15 October
American and Japanese naval aircraft trade attacks against forces attempting to reinforce Guadalcanal. While Navy and Marine aircraft from Henderson Field attack a convoy heading up the Slot, carrier planes from the Japanese carrier *Zuikaku* stage attacks against vessels of Task Units 62.4.5 and 62.4.6. Three Japanese cargo ships and the destroyer *Meredith* (DD 434) are sunk. Seven officers and fifty-six enlisted men from the destroyer's crew survive the sinking and subsequent three days drifting in shark-infested waters.

16 October
The submarine *Thresher* (SS 200) plants mines in the approaches to the harbor at Bangkok, Thailand, the first such operation performed by a U.S. Navy submarine during World War II.

Left: *Lieutenant A.C. "Al" Emerson depicted at the controls of his F4F Wildcat as he engages in air-to-air combat with Japanese fighters during the Battle of the Santa Cruz Islands, 26 October 1942. By the end of the battle he would add two more kill flags to the side of his cockpit. (Tom Lea, Army Art Collection, U.S. Army Center of Military History)*

18 October

Vice Admiral William F. Halsey, Jr., relieves Vice Admiral Robert L. Ghormley as Commander South Pacific Area and South Pacific Force at the direction of Admiral Chester W. Nimitz, who decides that "a more aggressive commander" is needed.

20 October

The heavy cruiser *Chester* (CA 27) is torpedoed by the Japanese submarine *I-176* while operating southeast of San Cristobal in the Solomon Islands. Hitting the ship amidships on the starboard side, the torpedo causes a blast that kills eleven sailors and wounds twelve others. The cruiser retires to Espiritu Santo for repairs.

25 October

Navy, Marine Corps, and Army Air Forces aircraft from Henderson Field damage one Japanese destroyer and bomb the light cruiser *Yura* to such an extent that she is abandoned. The Japanese sink the tug *Seminole* (AT 65) and district patrol vessel *YP 284* and damage the high-speed minesweeper *Zane* (DMS 14).

26 October

In the battle of the Santa Cruz Islands, the carriers *Enterprise* and *Hornet,* under the command of Rear Admiral Thomas C. Kinkaid, engage the Japanese flattops *Junyo, Shokaku, Zuiho,* and *Zuikaku* under the command of Vice Admiral Chuichi Nagumo. American aviators score hits on both *Zuiho* and *Shokaku* and

damage the heavy cruiser *Chikuma* and destroyer *Terutsuki.* However, Japanese pilots find both *Enterprise* and *Hornet,* damaging the latter to such an extent that she is abandoned. Attempts to scuttle *Hornet* fail and she is sunk by Japanese destroyers on 27 October. Enemy fliers also score hits on the battleship *South Dakota* (BB 57) and light cruiser *San Juan* (CL 54), and a damaged aircraft plunges into the destroyer *Smith* (DD 378). In addition, the destroyer *Hughes* (DD 410) collides with *Hornet* while fighting fires on board the carrier and taking off survivors, and the destroyer *Porter* (DD 356) is damaged by a torpedo that accidentally fires when a battle-damaged TBF Avenger torpedo bomber ditches in her vicinity. She is later scuttled. The action ends in a tactical victory for the Japanese.

29 October

A PBY Catalina of VP-11 sinks the Japanese submarine *I-172* off San Cristobal in the Solomon Islands.

4 November

Members of the Armed Guard detachment on board the U.S. freighter *John H.B. Latrobe* defend the ship against an attack by German He.115 aircraft east of Iceland. Their efforts, and the captain's skillful shiphandling, cause all seven torpedoes dropped by the enemy aircraft to miss the mark. Strafing wounds three men of the Armed Guard and damages the freighter to such an extent that she returns to Iceland for repairs.

Left: *Flight deck crewmen on board the carrier* Enterprise (CV 6) *hold up black boards that indicate the range and bearing of Japanese carriers for pilots about to launch during the Battle of the Santa Cruz Islands, 26 October 1942. (National Museum of Naval Aviation)*

Below: *Antiaircraft guns on board* Hornet (CV 8) *blast away at Japanese attackers during the Battle of the Santa Cruz Islands, 26 October 1942. ("The Fighting Hornet," Tom Lea, Army Art Collection, U.S. Army Center of Military History)*

5 November

U.S. Navy Captain Jerauld Wright temporarily commands the British submarine *Seraph* as she evacuates French General Henri-Honoré Giraud and his staff from occupied France.

A PBY Catalina of VP-84 sinks the German submarine *U-408* in the waters off Iceland.

8–10 November

U.S. Navy forces participate in Operation Torch, the invasion of North Africa, the first Allied offensive of the European war. Under the overall command of Admiral Sir Andrew B. Cunningham of the British Royal Navy, the naval element of the operation numbers three task forces, including the Western Naval Task Force commanded by Rear Admiral H. Kent Hewitt. U.S. Navy forces are active against defending Vichy French ships and shore installations contesting the landings. The heavy cruiser *Augusta* and destroyers *Ludlow* (DD 438) and *Wilkes* (DD 441) silence shore batteries in the Casablanca/Fedala areas. *Augusta* also joins the light cruiser *Brooklyn* (CL 40), heavy cruisers *Wichita* and *Tuscaloosa*, and battleship *Massachusetts* (BB 59) in turning back two attempts by the Vichy French fleet to disrupt the landings at Casablanca, driving the ships back into Casablanca Harbor, where they are bombed repeatedly by aircraft from U.S. Navy escort carriers. *Massachusetts* is damaged by shore batteries as she shells the defenses at Casablanca, damaging the French battleship *Jean*

Bart. The destroyers *Bernadou* and *Cole* (DD 155), along with the mechanized artillery transport *Lakehurst* (APM 9) land troops at the port of Safi, French Morocco, while the battleship *New York* (BB 34) and light cruiser *Philadelphia* (CL 41) silence the guns of the *Batterie Railleuse* on shore. On 10 November, after two failed attempts to enter the Sebou River in French Morocco, the destroyer *Dallas* (DD 199) manages to head upriver and land Army rangers to seize an airfield at Port Lyautey. In addition, carrier aircraft from *Ranger* bomb *Jean Bart*, causing heavy damage as she attempts a second sortie from Casablanca. Oran, Algeria, surrenders to the Allies on 10 November, followed by Casablanca the following day.

12 November

Rear Admiral Richmond Kelly Turner's Task Force 67 begins unloading reinforcements at Guadalcanal while eleven transports bearing 11,000 Japanese soldiers enter the Slot and set course for the embattled island escorted by two battleships, a cruiser, and eleven destroyers. Over the course of the next three days, the U.S. and Japanese navies wage two pivotal sea battles in the waters around Guadalcanal.

13 November

The Battle of Guadalcanal begins in the darkness just after midnight when two heavy cruisers, three light cruisers, and eight destroyers under the command of Rear Admiral Daniel J. Callaghan engage Japanese warships under the command of Vice Admiral Hiroaki

Abe. With the darkness creating confusion and searchlights crisscrossing the sky as ships maneuver radically, the U.S. Navy ships turn back the enemy vessels, which intended to fire their guns on Henderson Field. Four destroyers and the light cruiser *Atlanta* (CL 51) are sunk or scuttled, one of the hits on the cruiser coming inadvertently from the heavy cruiser *San Francisco* (CA 38), taking the life of Rear Admiral Norman Scott. On board *San Francisco*, enemy fire kills Rear Admiral Callaghan. Also among those killed on the ship are Boatswain's Mate First Class Reinhardt Keppler, who courageously battles fires and aids his wounded shipmates despite his own wounds. He receives a posthumous Medal of Honor. The light cruiser *Juneau* (CL 52) is damaged by enemy fire and later torpedoed by the Japanese submarine *I-26*. She sinks in twenty seconds. All but ten members of her crew perish, including the famous five Sullivan brothers serving in the ship. Japanese losses include the battleship *Hiei*, damaged by gunfire and sunk by aircraft from the carrier *Enterprise* and Henderson Field. Two destroyers are also sunk and six ships suffer damage.

14 November

Aircraft from the carrier *Enterprise* join planes from Henderson Field in attacking enemy ships in the Slot. In the first strike the heavy cruiser *Kinugasa* is sunk and five other ships are damaged. Later in the day airmen send seven transports and freighters to the bottom.

14–15 November

Shortly before midnight on 14 November the battleships *Washington* and *South Dakota* (BB 57) along with four destroyers under the command of Rear Admiral Willis A. Lee, Jr., engage in a night action with the battleship *Kirishima*, four cruisers, and nine destroyers under the command of Vice Admiral Nobutake Kondo. Japanese gunfire and torpedoes sink the destroyers *Preston* (DD 379) and *Walke* (DD 416), with the loss of 204 sailors combined. In subsequent action that carries into the following morning, the main batteries of *Washington* sink *Kirishima* and the destroyer *Ayanami*, while the U.S. destroyer *Benham* (DD 397) is so damaged that she is scuttled. On the afternoon of 15 November, planes

again hammer ships carrying Japanese reinforcements, sinking four transports. This marks the end of the Battle of Guadalcanal, the last time major Japanese naval forces enter the waters around the island. It is the beginning of the end for Japanese forces on the island, and on 31 December the Japanese command decides to evacuate Guadalcanal. Organized resistance on the island ends on 9 February 1943.

16 November

The destroyers *Woolsey* (DD 437), *Swanson* (DD 443), and *Quick* (DD 490) team up in a coordinated depth charge attack to sink the German submarine *U-173* in the waters off Casablanca, French Morocco.

Above: *("Battle of Guadalcanal," John Hamilton, U.S. Navy Memorial Foundation)*

Right: *A scoreboard on the battleship* South Dakota *(BB 57) records her exaggerated claim to have shot down thirty-two planes in the Battle of the Santa Cruz Islands, and the sinking of three Japanese cruisers in the naval battle of Guadalcanal. (Corbis)*

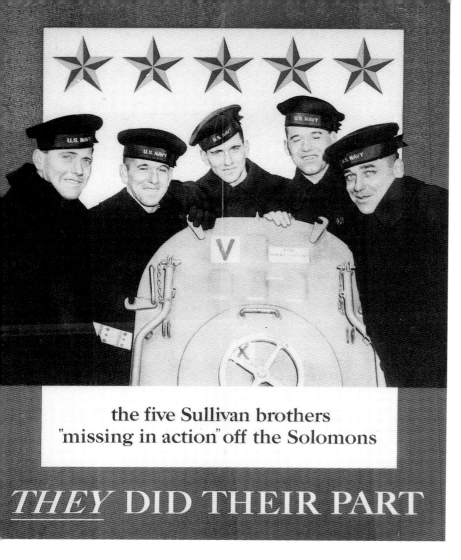

the five Sullivan brothers
"missing in action" off the Solomons

THEY DID THEIR PART

Above: *A wartime poster featuring the Sullivan brothers, all of whom perished when their ship, the light cruiser* Juneau *(CL 52) was sunk by a Japanese submarine off Guadalcanal on 13 November 1942. (Naval Historical Center)*

30 November

In the Battle of Tassafaronga, four heavy cruisers, one light cruiser, and six destroyers attack Japanese destroyers attempting to resupply troops on Guadalcanal. The Japanese quickly fire a spread of torpedoes that damage the heavy cruisers *Pensacola* (CA 24), *Northampton* (CA 26), *New Orleans*, and *Minneapolis* (CA 36). *Northampton* sinks the following day, as does the Japanese destroyer *Takanami*.

8 December

Eight motor torpedo boats, including one destined to be commanded by future President of the United States John F. Kennedy, turn back eight Japanese destroyers attempting to land reinforcements on Guadalcanal. The following night *PT-59* sinks the Japanese submarine *I-3* in the waters surrounding the island.

12 December

Five motor torpedo boats continue their actions against Japanese ships. The Japanese destroyer *Terutsuki* and *PT-44* are sunk.

15 December

VP-12 officially becomes known as a "Black Cat" squadron in reference to its employment of PBY Catalinas painted black in night attack missions in the Solomon Islands. Other squadrons also serve as "Black Cats," conducting highly effective strikes in the South Pacific campaigns.

Left: *Smoke rises from two enemy planes shot down during a Japanese air attack on U.S. ships off Guadalcanal, 12 November 1942. The view is from the transport* President Adams *(AP 38). The cargo ship at left (barely visible) is* Libra *(AK 53), and the one at right is* Betelgeuse *(AK 28). (Naval Historical Center)*

1943

5 January

With air raids against the island having commenced in December 1942, Navy surface ships of Task Force 67 under the command of Rear Admiral Walden L. Ainsworth bombard Munda, New Georgia, in the Solomon Islands. During an air attack against the task force, the light cruiser *Helena* (CL 50) becomes the first ship to employ projectiles equipped with proximity fuses in combat, downing a Japanese dive-bomber.

6 January

During a patrol off Brazil, a PBY Catalina of VP-83 sinks the German submarine *U-164*.

10 January

The transport submarine *Argonaut* (APS 1) attacks a Japanese convoy off New Britain. The escorting Japanese navy destroyers depth charge the submarine, forcing her bow to break the surface. The destroyers then pump shells into *Argonaut*, sinking her with the loss of all 105 crewmen on board.

11 January

Eleven motor torpedo boats attack a Japanese force of eight destroyers off Cape Esperance, Guadalcanal, damaging one of the enemy vessels. *PT-112* is sunk and *PT-43* is damaged.

13 January

PBY Catalinas of VP-83 send the German submarine *U-507* to the bottom off Brazil.

14–23 January

The Casablanca Conference between British Prime Minister Winston S. Churchill and President Franklin D. Roosevelt results in the decision to invade the island of Sicily; the outlining of a Pacific strategy with offensives through the central and southwest Pacific; a decision to send more troops to the China-Burma-India theater; support for a continued bombing campaign in Europe; and a commitment to the policy of "unconditional surrender" of the Axis powers.

20 January

Brennan (DE 13) becomes the first destroyer escort commissioned. Though her activity is confined to duty as a training ship off Miami, Florida, her successors

Right: *The heavy cruiser* Minneapolis *(CA 36) at Tulagi after being torpedoed in the Battle of Tassafaronga, 30 November 1942. This photo, taken on 1 December, shows that the work of cutting away the wreckage of her bow has begun.* Minneapolis *returned to service and participated in actions until the end of the war. (Naval Historical Center)*

THE U.S. NAVY AND AMPHIBIOUS OPERATIONS IN WORLD WAR II

by Dr. Donald Chisholm

When the United States entered World War II, it was already apparent that large-scale amphibious operations would be required for the Allies to reestablish their presence on the European mainland and to roll back the Axis powers. As anticipated by War Plan Orange, the defeat of Japan would also necessitate seizing a series of intermediate and advanced Pacific island bases before assaulting the Japanese home islands.

Amphibious assaults are the most complex of military operations, involving elements of sea, land, and air, and at least two services. Mounting successful amphibious operations requires solving a number of complex, interrelated problems. These included creating sound doctrine; establishing the types and organization of forces; setting the responsibilities of the services involved and arranging for coordination among them; devising effective command relations; acquiring, organizing, and training personnel to plan and execute the mission; providing logistics (especially dealing with time and distance issues); scheduling and synchronizing movements of forces; and specifying, designing, and converting/constructing amphibious shipping and lighterage for personnel and equipment. Problems specific to given operations include selection of locations, tides and currents, beach gradients, coastal/island defenses, etc. The enemy can also be expected to learn from initial operations and to adjust his defenses accordingly.

Fortunately, the Navy and Marine Corps had systematically contemplated the problems of amphibious operations since the Spanish-American War, though before World War II most amphibious actions conducted by U.S. forces had been relatively small-scale, ad hoc affairs. Although the solutions developed remained incomplete and untested by actual combat, a solid foundation was laid with the publication of manuals for landing operations and practice in interwar fleet exercises. By 1941, amphibious training commands were established on both coasts and training was underway in combat loading and unloading, boat handling, and joint communications. However, there was the problem of specialized vessels for amphibious operations. In 1940, the U.S. possessed virtually no ships, landing craft, or vehicles suitable for amphibious assaults. It began converting and producing these vessels in mid-1941, and by the end of World War II the number of all amphibious types exceeded 100,000, ranging from large attack transports to amphibious trucks and small craft. Wartime innovations included the development of the celebrated Underwater Demolition Teams (UDT) to clear beach obstacles, and amphibious tractors that could transport assault troops over reefs. Some problems were less amenable to solution, however. Interservice conflict was already evident in 1941 and would continue until the war's end over such issues as air support and command relations.

The Navy started the war with no trained and experienced amphibious planners, forces, or commanders. Much of its success may be attributed to the rapid blooding of all three. In Admirals Richmond Kelly Turner, Daniel Barbey, Henry Hewitt, Alan Kirk, and Richard Conolly, all drawn from its surface forces, the Navy found superior commanders who developed equally competent staffs. The amphibious operating forces, principally reserve officers and men, performed with remarkable aplomb.

World War II amphibious operations were conducted in three distinct areas—the Central Pacific, Southwest Pacific, and Europe—each with its own peculiar problems. Consequently, three distinct amphibious cultures developed. Pacific Fleet commander Admiral Chester W. Nimitz directed Central Pacific operations against the Japanese, mostly large-scale assaults consisting of overwhelming naval forces that focused on relatively small islands that could be effectively isolated, with little room for maneuver, little infrastructure, and in most cases few civilians. General Douglas A. MacArthur commanded Southwest Pacific operations against the Japanese, which before the campaign against the Philippines were primarily joint Army-Navy operations that were broken into many relatively small-scale endeavors on larger islands. Unlike the Central Pacific they had barely adequate shipping and difficulty isolating the immediate objectives. General Dwight D. Eisenhower's European and

Right: *Landing craft line the beach at Iwo Jima, Japan, discharging heavy equipment and unloading food and ammunition to sustain the Marines fighting ashore. Amphibious operations during World War II presented a challenge not only in putting troops ashore under fire and holding a beachhead, but also in the mammoth logistical effort to support them in the ensuing campaign. (Andrew Small, Naval War College)*

Mediterranean operations involved troops of several nations attacking continental objectives that were exceedingly difficult to isolate—with civilians to consider—and developed infrastructures. The amphibious doctrine developed prior to, and early in, the war proved flexible and effective in all three areas.

Each amphibious operation brought specific problems and taught its own lessons. The operational tempo was so high that deriving and absorbing those lessons was itself a challenge, but one largely met successfully. The U.S. Navy's first offensive in the Pacific came in August 1942 at Guadalcanal in the Solomon Islands, which revealed the importance of continuous air cover at the objective, well-organized logistics, shore parties to move supplies inland, and the necessity for clear-cut, effective command relations. The bloody assault against Tarawa in the Gilbert Islands in November 1943 produced lessons on naval gunfire support, the need for dedicated command ships, improved communications, more direct fire support, clearance of beach obstacles, more tracked amphibious vehicles to cross reefs under all tidal conditions, and the great danger of tying the fleet to a landing operation. The celebrated landings at Normandy on D-Day, 6 June 1944, particularly the experience of troops struggling to take Omaha Beach, demonstrated in dramatic fashion the importance of accurate, timely naval gunfire and the need for close air support. Operations in the Southwest Pacific demonstrated the value of maintaining a rapid operational tempo, even if

the shipping and forces committed were less than optimal. The Navy performed heroically here with very limited resources, making it possible for MacArthur to keep the Japanese perpetually off balance.

Amphibious assaults also confronted varying enemy tactics. Hitler's Fortress Europe, with its beach obstacles and fortifications, sought to defend all-out at the water's edge, which was mirrored by the Japanese until the invasion of Saipan in June 1944. There, the Japanese gave a hint of things to come when they focused their defensive efforts inland. It was a tacit recognition that they could not stop the invaders from taking any given island, but could hope to extract such a price that Japan could end the war on acceptable terms. This they raised to a high art at Peleliu, Iwo Jima, and Okinawa, the latter defense supported by waves of kamikazes that attacked the fleet supporting the operations on land.

As the war progressed, the scale of amphibious operations dramatically increased in both the Pacific and European theaters, straining shipping and landing craft, as well as command and control arrangements. Although they bent, they did not break, and such was the fierce operational pace in the Southwest and Central Pacific that the enemy was allowed no respite and little time to adjust defenses. The Pacific war ended before the Allies executed the largest amphibious operation ever planned on the Japanese island of Kyushu. It was a plan that embodied every lesson learned from preceding operations, each assault from the sea a stepping stone on the road to victory.

see action with Atlantic convoys and hunter-killer groups, and fight with distinction at the Battle of Leyte Gulf in October 1944.

24 January
Ships of Task Force 67 bombard Japanese fuel and ammunition dumps on the island of Kolombangara in the Solomon Islands. Aircraft from Henderson Field, Guadalcanal, bombard the targets later in the day.

Three survivors from the torpedoed Dutch motorship *Zaandam*, one of whom is Seaman First Class Basil D. Izzi, USNR, are rescued by the submarine chaser *PC-576* after spending eighty-three days in a raft, subsisting on a diet of raw fish, birds, and rainwater.

29–30 January
In the Battle of Rennell Island, Japanese land-attack planes strike U.S. Navy warships covering the movement of transports to Guadalcanal. The heavy cruiser *Chicago* is torpedoed on the night of 29 January. Taken under tow, she is attacked again the following day, sustaining four additional torpedo hits that sink her thirty miles east of Rennell Island.

1 February
Japanese aircraft sink the destroyer *DeHaven* (DD 469) as she covers the landing of Army troops in the Japanese rear on Guadalcanal. The first of three bomb hits causes the ship to go dead in the

water, and the second scores a direct hit on the bridge, killing the commanding officer. Meanwhile, the light minelayers *Montgomery* (DM 17), *Preble* (DM 20), and *Tracy* (DM 19) lay a minefield between Savo Island and Cape Esperance on Guadalcanal, which fatally damages the Japanese destroyer *Makigumo* the following day.

Above: Brennan *(DE 13), the first destroyer escort commissioned, underway off Florida, circa 1945, while serving as a training ship. (Naval Historical Center)*

Left: LCT-181 *comes alongside the destroyer* Fletcher *(DD 445) with survivors of* DeHaven *(DD 469) aboard.* DeHaven *had been sunk during a Japanese air attack off Guadalcanal on 1 February 1943, the day this photo was taken. (Naval Historical Center)*

7 February

In the early morning hours, Commander Howard Gilmore maneuvers his submarine *Growler* (SS 215) for a night surface attack against the Japanese stores ship *Hayasaki* off Rabaul. During the approach his quarry maneuvers to ram the submarine, prompting Gilmore to change course and ram *Hayasaki*. *Growler* hits the ship at a speed of seventeen knots, and her bridge soon raked by machine gun fire. Gilmore remains on deck while his crew goes below, but before he can reach the hatch he is mortally wounded. Knowing he cannot make it, he gives the order to "Take her down," thus saving his boat and her crew. Gilmore is posthumously awarded the Medal of Honor.

11 February

The destroyer *Fletcher* (DD 445), operating in concert with an SON Seagull floatplane of Cruiser Scouting Squadron (VCS) 9 off the light cruiser *Helena*, sinks the Japanese submarine I-18 in the Coral Sea.

12 February

The submarine *Grampus* (SS 207) sails from Brisbane, Australia, to begin her sixth war patrol. She is never heard from again and is declared lost at sea.

14 February

The submarine *Amberjack* (SS 219) sends her last radio transmission, reporting the capture of an enemy aviator and attacks by two enemy destroyers. She is never heard from again and is presumed lost at sea, probably the victim of attacks from the air and by the torpedo boat *Hiyo* and submarine chaser *Ch-18* off New Britain.

Above: *Commander Howard W. Gilmore, severely injured by Japanese machine gun fire, gives his last order, "Take her down," to the officer of the deck of* Growler *(SS 215) as the ship submerges beneath him, 7 February 1943. By diving rapidly,* Growler *was able to escape from the Japanese attack and return to Brisbane, Australia, where the boat was restored to its full combat capability after receiving an entirely new bow. (Fred Freeman)*

21 February

Ships of Task Unit 62.7.2 under the command of Captain Ingolf N. Kiland and carrier planes from *Saratoga* temporarily operating from Henderson Field, Guadalcanal, support successful landings in the Russell Islands, opening the campaign in the Central Solomon Islands.

22 February

The battleship *Iowa* (BB 61) is commissioned.

5 March

The auxiliary escort carrier *Bogue* (ACV 9), forming the centerpiece of a pioneer hunter-killer group, begins operations in the Atlantic, marking the first time that a ship of her type operates strictly in the antisubmarine role protecting convoys. All told, *Bogue*'s embarked aircraft and escorts send thirteen German U-boats to the bottom during World War II.

8 March

A PBY Catalina of VP-53 sinks the German submarine *U-156* off Trinidad.

10 March

The light cruiser *Savannah* (CL 42) and destroyer *Eberle* (DD 430) encounter the German blockade runner *Karin* in the South Atlantic. After crewmen from the destroyer board her in hopes of obtaining intelligence documents, scuttling charges set by *Karin*'s crew explode, killing seven and wounding two members of the boarding party. The surviving members of the boarding party continue their intelligence gathering until forced to abandon ship. They are picked up by *Eberle* along with the blockade runner's seventy-two man crew.

Left: *Wartime propaganda posters often featured stirring battle scenes that inspired those working on the home front to produce the necessary materials to provide weapons to those fighting abroad. (Corbis)*

Left: *A forgotten theater amidst the carrier battles and island beachheads of the Pacific war was the campaign in the Aleutian Islands. As evidenced by this image of ordnancemen loading bombs on a PBY Catalina at Cold Bay in November 1942, the bitter cold translated into one of the harshest environments in which the U.S. Navy fought during World War II. (National Museum of Naval Aviation)*

11 March

The submarine *Triton* (SS 201) reports sinking a Japanese army cargo ship on 6 March. This is the last transmission received from the sub, which is never heard from again and is presumed lost with all hands.

12 March

The destroyer *Champlin* (DD 601), while escorting convoy UGS 6 west of the Azores, obtains a radar contact ahead of the convoy. Racing to the contact point, she observes the surfaced German submarine *U-130*. The destroyer attempts to ram the sub, which makes a crash dive. *Champlin* drops depth charges into the swirl made by the submerging submarine, sinking it.

15 March

A system of numbering the Navy's fleets is instituted, assigning those in the Pacific odd numbers and those in the Atlantic even numbers.

23 March

The submarine *Kingfish* (SS 234), while operating in the waters near Formosa, undergoes an intense depth charge attack that damages the boat to such an extent that her crew destroys secret codes in preparation for abandoning ship. Damage to the sub's main piping causes an air bubble to rise to the surface, which confuses her attackers into thinking they have sunk her. *Kingfish* cuts short her patrol, is repaired, and conducts twelve war patrols during World War II.

25 March

The submarine *Wahoo* (SS 238) sends the Japanese cargo ships *Takaosan Maru*, *Teisho Maru*, and *Satsuki Maru* to the bottom in the Yellow Sea. Under the command of the legendary Lieutenant Commander D. W. "Mush" Morton, the sub attacks on the surface, on one occasion her crew throwing homemade "Molotov cocktails" at one of the cargo ships as the submarine pulls alongside. The unconventional submarine ordnance is the gift of Marines at Midway, where the boat stopped during her transit to the Yellow Sea.

26 March

In the Battle of the Komandorski Islands, Task Group 16.6 under the command of Rear Admiral Charles H. McMorris prevents a Japanese surface force from reinforcing their garrison on Kiska in the Aleutians.

The heavy cruiser *Salt Lake City* damages the Japanese heavy cruiser *Nachi* in the engagement despite suffering damage that briefly renders her dead in the water. The destroyers *Bailey* (DD 492) and *Coghlan* (DD 606) are also damaged by Japanese gunfire.

1 April

Naval Air Station Patuxent River, Maryland, is established. The base will eventually replace Naval Air Station Anacostia, Washington D.C., as the site of the Navy's flight testing and will become home to the Naval Test Pilot School.

5 April

The destroyer *O'Bannon* (DD 450) sinks the Japanese submarine *RO-34* operating on the surface near Russell Island in the Solomons.

7 April

A raid carried out against shipping off Guadalcanal by Japanese dive-bombers and fighters damages numerous U.S. Navy vessels. The destroyer *Aaron Ward* (DD 483) is hit by bombs and sinks with the loss of twenty-seven men. Bombs also start fires on board the oiler *Kanawha*, which is eventually beached, and sinks the following day.

9 April

The Navy reestablishes the rank of commodore.

15 April

The Navy begins playing a role in unconventional warfare in China with the establishment of the Sino-American Cooperative Organization (SACO) on this date. The deputy to the organization's leader, Lieutenant General Tai Li, is Commander Milton E. Miles. SACO is involved in training Chinese guerrillas, gathering intelligence, reporting the weather, and establishing a medical organization manned in part by U.S. Navy personnel.

A PBY Catalina of VP-83 sinks the Italian submarine *Archimede* off the coast of Brazil.

16 April

In a major change to uniform regulations, the color of the Navy's working uniform is changed to slate gray. "Grays" prove unpopular among the officer corps, and on 15 October 1946 khakis are reinstated as the working uniform for the Navy.

18 April

During an inspection of forward areas, Japanese Admiral Isoruku Yamamoto, Commander in Chief Combined Fleet, is killed when his plane is ambushed near Bougainville in the Solomons by Army Air Forces P-38 Lightnings. He is replaced by Admiral Mineichi Koga.

27 April

A PV-1 Ventura patrol-bomber of Bombing Squadron

(VB) 125 sinks the German submarine *U-174* while covering convoy SC 128 off Halifax, Nova Scotia.

11–13 May

Task Force 16 and Task Force 51 support the landing of the U.S. Army's Seventh Division on Attu in the Aleutian Islands. While surface ships, including the

Above: *A Japanese destroyer explodes in the background as a PT boat launches a torpedo at a target forward.* ("PT Boat," James Dietz)

the Japanese submarine *I-31*. The successful operation at Attu, which is declared secure on 30 May, influences the decision of the Japanese high command to evacuate Kiska, the last Japanese stronghold in the Aleutians.

14 May
The motor torpedo boats *PT-150* and *PT-152* sink the Japanese submarine *RO-182* in Vitiaz Strait, New Guinea.

15–25 May
The Trident Conference between British Prime Minister Winston S. Churchill, President Franklin D. Roosevelt and the Combined Chiefs of Staff in Washington, D.C., results in a reaffirmation of the "Germany first" strategy; decisions to invade Italy and plan for a cross-channel invasion of Europe; and approval for an offensive across the Central Pacific.

15 May
OS2U/OS2N Kingfisher aircraft of VS-62 join the Cuban submarine chaser *SC 13* in sinking the German submarine *U-176* in the waters off Cuba.

16 May
The destroyer *MacKenzie* (DD 614) executes two depth charge attacks against the German submarine *U-182* near the Madeira Islands, sinking the sub.

battleships *Pennsylvania* and *Idaho* (BB 42), provide gunfire support for the assault troops, aircraft from the auxilliary carrier *Nassau* (ACV 16) fly close air support missions, marking the first use of this type of direct support of an amphibious assault in the Pacific. Japanese submarines attempt to interfere with the landings, unsuccessfully attacking *Pennsylvania* and the light cruiser *Santa Fe* (CL 60). Subsequently, the destroyers *Edwards* (DD 619) and *Farragut* (DD 348) sink

Above: *A destroyer and cruiser fire on Vila Airfield, Kolombangara and Bairoko, New Georgia, during the bombardment of Munda-Vila, 13 May 1943. Photographed from the destroyer* Nicholas *(DD 449). (Naval Historical Center)*

Right: *The destroyer* Aaron Ward *succumbed to a Japanese air attack off Guadalcanal on 7 April 1943. (Naval Historical Center)*

Opposite: *With his twin .50-caliber machine guns at the ready, a PT boat crewman is ready for action during a patrol off New Guinea, July 1943. (National Archives)*

THE U.S. NAVY IN THE BATTLE OF THE ATLANTIC

by Dr. Kathleen Broome Williams

The Battle of the Atlantic was the longest battle of the Second World War, beginning at the outbreak of hostilities in 1939 and ending only with the German surrender in 1945. Failing to defeat Britain from the air, Germany turned to U-boats to starve the island nation into surrender by a war against trade. Dependent on imports, Britain—and Canada—waged an unrelenting antisubmarine campaign, developing vessels, aircraft, weapons, technical devices, intelligence, strategies, and tactics to keep the sea lanes open. The Atlantic conflict had an even broader significance than Britain's survival, however; in many ways the outcome of World War II in Europe hinged on its result. When Hitler attacked the Soviet Union in June 1941, and then declared war against the United States in the wake of the attacks on Pearl Harbor, Hawaii, Britain became a base for the shipment of war materiel to Russia, and for Allied operations in North Africa, the Mediterranean, and ultimately the invasion of Fortress Europe. Finally, the bulk of the Allied strategic bombing campaign against Germany was launched from British airfields. German

U-boats continued to threaten these operations to the end; without their defeat the Allied victory in Europe would have been in doubt.

In September 1941, with the battle already two years old, the U.S. Navy began to take an active part. By then U-boats operating in wolf packs were sinking merchant ships faster than they could be replaced, successfully breaching the defenses of convoys escorted by naval vessels. Although the United States was still neutral, its navy began providing protection for ships of every flag carrying supplies between the American continent and Iceland, joining the Royal Navy and the Royal Canadian Navy in convoy-escort duties. The opening of hostilities with Germany as well as Japan in December found the U.S. Navy committed to a two-ocean war. Its role in the Battle of the Atlantic was thus defined by the competing demands of the war in the Pacific and by the requirements of cooperation with the British and Canadians in a coordinated Allied operation.

The Atlantic campaign was, above all, a struggle between competing technologies, and the mobilization of American science coupled with the vast expansion of American productive capacity helped give the Allies the winning edge. Antisubmarine patrol and escort vessels and aircraft were armed with improved depth charges and new acoustic homing torpedoes. Equally important for antisubmarine warfare, aircraft and vessels were also equipped with a range of new and improved electronic devices. In addition to hydrophones—passive underwater listening devices—patrol vessels now used sonar, an active detection device based on the transmission and reflection of underwater sound waves. While U-boats operating on the surface, as they frequently did, were impervious to sonar, they could be detected by another new electronic device—radar. Radar transmits radio waves through the air in brief intermittent pulses and a receiver picks up the return echo when the wave bounces off an obstacle. By the end of the war, radars were small enough to mount on escort vessels and sensitive enough to detect submarine periscopes.

The U.S. Navy also made strides in radio intelligence. The U-boat's dependence on radio communications exposed them to interception of their coded messages. Ultra, the intelligence derived from breaking these intercepted messages, was particularly significant in diverting convoys away from gathering wolf packs. In conjunction with the British codebreaking effort, the U.S. Navy produced special-purpose computers, which proved invaluable for cryptanalysis. German radio messages were also intercepted by high-frequency direction finders (HF/DF), receiving devices capable of locating U-boats by their radio transmissions. Landbased HF/DF could locate U-boats thousands of miles away and this information was used strategically to divert convoys. Once the Allied navies deployed shipboard HF/DF, they could detect U-boats within striking distance of convoys and send escort vessels and aircraft to attack them directly.

The turning point of the Atlantic campaign came in March 1943, when U-boat successes peaked in a series of ferocious convoy battles. By May the U.S. Navy was ready to go on the offensive, wedding vessels and aircraft, weapons, radio intelligence, and electronic devices to effective tactics. Escort carrier task forces and hunter-killer groups waged a successful campaign against the U-boats in the U.S. Navy's area

of responsibility in the Central Atlantic. In May 1944, in one celebrated example of this final phase of the Battle of the Atlantic, the destroyer escort *Buckley* (DE 51), sailing with escort carrier *Block Island* (CVE 21) in Task Group 21.11, located, rammed, and sank *U-66* west of the Cape Verde Islands. The following month, Captain Daniel V. Gallery and his hunter-killer group, centered on the escort carrier *Guadalcanal* (CVE 60), captured *U-505*. The photograph of the triumphant skipper standing on her conning tower with the American flag flying overhead was a symbol of the Allied triumph in the bitterly contested Battle of the Atlantic.

Opposite: *Sailors man the 3-inch gun on the deck of the subchaser PC-565 as she patrols Atlantic waters in search of German U-boats. The sign on the bridge leaves little doubt about the ship's mission, which sank U-521 in the North Atlantic on 2 June 1943. (U.S. Naval Institute)*

Above: *Smoke rises from a German U-boat during an attack by TBF Avengers from the escort carrier Bogue (CVE 9). Operating in "hunter-killer" groups, surface ships and aircraft formed an effective team in combating German U-boats in the Atlantic. (National Museum of Naval Aviation)*

17 May

After being damaged in an attack by a PBM Mariner of VP-74, the German submarine *U-128* is sunk in the South Atlantic by 5-inch gunfire from the destroyers *Moffett* (DD 362) and *Jouett* (DD 396). Forty-seven of the sub's crew survive the sinking.

20 May

The Tenth Fleet is established with headquarters in Washington, D.C., to direct the antisubmarine warfare effort in the Atlantic.

22 May

While protecting convoy ON 184 in the Atlantic, TBF Avenger torpedo-bombers of Composite Squadron (VC) 9 from the escort carrier *Bogue* sink the German submarine *U-569* and damage *U-305*.

25 May

A PBY Catalina of VP-84 sinks the German submarine *U-467* in the waters off Iceland.

26 May

The submarine *Trout* lands a party on Basilan Island in the Philippines to establish a coastwatcher network, conduct surveys, and assist in supplying Filipino guerillas.

27 May

The submarine *Runner* (SS 275) departs Midway Atoll on her third war patrol. She is never heard from again and is presumed lost.

2 June

While operating off the Virginia Capes, the submarine chaser *PC-565* obtains an underwater sound contact on the German submarine *U-521*. A depth charge attack brings the sub to the surface, and gunners on board the submarine chaser batter her with 20mm fire, forcing her to submerge again. A second depth charge sinks *U-521* and only one member of her crew survives.

5 June

Having damaged three U-boats the previous day, TBF Avengers of VC-9 sink the German submarine *U-217* off the Canary Islands.

9 June

The United States Naval Academy Class of 1944 is graduated one year early due to the national emergency. Twenty-two members of this class are killed during World War II.

10 June

While escorting two vessels near Shemya Island in the Aleutians, lookouts on board the submarine chaser *PC-487* spot two periscopes, prompting her to increase speed and make a depth charge attack. The blasts force the Japanese submarine *I-24* to the surface. With guns blazing, *PC-487* rams the I-boat twice, causing her to eventually sink.

The German submarine *U-66* attacks the tanker *Esso Gettysburg* as she carries crude oil from Port Arthur,

Texas, to Philadelphia, Pennsylvania. The attack triggers fires that feed on the ship's cargo. Despite the flames, Ensign John S. Arnold II of the ship's Armed Guard detachment orders the forward gun manned and opens fire on the submarine. He receives the Navy Cross for his heroic actions. Arnold is one of fifteen of the seventy-two-man crew to survive.

12 June

Good hunting continues for the pilots and aircrewmen of VC-9 from the escort carrier *Bogue* as a TBF Avenger sinks the German submarine *U-118* near the Canary Islands.

The submarine *R-12* (SS 89) sinks while conducting training operations off Key West, Florida. All forty-two members of her crew perish in the accident.

13 June

While operating near Kiska in the Aleutians, *Frazier* (DD 607) spots a periscope and attacks. Gunfire hits the Japanese submarine *I-9* as she submerges and subsequent depth charge attacks sink her.

20 June

A PBY Catalina of VP-84 sinks the German submarine *U-388* and damages *U-420* in the waters off Iceland. A landmark event in antisubmarine warfare, this action marks the first employment of the Mark 24 homing torpedo, nicknamed Fido.

Right: *Landing craft put Army infantry and medics ashore on a New Georgia beach, summer 1943. The troops are to make their way through the jungle led by native guides. Though sea-going ships and submarines received much of the wartime glory, landing craft were perhaps the vessels most essential to ultimate victory. (Naval Historical Center)*

Left: *Flashes from gunfire on board the light cruiser* Helena *(CL 50) (center) illuminate the waters of the Kula Gulf during a night engagement with the Japanese, 5–6 July 1943. The next ship astern is* St. Louis *(CL 48). Moments after this photograph was taken,* Helena *was struck by torpedoes and began to sink. (Naval Historical Center)*

22 June

The destroyer *Monaghan* (DD 354) attacks and damages the Japanese submarine *I-7*, which later runs aground near Kiska. This marks *Monaghan*'s third brush with an enemy submarine, the first having come when she sank a midget submarine at Pearl Harbor, Hawaii, on the fateful morning of 7 December 1941.

23 June

The Japanese submarine *RO-103* sinks the cargo ship *Aludra* (AK 72) and damages the cargo ship *Deimos* (AK 78) to such an extent that she is scuttled. Both transports are en route to Guadalcanal when attacked.

30 June

U.S. naval forces are active on a variety of South Pacific fronts on this day, bombarding positions on Kolombangara and Bougainville in the Solomons, and laying mines off Bougainville and New Georgia. Task Force 31 under the command of Rear Admiral Richmond Kelly Turner and supported by land-based aircraft land Army troops and leathernecks of the Fourth Marine Raider Battalion on New Georgia. The Japanese mount some aerial opposition, torpedoing Turner's flagship, the attack transport *McCawley* (APA 4). Fire from shore damages the destroyer *Gwin* (DD 433). Meanwhile, off the coast of New Guinea tank landing ships and infantry landing craft of Task Force 76 under the command of Rear Admiral Daniel E. Barbey put Army troops ashore on Woodlark and Kiriwina Islands.

Unaware that he is an African-American, the Navy designates Ensign Oscar Holmes a naval aviator, making him the first man of color to receive the coveted wings of gold. Holmes' experience as a civilian pilot means that he is winged following completion of an instructor's course, rather than the entire Navy flight syllabus.

5–6 July

After bombarding positions on Kolombangara and New Georgia in the Solomon Islands, the ships of Task Group 36.1 under the command of Rear Admiral Walden L. Ainsworth engage Japanese destroyers in a night action. The Battle of Kula Gulf results in the sinking of the Japanese destroyer *Niizuki* and inflicts such damage upon the destroyer *Nagatsuki* that she is beached and abandoned. Three other destroyers are damaged. The U.S. Navy suffers the loss of the light cruiser *Helena* and the destroyer *Strong* (DD 467). Some of the cruiser's 900-man crew reaches the island of Vella Lavella, where they are aided by a coastwatcher and friendly natives. Taking to the jungle to avoid being spotted by Japanese patrols, the men are eventually rescued by U.S. Navy destroyers on the evening of 16 July. The engagement prevents four of the enemy destroyers from landing their cargoes of troops and supplies on Kolombangara.

6 July

A PB4Y-1 Liberator of Bombing Squadron (VB) 102 piloted by Lieutenant Commander Bruce A. Van

Right: *SS Robert Rowan's ammunition explodes after being hit by enemy air attack during the Allied landings at Sicily, 11 July 1943. (Naval Historical Center)*

Below: *A PB4Y-1 Liberator of Bombing Squadron 109, damaged during a raid against enemy installations, crash landed on Guadalcanal in 1943. In contrast to the high-altitude bombing of Army Air Forces Liberators, Navy PB4Y-1s made most of their attacks at treetop level. (National Museum of Naval Aviation)*

Voorhis makes a daring single-plane low-level attack on Japanese installations on Greenwich Island. The patrol bomber is shot down by Japanese seaplanes. Van Voorhis receives a posthumous award of the Medal of Honor for his actions.

9 July

A PBY Catalina of Patrol Squadron (VP) 94 sinks the German submarine *U-590* at the mouth of the Amazon River in Brazil.

While naval forces assemble for Operation Husky, the invasion of Sicily, a smoke pot ignites on a landing craft carried by *LST 375*. Ensign John J. Parle enters the craft, extinguishes a burning fuse and throws the smoke pot over the side. This saves his ship from

damage and prevents the burning smoke pot from giving advance warning of the landing. Seriously injured, Parle dies from his wounds eight days later. He is later awarded a posthumous Medal of Honor.

10 July

Naval forces under the overall command of Admiral of the Fleet Sir Andrew B. Cunningham of the British Royal Navy support Operation Husky, putting troops ashore on Sicily. The Western Naval Task Force, under the command of Vice Admiral H. Kent Hewitt, lands the U.S. Seventh Army while the Eastern Naval Task Force, under the command of British Vice Admiral Sir Bertram H. Ramsay, lands the British Eighth Army. Axis aircraft attempt to disrupt the landings by attacking the invasion force, bombing the destroyer *Maddox* (DD 622), which rolls over and sinks in just two minutes. German bombs also sink the tank landing ship *LST 313* and the minesweeper *Sentinel* (AM 113), which endures five separate air attacks. Fire from shore batteries damages the landing craft *LCT 242*.

11 July

Axis air attacks continue off the beaches of Sicily, damaging the tank landing ship *LST 158*, the attack transports *Barnett* (APA 5), *Joseph T. Dickman* (APA 13), and *William P. Biddle* (APA 8), and transport *Orizaba* (AP 24). However, the attacks cannot prevent naval forces from influencing the battle on shore as gunfire from U.S. Navy cruisers and destroyers slams into Axis tanks attempting to attack forces on the landing beaches at Gela. Naval gunfire accounts for thirteen tanks destroyed.

Man the GUNS Join the NAVY

13 July

In the Battle of Kolombangara three light cruisers and ten destroyers under Rear Admiral Walden L. Ainsworth engage one light cruiser and five destroyers under Rear Admiral Shunji Izaki. The pitched battle results in the sinking of the Japanese flagship *Jintsu*, with the loss of Admiral Izaki, and damage to the Japanese destroyer *Yukikaze*. Deadly torpedoes launched from Japanese destroyers damage all three light cruisers in Ainsworth's task group, and damage the destroyer *Gwin* (DD 433) to such an extent that she is scuttled. Two other destroyers are damaged in a collision while maneuvering during the battle.

A TBF Avenger of Composite Squadron 13 operating from the auxiliary aircraft carrier *Core* (ACV 13) sinks the German submarine *U-487* while operating in the Atlantic 720 miles from the Azores Islands.

14 July

TBF Avenger and F4F Wildcat aircraft of Composite Squadron (VC) 29 from the auxiliary aircraft carrier *Santee* (ACV 29) send the German submarine *U-160* to the bottom south of the Azores Islands.

15 July

A PBY Catalina of VP-92 assists three British warships in sinking the German submarine *U-135* west of the Canary Islands.

A TBF Avenger of VC-29 operating from the escort carrier *Santee* (CVE 29) sinks the German submarine *U-509* south of the Azores Islands.

12 July

The destroyer *Taylor* (DD 468) sinks the Japanese submarine *RO-107* in the waters off Kolombangara in the Solomon Islands.

Above: *Many of McClelland Barclay's recruiting posters focused on the individual sailor doing his duty. (Corbis)*

Left: *Shipfitter Third Class D. R. Cole looks through a hole in the light cruiser* Honolulu's *(CL 48) stern, caused by a hit by a Japanese torpedo that failed to explode during the Battle of Kolombangara, 13 July 1943. Mattresses were used to stop water from entering the hole. (Naval Historical Center)*

A PBM Mariner of VP-32 sinks the German submarine *U-159* in the Caribbean south of Haiti.

16 July
TBF Avengers from VC-13 operating from the escort carrier *Core* (CVE 13) sink the German submarine *U-67* in the Atlantic.

17–18 July
In two days of air strikes, U.S. Navy aircraft join those of the Marine Corps, Army Air Forces, and Royal New Zealand Air Force in striking targets on Bougainville in the Solomons, sinking one destroyer and damaging three others.

18 July
The blimp *K-74* is shot down by deck gunners on the surfaced German submarine *U-134* in the Florida Straits. This is the only loss of an airship to enemy action during World War II.

19 July
A PBM Mariner of VP-74 sends the German submarine *U-513* to the bottom off Brazil.

21 July
A PBY Catalina of VP-94 sinks the German submarine *U-662* off the mouth of the Amazon River in Brazil.

23 July
TBF Avengers of VC-9 operating from the escort carrier *Bogue* (CVE 9) sink the German submarine *U-527* south of the Azores Islands.

The destroyer *George E. Badger* (DD 196) sinks the German submarine *U-613* south of the Azores Islands.

PB4Y-1 Liberators of VB-107 sink the German submarine *U-598* off Brazil.

26 July
A PBM Mariner of VP-32 sinks the German submarine *U-359* off Haiti.

30 July
A PV-1 Ventura of VB-127 sinks the German submarine *U-591* while flying cover for convoy TJ 2 off Brazil.

TBF Avengers and F4F Wildcats of VC-29 from the escort carrier *Santee* (CVE 29) sink the German submarine *U-43* in the Atlantic.

The submarine chaser *PC-624* sends the German submarine *U-375* to the bottom off Tunisia.

31 July
A PBM Mariner of VP-74 joins Brazilian aircraft to sink the German submarine *U-199* off Rio de Janeiro, Brazil.

2 August
The motor torpedo boat *PT-109*, while engaged in a night patrol off Kolombangara in the Solomon Islands, is rammed and sunk by the Japanese destroyer *Amagiri*. Two sailors are killed and the survivors, including the boat's skipper Lieutenant (junior grade) John F. Kennedy, swim to a nearby island. The eleven survivors are rescued on 6 August. Kennedy later becomes the thirty-fifth President of the United States.

Above: *A destroyer fires on Japanese aircraft during operations off Vella Lavella in the central Solomon Islands, August–October 1943. Other ships are firing astern, lighting up the destroyer's wake. The ship may be the destroyer* Nicholas *(DD 449). (Naval Historical Center)*

3 August

A PBM Mariner of VP-205 sinks the German submarine *U-572* north of Dutch Guiana.

The destroyer *Buck* (DD 420) sinks the Italian submarine *Argento* off Tunisia.

5 August

While operating off Cape Henry, New Jersey, the gunboat *Plymouth* (PG 57) is sunk by the German submarine *U-566*.

6 August

The Battle of Vella Gulf, a night action between American and Japanese destroyers off Kolombangara in the Solomon Islands, results in the sinking of the Japanese vessels *Arashi*, *Hagikaze*, and *Kawakaze*. The Japanese ships are engaged in an attempt to deliver troops and supplies to the island.

7 August

A PB4Y-1 Liberator of VB-105 sinks the German submarine *U-84* in the North Atlantic.

7–11 August

F4F Wildcat fighters and TBF Avenger torpedo bombers of VC-1 operating from the escort carrier *Card* (CVE 11) sink the German submarine *U-117* while operating west of the Azores Islands. Two days later an Avenger from the squadron sends *U-664* to the bottom.

Previously damaged by air and surface attacks by U.S. forces, the German submarine *U-604* is scuttled in the South Atlantic by her crew.

Left: *Lieutenant John F. Kennedy, USNR (far right), with other crewmen of* PT-109, *circa 1943. The future President of the United States lost his boat on the night of 2 August 1943 when it was sliced in half by a Japanese destroyer. (Naval Historical Center)*

Right: *Contrails ring the fuselage of an F6F-3 Hellcat as it prepares to launch from the carrier* Yorktown *(CV 10), November 1943. Yorktown was one of the new Essex-class carriers that began joining the fleet in mid-1943. They would spearhead the central Pacific drive to Japan. (Naval Historical Center)*

15 August
Task Force 31, under the command of Rear Admiral Theodore S. Wilkinson, lands Seabees of the 58th Construction Battalion along with Marines and Army troops on Vella Lavella, which will become a vital Solomon Islands air base.

Naval forces under the command of Vice Admiral Thomas C. Kinkaid land U.S. Army and Canadian troops on Kiska in the Aleutians, only to find that the Japanese defenders have abandoned the island.

17–24 August
The Quadrant Conference between British Prime Minister Winston S. Churchill, President Franklin D. Roosevelt, and the Combined Chiefs of Staff at Quebec, Canada, results in the decisions to devote more effort to the Pacific theater, increase emphasis on defeating Italy, and work more closely with the U.S.S.R.

19 August
An OS2N Kingfisher of VS-57 and the New Zealand corvette *Tui* sink the Japanese submarine *I-17* off Australia.

25 August
The destroyer *Patterson* (DD 392) sinks the Japanese submarine *RO-35* southeast of San Cristobal Island in the Solomons.

27 August
The German submarine *U-847* is sunk in the Atlantic by F4F Wildcat fighters and TBF Avenger torpedo bombers of VC-1 from the escort carrier *Card*.

31 August
The carriers of Task Force 15, under the command of Rear Admiral Charles A. Pownall, strike Marcus Island, hitting installations ashore and sinking three Japanese small craft. The raid marks the combat debut of the *Essex*-class and *Independence*-class carriers, as well as the first combat action of the Navy's newest carrier fighter, the F6F Hellcat.

1 September
The Navy is given full responsibility for airborne antisubmarine warfare in the Atlantic Ocean.

During landings on Baker Island in the Central Pacific, *Ashland* (LSD 1) becomes the first dock landing ship employed in an actual operation.

3 September
The destroyer *Ellet* (DD 398) sinks the Japanese submarine *I-25* in the waters near Espiritu Santo.

4 September
The ships of Task Force 76, under the command of Rear Admiral Daniel E. Barbey, land Australian troops on the Huon Peninsula near Lae, New Guinea. The offensive

action prompts the Japanese to strike the invasion force by air, damaging the destroyer *Conyngham* (DD 371) and two tank landing ships. One of them is *LST-473*, which is hit by a bomb in the pilot house just as orders are given to turn the ship to avoid a torpedo. Despite his wounds, Seaman First Class Johnnie D. Hutchins grabs the wheel and turns his ship away from the oncoming torpedo, thus saving her. He receives the Medal of Honor posthumously for his heroic act

9 September
The submarine *Grayling* (SS 209) is lost in the South China Sea after being rammed by a Japanese transport.

Supported by the ships of Task Force 80 under the command of Vice Admiral H. Kent Hewitt, the Allied Fifth Army under the command of Lieutenant General Mark W. Clark goes ashore at Salerno, Italy. Fierce German counterattacks threaten the beaches and inflict damage on the ships supporting the invasion. Air attacks, fire from shore batteries, and mines sink one vessel and damage eight others.

11 September
In continuing action off the beachhead at Salerno, Italy, the destroyer *Rowan* (DD 405) sinks in just one minute after an engagement with German motor torpedo boats, taking 202 of her 273-man crew with her. Rocket bombs dropped by German Do. 217 aircraft score a direct hit on a gun turret on the deck of the light cruiser *Savannah*.

15 September
Operating in concert, the destroyer *Saufley* (DD 465) and a PBY Catalina of VP-23 sink the Japanese submarine *RO-101* in the waters east of San Cristobal in the Solomon Islands.

18 September
U.S. carrier aircraft from Task Force 15, under the command of Rear Admiral Charles A. Pownall, join Army Air Forces B-24 bombers in striking the Gilbert Islands.

22 September
Task Force 76, under Rear Admiral Daniel E. Barbey, puts Australian troops ashore at Finschhafen, New Guinea.

24 September
The German submarine *U-593* torpedoes the minesweeper *Skill* (AM 115) in the Gulf of Salerno. Italy. The minesweeper sinks in just twenty minutes with only 32 survivors among her 103-man crew.

27 September
While flying patrol off Brazil, a PBM Mariner of VP-74 attacks and sinks the German submarine *U-161*.

28 September
The submarine *Cisco* (SS 290) sinks in the Sulu Sea off Panay Island, probably the result of damage inflicted by a Japanese observation plane and gunboat.

Right: *Douglas SBD-5 dive bombers of Bombing Squadron (VB) 16 on Lexington's (CV 16) flight deck after returning from a raid on the Gilbert Islands, 18 September 1943. (Naval Historical Center)*

Below: *The light cruiser Savannah (CL 42) is hit by a German guided bomb while supporting Allied forces ashore in the Salerno area, 11 September 1943. A PT boat passes by in the foreground. (Naval Historical Center)*

3 October

The Japanese submarine *RO-108* sinks the destroyer *Henley* (DD 391) off eastern New Guinea.

4 October

The aircraft carrier *Ranger* launches attacks against German shipping in Norway in the only operation conducted by U.S. carriers in northern European waters. F4F Wildcat fighters of VF-4 splash two German aircraft that approach the carrier, while other

squadron Wildcats join SBD Dauntless and TBF Avenger aircraft in sinking four steamers and a transport and damaging five other vessels.

TBF Avengers and F4F Wildcats of VC-9 operating from the escort carrier *Card* spot four German U-boats engaged in a resupply operation north of the Azores Islands. The aircraft sink two of the boats, *U-460* and *U-422*.

A PV-1 Ventura of VB-128 sinks the German submarine *U-279* southwest of Iceland.

5–6 October

U.S. carrier aircraft from six flattops of Task Force 14 under the command of Rear Admiral Alfred E. Montgomery strike Wake Island.

6 October

In the Battle of Vella Lavella, the destroyers *O'Bannon*, *Chevalier* (DD 451), and *Selfridge* (DD 357) are damaged after engaging a superior Japanese force escorting troop-carrying barges. *Chevalier* and *Selfridge* both take torpedoes, but manage to torpedo and sink the Japanese destroyer *Yugumo*. *Chevalier* is later scuttled.

The submarine *Dorado* (SS 248) departs New London, Connecticut, bound for Panama. She is never heard from again and is declared lost at sea.

Left: Ranger *(CV 4)
launched the first U.S.
Navy carrier strikes in
Europe, her planes
attacking German shipping
in Bodo Harbor, Norway,
on 4 October 1943. (Naval
Historical Center)*

Below: *Pilots and
crewmen on board the
light carrier* Cowpens
*(CVL 25) look at bombs
that have been inscribed
with messages for the
targeted Japanese on Wake
Island, 5 October 1943.
(Naval Historical Center)*

7 October
The submarine *S-44* (SS 155) is sunk by the Japanese
escort destroyer *Ishigaki* in the northern Pacific east of
the Kamchatka Peninsula.

9 October
The destroyer *Buck* sinks after being torpedoed by the
German submarine *U-616* in the Gulf of Salerno, Italy.
She sinks in just four minutes with only ninety-seven
survivors.

11 October
While operating in the La Pérouse Strait between
Japan and Russia, the submarine *Wahoo* is sunk by
Japanese aircraft and surface ships.

13 October
A TBF Avenger of VC-9 operating from the escort
carrier *Card* sinks the German submarine U-*402*
north-northeast of the Azores Islands.

The German submarine *U-371* sinks the destroyer
Bristol (DD 453) off Algeria.

20 October
TBF Avengers of VC-13 operating from the escort
carrier *Core* (CVE 13) sink the German submarine
U-378 north of the Azores Islands.

21 October
The destroyer *Murphy* (DD 603), serving as an escort
for convoy UT 4, is accidentally rammed and cut in
two by the American tanker *Bulkoil* in the Atlantic.

Her bow section sinks; her after portion remains afloat
and is towed to New York. Fitted with a new forepart,
she returns to the fleet in time to support the landings
in Normandy.

31 October
The German submarine *U-584* is sunk by a TBF
Avenger of VC-9 operating from the escort carrier
Card north of the Azores Islands. *U-584* is on her

tenth patrol, an earlier one in June 1942 involving the landing of saboteurs at Jacksonville, Florida.

1 November

Task Force 31, under the command of Rear Admiral Theodore S. Wilkinson, puts Marines of the First Amphibious Corps ashore at Cape Torokina, Bougainville, in the Solomon Islands. Elsewhere in the Solomon Islands chain, light cruisers and destroyers of Task Force 39, under the command of Rear Admiral Aaron S. Merrill, shell a Japanese airfield on Shortland Island and bombard the Buka-Bonis area, joined in the latter by aircraft from the carriers *Saratoga* and *Princeton* (CVL 23).

2 November

A powerful Japanese surface force under the command of Rear Admiral Sentaro Omori, intent on disrupting the American landings at Bougainville in the Solomon Islands, runs into four light cruisers and eight destroyers of Task Force 39 under the command of Rear Admiral Aaron S. Merrill. In the resulting Battle of Empress Augusta Bay, U.S. destroyers sink the Japanse destroyer *Hatsukaze*, while gunfire sends the light cruiser *Sendai* to the bottom. Four other Japanese vessels are damaged. Task Force 39 loses no ships, but four suffer damage. Though the Japanese do attack the retiring task force by air, carrier raids against the Buka-Bonis area launched from *Saratoga* and *Princeton*

prevent the enemy from mounting serious air opposition.

The submarines *Seahorse* (SS 304), *Halibut* (SS 232), and *Trigger* (SS 237) attack the same Japanese convoy south of Honshu, Japan, with devastating results, sinking five transports and cargo ships.

5 November

Task Force 38, under the command of Rear Admiral Frederick C. Sherman, and including the aircraft carriers *Saratoga* and *Princeton*, strikes the Japanese bastion at Rabaul, New Guinea. The aircraft score hits on nine warships in Simpson Harbor. Six days later U.S. carrier aircraft hit Rabaul for a second time, with Task Force 38 aircraft joining those launched from Task Group 50.3 under the command of Rear Admiral Alfred E. Montgomery. The strike, which includes SB2C Helldivers on their first combat mission, sinks a destroyer and damages four other warships. Air strikes, primarily conducted by aircaft based at Solomon Islands airfields, continue to pound Rabaul, eventually making an invasion unnecessary.

PB4Y-1 Liberators of VB-107 join Army Air Forces B-25 Mitchell bombers of the First Composite Squadron in sinking the German submarine *U-848* in the waters southwest of Ascension Island.

Right: *Destroyers damaged during the Battle of Vella Lavella on 6–7 October 1943 lick their wounds. Pictured at left is* Selfridge *(DD 357), her bow mangled by a Japanese torpedo. Alongside is* O'Bannon *(DD 450), which suffered damage to her bow in a collision during the battle. (Naval Historical Center)*

Above: *Corpsmen and plane handlers remove casualties from the air group commander's TBF Avenger, just after it landed on* Saratoga *(CV 3) after being shot up over Rabaul, 5 November 1943. Gunner Kenneth Bratton was wounded in the plane, and Photographer's Mate First Class Paul Barnett was killed while photographing a Japanese Zero fighter making a head-on attack on the TBF. Commander Harold H. Caldwell is climbing from his cockpit after making a one-wheel landing with no flaps, ailerons, or radio. (Naval Historical Center)*

6 November

While escorting convoy KMF 25A bound for Naples, Italy, the destroyer *Beatty* (DD 640) is sunk by a torpedo dropped by a German aircraft, which also torpedoes the troop transport *Santa Elena*. The following day, *Santa Elena* collides with another transport and sinks.

10 November

PB4Y-1 Liberators of three Navy squadrons join British Royal Air Force aircraft in sinking the German submarine *U-966* in the Bay of Biscay.

12 November

President Franklin D. Roosevelt boards the battleship *Iowa* for his journey to conferences at Cairo, Egypt, and Tehran, Iran, the latter the first meeting of the so-called Big Three—Roosevelt, British Prime Minister Winston S. Churchill, and Soviet Premier Joseph Stalin. A close call occurs two days later when, during battle practice at sea, the destroyer *William D. Porter* (DD 579) accidentally launches a live torpedo at the battleship. *Iowa* receives a warning in time to avoid being hit.

A PB4Y-1 Liberator of VB-103 sends the German submarine *U-508* to the bottom in the Bay of Biscay.

16 November

The submarine *Corvina* (SS 216) is sunk by the Japanese submarine *I-176* in the waters off Truk in the Caroline Islands.

Left: *Planes from the carriers* Saratoga *(CV 3) and* Princeton *(CVL 23) hit shipping at Rabaul. One carrier at right center has been hit. This view is looking west, taken from a* Saratoga *plane. Cruisers and destroyers are standing out of Simpson harbor into Blanche Bay. Other landmarks include Vulcan Crater (upper left), Sulphur Point (lower right), and Matupi Island (right center) with flak overhead. (Naval Historical Center)*

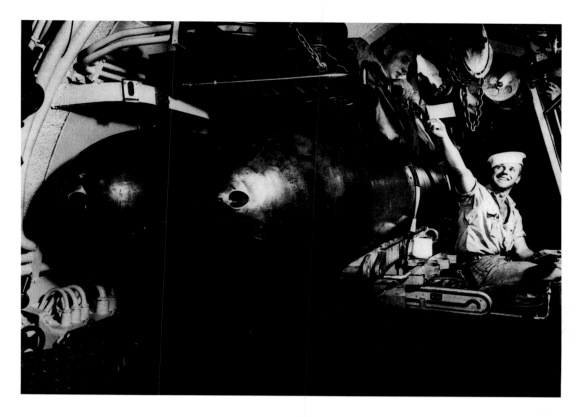

Right: *Men relax aboard the submarine* Cero *(SS 225) off New London, Connecticut, August 1943. The limited space on board a submarine meant that some crewmen bunked with torpedoes. (National Archives)*

17 November
Japanese aircraft attack a convoy carrying reinforcements to Bougainville in the Solomon Islands, sinking the high-speed transport *McKean* (APD 5) in a torpedo attack.

19 November
The submarine *Sculpin* (SS 191) is heavily damaged by the Japanese destroyer *Yamagumo* north of Truk in the Caroline Islands. Though he has time to escape the boat before she sinks, Captain John P. Cromwell, the commander of the submarine squadron of which *Sculpin* is a part, chooses to go down with the boat rather than face interrogation that might force him to reveal his knowledge of plans to seize the Gilbert Islands. For his selfless sacrifice, he receives a posthumous Medal of Honor.

20 November
Under the overall command of Vice Admiral Raymond A. Spruance, the ships of the Central Pacific Force support Operation Galvanic, the assault by Marines and Army troops against the Gilbert Islands. Task Force 54, under the command of Rear Admiral Richmond Kelly Turner, is responsible for the amphibious landings, and meets its greatest challenge at Tarawa Atoll, where a reef prevents many landing craft from carrying Marines all the way to the beach. While supporting the landings the aircraft carrier *Independence* (CVL 22) is torpedoed by a Japanese aircraft, and the destroyer *Ringgold* (DD 500) is damaged by shore batteries.

22 November
The destroyer *Frazier*, with the destroyer *Meade* (DD 602), depth charges the Japanese submarine *I-35* off the Gilbert Islands, forcing her to the surface. *Frazier* then rams the submarine, sinking her.

24 November
The Japanese submarine *I-175* penetrates the protective screen around the escort carrier *Liscome Bay* (CVE 56) and sinks her off the Gilbert Islands. A total of 702 crewmen are lost, including Rear Admiral Henry M. Mullinix, Commander Carrier Division 24. *Liscome Bay* is the first of six escort carriers lost in action during World War II.

25 November
In the early morning hours Destroyer Squadron 23, under the command of Captain Arleigh A. Burke, engages five destroyers under Captain Kiyoto Kagawa off Cape St. George, New Ireland. Burke's squadron, known as the "Little Beavers," sinks three enemy vessels and damages a fourth without suffering any damage.

The destroyer *Radford* (DD 446) sinks the Japanese submarine *I-19* north of the Gilbert Islands.

A PB4Y-1 Liberator of VB-107 sinks the German submarine *U-849* in the South Atlantic.

DESTRUCTION FROM THE DEPTHS: SUBMARINES IN WORLD WAR II

by Captain Edward L. Beach Jr., U.S. Navy (Retired)

Left: *The submarine* Wahoo *(SS 238) returns to Pearl Harbor, Hawaii, on 7 February 1943, after completing her third war patrol. The broom lashed to her periscope symbolizes a "clean sweep" of Japanese ships, and flags represent claims for the sinking of two Japanese warships and six merchantmen. Another flag proclaims "Shoot the sunza bitches," a slogan for the patrol. (Naval Historical Center)*

Below: *Crewmen on board a Navy submarine load a torpedo onto their boat at New London, Connecticut. Defective torpedoes that ran erratically and many times failed to explode hindered the U.S. Navy's undersea campaign against Japan during the early part of World War II. (National Museum of Naval Aviation)*

Opposite, center: *In the crowded confines of a submarine, all await the word of the skipper as he peers through the periscope at a target on the surface. A talker stands ready to receive information on settings and the ultimate command to fire, which he will quickly relay to the torpedo room. ("Up Periscope," Georges Schreiber, Navy Art Collection)*

It was during World War I that the vast potential of undersea warfare was first realized as German U-boats terrorized shipping in the Atlantic, but when the next global conflict erupted on 1 September 1939, all rules changed and the submarine came of age.

There were three major submarine forces deployed in the war—Germany, Japan, and the United States. With only a few effective U-boats available when the war began, the German navy soon had England on her knees. By war's end, Germany had built nearly 1,000 U-boats, but the tremendous power of Allied production, mostly based in the United States, converted about 800 of these into iron coffins for their crews, eternally dissolving them into the mud of the seabed. Japanese submarines sent three American flattops to the bottom and conducted the storied attack on the cruiser *Indianapolis* (CA 35), yet never posed a serious hindrance to Allied operations in the

Above: *The submarine* Barb *(SS 220) slices through the water on 23 January 1945, the flames of a burning convoy that she just attacked on the surface in Namkwan Harbor, China, lighting up the sky. Her skipper, Commander Eugene B. Fluckey, received the Medal of Honor for his actions on this patrol, which proved that even in protected waters Japanese ships could not hide from U.S. Navy submarines. ("The Galloping Ghost of the China Coast," Ted Wilbur, U.S. Naval Institute)*

Below: *Crewmen on board a U.S. Navy submarine gather for chow in a space that also served as the library. The limited room on board a World War II fleet boat translated into areas being used for multiple purposes. (U.S. Naval Institute)*

Pacific. Only the American submarine force, plagued as it was by criminally defective torpedoes, fulfilled the promise of undersea warships. The U.S. Navy's fleet boats were themselves of an inspired design, their skippers and crews equally so. At war's end, official tallies showed that they had destroyed almost two-thirds of Japan's merchant marine and one-third of her navy against a loss of about one-sixth of their own forces. Thus, less than two percent of the U.S. Navy inflicted half of the maritime war losses suffered by the Empire of Japan, an inspirational legacy for all those who have worn dolphins on their chest since 1945.

28–29 November

The submarines *Pargo* (SS 264) and *Snook* (SS 279) attack a Japanese convoy northwest of the Mariana Islands, sinking three ships.

29 November

The landing of the First Marine Parachute Battalion at Cape Torokina on Bougainville, Solomon Islands, encounters determined Japanese resistance. The destroyers *Fullam* (DD 474), *Lardner* (DD 487), and *Lansdowne* rush to the scene. Along with land-based aircraft, the three tin cans silence shore batteries and permit the extraction of the leathernecks.

4 December

The carriers of Task Force 50, under Rear Admiral Charles A. Pownall, launch air strikes against Japanese installations on Kwajalein and Wotje in the Marshall Islands. In addition to damage inflicted on land targets, the strike results in the sinking of four enemy vessels and damage to seven other ships, including two light cruisers. During the Japanese counterattack an aircraft puts a torpedo into the carrier *Lexington* (CV 16).

The submarine *Sailfish* (SS 192) sinks the Japanese escort carrier *Chuyo* in the waters off Honshu, Japan. The submarine's crew is unaware that their quarry carries survivors of their sister ship *Sculpin*, sunk the previous month.

9 December

President Franklin D. Roosevelt boards the battleship *Iowa* and returns to the United States after conferences in Cairo, Egypt, and Tehran, Iran.

13 December

The destroyer *Osmond Ingram* (DD 255) suffers damage in a gun battle with the German submarine *U-172* west of the Canary Islands. These are the only blows the German submarine strikes, for she is sent to the bottom by *Osmond Ingram*, *George E. Badger* (DD 196), *Clemson* (DD 186) and FM Wildcats of VC-19 from the escort carrier *Bogue*.

Following a thirty-two hour chase, the destroyer *Wainwright* (DD 419), operating with the British frigate *Calpe*, sinks the German submarine *U-593* off Algiers.

15 December

Task Force 76, under the command of Rear Admiral Daniel E. Barbey, lands Army troops on Arawe Peninsula in New Britain.

20 December

TBF Avengers and FM Wildcats of VC-19 from the escort carrier *Bogue* (VE 9) attack the German submarine *U-850* southwest of the Azores Islands. The sub engages in a gun battle with the aircraft but is sunk.

24 December

Attacked unsuccessfully the previous day, the antisubmarine task group led by the carrier *Card* suffers losses at the hands of German U-boats in the North Atlantic. Torpedoes sink the destroyer *Leary* (DD 158), with the loss of ninety-seven crewmen, but *Schenk* (DD 159) counters by sinking *U-645*.

26 December

Task Force 76, under the command of Rear Admiral Daniel E. Barbey, lands elements of the First Marine Division at Cape Gloucester, New Britain, with gunfire support from Task Force 74 under Rear Admiral Victor A.C. Crutchley. The Japanese contest the landings with air attacks that sink the destroyer *Brownson* (DD 518), which sinks in seventeen minutes, and damage five other ships.

28 December

A PB4Y-1 Liberator of VB-105 sights German destroyers and torpedo boats in the Bay of Biscay. Later in the day, Navy PB4Y-1s join two British light cruisers in attacking the force and sinking one destroyer and two torpedo boats.

29 December

Operating off Palau, the submarine *Silversides* (SS 236) sinks a Japanese transport and two cargo ships, and damages another cargo ship.

1944

2 January

While on patrol in the waters south-southwest of Ascension Island, PB4Y-1 Liberators of VB-107 spot the German blockade runner *Weserland*. She is intercepted by the destroyer *Somers* (DD 381), which fires one salvo that forces the enemy crew to abandon ship. *Weserland* subsequently explodes and sinks.

Above: *Commodore Arleigh A. Burke exudes confidence on the bridge of his flagship. ("Commodore Arleigh A. Burke, USN," Albert Murray, Naval Historical Center)*

Right: *Two sailors of the escort carrier* Liscome Bay *(CVE 56) are buried at sea from a Coast Guard–manned assault transport, November 1943. The baby flattop was torpedoed by a Japanese submarine off the Gilbert Islands and sank in just twenty-three minutes, taking 702 men with her. (National Archives)*

Above: *Commander Submarine Force, Pacific Fleet Rear Admiral Charles A. Lockwood, Jr., presents the Navy and Marine Corps Medal to Lieutenant John P. Bienia at Pearl Harbor, Hawaii, 21 March 1943. The medal was awarded for Bienia's part in the submarine* Silversides' *(SS 236) eventful fourth war patrol, from December 1942 to January 1943. (Naval Historical Center)*

Task Force 76, under Rear Admiral Daniel E. Barbey, lands Army troops at Saidor, New Guinea.

3 January
The submarine *Scorpion* (SS 278) departs Midway Atoll on what will be her final war patrol. After she conducts a rendezvous with *Herring* (SS 233) on 5 January, she will never be heard from again. She is presumed lost at sea with all hands.

4 January
The light cruiser *Omaha* (CL 4) and destroyer *Jouett* intercept the German blockade runner *Rio Grande* off the coast of Brazil, damaging her with gunfire to such an extent that she is scuttled by her crew. The pair of ships repeats the scenario the following day, sinking the German blockade runner *Burgenland*.

10–11 January
In a two-day attack against a Japanese convoy in the waters north of Okinawa, Japan, the submarine *Seawolf* (SS 197) sinks three cargo ships.

15 January
Service Squadron 10 is established at Pearl Harbor, Hawaii. Under the command of Captain Worrall R. Carter, the squadron's ships will provide vital mobile logistic support to the Central Pacific campaign.

Left: *During an engagement west of the Canary Islands on 13 December 1943, a destroyer races toward U-172, which was forced to the surface by depth charge attacks by U.S. Navy ships and aircraft. The German submarine was eventually sunk. By 1944 the noose was drawing tighter around Germany's once feared U-boat force. (Naval Historical Center)*

Right: *The submarine* Seawolf *(SS 197) off Hunters Point Naval Drydocks, San Francisco, California, 9 May 1944, less than four months after completing her eleventh war patrol.* Seawolf *completed three more patrols before being lost in the Pacific. (Naval Historical Center)*

16 January

A TBF Avenger of VC-13 flying from the escort carrier *Guadalcanal* (CVE 60) sinks the German submarine *U-544* in the Atlantic.

22 January

The Japanese submarine *RO-37* torpedoes the oiler *Cache* (AO 67) southeast of San Cristobal in the Solomon Islands, and is then sunk by the destroyer *Buchanan* (DD 484).

A naval force under the command of Rear Admiral Frank K. Lowry lands British and American troops at Anzio on the Italian coast, suffering the sinking of a minesweeper and damage to a large infantry landing craft. German air attacks and mines damage three more ships on 24 January, with the air attacks intensifying over the following days.

28 January

A PB4Y-1 Liberator of VB-103 sinks the German submarine *U-271* off the river Shannon estuary, Eire, Ireland.

29 January

Task Force 58, the Pacific Fleet's carrier striking force under Rear Admiral Marc A. Mitscher, begins launching air strikes against the Marshall Islands in preparation for U.S. landings. Commanded by the pioneer naval aviator throughout the entire war, Task Force 58 spearheads the Central Pacific offensive toward the Japanese home islands.

31 January

Following an intense bombardment the previous day and supported by carrier aircraft, Marines and Army troops go ashore at Kwajalein and Majuro in the Marshall Islands from ships under the command of Vice Admiral Raymond A. Spruance. Landings on Roi and Namur in the Marshalls occur on 1 February under the guns of Navy ships, which suffer damage only from operational accidents.

1 February

Amphibious Forces, Pacific Fleet is established with headquarters at Pearl Harbor, Hawaii, and placed under the command of Vice Admiral Richmond Kelly Turner.

2 February

The destroyer *Walker* (DD 517) sinks the Japanese submarine *RO-39* east of Wotje in the Marshall Islands.

5 February

The destroyer *Charrette* (DD 581) and destroyer escort *Fair* (DE 35) send the Japanese submarine *I-21* to the bottom north of Jaluit in the Marshall Islands.

Left: *Fifth Army troops wade ashore from the British LCI-281 during the first day of landings near Anzio, Italy, on 22 January 1944. The Royal Navy LCI-274 is extracting from the beach in center. Smoke at far right is from the burning U.S. LCI-20, victim of a German air attack. (Naval Historical Center)*

Below: *F6F-3 Hellcats are readied for launch on the deck of the light carrier* Cowpens *(CVL 25), known in the fleet as the "Mighty Moo." The target for the January 1944 raid is the Marshall Islands. (Naval Historical Center)*

6 February
PB4Y-1 Liberator of VB-107 sinks the German submarine *U-177* west of Ascension Island.

15 February
Lieutenant (junior grade) Nathan G. Gordon of VP-34 makes four landings under intense enemy fire off Kavieng, New Ireland, to rescue crews of three downed Army Air Forces bombers. All told, fifteen men are pulled into his PBY Catalina and flown to safety. Gordon receives the Medal of Honor for his heroism.

16 February
The destroyer *Phelps* (DD 360) and minesweeper *Sage* (AM 111) sink the Japanese submarine *RO-40* northwest of Kwajalein in the Marshall Islands.

17 February
Task Force 58 strikes the Japanese naval base at Truk in the Caroline Islands, causing heavy damage to shore installations and sinking thirty-three ships in the harbor and surrounding waters. The aircraft carrier *Intrepid* (CV 11) takes a torpedo during a Japanese counterattack. "The ship shook and shivered as tho (*sic*) a giant had hold of the stern," one crewman wrote in his diary describing the hit. Such would be *Intrepid*'s propensity for suffering battle damage during World War II that she would receive the nickname "Evil I." The attacks against Truk continue into the following day.

The destroyer *Nicholas* (DD 449) sinks the Japanese submarine *I-11* northwest of the Marshall Islands.

18–19 February
Task Group 51.11 supports the landing of Marines on Eniwetok in the Marshall Islands.

19 February
During operations in the South China Sea, the submarine *Jack* (SS 259) attacks a convoy of six tankers escorted by a lone destroyer, sending four of the tankers to the bottom.

22 February
In the first carrier strikes launched against the Marianas Islands, the flattops of Task Force 58 send

their air groups against Saipan, Tinian, Rota, and Guam. During two days of strikes, naval aviators sink three vessels and damage a fourth.

24 February

In the first employment of Magnetic Anomaly Detection (MAD) gear for tracking a submerged submarine, PBY-5A Catalinas of VP-63 join a PV-1 Ventura of VB-127 and British aircraft in attacking the German submarine *U-761* as she attempts to enter the Atlantic through the Straits of Gibraltar. The submariners abandon their heavily damaged boat and scuttle her. VP-63 is known throughout the remainder of the war as the "MAD Cats."

29 February

Task Group 76.1 ships, which include nine destroyers and three high-speed transports, land Army troops on Los Negros in the Admiralty Islands.

1 March

The destroyer escort *Bronstein* (DE 189) sinks the German submarine *U-603* in the North Atlantic and later in the day joins the destroyer escorts *Thomas* (DE 102) and *Bostwick* (DE 103) in sending *U-709* to the bottom.

9 March

The German submarine *U-255* torpedoes the destroyer escort *Leopold* (DE 319) in the North Atlantic, damaging the ship to such an extent that she sinks the following day. Only twenty-eight of her 199 crewmen survive the attack.

13 March

The submarine *Sand Lance* (SS 381) sinks the Japanese light cruiser *Tatsuta* and cargo ship *Kokuyo Maru* in the waters off Yokosuka, Japan, but pays a penalty for her success by spending more than eighteen hours submerged as Japanese escort vessels batter her with 105 depth charges.

Right: *Crewmen of a PBY Catalina pull a pilot shot down over Rabaul into their aircraft during 1944. For a downed airman floating in a rubber raft alone with nothing but water stretching to the horizons, the sight of an aircraft was akin to an angel from heaven. Flying "Dumbo" missions, U.S. Navy seaplanes rescued many a downed flier, often under fire, and also pull survivors of the heavy cruiser* Indianapolis *(CA 35) from the water in August 1945. (Corbis)*

In a truly joint effort, a TBF Avenger of VC-95 from the escort carrier *Bogue* joins U.S. and Canadian ships and a British patrol bomber in sinking the German submarine *U-575* in the North Atlantic.

16 March

A PBY Catalina of VP-63 employs Magnetic Anomaly Detection gear to detect the submerged German submarine *U-392* in the Straits of Gibraltar. The Catalina is joined by British ships in making attacks on the boat, with the British frigate *Affleck* delivering the blows that sink the sub.

17 March

TBF Avengers of VC-6 from the escort carrier *Block Island* (CVE 21) join the destroyer *Corry* (DD 463) and destroyer escort *Bronstein* in sinking the German submarine *U-801* west of the Cape Verde Islands.

19 March

A TBF Avenger and FM Wildcat of VC-6 from the escort carrier *Block Island* send the German submarine *U-1059* to the bottom in the Atlantic west-southwest of Dakar, Africa.

20 March

Task Group 31.2, under the command of Commodore Lawrence F. Reifsnider, lands the Fourth Marines on Emirau Island in the Bismarck Archipelago. Meanwhile, four battleships, two escort carriers, and destroyers of Task Force 37, under the command of Rear Admiral Robert M. Griffin, bombard Kavieng, New Ireland.

25 March

Operating south of Wotje, the destroyer escort *Manlove* (DE 36) and submarine chaser *PC-1135*, sink the Japanese submarine *I-32*.

26 March

A torpedo fired from the submarine *Tullibee* (SS 284) malfunctions, making a circular run and sinking the submarine in the waters north of the Palaus Islands.

30 March–1 April

Task Force 58 aircraft bombard Japanese airfields, repair facilities, and other installations at Palau, Yap, Ulithi, and Woleai in the Caroline Islands, sinking forty-one vessels of various sizes and classes. TBF Avengers from the carriers *Bunker Hill* (CV 17), *Hornet*

Right: *Personnel on board the carrier* Lexington *(CV 16) monitor radio traffic and plot the movements of ships and aircraft during strikes against the Gilbert and Marshall islands, December 1943. Air strikes from multiple carriers required detailed planing and coordination to ensure success over the target. (National Archives)*

(CV 12), and *Lexington* mine the approaches to the Palaus, the first time carrier aircraft participate in sowing a minefield during World War II.

7 April

The destroyer *Saufley* (DD 465) employs eighteen depth charges to sink the Japanese submarine *I-2* off New Hanover in the South Pacific.

The destroyer *Champlin* (DD 601) intentionally rams the German submarine *U-856* in the Atlantic. Although damaged, she joins with the destroyer escort *Huse* (DE 145) in sinking the sub. *Champlin's* commanding officer, Commander John J. Shaffer III, is wounded by shrapnel during the attack and dies the following day.

9 April

TBM Avengers and FM Wildcats of VC-58 from the escort carrier *Guadalcanal* join the destroyer escorts *Pillsbury* (DE 133), *Pope* (DE 134), *Flaherty* (DE 135), and *Chatelain* (DE 149) in sinking the German submarine *U-515* in the Atlantic off Madeira Island. VC-58 aircraft score another submarine kill the following day, sinking *U-68*.

16 April

The battleship *Wisconsin* (BB 64) is placed in commission.

17 April

While operating in the North Atlantic, the minesweeper *Swift* (AM 122) joins the submarine chaser *PC-619* in sinking the German submarine *U-986*.

18 April

The submarine *Gudgeon* (SS 211) is sunk southwest of Iwo Jima, Japan, probably by Japanese naval aircraft.

19 April

The aircraft carrier *Saratoga* and three escorting destroyers join ships of the British Eastern Fleet in conducting air attacks against Japanese installations and shipping at Sabang, Netherlands East Indies, the first joint offensive operations by the two nations in the Indian Ocean. Three vessels are sunk by aircraft from *Saratoga* and the British Royal Navy carrier *Illustrious*. In a message sent after the attack to the air group commander in *Saratoga*, the British fliers write, "We are very proud and pleased to have done it with you [and] your experienced chaps. It really has helped us to start our time out here."

20 April

The submarine *Seahorse* (SS 304) sinks the Japanese submarine *RO-45* off the Marianas.

An attack by German torpedo planes against convoy UGS 38 off Algeria sinks the destroyer *Lansdale* (DD 426), killing forty-seven members of her crew.

21 April

The submarine *Stingray* (SS 186) strikes an underwater pinnacle west of the Marianas and sinks.

22 April

With air support provided by the carriers of Task Force 58, Rear Admiral Daniel E. Barbey's Task Force 77 lands two Army divisions at the town of Aitape and at Tanahmerah Bay and Humboldt Bay, Hollandia, New Guinea.

26 April

Picking up a surface contact on radar off the Aleutian Islands, the destroyer escort *Gilmore* (DE 18) pursues what turns out to be the Japanese submarine *I-180*, which submerges. *Gilmore* launches a determined series of depth charge attacks that eventually sink the I-boat.

In the Atlantic north of the Canary Islands, four destroyer escorts—*Frost* (DE 144), *Huse* (DE 145), *Barber* (DE 161), and *Snowden* (DE 246)—sink the German submarine *U-488* with naval gunfire.

28 April

Secretary of the Navy Frank Knox dies in Washington, D.C. He is replaced by James V. Forrestal, who becomes the forty-eighth Secretary of the Navy on 19 May.

29 April–1 May

Task Force 58, under Vice Admiral Marc A. Mitscher, returns to the Caroline Islands, launching two days of strikes against Truk, which unfortunately is devoid of many shipping targets. However, a TBF Avenger from the light carrier *Monterey* (CVL 26) joins the destroyers *MacDonough* (DD 351) and *Stephen Potter* (DD 538) in sinking the Japanese submarine *I-174* with

Above: *Admiral Lord Louis Mountbatten talks with Captain John H. Cassady, commanding officer, and Commander Howard H. Caldwell, air officer, on board the carrier* Saratoga *(CV 3) at Colombo, Ceylon, in April 1944 shortly after* Saratoga *joined the British Eastern Fleet. (Naval Historical Center)*

Left: *Sailors launch a depth charge from a "Y" gun on a submarine chaser patrolling in the North Atlantic. (Corbis)*

Left: *During the island-hopping campaign across the Pacific, the Navy's construction battalions landed on the heels of the combat forces to begin work constructing airfields. The efforts of the Seabees had planes in the air often while enemy forces still fought, a testament to their skill and spirit. (National Museum of Naval Aviation)*

Below: *One of Admiral William F. Halsey's orders issued to the forces under his command during the war inspired this poster. (Naval Historical Center)*

depth charges. In addition, battleships, cruisers and destroyers, under the command of Rear Admiral Jesse B. Oldendorf and Vice Admiral Willis A. Lee, Jr., bombard Satawan Island and Ponape in the Carolines.

4 May
In a coordinated attack against a Japanese convoy in the Luzon Strait, Philippines, the submarines *Bang* (SS 385), *Parche* (SS 384), and *Tinosa* (SS 283) sink five freighters.

6 May
Pursuing the German submarine *U-66* west of the Cape Verde Islands, the destroyer escort *Buckley* (DE 51) evades enemy torpedoes and gunfire and rams the U-boat. After the destroyer escort backs off, the sub slams into her starboard side, opening a hole. There ensues a pitched battle at close quarters that ends when *U-66* sinks as a result of the damage she has sustained.

13 May
The destroyer escort *Francis M. Robinson* (DE 220) sinks the Japanese submarine *R-501* en route from Germany to Japan, south-southwest of the Azores.

15 May
PBY Catalinas of VP-63 join British ships in sinking the German submarine *U-731* off Tangiers.

16 May
The destroyers *Franks* (DD 554), *Haggard* (DD 555), and *Johnston* (DD 557) send the Japanese submarine *I-176* to the bottom north of the Solomon Islands.

17 May
The carrier *Saratoga* and the British flattop *Illustrious* attack the harbor at Surabaya, Java, in an operation that coincides with the landing of Army troops in the Wakde-Toem area of New Guinea by Task Force 77 under Rear Admiral William M. Fechteler.

Eight U.S. Navy destroyers join a British bomber in damaging the German submarine *U-616* off the coast of Algeria, forcing her crew to scuttle the U-boat.

19 May

Assisted by radio intelligence that pinpoints the operating area for Japanese submarines in the waters around New Ireland, the destroyer escort *England* (DE 635) sinks *I-16*, the first of six enemy subs that the ship sends to the bottom in one week. Subsequent sinkings are *RO-106* on 22 May, *RO-104* on 23 May, *RO-116* on 24 May, *R-108* on 26 May, and, with the assistance of other ships, *R-105* on 30 May.

The destroyers *Niblack* (DD 424) and *Ludlow* (DD 438) join British aircraft in sinking the German submarine *U-960* off Algeria.

27 May

Task Force 77, under Rear Admiral William M. Fechteler, lands Army troops on Biak in the Schouten Islands off New Guinea.

Right: *Stern view of the destroyer escort* England *(DE 635) as she steams off San Francisco, California, February 1944. Visible on deck are the racks for launching depth charges, which* England's *crew used with great effectiveness to sink six Japanese submarines in one week. (Naval Historical Center)*

29 May

The German submarine *U-549* slips through a screen of escorts and torpedoes the escort carrier *Block Island* (CVE 21), and sinks her, the only U.S. Navy aircraft carrier lost in the Atlantic theater. The destroyer escorts *Ahrens* (DE 575) and *Eugene E. Elmore* (DE 686) subsequently attack *U-549* and sink her.

31 May

The submarines *Barb* (SS 220) and *Herring* combine to sink all five ships of convoy NE off Matsuwa in the Kurile Islands, Japan. The next day, after *Herring* sinks the Japanese freighter *Hiburi Maru*, shore batteries sink the American submarine.

4 June

In the first capture of an enemy vessel on the high seas by a U.S. Navy warship since 1815, Task Group 22.3, a hunter-killer group that includes the escort carrier *Guadalcanal* and five destroyer escorts under the command of Captain Daniel V. Gallery, drive the German submarine *U-505* to the surface off Africa.

Subsequently, the destroyer escort *Pillsbury* puts a boarding party aboard the captured submarine. Lieutenant (junior grade) Albert L. David receives the Medal of Honor for leading the men to enter the sub despite the danger of scuttling charges exploding. *U-505* is kept afloat and eventually towed to Trinidad. She is now on display in the Museum of Science and Industry in Chicago, Illinois, the hometown of Daniel V. Gallery.

6 June

The U.S. Navy supports the launching of what General Dwight D. Eisenhower calls the "Great Crusade," the liberation of Europe. The naval aspect of the landings at Normandy, France, codenamed Operation Neptune, includes the American Western Task Force under the command of the Rear Admiral Alan G. Kirk, which provides gunfire support and lands Army troops at Omaha and Utah beaches. Off Omaha, destroyers close the beach, firing at point blank range, running the risk of grounding in an effort to support the troops ashore. "Thank God for the United States Navy," is the message sent by Major General Leonard Gerow when he arrives on shore to establish his V Corps headquarters. Off Utah, mines sink the destroyer *Corry* (DD 463) and destroy 18 landing craft, while 3 others are sunk by shore batteries. In addition, 114 landing craft are wrecked on the beaches. Largely unheralded, Navy demolition teams, Seabees, and naval beach battalions hit the beaches, suffering heavy casualties alongside their Army counterparts as they clear obstacles and direct the flow of landing craft unloading assault troops. For days, Navy ships continue the mission of transporting men and equipment ashore, and provide much-needed gunfire support to advancing troops. In addition, doctors and corpsmen provide critical medical care for casualties evacuated from the beaches. These efforts do

Opposite, top: *Senior officers view the Normandy landings from the cruiser* Augusta *(CA 31). Pictured from left to right are Rear Admiral Alan G. Kirk, Army Lieutenant General Omar N. Bradley, Rear Admiral Arthur D. Struble, and Major General Hugh Keen. (Naval Historical Center)*

Opposite, bottom: *Landing craft maneuver through geysers from near misses by enemy gunners ashore as they transport troops to Omaha Beach in Normandy on D-Day, 6 June 1944. With few tanks getting ashore, Navy destroyers like* Emmons *(DD 457) maneuvered close to the beach to provide welcome fire support. ("The Battle for Fox Green Beach," Dwight C. Shepler, Navy Art Collection)*

Right: *With the lives of the troops on board and the success of their mission at stake, a landing craft coxswain keeps one hand on the throttle and the other on the wheel as he braves enemy fire to take his boat ashore. ("Assault Wave Cox'n," Dwight C. Shepler, Navy Art Collection)*

not come without cost; during the period 6–25 June combat losses suffered by the U.S. Navy include 165 ships and craft lost, ranging from transports and destroyers to landing craft.

7 June

The construction of artificial harbors, necessary because of the lack of port facilities on the Normandy coast, begins with the sinking of blockships and concrete caissons.

The United States Naval Academy Class of 1945 is graduated a year early due to the national emergency. Sixteen members of the class are killed during the remaining months of World War II.

8 June

Task Forces 74 and 75, which include the U.S. light cruisers, *Boise* (CL 47) and *Phoenix* (CL 46), along with an Australian cruiser and fourteen Allied destroyers finish the work begun by Army Air Forces medium bombers and turn back a Japanese convoy carrying reinforcements bound for Biak, New Guinea.

A mine damages the destroyer *Glennon* (DD 620) off Normandy. As the destroyer escort *Rich* (DE 695) maneuvers close by to assist her, three mines detonate nearby in quick succession, one blowing off fifty feet of the destroyer escort's stern. *Rich* sinks with the loss of 27 killed, 73 wounded, and 62 missing.

Left: *Equipped with searchlight, bullhorn, and radios, and protected by sandbags, a Navy communication command post established on the beach in Normandy is ready to relay fire support requests to ships offshore, June 1944. (National Museum of Naval Aviation)*

Below: *The carrier Lexington (CV 16) as seen from the back seat of an SBD Dauntless dive bomber, which has just taken off to strike targets in the Mariana Islands, 13 June 1944. (Naval Historical Center)*

9 June

The submarine *Harder* (SS 257) completes four days of operations in the vicinity of the Japanese fleet anchorage at Tawi Tawi, Philippines, during which she sinks three enemy destroyers, survives a determined depth charge attack, and evacuates coastwatchers from the nearby island of Borneo. The boat's skipper, Commander Samuel D. Dealey, will receive a posthumous Medal of Honor for his actions during this time period.

The destroyer *Meredith* (DD 726) sinks off Normandy from damage incurred after striking an enemy mine off Utah Beach on 7 June.

10 June

The destroyer *Taylor* (DD 468) sinks the Japanese submarine *RO-111* north-northeast of Kavieng, New Ireland.

The destroyer escort *Bangust* (DE 739) sinks the Japanese submarine *RO-42* northeast of Kwajalein.

Off Normandy the destroyer *Glennon*, having already been damaged by a mine on 8 June, sinks after being hit by German artillery fire.

11 June

The battleship *Missouri* (BB 63) is commissioned, the last American battleship to enter active service.

11–12 June

Gunfire from U.S. Navy battleships operating off Normandy provide much-needed support to paratroopers of the 101st Airborne Division in their capture of Carentan.

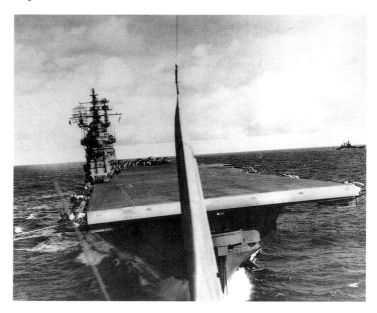

11–14 June

F6F Hellcats from Task Force 58 open four days of strikes preparatory to landings in the Mariana Islands, conducting a massive fighter sweep of enemy airfields that decimates Japanese air power. Subsequent missions strike installations ashore and attack two convoys near the islands, sinking nineteen ships.

13 June

The destroyer *Melvin* (DD 680) sinks the Japanese submarine *RO-36* in the waters east of Saipan.

13–15 June

On 13 June, battleships, cruisers, and destroyers of Task Group 58.7 under the command of Vice Admiral Willis A Lee, Jr., conduct a day-long bombardment of Saipan and Tinian preparatory to landings in the Mariana Islands. Task Groups 52.17 under Rear Admiral Jesse B. Oldendorf and 52.18 under Rear Admiral Walden L. Ainsworth begin their bombardment of Saipan and Tinian on 14 June and continue fire support during and after the landings the following day.

The submarine *Golet* (SS 361) sinks off Honshu, Japan, probably succumbing to attacks by Japanese ships and aircraft.

15 June

Task Force 52, under the command of Vice Admiral Richmond Kelly Turner, lands Marines on Saipan in the Mariana Islands. Naval gunfire and carrier aircraft support the leathernecks ashore, and flattops also launch strikes in the Bonin Islands and against Iwo Jima, Japan, through the next day to prevent Japanese air power there from interfering with the invasion. U.S. Navy ships suffer minor damage during the first day of the invasion.

TBF Avengers and FM Wildcats of VC-9 operating from the escort carrier *Solomons* (CVE 67) sink the German submarine *U-860* in the South Atlantic.

16 June

The destroyers *Melvin* and *Wadleigh* (DD 689) sink the Japanese submarine RO-114 off Tinian in the Marshall Islands, while the destroyer escort *Burden R.*

Right: *A New Mexico-class battleship, fires her guns in support of the landings on Saipan in the Mariana Islands, June 1944. A sister ship appears astern and the battleship* Pennsylvania *(BB 38) appears in the far background. Note that the middle gun in the #3 turret is in recoil position. The Mariana Islands represented the gateway to Japan's inner defensive circle and were a prized target. (Naval Historical Center)*

Left: *Landing craft and vehicles of all shapes and sizes pictured on a beach at Saipan in the Mariana Islands, June 1944. Not only did they put the first waves of assault troops ashore, but these vessels served as a vital link from ship to shore for the transfer of supplies and wounded. (National Museum of Naval Aviation)*

Hastings (DE 19) sends the Japanese submarine *RO-44* to the bottom off Eniwetok.

17 June
A PB4Y-1 Liberator of VB-109 sinks the Japanese submarine *RO-117* off Truk in the Caroline Islands.

19 June
A TBM Avenger of Torpedo Squadron (VT) 60 off the escort carrier *Suwanee* (CVE 27) sinks the Japanese submarine *I-184* in the waters off Guam.

19–20 June
In an effort to disrupt the landings at Saipan in the Mariana Islands, a Japanese carrier force consisting of nine flattops supported by five battleships and numerous cruisers and destroyers enters the Philippine Sea. Beginning what becomes known as the Battle of the Philippine Sea, the force launches a mass air strike against the ships of the Fifth Fleet, hoping the aircraft can land at airfields in the Marianas, where they can be refueled and rearmed for repeated attacks. The Japanese attackers, largely inexperienced pilots, run into a determined combat

Right: *An F6F-3 Hellcat flown by Lieutenant (junior grade) Ray Hawkins battles a Japanese Zero on the first day of the Battle of the Philippine Sea, 19 June 1944. His kill was one of nearly 300 enemy planes to fall in what became known as the "Great Marianas Turkey Shoot." (Robert L. Rasmussen)*

Right: *The Japanese carrier* Chiyoda *is hit aft and near-missed several times during air attacks by Task Force 58 planes during the Battle of the Philippine Sea, 20 June 1944. The aircraft launched at extended range to attack the Japanese fleet, returning to their carriers at night, desperately low on fuel. (Naval Historical Center)*

air patrol over the Fifth Fleet. In an engagement later called the Great Marianas Turkey Shoot, F6F Hellcats decimate the Japanese strike group, shooting down nearly 300 aircraft. Many pilots achieve multiple kills, with Commander David McCampbell, Commander Air Group 15 on board *Essex* (CV 9), splashing nine enemy aircraft. Meanwhile, the submarines *Albacore* (SS 218) and *Cavalla* (SS 244) sink the Japanese carriers *Taiho* and *Shokaku*. Fearing an attempt by Japanese surface forces to go around his ships and descend on the invasion force, Fifth Fleet commander Vice Admiral Raymond A. Spruance chooses to keep the carriers of Task Force 58 in the vicinity of Saipan on the evening of 19 June rather than allow them to pursue the Japanese fleet to the west. When Vice Admiral Marc A. Mitscher's flattops are released the following day, aerial scouts do not spot the enemy carriers until late in the afternoon, necessitating a strike launched at extreme range with pilots having to return after nightfall. In the ensuing mission carrier aircraft sink the Japanese carrier *Hiyo*, damage two oilers to such an extent that they are scuttled, and damage three carriers, a battleship, and four other ships. The strike aircraft are assisted in finding their way back to their carriers by Vice Admiral Mitscher's order to turn on the lights of Task Force 58's ships as a guide to the returning pilots.

21 June

The destroyer *Newcomb* (DD 586) and the high-speed minesweeper *Chandler* (DMS 9) sink the Japanese submarine *I-185* north of Saipan in the Marianas.

24 June

The submarine *Tang* (SS 306), attacking a Japanese convoy leaving the Koshiki Straits, Japan, sinks three cargo ships and a tanker.

A TBM Avenger of VC-69 off the escort carrier *Bogue* sinks the Japanese submarine *I-52* southwest of the Azores Islands.

25 June

Ships of Task Force 129 engage in a gun battle with German shore batteries at Cherbourg, France, with three destroyers and the battleship *Texas* (BB 35) suffering damage during the action. Straddled sixty-five times by enemy fire, the battleship is hit twice by shells, including one that strikes the fire control tower. German defenders at Cherbourg surrender the following day.

2 July

Task Force 77, under the command of Rear Admiral William M. Fechteler, puts Army troops ashore on Noemfoor Island, where they soon capture three airstrips that benefit subsequent operations in New Guinea.

A TBM Avenger of VC-58 off the escort carrier *Wake Island* (CVE 65) sinks the German submarine *U-543* in the waters southeast of the Azores Islands.

3 July

The destroyer escorts *Frost* and *Inch* (DE 146) sink the German submarine *U-154* in the Atlantic Ocean off Madeira.

FLEET ADMIRAL CHESTER W. NIMITZ

by John B. Lundstrom

On 31 December 1941, barely three weeks after the worst naval disaster in U.S. history, Admiral Chester W. Nimitz took command of a Pacific Fleet hard hit by the surprise Japanese carrier air attack on Pearl Harbor, Hawaii. President Franklin D. Roosevelt's only instructions were to "get the hell out to Pearl and stay there till the war is won." And Nimitz did just that. An 1905 Naval Academy graduate, pioneer submariner, and diesel propulsion expert, he broadened his career to cruisers and battleships, but made his reputation as an administrator. His gracious, cheerful personality and optimistic outlook seemed just the thing to restore sagging morale in Hawaii, though whether the new Commander in Chief of the Pacific Fleet (Cincpac) with his sunny disposition and piercing blue eyes was really a fighter, only time would tell. Nimitz wrote his wife on 28 December 1941: "I am not discouraged and will do my best—but everyone must be very, very patient."

Nimitz, though, received very little time and no patience. In short order Japan conquered Southeast Asia and the Philippines, rampaged into the Indian Ocean, and threatened Australia. Nimitz could only counter with pinprick carrier attacks, the most spectacular being the Doolittle Raid on Tokyo, Japan, in April 1942. Later that month, inspired by growing trust in his radio intelligence and confidence in his fleet, he boldly committed two carriers to stop an offensive against distant Port Moresby in eastern New Guinea. Thus in early May during the Battle of the Coral Sea, Japan suffered its first strategic check of the war. Then Nimitz learned from his codebreakers that the Combined Fleet had set its sights on tiny Midway Island, the gateway to Hawaii. Of all likely enemy moves, that posed the gravest threat to the Pacific Fleet. Nevertheless Nimitz had strong reasons for optimism that certainly warranted taking a "calculated risk" with his

few carriers and cruisers. To advance to Midway, Japan must expose its own precious carriers to several kinds of counterattack strongly abetted by the element of surprise. Their destruction would pay enormous dividends. Nimitz explained to Washington: "We are very actively preparing to greet our expected visitors with the kind of reception they deserve, and we will do the best we can with what we have." Indeed, the decisive victory of 4–6 June 1942 at Midway cost Japan four of its best carriers as well as the strategic initiative. The way was open for Allied counteroffensives in the Pacific.

Never again did Nimitz exercise such direct personal influence over the course of the war as from April to June 1942. Like World War I British Admiral Sir John Jellicoe, he literally could have lost the war in an afternoon. From then on Nimitz worked within the tight framework of policy and strategy formulated by the Joint Chiefs of Staff. Yet once a plan was proposed, he did not hesitate to offer his informed opinion. Like Midway, complete success in the bitter 1942–1943 Guadalcanal campaign provided another watershed of the Pacific War. Thereafter, enjoying increasing superiority in men and materiel, the Allies went irrevocably on the offensive all the way to Japan. On 2 September 1945, Fleet Admiral Nimitz was present for the unconditional surrender of Japan. No other single person did more to ensure the final Pacific victory. Serving two years as Chief of Naval Operations, Nimitz helped usher the Navy into the nuclear age.

History vindicated the brilliance of Roosevelt's choice of Chester Nimitz. Few other military leaders were as successful and as beloved. Not wedded to any particular faction in the Navy, Nimitz had approached his daunting task with an open mind and realized sooner even than the celebrated Japanese Admiral Isoroku Yamamoto that carriers had completely usurped the role of battleships as the

decisive instrument of naval warfare. Moreover, Nimitz displayed a surprising degree of aggressiveness in fighting despite heavy odds and great boldness in relying on radio intelligence. His congenial manners concealed a will of steel that he rarely needed to reveal except in times of extreme crisis, such as the spring of 1942, the Guadalcanal campaign, and, in 1945, at Okinawa.

After 1942, as the strength of the Pacific Fleet grew in geometric progression, Nimitz's managerial skills shone forth. His Pacific Ocean Area became the most efficient wartime organization of such size and complexity. It is fitting in so many ways that Chester W. Nimitz was the last officer of the United States Navy ever to wear the five-star insignia of Fleet Admiral.

Left: *Vice Admiral Marc A. Mitscher on board his flagship, the carrier* Lexington *(CV 16), June 1944. A less than stellar student at the Naval Academy, Mitscher overcame a rough beginning to his naval career and became a pioneer naval aviator after receiving his wings in 1916. The skipper of the carrier* Hornet *(CV 8) when she launched the Doolittle Raiders in April 1942, he eventually rose to flag rank. In command of the famed Task Force 58, he led the fast carriers in wide-ranging attacks that took them to the Japanese home islands. (Naval Historical Center)*

4 July

Attacks by carrier-based aircraft against the Volcano and Bonin Islands result in damage to installations and the sinking of ten vessels.

The destroyer *David W. Taylor* (DD 551) and the destroyer escort *Riddle* (DE 185) sink the Japanese submarine *I-10* off Saipan in the Mariana Islands.

The submarine *S-28* (SS 133) is lost with all hands during a training exercise off Oahu, Hawaii.

5 July

Off Nova Scotia, Canada, the destroyer escorts *Thomas* and *Baker* (DE 190) attack the German minelaying submarine *U-233*. A depth charge attack by *Baker* forces the submarine to the surface, after which *Thomas* sets a collision course and bears down on the submarine with all guns firing. She slices through *U-233*'s pressure hull about twenty feet aft of the submarine's conning tower, causing the U-boat to sink in less than a minute.

8 July

While moored at the Naval Advance Amphibious Base at Deptford, England, the tank landing ships *LST-312* and *LST-384* become the first naval vessels damaged by German V-1 missiles.

12–17 July

Submarines of Task Group 17.16, under Captain William V. O'Regan, attack Japanese shipping off Luzon, Philippines, sinking nine ships.

14 July

The destroyer escort *William C. Miller* (DE 259) joins the high-speed transport *Gimer* (APD 11) in sinking the Japanese submarine *I-6* off Tinian in the Mariana Islands.

17 July

During the loading of ammunition into the holds of the merchant vessels *Quinault Victory* and *E. A. Bryan* at the Port Chicago Naval Magazine in California, something triggers a series of explosions that ignites nearly 5,000 tons of munitions. *E. A. Bryan* is literally blown to pieces and the adjacent pier disintegrates. The force of the explosions causes damage in San Francisco forty-eight miles away. A total of 320 men working on the loading parties are killed instantly, 202 of them African-Americans. In the wake of the disaster, surviving black munitions loaders refuse to

Right: *Amphibious ships off Guam during the invasion of the island, July 1944. (Naval Historical Center)*

Below: *The German submarine* U-233 *sinks after being rammed by the destroyer escort* Thomas *(DE 102) in the North Atlantic, 5 July 1944. Note mine chutes on the submarine's foredeck, a feature of the type XB U-boat. (Naval Historical Center)*

obey orders directing them to perform the hazardous duty, and 258 of them face courts-martial. In January 1946 all of the men are given clemency and the opportunity to receive honorable discharges.

17–20 July
Underwater demolition teams, supported by destroyers and landing craft infantry (gunboats) successfully remove some 940 beach obstacles in preparation for landings on Guam in the Mariana Islands.

19 July
The destroyer escort *Wyman* (DE 38) sinks the Japanese submarine *RO-48* off Tinian in the Marianas.

21 July
Task Force 53, under Rear Admiral Richard L. Conolly, supported by naval gunfire and carrier aircraft, lands Marines and Army troops on Guam in the Mariana Islands.

24 July
Task Force 52, under Rear Admiral Harry W. Hill, puts Marines ashore on Tinian in the Mariana Islands with the support of naval gunfire and aircraft operating from Saipan and carriers offshore. Once captured, Tinian becomes an important base for the strategic bombing of Japan by Army Air Forces B-29 Superfortesses.

25–27 July
The carriers of Task Force 58 launch a series of air strikes against the Caroline Islands, hitting Yap, Ulithi, Fais, Ngulu, Sorol, and Palau.

26 July
Arriving at Pearl Harbor, Hawaii, on board the heavy cruiser *Baltimore* (CA 68), President Franklin D. Roosevelt begins a four-day conference with senior military advisor Admiral William D. Leahy and Admiral Chester W. Nimitz and General Douglas A.

MacArthur, the principal American commanders in the Pacific. The conference results in the decision to liberate the Philippines, a move opposed by many as detracting from the offensive toward the Japanese home islands.

28 July
The destroyer escorts *Wyman* and *Reynolds* (DE 42) sink the Japanese submarine *I-55* east of Tinian in the Mariana Islands.

30 July
Task Force 77, under Rear Admiral William M. Fechteler, puts Army troops ashore near Cape Opmari in northwest New Guinea and on the nearby islands of Amsterdam and Middleburg. On the following day Task Force 77 lands troops at Cape Sansapor, New Guinea.

31 July
A submarine group under Commander Lewis S. Parks attacks Japanese convoy MI 11 near Bashi Channel south of Formosa, sinking four ships and damaging three others. During the operation the submarine

Parche (SS 384) engages in a daring predawn surface attack against the convoy, torpedoing four ships. Despite the flames from the burning convoy ships illuminating *Parche* and drawing fire from the convoy's escorts, skipper Commander Lawson P. Ramage presses home the attacks and skillfully avoids an enemy ship about to ram him. For his heroism, Lawson receives the Medal of Honor.

2 August
The German submarine *U-804* sinks *Fiske* (DE 143) east of Newfoundland, Canada, the destroyer escort breaking in two after being hit amidships.

3 August
The Office of the General Counsel is established in the Navy Department.

4 August
Task Group 58.1, under Rear Admiral Joseph J. Clark, attacks Japanese convoy 4804 off the Bonin Islands. Naval gunfire and carrier aircraft sink eight Japanese vessels. The force attacks the Bonin Islands the following day along with Task Group 58.3 under Rear Admiral Alfred E. Montgomery.

13 August
The submarine *Flier* (SS 250) strikes a mine north of Borneo and is sunk.

15 August
Covered by naval gunfire and aircraft, including planes from escort carriers, Allied troops go ashore in southern France during Operation Dragoon. German mines, underwater obstructions, and artillery fire damage nineteen landing craft, but the operation, under Vice Admiral H. Kent Hewitt, overwhelms the light enemy defenses and successfully puts three

Opposite, top: *The deck of the battleship* New Mexico *(BB 40) is lined with 14-inch shells as she replenishes her ammunition stores prior to the next operation. (U.S. Naval Institute)*

Opposite, bottom: *President Franklin D. Roosevelt, General Douglas A. MacArthur, and Admiral Chester W. Nimitz during the president's visit to Hawaii, 26 July–10 August 1944. (Naval Historical Center)*

Right: *U.S. Army DUKWs (amphibious trucks) land on Alpha Red beach in Cavalaire Bay during the invasion of southern France, 6 June 1944. (U.S. Naval Institute)*

divisions ashore. Subsequently, Hewitt's Western Naval Task force provides naval gunfire support for forces inland, including Army Air Forces observation aircraft launching from tank landing ships to spot gunfire, and continues landing equipment and supplies. German air and surface attacks cause only minor damage to ships of the invasion force.

18 August

In an attack on the Japanese convoy HI 71 in the waters off Luzon, Philippines, the submarine *Rasher* (SS 269) sinks four ships and damages a fifth, and the submarine *Redfish* (SS 395) damages one vessel.

20 August

TBM Avengers and FM Wildcats of VC-42 from the escort carrier *Bogue* sink the German submarine *U-1229* in the North Atlantic.

21–24 August

U.S. submarines attack Japanese convoys off the Philippines, sinking eight ships. Among the attacking boats is *Harder* (SS 257) under the command of Commander Samuel D. Dealey, the most decorated submarine officer of World War II. On 24 August *Harder* is sunk by an enemy coast defense vessel off Luzon.

31 August–2 September

Carrier aircraft from flattops of Task Group 38.4, under Rear Admiral Ralph E. Davison, attack Iwo Jima and Chichi Jima, Japan. On 2 September a TBM Avenger of VT-51 from the light carrier *San Jacinto* (CVL 30) is shot down over Chichi Jima. The pilot, Lieutenant (junior grade) George H.W. Bush, successfully parachutes from his aircraft and is subsequently rescued by the submarine *Finback* (SS 230). Bush eventually becomes the forty-first President of the United States.

6–8 September

Task Force 38, under Vice Admiral Marc A. Mitscher, launches air strikes against the western Caroline Islands, with surface ships supplementing the aerial attacks with shore bombardment. The action includes the aircraft carrier *Independence* (CVL 22), the first flattop in the U.S. Navy specially equipped to carry out night operations.

9 September

Carrier planes of Task Force 38 strike port facilities and airfields at Mindanao, Philippines, and also sink seventeen vessels. The attacks continue the following day.

Left: *President Franklin D. Roosevelt and British Prime Minister Winston Churchill pose atop the Quebec Citadel with their principal military and naval advisors during the Second Quebec Conference in Canada, 11–16 September 1944. (Naval Historical Center)*

Opposite, top: *The high-speed minesweeper* Perry *(DMS 17) is abandoned after striking a mine off Angaur during the Palaus Operation, 13 September 1944. The destroyer minesweeper* Preble *(DM 20) is standing by. (Naval Historical Center)*

11–16 September

President Franklin D. Roosevelt and British Prime Minister Winston S. Churchill, along with the Combined Chiefs of Staff, meet at the Second Quebec Conference, with the discussions centering mainly on the British Royal Navy's role in the campaign against Japan. In addition, Admiral William F. Halsey, Jr.'s, suggestion to push the invasion of Leyte ahead, which is based in part on intelligence gathered from Filipino rescuers by a fighter pilot shot down off Leyte, is approved.

12 September

Aircraft launched from the carriers of Task Force 38 attack the Visayas, Philippines, causing heavy damage to airfields and sinking thirty-eight enemy vessels in surrounding waters. Over the following two days carriers attack Cebu, Negros, and Legaspi in the Philippines.

13 September

The high-speed minesweeper *Perry* (DMS 17) strikes a mine off Anguar in the Palau Islands and sinks.

15 September

Ships of the Third Amphibious Force, under Vice Admiral Theodore S. Wilkinson, land the First Marine Division (Reinforced) on the coral-strewn island of Peleliu in the Palau Islands. On this same day Task Force 77, under Rear Admiral Daniel E. Barbey, lands Army troops on the island of Morotai, on which

an airfield is constructed to support the forthcoming invasion of Leyte, Philippines.

16 September

Lieutenant Arthur M. Preston leads the motor torpedo boats *PT-489* and *PT-363* through sixty miles of heavily mined waters and, despite being repeatedly fired on by Japanese shore batteries, presses forward through an eleven-mile channel into Wasile Bay, Halmahera Island, East Indonesia. There, within 150 yards of enemy guns on shore, Preston's PTs pull downed fighter pilot Ensign Harold A. Thompson from the water. During their high-speed retirement the PTs sink a small cargo vessel. Under almost continuous fire for two and one-half hours, Preston and his men successfully execute a mission deemed "suicidal in its tremendous hazards." For heroism above and beyond the call of duty, Preston receives the Medal of Honor.

In an attack against a Japanese convoy southeast of Hong Kong, the submarine *Barb* (SS 220) sinks the 20,000-ton carrier *Unyo* and a tanker.

The submarine *Sea Devil* (SS 400) sinks the Japanese submarine *I-364* off Yokosuka, Japan.

17 September

Task Group 32.1, under Rear Admiral William H.P. "Spike" Blandy, lands Army troops on the island of

Angaur in the Palaus, where an airfield is established to support offensive operations in the Philippines.

21 September
Carrier planes from Task Force 38 strike enemy airfields and shipping in the vicinity of the Philippine capital of Manila and at Subic Bay. All told, twenty-eight enemy vessels are sent to the bottom in the protected waters of Manila and Subic bays and during an attack against a convoy off Luzon.

22 September
Carrier aircraft from Task Force 38 sink nine enemy ships in the waters off Cebu and San Fernando, Luzon in the Philippine Islands.

23 September
Task Group 33.19 lands Army troops on Ulithi in the Caroline Islands, an undefended atoll that becomes the forward base for the Pacific Fleet during the final campaigns of the war.

The battleship *West Virginia* (BB 48) rejoins the Pacific Fleet at Pearl Harbor, Hawaii, the last veteran of the 7 December 1941 attack to return to active service.

24 September
Carrier planes of Task Force 38 continue their aerial onslaught against Japanese shipping off the Philippines, sinking fifteen vessels.

25 September
While operating off Le Havre, France, the minelayer *Miantonomah* (CM 10) strikes an enemy mine and sinks in twenty minutes with the loss of fifty-eight crewmen.

Right: *Elements of the First Marine Division head for the beach, as their LCTs churn past the offshore line of LCI gunboats, at Peleliu, 15 September 1944. Note gunner saluting from the LCT in the foreground. Nearest is LCIG-452. An* Idaho-*class battleship is firing in the left distance. (Naval Historical Center)*

Left: *Navy Chaplain Rufus W. Oakley holds services within a few hundred yards of Japanese positions, well within range of their mortars if they had chosen to fire them, on Peleliu, September 1944. The comforting words of a chaplain are always welcome in the battle zone. (National Archives)*

Below: *A Japanese cargo ship under attack in Masbate Harbor, Philippine Islands, by planes from the carrier* Langley *(CVL 27), September 1944. (Naval Historical Center)*

27 September
On Bougainville in the Solomon Islands, Special Air Task Force 1 carries out its first operational missions employing TDR-1 drones controlled from specially modified TBM Avenger aircraft. Four of the primitive guided missiles are launched and two strike their target, a beached Japanese freighter that contains an enemy antiaircraft emplacement.

29 September
PB4Y-1 Liberators of VP-107 sink the German submarine *U-863* in the South Atlantic.

30 September
The destroyer escort *Fessenden* (DE 142) sinks the German submarine *U-1062* west of the Cape Verde Islands.

1 October
Vice Admiral Richard S. Edwards is named to the new posts of Deputy Commander in Chief, U.S. Fleet and Deputy Chief of Naval Operations.

3 October
While operating off Morotai, the destroyer escort *Shelton* (DE 407) is sunk by the Japanese submarine *RO-41*. The destroyer escort *Richard M. Rowell* (DE 403) pursues the submarine but, unmindful of the fact that U.S. submarines are operating in the vicinity, sinks *Seawolf* with the loss of all hands.

The destroyer escort *Samuel S. Miles* (DE 183) sinks the Japanese submarine *I-177* in the waters off Angaur in the Palau Islands.

10 October
Shifting its operations to the west, Task Force 38 launches air strikes against Okinawa, Japan, destroying Japanese military installations and sinking thirty vessels in the surrounding waters.

Right: *The light cruiser Houston (CL 81) under tow after being torpedoed off Formosa, October 1944. It took almost two weeks for her to reach Ulithi for makeshift repairs to enable her to return to the United States. She never fought again. (Naval Historical Center)*

12–15 October

Task Force 38 attacks the heavily defended island of Formosa (now Taiwan), bombing industrial targets and airfields and conducting fighter sweeps. Naval aviators also sink seventeen Japanese vessels in the waters around Formosa. Despite the heavy damage sustained on Formosa, the Japanese launch determined aerial counterattacks against Task Force 38 on 13 October, damaging the carrier *Franklin* (CV 13) and putting a torpedo into the side of the heavy cruiser *Canberra* (CA 70), which is taken under tow. On 14 October enemy aircraft damage the carrier *Hancock* (CV 19), light cruisers *Houston* (CL 81) and *Reno* (CL 96), and destroyer *Cassin Young* (DD 793). *Houston* is taken under tow. In an effort to draw the Japanese fleet into action in hopes of finishing off the damaged ships, Third Fleet commander Admiral William F. Halsey, Jr., directs two carrier task groups to withdraw to the east, from where they can launch air strikes against any attackers. Enemy surface units do not sortie, but torpedo planes again damage *Houston* on 15 October.

18–19 October

Task Force 38 launches air strikes against targets in the Philippines, hitting airfields around Manila and sinking eight ships in Manila Bay, and sending twelve enemy vessels to the bottom off Luzon. Seventh Fleet aircraft also attack Japanese shipping, sinking twelve ships off Cebu.

20 October

The Seventh Fleet, under Admiral Thomas C. Kinkaid, lands four Army divisions on Leyte, with carrier aircraft and fast battleships of the Third Fleet joining Seventh Fleet battlewagons and escort carriers in supporting the amphibious assault. During the day General Douglas MacArthur disembarks from a landing craft and once again sets foot in the Philippines, thus fulfilling his famous promise "I shall return." Japanese counterattacks against the ships supporting the landing are fierce, with enemy bombers damaging the escort carrier *Sangamon* (CVE 26), the light cruiser *Honolulu* (CL 48), and a salvage vessel. Fire from shore batteries damages a destroyer and a tank landing ship.

23 October

In the first stage of the Battle of Leyte Gulf, the largest naval battle in history, the submarine *Darter* (SS 227) detects a sizeable Japanese surface force heading toward Leyte, Philippines. *Darter* joins with *Dace* (SS 247) in sinking the heavy cruiser *Atago*, the flagship of Vice Admiral Takeo Kurita, and the heavy cruiser *Maya*. *Darter* also torpedoes the heavy cruiser *Takao*, damaging her to such an extent that she withdraws under the escort of two destroyers.

24 October

Carrier planes of Task Force 38 strike ships of a Japanese surface force under the command of Vice Admiral Takeo Kurita as they enter the Sibuyan Sea, Philippines. Japanese land-based aircraft launch from the Philippines against the task force's carriers, hitting the light carrier *Princeton*. As surface ships assist the stricken flattop, fires reach her after magazines, triggering a massive explosion that damages three destroyers and the light cruiser *Birmingham* (CL 62),

Left: *The light carrier* Princeton *(CVL 23) suffers another tremendous explosion soon after being hit by a Japanese air attack off the Philippines, 24 October 1944. She was the only Independence-class carrier lost during World War II. (Naval Historical Center)*

Below: *This ribbon-bedecked tunic belonged to Admiral Thomas C. Kinkaid, who commanded the Seventh Fleet during the latter part of World War II. (Alex Weyers)*

which loses 229 men killed, 4 missing, and 426 wounded. *Princeton* is later scuttled. The enemy air attacks do not deter American pilots from attacking Kurita's ships, which, devoid of air cover, suffer heavy damage. The battleship *Musashi*, hit by nineteen torpedoes and seventeen bombs, sinks and two other battleships, two heavy cruisers, and three destroyers are damaged, prompting Kurita to reverse course. In the meantime, carrier aircraft of Task Force 38 also attack another Japanese surface force under the command of Vice Admiral Shoji Nishimura as it approaches Leyte through the Sulu Sea, damaging two battleships and sinking a destroyer.

During the aerial action in the skies over Leyte, Commander David McCampbell, air group commander aboard the aircraft carrier *Essex*, along with one wingman attacks a formation of sixty Japanese aircraft heading for the ships of the Third Fleet. The pair breaks up the enemy formation, with McCampbell splashing nine of the attackers. For this action and his performance in the Battle of the Philippine Sea in June, McCampbell receives the Medal of Honor. He finishes the war as the U.S. Navy's leading fighter ace with thirty-four kills to his credit.

The day's actions mark the first attacks by kamikazes (Japanese suicide planes) that hit the freighters *Augustus Thomas* and *David Dudley Field* off Leyte.

U.S. submarines attack Japanese shipping in the South China Sea, sinking eight ships. However, depth

charges dropped from the escorting destroyer *Harukaze* sink the submarine *Shark* (SS 314). In other actions involving submarines, *Darter* runs aground on Bombay Shoal, Palawan Passage, in the Philippine Islands, and is scuttled by the submarine *Nautilus* to prevent her capture. Meanwhile, during operations in

the Formosa Strait, Commander Richard O'Kane leads his submarine *Tang* in a surface attack against a Japanese convoy, sinking two freighters before one of his submarine's own torpedoes makes a circular run and sinks the boat. Only nine crewmen, including O'Kane, survive the sinking of *Tang* and are taken prisoner. For his actions in command of the submarine, O'Kane receives the Medal of Honor.

The destroyer escort *Richard M. Rowell* sinks the Japanese submarine *I-54* east of Surigao Strait, Philippines.

25 October
The Battle of Leyte Gulf reaches its climax, with three distinct naval engagements occurring in the waters around the Philippines. Task Group 77.2, under the command of Rear Admiral Jesse B. Oldendorf, augmented by Task Group 77.3 and thirty-nine motor torpedo boats, attacks Vice Admiral Shoji Nishimura's surface force in the Battle of Surigao Strait. PT boats and destroyers open the battle by launching torpedoes against the Japanese, sinking four ships, including the battleship *Fuso*, and damaging three others, including the battleship *Yamashiro*. Following this onslaught, the Japanese surface force faces the guns of Oldendorf's ships, which include some repaired battleships damaged during the attack on Pearl Harbor, Hawaii, in 1941. The

U.S. Navy gunners pound their adversaries to such an extent that only one destroyer survives the engagement.

In one of the most controversial decisions of World War II, Third Fleet commander Admiral William F. Halsey, Jr.,—with reports of Japanese carriers operating to the north of the Philippines and believing his pilots have successfully turned back Admiral Takeo Kurita's surface force with their attacks the previous day— heads north with his fast carriers. Though the previous day he had issued a contingency plan for creating Task Force 34, consisting of some fast battleships, cruisers, and destroyers from his carrier screen, he does not execute an implementing order for the force to remain behind and cover the invasion force off Leyte. Thus, while Halsey's fliers strike the enemy carriers under the command of Vice Admiral Jisaburo Ozawa, sinking four of them (one with the assistance of naval gunfire), the only force guarding the northern approach to Leyte Gulf consists of escort carriers,

Above: *Commander David McCampbell and his wingman, Lieutenant (junior grade) Roy Rushing, prepare to battle a numerically superior Japanese formation on 24 October 1944 during the Battle of Leyte Gulf. The pair splashed fifteen enemy planes. ("High Side Attack over Leyte Gulf," Ted Wilbur, U.S. Naval Institute)*

destroyers, and destroyer escorts. They soon discover that Admiral Kurita's force has reversed course when the masts of his ships appear on the horizon heading toward them after passing through San Bernardino Strait. Unleashing their heavy guns, the Japanese ships wreak havoc on the thin-skinned escort carriers and the destroyers and destroyer escorts of their screens, sinking *Hoel* (DD 533), *Johnston* (DD 557), and *Samuel B. Roberts* (DE 413). Before they go down, *Johnston*, led by her wounded skipper Commander Ernest E. Evans, closes the enemy and damages a light cruiser and a heavy cruiser, while *Samuel B. Roberts* stages a daylight torpedo attack. Evans receives a posthumous Medal of Honor for his actions. Carrier aircraft, their pilots used to dropping ordnance in close air support missions, torment the Japanese ships, making dummy runs when their ammunition is depleted in an effort to ward off the attackers. Despite these efforts and the laying down of smoke screens, Japanese gunfire reaches the escort carriers, damaging *Fanshaw Bay* (CVE 70) and *Kalinin Bay* (CVE 68) and sinking *Gambier Bay* (CVE 73). Miraculously, despite being outgunned, the heroic men of Task Forces 2 and 3 force Admiral Kurita to retire. However, Japanese suicide planes continue to make life miserable for the escort carrier sailors, damaging *Suwanee*, *Santee*, *Kalinin Bay*, and *Kitkun Bay* (CVE 71) and sinking *St. Lo* (CVE 63).

Aircraft from escort carriers and Task Force 38 descend on the retiring Japanese surface forces, damaging the battleships *Nagato*, *Yamato*, and *Haruna*, damaging three heavy cruisers to such an extent that they are scuttled, and scoring hits on four other ships. U.S. Navy submarines claim a light cruiser and destroyer, and naval gunfire sinks a destroyer.

26 October
Carrier aircraft and land-based Army Air Forces bombers attack the retiring remnants of the Japanese fleet following the Battle of Leyte Gulf, sinking five ships. In addition, Task Group 34.5 sinks a destroyer off Panay.

28 October
The destroyers *Helm* (DD 388) and *Gridley* (DD 380), assisted by a TBF Avenger from the light carrier *Belleau Wood* (CVL 24), sink the Japanese submarine *I-46* in Philippine waters.

The Japanese submarine *I-45* torpedoes and sinks the destroyer escort *Eversole* (DE 404) off Leyte, Philippines, and is subsequently sunk by the destroyer escort *Whitehurst* (DE 634).

29–30 October
Task Force 38 carriers, while launching strikes against

Opposite: *Splashes from near misses straddle the escort carrier* Gambier Bay *(CVE 73) during the Battle of Leyte Gulf on 25 October 1944. The enemy gunners soon found their mark, and sent her to the bottom. ("USS* Gambier Bay," *U.S. Naval Institute)*

Right: *Ships of Carrier Division 25 under fire during the battle off Samar, 25 October 1944. Their determined resistance turned back a powerful Japanese surface force. (Naval Historical Center)*

the Philippines, endure repeated kamikaze attacks that damage *Intrepid*, *Franklin*, and *Belleau Wood*.

1 November
Kamikaze attacks in the waters off Leyte, Philippines, sink the destroyer *Abner Read* (DD 526) and combined

with conventional bombing attacks inflict damage on five other destroyers.

5–6 November
Task Force 38, under Vice Admiral John S. McCain, strikes airfields on Luzon, Philippines, and shipping in surrounding waters, sinking four vessels including the heavy cruiser *Nachi*.

7 November
The submarine *Albacore* (SS 213) strikes a mine north of Honshu, Japan, and sinks.

8 November
The submarine *Growler* (SS 215) is sunk off Mindoro in the Philippine Islands by Japanese surface ships.

10 November
While anchored in Seeadler Harbor, Manus, Admiralty Islands, the ammunition ship *Mount Hood* (AE 11) is

Left: *Commander Richard O'Kane was the most successful American submarine skipper of the war. As commanding officer of* Tang *(SS 305), he was credited with sinking twenty-four Japanese ships. His operations were cut short when a circular run by one of* Tang's *own toredoes sank the submarine in October 1944. O'Kane—along with the handful of shipmates who escaped—spent the rest of the war as prisoners of the Japanese. (U.S. Naval Institute)*

blown apart and all on board are killed when the 3,000 tons of munitions she is carrying explode. Thirty-six vessels in the vicinity, ranging in size from an escort carrier to a fuel oil barge, suffer damage.

With intelligence predicting the position of her target, the submarine *Flounder* (SS 251) sinks the German submarine *U-537* in the Java Sea.

11 November
Carrier planes from Task Force 38 attack a Japanese convoy as it enters Ormoc Bay on Leyte in the Philippines, sinking a total of nine ships.

12 November
The destroyer *Nicholas* (DD 449) sinks the Japanese submarine *I-37* south of Yap in the Caroline Islands.

13 November
The minesweeper *Ardent* (AM 340) and the frigate *Rockford* (PF 48) sink the Japanese submarine *I-12* between California and Hawaii.

13–14 November
Aircraft of Task Force 38 strike targets in and around Manila, Philippines, sinking a total of twenty-five enemy vessels.

17 November
TBM Avengers of VC-82 from the escort carrier *Anzio* (CVE 57) join the destroyer escort *Lawrence C. Taylor* (DE 415) in sinking the Japanese submarine *I-26* in the Philippine Sea. The squadron and destroyer escort team up again the following day to send *I-41* to the bottom.

17–18 November
In two days of attacks against Japanese convoy MI 27 in the East China Sea, U.S. submarines sink five enemy vessels.

19 November
The destroyer escorts *Conklin* (DE 439) and *McCoy Reynolds* (DE 440) sink the Japanese submarine *I-37* west of the Palau Islands.

21 November
The submarine *Sealion* (SS 315) attacks a Japanese task force off Formosa, sinking the battleship *Kongo* and the destroyer *Urakaze*.

25 November

While carrier planes from Task Force 38 strike enemy shipping off Luzon, Philippines, sinking eight enemy vessels, kamikazes inflict damage on the flattops, including *Essex*, *Intrepid*, and *Hancock*.

27–29 November

During three days of operations off Leyte, Philippines, one vessel and six ships are damaged by kamikaze aircraft.

28 November

The destroyers *Saufley Waller* (DD 466), *Pringle* (DD 477), and *Renshaw* (DD 499) sink the Japanese submarine *I-46* in the Leyte Gulf, Philippines.

29 November

The submarine *Archerfish* (SS 311) claims the biggest prize of the war, torpedoing the 64,000-ton Japanese carrier *Shinano* southwest of Tokyo Bay, Japan. The sinking marks the end of *Shinano's* maiden voyage.

2–3 December

The tin cans of Destroyer Division 120 enter Ormoc Bay on Leyte in the Philippines and engage in a night action with the enemy. *Cooper* (DD 695) sinks after being struck by a torpedo, but not before joining other ships in sinking the Japanese escort destroyer *Kuwa*. *Allen M. Sumner* (DD 692) and *Moale* (DD 693) are damaged in the engagement.

Opposite, top: *The light carrier* Belleau Wood *(CVL 24) afire astern after being hit by a kamikaze off the Philippines, 30 October 1944. Flight deck crews are moving undamaged TBM bombers away from the flames. In the background, another carrier is also afire after a kamikaze hit. (Naval Historical Center)*

Opposite, bottom: *Sailors cling to rope ladders as they reach out to pull survivors from ships sunk off Samar during the Battle of Leyte Gulf to safety, October 1944. (Naval Historical Center)*

Right: *Smoke rises above the ammunition ship* Mount Hood *(AE 11) after she explodes in Seeadler Harbor, Manus, Admiralty Islands, 10 November 1944. (Naval Historical Center)*

6–7 December

Two days of attacks by U.S. submarines against the Japanese convoy TAMA 34 in Philippine waters result in the sinking of four ships and the forced grounding of another.

7 December

Task Group 78.3 puts Army troops ashore at Ormoc Bay on Leyte in the Philippines, drawing the attention of kamikazes that damage the destroyers *Lamson* (DD 367) and *Mahan* (DD 364) and the high-speed transport *Ward* (APD 16). *Mahan* and *Ward* are damaged so heavily that they are scuttled.

11 December

While en route to resupply American forces at Ormoc Bay on Leyte, Philippines, a convoy is attacked by kamikazes, which sink the destroyer *Reid* (DD 369).

14 December

The rank of Fleet Admiral is established. The following day Admirals William D. Leahy, Ernest J. King, and Chester W. Nimitz receive their fifth stars.

15 December

Army troops land at Mindoro, Philippines, the men ashore and the ships of Task Group 78.3 under Rear Admiral Arthur D. Struble receiving air support from escort carriers. Kamikazes attack the invaders,

damaging two tank landing ships to such an extent that they are scuttled, and damaging the escort carrier *Marcus Island* (CVE 77), two destroyers, and a motor torpedo boat.

16 December

Task Force 38 aircraft sink the Japanese freighter *Oryoku Maru* in Subic Bay, Philippines, unaware that she is carrying more than 1,600 Allied prisoners of war en route to Japan.

18 December

A typhoon decimates the ships of the Third Fleet, under Admiral William F. Halsey, Jr., as they operate east of the Philippines. The destroyers *Hull*, *Monaghan* (DD 354), and *Spence* (DD 512) capsize with heavy loss of life, and twenty-one other ships suffer damage.

19 December

The submarine *Redfish* (SS 395) sinks the Japanese carrier *Unryu* southeast of Shanghai, China, but the resulting depth charge attacks by the flattop's escorts cause such damage that the submarine terminates her war patrol.

26 December

A Japanese surface force consisting of a heavy cruiser, a light cruiser, and destroyers under Rear Admiral Masanori, intent on disrupting the American landings at Mindoro, Philippines, encounters determined attacks from land-based aircraft and motor torpedo boats. Though the Japanese succeed in bombarding the Mindoro beachhead, they lose one destroyer sunk and five ships damaged.

The submarine *Swordfish* departs on her thirteenth and final war patrol. She never returns and is declared missing with the loss of all hands.

28–30 December
Attacks by kamikazes against a convoy steaming to support the assault on Mindoro result in the sinking of two freighters and damage to five other ships, including the destroyers *Pringle* and *Gansevoort* (DD 608). Another freighter sinks after being hit in a conventional bombing attack. *LST 750*, hit by a suicide plane and later by an aircraft torpedo, is scuttled.

1945

1 January
During the last year of World War II, Navy personnel strength reaches a wartime high of 3,405,525.

3–4 January
Aircraft from the carriers of Task Force 38, under Vice Admiral John S. McCain, strike airfields on Formosa and attack shipping off shore, sinking ten ships and damaging eight others.

3–8 January
U.S. Navy ships bound for Lingayen Gulf, Philippines, come under attack by kamikaze aircraft. The escort carrier *Ommaney Bay* (CVE 79) takes a hit that ignites fueled aircraft on the hangar deck, and is scuttled with the loss of ninety-five of her crew. The most intense day of attacks occurs on 6 January, when the battleships *California* (BB 44) and *New Mexico* (BB 40) and the heavy cruiser *Louisville* (CA 28) and light cruiser *Columbia* (CL 56) suffer damage. Among the five destroyers hit, *Walke* (DD 723) suffers the most damage as four suicide aircraft set their sights on her. The ship's antiaircraft gunners splash three of the attackers, but one enemy aircraft scores a direct hit on the bridge, which ignites in flames that seriously wound and burn its occupants, including skipper Commander George F. Davis. Despite his painful wounds he continues to conn the ship and direct her defenses until assured his command is safe. He dies

Above: *Fleet Admiral William D. Leahy, senior member of the Joint Chiefs of Staff and aide to President Roosevelt. (Naval Historical Center)*

Left: *A sky lookout searches for the enemy, 1944. (U.S. Naval Institute)*

8 January

The submarines of Task Group 17.21, under Commander Charles E. Loughlin, attack the Japanese convoy MOTA 30 off the coast of Formosa, sinking three ships and damaging three others.

9 January

Task Force 77, under Admiral Thomas C. Kinkaid, supported by naval gunfire and carrier aircraft, lands Army troops at Lingayen Gulf, Philippines. Kamikazes descend on the invasion force, hitting four ships, including the battleship *Mississippi* (BB 41). For days, suicide aircraft continue to plague the ships supporting the landings, which are also attacked by Japanese assault demolition boats.

hours later and receives the Medal of Honor posthumously. On 8 January suicide aircraft damage the escort carriers *Kitkun Bay* and *Kadashan Bay*, and the Australian heavy cruiser *Australia*. All told, twenty-nine ships are sunk or damaged by kamikazes, prompting the fast carriers of Task Force 38 to begin concentrated strikes against Japanese airfields in the Philippines on 6 January.

Above: *PBY Catalinas of the Seventh Fleet Air-Sea Rescue squadron arrive over Lingayen Gulf, Philippines, 10 January 1945. Note ships of the invasion force below. (Naval Historical Center)*

Below: *The escort carrier* Ommaney Bay *(CVE 79) burning after a kamikaze hit in the Sulu Sea off Luzon, Philippines, on 4 January 1945, during the Lingayen operation. A destroyer is standing by with fire hoses ready to assist the stricken flattop. (Naval Historical Center)*

6 January

The first contingent of WAVES arrives in Hawaii. Eventually 4,009 women serve there, the only post outside the continental United States to which women are permanently assigned during World War II.

12 January

Task Force 38, under Vice Admiral John S. McCain, strikes targets in French Indochina, a location where the admiral's grandson will fly combat missions twenty-two years later during another war. All told, thirty-one enemy vessels are sent to the bottom by the carrier planes. Over the course of the ensuing days Task Force 38 hits shipping and installations at Hong Kong and shipping off the coast of China.

13 January

The destroyer escort *Fleming* (DE 32) sinks the Japanese submarine *I-362* northeast of Truk in the Carolines.

16 January

Four destroyer escorts—*Otter* (DE 210), *Hubbard* (DE 211), *Hayter* (DE 212), and *Varian* (DE 798)—send the German submarine *U-248* to the bottom off the Azores Islands.

Below: *A WAVE ground crew services an F4U Corsair fighter at a Pacific naval base. Women expanded their roles in World War II to include most ratings and jobs. ("Grooming the Dogs of War," Howard Baer, Navy Art Collection)*

Left: *Pilots on board the carrier* Hornet *(CV 12) study the target area prior to strikes on Hong Kong in one of the carrier's ready rooms.* Hornet's *planes raided Hong Kong on 16 January 1945. Note the China-Burma-India (CBI) theater insignia on their flight suits, and the bone-handled revolver carried by man in center. Also note the recognition sheets for Japanese shipping at left. (Naval Historical Center)*

21–22 January

Task Force 38 strikes targets on Formosa and in the Ryukyus. Kamikazes attack the carriers, damaging *Ticonderoga* (CV 14) and the destroyer *Maddox* (DD 731). In addition, an aerial bomb scores a hit on the light aircraft carrier *Langley* (CVL 27). Carrier planes sink twenty-three ships in the two-day operation.

23 January

President Franklin D. Roosevelt boards the heavy cruiser *Quincy* (CA 71), which will carry him to Malta on the first leg of his trip to Yalta in the Crimea for conferences with British Prime Minister Winston S. Churchill and Soviet Premier Joseph Stalin.

The destroyer escorts *Conklin*, *Corbesier* (DE 438), and *Raby* (DE 698) sink the Japanese submarine *I-48* off Yap in the Caroline Islands.

30–31 January

Task Groups 78.3 (Rear Admiral Arthur D. Struble) and 78.2 (Rear Admiral William M. Fechteler) land Army troops in Subic Bay and Manila Bay, Philippines, in an effort to outflank the Japanese forces defending the Philippine capital.

1 February

The destroyers *Jenkins* (DD 447), *O'Bannon* (DD 450), and *Bell* (DD 587) join the destroyer escort *Ulvert M. Moore* (DE 442) in sinking the Japanese submarine *RO-115* southwest of Manila, Philippines.

4–11 February

The Yalta Conference, the last of the meetings with British Prime Minister Winston S. Churchill and Soviet Premier Joseph Stalin attended by President Franklin D. Roosevelt, discusses the timing of the entry of the U.S.S.R. into the war against Japan. In

Right: *SB2C-1C Helldivers, the white bars on their tails indicating their assignment to the carrier* Yorktown *(CV 10), in flight. Popularly known as the "Beast," pilots and mechanics alike swore that SB2C stood for "Son-of-a-Bitch Second Class."* (Naval Historical Center)

Below: *The carrier* Essex *(CV 9) receives supplies, 27 April 1945. The ability to replenish ships at sea enabled the Pacific Fleet to maintain constant pressure on the Japanese.* (Naval Historical Center)

addition, the conference focuses on postwar issues, including the division of Germany, the future of Poland, and the Soviet influence in Europe, that greatly impact East-West relations.

4 February
Japanese aircraft sink the submarine *Barbel* (SS 316) in the South China Sea. There are no survivors.

7 February
The destroyer escort *Thomason* (DE 203) sinks the Japanese submarine *RO-55* off Luzon, Philippines.

13 February
The submarine *Batfish* (SS 310) sinks the Japanese submarine *RO-113* off the Babuyan Islands, Philippines.

14 February
During minesweeping operations off Corregidor in the Philippines, gunfire from Japanese shore batteries sinks the motor minesweeper *YMS-48* and damages escorting destroyers *Hopewell* (DD 681) and *Fletcher* (DD 445). Hot shell fragments penetrate one of *Fletcher*'s magazines and ignite some powder charges. Watertender First Class Elmer C. Bigelow enters the space and extinguishes the flame before it can detonate the entire magazine. He succumbs to smoke inhalation the following day and is posthumously awarded the Medal of Honor.

15 February
Task Group 78.3, under Rear Admiral Arthur D. Struble, lands Army troops near Mariveles Harbor, Bataan, Luzon in the Philippines. The following day

Army forces go ashore on Corregidor and, between 16 and 28 February, a support force of six destroyers under Captain Robert W. Cavenaugh provides accurate fire support for the troops on Corregidor.

16–17 February
Task Force 58, under Vice Admiral Marc A. Mitscher, strikes Tokyo, Japan, marking the first time that carrier aircraft attack the home islands. The strikes prove successful, with the destruction of numerous shore installations and port facilities.

17 February

Underwater demolition teams (UDT) reconnoiter the landing beaches at Iwo Jima, Japan, under enemy fire. One supporting landing craft infantry (gunboat) is sunk by shore battery fire and eleven are damaged, including *LCI(G)-449* under the command of Lieutenant Rufus G. Herring. Although he is badly wounded, Herring personally maintains the position of his craft close to shore in support of the UDT operations. For his heroism, he receives the Medal of Honor.

Boatswain's Mate Second Class Owen F.P. Hammerberg, while participating in underwater salvage operations on a tank landing ship sunk in Pearl Harbor, Hawaii, by an ammunition explosion on 21 May 1944, rescues two fellow divers trapped in the wreckage. However, he is injured during the rescue and dies. For his heroism the Navy diver is awarded the Medal of Honor posthumously.

19 February

Supported by naval gunfire and aircraft, the Fourth and Fifth Marine Divisions under Lieutenant General Holland M. Smith land on Iwo Jima, Japan, marking the beginning of one of the bloodiest battles in the Pacific war. Japanese shore batteries and mortar fire damage a destroyer and four medium landing ships.

21 February

Kamikazes attack the invasion fleet assembled off Iwo Jima, Japan. Two suicide planes hit the escort carrier *Bismarck Sea* (CVE 95), starting

uncontrollable fires and triggering the explosion of ammunition. She sinks in ninety minutes with the loss of 318 members of her crew. The aircraft carrier *Saratoga* is hit by five kamikazes and also by an aerial bomb, wrecking the forward part of her flight deck and starting fires in the hangar deck. She is forced to return to the United States for repairs, ending her combat service. Suicide planes also damage the escort carrier *Lunga Point* (CVE 94), the net cargo ship *Keokuk* (AKN 4), and the tank landing ships *LST-477* and *LST-809*. An aerial bomb damages the light aircraft carrier *Langley*.

23 February

Marines raise a small flag, obtained from the attack transport *Missoula* (APA 211), atop Mount Suribachi on

Above: *The submarine* Balao *(SS 285) returns to port after a war patrol, early 1945. The Japanese flag flying from her conning tower is testament to her success. (Naval Historical Center)*

Left: *Tracked landing vehciles (LVTs) circle a battleship during the bombardment of Iwo Jima just before the landing, 19 February 1945. Note the 40mm quad-mount gun in foreground. (Naval Historical Center)*

Iwo Jima, Japan. Later in the day the decision is made to raise a larger flag, an eight-foot ensign from the tank landing ship *LST-779*, atop the mountain. As they struggle to raise this second flag, five Marines and one Navy corpsman, Pharmacist's Mate Second Class John H. Bradley, are captured on film by Associated Press photographer Joe Rosenthal in perhaps the most famous photograph of the twentieth century.

25 February
Task Force 58 returns to the waters around the Japanese home islands, launching strikes against factories and airfields before the onset of bad weather in the afternoon forces the cancellation of the operation.

26 February
TBM Avengers of VC-82 from the escort carrier *Anzio*, in concert with the flattop's escorts, sink the Japanese submarines *I-368* and *RO-43* off Iwo Jima, Japan. Meanwhile, the destroyer escort *Finnegan* (DE 307) sends the Japanese submarine *I-370* to the bottom south of Iwo Jima, Japan.

27 February
A PB4Y-1 Liberator of Patrol Bombing Squadron (VPB) 112 teams with British ships in sinking the German submarine *U-327* in the English Channel.

28 February
Task Group 78.2, under Rear Admiral William M. Fechteler, with gunfire support from Task Group 74.2 under Rear Admiral Ralph S. Riggs, lands Army troops on Puerto Princesa, Palawan Island in the Philippines.

During the fighting on Iwo Jima, Japan, Pharmacist's Mate First Class John H. Willis, having sneaked back to the front lines after being wounded earlier, rushes to treat a wounded Marine in a shell hole while his platoon fights off a Japanese counterattack. While Willis administers aid, nine Japanese hand grenades are lobbed into the shell hole. The corpsman throws eight of them out, but the ninth one explodes in his hand, killing him. His actions inspire the men of his platoon to press forward. Willis is awarded the Medal of Honor posthumously.

1 March
Task Force 58, under Vice Admiral Marc A. Mitscher, strikes Japanese airfields and installations on Okinawa, Japan, and sinks fifteen vessels in surrounding waters.

3 March
On Iwo Jima, Japan, Pharmacist's Mate Third Class Jack Williams, despite being wounded and in a partial state of shock, rushes to the side of a wounded Marine, shielding the fallen leatherneck with his own body as he administers aid. He then treats another wounded Marine. While making his way to the rear to have his own wounds treated, Williams is shot and killed. He is posthumously awarded the Medal of Honor.

During fighting on Iwo Jima, Japan, Pharmacist's Mate Second Class George E. Whalen, having previously been wounded aiding fallen Marines under enemy fire, is hit again while treating casualties. Unable to walk, he crawls fifty yards to render medical attention to another leatherneck. For his actions on this and previous days, Whalen receives the Medal of Honor.

Above: *Pharmacist's Mate First Class John Harlan Willis was awarded the Medal of Honor for heroism during the battle for Iwo Jima, 28 February 1945. The destroyer escort* John Willis *(DE 1027) was named in his honor. (Naval Historical Center)*

NAVY MEDICINE IN PEACE AND WAR

by Jan K. Herman

Since the Continental Congress first authorized the hiring of surgeons and surgeons' mates in 1775, Navy medicine has distinguished itself in peace and war supporting both the Navy and Marine Corps.

Medicine in the square-rigged Navy was a frightening experience for patients and doctors. Never mind what damage cannonballs, musket fire, and cutlasses could inflict. War wounds were insignificant compared to the ills caused by a seagoing diet of salt meat and weevily biscuits, which included deficiency diseases, with scurvy topping the list. Poor ventilation, a lack of hygiene, and injuries resulting from floggings and accidents gave Navy medicine's earliest practitioners enough business to keep them occupied.

As the Navy entered the ironclad era during the Civil War, and then made the transition to steel and steam, new hazards arose—horrific scald injuries caused by ruptured steam pipes and boilers, and penetrating shrapnel wounds resulting from large-caliber, breech-loading naval guns. Navy medicine also concerned itself with new environmental and occupational concerns in the form of inadequate ventilation and hell-hot engine rooms that were commonplace in the steel navy. The turn of the twentieth century also marked the rise of the United States as a world power, her reach extending into the vast Pacific and Caribbean. Sailors on far-flung cruises were exposed to tropical diseases Navy medical personnel had never seen—dengue, yaws, leishmaniasis, leprosy, yellow fever, filariasis, and malaria among them, in addition to the ubiquitous venereal maladies sailors acquired in exotic liberty ports.

When the United States entered World War I, and the Marines deployed to France, physicians, dentists, hospital corpsmen, and nurses went with them. What they encountered were the frightful realities of trench warfare and the terrifying results of poison gas, not to mention conventional war trauma. They confronted the horrors of war with a devotion to saving lives, and of the twenty-eight Medals of Honor awarded to naval personnel during the Great War, six went to corpsmen and doctors. Since the combatants extensively used airplanes and submarines, the birth of aviation medicine and undersea medicine should have come as no surprise. The new technologies kept Navy medical personnel busy between the wars learning how to protect the human body while in flight and beneath the sea.

As the attack on Pearl Harbor, Hawaii, galvanized an unprepared nation into action, so too did Navy medicine respond to yet another world war. In 1941, the Navy had approximately 13,500 physicians, dentists, nurses, hospital corps officers, and corpsmen. By 1945, the ranks had swollen to about 169,000 personnel, a staggering growth of 1,252 percent! These men and

Opposite: *This "Tiffany Cross" Medal of Honor, created to award combat heroism, was awarded posthumously to Lieutenant (j.g.) Weedon E. Osborne, DC, for action in France, 6 June 1918. (Alex Weyers)*

Right: *Using the fallen leatherneck's rifle to hold a plasma bag, a Navy corpsman provides medical attention to a wounded Marine on an embattled beach during the invasion of Tarawa in the Gilbert Islands. The quick work of corpsmen under fire has earned the respect of the Marines they serve. ("Aid Station," Kerr Eby, Navy Art Collection)*

women supported the fleet and Marine Corps in all theaters, but most prominently in the Pacific, where corpsmen saved lives on such hallowed battlefields as Guadalcanal, Iwo Jima, and Okinawa, and shipboard medical personnel confronted the mass casualties that were a part of modern combat, particularly with the introduction of the kamikazes.

In the battles of the Cold War, Navy medicine was always ready. When North Korean forces poured across the 38th Parallel in 1950, medical personnel supported the Navy and Marines on board three hospital ships on station. For the first time, helicopters brought the wounded to hospital ships and other medical facilities shortly after they had incurred their injuries, ones that would have resulted in death in previous wars. The war in Vietnam saw further refinement of air evacuation and surgical techniques, especially aboard two hospital ships where surgical teams performed definitive surgery on patients rushed there by helicopter. The Gulf War presented the opportunity to deploy two new hospital ships and several fleet hospitals—prefabricated facilities erected, equipped, and manned in Saudi Arabia. Navy medicine also prepared to confront another challenge, the threat of biological and chemical warfare.

If Navy medicine's primary duty is to keep sailors and Marines healthy and ready for war, Navy medical personnel have continued to support "missions other than war." Navy medical researchers have made a

significant impact on medicine. In the mid-nineteenth century a young Navy surgeon, Edward R. Squibb, pioneered the manufacture of pure drugs. In 1934 the first experimental tetanus trials took place in the hospital ship *Relief*, where a Navy physician determined the proper interval between injections and the number of injections required for successful immunization, conquering the scourge of lockjaw. And too, it was another Navy physician, Captain Robert Phillips, who developed a simple oral therapy that is now the standard treatment for cholera throughout the world. Navy medical personnel have had a significant impact on deep sea diving as well by helping to develop data used by divers to work more safely and prevent serious injury and death from the bends.

The race for space saw Navy medical participation in Projects Mercury, Gemini, Apollo, and the Space Shuttle program. In 1973 a Navy flight surgeon became the first American physician in space. Other Navy physician-astronauts have flown Space Shuttle missions (including the tragic final flight of *Columbia* in 2003), served as crewmembers aboard the Russian space station *Mir*, and are helping to build the International Space Station. As the United States fights the international war against terrorism, Navy medicine continues to support the Navy and Marine Corps mission anywhere in the world.

Left: *An R5D Skymaster assigned to the Naval Air Transportation Service (NATS) unloads its cargo at an unidentified location. Established during the war, NATS transported people and supplies from the U.S. to the Pacific and Europe. (National Museum of Naval Aviation)*

Below: *As the fleet moved closer to Japan and the kamikaze threat increased, the chance for rest became even more rare, and sailors like this one on board the battleship* New Jersey *(BB 62) had to sleep whenever and wherever they could. (National Archives)*

6 March

Navy nurse Ensign Jane Kendeigh arrives at Iwo Jima, Japan, and the plane on which she is flying comes under mortar fire as it lands. She is the first Navy flight nurse to serve in a combat zone.

8 March

Phyllis Daley becomes the first African-American woman commissioned as an ensign in the Navy Nurse Corps.

10 March

Task Group 78.1, under Rear Admiral Forrest B. Royal, lands Army troops on Mindanao, Philippines. Though four landing craft are sunk by Japanese shore batteries, the troops meet little resistance on shore.

The submarine *Kete* (SS 369) sinks a Japanese transport and two army cargo ships in the waters off Okinawa, Japan. Following this action no word is received from the boat, and she is declared lost at sea.

11 March

Though normally used in the surf of an ocean shore, U.S. Navy landing craft are hauled on trucks from the Atlantic to the Rhine River, where sailors ferry Army troops across the river and assist in building a pontoon bridge at Remagen, Germany. On 17 March the landing craft ferry 2,500 soldiers across the Rhine.

A PB4Y-1 Liberator of VPB-103 sinks the German submarine *U-681* off the Isles of Scilly.

In a most unlikely long-range attack, land-based bombers fly from Japan to the U.S. Navy fleet anchorage at Ulithi in the Caroline Islands. One Japanese aircraft crashes into the anchored aircraft carrier *Randolph* (CV 15), killing 25 members of the crew and wounding 106.

15 March

An accident involving improper operation of the torpedo tube doors on board the submarine *Lancetfish* (SS 296) results in the sinking of the boat at the Boston Navy Yard, Massachusetts.

15–16 March

In the last days of fighting on Iwo Jima, Japan, on 15 March, Pharmacist's Mate Second Class Francis J. Pierce is leading a stretcher party to an aid station when it is taken under fire, wounding members of the party. After treating the wounded, Pierce draws his pistol and covers his comrades as they dash to safety, killing one enemy soldier. He then twice carries wounded Marines 200 yards to safety under enemy fire. The following day, Pierce is wounded while directing the treatment of a wounded leatherneck from a platoon patrolling the forward lines. Refusing treatment, he draws his pistol and fires it so that enemy guns concentrate on his position while the wounded man is carried to safety. For his actions Pierce receives the Medal of Honor.

18 March

The destroyer escorts *Menges* (DE 320), *Mosley* (DE 321), *Pride* (DE 323), and *Lowe* (DE 325) sink the German submarine *U-866* in the waters off Nova Scotia, Canada.

18–19 March

Task Force 58, under Vice Admiral Marc A. Mitscher, strikes targets on the Japanese home islands of Kyushu and Honshu, devastating airfields and inflicting great damage on shipping, including hits on the battleships , *Haruna, Hyuga,* and *Yamato* and carriers *Amagi, Hosho, Ikoma, Kaiyo, Katsuragi,* and *Ryuho.* Kamikazes exact revenge, scoring a hit on the aircraft carrier *Intrepid.* Conventional bombing attacks damage the venerable carrier *Enterprise,* along with *Yorktown* and *Wasp.* However, the worst damage is inflicted on *Franklin* on 19 March, with two bombs triggering a series of explosions that turn her flight and hangar decks into a blazing inferno. In the bowels of the ship, Lieutenant (junior grade) Donald A. Gary leads a group of shipmates trapped below through dark passageways to safety, and

Right: *With the Remagen railroad bridge collapsed into the Rhine River, Navy landing craft were transported overland to Germany to ferry Army troops across strategic waterways. Here an LCVP landing craft carries a Jeep upstream. (U.S. Naval Institute)*

AFRICAN AMERICANS IN THE NAVY

by Bernard C. Nalty

When Japanese aircraft attacked Pearl Harbor, Hawaii, on 7 December 1941, a sailor on board the battleship *West Virginia* (BB 48), Doris Miller, helped carry his fatally wounded captain from the bridge. Miller then manned a machine gun, even though he was trained as a steward to wait on the ship's officers. Miller's heroism earned him the Navy Cross, as he became another link in a chain of tradition forged over the years by African-American sailors.

Black sailors helped man the warships of Britain's North American colonies and fought for American independence. The United States Navy, when established in 1798, ignored their contributions and attempted to ban African-Americans, both slaves and freemen. However, the need for sailors to fight a two-year undeclared naval war against France and the War of 1812 against Britain compelled the Navy to accept free blacks. Soon, however, political pressure from the

slave-holding states forced the Navy to specify that only five percent of recruits could be men of color. The willingness of African-Americans to reenlist, and a scarcity of white volunteers, increased the proportion of black sailors well beyond five percent. During the Civil War, the Union Navy continued to recruit blacks, especially escaped or liberated slaves, to man gunboats on the Mississippi River.

Although the Navy refused to commission blacks, their numbers in the enlisted force hovered around ten percent by the 1880s, with blacks and whites messing and berthing together. Racial segregation returned in the mid-1890s after the Navy completed its transition from sail to steam. The new warships required new abilities; sailors now had to be capable of handling steam and electricity rather than furling or spreading canvas aloft. African-Americans, often deprived of even a basic education, tended to lack the skills the new Navy demanded. Thus, to man its new warships, the Navy relied on whites who, as racial segregation gripped American society, proved increasingly unwilling to serve alongside blacks. The Navy therefore concentrated its black sailors in easily segregated specialties like messman or coal passer.

A racially segregated Navy fought World War I and afterward channeled its few black recruits into the Messmen Branch. The demands of World War II, however, forced the services to rely on the Selective Service System to promote the efficient use of manpower. Instead of adopting its own arbitrary quota, in February 1943 the Navy began to accept a designated share of the African-Americans drafted for military service. At first, it tried to employ them in an expanded Messmen Branch, but when the number proved too great, the Navy began assigning them to construction battalions and other racially segregated labor units. Even so, black manpower was being wasted, since men were assigned solely because of race, rather than by matching their skills to the needs of the Navy. After experimenting with ships manned by black crews—and commissioning its first black officers—the service began assigning black sailors to the crews of

Opposite: *Only a generation removed from a time when African-American sailors were restricted to duty as stewards, Seaman Daniel J. Lewis scans the horizon as he stands a watch on the bridge of the ballistic missile submarine* John Adams *(SSBN 625) during the 1960s. (Naval Historical Center)*

Right: *Mess Attendant Second Class Doris Miller proudly displays the Navy Cross presented to him by Admiral Chester W. Nimitz for his actions on board the battleship* West Virginia *(BB 48) during the Japanese attack on Pearl Harbor, Hawaii. He lost his life on board the escort carrier* Liscome Bay *(CVE 56) when she was torpedoed off the Gilbert Islands on 24 November 1943. (Naval Historical Center)*

fleet auxiliaries, though the number of African-Americans could not exceed ten percent of any crew.

After Japan surrendered, the Navy contracted to peacetime size and could not maintain even this degree of racial integration. Too many blacks, both officers and sailors, left the Navy, and those who remained tended to be enlisted stewards. The reserve officers who left active duty included Samuel L. Gravely, Jr., who would return, join an increasing number of blacks holding regular commissions, and in 1971 become the first black to be promoted to rear admiral. When in July 1948 President Harry S. Truman directed the armed forces to provide equal treatment and opportunity regardless of race, the Navy had very few blacks serving as officers or in enlisted specialties other than the Messmen Branch. The President's goal of racial integration seemed distant at best.

The Navy succeeded, however, in attracting African-Americans to reserve officer training programs and to the Naval Academy, where Wesley A. Brown became the first black graduate in 1949. It also encouraged newly enlisted blacks to train for specialties outside the Messmen Branch. Gradually, the officer corps and the enlisted force came to reflect more closely the racial composition of American society. Emphasis then shifted from mere numbers to the more difficult tasks of eliminating the remaining effects of segregation, incorporating blacks into a smoothly functioning Navy and making full use of their talents and training. Despite instances of racial friction during the Vietnam War, including violent unrest aboard ships, the Navy hewed to this course and achieved genuinely equal treatment and opportunity.

Roman Catholic chaplain, Commander Joseph T. O'Callahan, ChC, brings an air of calm to the wounded and dying and also mans hoses to fight fires and lends a hand throwing ammunition over the side. Both Gary and O'Callahan receive the Medal of Honor.

23 March
Navy landing craft of Task Unit 122.5.1 ferry over 4,000 men of General George S. Patton's Third Army across the Rhine River, continuing the operation on 24 and 26–27 March, the latter crossings occurring under heavy enemy fire.

Task Force 58 begins launching air strikes against Okinawa, Japan, in preparation for the 1 April assault on the island, while Task Force 54, under Rear Admiral Morton L. Deyo, begins bombarding Okinawa from the sea on 25 March.

The destroyer *Haggard* spots the Japanese submarine *I-371* on the surface in the Philippine Sea and rams her, sinking the sub.

later takes charge of firefighting parties in combating the flames on the hangar deck. He also helps raise steam in one of the boilers in an effort to get the crippled flattop underway. Meanwhile, on the flight deck the carrier's

26 March
Off Okinawa, Japan, kamikazes damage the battleship *Nevada* (BB 36), the light cruiser *Biloxi* (CL 80), three destroyers, two auxiliaries, and two transports.

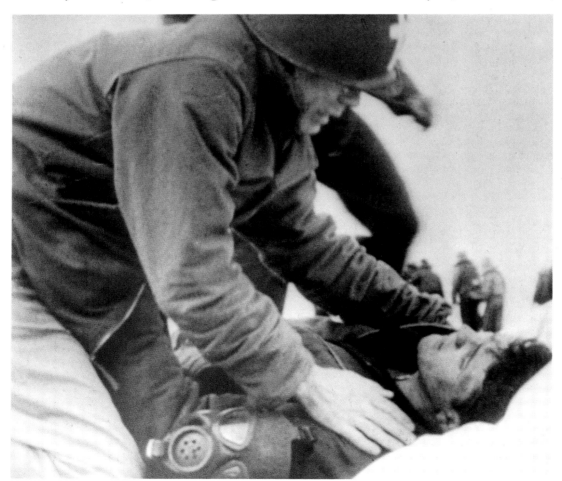

Above: *Planes from the carrier* Essex *(CV 9) attack two Japanese aircraft carriers at Kure, Japan, 19 March 1945. The ship at bottom is either* Katsuragi *or* Amagi. *The other carrier is* Kaiyo. *Note the SB2C Helldiver at right with* Essex *markings. (Naval Historical Center)*

Left: *Chaplain Commander Joseph T. O'Callahan ministers to an injured man aboard the carrier* Franklin *(CV 13) after she was hit by enemy bombs on 19 March 1945. (Naval Historical Center)*

Right: *The medium rocket landing ships LSMR-196, LSMR-198, and LSMR-199 unleash waves of rockets on Pokishi Shima, near Okinawa, Japan, five days before the landing there in March 1945. Each landing in the Pacific brought tough lessons, among them the fact that there was no such thing as too much fire support for troops going ashore. (Naval Historical Center)*

Task Group 51.1, under Rear Admiral Ingolf N. Kiland, lands Army troops on Kerama Retto, Ryukyus, while further south Task Group 78.2, under Captain Albert T. Sprague, Jr., puts Army troops ashore on Talisay Point, Cebu, Philippine Islands.

29 March
Two carrier task groups of Task Force 58 strike targets in the Kagoshima Bay area off Kyushu, Japan, sinking twelve enemy vessels.

31 March
The destroyers *Morrison* (DD 560) and *Stockton* (DD 646) combine to sink the Japanese submarine *I-8* off Okinawa, Japan.

Off Okinawa, Japan, the heavy cruiser *Indianapolis* (CA 35), flagship of Fifth Fleet commander Admiral Raymond A. Spruance, is damaged by a kamikaze, necessitating her return to the United States for repairs. The admiral shifts his flag to the battleship *New Mexico*.

1 April
Easter Sunday brings the assault on Okinawa, Japan, with naval gunfire and aircraft supporting the landing of Army troops and Marines under the command of Army Lieutenant General Simon Bolivar Buckner. By nightfall some 65,000 men are ashore. Kamikazes damage the battleship *West Virginia* and two attack transports, and in the coming days the "divine wind" strikes the ships operating off Okinawa with increasing deadliness.

Task Group 78.4, under Captain Homer F. McGee, puts Army troops ashore near Legaspi in southern Luzon, Philippine Islands.

The submarine *Queenfish* (SS 393) mistakenly sinks *Awa Maru*, a Japanese ship carrying Red Cross supplies to Allied prisoners of war in Singapore. She is marked and illuminated in a manner identifying her as a vessel on a humanitarian mission, but foggy weather prevents the sub's skipper, Lieutenant Commander Charles E. Loughlin, from discerning the markings. For his actions

that day in the Formosa Straits, Loughlin is eventually court-martialed and relieved of his command.

5 April
The destroyer *Hudson* (DD 475) sinks the Japanese submarine *RO-41* off Okinawa, Japan.

6 April
The first large-scale air assault by the Japanese against Allied ships operating off Okinawa, Japan, begins. About half of the 699 aircraft targeting the ships of the invasion force are kamikazes. Four suicide planes cause extensive damage to the destroyer *Colhoun* (DD 801), which is later scuttled, and kamikazes also send the tank landing ship *LST-347* to the bottom. Two freighters carrying ammunition for the men fighting ashore are sunk, and twenty-six other vessels ranging in class from the light carrier *San Jacinto* to a motor minesweeper are damaged during the air attack.

7 April
Carrier aircraft of Task Force 58 attack the Japanese battleship *Yamato*, which steams for Okinawa, Japan, with a light cruiser and eight destroyers. A total of 386 carrier planes score repeated hits on the Japanese ships, sending *Yamato*, the light cruiser *Yahagi,* and four destroyers to the bottom of the East China Sea.

Off Okinawa, Japan, Japanese suicide planes damage six ships, including the carrier *Hancock* and battleship *Maryland* (BB 46).

8 April
Following a rendezvous with the submarine *Tigrone* (SS 419), the submarine *Snook* (SS 279) is not heard from again, and she is later presumed lost with all hands.

9 April
The destroyers *Mertz* (DD 691) and *Monssen* (DD 798) sink the Japanese submarine *RO-56* off Okinawa, Japan.

11 April
Kamikaze attacks off Okinawa, Japan, damage six ships, including the battleship *Missouri* and the aircraft carrier *Enterprise*. Conventional bombing and strafing attacks by Japanese aircraft damage the carrier *Essex*, three destroyers, a tank landing ship, and a large support landing craft.

12 April
On the day that their Commander in Chief, President Franklin D. Roosevelt, dies in Warm Springs, Georgia, sailors fight for their lives against Japanese suicide attacks off Okinawa, Japan. Some 380 aircraft, in addition to piloted bombs known as

bakas, attack U.S. ships, the latter weapon scoring its first sinking by sending the destroyer *Mannert L. Abele* (DD 733) to the bottom. In addition, the large support landing craft *LCS(L)-33* is sunk by a kamikaze, while suicide planes and bombing attacks inflict damage on eighteen vessels.

14 April

While operating in the approaches to the Yellow Sea, the submarine *Tirante* (SS 420), commanded by Lieutenant Commander George L. Street III, boldly attacks the Japanese convoy MOSI 02 on the surface despite the presence of mines and numerous shoals in the water. *Tirante* sinks three ships and Street receives the Medal of Honor for his actions that day.

15 April

The destroyer escorts *Frost* and *Stanton* (DE 247) sink the German submarine *U-1235* west of the Azores Islands. The pair scores another kill there the following day, sending *U-880* to the bottom.

The destroyer *Laffey* (DD 724) is the target of twenty-two separate kamikaze attacks while she operates on radar picket duty off Okinawa, Japan. For over an hour her crew braves the onslaught, shooting down six of the attackers, while the ship is

Left: *U.S. ships put up a heavy antiaircraft barrage against Japanese planes coming in just above the water on the seaward side of Kerama Retto at dusk, 6 April 1945. The bright flash in the center may be a plane exploding on the water. (Naval Historical Center)*

crashed by suicide planes six times and holed by bombs twice. Amazingly, *Laffey* survives the attack and is towed to safety.

16 April
Kamikaze attacks off Okinawa, Japan, sink the destroyer *Pringle* and damage nine other vessels,

including the battleship *Missouri* and the aircraft carrier *Intrepid*. *Pringle* breaks in two and sinks in five minutes with the loss of sixty-two of her crew.

18 April
Four destroyers, assisted by a TBM Avenger of VT-47 from the light carrier *Bataan* (CVL 29), sink the Japanese submarine *I-56* off Okinawa, Japan.

The submarine *Sea Owl* (SS 405) sinks the Japanese submarine *RO-46* just 500 yards off the beach at Wake Island.

19 April
While operating off Halifax, Nova Scotia, Canada, the destroyer escorts *Buckley* and *Reuben James* (DE 153) sink the German submarine *U-548*.

22 April
The destroyer escorts *Carter* (DE 112) and *Neal A. Scott* (DE 769), operating off the Azores, sink the German submarine *U-518*.

23 April
The submarine *Besugo* (SS 321) sinks the German submarine *U-183* in the Java Sea.

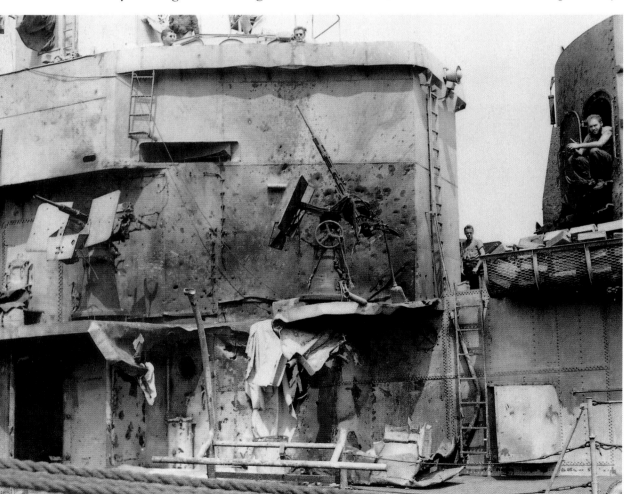

Above: *Ordnancemen load aerial mines into the yawning bomb bay of a TBF Avenger on the flight deck of the carrier* Lexington *(CV 16). (National Museum of Naval Aviation)*

Left: *Damage where the destroyer* Laffey *(DD 724) took one of the four bombs and five kamikazes that hit her off Okinawa, Japan, on 16 April 1945. Picket destroyers positioned to warn the fleet of approaching formations of suicide planes off Okinawa bore the brunt of many attacks by the "divine wind." (Naval Historical Center)*

Opposite: *An F6F Hellcat takes off from* Hornet *(CV 12) to strike targets on 4 May 1945. ("Kyushu Strike," Dwight C. Shepler, Naval Historical Center)*

PB4Y-2 Privateers of VPB-109 attack Japanese shipping off Balikpapan, Borneo, using "Bat" missiles, the first employment of the only automatic homing missiles used during World War II.

24 April
The German submarine *U-546* sinks the destroyer escort *Frederick C. Davis* (DE 136) east of Newfoundland, Canada. Seven other destroyer escorts avenge their sister ship, sending *U-546* to the bottom.

25 April
A PB4Y-1 Liberator of VPB-103 sinks the German submarine *U-326* in the waters off Brest, France.

28–30 April
Kamikazes and conventional air attack damage fifteen ships off Okinawa, Japan.

29 April
A TBM Avenger of VC-92 operating from the escort carrier *Tulagi* (CVE 72), sinks the Japanese submarine *I-44* off Okinawa, Japan.

30 April
While conducting an antisubmarine patrol off the Virginia Capes, the destroyer escorts *Thomas* (DE 102), *Bostwick* (DE 103), and *Coffman* (DE 191) along with the frigate *Natchez* (PF 2) sink the German submarine *U-879*.

A PBY Catalina of VP-63 sinks the German submarine *U-1107* off Brest, France.

1 May
Task Group 78.1, under Rear Admiral Forrest B. Royal, puts Australian troops ashore on Tarakan Island, Borneo, under the guns of Task Group 74.3 commanded by Rear Admiral Russell S. Berkey.

2 May
During the bitter ground fighting on Okinawa, Japan, Hospital Apprentice Second Class Robert E. Bush is administering plasma to a wounded Marine when Japanese soldiers attack his position. Using his pistol and a carbine he finds nearby, the corpsman beats back the enemy, killing six attackers despite losing an eye in the engagement. He refuses treatment for his own wounds until sure the Marine he tended is evacuated. For his actions above and beyond the call of duty, Bush is awarded the Medal of Honor.

3 May
Kamikazes sink the destroyer *Little* (DD 803) and the medium landing ship *LSM-195* off Okinawa, Japan. Four other vessels suffer damage at the hands of suicide planes.

The Japanese minelayer *Hatsutaka* sinks the submarine *Lagarto* (SS 371) in the Gulf of Siam.

4 May
An intense attack by kamikaze aircraft off Okinawa, Japan, sinks four ships and damages twelve others. The ships sunk include the destroyers *Luce* (DD 522), which goes down in four minutes with the loss of 149 members of her crew, and *Morrison*, which is hit four times and sinks with the loss of 153 officers and men.

4–10 May
Patrol planes of Fleet Air Wing 1 fly sweeps off Korea and in the Tsushima Strait, sinking twenty-one ships.

6 May
While operating near Block Island off New England, the destroyer escort *Atherton* (DE 169) and frigate *Moberley* (PF 63) sink the German submarine *U-853*.

In the last sinking of a German submarine by American forces, the destroyer escort *Farquhar* (DE 139) sinks *U-881* in the North Atlantic. The following day Germany surrenders to the Allies, and Victory-in-Europe Day is declared on 8 May.

11 May
Kamikazes attacking the ships operating off Okinawa, Japan, reach the carriers, with two crashing into *Bunker Hill* (CV 17), forcing Task Force 58 commander

Left: *Crew members of the frigate* Moberly *(PF 63) watch the hedgehog pattern ahead of the ship during the attacks that led to the sinking of* U-853 *off Block Island in New York's Long Island Sound, 6 May 1945. Hedgehog, the name for the projector that launched twenty-four depth charges ahead of the ship, overcame the problem of "blindness" in tracking an enemy submarine when it was too close to be spotted by sonar. (Naval Historical Center)*

Vice Admiral Marc A. Mitscher to transfer his flag to the carrier *Enterprise*. Three days later the admiral must shift his flag again when the "Big E" is damaged by a suicide plane off Honshu.

During the fighting on Okinawa, Japan, Pharmacist's Mate Second Class William D. Halyburton, Jr., rushes to the aid of a wounded Marine, shielding the leatherneck's body with his own while tending to his injuries. The corpsman is mortally wounded and receives the Medal of Honor posthumously for his heroic sacrifice.

13–14 May
In an effort to blunt kamikaze attacks against the fleet off Okinawa, Japan, the carriers of Task Force 58 strike Japanese airfields on Kyushu.

18 May
Japanese shore batteries on Naha, Okinawa, Japan, zero in on the destroyer *Longshaw* (DD 559) after she runs aground, hitting her repeatedly and exploding her forward magazine. Eighty-six of her crew are lost.

25 May
The high-speed transport *Bates* (APD 47) and the medium landing ship *LSM-135* are sunk by kamikazes off Okinawa, Japan.

28 May
The destroyer *Drexler* (DD 741) comes under attack off Okinawa, Japan. Hit by one suicide plane, she continues firing her guns until hit in her superstructure by another kamikaze. Following a tremendous explosion, she rolls over and sinks in less than a minute with the loss of 168 dead and 52 wounded.

30 May

A TBM Avenger of VC-82 operating from the escort
carrier *Anzio* sinks the Japanese submarine *I-361* off
Okinawa, Japan.

5 June

A typhoon batters the Third Fleet off Okinawa, Japan,
causing damage to 4 battleships, 8 carriers, 7 cruisers, 11
destroyers, 3 destroyer escorts, and 3 fleet auxiliaries.
Heavy seas collapse the bow section of the flight decks
of the carriers *Hornet* and *Bennington* (CV 20),
necessitating the launching of aircraft over the stern until
the carriers can be detached for repairs. In addition, the
heavy cruiser *Pittsburgh* (CA 72) loses her bow, which is
later recovered. Third Fleet commander Admiral
William F. Halsey, Jr., and Task Force 38 commander
Vice Admiral John S. McCain are found negligent in
not taking the proper actions to avoid the typhoon.

6 June

The U.S. Naval Academy Class of 1946 graduates one
year early due to the national emergency.

8 June

As Marines continue the offensive on Okinawa, Japan,
Hospital Apprentice First Class Fred F. Lester rushes
beyond the front lines to render aid to a wounded
Marine. Wounded by enemy fire, which paralyzes him
on his right side, Lester nevertheless manages to drag
the Marine to safety and refuses aid himself, instead

directing the treatment of the wounded until he dies.
Lester receives the Medal of Honor posthumously.

9–23 June

Task Group 17.21, a submarine attack group
consisting of nine boats and commanded by
Commander Earl T. Hydeman, operates against
Japanese shipping in the Sea of Japan. Over the
course of fifteen days, U.S. submarines sink thirty-
three Japanese vessels, losing one boat when *Bonefish*

Right: *An F4U Corsair of Bombing Fighting Squadron (VBF) 83 traps on board the carrier Essex (CV 9) in 1945. Initially not suitable for operations at sea, improved versions of the "U-bird" proved a valuable addition to carrier air groups in the war's latter stages. (National Museum of Naval Aviation)*

(SS 223) goes down after being attacked by a Japanese destroyer and coast defense vessels.

10 June
Following bombardment by cruisers and destroyers of Task Group 74.3 under Rear Admiral Russell S. Berkey, the ships of Rear Admiral Forrest P. Royal's Task Group 78.1 land Australian troops at Brunei Bay, Borneo.

A kamikaze near misses the destroyer *William D. Porter* (DD 579) off Okinawa, Japan, causing her to burn fiercely. In command of the nearby large support landing craft *LCS(L)-122*, Lieutenant Richard M. McCool, Jr., places his vessel alongside the stricken destroyer to take off members of her crew before the destroyer sinks. The following day, when a suicide plane crashes into his ship, McCool is wounded, but musters the strength to personally free men trapped in a compartment. For his heroic actions on these two days, McCool is awarded the Medal of Honor.

16 June
The Naval Air Test Center is established at Patuxent River, Maryland.

In the waters off Okinawa, Japan, an aerial torpedo sinks the destroyer *Twiggs* (DD 591).

21 June
The Japanese island of Okinawa is officially declared secure, though kamikaze attacks on this day sink one vessel and damage four others. All told, in eighty-nine days at sea off Okinawa, the U.S. Navy loses 36 vessels sunk and 243 damaged. Over 4,900 sailors give their lives and 4,824 are wounded.

27 June
A PV-1 Ventura of VPB-142 sinks the Japanese submarine *I-16* in the waters east of Saipan.

1 July
In the final amphibious assault on Borneo, Rear Admiral Albert G. Noble's Task Group 78.2 lands Australian troops at Balikpapan.

2 July
In the first employment of bombardment rockets by a submarine, *Barb* attacks shore installations at Kaiyho Island in the Kuriles.

7 July
President Harry S. Truman embarks in the heavy cruiser *Augusta* (CA 31) for the first leg of his trip to a conference with British Prime Minister Winston S. Churchill and Soviet Premier Joseph Stalin at Potsdam, near Berlin, Germany.

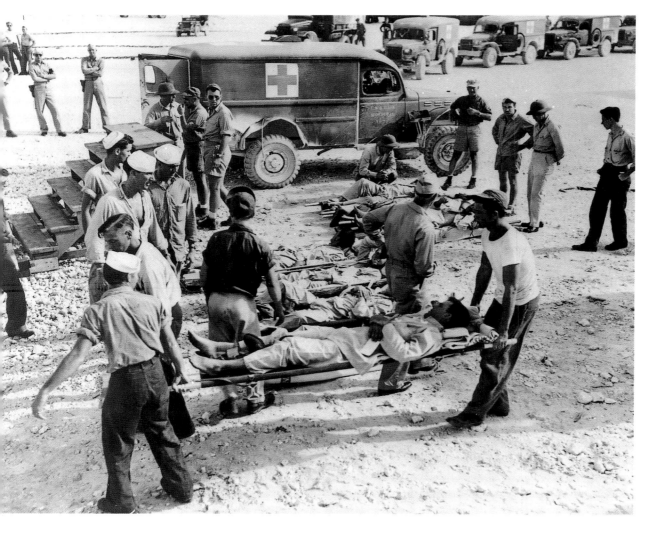

Left: *Ravaged by sun and sharks, survivors of the cruiser* Indianapolis *(CA 35) are loaded on board ambulances at Guam, August 1945. One of the great tragedies of World War II, the cruiser's sinking sparked debate in later years over the court-martial of her skipper, Captain Charles B. McVay III. (Naval Historical Center)*

10 July

The carriers of Task Force 38, under Vice Admiral John S. McCain, launch air strikes against Japanese airfields around Tokyo.

14–15 July

In attacks against enemy shipping in northern Honshu and Hokkaido, Japan, aircraft from Task Force 38 sink forty-six enemy vessels. At the same time battleships, cruisers, and destroyers of Task Units 34.8.1 and 34.8.2—commanded by Rear Admiral John F. Shafroth and Rear Admiral Oscar P. Badger, respectively— conduct bombardments of Kamaishi, Honshu, and Muroran on the coast of Hokkaido. Air attacks and surface bombardment of the Japanese home islands continue into August.

16 July

A TBM Avenger of VC-13 from the escort carrier *Anzio* (CVE 57), operating with the destroyer escort *Lawrence C. Taylor* (DE 415), sinks the Japanese submarine *I-13* in the waters off Yokohama, Japan.

17 July–2 August

The Potsdam Conference, during which Winston S. Churchill is replaced by newly elected Prime Minister Clement Attlee, results in a declaration calling for the unconditional surrender of Japan.

24 July

In strikes against airfields and the Kure naval base in Japan, pilots from Task Force 38 sink the "battleship-carrier" *Hyuga*, heavy cruiser *Tone*, and two other vessels. Sixteen Japanese ships are damaged in the strikes.

The destroyer escort *Underhill* (DE 682) is scuttled after being damaged by kaitens—one-man torpedoes—from the Japanese submarine *I-53* in the waters off Luzon, Philippines.

28 July

In strikes against the Kure naval base in Japan and shipping in the Inland Sea, carrier aircraft from Task Force 38 sink the battleship *Haruna*, "battleship-carrier" *Ise*, and nineteen other ships and craft.

The destroyer *Callaghan* (DD 792) is hit by a kamikaze off Okinawa, Japan. She becomes the last ship sunk by the "divine wind" during World War II.

Right: *Fleet Admiral Chester W. Nimitz signs the surrender document on behalf of the United States during ceremonies on board the battleship* Missouri *(BB 63), 2 September 1945. Behind him stand (left to right) General of the Army Douglas A. MacArthur, Admiral William F. Halsey, and Rear Admiral Forrest P. Sherman. (Naval Historical Center)*

Below: *The battleships* Missouri *(BB 63) and* Iowa *(BB 61) steam off the coast of Japan in August 1945, symbols of ultimate victory in World War II. (Naval Historical Center)*

30 July

After delivering top-secret components for the atomic bomb to Tinian in the Marianas, the heavy cruiser *Indianapolis* steams for Leyte, Philippines. On the evening of 30 July a torpedo fired from the Japanese submarine *I-58* sinks the ship in just twelve minutes. Over 800 members of the crew are able to abandon ship, though the cruiser's last distress signals are not heard. Aircraft do not spot the survivors of *Indianapolis* until 2 August, and by that time sharks and the elements have reduced their number to 316 emaciated men. Captain Charles B. McVay III is convicted by court-martial for "suffering a vessel to be hazarded through negligence" by failing to zigzag, the only skipper during World War II to receive such punishment.

6 August

The Army Air Forces B-29 Superfortress "Enola Gay" drops the first atomic bomb on Hiroshima, Japan. The weapon is actually armed by Navy Captain William S. "Deke" Parsons. Among those killed in the blast at Hiroshima are two Navy prisoners of war being held in the city, Lieutenant (junior grade) Raymond Porter and Aviation Radioman Third Class Normand Brissette, a VB-87 crew shot down in late July.

The submarine *Bullhead* (SS 332) is sunk in the Java Sea, apparently by Japanese aircraft.

9 August

The Army Air Forces B-29 Superfortress "Bock's Car" drops the second atomic bomb on Nagasaki, Japan, with Commander Frederick L. Ashworth arming the weapon on the mission.

14 August

Japan agrees to the terms of unconditional surrender.

The submarine *Spikefish* (SS 404) sinks the Japanese submarine *I-373* in the waters southeast of Shanghai, China.

21 August

In the last surface action of World War II, two Chinese junks commanded by U.S. Navy Lieutenant Livingston Swentzel, Jr., and manned by Americans and Chinese guerrillas are attacked by a Japanese junk between Haimen and Shanghai, China. The Chinese vessels, their crews firing bazookas and machine guns and lobbing grenades, soundly defeat the Japanese junk. Swentzel receives the Navy Cross for his extraordinary heroism during the engagement.

27 August

Ships of the Third Fleet under the command of Admiral William F. Halsey, Jr., enter Sagomi Wan outside the entrance to Tokyo Bay, Japan.

29 August

Landing craft arrive at Omori, the first prisoner of war camp in Japan liberated by the Allies.

2 September

The instrument of the Japanese surrender is signed on the deck of the battleship *Missouri* in Tokyo Bay, Japan, as mass formations of carrier planes and B-29 Superfortresses fly overhead in triumph. Fleet Admiral Chester W. Nimitz signs the document for the United States. This is proclaimed Victory-in-Japan Day.

10 September

Midway (CVB 41), the first of the large aircraft carriers built reflecting wartime experience, is placed in commission. In terms of displacement, she is the largest warship built by the U.S. Navy to date.

11 September

Operation Magic Carpet, in which U.S. Navy warships serve as makeshift transports returning U.S. servicemen to the United States, commences.

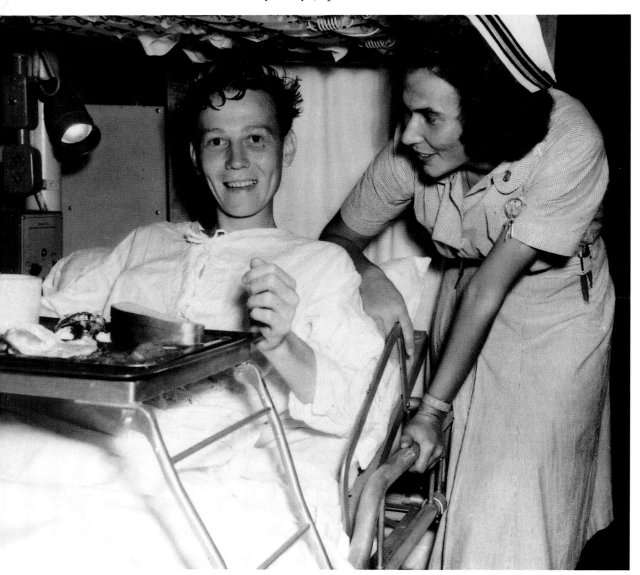

Left: *A repatriated prisoner of war appears in good hands as he rests on board the hospital ship* Benevolence *(AH 13), 30 August 1945, after enduring months of brutal captivity at the hands of Japanese guards. (Naval Historical Center)*

Right: *A sailor kisses a nurse passionately in Manhattan's Times Square as New York City celebrated the surrender of Japan on 14 August 1945. Kissing strangers was a common elated reaction to the news of the end of World War II. (Corbis)*

23 September

A reorganization of the Navy Department results in the creation of an Office of Naval Material and billets for five Deputy Chiefs of Naval Operations for Personnel, Administration, Naval Operations, Logistics, and Aviation.

29 September

An executive order eliminates the post of Commander in Chief, U.S. Fleet.

27 October

The aircraft carrier *Franklin D. Roosevelt* (CVB 42) is placed in commission with President Harry S. Truman present for the ceremony.

5 November

An FR-1 Fireball piloted by Ensign Jake West makes the first successful landing of a jet aircraft on board a U.S. Navy carrier, landing the combination piston-engine jet-powered aircraft on the flight deck of the escort carrier *Wake Island*.

15 November

While monitoring shipping activity off the coast of Manchuria near Port Arthur, a PBM Mariner is fired upon by a Soviet fighter plane, an event symbolic of the beginning of the Cold War for the U.S. Navy.

5 December

Flight 19, consisting of five TBM Avengers, takes off from Naval Air Station Fort Lauderdale, Florida, on a routine training flight. Although contact is maintained with the aircraft for a time, the radios eventually go silent and the aircraft are never seen again, spawning theories about their disappearing over the Bermuda Triangle.

1 December

Fleet Admiral Chester W. Nimitz, the leader of the U.S. Navy in the Pacific during World War II, becomes the tenth Chief of Naval Operations.

HOT TO COLD

1946-1963

HOT TO COLD

1946-1963

At the end of World War II, the U.S. Navy was truly a navy second to none. In concert with allied forces, its ships and aircraft had swept the enemy from the sea. Yet, with victory came a period of uncertainty for the world, as well as America's sea service. As British Prime Minister Winston S. Churchill stated in his famous speech at Westminster College in Fulton, Missouri, an "Iron Curtain" descended over Europe, part of the Cold War that pitted the Soviet Union against the West. Since World War II ended with the unleashing of nuclear weapons on Japan, many believed the nature of warfare had changed forever, with bombers wielding atomic bombs the purveyors of future conflicts. No longer, in the minds of airpower advocates, was the Navy the nation's first line of defense. Accordingly, its size was dramatically reduced in the postwar years. By June 1950, the number of active ships had decreased from a wartime level of 6,768 to 634. In the Western Pacific, where the carriers of Task Force 58 once roamed with impunity, there was assigned only one flattop. Such was the situation when North Korean tanks rolled across the 38th parallel into South Korea, catching the world off guard.

The war in Korea represented the limited conventional conflicts that combined with the nuclear arms race to form a central element of the Cold War. In this new arena, the U.S. Navy was destined to play an important role, though one that did not include the great sea battles experienced in World War II. Power projection ashore—whether through amphibious landings of Marines, like that demonstrated at Inchon in September 1950, or carrier strikes that provided close air support, interdicted transportation networks, and bombed strategic targets—was the central component of naval operations in the Korean War. Though the Korean War was fought largely with men

and machines that were veterans of World War II, the war also represented a technological revolution, particularly with respect to aviation as the Navy's early generation of jet aircraft entered combat.

At the end of that conflict, the Navy maintained a sizeable presence in the western Pacific, with forces being dispatched to the Taiwan Straits on more than one occasion during the 1950s in response to shows of force by Communist China against the island nation. In the Mediterranean, ships of the U.S Sixth Fleet were on station during the Suez Crisis and landed Marines in Beirut, Lebanon, in response to unrest in that country. When aerial reconnaissance of Cuba revealed the presence of Soviet nuclear missiles in the Caribbean nation in October 1962, President John F. Kennedy chose a naval blockade of the island to prevent the delivery of further missiles and equipment to Cuba. Eventually, the Cuban Missile Crisis, which took the United States and Soviet Union to the brink of nuclear war, was resolved peacefully in part thanks to the effectiveness of naval forces and their quarantine of the island.

Other weapons that would come to represent the premier striking arms of the Navy entered service. On 30 September 1954 the world's first nuclear-powered submarine, *Nautilus* (SSN 571), was commissioned, representing a revolution in undersea warfare in that the boats of the silent service could now operate submerged for longer periods of time at extended ranges. When coupled with the Polaris missile, which made the first successful launch from a submerged submarine in 1960, nuclear submarines assumed a prominent role in the nation's strategic arsenal. The same year that *Nautilus* joined the fleet, the Navy commissioned *Forrestal* (CVA 59), the nation's first supercarrier, which was joined in 1961 by *Enterprise* (CVAN 65), the world's first nuclear-powered aircraft

carrier and, at the time, the largest warship afloat. These first generations of large-deck carriers provided the Navy with versatile platforms from which to operate an increasingly sophisticated stable of jet aircraft, and the carrier remains a mainstay of naval operations in the twenty-first century.

The years immediately following World War II shaped the Navy for the postwar world, one in which U.S. forces would be called upon to contain Communist expansion in crisis areas throughout the world and maintain a leading edge in the ability to deliver nuclear weapons. "Control of the seas means security," proclaimed President John F. Kennedy to crewmen on board the carrier *Kitty Hawk* (CVA 63) just months before his death. "Control of the seas means peace. Control of the seas can mean victory. The United States must control the sea if it is to protect our security."

Above: George Washington *(SSBN 598), the first nuclear-powered submarine designed to launch Polaris ballistic missiles while submerged, takes to the water at Groton, Connecticut, in June 1959. George Washington was built quickly by cutting an attack submarine in half on the building ways and adding a missile compartment. The submarine hull had been intended to be* Scorpion, *which became the only ship to have its keel laid twice. (U.S. Naval Institute)*

Pages 528–529: *Tank landing ships (LSTs) unload men and equipment on the beach during the amphibious invasion of Inchon, Korea, 15 September 1950. Ships present include (left to right):* LST-611, LST-845, *and* LST-715. *(Naval Historical Center)*

HOT TO COLD

1946-1963

1946

1–22 March

The aircraft carrier *Midway* (CVB 41) steams to the Davis Strait off Greenland north of the Arctic Circle where she conducts cold-weather operations as part of Operation Frostbite, evaluating the viability of operating naval assets in the northern regions of the globe.

5–14 April

The battleship *Missouri* (BB 63) arrives in the Mediterranean Sea ostensibly to return the remains of Turkey's wartime ambassador to the United States, who died in Washington, D.C., in 1944, to his homeland. In reality, her presence marks a show of twentieth-century gunboat diplomacy, a symbol of American interest in the Mediterranean in response to Communist activity in both Turkey and Greece.

1 July

Operation Crossroads, atomic weapons tests conducted to determine the survivability of warships in the nuclear age, begins at Bikini Atoll in the Marshall Islands with the detonation of an atomic bomb over a target array of ships centered on the battleship *Nevada* (BB 36). In Test Baker on 25 July, an underwater detonation of an atomic bomb sends water nearly 6,000 feet into the air and sinks or damages seventy-five vessels of various sizes.

21 July

In the first landing of a pure jet on board a U.S. Navy aircraft carrier, Lieutenant Commander James J. Davidson traps on board *Franklin D. Roosevelt* (CVB 42) in an XFD-1 Phantom, the first jet procured for operational service by the U.S. Navy.

8 August

The aircraft carrier *Franklin D. Roosevelt* (CVB 42) departs on a cruise that takes her to the Mediterranean Sea, where she makes a port call at Athens in support of the Greek government's efforts to stem the tide of communism in the nation. The carrier departs the Med on 4 October.

13 August

President Harry S. Truman approves the Holloway Plan, named for Rear Admiral James L. Holloway II, who chaired the board that drew up the plan. It preserves the structure of the U.S. Naval Academy and bolsters the Naval Reserve Officer Training Corps. One of the programs espoused by Holloway is called the Flying Midshipmen, whose graduates include Neil Armstrong, the first man to walk on the moon.

21 August

The Office of Naval Research is established to plan and engage in scientific research.

29 September

A P2V-1 Neptune nicknamed the *Truculent Turtle* and flown by Commander Thomas Davies and a crew of three completes a record-setting long-distance flight of 11,235.6 miles from Perth, Australia, to Columbus, Ohio, in a time of 55 hours and 17 minutes. P2V Neptunes serve in Navy patrol squadrons into the 1960s, and also operate from aircraft carriers as interim nuclear strike aircraft.

Opposite: Missouri's (BB 63) Marine detachment stands at attention as the body of the late Munir Ertegun, former Turkish Ambassador to the U.S., is lowered over the side at Dolmabahce, Turkey, 5 April 1946. Note smoke from gun salutes in the background. (Naval Historical Center)

Right: "Baker Day" atomic bomb test at Bikini Atoll, Marshall Islands, 25 July 1946. Frame 7 of a series of ground level views, taken about six seconds after detonation. Identifiable ships are (l–r): Pennsylvania, New York, Salt Lake City, Nagato (ex-Japanese BB), and Nevada. The dark area on the right side of the water column marks the location of Arkansas. (Naval Historical Center)

1 October
Reflecting the development of guided missile technology, the Navy establishes the Naval Air Missile Test Center at Point Mugu, California.

The growing importance of maintaining naval forces in the Mediterranean Sea prompts the establishment of U.S. Naval Forces, Mediterranean, which eventually becomes the Sixth Fleet. The following month the aircraft carrier *Randolph* (CV 15) embarks on a cruise to the Med, beginning a regular schedule of deployment of U.S. flattops to the region.

6 December
Attack Squadron (VA) 19A takes delivery of the Navy's first AD Skyraiders. Called the finest close air support platform ever built, the Skyraider serves naval aviation in a multitude of roles from attack to electronic countermeasures into the late 1960s, and is also operated by the U.S. Air Force and foreign air forces.

1947

1 January
Admiral John H. Towers, the Navy's third aviator, assumes the duties of the newly created post of Commander in Chief Pacific Command. He also serves as Commander in Chief Pacific Fleet, the first aviator to do so.

11 January
The XF2H-1 Banshee, which serves as a fighter and also a capable photoreconnaissance platform during the Korean War, makes its first flight.

29 January
As part of Operation Highjump under the command of Rear Admiral Richard E. Byrd, six R4D Skytrain transport aircraft launch from the aircraft carrier *Philippine Sea* (CV 47) for a flight to Little America in the Antarctic. Equipped with skis to facilitate

operating from the ice cap, the aircraft conduct aerial mapping flights covering some 150,000 square miles, completing their work in March.

12 February
Cusk (SS 348) launches a Loon missile—the American adaptation of Germany's V-1 rocket of World War II—becoming the first U.S. submarine to launch a guided missile.

12 March
President Harry S. Truman, in an address to a joint session of Congress requesting financial aid be provided for the governments of Turkey and Greece to thwart Communist incursions, outlines what becomes known as the Truman Doctrine, calling for America to support all free people resisting outside forces attempting to subjugate them. Combined with the publication of the famous "X article" by foreign service officer George F. Kennan in the July 1947 issue of *Foreign Affairs*, which calls for a policy of containment against inevitable Soviet expansion, the Truman Doctrine forms a basis for U.S. foreign policy during the Cold War.

15 March
Though African-Americans, led by the famous "Golden Thirteen," received commissions as reserve officers during World War II, the commissioning of Ensign John W. Lee on this date marks the first time a black officer receives a commission in the regular Navy.

Above: *Test pilots Commander Turner F. Caldwell (right) and Major Marion Carl, USMC, pose by the tail of the Douglas D-558-1 Skystreak research plane, circa 1948. (Naval Historical Center)*

Right: *James Forrestal is sworn in as the first Secretary of Defense by Chief Justice Fred M. Vinson, in the office of the Secretary of the Navy, 17 September 1947. Also present are (l–r): Unidentified man, Secretary of the Army Kenneth C. Royall, General of the Army Dwight D. Eisenhower, Secretary of the Navy, John L. Sullivan, Fleet Admiral Chester W. Nimitz, Secretary of the Air Force Stuart Symington, and General Carl Spaatz. Forrestal's tenure was marked by bitter interservice struggles. (Naval Historical Center)*

5 June

In a speech at Harvard University, Secretary of State George C. Marshall outlines a program in which the United States will provide economic aid to the war-torn nations of Europe. The effort, which rebuilds the economic infrastructure of Western Europe, is called the Marshall Plan.

26 July

The National Security Act of 1947 becomes law with the signature of President Harry S. Truman. A far-reaching document largely opposed by the Navy, the act unifies the U.S. armed forces into a National Military Establishment under a Secretary of Defense, who replaces the Secretaries of War and Navy in the cabinet. The act also renames the War Department the Department of the Army, and creates an independent U.S. Air Force. President Truman taps Secretary of the Navy James Forrestal as the first Secretary of Defense.

20 August

Flying the D-558-1 Skystreak, a high-speed research aircraft developed under the auspices of the National Advisory Committee for Aeronautics and the Navy, Commander Turner F. Caldwell establishes a new

world's speed record of 640.663 miles per hour over Muroc, California. The mark is broken five days later by Marine Lieutenant Colonel Marion Carl flying the same aircraft.

18 September

John L. Sullivan, a lawyer from New Hampshire and former Assistant Secretary of the Navy for Air, becomes the forty-ninth Secretary of the Navy.

21 November

The XF9F-2 Panther, prototype for naval aviation's front-line fighter aircraft of the Korean War and a continuation of Grumman's famed "Cat" series of fighters, makes its first flight.

1 December

Admiral William H.P. Blandy becomes the first Commander in Chief Atlantic Command. He also serves as Commander in Chief Atlantic Fleet.

15 December

Admiral Louis Denfeld, a former Chief of Naval Personnel, becomes the eleventh Chief of Naval Operations.

CAPTAIN JOY BRIGHT HANCOCK

by Dr. Kathleen Broome Williams

Joy Bright Hancock (1898–1986) had a long association with the U.S. Navy. Her energy, ability, and dedication, instrumental in shaping the conditions under which women serve in the Navy today. Before World War II, women were only periodically and temporarily admitted to the sea service, and their positions and numbers were restricted. Now, largely due to Hancock's pioneering efforts, women are an integral part of naval operations in the air, at sea, and ashore.

One of six children of a New Jersey real estate and insurance agent, there was little in Joy Bright's childhood to suggest a naval career. After high school she took a secretarial course before enlisting in the naval reserve in 1918. Since there was no legislation banning women from the Navy, they were admitted for the duration to cope with the manpower shortages of World War I. Bright became a yeoman (F), one of 11,275 enlisted women, most of whom filled clerical positions. No women were allowed to be officers, however, and all were separated at war's end.

During the war, Bright was assigned to Naval Air Station Cape May, New Jersey, and became profoundly attached to naval aviation. For most of the next twenty-three years she worked for the Navy as a civilian, much of the time at the Bureau of Aeronautics, where beginning in 1930 she headed the General Information Section.

During these years Bright's life was marked by extraordinary tragedy. She was married twice, briefly, to naval aviators, both of whom were killed in airship accidents. Keeping her second husband's name—Hancock—she remained a widow from 1924 until she married naval aviator Vice Admiral Ralph A. Ofstie in 1954. He, too, died a year later. One measure of Hancock's great strength is her life of accomplishment in the face of such adversity.

By 1942, the demands of World War II required the Navy to accept the services of women once again,

this time in far greater numbers than before, and as officers as well as enlisted personnel. When the Women's Reserve, or WAVES (Women Accepted for Voluntary Emergency Service), was created that July, its structure was based, in part, on recommendations presented by Hancock in her report on the organization of the Women's Division, Royal Canadian Air Force. Eventually, more than 100,000 women served in the wartime WAVES, Hancock among them. She was sworn in as a lieutenant in October 1942 and spent the war in the office of the Deputy Chief of Naval Operations (Air), achieving the rank of commander in 1945. Hancock worked to expand the range of specialties and ratings open to women, insisting that they be allowed to train alongside men in aviation schools and to qualify for technical ratings such as aviation machinist's mate.

At the end of the war, Hancock pressed for a permanent position for women in the Navy. In July 1946 she became the director of the WAVES and was promoted to captain. For the next two years she lobbied for legislation to admit women to the regular Navy, helping to pass the Women's Armed Forces Integration Act of June 1948. That October, Hancock was among the first 8 of the 288 women officers sworn into the regular Navy. An additional 128 reserve officers were admitted, as were some 1,500 enlisted women, regular and reserve. By 1952 these numbers had jumped to 1,000 women officers and 8,500 enlisted women, the Korean War quickly validating the decision to make a permanent place for women in the Navy.

As the first director of women in the regular Navy, Hancock's role was pivotal in clearing the way for their ever-increasing participation. By pressing for equality of treatment—and training—with men, she demonstrated that women could meet the highest professional standards. She advocated the admission of women officers to the General Line School at Newport, Rhode Island, and enabled

enlisted women to attend all specialists' schools. When she retired as WAVES director in July 1953, Hancock was awarded the Legion of Merit for her years of service.

Drawing on her intimate knowledge of the Navy as a World War I yeoman, as a Navy wife, as a civilian at the Bureau of Aeronautics, and as a WAVE officer, Hancock worked for reform from within the system to accomplish her objectives. Under her guidance, opportunities for women in the Navy continued to expand, paving the way for their essential role today.

Above: *Captain Joy Bright Hancock inspects women recruits at the Great Lakes Naval Training Center in Illinois, circa 1948. A veteran of two world wars, Hancock's successful efforts in integrating women into the Navy laid the foundation for the modern era, in which women wear the stars of admirals and fly combat missions. (Naval Historical Center)*

1948

11 March
Interservice conflict over roles and missions prompts Secretary of Defense James Forrestal to convene meetings of the Joint Chiefs of Staff at Key West, Florida, resulting in concessions by both the Navy and the Air Force. The Navy gives the Air Force primacy in strategic bombing, while the Air Force agrees to put aside its opposition to the construction of a large, flush-deck carrier (one without an island superstructure).

1 April
The Navy commissions its first helicopter squadron, Helicopter Utility Squadron (HU) 1, at Naval Air Station Lakehurst, New Jersey.

30 April
The XP5M-1 Marlin flying boat makes its first flight.

5 May
Operating the FH-1 Phantom, the first jet procured by the Navy, Fighter Squadron (VF) 17A begins three days of carrier qualifications on board *Saipan* (CVL 48), thus becoming the Navy's first operational jet squadron.

24 June
Soviet military forces initiate a blockade of Berlin, Germany, cutting off all road, rail, and waterborne traffic into the city. This action prompts the initiation of the Berlin Airlift, a massive airlift of supplies into the city by American aircraft, codenamed Operation Vittles. Two U.S. Navy transport squadrons, VR-6 and VR-8, commence flights into Berlin on 9 November. They conclude their operations on 31 July 1949, logging a total of 45,990 flight hours and carrying 129,989 tons of cargo.

20 August
Secretary of Defense James Forrestal convenes a second conference with the Joint Chiefs of Staff at the Naval War College in Newport, Rhode Island, in an effort to solidify the respective roles and missions of the armed forces, which results in the Air Force being given temporary control of the atomic bomb.

Above: *The cruiser* Salem *(CA 139) underway in the Mediterranean Sea, 16 June 1952. (Naval Historical Center)*

Left: *Members of a Navy transport crew participating in the Berlin Airlift receive an intelligence briefing by an Air Force captain, who provides intelligence on Russian activity in the corridor, the weather expected enroute, and any special route instructions, 5 October 1949. (Naval Historical Center)*

Right: *James V. Forrestal, Secretary of Defense, poses with the Joint Chiefs of Staff and other senior officers at the Naval War College, Newport, Rhode Island, August 1948. Present include (l–r): Lieutenant General Lauris Norstad, USA; General Hoyt Vandenberg, USAF; Lieutenant General Albert Wedemeyer, USA; General Omar Bradley, USA; Forrestal; Admiral Louis Denfeld, USN; Vice Admiral Arthur W. Radford, USN; and Major General Alfred M. Gruenther, USA. (Naval Historical Center)*

9 September

The Navy, in an effort to provide its carriers with strategic capability, establishes Composite Squadron (VC) 5. Equipped with modified P2V Neptune patrol planes, the squadron develops tactics and procedures for the delivery of nuclear weapons from the decks of aircraft carriers. The following March a squadron aircraft demonstrates this capability in dramatic fashion, launching from the aircraft carrier *Coral Sea* (CVB 43) off the Atlantic coast and logging a flight of nearly twenty-three hours to "bomb" a West Coast target before returning to land at Naval Air Station Patuxent River, Maryland.

1 October

The seaplane tender *Norton Sound* (AV 11) completes conversion to a guided missile test ship. She is redesignated AVM 1 IN 1950.

16 November

The heavy cruiser *Des Moines* (CA 134) is placed in commission at the Boston Navy Yard, Massachusetts, the first of a class of three ships featuring fully automatic 8-inch guns, the largest cruisers ever built. *Salem* (CA 139), the final *Des Moines*-class cruiser and the last all-gun cruiser built for the U.S. Navy, is commissioned on 14 May 1949.

1949

23 April

Secretary of Defense Louis Johnson, having replaced James Forrestal on 28 March, abruptly cancels construction of the aircraft carrier *United States* just five days after the laying of her keel at Newport News, Virginia. This decision is made without consulting either the Chief of Naval Operations or the Secretary of the Navy. Six days later Secretary of the Navy John L. Sullivan resigns in protest.

25 May

Francis P. Matthews, who admits to having never in his life been on board a floating vessel larger than a rowboat, takes office as the fiftieth Secretary of the Navy.

3 June

Ensign Wesley Brown becomes the first African-American to graduate from the U.S. Naval Academy. He enters the Civil Engineering Corps and eventually retires as a commander.

1 August
The Seventh Task Fleet is reestablished as the forward-deployed U.S. naval force in the Western Pacific.

9 August
While flying over South Carolina in an F2H Banshee, Lieutenant J. L. Fruin of VF-171 experiences an in-flight emergency and ejects from his aircraft. This is the first operational use of an ejection seat in the United States.

25 August
While conducting surveillance operations with the submarine *Tusk* (SS 426) in the Greenland Sea, the submarine *Cochino* (SS 34) suffers a battery explosion while submerged. She is able to make it to the surface, where a second explosion finally sinks her. Her crew transfers to *Tusk*. One civilian technician on board *Cochino* and six *Tusk* sailors die during the sinking and subsequent rescue operation.

1 October
The Military Sea Transportation Service, which eventually includes both Army and Navy cargo ships and transports, is established within the Navy.

5 October
Congress opens hearings on the roles and missions of the armed forces, with testimony from an array of high-ranking officers. Admiral Arthur W. Radford spearheads the Navy's witnesses, speaking out against

the Air Force's B-36 bomber and the all-or-nothing concept of future warfare. On 17 October Chief of Naval Operations Louis Denfeld, over the objections of the Secretary of Defense and Secretary of the Navy, supports the statements of preceding witnesses against the B-36 bomber and the limitations on naval forces. This act prompts his removal from office on 1 November. The controversial stand taken by some of the Navy's top brass becomes known as the "Revolt of the Admirals," and results in Congress preserving an important role for the Navy and Marine Corps in the postwar defense establishment.

2 November
The day after Admiral Louis Denfeld's relief, Admiral Forrest P. Sherman becomes the twelfth Chief of Naval Operations. Sherman, who served as Fleet Admiral Chester W. Nimitz's wartime deputy, is the youngest man to hold the office to date.

1950

17 January
The battleship *Missouri* runs aground at Hampton Roads, Virginia, resulting in the courts-martial of her commanding officer, navigator, operations officer, and combat information officer.

12 February
The Sixth Task Fleet and Seventh Task Fleet are renamed the Sixth Fleet and Seventh Fleet, respectively.

Left: *The advent of nuclear weapons prompted the Navy to procure long-range aircraft capable of delivering them from the decks of aircraft carriers. The AJ-1 Savage, pictured here trapping on board the carrier* Midway *(CVB 41) in 1951, was the first Navy aircraft specifically built for this purpose. In addition to the two reciprocating engines, the Savage incorporated a jet engine in its tail and had a range of 1,630 miles. (National Museum of Naval Aviation)*

16 March–5 April

The submarine *Pickerel* (SS 524) completes a record underwater voyage between Hong Kong and Pearl Harbor, Hawaii, employing a snorkel to remain submerged for over twenty-one days while covering a distance of 5,194 nautical miles.

8 April

Soviet fighters shoot down an unarmed PB4Y-2 Privateer of Patrol Squadron (VP) 26 flying an electronic reconnaissance mission over the Baltic Sea. The aircraft's ten-man crew is never accounted for and is presumed killed in action.

21 April

An AJ-1 Savage, the first aircraft designed for employment as a carrier-based atomic bomber, makes its first carrier takeoff, launching from the deck of *Coral Sea*.

25 June

North Korean troops and tanks cross the 38th parallel into South Korea, marking the beginning of the Korean War. A United Nations Security Council resolution condemning the action is adopted that day. President Harry S. Truman authorizes the use of American forces to support South Korea two days later.

26 June

The destroyers *Mansfield* (DD 728) and *De Haven* (DD 727) support the evacuation of 700 Americans and friendly foreign nationals from Inchon, South Korea.

29 June

The antiaircraft light cruiser *Juneau* (CLAA 119) fires on shore targets in the vicinity of Samchok, Korea, marking the first naval gunfire support mission of the

Above: *The submarine* Cochino *(SS 345) prepares to get underway from the United Kingdom in July 1949, one month before battery explosions caused a fire that sent her to the bottom in waters north of Norway. At the time she was gathering intelligence on Soviet military activities, a highly secret and sometimes deadly mission carried out by Navy ships and aircraft during the Cold War. (Naval Historical Center)*

Below: Pickerel *(SS 524) surfaces from a depth of 150 feet at a 48-degree up angle during tests off Oahu, Hawaii, on 1 March 1952. (Naval Historical Center)*

THE REVOLT OF THE ADMIRALS

by Dr. Jeffrey G. Barlow

The "Revolt of the Admirals" (a term actually conjured up by *Time* magazine to headline one of its stories) refers to a series of events in 1949 closely connected to the long-term fate of U.S. naval aviation. In March of that year, Secretary of Defense James V. Forrestal resigned and was succeeded by Louis A. Johnson, a well-connected Democratic Party fundraiser and long-time supporter of Army (i.e., Air Force) aviation. During Forrestal's term as Defense Secretary, the Navy had staked most of its hopes for acquiring an atomic bombing capability on the construction of a large, flush-deck aircraft carrier designed to operate long-range aircraft capable of carrying the heavy atomic bombs of the period. Within less than a week after the carrier's keel plate was laid in April 1949, Johnson cancelled the ship's construction without seriously talking with the Navy's senior leaders about the decision.

In the aftermath of this action, Navy Secretary John L. Sullivan resigned in protest and was quickly replaced by an inexperienced politician named Francis P. Matthews, who admitted to reporters that his only familiarity with his new responsibilities was the fact that he had owned a rowboat at his vacation home in Minnesota. The events that led to the "revolt" began when two individuals working in the Navy Department Secretariat—former journalist Cedric R. Worth and Commander Thomas D. Davies, a noted naval aviator—decided that something had to be done to bring naval aviation's plight in Johnson's Pentagon to the attention of Congress. Together they drafted a document based primarily on aircraft industry gossip and innuendo that discussed the weaknesses of the U.S. Air Force's vaunted B-36 intercontinental bomber program. The Anonymous Document (as it came to be known), which asserted that Defense Secretary Johnson and

Air Force Secretary W. Stuart Symington had supported the plane because they had personal financial stakes in the program, was surreptitiously passed to important members of Congress. When the document's charges became publicly known, Congressman Carl Vinson, chairman of the House Armed Services Committee, was forced to hold public hearings on the B-36 program. Army, Navy, and Air Force leaders were notified that they were also expected to testify before the committee on the larger issues relating to the state of the country's military aviation. Captain Arleigh A. Burke and the staff of his Navy office, designated OP-23, eventually were tasked with assembling the Navy's testimony for delivery before Vinson's committee.

At these August 1949 hearings Air Force leaders successfully proved that the B-36 program, though it had experienced development problems, had not been influenced by matters of personal financial gain. In the final days of testimony, however, Cedric Worth's role in producing the Anonymous Document came to light, blackening the Navy's reputation by implication. When the B-36 hearings recessed, Navy witnesses had not yet been heard, and there were indications that the Armed Services Committee wished to conclude the hearings without going into other aviation issues of Navy concern. In part due to the publicity efforts of Captain John G. Crommelin, a noted naval aviator determined to get the hearings reopened even at the cost of his own career, Vinson's committee began a new series of hearings on unification and strategy. Navy Secretary Matthews led off the Navy testimony, asserting that his service, and naval aviation in particular, was doing well. The rest of the Navy witnesses, spearheaded by Admiral Arthur W. Radford, the sea service's commander in the Pacific, disputed this rosy assessment. They argued strongly that the country's

existing defense policies, centered around the intercontinental atomic bombing of enemy cities by Air Force bombers exemplified by the already obsolete B-36, were misguided and that naval aviation's valuable role in national defense was being badly diminished by Louis Johnson's actions.

The final Navy witness was Chief of Naval Operations (CNO) Admiral Louis Denfeld. When he testified in agreement with his service colleagues, Matthews and Johnson were livid with anger and quickly removed Denfeld as CNO. Also in the aftermath of the testimony, Secretary Matthews struck Captain Burke's name from the flag promotion list. Luckily, President Harry S. Truman, when apprised of the injustice, reinstated this highly regarded officer, who himself later became CNO.

Although it was not apparent at the time, the Navy's effective testimony convinced vital congressmen of the importance of naval aviation. This, in turn, helped set the stage for a revival of its fortunes the following year, when the Navy's flattops were called to action in Korea.

Above: *Admiral Arthur W. Radford, Commander in Chief, Pacific and Pacific Fleet, delivers his statement to the House Armed Services Committee during hearings on unification and service roles and missions, 7 October 1949. The veteran aviator was a leading figure in the "Revolt of the Admirals." (AP/Wide World Photos)*

Left: *The cruiser* Juneau *(CLAA 119) replenishes her ammunition and fuel in a Japanese harbor after bombarding Korean targets in the early days of the Korean War, 15 July 1950. (Naval Historical Center)*

Opposite, top: *An F9F Panther of Fighter Squadron (VF) 154 conducts a mission over North Korea. Their battles with enemy MiG fighters infrequent, Navy jet pilots primarily flew interdiction missions that represented the primary role of naval aviation during the Korean War. (National Museum of Naval Aviation)*

Korean War and the first action involving the U.S. Navy. On 2 July the cruiser engages in the only purely naval action of the war when, while operating with two British ships, she is attacked by North Korean torpedo boats. Three enemy craft are sunk without damage to the allied warships.

3 July

The aircraft carrier *Valley Forge* (CV 45), the only U.S. Navy flattop operational in the Western Pacific at the outbreak of the war in Korea, joins the British carrier *Triumph* in launching the first naval air strikes of the war. In two days of attacks, aviators strike military installations around the North Korean capital of Pyongyang, with pilots of VF-51 splashing two YAK-9 fighters, naval aviation's first kills in the skies over Korea.

11 July

A landing party consisting of ten sailors and Marines under Commander W. B. Porter from the cruiser *Juneau* goes ashore under the cover of darkness and destroys a railroad tunnel at Rashin, North Korea.

18 July

Carrier-based aircraft from Task Force 77 strike targets at Wonsan, North Korea, destroying airfields, railroads, factories, and an oil refinery.

18–19 July

Under the command of Rear Admiral James H. Doyle, the ships of Amphibious Group 1 land elements of the First Cavalry Division at Pohang, South Korea, to take part in defending the Pusan perimeter.

19 July

Ensign Donald E. Stevens of Attack Squadron (VA) 55 crashes in an AD Skyraider during a strafing run against an enemy truck in Kangmyong-ni, North Korea, becoming the first naval aviator lost in combat during the Korean War.

25 July

Recommissioned to handle expected casualties from the Korean War, the hospital ship *Benevolence* (AH 13) collides with SS *Mary Luckenbach* off San Francisco, California, and sinks with the loss of 13 lives.

3 August

Marine Fighter Squadron (VMF) 214, embarked in the escort carrier *Sicily* (CVE 118), attacks Chinju, South Korea, with rockets and incendiary bombs, the first of many strikes by Marine carrier-based squadrons. During the war, leatherneck squadrons log twelve deployments on board baby flattop during the war, providing vital close air support to their fellow Marines ashore.

15–16 August

Navy Underwater Demolition Team personnel and Marines from the high-speed transport *Bass* (APD 124) stage night raids along the east coast of Korea, destroying railroad bridges and tunnels.

16 August

Task Element 96.51, consisting of four landing ships, the cruiser *Helena* (CA 75), and escorting destroyers evacuate the Third Division of the Republic of Korea (ROK) Army from Yonghae, South Korea.

21 August

Signaling the intensification of the air war over Korea, aircraft from the carriers *Valley Forge* and *Philippine Sea* set new records for operations, completing 202 sorties in one day in the Pyongyang, North Korea, area.

14 September

The battleship *Missouri* arrives in South Korean waters and bombards a bridge near Samchok, unleashing fifty 16-inch projectiles that demolish the bridge.

15 September

In one of the most daring operations in military history, the ships of Task Force 90 under the command of Rear Admiral James H. Doyle pass through a narrow channel and land the First Marine Division at Inchon, South Korea. The first action occurs at heavily fortified Wolmi-Do Island, which had been shelled by destroyers and bombed by carrier aircraft during the previous days, and the Marines plant the American flag after just forty-five minutes of fighting. In the afternoon leathernecks begin the assault against Inchon, with tank landing ships supplying them through the night as they secure the city. Writes General of the Army Douglas MacArthur in a message to Commander Seventh Fleet Vice Admiral

Arthur Struble, "The Navy and the Marines have never shone more brightly than this morning."

25–29 September

After striking mines in Korean waters, the destroyers *Brush* (DD 745) and *Mansfield* suffer extensive damage and the minesweeper *Magpie* (AMS 25) is sunk. At this juncture in the war, intelligence estimates that some 3,500 enemy mines are in the waters around Korea, posing a serious problem to the U.S. Navy.

Right: *A U.S. Navy underwater demolition team (UDT) "frogman" affixes a demolition pack to a beach obstacle, clearing the way for landing craft to reach the shore in an amphibious assault. During the early 1960s the UDT mission was expanded to include beach reconnaissance, couterinsurgency, and raids, and the frogmen received a new name—the SEALs. (U.S. Naval Institute)*

THE LANDING AT INCHON

by Curtis A. Utz

The amphibious assault at Inchon, South Korea, was one of the most significant and difficult operations of the Korean War, and one of the most daring operations in the history of warfare. The U.S. Far East Command (FECOM) planned and executed the operation in a little over two months despite numerous handicaps. FECOM lacked almost everything needed to mount such an operation, including amphibious, escort, and cargo ships, logistic vessels, a trained landing force, and landing site intelligence. General of the Army Douglas A. MacArthur, commander of FECOM and United Nations (UN) troops in Korea, relied on the expertise and skill of the Navy and the Marine Corps to execute this risky assault.

MacArthur began considering a counteroffensive against the Communists less than a week after the North Korean Peoples' Army (NKPA) crossed the 38th parallel on 25 June 1950. U.S. forces destroyed most of the North Korean air force and navy within days of intervention, and MacArthur wanted to use his sea and air advantages to the fullest. He concluded that his enemy was most vulnerable to a landing on Korea's west coast at Inchon. The capture of this port and nearby Kimpo airfield would enable the UN to mount a major attack on Seoul, the South Korean capital and the key road and rail link in the NKPA's supply line. The Inchon landing force would then serve as an anvil on which an offensive from the Pusan perimeter would shatter the enemy army. MacArthur's objectives were the utter destruction of the NKPA and the recovery of all of South Korea.

Inchon had several advantages as a strategic target, but many disadvantages as a landing site. The approaches to the city were narrow and the current was dangerously swift. The waterways and harbor could be easily mined. The port's small anchorage and limited facilities would hinder follow-up support. There were no true landing beaches, only seawalls, piers, and "rocks, with patches of sand." Wolmi-do, an island that divided the harbor from the Sale River, had to be taken to protect the flanks of the main landing

areas. The most critical factor was Inchon's extreme tidal range of thirty-two feet. Low tide exposed extensive mud flats and other hazards in the harbor and the approaches. The need for a daylight extreme high tide limited the operation to only several days each month. One naval staff officer commented, "We drew up a list of every natural and geographic handicap—and Inchon had 'em all." The site's difficulties, however, could be advantageous. The apparent impossibility of an amphibious landing at Inchon led MacArthur to conclude that the port would be poorly defended and that the NKPA would be taken by surprise.

Military leaders in Washington had misgivings about a landing at Inchon, as did many naval officers in theater. Some amphibious planners recommended a more viable landing site, such as Kunsan. There was a meeting on 30 August 1950 at MacArthur's Tokyo, Japan, headquarters to discuss the issue with the amphibious commanders and representatives from Washington, including Chief of Naval Operations Admiral Forrest Sherman. After hearing the concerns of several officers, MacArthur spoke to the strategic importance of Inchon and a quick end to the war, and commented to Sherman, "The Navy has never let me down in the past and they will not let me down this time." He summed up his presentation with his trademark dramatic flair: "We will land at Inchon and I shall crush them!"

Assembling the necessary men and materiel proved a daunting task. Rear Admiral James Doyle, the capable commander of Amphibious Group 1, pulled vessels from as far away as the Mediterranean. He even recalled fifty-seven tank landing ships from merchant service in occupied Japan—still manned by Japanese crews—for use in the operation. Marines, both active and reserve, streamed to the First Marine Division from all over the U.S. to bring it up to strength for the landings. The follow-up force, the Army's Seventh Infantry Division, had been stripped of many men to reinforce the Pusan perimeter, and received several thousand South Korean recruits to help fill the ranks.

The landing was set for 15 September and the execution of the final plan would require timing, skill, and luck. A bombardment group would shell Inchon, and carrier-based Navy and Marine planes would strike starting 13 September. There would be two landings on the day of the assault. Wolmi-do, which overlooked the other two landing areas, would be seized on the morning high tide by a battalion of the 5th Marines. At the next high tide, almost twelve hours later, the 1st Marines would hit Blue Beach and the rest of the 5th Marines would land at Red Beach. These units would seize key objectives to protect the beachhead overnight while tank landing ships, stranded by the receding tide, would provide supplies. The next day, the Marines would take the rest of the city, receive reinforcements, and begin advancing toward Seoul. The units in the Pusan perimeter would then attack, smashing the retreating NKPA against the Inchon force.

Doyle's assault force sortied from Japan on 11 September and encountered the heavy seas and winds of a typhoon. These ships, and those bringing the Marines from Pusan, steamed toward Inchon through the gales. With their objective blasted by carrier aircraft and ships' gunfire, the amphibious force steamed into the treacherous approaches to Inchon during the night of 14 September. The following morning the signal "Land the landing force" sent the landing craft toward Wolmi-do, which was secured within an hour. Similarly, at Blue Beach, Marines began moving inland within thirty minutes of hitting the beach. However, at Red Beach the leathernecks faced greater resistance. The landing craft, with makeshift ladders in the bows, came under fire as they headed for the seawall. Once they hit, Marines threw grenades over the wall and then clambered up the ladders to attack the enemy. Communist fire pinned down several platoons, but these strongpoints soon fell. The Marines only had two hours of daylight to seize three hills that overlooked the landing area. They took the first quickly, but there was sharp fighting on the other two. As darkness loomed, the Marines completed taking the hills, securing the beachhead.

When the assault force moved inland to seize its objectives, the Korean War entered a new phase, one begun by the Navy and Marines in one of the most incredible and improbable successes in modern warfare.

Above: *Wakes mark the trails of landing craft heading ashore to disembark the First Marine Division at Inchon, the smoke rising skyward the result of damage to enemy positions from aircraft and the guns of the bombardment force. The daring amphibious assault in September 1950 changed the course of the Korean War. ("Inchon," Herbert C. Hahn, Navy Art Collection)*

Left: *Missouri (BB 63) fires a salvo of 16-inch shells at enemy forces at Chongjin, North Korea, 21 October 1950, in efforts to cut North Korean communications. The "Mighty Mo's" main battery proved highly effective. (Naval Historical Center)*

Below: *Landing craft from Union (AKA 106) circle in the transport area prior to assembling at the line of departure off Inchon, 15 September 1950. A Japanese-manned tank landing ship is in the background. (Naval Historical Center)*

9 October

The aircraft carrier *Leyte* (CV 32), transferred from the Atlantic Fleet, arrives in Korean waters.

12 October

While operating off Wonsan, North Korea, the minesweepers *Pirate* (AM 275) and *Pledge* (AM 277) strike mines and sink. *Pirate* is taken under fire by enemy shore batteries after striking a mine, and *Pledge* strikes a mine as she maneuvers to avoid enemy fire. U.S. Navy efforts to clear the underwater weapons at Wonsan are ultimately successful and elements of the First Marine Division land at the harbor on 26 October.

9 November

In the first jet-versus-jet combat in the history of naval aviation, F9F Panthers of VF-111 from the carrier *Philippine Sea* engage Chinese MiG-15 fighters. Lieutenant Commander William T. Amen becomes the first naval aviator to shoot down a jet.

25–27 November

Some 300,000 Chinese troops pour across the Yalu River into North Korea, attacking U.S. Army troops in the north and descending upon the First Marine Division, which on 27 November confronts eight Chinese divisions around the Chosin Reservoir. U.S. Navy aircraft join Marine planes in providing vital close air support to the embattled leathernecks.

4 December

While flying a mission near Hagaru-Ri in the Chosin Reservoir, North Korea, the F4U Corsair flown by Ensign Jesse Brown of VF-31 from the carrier *Leyte* is hit by enemy fire. The pilot makes a forced landing and is pinned in the cockpit. Squadronmate Lieutenant (junior grade) Thomas J. Hudner purposefully crash lands his own aircraft and makes his way to Brown's crashed plane. Despite Hudner's repeated efforts to save Brown— who is the first African-American designated a naval aviator after completing the Navy's flight training program—he eventually dies. Hudner is rescued by a helicopter and subsequently awarded the Medal of Honor for his actions.

Right: *Ensign Jesse L. Brown (left, front) and Ensign R. G. Rider play a game of "acey-deucy" in the Fighter Squadron 32 ready room on board* Leyte *(CV 32), 12 April 1949. Brown, the first African-American to complete the Navy's flight training program, was killed in action when his F4U Corsair crashed in North Korea after being hit by antiaircraft fire on 4 December 1949. (Naval Historical Center)*

10 December

U.S. Navy ships of Task Force 90 under the command of Rear Admiral James H. Doyle begin evacuating personnel and equipment from Hungnam, North Korea. The two-week effort results in 105,000 American and South Korean troops, 91,000 civilians, and 350,000 tons of supplies and equipment being taken aboard ship. Once the evacuation is completed, demolition charges are triggered, destroying Hungnam's harbor installations to deny their use to the enemy.

18 December

In a war in which so-called "weekend warriors" play a highly important role, Patrol Squadron (VP) 892 becomes the first recalled Naval Air Reserve squadron to begin operations in the Korean War zone.

1951

2 February

The minesweeper *Partridge* (AMS 31) strikes a mine while operating near Wonsan, North Korea, sinking with the loss of eight of her crew killed and six wounded. She is the last minesweeper lost during the Korean War.

5 February

In the first successful flight of carrier aircraft across the Atlantic, five AJ Savages of VC-5 fly from Norfolk, Virginia, to Port Lyautey, French Morocco. The nuclear strike aircraft deploy on board *Midway*-class carriers, which carry atomic weapons. The flight, which includes three squadron P2V Neptunes and is completed in stages, ends on 8 February.

16 February

United Nations forces begin a naval siege of Wonsan, North Korea's principal port, which lasts until the end of the war. The harbor becomes an important haven for aircraft damaged by enemy fire over North Korea, with helicopters pulling downed airmen from the water to fight another day.

14–19 March

Over the course of five days, gunfire from the battleship *Missouri* (BB 63) operating off Kyojo Wan, Songjin, Chaho, and Wonsan, North Korea, destroys eight railroad bridges and seven highway bridges.

29 March

Carrier Air Group (CVG) 101, the first all-Reserve carrier air group to deploy to Korean waters, begins flying combat missions from the aircraft carrier *Boxer* (CV 21).

dashes four times through a fire-swept area to treat four wounded leathernecks, dragging two of them to safety despite suffering two wounds himself. He is mortally wounded while treating the fourth wounded Marine and receives the Medal of Honor posthumously for his actions.

1 May

In one of the most unique aerial operations conducted during the Korean War, eight AD Skyraiders from Attack Squadron (VA) 195 and Composite Squadron (VC) 35 launch a torpedo attack against the Hwachon Dam in North Korea, the first such operation carried out since World War II. The squadrons score hits on the dam, flooding the Han and Pukhan River valleys. To this day VA-195, now Strike Fighter Squadron (VFA) 195, is nicknamed the "Dambusters."

20 May

Heavy shore batteries at Wonsan, North Korea, take the destroyer *Brinkley Bass* (DD 887) under fire and score one hit on the ship, killing one man and wounding nine others. The ship maneuvers out of range without serious material damage, delivering counterbattery fire.

21 May

One day after beginning fire support operations off the coast of Korea, the battleship *New Jersey* (BB 62) is hit by a shore battery, suffering slight damage with the loss of one sailor killed and three wounded.

2 April

In the first use of jet aircraft as bombers, F9F Panthers of Fighter Squadron (VF) 191 off the aircraft carrier *Princeton* (CV 45) bomb the bridge at Songjin, North Korea. The core of this squadron consists of pilots of the Blue Angels Flight Demonstration Team, which was disbanded for service in the Korean War.

5 April

During an engagement between elements of the First Marine Division and an enemy force in Korea, Hospital Corpsman Richard D. DeWert bravely

Above: *As the transport Begor (APD 127) stands by offshore, military stores are destroyed in dramatic fashion to deny their use to the enemy following the evacuation of Hungnam, North Korea, 24 December 1950. (Naval Historical Center)*

Left: *The Republic of Korea minesweeper YMS-516 strikes a mine during operations to open and clear Wonsan Harbor on 18 October 1950. She was formerly the U.S.-built YMS-148, which served with the Royal Navy in World War II. (Naval Historical Center)*

5 June

In the continuing effort to interdict the flow of supplies to Communist troops on the front lines, carrier-based aircraft of Task Force 77 begin participating in strikes as part of Operation Strangle, joining U.S. Air Force planes and those of the First Marine Aircraft Wing (MAW) in attacking eight supply routes. The operation lasts until 20 September, when it is determined to have been only minimally successful. "Most of our flying is what they call 'armed reconnaissance,' which is the searching out and destroying of ground targets. Such as trucks, trains, supply centers, ammo dumps, troops, gun emplacements, tanks, etc.," a Navy pilot describes in a letter to a friend in the United States. "Due to their expert camouflaging, targets are very difficult to find. On my last hop we caught two trucks on the road—burned one, knocked out or badly damaged the other one. They were camouflaged with large, freshly cut tree boughs."

12 June

The destroyer *Walke* (DD 723) strikes a mine while operating off Hungnam, North Korea. The blast kills twenty-six members of her crew and wounds thirty-five others.

14 June

The destroyer minesweeper *Thompson* (DMS 38) is hit fourteen times by enemy shore batteries off Songjin, North Korea. Three sailors are killed and four others wounded.

18 June

Admiral Robert B. Carney assumes his duties as the first Commander, Allied Command Southern Europe.

3 July

Despite the fact that darkness is approaching, Lieutenant (junior grade) John K. Koelsch volunteers to attempt a helicopter rescue of a downed Marine pilot in North Korea. Arriving inland with a solid overcast developing, Koelsch descends into a mountainous area without the benefit of fighter escort. Locating the position of the downed flier, who is

Above: *In one of the most successful and unconventional air strikes of the Korean War, Commander "Swede" Carlson led AD Skyraiders of Attack Squadron (VA) 195 and Composite Squadron (VC) 35 in launching aerial torpedoes that knocked out flood gates of the Hwachon Dam in North Korea. The aviators ran a gauntlet of antiaircraft fire as they exited the target area. (R.G. Smith)*

suffering from painful burns, Koelsch maneuvers his HO3S into position for his aircrewman to lower the rescue hoist. While in the process of bringing the Marine aboard, the helicopter is hit by enemy fire and crashes. The three men depart the crash site and avoid capture for nine days. Once captured, Koelsch displays fortitude and inspires his fellow prisoners in his refusal to aid his captors. He dies in captivity and for his actions in the air and in a POW camp, he is awarded the Medal of Honor posthumously.

10 July
The first truce talks between the opposing forces in Korea commence at Kaesong, on the border between North and South Korea. The chief United Nations delegate is Vice Admiral C. Turner Joy, Commander, U.S. Naval Forces, Far East, who is joined at the conference table by Rear Admiral Arleigh A. Burke, Commander, Cruiser Division 5.

22 July
Chief of Naval Operations Admiral Forrest P. Sherman suffers a heart attack and dies while visiting Naples, Italy.

28 July
The cruiser *Los Angeles* (CA 135) enters Haeju-Man channel and engages unsuspecting North Korean shore batteries, demonstrating United Nations control of the Ongjin Peninsula area.

31 July
Dan A. Kimball, an Army pilot during World War I and former Assistant Secretary of the Navy for Air, takes office as the fifty-first Secretary of the Navy.

11 August
The minesweepers *Dextrous* (AM 341) and *Redstart* (AM 378) come under fire by shore batteries while conducting check sweep operations in the vicinity Hodo-pando, North Korea. *Dextrous* suffers two direct hits that cause moderate damage, killing one sailor and wounding three others.

16 August
Admiral William M. Fechteler, a battleship skipper and leader of amphibious operations as part of the Seventh Fleet during World War II, becomes the thirteenth Chief of Naval Operations.

25 August
U.S. Navy carrier aircraft support long-range strikes by U.S. Air Force B-29 bombers as F2H Banshees and F9F Panthers off the aircraft carrier *Essex* (CV 9) escort a mission against the railroad marshalling yards at Rashin, North Korea.

7 September
In its first shipboard evaluation, a Terrier missile is fired from the missile test ship *Norton Sound* (AVM 1) and intercepts an F6F target drone.

3 October
Rotary-wing aircraft formally enter the arena of antisubmarine warfare with the establishment of Helicopter Antisubmarine Squadron (HS) 1, the first squadron of its type in the U.S. Navy, at Naval Air Station Key West, Florida.

29 October
Based on an intelligence report, VF-54 AD Skyraiders from the carrier *Essex* (CV 9) attack the Communist Party headquarters building in Kapsan, North Korea, eliminating more than 500 Party officials.

6 November
While conducting weather reconnaissance over the Sea of Japan, a P2V Neptune of VP-6 is attacked by Soviet fighter planes and shot down. All ten crewmembers are reported as missing and presumed dead.

21 November
The cruiser *Los Angeles* is detached from Task Force 77 and speeds to the waters off Kojo, North Korea, where

Opposite: *Chief of Naval Operations (CNO) Admiral Forrest P. Sherman (left) confers with Admiral Robert B. Carney, Commander in Chief, Allied Forces, Southern Europe, after arriving in Naples, Italy, on 20 July 1951. At that time the youngest man to ever hold the post of CNO, Sherman died of a heart attack two days later and was succeeded by Admiral William M. Fechteler. (Naval Historical Center)*

Right: *A Western Union telegram relaying the dreaded news to the family of Lieutenant (junior grade) John K. Koelsch that he died while in captivity in North Korea. Koelsch, who volunteered for a hazardous rescue mission in July 1951, was the first helicopter pilot to ever receive the Medal of Honor. (National Museum of Naval Aviation)*

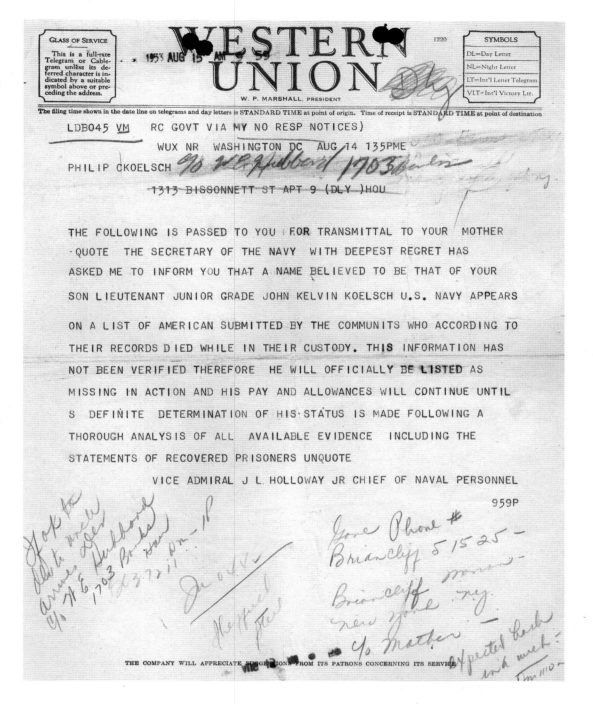

she bombards enemy forces threatening to cut off the First Republic of Korea Corps. The naval gunfire is successful in driving the Communist troops back.

1952

11 January
In an effort to interdict the flow of men and materiel, ships of Task Force 95 and aircraft of Task Force 77 begin a sustained offensive against North Korea's coastal rail network under the codenames Project Package and Project Derail.

30 January
Vice Admiral Lynde D. McCormick is named the North Atlantic Treaty Organization's (NATO) first Supreme Allied Commander Atlantic. The command becomes operational on 10 April.

February
As forty-five North Korean sampans attempt to capture the islands of Kil-chu and Myongchon off the city of Songjin, North Korea, the destroyer *Shelton* (DD 790) and destroyer minesweeper *Endicott* (DMS 35) join the New Zealand frigate *Taupo* in breaking up the attack with gunfire. Several sampans reach Kil-chu, but their occupants are defeated by the island's South Korean Marine defenders.

Left: *Anxious for news on the progress of negotiations, war correspondents surround Rear Admiral Arleigh A. Burke, a United Nations delegate to the armistice talks at Kaesong, 12 July 1951. Not until July 1953 would a cease-fire end the stalemate in Korea. (Naval Historical Center)*

21 April

While providing naval gunfire in support of operations in Korea, a turret explosion on board the cruiser *St. Paul* (CA 73) kills thirty crewmen.

26 April

In one of the worst operational accidents at sea since World War II, the aircraft carrier *Wasp* (CV 18) and destroyer minesweeper *Hobson* (DMS 26) collide in the North Atlantic. *Hobson* is cut in half and goes down quickly, taking 176 of her crew with her.

8 May

The Navy establishes the Fleet Air Gunnery Unit to provide aerial gunnery training for Pacific Fleet squadrons.

14 June

The Navy's atomic era is born as the keel of the submarine *Nautilus* (SSN 571) is laid at the Electric Boat Company in Groton, Connecticut. Once commissioned in 1954, the submarine becomes the first nuclear-powered vessel in the world.

23–24 June

In a series of air strikes involving Navy, Marine Corps, and Air Force aircraft that are the largest since the end of World War II, American pilots log over 1,200 sorties in attacking the hydroelectric plants at Suiho, Chosen, Fusen, and Kyosen, North Korea.

1 July

The Navy establishes the Naval Guided Missile School at the Fleet Air Defense Training Center at Dam Neck, Virginia, and the Naval Air Guided Missile School (Advanced) at the Naval Air Technical Training Center at Naval Air Station Jacksonville, Florida.

11–12 July

American Marine, Navy, and Air Force aircraft join those of Great Britain and Australia to bomb railroad yards and industrial facilities at Pyongyang, North Korea. Allied air assets return to the city to attack supply concentrations on 29 August.

14 July

The keel for the Navy's first supercarrier, *Forrestal* (CVB 59), is laid at Newport News Shipbuilding and Dry Dock Company in Norfolk, Virginia.

6 August

A hangar deck fire on board *Boxer* operating off Korea kills eight crewmen, but does not necessitate the carrier's withdrawal from the combat zone.

13 August

With his company under attack while defending a hill well forward of the main line of resistance in Korea, Hospital Corpsman John E. Kilmer braves enemy fire while moving from position to position to treat the wounded. He continues his work despite being hit by

mortar fragments. While treating a wounded Marine, he shields the man from enemy fire with his own body and is mortally wounded. He receives the Medal of Honor posthumously for his actions.

28 August
Guided Missile Unit 90 attacks a railroad bridge at Hungnam, North Korea, launching an explosives-laden F6F drone from the aircraft carrier *Boxer*.

1 September
U.S. Navy forces, including the carriers *Midway* and *Franklin D. Roosevelt* and battleship *Wisconsin* (BB 64), join ships of other allied nations participating in Operation Mainbrace in the North Atlantic, NATO's first major naval exercise.

Carrier-based aircraft from Task Force 77 strike the North Korean oil refinery at Aoji, eight miles from the Soviet border.

3 September
The first firing of a Sidewinder air-to-air missile occurs at the Naval Ordnance Test Station in Inyokern, California.

5 September
During a night attack against elements of the First Marine Division in Korea, Hospital Corpsman Third Class Edward C. Benford leaves his protected position and advances to an exposed ridgeline to ascertain the condition of two Marines huddled in a bomb crater. He unhesitatingly grabs two enemy grenades that land in the crater, and charges two oncoming enemy soldiers, pushing the grenades into their chests and killing them. Benford is mortally wounded and is awarded the Medal of Honor posthumously.

Above: *A sailor operates a winch on board the minesweeper* Mockingbird *(AMS 27) off Korea in 1950. The Korean War marked the first significant combat action following President Harry S. Truman's desegregation of the armed forces. (Naval Historical Center)*

Right: *A ring of fire marks the firing of 5-inch guns on board the cruiser* Los Angeles *(CA 135) during a bombardment of Wonsan Harbor in 1951. With the North Korean navy virtually nonexistent, ship-versus-ship actions were few; U.S. Navy ships spent much of their time on station in Korea bombarding targets on shore. (Naval Historical Center)*

Left: *Planes of Carrier Air Group (CVG) 2 ready for launch from* Philippine Sea *(CV 47) operating off Korea, circa 1950. Though jets made their combat debut in Korea, propeller-driven aircraft, including the World War II-era F4U Corsair pictured in the foreground, flew the bulk of the strike missions. (National Museum of Naval Aviation)*

Below: *Crewmen handle ammunition at pierside in preparation for loading the cruiser* Toledo *(CA 133). (Naval Historical Center)*

16 September

The destroyer *Barton* (DD 722) strikes a mine while operating in the waters some ninety miles east of Wonsan, North Korea, killing five members of her crew.

9 October

"Cherokee strikes," so named because of the Native American ancestry of Seventh Fleet Commander Vice Admiral Joseph J. Clark, commence with carrier aircraft striking targets along the front lines that are beyond the range of United Nations artillery.

28 October

The XA3D-1 Skywarrior, the largest aircraft to ever operate from the deck of an aircraft carrier and a long-lived design that operates into the 1980s, makes its first flight. Though initially designed as a nuclear strike aircraft, the aircraft known as the "Whale" also serves as a tanker, reconnaissance, and electronic warfare platform.

3 November

The missile test ship *Norton Sound* launches a Regulus assault missile off the coast of California in the missile system's first shipboard demonstration.

18 November

Seven Soviet MiG-15 fighters approach Task Force 77, which is launching strikes against North Korea from the waters near the Soviet naval base at Vladivostok. Three F9F Panthers of Fighter Squadron (VF) 781, flying combat air patrol, engage the Soviet planes, shooting down two of them and damaging a third.

4 December

The XS2F-1 Tracker, prototype of the first carrier-based aircraft designed specifically for antisubmarine warfare, makes its first flight.

Right: *Perched on the folded wing of an F4U Corsair, an ordnanceman arms high-velocity aircraft rockets on the deck of the carrier* Bon Homme Richard *(CVA 31), November 1952. In production longer than any piston-engine fighter in history, the venerable F4U served at sea and ashore, scoring air-to-air kills both day and night and continuing its sterling World War II reputation as a capable ground attack platform, especially in providing close air support for troops on the front lines. (National Museum of Naval Aviation)*

1953

12–16 January

Testing of the angled flight deck on board the aircraft carrier *Antietam* (CVA 36) occurs with six types of aircraft conducting operations from the carrier in various wind conditions day and night. The angled deck becomes a feature on all Navy carriers, greatly diminishing the accident rate.

18 January

While flying a patrol over the Formosa Strait, a P2V Neptune of VP-22 is shot down off Swatow, China, by Communist Chinese antiaircraft fire. Eleven of the thirteen crewmen escape the aircraft and are recovered by a Coast Guard PBM Mariner, which crashes during takeoff in heavy seas. Eventually, the destroyer *Halsey Powell* (DD 686) braves enemy fire to pull ten men from the sea. Eleven Navy and Coast Guard personnel are lost.

4 February

Texas attorney Robert B. Anderson becomes the fifty-second Secretary of the Navy.

9–10 February

Aircraft from the carriers of Task Force 77 strike supply concentrations and the transportation network from Wonsan through Songjin to Chongjin, North Korea.

MINE WARFARE IN KOREA

by Dr. Malcom Muir, Jr.

Ever since its employment in the American Civil War, the mine has proven the most effective weapon of the lesser naval power. Inexpensive and lethal, it is the great leveler, capable of inflicting appalling damage on the largest warships and of sinking smaller vessels outright. So potent is the mine that it can close waters to the strongest fleet, thereby canceling the advantages usually conferred by superior sea power in blockade and power projection.

Following the Civil War, U.S. Navy interest in mine warfare ebbed and flowed. In 1945, American minecraft numbered approximately 550, but with the drawdown of the postwar years, almost all these vessels went into reserve or were sold for scrap. By 1950, only seven U.S. mine countermeasures ships served in the Pacific, the few sailors still assigned to minesweeping duty finding most of their work honing their antisubmarine skills and towing targets. However, events soon vaulted the unheralded art of mine warfare to the fore once again.

The outbreak of the Korean War confounded Defense Department soothsayers in many respects, not least in the neglected area of mine warfare. In October 1950, General of the Army Douglas MacArthur tried to follow up his great success at Inchon by putting a landing force across the path of the retreating North Koreans at Wonsan. Soviet mines, many of Tsarist vintage, laid by North Korean sampans and other small craft, thwarted his powerful amphibious thrust. American intelligence regarding the threat was minimal, but its extent became shockingly evident on 12 October, when three U.S. minecraft, just starting to clear Wonsan waters, brought thirteen mines to the surface within minutes. Two of the sweepers, *Pirate* (AM 275) and *Pledge* (AM 277), unable to extricate themselves from the field, struck mines and sank. During the next two weeks, Marines and soldiers steamed back and forth in transports offshore (in the sardonically dubbed "Operation Yo-Yo"), while sweepers laboriously cleared channels through the massive field. The timetable for the landings was delayed by ten days. As Rear Admiral Allan E. Smith exclaimed in frustration, "We have lost control of the seas to a nation without a navy, using pre–World War I weapons, laid by vessels that were utilized at the time of the birth of Christ." Smith recommended that mine countermeasures be given the priority accorded antiaircraft and antisubmarine warfare.

Over the course of the war, mines remained the most potent Communist naval weapons. Of the five U.S. warships lost in Korean waters, all were sunk by mines, and five additional U.S. naval vessels suffered damage. Fortunately, the Soviet Union generally supplied its allies with only contact mines but, on occasion, more advanced magnetic types were provided. These weapons and the specter of sophisticated pressure mines forced the United Nations command to take constant countermeasures along much of the North Korean coast.

Sweeping was tedious and dangerous, especially at night. The minecraft were mostly small wooden vessels (the 136-foot AMS) that gave a rough ride. Lanes had to be marked methodically and swept continually because the Communists would frequently "freshen" their fields. Since the sweepers were small warships, enemy coastal defense batteries frequently took them under fire, and thus the minecraft needed a larger destroyer, cruiser, or battleship to "ride shotgun."

By 1951 the minesweepers were back on top of their game. The Pacific Fleet's minesweeping command, eliminated following World War II, was resurrected early that year; forces were augmented with vessels taken from reserve or from the building yards. By the end of the war, 125 new minesweepers were in commission or under construction. Although shipboard techniques and equipment remained

Right: *Sailors on board* Mockingbird *(AMS 27) deploy an acoustic hammer box prior to commencing minesweeping operations in Korean waters. The long-serving minesweeper helped pave the way for amphibious landings at Pohang and Inchon in South Korea, and served throughout the war, receiving ten battle stars for her service. (Naval Historical Center)*

reminiscent of World War II, minehunters adopted new technology in the form of helicopters to assist in spotting mines. The increased effectiveness of these measures can be judged by a simple comparison. In the first year of the war, minesweepers disposed of about 200 enemy mines at a cost of five sweepers. Over the next two years, the minehunters removed almost 900 mines while suffering no losses. Thus,

the minecraft sailors could be justly proud of one assessment praising them for their "high state of efficiency and effectiveness." Public recognition, usually a rarity for those who worked so far from the limelight, came in the form of Presidential Unit Citations. Ten U.S. Navy warships were decorated with the coveted award during the Korean conflict; all of these were minesweepers.

13 February

The Sparrow III missile makes its first full guidance flight at the Naval Missile Test Center, Point Mugu, California.

1 March

Carrier aircraft launched from Task Force 77 score numerous hits on the hydroelectric plant at Chosen, North Korea, causing heavy damage. They strike the same target on 5 March.

6 March

The submarine *Tunny* (SSG 284), refitted to launch the Regulus surface-to-surface missile, is commissioned. She conducts her first test firing of the missile on 15 July. A recipient of two Presidential Unit Citations for her World War II service, the submarine remains a missile boat until 1965, at which time she begins conversion to a troop-carrying submarine. Engaging in unconventional warfare operations off Vietnam, she receives five battle stars before being decommissioned in 1969.

Hospital Corpsman Francis C. Hammond is seriously wounded when the enemy counterattacks. He continues to treat the wounded over the course of a four-hour period until his platoon is ordered to withdraw. While supervising the evacuation of casualties and assisting the corpsmen of the relieving unit, he is killed by enemy fire. Hammond is awarded the Medal of Honor posthumously.

27 March

In action with an enemy force in Korea, Hospital Corpsman Third Class William R. Charette performs numerous acts of courage—throwing himself on the body of a wounded Marine to shield him from the blast of an enemy grenade that lands a few feet away; removing his own protective vest and giving it to another wounded Marine; and exposing himself to enemy fire by standing up in a trench in order to better treat a leg wound suffered by another man. For his actions, Charette receives the Medal of Honor.

19 March

Carrier aircraft from Task Force 77 strike industrial targets in Chongjin, North Korea.

26–27 March

Serving in a platoon of the First Marine Division in Korea during an attack against an enemy force,

11 June

During the Korean War the Navy executes numerous evacuations of civilian personnel, culminating on this date with the completion of the evacuation of 19,425 civilians from islands on the west coast of Korea north of the 38th parallel.

Right: *Dramatic air-sea rescue of Ensign E. H. Barry, pilot of an AF Guardian that he was forced to ditch immediately after launching from the carrier* Block Island *(CVE 106) circa 1952. Barry's parachute has opened and partially filled with water, putting a strain on shroud lines and creating a "tug-of-war" situation between the parachute and the HUP helicopter with the pilot in the middle. The photo was taken by a Navy photographer on the bridge of the destroyer* Bears *(DD 654). (Naval Photographic Center)*

Left: *President Dwight D. Eisenhower poses with two soldiers and a Navy corpsman to whom he has just presented the Medal of Honor for conspicuous gallantry against the enemy in Korea, 12 January 1954. Shown are (l–r): First Lieutenant Edward R. Showalter, Jr., USA; Private First Class Ernest E. West, USA; President Eisenhower; and Hospital Corpsman Third Class William R. Charette, USN. (Naval Historical Center)*

16 July

Lieutenant Guy P. Bordelon, Jr., operating as part of a Composite Squadron (VC) 3 detachment temporarily based ashore to combat nocturnal raids against Seoul, South Korea, shoots down a North Korean PO-2, his fifth kill of the war. Bordelon is the only Navy ace of the Korean War.

27 July

The signing of an armistice between United Nations and Communist negotiators at Panmunjom, South Korea, ends hostilities in Korea. On the final day of the war Navy aircraft from Task Force 77 destroy or damage 23 railroad cars, 11 railroad bridges, one railroad tunnel, and nine highway bridges.

12 August

The experimental ship *Mississippi* (EAG 128), formerly (BB 41), conducts the first successful shipboard launch of a fully guided Terrier missile, which successfully intercepts an F6F drone.

17 August

Admiral Robert B. Carney—chief of staff to Admiral William F. Halsey, Jr., during the latter part of World War II and a NATO commander in Southern Europe—becomes the fourteenth Chief of Naval Operations.

3 October

An F4D Skyray flown by Lieutenant Commander James F. Verdin establishes a new world's speed record, covering the 3-kilometer course at Muroc, California, at 752.943 miles per hour.

16 October

While the aircraft carrier *Leyte* (CVS 32) undergoes an overhaul in the Boston Navy Yard, Massachusetts, an explosion and fire in the vicinity of the portside catapult control room kills thirty-two crewmen and five civilian yard workers.

30 October

The adoption of National Security Council directive Number 162 reflects President Dwight D. Eisenhower's so-called "New Look" defense policy that places an emphasis on strategic warfare.

1954

4 January

The aircraft carrier *Leyte* (CVS 32) begins operations as the first antisubmarine warfare (ASW) carrier. The new concept employs flattops as centerpieces of task groups that include destroyers and, sometimes, submarines in an effort to combat the growing Soviet submarine menace.

Right: *A Terrier surface-to-air missile streaks skyward after being launched from the experimental auxiliary ship* Mississippi *(EAG 128) during at-sea tests, circa 1954. In the years following World War II, the Navy devoted much attention to the development of guided missiles for use aboard ship. (Naval Historical Center)*

3 May
Charles S. Thomas, a naval reservist during World War I and former Under Secretary of the Navy, takes office as the fifty-third Secretary of the Navy.

25 May
A ZPG-2 airship under the command of Commander Marion H. Eppes lands on this day after a record-setting flight lasting eight days and eight hours.

26 May
While conducting flight operations in the North Atlantic, the aircraft carrier *Bennington* (CVA 20) suffers a catapult explosion that kills 103 of her crew and embarked air group and injures 201 others.

27 May
To keep World War II-era carriers capable of operating increasingly larger and more powerful jet aircraft, the Chief of Naval Operations approves a plan to add angled flight decks and an enclosed hurricane bow to *Essex*-class carriers.

1 June
In the initial trials of the first steam catapult installed on board a U.S. Navy carrier, an S2F Tracker successfully launches from the aircraft carrier *Hancock* (CVA 19). Through the remainder of the month, a variety of aircraft make 254 successful launches.

22 June
The XA4D-1 Skyhawk, a light attack aircraft that becomes a mainstay in Vietnam and serves as a training aircraft into 2003, makes its first flight.

26 July
While engaged in a search for survivors of a British Cathay Airlines plane shot down by Chinese fighter aircraft off Hainan Island on 22 June, two AD Skyraiders from the aircraft carrier *Philippine Sea* (CVA 47) are attacked by a pair of Chinese La-7 fighters. The Navy planes return fire and shoot down both of the attackers.

Below: *General Mark Clark, USA, signs the armistice agreement at the Panmunjom negotiation table, 27 July 1953, bringing an end to the Korean War. Also present are (l–r): Vice Admiral Robert P. Briscoe, Commander Navy Forces, Far East, and Vice Admiral J. J. Clark, Commander Seventh Fleet. (Naval Historical Center)*

Left: Essex *(CVA 9) plows through heavy ocean swells in 1961. Leading the Navy to victory in World War II, the* Essex-*class carriers formed a significant part of the Navy's postwar carrier fleet, with modernizations such as the installation of angled and reinforced flight decks and hurricane bows enabling them to keep pace with the rapidly advancing technology of jet aircraft. (Naval Historical Center)*

16 August
Operation Passage to Freedom, which will last into May 1955, begins. The operation involves U.S. Navy ships supporting a provision of the Geneva Accords that ended the French Indochina War, which permits Vietnamese living in North Vietnam to move to South Vietnam. All told, the Navy transports 293,002 civilians and 17,846 military personnel.

4 September
While operating off the coast of Siberia, a P2V Neptune of VP-19 is shot down by Soviet MiG-15 fighter aircraft. One crewman is lost in the engagement, but a Coast Guard aircraft rescues the nine that survive the encounter.

30 September
Nautilus, the world's first nuclear-powered submarine, is placed in commission.

Left: *Chinese Nationalist soldiers come over the side of* Lenawee *(APA 195) during the evacuation of the Tachen Islands, 2 March 1955. (Naval Historical Center)*

Opposite: *Nautilus (SSN 571) underway in 1955. Reactor plants gave submarines unlimited range and the ability to operate virtually without detection. The combination of endurance, stealth, and ballistic missile launch capabilities eventually shifted most of America's strategic deterrence force to the Navy. (Naval Historical Center)***Above:** *Boston (CAG 1), commissioned during*

1955

17 January
With her skipper, Commander Eugene P. Wilkinson, radioing the message "underway on nuclear power," the submarine *Nautilus* proceeds down Long Island Sound into the Atlantic for sea trials.

6 February
The Seventh Fleet, under Vice Admiral Alfred M. Pride, begins a weeklong evacuation of Nationalist Chinese civilians and military personnel from the Tachen Islands. Carrier aircraft provide cover for the operation, which involves the movement of some 29,000 soldiers and civilians.

25 March
The XF8U-1 Crusader makes its first flight, breaking the sound barrier. It will become a front-line fighter and photoreconaissance platform in Vietnam.

22 June
An attack by Soviet MiG-15 aircraft against a P2V Neptune of VP-9 results in one of the patrol plane's engines catching fire. It makes a forced landing on St. Lawrence Island in the Bering Sea with no fatalities.

17 August
Famed World War II destroyerman Admiral Arleigh A. Burke becomes the fifteenth Chief of Naval Operations.

22–24 August
Pilots of Experimental Squadron (VX) 3 evaluate the mirror landing system on board the aircraft carrier *Bennington*. The system, which replaces the paddle-waving landing signal officers, soon becomes standard on board U.S. Navy flattops.

1 October
The aircraft carrier *Forrestal* (CVA 59) is commissioned, the largest carrier built for the U.S. Navy to date.

1 November
Boston (CAG 1) is placed in commission at the Philadelphia Naval Shipyard, Pennsylvania. She is the world's first guided missile cruiser, featuring two launchers capable of firing Terrier surface-to-air missiles.

17 November
The Secretary of the Navy establishes a Special Projects Office to conduct work on the development of shipboard launching systems for ballistic missiles.

ADMIRAL ARLEIGH A. BURKE

by Dr. David A. Rosenberg

Admiral Arleigh A. Burke was the most junior officer ever appointed to the post of Chief of Naval Operations (CNO). He completed three two-year terms as CNO from 1955 to 1961, the longest anyone has served in that position. Burke is best remembered as the U.S. Navy's most famous surface warfare officer as a result of his exploits leading destroyer units World War II, but his impact on the service continues into the twenty-first century in multiple ways.

Burke was born on the family farm near Boulder, Colorado, on 19 October 1901, the grandson of a Swedish immigrant and son of a farmer and a teacher. The 1918 flu epidemic prevented him from completing high school, but he won appointment to the U.S. Naval Academy in 1919. He graduated on 7 June 1923, and married Kansas native Roberta "Bobbie" Gorsuch the same day. After five years in the battleship *Arizona* (BB 39), Burke was selected for an ordnance specialty, one of the most influential in the U.S. Navy between the world wars. He earned a master's degree in chemical engineering from the University of Michigan in 1931 and served as a design and production specialist in explosives at the Bureau of Ordnance and as a gun mount inspector at the Naval Gun Factory.

Although he came late to destroyer service in 1937, Burke's first command, *Mugford* (DD 389), won the Destroyer Gunnery Trophy in 1939, and it would be in the "greyhounds of the fleet" that he would receive national acclaim during World War II. Arriving in the South Pacific in early 1943, he proved a skilled combat surface force commander and tactical innovator. He received the nickname "31 Knot Burke" in November 1943 when his Destroyer Squadron 23 decisively defeated a Japanese force in the Battle of Cape St. George in the Solomon Islands. Burke subsequently served as Vice Admiral Marc A. Mitscher's chief of staff with the fast carriers during the Marianas, Philippines, Iwo Jima, and Okinawa campaigns.

After the war, Captain Burke continued to serve under Mitscher while the admiral commanded the Eighth Fleet and Atlantic Fleet. Burke developed the Navy's first postwar long-range plan for the Secretary of the Navy as a member of the General Board, and helped coordinate the service's testimony before Congress during the 1949 hearings on defense unification and strategy. At the direction of CNO Admiral Forrest Sherman, Burke directed an expanding operational staff and served as the top planner for Commander Naval Forces, Far East, during the first year of the Korean War. He also was a member of the first United Nations Truce Negotiation Team during the Korean War in the last half of 1951 and subsequently directed the Navy's strategic plans division into 1954.

Rear Admiral Burke was serving as Commander, Destroyer Force, U.S. Atlantic Fleet in 1955 when President Dwight Eisenhower appointed him over ninety-two senior admirals to become Chief of Naval Operations. As CNO, Burke fought against increased unification and restriction of command authority in the armed forces, and for maintenance of a balanced, flexible fleet capable of responding quickly and effectively to crises and limited wars. He played a key role in planning military responses to Cold War crises over Suez, Lebanon, Indonesia, the Taiwan Straits, Berlin, and Cuba.

Burke possessed instincts for the potential of technology and the requirements of future combat that enabled him to build a Navy suited not only for his time, but also for decades to come. He was the critical leader who overruled advisors concerned about cost and feasibility to champion the development of the Polaris submarine-based ballistic missile, deployed in 1960, as a national nuclear deterrent system. Burke believed that a small, relatively invulnerable force of missile submarines could deter war and ensure a controlled response to Soviet attack. Burke's strategy of "finite deterrence, controlled retaliation" was tied to the need to prepare for limited as well as general war. He led one of the few serious challenges to massive retaliation and nuclear build-up during the Eisenhower years. His vision for a sea-based national strategic deterrent system continues in the Trident submarine force of the twenty-first century.

As CNO, Burke also promoted new technologies to enable the Navy to communicate and coordinate its

intrigued by the new tactics for "vertical envelopment" using helicopters, oversaw Navy procurement for the first classes of helicopter assault ships, and directed the successful Marine landing in Lebanon in 1958.

Burke was above all a sailor. He felt a bond with naval officers everywhere based on a shared experience of the sea. During his year in Japan in 1950–1951, Burke developed lifelong friendships with Japanese officers, and helped found the Japanese Maritime Self-Defense Force. As CNO, he cultivated close relationships with his counterparts in England, Germany, France, Japan, and Australia. He initiated a program, still in operation, which enabled naval officers from around the world to attend a year-long senior Naval Command Course at the Naval War College in Newport, Rhode Island. Believing that every naval officer was a member of "the fraternity of the blue uniform," he helped lay the groundwork for international cooperation in global coalition naval operations.

Burke's unquestioned integrity and self-discipline, and his legendary capacity for hard work, enabled him to achieve great things, yet he was also a man of genuine humility, and a generous sense of humor. His leadership was grounded in the Navy tradition of loyalty to seniors and subordinates: "loyalty up and down." He believed in broad delegation of authority and responsibility as a means of encouraging individual initiative and as a sign of great confidence in his subordinates. Burke understood well the great uncertainties of combat and repeatedly told shipmates that the difference between a successful officer and an unsuccessful one was "ten seconds." Further, "when you have anything to do, the time to do it is right now. If you've got power, use it and use it fast, and the time to make a decision is as soon as the problem presents itself."

Arleigh Burke retired from the Navy in August 1961. He had a long and distinguished post-CNO career on corporate boards, in founding the Center for Strategic and International Studies, and in public service with institutions such as the USO and the Boy Scouts of America. Admiral Burke died 1 January 1996 and was buried in the cemetery at the U.S. Naval Academy. On his tombstone is the single word epitaph: SAILOR.

operations tactically and around the globe. He fostered the introduction of computer-based command and control at sea in the Naval Tactical Data System and approved the nation's first space-based intelligence system, the GRAB electronic intelligence satellite. His successful innovations in night battle tactics in World War II led him to emphasize a variety of technologies and weapons systems to support all-weather and nighttime operations as CNO, including the F4H (F-4) Phantom II fighter and A2F (A-6) Intruder attack aircraft. He also championed a new form of one-stop combat support ship—the AOE—that remains the mainstay of U.S. Navy underway replenishment and rearmament. He was a powerful advocate of nuclear propulsion for surface ships, including aircraft carriers and surface combatants, and ordered that all submarines built after 1956 be nuclear-powered. He controlled the Navy's use of submarines as reconnaissance platforms and sent *Nautilus* (SSN 571) under the North Pole in 1958, and *Triton* (SSRN 586) on the first submerged circumnavigation of the globe in 1960. As a midshipman Burke had toyed with the idea of becoming a Marine, and in the 1930s had witnessed the creation of the Fleet Marine Force. As CNO he took a great interest in amphibious operations. He was

Above: *Admiral Arleigh A. Burke's World War II service included command of destroyers and duty as chief of staff to Vice Admiral Marc A. Mitscher, planning carrier operations during 1944–1945. This foundation of experience combined with his visionary advocacy of new technology made him an excellent leader of the sea service during the period 1955–1961. His legacy still influences the Navy of the modern era. (Corbis)*

1956

10 January
The Navy establishes its first nuclear power school at the submarine base at New London, Connecticut.

12 March
VA-83 becomes the first missile-equipped squadron to make a deployment on board an aircraft carrier. Flying F7U Cutlass aircraft capable of launching Sparrow missiles, the squadron operates from *Intrepid* (CVA 11). VA-46, equipped with Sidewinder missiles, deploys in June.

20 July
Thetis Bay (CVHA 1), the Navy's first amphibious assault ship, is commissioned. Her designation is changed to LPH 6 in 1959. She never supports a combat landing during her service, which ends with her decommissioning in 1964.

21 August
An F8U Crusader piloted by Commander Robert W. Windsor sets a new national speed record of 1,015.428 miles per hour over a 15-kilometer course at the Naval Ordnance Test Station in China Lake, California. The F8U becomes the first operationally equipped aircraft to exceed 1,000 miles per hour.

22 August
A P4M Mercator of Electronic Countermeasures Squadron (VQ) 1 is shot down by hostile aircraft off the coast of China. All sixteen men aboard are killed.

11 October
An R6D Skymaster of VR-6 crashes in the Atlantic with the loss of fifty-nine passengers and crewmen.

29 October
Israeli forces invade the Sinai Peninsula and advance toward the Suez Canal. In response, ships of the Navy's Sixth Fleet begin evacuating U.S. nationals from the area. All told, 2,213 people are evacuated by air and sea.

Above: Boston *(CAG 1), commissioned during World War II, was converted to a guided missile heavy cruiser in 1955, her after gun batteries replaced by Terrier missiles. ("USS* Boston," *Rod Claudius, Naval Historical Center)*

31 October

An R4D Skytrain named "Que Sera Sera" piloted by Lieutenant Commander Conrad Shinn and carrying Rear Admiral George Dufek and five crewmen lands at the South Pole. The men are the first to stand at the spot since British Royal Navy Captain Robert F. Scott in 1912.

3 December

Gyatt (DDG 712), the first destroyer equipped with the Terrier surface-to-air missile, is commissioned. The ship is also the first fitted with the Denny-Brown stabilization system, which consists of two, forty-five-square-foot retractable fins extending out from amidships well below the waterline to greatly reduce pitch and roll on the sea. In recognition of her pioneering role as a missile destroyer, she is redesignated DDG 1 in May 1957.

8 December

The Navy receives authorization to proceed with development of the solid-fuel missile for operations from submarines, under the Special Projects Office. A deadline is set for 1965, but is accelerated to 1960 by the Secretary of Defense.

1957

4–15 March

Commander Jack R. Hunt commands a ZPG-2 airship on a record-setting 264-hour endurance flight from the continental United States to the African coast and back.

17 March

Vanguard, the U.S. Navy's first satellite, is launched from Cape Canaveral, Florida. It weighs just three and one-half pounds.

21 March

In a round-trip coast-to-coast flight between Los Angeles and New York, an A3D Skywarrior flown by Commander Dale Cox establishes new west-to-east (9 hours, 31 minutes, 35.4 seconds) and east-to-west (5 hours, 12 minutes, 39.24 seconds) transcontinental speed records.

1 April

Thomas S. Gates, a decorated World War II naval officer and former Under Secretary of the Navy, becomes the fifty-fourth Secretary of the Navy.

12 August

Lieutenant Commander Don Walker, in a test of the automatic carrier landing system on board the carrier *Antietam* (CVS 36), makes the first "hands off" carrier landing.

23 December

Skate (SSN 578), the lead boat for the first class of nuclear-powered submarines, is commissioned.

1958

4 February

The keel for *Enterprise* (CVAN 65), the world's first nuclear-powered aircraft carrier, is laid at Newport News, Virginia.

7 March

Grayback (SSG 574), the first submarine designed from the keel up with the capability to launch Regulus guided missiles, is commissioned. She completes nine deterrent patrols, spending over twenty months at sea and covering a distance of more than 130,000 miles before decommissioning on 25 May 1964 for conversion to a submarine troop transport.

Above: *Admiral Arthur W. Radford pictured on 17 March 1954 during the first of his two terms as Chairman of the Joint Chiefs of Staff. (Naval Historical Center)*

Left: *Sir Edmund Hillary, Doctor Vivian Fuchs, and Rear Admiral George Dufek at a meeting two miles from the South Pole, Antarctica, 20 January 1958. Dr. Fuchs and his British Commonwealth trans-Antarctic expedition were at the end of a 950-mile transverse from the Weddell Sea Coast en route to McMurdo Sound. (Naval Historical Center)*

27 May
The XF4H-1 Phantom II, prototype of perhaps the most successful fighter aircraft ever built, makes its maiden flight.

28 May
The destroyer escort *Silverstein* (DE 534) collides with the submarine *Stickleback* (SS 415) off Pearl Harbor, Hawaii. The submarine, which broaches the surface just 200 yards in front of the destroyer after losing power during an ascent, sinks despite efforts to put her under tow. All members of her crew are rescued.

The guided missile cruiser *Galveston* (CLG 3), the first warship equipped with the Talos surface-to-air missile, called by Chief of Naval Operations Admiral Arleigh Burke "the best antiaircraft missile in any arsenal in the world," is placed in commission.

1 July
Submarine Squadron 14 is established, the first Fleet Ballistic Missile Submarine Squadron.

15 July
With the government of Lebanon threatened by civil war, President Camille Chamoun requests American

intervention. In response, on this day ships of the Sixth Fleet put Marines ashore at Beirut under the air cover of carrier aircraft from *Saratoga* (CVA 60) and *Essex* (CVA 9). Navy and Marine forces are soon bolstered by elements of the Army and Air Force. Negotiations end the civil war, and an American military presence remains in Lebanon until October.

3 August
The nuclear-powered submarine *Nautilus* becomes the first ship to reach the North Pole, reaching the pole while submerged under the polar ice cap.

11 August
As part of an exploratory voyage to the Arctic region of the globe, the nuclear-powered *Skate* becomes the first submarine to surface at the North Pole when her sail tower breaks through the ice.

Above: *The submarine* Grayback *(SSG 574) enters San Diego harbor with a Regulus I Medium range surface-to-surface missile on deck, 12 December 1958. (Naval Historical Center)*

UNDERWAY ON NUCLEAR POWER

by Rear Admiral W. J. Holland, Jr., U.S. Navy (Retired)

In the message, "Underway on nuclear power," the submarine *Nautilus* (SSN 571) announced a revolution in maritime warfare. When she first put to sea on 17 January 1955, it marked the culmination of technical triumphs and bureaucratic innovations that began on St. Patrick's Day 1939, even before the first self-sustaining nuclear fission reaction took place. Ross Gunn, technical advisor at the Naval Research Laboratory, after meeting with Enrico Fermi, father of the atom bomb, and recognizing nuclear energy could power a true submarine, began efforts then to create that capability. These submarines, when deployed in the 1950s and 1960s, changed the nature of naval warfare.

The Manhattan Project's focus on nuclear energy as an explosive essentially froze efforts on controlled fission, but in November 1944, the Deputy Commander of the Bureau of Ships (BUSHIPS), Rear Admiral Earle W. Mills, ensured that postwar plans for development of atomic energy included development of nuclear propulsion for the Navy. While these plans recommended developing nuclear-powered submarines, that road seemed to most officers and scientists a long and difficult one. In 1946, two events coincided to provide the impetus: the Oak Ridge Laboratory invited service representatives to learn about nuclear energy, and the Navy's General Board recommended immediate efforts to develop nuclear propulsion for submarines. Admiral Mills, now Chief of BUSHIPS, selected Captain Hyman G. Rickover to lead the Navy's team.

Though the stage was set, many organizational hurdles remained to be overcome by the energy, intelligence, and perseverance of Rickover and his cohorts. Typical was the November 1947 report of the General Advisory Committee, a board of scientists that advised the new Atomic Energy Commission (AEC), declaring that a nuclear submarine project was premature. Within a month, in documents drafted by Rickover and maneuvered by submarine officers including Commander Edward L. "Ned" Beach, the Navy demanded the AEC build a nuclear power plant for a submarine.

Still, little happened as the AEC's scientists studied the problem rather than seeking a solution. After months of fruitless badgering, Rickover proposed a joint AEC-Navy project similar to that used in the Bikini atom bomb tests. In August 1948, Mills established the Nuclear Power Branch in the Bureau of Ships, and shortly thereafter the Naval Reactors Branch of the Division of Reactor Development of the Atomic Energy Commission came into being. Rickover headed both. While the rest of the AEC dithered, Rickover convinced the Westinghouse Corporation to establish an atomic power division and by December 1948 the design contract for the prototype submarine reactor was in place. Thus, the organization that would produce the largest number of reactor plants in the world was in operation. Naval nuclear power and Rickover would be synonymous for the next thirty-four years.

Rickover selected materials and established methods that became the basis of the design and construction of nuclear power plants, civilian and military. The Navy program fostered technical developments and created industrial suppliers. His emphasis on training pervaded the program. High standards of performance and capital investment were hallmarks of this Navy program that carried over into successful civilian industrial organizations, many led by graduates of Rickover's programs.

Successes followed, pushed by the endless energy of Captain, and later Admiral Rickover. On 14 January 1952, President Harry Truman laid the keel of *Nautilus* and the following June a contract for the nuclear power plant for the carrier *Enterprise* (CVAN 65) was announced. On 30 March 1953, the Submarine Thermal Reactor, the world's first practical nuclear power plant, went critical.

Nautilus's initial operating period confirmed the advantages of nuclear propulsion. In April 1957 the submarine returned to the shipyard to refuel after

Right: Nautilus *(SSN 571), the submarine that changed the face of undersea warfare forever, nears completion at the Electric Boat Company in Groton, Connecticut, 1954. The historic ship is now on display at the Submarine Force Museum. (Hulton-Deutsch Collection/Corbis)*

more than two years at sea, the following year venturing under the North Pole. Also in 1958, *Seawolf* (SSN 575), the second nuclear-powered submarine, completed a sixty-day submerged voyage—a startling feat then, duplicated many times since. Reactor plants for new classes of submarines, aircraft carriers, and other surface ships followed. While costs lured surface warships to gas turbines, naval aviators never endorsed conventionally powered ships after *Enterprise* proved nuclear power's worth. Rickover's reactor plants grew more powerful and longer-lived until, by the time he retired in 1982, cores were configured to last the life of a ship—some thirty years.

The reputation for safe operation, reliability, and performance of naval reactors continues—an enviable record with few equals in or outside the service.

19 August

The XP3V-1, prototype for the P-3 Orion maritime patrol aircraft that remains operational to this day, makes its maiden flight.

The Tartar surface-to-air missile makes its first successful flight at the Naval Ordnance Test Station China Lake, California, successfully intercepting an F6F drone.

23 August

Communist Chinese artillery batteries begin shelling Nationalist Chinese forces on the offshore islands of Matsu and Quemoy, prompting President Dwight D. Eisenhower to dispatch elements of the Seventh Fleet to the region to support the transport of supplies from Formosa to Nationalist troops on Quemoy. He also orders six aircraft carriers to the waters around Formosa. The show of resolve ends the crisis by December.

25 August

Commander Forrest S. Petersen makes his first flight in the National Aeronautics and Space Administration's (NASA) X-15 high-speed research aircraft. Petersen is the only active-duty naval aviator assigned to the program.

15 September

While at the controls of an F8U-3 Crusader, Lieutenant William P. Lawrence becomes the first naval aviator to fly at twice the speed of sound in an operational-type airplane.

12 December

With the emphasis placed on development of the Polaris missile, the Secretary of the Navy cancels the Regulus II missile program less than three months after its successful launch from a submarine.

1959

11 March
The XHSS-2, prototype for the successful Sea King antisubmarine warfare helicopter, makes its first flight.

9 April
America's first seven astronauts selected by the National Aeronautics and Space Administration include four naval aviators—Lieutenant Malcolm Scott Carpenter, Marine Lieutenant Colonel John H. Glenn, Jr., Lieutenant Commander Walter M. Schirra, and Lieutenant Commander Alan B. Shepard, Jr.

20 April
A major milestone in the Polaris missile program occurs with the first successful flight test of a Polaris test vehicle at Cape Canaveral, Florida.

25 April
VA-212 deploys on the carrier *Lexington* (CVA 16), marking the first operational deployment of the Bullpup air-to-surface missile.

8 June
William B. Franke, former Assistant Secretary and Under Secretary of the Navy, becomes the fifty-fifth Secretary of the Navy.

16 June
While operating over the Sea of Japan off Korea, a P4M Mercator of VQ-1 is attacked by a pair of MiG fighters, rendering the patrol plane's two starboard engines inoperative and wounding the tail gunner. The P4M makes an emergency landing in Japan.

Opposite: *Marines disembark from a landing craft launched by* Chilton *(APA 38) on Red Beach, Beirut, Lebanon, 16 July 1958, as part of the Lebanon intervention force. (Naval Historical Center)*

Above: *The destroyer* Silverstein *(DE 534) and the submarine* Stickleback *(SS 415) collide nineteen miles off Barbers Point, Oahu, Hawaii, 29 May 1958.* Stickleback *sank soon thereafter. (Naval Historical Center)*

Left: *Lieutenant Commander Malcolm Scott Carpenter, one of four naval aviators selected as America's first astronauts. (Naval Historical Center)*

19 June
The first ZPG-3W airship, the largest nonrigid airship ever built, is delivered to Naval Air Station Lakehurst, New Jersey.

21 September
The submarine *Barbero* (SSG 317), equipped with Regulus I missiles, makes the first deterrent patrol to the North Pacific.

6 October
The aircraft carrier *Kearsarge* (CVS 33) completes humanitarian operations at Nagoya, Japan, in the aftermath of a typhoon. Some 6,000 people are evacuated and upwards of 200,000 pounds of medicine and supplies are provided to the population of the city.

1 December
A merging of the Bureau of Ordnance and Bureau of Aeronautics results in the establishment of the Bureau of Naval Weapons. The new bureau's first chief is Vice Admiral P. D. Stroop.

6 December
Commander Larry E. Flint establishes an altitude record of 98,560 feet in an F4H-1 Phantom II, marking the beginning of an amazing period lasting until 12 April 1962 in which the aircraft establishes twelve speed, altitude, and time-to-climb marks.

31 December
George Washington (SSBN 598), the Navy's first fleet ballistic missile submarine, is commissioned. The submarine was originally *Scorpion* (SSN 589), which was modified with the addition of a 130-foot missile section and renamed *George Washington*.

1960

January
Piloted by Lieutenant Don Walsh and civilian Jacques Piccard as part of Project Nekton, the bathyscaph *Trieste* reaches a depth of 35,800 feet off the Mariana Islands, the deepest known spot on earth.

25 February
An R6D Liftmaster carrying members of the Navy Band collides with a Brazilian airliner over Rio de Janiero. Sixty-four people, including thirty-eight on board the Navy aircraft, are killed. The only survivors are three Navy men.

Above: *The F4H-1 Phantom II in which Commander Lawrence E. Flint, Jr., established a world altitude record of 98,560 feet on a flight from Edwards Air Force Base, California, 6 December 1959. (Naval Historical Center)*

Right: *Captain Edward L. Beach, Jr., skipper of* Triton *(SSRN 586), peers through the periscope during the nuclear-powered submarine's shakedown cruise, a dramatic voyage in which she became the first submarine to circumnavigate the globe while submerged. The cruise lasted eight-four days and was a far cry from Beach's initial service in submarines, when frequent time on the surface to recharge batteries was required. (Corbis)*

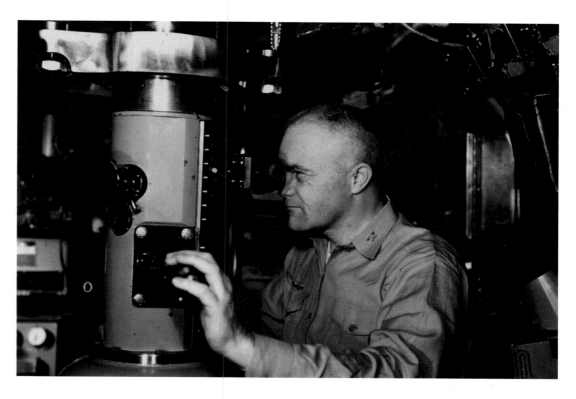

13 April

The Navy's Transit 1B, the United States' first navigational satellite, enters orbit after launch from Cape Canaveral, Florida.

19 April

The YA2F-1 makes its first flight. It is the prototype for the A-6 Intruder all-weather attack aircraft that enters service in Vietnam and flies combat missions during the Gulf war.

6 May

The submarine *Sea Poacher* (SS 406), operating in the San Nicholas Channel off Cuba, takes fire from the Cuban cutter *Oriente*.

10 May

The nuclear-powered submarine *Triton* (SSRN 586) completes an epic eighty-four-day voyage in which she becomes the first submarine to circumnavigate the globe submerged. Her sail breaks the surface

Left: *Task Force Alfa, with the aircraft carrier* Randolph *(CVS 15) flanked by destroyers and submarines, 29 March 1963. To combat the increasing Soviet submarine force, the Navy redesignated a number of* Essex-*class carriers as antisubmarine warfare carriers (CVS) to deploy in special task groups. (National Museum of Naval Aviation)*

CONFRONTATION IN THE TAIWAN STRAITS

by Dr. Edward J. Marolda

Throughout the 1950s, the U.S. Navy served as a major instrument of American foreign policy with regard to China. At the outset of the Korean War in June 1950, President Harry S. Truman ordered ships of the U.S. Seventh Fleet to the Straits of Taiwan (Formosa) in an effort to prevent the spread of conflict throughout the Far East. From 1950 to 1953, the United States and the People's Republic of China (PRC) under Mao Tse-tung fought a bloody, three-year conventional war, but the two nations restricted the heavy fighting to the Korean peninsula. American and Chinese military forces, however, did engage in lesser hostilities along the entire coast of China and among its thousands of offshore islands for most of that tumultuous decade.

Another reason Truman deployed the fleet into the straits in June 1950 was recognition by his administration that the PRC and other Asian Communist nations, supported politically and militarily by the Soviet Union, were intent on forcefully overturning the existing order in the Far East. Truman and his advisors also understood that to contain these militant Communist states, the United States would have to employ political, economic, and military power. Deterring or defeating Communist aggression would also depend on a clear and demonstrable American commitment to the defense of threatened governments in the region.

As the war raged in Korea, U.S. Navy surface ships, submarines, seaplanes, and other patrol planes operating from Japan, the Philippines, Okinawa, and Taiwan, the latter occupied by Chiang Kai-shek's Republic of China government, kept watch on the long coast of China. Twice during the war, Seventh Fleet carrier task forces left the Korean theater to mount "shows of force" off China as far south as Hainan Island, their planes overflying Chinese coastal cities.

In addition, the Truman and later Eisenhower administrations provided substantial material assistance to Nationalist Chinese military forces and accepted Chiang's garrisoning of numerous islands off the PRC-held coast. Sizeable Nationalist and Communist ground, air, and naval forces battled for control of these islands beginning in 1949. That year, Chiang's troops defeated a large Communist amphibious assault on Quemoy Island, and the following year Mao's Communists overwhelmed the Nationalist defenders of Hainan Island. Minelaying, naval bombardment, and air strike operations frequently occurred during this period.

Despite the enormous expenditure of Chinese lives and treasure in the Korean War, Mao concluded afterward that, because of that effort, the United States had learned to fear and respect China. He also used the nationalistic fervor generated by the war to strengthen Communist Party control at home and deflect criticism of his government's many failings.

In 1954, one year after the end of the Korean War, Mao directed his military forces to seize those Nationalist-held offshore islands that were most vulnerable. In September, PRC artillery on the mainland opened a bombardment of Quemoy and a Communist naval unit torpedoed and sank the Nationalist destroyer escort *T'ai Ping*. Then, in January 1955, Communist amphibious forces stormed Ichiang Island in the Tachen group 200 miles north of Taiwan.

Mao Tse-tung, however, did not order a full assault on Nationalist positions along the periphery of China because he knew that the United States could bring overwhelming naval power to bear in support of Chiang's forces. This perception had discouraged the Communist dictator from ordering an invasion of Taiwan during the Korean War. And, indeed, by early 1955, the U.S. Navy had assembled off China a powerful armada of five aircraft carrier task groups.

President Dwight D. Eisenhower did not want a major war with China, so he decided not to contest Communist occupation of Ichiang and the other Tachens. He did, however, persuade Congress to pass a resolution in support of military action if the Communists continued their hostile acquisitions. The United States also entered into a mutual defense treaty with the Nationalist government. Mao refrained from seizing other islands and the 1954–1955 crisis quickly ebbed.

In the summer of 1958, when Mao wanted to promote his radical "Great Leap Forward" collectivization program in China, he engineered another "foreign threat" to rally domestic support. He called for the "liberation" of Taiwan and ordered the shelling of Quemoy and Matsu islands. The Communist leader believed that Quemoy, located only a few miles from the mainland, could be cut off from supplies and forced to surrender by a massive and continuous artillery bombardment. He also concluded that since the United States was heavily involved in a crisis over Lebanon in the Mediterranean, it would have neither the will nor sufficient military strength in the Pacific to counter his actions. He was wrong on all counts.

Admiral Arleigh Burke, the Chief of Naval Operations, immediately deployed the Seventh Fleet to the China coast and ordered reinforcements from the Mediterranean to the Far East. As directed by the Eisenhower administration, U.S. warships then escorted Nationalist resupply convoys to and from Quemoy. Eventually, aircraft from six American carriers provided overhead cover for the surface ship convoys, as did land-based Nationalist squadrons (in this crisis, Nationalist squadrons equipped with the new U.S. Navy-developed Sidewinder weapons made the world's first air-to-air missile "kills").

Mao allowed his forces to fight the Nationalists, but strictly prohibited attacks on American units. He knew that the United States possessed nuclear weapons and

doubted that he could rely on his nuclear-armed Soviet ally in a major conflict with the United States. Once Mao also understood that the blockade of Quemoy would not succeed, because supply convoys were getting through, he ended the confrontation. He directed his coastal artillery forces to shell Quemoy only every other day, which in effect allowed the Nationalists to resupply the island unhindered.

Hence, during the 1950s, the fighting strength, forward presence, and mobility of American sea power provided the U.S. government with great flexibility to execute its policies. America's nuclear readiness discouraged Mao from action at that level and its conventional naval capability enabled the United States and its Nationalist ally to mount successful operations on the very shores of Communist China. Because the United States stood firm in the 1950s confrontations, and has kept its naval deterrent in place since then, the People's Republic of China has explored options other than the use of force to resolve its territorial differences with the Republic of China.

Above: *Vice Admiral Austin K. Doyle, Commander, Taiwan Defense Command, receives a briefing during an inspection of a Nationalist Chinese Air Force photoreconnaissance squadron, circa 1957. Supporting the island nation in the face of aggression from Communist China has been a key element of American policy in the Far East. (National Museum of Naval Aviation)*

Left: *The destroyer* Collett's *(DD 730) shattered bow is testament to the force of the collision with* Ammen *(DD 527) off Long Beach, California, on 19 July 1960.* Collett *made port under her own power. Her bow was removed and replaced with that of* Seaman *(DD 791), an uncompleted destroyer in the Reserve fleet. (Naval Historical Center)*

only once during her time at sea, to transfer a sick sailor to the cruiser *Macon* (CA 132). *Triton* receives the Presidential Unit Citation for the voyage, which is recounted in the 1962 book *Around the World Submerged* by the submarine's skipper, Captain Edward L. Beach, Jr.

19 July

The destroyers *Ammen* (DD 527) and *Collett* (DD 730) collide during maneuvers off Long Beach, California. *Ammen* is damaged beyond repair, and loses eleven crewmen killed and twenty injured.

20 July

The fleet ballistic missile submarine *George Washington* conducts two successful launchings of Polaris A-1 ballistic missiles off Cape Canaveral, Florida, marking the first time that a missile is fired from a submerged U.S. Navy submarine. A message from the submarine's skipper to President Dwight D. Eisenhower proclaims, "George Washington Sends—Polaris—from out of the deep to target—perfect." *George Washington* is ready for operational service later in the year, departing on her first deterrent patrol on 15 November.

10 September

Charles F. Adams (DDG 2) is commissioned, becoming the first "keel up" missile destroyer built for the U.S. Navy. She is the first of a class of sixteen ships.

21 October

The W2F-1, prototype for the E-2 Hawkeye carrier-based airborne early warning aircraft still in service today, makes it maiden flight.

13 December

An A3J-1 Vigilante, piloted by Commander Leroy A. Heath and carrying a payload of 454.5 pounds, reaches an altitude of 91,450.8 feet over Edwards Air Force Base, California, establishing a new world altitude record.

19 December

Fifty workers die and 150 are injured when fire breaks out on board the aircraft carrier *Constellation* (CVA 64), under construction at the New York Naval Shipyard.

1961

20 January

Texan John B. Connally, Jr., a fighter director officer on board the carrier *Essex* (CV 9) during World War II, becomes the fifty-sixth Secretary of the Navy.

17–20 April

In a debacle that marks a foreign policy blow to the new administration of President John F. Kennedy, some 1,400 Cuban exiles trained by the Central Intelligence Agency (CIA) land at the Bay of Pigs in Cuba in an effort to overthrow the Communist government of Fidel Castro. The force is overwhelmed

by the Cuban military. Six aircraft from the aircraft carrier *Essex* (CVA 9) operating offshore are reluctantly committed to the operation to protect CIA propeller-driven B-26 Marauder bombers from attacking Cuban fighters. The CIA aircraft arrive over the target area before the covering jets do, and two B-26s are shot down.

29 April
Kitty Hawk (CVA 63), the first of a new class of aircraft carriers, is placed in commission. She is still operational today.

4 May
Commander Malcolm D. Ross and Lieutenant Commander Victor A. Prather, MC, achieve a record altitude of 113,740 feet after being launched in a balloon from the deck of the carrier *Antietam* (CVS 36) operating in the Gulf of Mexico. Prather falls while being recovered from the water by a helicopter and subsequently dies.

5 May
Lieutenant Commander Alan B. Shepard, Jr., becomes the first American in space when his Mercury space capsule, Freedom 7, reaches an altitude of 116.5 miles after being launched from Cape Canaveral, Florida.

1 August
Veteran naval aviator Admiral George W. Anderson, Jr., becomes the sixteenth Chief of Naval Operations.

13 August
The Soviets and East Germans begin building a wall to separate East and West Berlin. The Berlin Wall becomes a symbol of the Cold War standoff between the United States and the Soviet Union.

26 August
Iwo Jima (LPH 2), the first of a class of amphibious assault ships capable of launching landing craft and operating helicopters for the transport of Marines, is commissioned.

Left: *The amphibious assault ship* Iwo Jima *(LPH 2). (Naval Historical Center)*

Below: *The nuclear aircraft carrier* Enterprise *(CVAN 65), the guided missile cruiser* Long Beach *(CGN 9), and the guided missile frigate* Bainbridge *(DLGN 25) steam in formation through the Mediterranean in the mid-1960s. Because of their nuclear propulsion, these ships could remain on station far from the United States for long periods, a clear advantage during the protracted Cold War. (Naval Historical Center)*

Right *President John F. Kennedy inspects a Navy underwater demolition team (UDT), pausing to speak with one of its members. From this cadre of UDTs the Navy created the first SEAL teams, highly trained counterinsurgency and unconventional warfare specialists that proved valuable in the war in Vietnam. (Naval Historical Center)*

10 September
The cruiser *Long Beach* (CGN 9) is commissioned. She is the world's first nuclear-powered surface warship and the first warship armed entirely with missiles.

23 October
Operating in the Atlantic Ocean, the fleet ballistic missile submarine *Ethan Allen* (SSBN 608) accomplishes the first submerged launch of a Polaris A-2 missile.

25 November
Enterprise, the world's first nuclear-powered aircraft carrier and the largest warship built to date, is commissioned.

1962

1 January
Reflecting President John F. Kennedy's emphasis on unconventional warfare and counterinsurgency operations, the Navy creates two Sea Air Land (SEAL) teams. The SEALs are successors to the Underwater Demolition Teams formed during World War II.

4 January
Fred Korth, a Texas attorney and former Assistant Secretary of the Army, becomes the fifty-seventh Secretary of the Navy.

20 February
Lieutenant Colonel John H. Glenn, Jr., completes the U.S. space program's first orbital flight,

Above: *Lieutenants Gerald L. Coffee (left) and Arthur R. Day, two naval aviators from Light Photographic Squadron (VFP) 62, debrief Rear Admiral Joseph M. Carson, Commander Fleet Air, Jacksonville, Florida, following reconnaissance flights over Cuba during the Cuban Missile Crisis. The squadron received the Navy Unit Commendation for its actions. Lieutenant Coffee was later shot down in North Vietnam and held as a prisoner of war. (Naval Historical Center)*

completing three orbits around the Earth in his Mercury space capsule, Friendship 7.

12 April
Amphibious ships of the Seventh Fleet—the amphibious assault ship *Valley Forge* (LPH 8), the attack transport *Navarro* (APA 215), and the dock landing ship *Point Defiance* (LSD 31)—put Marines ashore in Thailand to support that nation's independence.

24 May
Lieutenant Commander Malcolm Scott Carpenter completes three orbits of the Earth in his Mercury spacecraft, Aurora 7.

26 June
The fleet ballistic missile submarine *Ethan Allen* departs Naval Base Charleston, South Carolina, the first patrol of a submarine carrying the Polaris A-2 missile.

17 August
The Navy's first hydrofoil patrol craft, *Long Point* (PC(H) 1), is launched at Seattle, Washington.

31 August
Following the decision of 30 November 1961 to end the Navy's operation of lighter-than-air craft, which dates from before World War I, on this date the Navy's last airship makes its final flight at Naval Air Station Lakehurst, New Jersey.

8 September
The first of a class of amphibious transport docks, *Raleigh* (LPD 1), is commissioned.

3 October
The Mercury spacecraft Sigma 7, flown by Commander Walter M. Schirra, Jr., completes six orbits around the earth in a flight lasting over ten hours.

6 October
Bainbridge (DLGN 25), the world's first nuclear-powered guided missile frigate, is commissioned.

15 October
Navy RF-8A Crusaders of Light Photoreconnaissance Squadron (VFP) 62 based at Naval Air Station Jacksonville, Florida, join Air Force aircraft in flying photoreconnaissance missions over Cuba. The squadron eventually receives the Navy Unit Commendation from President John F. Kennedy.

Opposite, bottom:
Insignia of the nuclear submarine Thresher *(SSN 593) adopted in 1960.*

Right: *Commander Sixth Fleet Vice Admiral David L. McDonald (left) aboard his flagship* Springfield *(CLG 7) discusses the progress and operations of the fleet during the past months with Chief of Naval Operations (CNO) Admiral George W. Anderson, 1 June 1962. McDonald succeeded Anderson as CNO in 1963. (Naval Historical Center)*

24 October

A U.S. naval quarantine of Cuba begins in response to reconnaissance photographs showing Soviet nuclear missile sites under construction there. Carrying out the quarantine is Task Force 136, under Vice Admiral Alfred G. Ward, consisting of the antisubmarine warfare carrier *Essex* (CVS 9), two heavy cruisers, and numerous destroyers and support ships. Two carrier divisions centered on *Enterprise* (CVAN 65) and *Independence* (CVA 62) also operate in the area. The Cuban Missile Crisis, which takes the world to the brink of nuclear war, ends when the Soviet Union agrees to pull its offensive missiles out of Cuba in exchange for the United States agreeing not to invade the island nation and removing missiles from Turkey. The naval quarantine lasts until 20 November.

1963

10 April

The nuclear-powered submarine *Thresher* (SSN 593), while diving to her test depth of 1,300 feet east of Cape Cod, Massachusetts, sinks with the loss of 129 officers, men, and civilian technicians.

1 August

Admiral David L. McDonald, former Sixth Fleet commander and Commander in Chief U.S. Naval Forces, Europe, becomes the seventeenth Chief of Naval Operations.

25 October

Navy ships conclude two weeks of relief operations in Haiti in the wake of Hurricane Flora, having joined with Air Force aircraft to deliver almost 375 tons of food, clothing, and medical supplies.

26 October

The fleet ballistic missile submarine *Andrew Jackson* (SSBN 619) conducts the first shipboard launch of a Polaris A-3 missile, which weighed 4,000 pounds more than the A-2 and boasted a range of some 2,500 nautical miles.

29 November

Paul H. Nitze, a veteran of past service in the Navy, State, and Defense departments, becomes the fifty-eighth Secretary of the Navy.

THE LONGEST WAR

1964-1980

THE LONGEST WAR

1964-1980

On 11 January 1945, thee ships of Task Force 38 entered the South China Sea and the following morning commenced launching some 850 carrier planes at Japanese shipping and installations in French Indochina, focusing much of their effort against the capital city of Saigon. Among the carriers off shore that day was *Ticonderoga* (CV 14) and the destroyers escorting the flattops included *Maddox* (DD 731). No one aboard either ship could have imagined that less than twenty years later, both ships would again be engaged in combat in the same waters, this time against a different enemy in a land called Vietnam. Yet, such was the case on 2 August when, in response to attacks by torpedo boats against *Maddox*, aircraft from *Ticonderoga* joined the destroyer's guns in knocking out two of the enemy vessels. Two days later, *Maddox* and *Turner Joy* (DD 951) reported more approaching torpedo boats, and this alleged attack prompted President Lyndon B. Johnson to order a retaliatory strike against North Vietnam on 5 August 1964, marking the escalation of American involvement in Southeast Asia.

Vietnam proved a watershed event for the U.S. Navy and the country it served. Thousands of sailors and hundreds of ships, small craft, and airplanes deployed to the western Pacific during the period 1964–1975, steaming on "Yankee Station" in the Gulf of Tonkin or patrolling the Mekong Delta. The nature of the war presented challenges for those waging it, some the result of enemy tactics and others products of American policy and social changes on the home front. The North Vietnamese and Viet Cong fought an unconventional war, prompting the Navy to adopt weapons and tactics to meet the new threat. The Sea-

Air-Land (SEAL) teams proved their worth in Southeast Asia against an enemy that fought in the shadows. In addition, just like their predecessors who went into harm's way aboard PT-boats in World War II, the sailors in black berets who manned the over 700 small craft of the "brown water Navy" effectively combated the enemy on the inland waterways of South Vietnam. Aircraft carriers, just as they had done in Korea, were able to operate at will without the threat of attack by enemy surface ships or aircraft. Flying into a deadly array of antiaircraft defenses, pilots and aircrewmen engaged in dramatic dogfights with enemy MiG fighters and pressed home attacks against the enemy transportation network in an attempt to interdict the flow of supplies into South Vietnam. Yet, the greatest obstacle they faced was the restrictive rules of engagement and periodic bombing halts that governed the air campaign, diminishing its effectiveness. And as the war progressed and became increasingly unpopular at home, the Navy's leadership faced racial unrest and sailors resistant to the traditional disciplinary standards of the past, which prompted the controversial measures taken by Admiral Elmo Zumwalt during his time as Chief of Naval Operations.

Even after the last helicopters departed the U.S. Embassy in Saigon in 1975 just ahead of North Vietnamese troops, the specter of Vietnam continued to haunt the Navy. Its fleet in need of modernization that the war had placed on hold, the Navy faced difficult decisions on what types and numbers of ships to build to meet projected threats. It did so in an era in which politicians sought to reduce defense spending and conduct a retrenched foreign policy that avoided the threat of involvement in another war. Debates over weapons procurement included President Jimmy

Carter, a Naval Academy graduate, seeking to end the construction of nuclear carriers. Nevertheless, weapons that would play a prominent role in naval operations in ensuing decades—the *Nimitz*-class carrier, the F/A-18 Hornet, the Tomahawk cruise missile, and the *Los Angeles*-class attack submarine—were in development or put to sea during the post-Vietnam War years.

While the Navy looked to the future, the present still required its attention. The traditional Cold War enemy, the Soviet Union, continued to occupy the attention of strategists and foreign policy makers, and threats to world peace and national security emerged throughout the world. This was particularly true in the Middle East where a fundamentalist regime in Iran took Americans hostage in November 1979. The aircraft carrier *Nimitz* (CVN 68) played a supporting role in the failed attempt to rescue them, which was symbolic of the decline of the U.S. military in the aftermath of Vietnam. In an ultimate insult, Iran released the hostages in January 1981 on the day

Ronald Reagan took the oath as President of the United States, which marked the end of a troublesome time in the nation's history and the beginning of a new era that would mark the resurgence of the U.S. Navy.

Pages 586–587: *The bow of the aircraft carrier* Enterprise *(CVN 65) slices through the ocean during a deployment in the late 1970s. The radar and electronic suites on the carrier's island superstructure, later removed during a conversion, gave the ship a futuristic appearance when commissioned in 1961, which befitted the world's first nuclear-powered carrier. (National Museum of Naval Aviation)*

Above: *The machine gun on the bow of a river patrol boat (PBR) spits fire as the boat is straddled by enemy fire during a nighttime fight in Vietnam's Mekong Delta. Manned by a crew of four, PBRs were widely used in the "brown water Navy," with almost 300 operating in country by the end of 1970. ("Fire Fight, Mekong Delta," R. G. Smith, Navy Art Collection)*

THE LONGEST WAR
1964-1980

13 January
The destroyer *Manley* (DD 940) evacuates fifty-five American citizens and thirty-six others in the wake of revolution on the island of Zanzibar in the Indian Ocean off Africa.

6 February
Cuba cuts off the supply of fresh water to the naval base at Guantanamo Bay in retaliation for the American seizure of four Cuban fishing boats off Florida. The United States responds by making the Caribbean base self-sufficient by constructing saltwater conversion plants, which are completed by the end of the year.

6 June
During "Yankee Team" operations involving photoreconnaissance missions over Laos, an RF-8A Crusader of Photographic Reconnaissance Squadron (VFP) 63 off the carrier *Kitty Hawk* (CVA 63) is shot down over the Plaine des Jarres. Lieutenant Charles F. Klusmann ejects from his crippled aircraft and is captured by the Pathet Lao and held captive until he escapes on 1 September.

7 June
An F-8 Crusader from Fighter Squadron (VF) 111 off the carrier *Kitty Hawk* is shot down over Laos. The pilot, Commander Doyle W. Lynn, ejects from his aircraft and is rescued by a helicopter.

31 July
Consisting entirely of nuclear-powered ships—the carrier *Enterprise* (CVAN 65), guided missile cruiser *Long Beach* (CGN 9), and guided missile frigate *Bainbridge* (DLGN 25)—Task Force 1 departs Gibraltar on a round-the-world cruise called Operation Sea Orbit. The three ships complete the cruise on 3 October neither having refueled nor replenished for sixty-four days.

2 August
North Vietnamese torpedo boats execute a night attack against the destroyer *Maddox* (DD 731), which is engaged in intelligence gathering in international waters in the Gulf of Tonkin. The destroyer, with the

Left: *Captain John Herrick (left) was the on-scene commander during North Vietnamese torpedo boat attacks in the Tonkin Gulf in August 1964, which involved the destroyer* Maddox *(DD 731), whose skipper was Commander Herbert L. Ogier (right). The action on the high seas precipitated air strikes against North Vietnam, the beginning of an escalation of U.S. involvement in Southeast Asia. (Naval Historical Center)*

Right: *Commander James B. Stockdale leads the first American strike on North Vietnam, an attack on the oil facilities at Vinh on 5 August 1964. Stockdale was later shot down and became a prisoner of war. Awarded the Medal of Honor for bravery, exemplary conduct, and inspirational leadership as a prisoner, he returned to serve as a vice admiral and Naval War College president. ("Operation Pierce Arrow," R.G. Smith, Navy Art Collection)*

assistance of VF-51 F-8 Crusaders from the carrier *Ticonderoga* (CVA 14), drives off the attackers.

4 August

The destroyers *Maddox* (DD 731) and *Turner Joy* (DD 951) are allegedly attacked by North Vietnamese torpedo boats while operating in international waters in the Gulf of Tonkin. They return fire on the radar contacts, claiming to have possibly sunk two of the enemy craft. Bad weather hampers the operations of F-8 Crusaders sent from the carrier *Ticonderoga* to assist the destroyers, preventing a visual sighting of the torpedo boats and causing speculation over whether any actually attacked.

5 August

President Lyndon B. Johnson orders the U.S. Navy into action, launching Operation Pierce Arrow from the carriers *Ticonderoga* and *Constellation* (CVA 64). Carrier-based aircraft strike petroleum storage facilities and naval assets at Vinh, PhucLoi, Loc Chao, Hon Gay, and Quang Khe, North Vietnam. Two aircraft are lost during the attacks: the A-1H Skyraider flown by Lieutenant (junior grade) Richard A. Sather, and the A-4 Skyhawk flown by Lieutenant (junior grade) Everett Alvarez. Sather is killed in action, while Alvarez is captured, becoming the first American prisoner of war in North Vietnam. He is held captive until February 1973.

7 August

Congress overwhelmingly passes the Tonkin Gulf Resolution, giving President Lyndon B. Johnson

virtually unlimited authority to conduct military operations in Vietnam.

28 September

In the first deployment of the Polaris A-3 missile, the fleet ballistic missile submarine *Daniel Webster* (SSBN 626) departs the naval base at Charleston, South Carolina.

26 December

The fleet ballistic missile submarine *Daniel Boone* (SSBN 629) departs Guam, marking the first Pacific Ocean patrol of a submarine carrying Polaris missiles.

1965

7 February

In response to an attack by Viet Cong guerillas against an American barracks at Pleiku, South Vietnam, which kills 8 and wounds 126 Army personnel, Navy carrier aircraft execute Operation Flaming Dart I. Aircraft from *Hancock* (CVA 19), *Coral Sea* (CVA 43), and *Ranger* (CVA 61) strike military barracks at Dong Hoi, North Vietnam. This marks the first combat action for *Coral Sea*, which eventually makes the most deployments to Vietnam of any carrier.

11 February

In the aftermath of the Viet Cong bombing of an Army enlisted barracks at Qui Nhon, South Vietnam, which kills twenty-three Americans and injures twenty-one others, carrier aircraft again strike targets in North

ADMIRAL THOMAS H. MOORER

by Dr. Edward J. Marolda

Admiral Thomas H. Moorer was a pivotal figure in the national security establishment of the United States during the long and contentious Vietnam War. A man of firm convictions, intellectual rigor, and forthrightness, the Navy admiral strongly influenced the wartime policies of two presidential administrations during a key period of American history.

Thomas Hinman Moorer was born in Willing, Alabama, on 9 February 1912, attended local schools from which he graduated with distinction, and in 1929 entered the U.S. Naval Academy in Annapolis, Maryland, where four years later his classmates concluded in the *Lucky Bag* yearbook that "Tom will surely be a credit to his profession." He would more than fulfill their expectation.

Following graduation and commissioning as an officer in the U.S. Navy, Moorer entered the new and exciting, but dangerous field of military endeavor: naval aviation. He became one of the Navy's aviation pioneers, operating fighter aircraft from the first carrier, *Langley* (CV 1). In the desperate months after the 7 December 1941 Japanese attack on Pearl Harbor, Hawaii, he flew PBY flying boats in the South Pacific. Wounded during a 19 February 1942 mission when Japanese Zero fighters shot his aircraft down, the young officer received the Distinguished Flying Cross for his courage and professional skill in numerous South Pacific battles. Moorer broadened his experience with training and staff duties in the Atlantic Fleet for the remainder of the war. Recognizing his potential, the Navy promoted him to commander in 1945. During the 1950s, the hard-charging officer completed instruction at the Naval War College, performed with distinction as commanding officer of the seaplane tender *Salisbury Sound* (AV 13), and directed the Navy's strategic planning office as a rear admiral.

When the Navy named him Commander, Seventh Fleet, in 1962, Moorer began a long association with the conflict in Southeast Asia. During his watch, naval advisors and Sea-Air-Land (SEAL) teams deployed to Vietnam in increasing numbers. In the eventful year of 1964, Admiral Moorer, now with four stars, took charge of the U.S. Pacific Fleet, which directed the operations of the First Fleet in the eastern Pacific and the Seventh Fleet in the Far East. Even in these early days of the war, Moorer complained through channels about Washington's micromanagement of air operations. He objected when Secretary of Defense Robert McNamara personally decided from afar the type and number of aircraft, bomb loads, approach altitudes, and other operational requirements for one or two-plane reconnaissance missions over Laos.

When Communist North Vietnamese torpedo boats attacked *Maddox* (DD 731) in the Gulf of Tonkin on 2 August 1964, the destroyer (and supporting carrier aircraft) shot up the assailants and withdrew from the hostile waters. Commander John J. Herrick, the officer in charge of *Maddox*'s intelligence-gathering operation, was reluctant to reenter the gulf. Admiral Moorer, however, irate that the Communists had attacked a U.S. warship on the high seas in broad daylight, ordered *Maddox* to resume the patrol, accompanied by the destroyer *Turner Joy* (DD 951). When Moorer and other officers in the Pacific chain of command concluded that Communist naval units had carried out a second attack on American ships (later discounted), on the night of 4 August, they recommended retaliatory air strikes on North Vietnam. President Lyndon B. Johnson concurred, and ordered the reprisal missions that destroyed North Vietnamese naval vessels and fuel storage facilities on 5 August.

One month after the Seventh Fleet landed U.S. Marines at Danang, South Vietnam, in March 1965, Moorer took command of U.S. and NATO naval forces in the Atlantic. President Johnson, impressed with Moorer's honest, straightforward military manner, and no doubt his Southern background (Johnson was a Texan), appointed him Chief of Naval Operations in 1967. The admiral oversaw the deployment to Vietnam and offshore waters of carrier, naval gunfire, coastal patrol, river assault, and river patrol forces that fought in operations Rolling Thunder, Market Time, and Game Warden.

In 1970 President Richard M. Nixon, who was comfortable with Moorer's general conservatism and loyal support of the administration's war effort, named the admiral Chairman of the Joint Chiefs of Staff. While his views were not always welcomed in the White House, Moorer led those who called for

stronger military action in Southeast Asia. He favored heavier bombing of the Communists and a slower withdrawal of U.S. forces from South Vietnam, so that "Vietnamization" of the war could succeed. He also advocated cutting off the flow of war material to North Vietnam. In 1972, when the Communists repeatedly caused delay in negotiations to end the war, Moorer and other officials recommended inauguration of a major bombing campaign and the mining of North Vietnam's ports. The President agreed and ordered Operation Linebacker, which helped compel Hanoi to sign the Paris agreement of January 1973. That agreement ended direct U.S. involvement in the war and brought American prisoners of war home.

Even though he devoted much of his time to the war in Southeast Asia, Admiral Moorer worked to ensure that U.S. nuclear and conventional forces were strong enough to counter Soviet threats in other regions of the world. He helped keep modernization of the Navy's attack and ballistic missile submarine fleets on track. He stood out as a hard-liner with regard to proposed U.S. concessions to the USSR in the Strategic Arms Limitation Talks of 1972. Moorer was a strong voice for employing military might to

back up America's international commitments. At the same time, he recognized that U.S. involvement in the Vietnam War, which put a heavy strain on national resources, limited what could be accomplished globally. During the Yom Kippur War of 1973 in the Middle East, Moorer spoke clearly and forthrightly in the councils of government about what U.S. military forces could and could not do to counter aggressive Syrian and Soviet actions.

In July 1974, Admiral Thomas H. Moorer retired as Chairman of the Joint Chiefs of Staff, completing forty-one years of distinguished service to the United States. Throughout his service he had exhibited moral and physical courage, a strong will, and a balanced appreciation of military power in the modern world. Admiral Moorer died on 5 February 2004.

Above: *Chief of Naval Operations Tom Moorer, sporting the black beret of Task Force 116, the "brown water Navy," receives a briefing from Rear Admiral William R. Flanagan, Deputy Commander, U.S. Naval Forces, Vietnam, August 1969. Captain Joseph R. Faulk, Commander River Patrol Force and River Patrol Flotilla 5, stands behind the CNO. (U.S. Navy)*

Vietnam. Operation Flaming Dart II, launched from the decks of *Hancock*, *Coral Sea*, and *Ranger*, hits North Vietnamese barracks near Chan Hoa.

2 March

The United States initiates Operation Rolling Thunder, the sustained bombing of North Vietnam that lasts until President Lyndon B. Johnson calls a bombing halt in October 1968. Rolling Thunder is designed to strike targets incrementally and with gradually increasing intensity in response to the actions of the North Vietnamese in hopes of discovering their breaking point. It does not prove successful.

8 March

The amphibious transport dock *Vancouver* (LPD 2), amphibious force flagship *Mount McKinley* (AGC 7), attack transport *Henrico* (APA 45), and attack cargo ship *Union* (AKA 106) support the landing of the 9th Marine Expeditionary Brigade at Da Nang, South Vietnam, which becomes a major American air base during the war. On 1 April the leathernecks receive authorization to actively engage North Vietnamese and Viet Cong forces.

11 March

The discovery of a North Vietnamese trawler unloading munitions in South Vietnam prompts the initiation of a wide-ranging operation called Market Time, which involves warships, and, later, patrol aircraft in the observation and inspection of native

Right: *The destroyer* Wedderburn *(DD 684) is trailed by* Porterfield *(DD 682) and another unidentified destroyer as they conduct a shore bombardment of North Vietnam, 21 August 1964. Like many "tin cans" serving in Vietnam, these destroyers had served in combat in Word War II and Korea. (Naval Historical Center)*

junks in an effort to stem the flow of supplies to enemy forces fighting in South Vietnam. Eventually, Task Force 71 is established specifically to control Market Time operations.

23 March

In the first manned space mission of Project Gemini, Lieutenant Colonel Virgil I. "Gus" Grissom, USAF, and Lieutenant Commander John W. Young complete three orbits of the earth before splashing down in the Atlantic Ocean.

3 April

Aircraft from the carriers *Hancock* and *Coral Sea* strike the North Vietnamese transportation network for the first time, destroying the Dong Phuong highway bridge south of the North Vietnamese capital of Hanoi. During this strike naval aviators make their first observation of airborne enemy MiG fighters.

15 April

In the first air strike of the Vietnam War involving all services, carrier-based aircraft from *Midway* (CVA 41) and *Coral Sea* join planes from the Marine Corps, Army, and Air Force in attacking Viet Cong positions in South Vietnam.

27 April

The amphibious assault ship *Boxer* (LPH 4) puts Marines ashore in the Dominican Republic in the face of a potential revolt in the island nation. Marine helicopters from *Boxer* also begin the evacuation of 1,000 American citizens.

10 May

The tank landing ship *Tioga County* (LST 1158) conducts the first shipboard launching of Seaspar, a surface-to-air version of the Sparrow air-to-air missile, off the coast of California. Seaspar is later renamed Sea Sparrow.

20 May

Seventh Fleet destroyers begin bombardment of enemy positions along the coast of South Vietnam in the first naval gunfire support missions of the Vietnam War.

10 June

While serving in Seabee Team 1104 at Dong Xoai, South Vietnam, Construction Mechanic Third Class Marvin G. Shields, despite being wounded, remains in the defensive lines for seven hours as a Viet Cong regiment attacks the American position. Wounded a second time, he volunteers for a two-man mission forward of the front lines to attempt to destroy an enemy machine gun emplacement. The effort is successful, but Shields is mortally wounded while returning to friendly lines. For his heroism he is awarded a posthumous Medal of Honor.

17 June

In the first confirmed air-to-air kills of enemy aircraft during the Vietnam War, two F-4B Phantom II aircraft of VF-21 from the carrier *Midway* shoot down two North Vietnamese MiG-17s with Sidewinder air-to-air missiles.

Left: *"Swift boats" were one of the Navy's most versatile vessels in Vietnam, serving along the coast in Operation Market Time and far upriver in the Mekong Delta. (Naval Historical Center)*

Below: *An F-4J Phantom II of Fighter Squadron (VF) 84 shows the scars from antiaircraft artillery (AAA). Though Soviet-made SA-2 surface-to-air missiles were frightening, it was conventional AAA that downed the majority of the some 900 Navy aircraft shot down during the Vietnam War. (National Museum of Naval Aviation)*

11 August

An A-4E Skyhawk of Attack Squadron (VA) 23 from the aircraft carrier *Midway* is shot down over North Vietnam, the first confirmed loss of a Navy aircraft to a surface-to-air missile.

18 August

Operation Starlite, one of the more successful amphibious operations of the Vietnam War, commences as the Seventh Fleet Amphibious Ready Group lands Marines near Chu Lai, South Vietnam,

Right: *Pilots of Attack Squadron (VA) 216 receive final instructions on the approach to a target prior to launching from the carrier* Hancock *(CVA 19) for a strike against North Vietnam, May 1965. (National Museum of Naval Aviation)*

to thwart a Viet Cong regiment's attempt to take the city. The cruiser *Galveston* (CLG 3) and two destroyers provide gunfire support, and some leathernecks are put ashore by helicopters from the amphibious assault ship *Iwo Jima* (LPH 2). The weeklong battle results in the death of over 964 enemy troops.

21 August
Gemini V, carrying Colonel Leroy Gordon Cooper, USAF, and Commander Charles C. "Pete" Conrad, launches from Cape Kennedy, Florida, beginning an eight-day mission.

28 August
In an experiment designed to determine the capacity of humans to spend extended periods of time living and working underwater, a ten-man group that includes astronaut Commander Malcolm Scott Carpenter enters the Sealab II capsule on the seafloor off La Jolla, California. Three teams of ten men each spend fifteen days in the capsule, though Carpenter spends one period of thirty successive days underwater.

27 September
The A-7 Corsair II, a light attack plane that sees its first combat in Vietnam and last over the sands of Iraq in 1991, makes its first flight.

15 October
U.S. Naval Support Activity Da Nang, responsible for logistical support for forces in South Vietnam, is established.

17 October
Northeast of Hanoi, North Vietnam, A-6 Intruders and A-4 Skyhawks from the carrier *Independence* (CVA 62) conduct the first successful attack against a mobile surface-to-air missile site.

26 October
Off Vietnam, a powder charge ignites in one of the 5-inch gun mounts of the destroyer *Turner Joy*, killing three sailors and wounding three others.

31 October
The first "swift boats" (PCF) arrive in South Vietnam to support Operation Market Time.

26 November
The carrier *Enterprise* and the guided-missile frigate *Bainbridge* arrive off Vietnam. On 2 December the "Big E" launches her first air strikes against Viet Cong positions in South Vietnam, becoming the first nuclear-powered ship to participate in combat operations.

SAILORS IN THE SHADOWS: THE U.S. NAVY SEALS

by M. Hill Goodspeed

In the beginning they were called "frogmen," masked sailors who stealthily made their way ashore to clear beaches of obstacles so that invading troops could successfully land on hostile beaches. Part of Navy Combat Demolition Units and Underwater Demolition Teams, they swam ashore at Normandy, France, in the early morning hours of D-Day in 1944 and supported the island-hopping campaign across the Pacific. In Korea, they foreshadowed future actions by expanding their operations to inland areas, and in 1962 they formed the cadre of what became the Navy's most specialized and highly trained force, the legendary Sea-Air-Land teams (SEALs). From the jungles of Vietnam, where they received three Medals of Honor, to Grenada, Panama, Afghanistan, Iraq, and countless classified locations, the SEALs have performed a variety of specialized missions ranging from counterinsurgency and special reconnaissance to combating terrorism and recovering personnel. The only element of the nation's special operations forces trained to strike from the sea and return to the sea, they are the Navy's elite force.

Left: *A Navy SEAL, camouflaged amidst the jungle foliage of the Mekong Delta of South Vietnam, keeps a sharp look out for any sign of the enemy while on patrol in 1968. The SEALs specialized in counterinsurgency operations and unconventional warfare and proved indispensable during the war in Southeast Asia. (Bettman/Corbis)*

Above: *Members of SEAL Team 2 conduct SEAL Delivery Vehicle (SDV) training in the warm waters of the Caribbean, 2 October 1997. This evolution marks a continuation of the mating of two weapons that rely on stealth—submarines and special operations forces—to conduct clandestine missions. (U.S. Navy)*

Opposite, top left: *Members of Basic Underwater Demolition (BUD/S) SEAL Class 244 carry their inflatable boat to the shoreline while conducting exercises as part of the training at the Naval Amphibious Base at Coronado, California. This initial phase of the arduous process of becoming a SEAL tests not only the individual's fortitude, but also his ability to work as part of a team. (U.S. Navy)*

Below: *A key element of the Navy's special operations forces are the boat crews that transport SEAL teams into combat and extract them upon completion of a mission. This rigid hull inflatable boat (RHIB) provides a high-speed platform for the mission, and is armed to support the men on the ground in the event of trouble. (U.S. Navy)*

Above: *A SEAL provides cover for a teammate while advancing on a suspected location of al Qaeda and Taliban forces in Afghanistan, 24 January 2002. The nature of the war on terrorism makes special operations and their unique capabilities an important weapon in the war on terrorism. (U.S. Navy)*

7 December
A fire in the machinery room on board the carrier *Kitty Hawk* operating in the South China Sea kills two sailors and injures twenty-eight others.

15 December
In the first docking of two manned spacecraft in orbit Gemini VII, flown by Commander James A. Lovell, Jr., and Lieutenant Colonel Frank Borman, USAF, executes a rendezvous with Gemini VIII flown by Captain Walter M. Schirra, Jr., and Major Thomas P. Stafford, USAF.

18 December
The establishment of the U.S. Navy River Patrol Force (Task Force 116) signals the beginning of the "Brown Water Navy," the nickname given to naval forces that operate in the Mekong Delta in Operation Game Warden. River patrol craft begin arriving in theater on 10 April 1966.

22 December
In the first raid on an industrial target in North Vietnam, planes from the carriers *Enterprise*, *Kitty Hawk*, and *Ticonderoga* attack the power plant at Uong Bi.

1966

28 January
In Operation Double Eagle, the largest amphibious operation to date in South Vietnam, the Seventh Fleet Amphibious Ready Group executes a landing near Quang Ngai City and Tam Ky in what turns out to be a fruitless search for Viet Cong units.

14 February
While operating in the Gulf of Thailand off South Vietnam, *PCF-4* is sunk by an underwater explosion, killing four of her six crewmen. She is the first swift boat lost in action.

26 March
The Seventh Fleet Amphibious Ready Group lands U.S. and South Vietnamese Marines thirty-five miles south of Saigon, South Vietnam. This is the first amphibious operation conducted in the Mekong Delta, though no sizeable Viet Cong force is encountered.

29 March
As part of her training in aviation experimental psychology, Ensign Gale Ann Gordon, MC, makes a solo flight at Naval Air Station Pensacola, Florida, the first woman to ever fly a Navy aircraft.

31 March
Lieutenant Marcus A. Arnheiter is relieved of command of the escort *Vance* (DER 387) operating off Vietnam. The controversial Arnheiter points to disloyal junior officers as the reason behind his relief.

1 April
U.S. Naval Forces Vietnam, responsible for all naval forces in South Vietnam and some offshore units, is established with Rear Admiral Norvell G. Ward commanding.

1 May
The entrenched bureau system in the Navy Department, first established in 1842, ends with a reorganization that places the Bureau of Naval Personnel and Bureau of Medicine and Surgery directly under the Chief of Naval Operations. The

Right: *The constant threat of enemy sappers affixing mines to ships at anchor in the harbors of South Vietnam prompted heightened security, including the employment of explosive ordnance disposal (EOD) teams to monitor the waters. (Naval Historical Center)*

Below: *Sporting a fearsome paint scheme, a patrol air cushion vehicle (PACV) splashes through the waters of the Mekong Delta. The Navy operated only three PACVs in South Vietnam, the type proving too mechanically difficult in the harsh conditions. (Corbis)*

Bureaus of Naval Weapons; Yards and Docks; Supplies and Accounts; and Ships are rearranged into six systems commands under the Chief of Naval Material.

9 May
Patrol air-cushion vehicles begin support of Operation Market Time in South Vietnamese waters, while river patrol boats launch their first combat operations on the Bassac River in the Mekong Delta.

11 May
A North Vietnamese freighter attempting to deliver supplies to Viet Cong forces in South Vietnam is sunk

by Navy and South Vietnamese Air Force aircraft in combination with the escort ship *Brister* (DER 327), minesweeper *Vireo* (MSC 205), and Coast Guard patrol vessel *Point Grey* (WPB 82324).

12 May
The first successful guided firing tests of the Phoenix missile, which in future years is carried by the F-14 Tomcat, are conducted on the Pacific Missile Range in the waters off Point Mugu, California.

22 May
While operating in the Dinh Ba River in South Vietnam, the patrol boat *PCF 41* is taken under fire and sunk.

23 May
The nuclear-powered cruiser *Long Beach* scores the first shootdown of an enemy aircraft by surface-to-air missiles during the Vietnam War when a Talos missile launched from her deck destroys a MiG fighter over the Tonkin Gulf.

3 June
While orbiting the earth in the Gemini IX spacecraft with Lieutenant Colonel Thomas P. Stafford, USAF, Lieutenant Commander Eugene A. Cernan becomes the second American astronaut to walk in space.

Left: *Smoke, dust, and mud boil skyward as Navy A-4 Skyhawks from the carrier* Oriskany *(CVA 34) press their attack on the Phuong Dinh railroad bypass bridge, North Vietnam, 10 September 1967. (National Museum of Naval Aviation)*

Below: *Mechanics prepare a Helicopter Attack (Light) Squadron 3 UH-1B for a mission. The Seawolves provided air support for riverine missions. (National Museum of Naval Aviation)*

16 June

Carrier aircraft begin a sustained effort to destroy North Vietnamese petroleum facilities with a strike at Thanh Hoa by planes from *Hancock*. This strike is followed up by an attack against the petroleum facilities near the major cities of Haiphong and Hanoi.

1 July

In the North Vietnamese Navy's first offensive action against Navy ships since the Tonkin Gulf incident in August 1964, three torpedo boats attempt to attack the frigate *Coontz* (DLG 9) and the destroyer *Rogers* (DD 876) only to be sunk by carrier aircraft. Five days later carrier aircraft exchange fire with enemy torpedo boats off Haiphong.

Mine Squadron 11, Detachment Alfa is established to keep the Long Tau River channel to Saigon, South Vietnam, swept of mines.

16 July

Opening Operation Deck House II, the Seventh Fleet Amphibious Ready Group lands Marines in Quang Tri Province north of Hue in South Vietnam.

18–21 July

Gemini X astronauts Commander John W. Young and Major Michael Collins, USAF, make forty-three orbits around the earth and dock with an Agena space vehicle.

6 August

The Navy commissions the first of a new class of patrol gunboats, *Asheville* (PGM 84). With small ships and craft playing an important role in naval operations in Vietnam, the PGMs see extensive service in Southeast Asia.

Right: *The Seventh Fleet Amphibious Ready Group, led by* Iwo Jima (LPH 2), *steams in the South China Sea. Other ships are* Thomaston (LSD 28) *and* Vancouver (LPD 2). *This force provided the Navy the flexibility to put troops ashore by landing craft or helicopter in trouble spots along the coast of South Vietnam. (National Museum of Naval Aviation)*

22 August
The amphibious assault ship *Iwo Jima* lands Marines 100 miles east of Saigon, South Vietnam, as part of Operation Deckhouse III, with the leathernecks joining U.S. and South Vietnamese paratroopers in an operation against Viet Cong forces in the region.

30 August
Taking over from Army pilots, naval aviators begin flying UH-1B "Huey" helicopters in support of riverine forces participating in Operation Game Warden. The success of the helicopter missions results in the

eventual establishment of Helicopter Attack (Light) Squadron (HAL) 3. Called the Seawolves, HAL-3 is one of the most highly decorated Navy squadrons of the Vietnam War.

11 September
The first fatality of Operation Game Warden occurs when Viet Cong forces ambush two river patrol boats on the Co Chien River in South Vietnam, killing one crewman.

orbits and includes a spacewalk by Gordon and docking with an Agena space vehicle.

15 September
Seventh Fleet Amphibious Ready Group vessels put Marines ashore in Quang Tri Province, South Vietnam, as part of Operation Deckhouse IV.

16 September
Helicopters from the aircraft carrier *Oriskany* (CVA 34) rescue forty-four crewmen from the merchant ship *August Moon*, aground and breaking up on the Pratas Reef southeast of Hong Kong.

22 September
In the first combat action involving Navy minesweeping craft during the Vietnam War, Viet Cong gunners ambush two minesweeping boats, hitting *MSB-15* in the pilot house, killing one of her crew and wounding eleven others.

29 September
In the wake of Hurricane Inez, the amphibious ships *Boxer* (LPH 4), *Rankin* (AKA 103), *Plymouth Rock* (LSD 29), *Ruchamkin* (APD 89), and *Suffolk County* (LST 1173) begin relief operations in the Dominican Republic and Haiti.

12–15 September
The Gemini XI mission consisting of the all-Navy crew of Lieutenant Commander Richard Gordon and Commander Charles C. Conrad completes forty-four

25 October
Seventh Fleet ships commence Operation Sea Dragon, a complement to the air campaign over Vietnam, by

Above: *Boatswain's Mate First Class James E. Williams exemplified the heroism of those who fought in the "brown water Navy," receiving the Medal of Honor for actions on 31 October 1966. (Naval Historical Center)*

Left: *The carrier Oriskany (CVA 34) in flames off North Vietnam, 26 October 1966. (Robert L. Rasmussen, National Museum of Naval Aviation)*

Right: *Gunners on board riverine patrol boats faced danger at every turn. The jungle lining the riverbanks of the Mekong Delta was a haven for Viet Cong guerillas. Firefights involved heated, close-quarters combat in which every ounce of firepower was employed against the enemy. ("Firefight—Swift on Soi-Rap," John Steel, Navy Art Collection)*

unleashing naval gunfire against enemy coastal batteries, radar sites, and transportation routes. Ships ranging in size from destroyers to a battleship will participate in Sea Dragon.

26 October
In the first of three disastrous fires on board aircraft carriers during the Vietnam War, a fire in a flare locker on board *Oriskany* takes the lives of forty-four men from the ship's crew and embarked air wing.

31 October
In the most successful Operation Game Warden action thus far during the Vietnam War, the patrol boats *PBR-105* and *PBR-107*, later joined by UH-1B helicopters, sink or capture fifty-seven junks and sampans during a three-hour engagement in the Mekong River. During the action Boatswain's Mate First Class James E. Williams, on board *PBR-105*, displays inspiring leadership and courage, exposing himself to withering enemy fire in directing attacks against the numerically superior enemy force. In gathering darkness he orders the boats' searchlights turned on to provide better visibility for his gunners and the attacking helicopters, knowing that this would make the patrol boats more visibile. For his actions Williams receives the Medal of Honor.

In the first sinking of a minesweeping craft during the Vietnam War, *MSB-54* is sent to the bottom of the Long Tau River after striking a mine. Two crewmen are reported missing and four are wounded by the explosion.

4 November
A fire in an oil and hydraulic fluid storage area on board the carrier *Franklin D. Roosevelt* (CVA 42) is contained, and the carrier continues flight operations in the South China Sea uninterrupted. Seven crewmen are killed and four are injured in the blaze.

11–15 November
Gemini XII, the last flight of Project Gemini, includes fifty-nine orbits, a spacewalk, and practice docking with an Agena space vehicle. The astronauts are Commander James A. Lovell, Jr., and Lieutenant Colonel Edwin E. Aldrin, Jr., USAF.

23 November
A highly successful intercept as part of Opeation Sea Dragon occurs when the destroyers *Mullany* (DD 528) and *Warrington* (DD 843) sink or damage forty-seven enemy supply barges off the coast of North Vietnam.

5 December
Enemy shore batteries fire on the destroyer *Ingersoll* (DD 652) northeast of Dong Hoi, North Vietnam, and fragments from near misses slightly damage the ship.

11 December
Two river patrol boats operating in the Mekong River trail a sampan to a canal, where their crews discover forty more sampans and numerous Viet Cong troops. Opening fire, the PBRs kill nine enemy soldiers and destroy twenty-eight sampans.

Left: *The cruiser Canberra (CAG 2) bombarding North Vietnam, March 1967. (Naval Historical Center)*

Below: *A bluejacket prepares to drop a round down the tube of an 81mm mortar as his shipmate stands by to receive communications via earphones from the vessel's commander. The dual-mounted mortar and .50-caliber machine gun was an effective weapon on board swift boats of the coastal/river patrol force. (Naval Historical Center)*

23 December
North Vietnamese gunners find their mark when a shore battery scores a direct hit on the destroyer *O'Brien* (DD 725) operating in the Tonkin Gulf. Two crewmen are killed and four are wounded.

1967

13 January
Master Chief Gunner's Mate Delbert D. Black is appointed the Navy's first Senior Enlisted Advisor, a billet that is soon renamed Master Chief Petty Officer of the Navy (MCPON). The MCPON advises the Chief of Naval Operations on all matters pertaining to enlisted personnel in the Navy.

27 January
During a ground test at Cape Kennedy, Florida, a fire caused by a spark in the pure-oxygen environment of the Apollo I space capsule kills three astronauts, including Lieutenant Commander Roger B. Chaffee.

4 February
A Viet Cong grenade sets fire to the river patrol boat *PBR-113* on patrol in the Co Chien River. The boat is salvaged and used for spare parts.

15 February
The Navy's minesweeping effort in the channel waters leading to Saigon, South Vietnam, suffers a setback as *MSB-45* is destroyed by a mine and *MSB-49* is heavily damaged by recoilless rifle fire from ashore. One American is killed and sixteen are wounded.

Right: *An F-8E Crusader from Fighter Squadron (VF) 162 makes an arrested landing on board the carrier* Oriskany *(CVA 34) after completing a combat mission over North Vietnam, December 1967. The "last of the gunfighters," the F-8 splashed eighteen North Vietnamese MiGs during the war. (National Museum of Naval Aviation)*

16 February

River Assault Flotilla One launches its first offensive operations supporting Army troops in the Rung Sat Special Zone of South Vietnam.

26 February

A-6 Intruders from the carrier *Enterprise* conduct the first aerial mining of the Vietnam War, planting the underwater weapons in the mouths of the Song Ca and Song Giang rivers in an effort to stop the flow of enemy supplies into South Vietnam.

The cruiser *Canberra* (CAG 2) joins the destroyers *Benner* (DD 807) and *Joseph Strauss* (DDG 16) in bombarding sixteen targets near Thanh Hoa in North Vietnam, the first time that naval gunfire has been employed without being provoked by the enemy. On 1 March enemy shore batteries score hits on *Canberra*, damaging her slightly.

28 February

The Mobile Riverine Force (Task Force 117) is established to employ armored riverine craft to seek out and destroy enemy units in the Mekong Delta.

6 March

While serving as a machine gunner on board the river patrol boat *PBR-124*, Seaman David G. Ouellet observes suspicious activity along a bank of the Mekong River. His boat moves in closer to shore and a grenade is thrown at it. Ouellet leaves his machine

gun, dashes to the rear of the boat and pushes the boat captain aside, placing his body between his skipper and the grenade. The subsequent blast kills him. For his uncommon devotion to his shipmates, Ouellet is awarded the Medal of Honor posthumously.

7 March

The number of Women Accepted for Voluntary Emergency Service (WAVES) is increased by twenty percent to 600 officers and 6,000 enlisted.

11 March

Operating off Vinh, North Vietnam, the destroyer *Keppler* (DD 765) takes a hit from an enemy shore battery in her forward 5-inch mount, injuring six members of her crew.

14 March

A North Vietnamese trawler attempting to deliver arms to Communist forces in South Vietnam is spotted by a P-2 Neptune patrol plane and is forced to beach by the radar picket escort ship *Brister* (DER 327), the patrol boat *Point Ellis* (WPB 82330), and *PCF-78*.

17 March

The destroyer *Stoddard* (DD 566) is hit by enemy fire from shore as she joins another destroyer in attempting to rescue a downed naval aviator off the coast of Vietnam. She silences her attacker and ultimately makes a successful rescue.

20 March

The amphibious ships *Monticello* (LSD 35), *Ogden* (LPD 5), and *Princeton* (LPH 5) put the Seventh Fleet's Special Landing Force ashore just south of the Demilitarized Zone as part of Operation Beacon Hill I.

1 April

In the largest single-day bombardment of the Vietnam War, the cruiser *Providence* (CLG 6) and four destroyers unleash their guns on targets along the coast of North Vietnam.

Will Rogers (SSBN 659), the last of the Navy's twenty-six Polaris submarines, is placed in commission.

20, 26 April

While serving as a pilot in Attack Squadron (VA) 192 on board the aircraft carrier *Ticonderoga* (CVA 14), Lieutenant Commander Michael J. Estocin participates in Iron Hand missions against enemy surface-to-air missile (SAM) sites near Haiphong, North Vietnam. On 20 April he personally neutralizes three SAM sites and stays in the target area despite heavy damage and dwindling fuel. Conducting in-flight refueling for a distance of 100 miles back to ship, he manages to bring his crippled A-4 Skyhawk aboard. On 26 April Estocin is again involved in an attack against Haiphong, and despite the fact that his aircraft is hit and in flames,

he attacks a SAM site. He then crashes and is killed. For his heroism in the face of a determined enemy, he receives the Medal of Honor posthumously.

21 April–12 May
The Seventh Fleet's Special Landing Force operates against the Viet Cong in Thua Thien Province, South Vietnam, as part of Operation Beacon Star.

Above: *Established to carry out guerrilla and anti-guerrilla operations in harbors, inland waters, and their adjacent land areas, Sea, Air, Land (SEAL) teams usually operated in six-man units to gather intelligence and conduct raids, reconnaissance patrols, salvage dives, and, as depicted here, ambushes of enemy forces. ("Seals on Ambush, Mekong Delta," Marbury Brown, Navy Art Collection)*

Right: *Navy Lieutenant Commander Frederick E. Whitaker, CHC, delivers a sermon to battle-weary Marines, a moment of peace amidst the violence of war. (U.S. Marine Corps)*

8 June
Claiming a case of misidentification and misinformation, Israeli aircraft and torpedo boats attack the intelligence collection ship *Liberty* (AGTR 5) in international waters north of the Sinai Peninsula, killing 34 sailors and wounding 171. *Liberty*'s skipper, Commander William L. McGonagle, is wounded in the initial attack, but steadfastly remains on the bridge for seventeen hours directing her defense. He receives the Medal of Honor for his actions.

25 June
PCF-97 is sunk by enemy fire off the Ca Mau Peninsula, South Vietnam. One man is wounded in the attack.

1 July
A Navy Department reorganization results in the establishment of the U.S. Naval Intelligence Command under the command of the Director of Naval Intelligence.

21 July

F-8 Crusaders of VF-24 and VF-211 from the carrier *Bon Homme Richard* (CVA 31) shoot down three MiG-17s in aerial combat over North Vietnam.

29 July

While *Forrestal* (CVA 59) prepares to launch her second strike of the day off Vietnam, a Zuni rocket ignites and shoots across the carrier's flight deck, detonating a bomb beneath an aircraft and causing a series of explosions that rock the ship. Fire engulfs the after end of the flight deck and spreads below decks. Only the determined efforts of her crew save the Navy's first supercarrier, though not without cost. All told, 134 members of her crew and embarked air wing are killed and sixty-two more are injured. Twenty-one aircraft are destroyed. The incident ends *Forrestal*'s combat deployment after just five days.

1 August

Admiral Thomas H. Moorer, a former commander of both the Pacific and Atlantic fleets, becomes the eighteenth Chief of Naval Operations.

4 September

During heavy fighting in the Quang Tin Province of South Vietnam, Navy chaplain Lieutenant Vincent R. Capodanno voluntarily leaves the relative safety of a battalion command post and rushes to the front lines where a platoon is in danger of being overrun. He performs last rites for dying Marines and administers aid to the wounded, even after he loses a portion of

one hand when a mortar explodes near him. He is killed going to the aid of a wounded corpsman. For his inspiring example and heroism, he receives the Medal of Honor.

31 October

Currituck (AV 7), the Navy's last seaplane tender, is decommissioned at Mare Island, California. Six days later an SP-5B Marlin of Patrol Squadron (VP) 40 makes the last operational flight of a U.S. Navy seaplane at Naval Air Station North Island, California. For the first time since 1911 the Navy will not have a seaplane flying in its active inventory.

1968

21 January

The Marine garrison at Khe Sanh, South Vietnam, is effectively cut off from ground reinforcements and surrounded by North Vietnamese troops. The ensuing siege is one of the epic engagements in the history of the Marine Corps. The men of Naval Construction Battalion Maintenance Unit 301, Detail Bravo, play an instrumental role in the defense of Khe Sanh, which earns the unit the Presidential Unit Citation. Seabees are largely responsible for reopening land communication with the beleaguered base.

22 January

While she operates in international waters off the east coast of North Korea, the intelligence collection ship *Pueblo* (AGER 2) is attacked and captured by North

Right: *A Navy chaplain trails the casket of Duane Hughes, the only sailor killed during the attack and capture of intelligence collection ship* Pueblo *(AGER 2), on 22 January 1968. (Bettmann/Corbis)*

Below: *Men of Construction Battalion Maintenance Unit 301, Detail Bravo, proudly display the Presidential Unit Citation streamer awarded their unit for exceptional service during the long North Vietnamese siege of Khe Sanh. (Naval Historical Center)*

Korean patrol boats. Enemy fire mortally wounds one crewman and wounds three others, including the skipper, Commander Lloyd Bucher. The crew is taken prisoner and held captive for over eleven months.

30 January
Though in previous years an informal truce has been observed during Tet, the Vietnamese New Year, on this day the North Vietnamese launch a massive offensive throughout South Vietnam. The Tet Offensive results in some 32,000 enemy casualties, but succeeds in turning American public opinion against the war.

31 March
President Lyndon B. Johnson calls a halt to bombing in North Vietnam north of the 20th parallel and informs the nation that he will not seek reelection.

6 April
The battleship *New Jersey* (BB 62) is recommissioned for service in Vietnam. She unleashes her 16-inch guns on targets in Vietnam beginning on 29 September.

3 May
The Naval Safety Center is established with headquarters at Norfolk, Virginia.

16 May
When his company comes under attack by North Vietnamese forces in Quang Tri Province, South Vietnam, Hospital Corpsman Third Class Donald E. Ballard braves enemy fire to reach a wounded Marine. As the man is being placed on a stretcher, an enemy

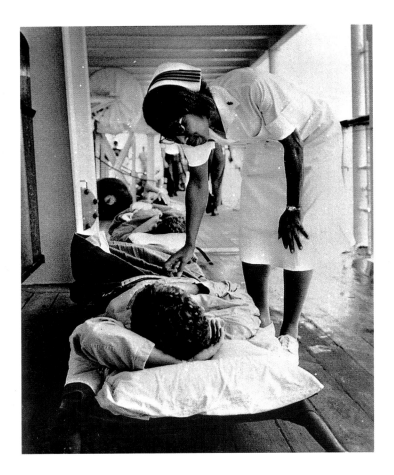

the loss of all ninety-nine members of her crew. A survey of the wreckage results in the opinion that the cause of her sinking is a torpedo that begins running in its tube, is launched, and circles back to hit the submarine.

25 May

The prototype of the EA-6B Prowler, a carrier-based electronic countermeasures aircraft that is still a mainstay of carrier aviation, makes its first flight.

16 June

In a case of friendly fire, the missile cruiser *Boston* (CAG 1) and the Australian missile destroyer *Hobart* are damaged and the patrol craft *PCF-19* is sunk by Air Force planes off the coast of Vietnam.

19 June

Venturing deep into North Vietnam at night to rescue the crew of a downed Navy F-4 Phantom II, Lieutenant (junior grade) Clyde E. Lassen maneuvers his UH-2 Seasprite helicopter into position for a recovery when he begins taking enemy fire. Lifting off again, he ignites flares to illuminate the wooded area, but when they are extinguished his helicopter collides with a tree. Lassen rights his craft and makes two more rescue attempts, on the second turning on his landing lights despite the danger of enemy fire. Taking the survivors aboard, Lassen skillfully flies his helicopter to a ship off shore, landing with fuel for only five minutes of flight remaining. For his heroic actions in the air, Lassen receives the Medal of Honor.

soldier throws a grenade that lands nearby, and Ballard unhesitatingly hurls himself upon it. Luckily, it doesn't detonate and he continues treating casualties. For his willingness to risk his life for his comrades in arms, he receives the Medal of Honor.

21 May

The nuclear-powered submarine *Scorpion* (SSN 589) sinks 400 miles southwest of the Azores Islands with

Above: *A Navy nurse provides a comforting touch and kind word to a wounded man on board the hospital ship* Repose *(AH 16) off Vietnam, 1967. A total of 425 female nurses served afloat and ashore during the war. (Naval Historical Center)*

Left: *This HC-7 crew made a daring night rescue of two downed aviators in North Vietnam on 19 June 1968. Pilot Lieutenant (j.g.) Clyde E. Lassen is at left. (National Museum of Naval Aviation)*

Right: *American and Vietnamese river patrol force sailors fire at enemy troops concealed in thick vegetation ashore during a SEALORDS operation. U.S. Army soldiers are among those aboard. As the war progressed, South Vietnamese forces were increasingly integrated into operations under the policy of Vietnamization of the war. (Naval Historical Center)*

9 July

The Army-Navy Mobile Riverine Force shifts its operations to the Co Chien River in South Vietnam.

28 July

When his platoon comes under attack while in an open rice field in Quang Nam Province, South Vietnam, Hospital Corpsman Third Class Wayne M. Caron rushes to the aid of a wounded Marine and, though himself wounded by enemy fire, renders valuable aid. En route to a second casualty Caron is hit in the leg, but crawls the remaining distance to the wounded Marine. While attempting to reach yet another wounded leatherneck, the intrepid corpsman is killed by an enemy rocket round. He is posthumously awarded the Medal of Honor.

29 July

Operation Game Warden is expanded to include the entire Mekong Delta from the Cambodian border to the South China Sea.

17 August

Dolphin (AGSS 555), the Navy's only operational, diesel-electric, deep-diving, research and development submarine, is commissioned. Able to support missions such as acoustic deep-water and littoral research, near-bottom and ocean surveys, weapons launches, sensor trials, and engineering evaluations, she remains operational today.

18 September

While operating in Quang Tin Province in South Vietnam, the fast patrol boat *PCF-21* attacks an assembly of Viet Cong small craft, destroying forty-four junks and four sampans.

11–22 October

Apollo VII, the first manned mission of the space program that eventually lands a man on the moon, completes 163 orbits around the earth. The commander of the three-man crew is Captain Walter M. Schirra, Jr., the only astronaut to fly missions in the Mercury, Gemini, and Apollo programs.

15 October

Developed by Commander Naval Forces, Vietnam Vice Admiral Elmo R. Zumwalt, Jr., SEALORDS (Southeast Asia Lake, Ocean, River, and Delta Strategy) operations begin with the goal of cutting off North Vietnamese and Viet Cong supply lines from Cambodia. In the first year of operations, SEALORDS results in the capture or destruction of 500 tons of supplies and ammunition and the death or capture of some 3,300 Communist soldiers. Navy, Army, and South Vietnamese Navy forces participate in SEALORDS.

29 October

In a surprise attack in the Lon-Bo De River area of South Vietnam, Navy patrol boats join South Vietnamese

Air Force A-1 Skyraiders, the tank landing ship *Washoe County* (LST 1165) and the Coast Guard cutter *Wachusett* (WHEC 44) in destroying 242 enemy watercraft and 167 structures during a period of five hours.

6 December
Navy riverine forces begin regular patrols on the Vam Co Dong and Vam Co Tay rivers west of Saigon, South Vietnam, as part of Operation Giant Slingshot, an effort to stem the flow of supplies from the so-called Parrot's Beak area of Cambodia. The operation is turned over to the South Vietnamese completely on 5 May 1970 after 1,200 firefights with the enemy.

21–27 December
Apollo VIII, whose three-man crew includes Commander James A. Lovell, Jr., is the first space mission to venture to the moon, circling it before returning to the earth.

23 December
Four patrol boats supported by Army helicopter gunships destroy or damage 167 sampans, 125 structures, and eight bunkers in An Xuyen Province, South Vietnam.

1969

3 January
The Navy establishes Attack Squadron (Light) (VAL) 4, the first squadron of its kind, at Naval Air Station

North Island, California. Flying OV-10 Bronco aircraft, the "Black Ponies" provide support for riverine forces operating in South Vietnam.

13 January–9 February
In the largest amphibious assault of the Vietnam War, the Seventh Fleet Amphibious Ready Group, supported by naval gunfire that includes the 16-inch

Right: *Recommissioned to lend the massive fire support of her 16-inch guns to ground forces, the battleship* New Jersey *(BB 62) served one combat tour during 1968–1969 before again being withdrawn from service. (Naval Historical Center)*

guns of the battleship *New Jersey*, puts 2,500 Marines ashore on the Batangan Peninsula, South Vietnam. Operating in concert with U.S. and South Vietnamese Army troops, the leathernecks screen some 12,000 Vietnamese civilians and kill 239 Viet Cong.

14 January

While steaming off Hawaii before deploying to Vietnam, the nuclear-powered carrier *Enterprise* suffers a costly fire when a rocket ignites on the flight deck and triggers explosions in armed aircraft. Though the flames are brought under control in less than an hour, 27 crewmen are dead, 344 are injured, and 14 aircraft are destroyed.

31 January

John H. Chafee, a Marine combat veteran of World War II and Korea, becomes the sixtieth Secretary of the Navy.

14 March

While in command of a SEAL team in an assault on an island in Nha Trang Bay, South Vietnam, Lieutenant (junior grade) Joseph R. Kerrey is severely wounded by a grenade. He maintains control of the operation, calling in fire support and ordering the members of his team to secure an extraction site. For his heroism Kerrey is awarded the Medal of Honor.

19 March

While serving with a Marine howitzer battery in Quang Nam Province, South Vietnam, Hospital Corpsman Second Class David R. Ray springs into action when enemy forces launch a determined assault against the battery's position. Although seriously wounded himself, Ray administers aid to wounded Marines, fighting off two enemy soldiers while caring for one fallen comrade. His final act, before sustaining fatal wounds, is covering the body of a wounded Marine when an enemy grenade lands nearby. Ray receives a posthumous Medal of Honor for his heroic actions.

14 April

North Korean aircraft shoot down an EC-121 Warning Star electronic surveillance aircraft over the Sea of Japan. All thirty-one crew members are lost. In response to the shootdown, the Navy establishes Task Force 71, consisting of four carriers and their escorts, to make a show of force in the Yellow Sea.

18–26 May

Apollo X, the last mission launched preparatory to a moon landing, includes naval aviators Captain John W. Young and Commander Eugene A. Cernan. During the mission, Cernan joins Colonel Thomas P. Stafford in making a trial descent in a lunar landing vehicle to within nine and one-half miles of the lunar surface.

2 June

While engaged in Southeast Asia Treaty Organization exercises in the South China Sea, the Australian carrier *Melbourne* strikes the destroyer *Frank E. Evans* (DD 754), cutting her in two. The destroyer's bow section sinks within minutes, while *Melbourne's* crew secures the after section alongside the carrier. Seventy-four crewmen from *Frank E. Evans* die in the tragic mishap, for which the destroyer's skipper and officer of the deck are court-martialed.

15 June

While in command of eight river assault craft extracting Army troops on a bank of the Ong Muong Canal, South Vietnam, Lieutenant Thomas G. Kelley receives word that one of the craft under his command is experiencing mechanical difficulties. When Viet Cong forces open fire from the opposite bank of the canal, Kelley places his craft in the line of fire to shield the others. Despite suffering severe head injuries, he maintains control of the situation and provides inspirational leadership for which he receives the Medal of Honor.

Right: *An RA-5C Vigilante of Reconnaissance Attack Squadron (RVAH) 11 flies a photoreconnaissance mission over North Vietnam from the carrier* Constellation *(CVA 64). The sleek aircraft began its life as a nuclear weapons delivery platform, but with the elimination of the heavy attack mission from carrier air wings it found a role as a capable reconnaissance plane. (National Museum of Naval Aviation)*

21 July

During the Apollo XI mission to the moon, astronaut Neil Armstrong steps down the ladder of the lunar lander Eagle onto the surface of the moon, uttering the famous words, "That's one small step for man, one giant leap for mankind." Armstrong is a former naval aviator who flew combat missions over Korea.

5 August

Five years after taking their first prisoner of war, the North Vietnamese release three POWs, including Lieutenant Robert F. Frishman and Seaman Douglas B. Hegdahl, who became an unlikely POW after falling overboard from the cruiser *Canberra* (CAG 2). The three report the torturing of prisoners. Hegdahl, having memorized the names of those in captivity, verifies that many pilots feared killed in action are, in fact, alive.

4 September

Captain James B. Stockdale, having already been subjected to extreme torture and deprivation during his captivity in North Vietnam, is caught attempting to communicate covertly with fellow prisoners. Rather than submit to the North Vietnamese, he attempts to commit suicide as a symbol of his defiance, prompting his captors to revive him and abate their torture. For his actions Stockdale receives the Medal of Honor.

27 October

NR-1, the first deep submergence vessel using nuclear power, enters service. Capable of performing underwater search and recovery, oceanographic research missions and installation and maintenance of underwater equipment, the *NR-1* becomes a key asset in the recovery of wreckage following the explosion of the Space Shuttle Challenger in 1986.

14–24 November

The all-Navy crew of Apollo XII—Commanders Charles C. Conrad and Richard F. Gordon and Lieutenant Commander Alan Bean—make the second landing on the moon, with Conrad and Bean spending 31 hours on the lunar surface.

1970

28 March

The destroyer *Orleck* (DD 886) bombards enemy positions near Rach Gia, South Vietnam, in support of South Vietnamese Army troops, damaging or destroying forty-four structures.

11 April

The Apollo XIII mission, which is commanded by Captain James A. Lovell, Jr., experiences an in-flight explosion en route to the moon. National Aeronautics and Space Administration (NASA) engineers and the

astronauts devise solutions that keep the men alive and return them safely to earth after over five days in space.

16 April
Strategic Arms Limitation Talks begin between the United States and the Soviet Union in Vienna, Austria. This comes a month after the Non-Proliferation Treaty signed between the two superpowers in July 1968 takes affect.

6 May
In the aftermath of the 4 May invasion of Cambodia by U.S. and South Vietnamese forces, forty U.S. Navy river patrol craft enter that nation on the Kham Span River and come under attack. Two days later 100 American and South Vietnamese craft enter Cambodia by way of the Mekong River.

12 May
As part of the continuing effort to cut off North Vietnamese and Viet Cong vessels from Cambodia, American and South Vietnamese ships and small craft establish a blockade of the Cambodian coast from the Vietnam border west to the city of Sihanoukville.

1 July
Admiral Elmo R. Zumwalt, Jr., becomes the nineteenth Chief of Naval Operations, the youngest man to hold the post and youngest to achieve four-star rank. With his espousing of liberal policies regarding the discipline and dress of sailors, he becomes one of the most controversial Chiefs of Naval Operations in history.

22 July
As part of the Vietnamization of the war, sixty South Vietnamese are commissioned in their navy following graduation from Officer Candidate School in Newport, Rhode Island. Some of these men end up manning the 525 ships and small craft transferred to the South Vietnamese Navy by the United States.

1 August
The Military Sea Transportation Service is renamed the Military Sealift Command with control remaining with the Navy.

3 August
The fleet ballistic missile submarine *James Madison* (SSBN 627), the first ship converted to operate the Poseidon C-3, conducts the first submerged launch of that missile off Cape Kennedy, Florida.

21 November
Navy aircraft from the carriers *Hancock*, *Oriskany*, and *Ranger* join Marine and Air Force planes in striking missile and antiaircraft artillery sites below the 19th parallel in response to attacks on American reconnaissance aircraft.

21 December
The prototype for the F-14 Tomcat fighter, a veritable symbol of naval aviation during the latter quarter of the twentieth century, makes its maiden flight.

Above: *A river monitor, converted from a landing craft and armed to support ground troops, uses a flame thrower to destroy riverbank foliage that might conceal an enemy ambush. (Naval Historical Center)*

Right: *Admiral John S. McCain, Jr., Commander in Chief, Pacific, discusses Vietnam War strategy with President Richard M. Nixon, 1970. (Corbis)*

Below: *(Left to right): Ensign Le Cuy Dang, VNN, Lieutenant Taylor Field, USN, and Lieutenant (jg) Phu, VNN, observe maritime activity while on patrol with the Coastal Force along the littoral of South Vietnam. (Naval Historical Center)*

1971

14 January
President Richard M. Nixon signs into law a bill passed by Congress repealing the Tonkin Gulf Resolution.

22 January–8 February
A P-3 Orion flown by Commander Donald H. Lilienthal establishes eight world distance, speed, and time-to-climb records for turboprop aircraft, including a record distance flight of 5,963 nautical miles from Naval Air Station Atsugi, Japan, to Naval Air Station Patuxent River, Maryland.

31 January–9 February
During the Apollo XIV mission to the moon, Captain Alan B. Shepard, Jr., the first American in space, becomes the seventh man to walk on the lunar surface almost a decade after his first spaceflight in the Mercury spacecraft.

5 March
Under a reorganization plan espoused by Chief of Naval Operations Admiral Elmo Zumwalt, the offices of the Deputy Chief of Naval Operations for Air Warfare, Surface, and Submarine are established. The Air Warfare post, created in 1944, involves only a name change.

16 March
The SH-2D Seasprite Light Airborne Multipurpose System helicopter makes its maiden flight. Fitted with advanced sensors and processors, the helicopter effectively extends the range at which surface ships can detect and attack surface and subsurface targets.

31 March
On the same day that the fleet ballistic missile submarine *James Madison* departs on the first submarine patrol with the Poseidon C-3 missile, the Navy establishes the office responsible for the development of its successor, the Undersea Long-Range Missile System, later called Trident.

ADMIRAL ELMO R. ZUMWALT, JR.'S INFLUENCE ON THE MODERN U.S. NAVY

by Lieutenant Commander Thomas J. Cutler, U.S. Navy (Retired)

Admiral Elmo R. Zumwalt, Jr., summed up his tenure as the nineteenth Chief of Naval Operations (1 July 1970–1 July 1974) when he told an audience, "I have a wonderful list of friends and a wonderful list of enemies, and am very proud of both lists." Probably the best-known admiral since Halsey and Nimitz, he was also one of the most controversial to ever head the Navy. His opponents saw him as the instigator of permissiveness and the destroyer of discipline, while his advocates called him the "man of the hour" and the "savior of the Navy."

Zumwalt's career included service in World War II, command of several ships, attendance at both the Naval and National War Colleges, and two tours in Washington, one as an aide to the Assistant Secretary of the Navy for Personnel and the other in the Bureau

of Naval Personnel. As Commander of Naval Forces in Vietnam, he revitalized the strategy and the morale of the so-called "brown water Navy" and presided over the extrication of U.S. forces from Vietnam. He also made the decision to use chemical defoliants to remove enemy hiding places along the waterways of the Mekong Delta. Evidence would later suggest that those chemicals had been carcinogenic. When his son who had served in Vietnam as part of the brown water navy succumbed to cancer, the admiral was faced with the terrible possibility that he may have played a role in the death of his own son.

Zumwalt's three decades of experience had taught him that traditional methods of change often led to the slow death of an initiative, killed by the reluctance of conservative senior commanders. He came to believe that ideas that went against the grain of tradition could only survive if they were suddenly brought into the open where they could not be ignored. This philosophy brought unprecedented changes to the Navy but had the corollary effect of creating vehement factions.

Most controversial of Zumwalt's methods were his so-called "Z-Grams," most of which were designed to counter personnel retention problems in the Navy. Determined to "bring the Navy into the modern age" and keeping to his philosophy that unconventional changes needed unconventional methods of implementation if they were to succeed, he used the Z-gram method as a means of simultaneously communicating his changes directly to all personnel in the Navy.

Although the changes wrought by the Z-grams were generally popular among the younger officers and enlisted men, they were less so among more senior officer and petty officers, many of them believing that the method and the content of the Z-grams had undermined their authority. The results were indisputable, however. Never, in the history of the Navy, had such sweeping changes taken place. Gone were many of the so-called "chicken-regs" that had long been a prickly point of contention among naval

Right: *One of the steps taken by Admiral Elmo R. Zumwalt, Jr., during his time as Chief of Naval Operations was issuing his famous "Z-Grams" to the fleet, thus establishing a more direct communication with the common sailor. (Naval Historical Center)*

Opposite: *Admiral Elmo R. Zumwalt, Jr., addresses sailors on board the destroyer* Newman K. Perry *(DD 883), a familiar spot given the fact that much of his time at sea during a long naval career was spent on board destroyers. (Naval Historical Center)*

personnel. Suddenly the family and the individual had taken on a new significance, and in Zumwalt's first year in office, first-term reenlistments rose from ten to seventeen percent. During his tenure as CNO, he succeeded in transforming the Navy from its image of a "humorless, tradition-bound, starchy institution."

One of the high points of his career came when he took aim at racial discrimination with Z-gram number 66, entitled "Equal Opportunity in the Navy." Z-66 acknowledged that the Navy had problems in this area and went on to establish a number of measures to alleviate the situation. This ground-breaking Z-gram concluded with the words, "there is no black Navy, no white Navy—just one Navy—the United States Navy."

Zumwalt was CNO at a time when all of American society was in turmoil, when terms such as "counter-cultural revolution" were commonplace, when racial tensions and dissension over the Vietnam War had skewed perceptions and erected barriers to reasoned debate. Because of that milieu, and despite it, he was able to transform the Navy, removing many of the barnacles that were retarding its progress and altering its course in the process.

"Bud" Zumwalt is remembered for his innovation and for his disruption. His death on 2 January 2000 did not diminish his lists of friends and enemies, but few on either list will deny that he sailed in harm's way—both literally and figuratively—and changed the Navy in the process.

Left: *The destroyer* de Haven *(DD 727) plows through the Tonkin Gulf while screening the carrier* Coral Sea *(CVA 43). The winter monsoon in Southeast Asia, characterized by consistent heavy clouds and rainfall, made operations difficult. ("Sudden Squall," R. G. Smith, Navy Art Collection)*

1 April

Helicopter Mine Countermeasures Squadron (HM) 12 is established at Naval Air Station Norfolk, Virginia, the first squadron of its kind in the U.S. Navy. Its importance will be revealed in the coming years in the waters off Vietnam.

28 April

Among the names of forty-nine captains on the promotion list to rear admiral released on this date is that of Samuel L. Gravely, Jr., the first African-American to rise to flag rank.

31 December

The end of this year signals the end of a 147-year tradition at the Boston Naval Shipyard with the closing of the ropewalk that, since the administration of President Andrew Jackson, manufactured all of the rope used by Navy ships and stations.

1972

21 January

The prototype of the S-3 Viking, the Navy's first jet-powered antisubmarine warfare airplane, makes its first flight.

1 April

Attack Squadron Light (VAL) 4 is withdrawn from South Vietnam, becoming the last U.S. Navy combat unit to operate in-country during the Vietnam War. The withdrawal comes a day after North Vietnamese forces launch the so-called Easter Offensive across the demilitarized zone into South Vietnam.

6 April

In response to the recent North Vietnamese offensive, President Richard M. Nixon reinstitutes the bombing campaign against North Vietnam, with Navy and Air Force aircraft launching massive air strikes on this date, the prelude to some of the most intense air actions of the Vietnam War. Over the course of the following week, naval aircraft flying from four carriers average 191 combat sorties per day. In addition, surface forces operating off the coast bombard advancing North Vietnamese troops, in one month firing 117,000 rounds.

10–13 April

While serving as an advisor to South Vietnamese forces, SEAL Lieutenant Thomas R. Norris twice leads teams into enemy territory to recover two downed pilots. The first rescue on 10 April involves penetration over one mile into enemy territory. During

the second rescue mission, Norris and one South Vietnamese disguise themselves as fishermen and make their way to the injured pilot under the cover of darkness. Covering him with bamboo and vegetation, the pair returns to their base through enemy lines. Both pilots were recovered. Norris receives the Medal of Honor for his actions.

16–27 April
The Apollo XVI mission includes among its three astronauts naval aviators Captain John W. Young and Lieutenant Commander Thomas K. Mattingly, II. Young and Lieutenant Colonel Charles F. Duke, Jr., USAF, walk on the lunar surface during the mission, which concludes with a splashdown in the Pacific Ocean.

25 April
Virginian John W. Warner, a Navy veteran of World War II and Marine Corps veteran of the Korean War, becomes the sixty-first Secretary of the Navy.

27 April
Among the fifty captains selected for promotion to flag rank is Alene B. Duerk, NC, the first female to reach the rank of rear admiral.

THE U.S. NAVY'S ROLE IN STRATEGIC DETERRENCE

by Dr. Jeffrey G. Barlow

From almost the outset of the postwar era, U.S. naval leaders were interested in obtaining for their service a role in the delivery of atomic weapons, whose awesome destructive power had been demonstrated in the closing days of World War II. After several months of uncertainty as to whether the Navy was allowed to pursue such an effort, Acting Secretary of the Navy John L. Sullivan wrote a letter to President Harry S. Truman in July 1946 requesting that he authorize the service to begin preparations for the delivery of atomic bombs in an emergency. Upon determining that Truman had already given such authorization to Navy Secretary James V. Forrestal, the service began planning to equip its ships and aircraft for atomic operations.

The first action was to modify the design of its new XAJ-1 heavy attack aircraft to enable it to carry an atomic bomb. The second step was to move forward with the planning for a flush-deck aircraft carrier capable of operating long-range atack planes weighing

up to 100,000 pounds. Yet, the construction of a carrier of such magnitude took time, and thus in early 1948 the Deputy Chief of Naval Operations (Air) decided that an interim atomic capability for existing carriers was needed. Accordingly, two P2V Neptune land-based patrol planes were modified and flown off a *Midway*-class carrier to demonstrate the feasibility of the plan. Thus proven, the Navy paid for the construction of twelve P2V-3C aircraft specifically designed for the atomic mission.

Under the tutelage of Op-36, the Atomic Energy Division in the Office of the Chief of Naval Operations, plans were drawn up for the establishment of the Navy's first heavy attack squadrons to undertake the atomic delivery role. The first such squadron, designated Composite Squadron (VC) 5, was established at Naval Air Station Moffett Field, California, in September 1948. It received its complement of specially modified P2V-3Cs two months later. In January 1950, VC-5, now equipped with a complement of new AJ-1 Savage heavy attack aircraft, was split in two and a second squadron, VC-6, was established. Three additional squadrons became operational during the next several years and were transferred to the East Coast. In February 1951, Heavy Attack Wing (HATWING) 1 was established at Norfolk, Virginia, to outfit and train all VC squadrons in the heavy attack mission. That same month, a detachment of planes from VC-5 flew to Port Lyautey, French Morocco, to begin operating with the Sixth Fleet in the Mediterranean.

By the late 1950s, all of the Navy's attack aircraft carriers (CVAs), including the new *Forrestal*-class supercarriers, were equipped to store, arm, and load nuclear weapons on their nuclear-capable aircraft. In addition to the all-weather, heavy attack (VAH) squadrons or detachments—equipped with long-range, all-jet A3D Skywarriors—that were on board each carrier deployed in the Mediterranean or the western Pacific, these ships also carried light attack planes and specially modified fighter aircraft capable of delivering the new, lighter weight nuclear weapons.

Thus, aircraft carriers forward-deployed with the Sixth and Seventh fleets provided a significant portion of the nuclear forces that served to deter possible Soviet and Communist Chinese military actions in Europe, the Middle East, and Asia.

In mid-1955, Admiral Arleigh A. Burke, the new Chief of Naval Operations, decided that the Navy would be able to significantly strengthen its strategic deterrent role if it could design and deploy a sea-based intercontinental ballistic missile (IRBM). The first goal of the effort was to acquire a liquid-fueled missile capable of being fired from surface ships. The long-term plan, however, was to obtain a smaller, solid-fueled IRBM that could be used in both surface ships and submarines. After initially partnering with the Army in its Jupiter missile program, the Navy was granted permission to set out on its own in December 1956 with the fleet ballistic missile (FBM) program, designated Polaris. A year later the Eisenhower administration sped up the Polaris program in order to have a missile with a 1,200-mile range and three FBM submarines operational in 1960. The effort proved a tremendous success, and the fleet ballistic missile submarine *George Washington* (SSBN 598)—the first of

forty-one nuclear-powered Polaris missile submarines eventually built—went to sea on her first submerged nuclear deterrent patrol in November 1960.

Although the Navy's carriers eventually were replaced in the strategic deterrent role, Trident missile submarines, successors to the Navy's initial FBM fleet, continue to carry out their vital nuclear responsibilities today in waters around the globe. Their stealthy submerged patrols serve to dissuade potential enemies from using their own arsenals of nuclear weapons.

Opposite: *Until the early 1960s, carrier aviation's atomic punch consisted of the A3D Skywarrior—a heavy attack plane affectionately known as the "Whale" because it was the largest aircraft to ever operate from a U.S. Navy carrier—and the A4D Skyhawk, which could effectively deliver tactical nuclear weapons. These aircraft are from the carrier* Oriskany *(CVA 34). (U.S. Navy)*

Above: *An aerial view of the Electric Boat Division of the General Dynamics Corporation showing the fleet ballistic missile submarine* Michigan *(SSBN 727), the doors to her launch tubes open, circa 1982. (U.S. Navy)*

6 May
Navy F-4 Phantom II fighters of VF 111 and VF 57 from the carrier *Coral Sea* and VF-114 from the carrier *Kitty Hawk* splash two MiG-17s and two MiG-21s in combat over North Vietnam.

8 May
Operation Pocket Money begins as U.S. Navy A-7 Corsair II aircraft and Marine Corps A-6 Intruders drop thirty-six Mk 52-2 magnetic-acoustic sea mines in the approaches to Haiphong, North Vietnam. Some 11,000 mines are sown in North Vietnamese waters during the following eight months.

10 May
In the most intense day of air-to-air combat over North Vietnam, Navy fighters shoot down eight enemy MiGs. Five kills are scored by two VF-96 F-4 Phantom II aircrews from the carrier *Constellation* (CV 64)—two by Lieutenant Matthew J. Connelly III and Lieutenant Thomas J.J. Blonski, and three by Lieutenant Randall H. Cunningham and Lieutenant (junior grade) William P. Driscoll.

After their third kill, Cunningham and Driscoll's F-4 Phantom II is hit by a surface-to-air missile, forcing them to eject over the Tonkin Gulf. They both receive the Navy Cross for their actions on this day. Having scored two kills previously, they are the first aces of the Vietnam War, and the Navy's only aces of the conflict.

23 May
The VF-161 crew of Lieutenant Commander Ronald E. McKeown and Lieutenant John C. Ensch from the carrier *Midway* shoots down two North Vietnamese MiG-17 fighters over North Vietnam. This concludes a month in which Navy aircraft score seventeen kills.

25 May
Meeting in Moscow, Secretary of the Navy John W. Warner and Soviet Admiral of the Fleet Sergei G. Gorshkov conclude the Incidents at Sea Agreement, which sets guidelines for the conduct of navies of the United States and the Soviet Union in an effort to reduce accidents on the high seas.

Right: *The signing of the Memorandum of Understanding in Washington, D.C., which set the stage for the 1972 Incidents at Sea Agreement. (Senator John Warner)*

Below: *Admiral Elmo Zumwalt, Jr., Chief of Naval Operations, listens to men of the Seventh Fleet discuss racial tensions. The Navy mirrored American society with respect to social issues, prompting Admiral Zumwalt to institute controversial measures in an effort to alleviate a number of problems. (Naval Historical Center)*

26 May

United States and Soviet negotiators conclude the Strategic Arms Limitation Talks with agreements to limit each nation to the construction of two antiballistic missile systems and establish limits on the numbers of land-based and submarine-launched missiles each nation can deploy in the ensuing five years. The agreement takes effect on 3 October 1972.

11 August

In the wake of a change in policy permitting women not part of the Nurse Corps to go to sea as part of a ship's crew, Ensign Rosemary E. Nelson, SC, and Lieutenant (junior grade) Ann Kerr are assigned to the hospital ship *Sanctuary* (AH 17) as supply officer and personnel officer, respectively.

11 October

A turret explosion on board the cruiser *Newport News* (CA 148) off the coast of Vietnam kills nineteen sailors, mortally wounds one, and injures nine others.

12 October

Reflecting the turbulence in American society during the Vietnam era, a race riot breaks out on board the carrier *Kitty Hawk* while she operates off the coast of North Vietnam. Nine black sailors beat up a white sailor, which leads to unrest that lasts into the following day. All told, sixty men of *Kitty Hawk* are injured.

16 October

Twelve black sailors, members of the crew of the fleet oiler *Hassayampa* (AO 145), announce their intention to stay behind when she puts to sea from Subic Bay in the Philippines. Their action is in protest of white sailors allegedly stealing money from them. African-American and white sailors brawl later in the day, but a detachment of Marines restores order to the ship in time for her departure.

17 October

The Harpoon antiship missile makes its first test flight. With a range of over sixty nautical miles, it can be launched from ships, submarines, and aircraft.

31 October

While serving as a SEAL advisor, Engineman Second Class Michael E. Thornton participates in an intelligence-gathering mission against a North Vietnamese naval river base. His five-man patrol comes under fire by a numerically superior force, which results in a vicious firefight. As they withdraw, Thornton learns that the patrol's leader, a SEAL lieutenant, is hit and believed dead. In the face of enemy gunfire, he returns to the officer's last position and discovers that he is unconscious, but still alive.

Killing two enemy soldiers about to overrun his position, Thornton moves the lieutenant to safety. Inflating the wounded man's lifejacket, he then pulls him through the water for two hours until picked up by a support craft. For his heroism, Thornton receives the Medal of Honor.

7–19 December

Following a night launch from Cape Kennedy, Florida, the Apollo XVII space capsule commanded by Captain Eugene A. Cernan and including Commander Ronald E. Evans and geologist Harrison H. Schmidt sets course for the moon. Cernan and

Schmidt become the last men to set foot on the lunar surface, and the twelve-day mission concludes with splashdown in the Pacific. Of the seven Apollo missions to the moon, naval aviators command six.

19 December

On 26 October negotiations between representatives of the United States and North Vietnam are promising enough to prompt Secretary of State Henry Kissinger to announce that "peace is at hand." However, the decision of the North Vietnamese delegation to walk out of the peace talks in Paris, France, on 18 December prompts President Richard M. Nixon on this day to commence Operation Linebacker II, a series of devastating raids on North Vietnam by carrier aircraft and Air Force planes, among them B-52 bombers. The so-called Christmas Bombings last until 30 December, when President Nixon calls a bombing halt above the 20th parallel in anticipation of the resumption of peace talks.

1973

12 January

An F-4 Phantom II flown by Lieutenant Victor T. Kovaleski and Lieutenant James A. Wise of VF-161 from the carrier *Midway* shoots down a MiG-17 over the Tonkin Gulf, the last air-to-air kill scored by Navy aircraft during the Vietnam War.

27 January

Twenty-four days after the resumption of peace talks in Paris, France, United States and North Vietnamese negotiators sign an agreement declaring a cease-fire. The terms of the agreement also include the return of all Americans held as prisoners of war and the withdrawal of the remaining American forces in South Vietnam within sixty days.

On this last day of hostilities, an F-4 Phantom II of VF-143 from the carrier *Enterprise* is shot down over South Vietnam. The radar intercept officer is rescued, but pilot Commander Harley H. Hall, a former leader of the Navy's Blue Angels flight demonstration squadron, is eventually declared killed in action.

28 January

Though a cease-fire is in effect in Vietnam, carrier aircraft from *Ranger* and *Enterprise* fly combat missions against Communist positions in Laos in support of the Laotian government. U.S. aircraft later conduct combat sorties over Cambodia, which end on 15 August 1973.

6 February

Operation End Sweep commences as the Seventh Fleet's Mine Countermeasures Force (Task Force 78), under the command of Rear Admiral Brian McCauley, begins minesweeping operations in the waters off

Right: *The ocean minesweepers (front to back)* Force *(MSO 445),* Engage *(MSO 433),* Impervious *(MSO 449), and* Fortify *(MSO 446) depart Subic Bay, Philippines, for Operation End Sweep in Vietnam, February 1973. (U.S. Navy)*

SUBMARINES: HOT MISSIONS IN THE COLD WAR

by Rear Admiral William J. Holland, Jr., U.S. Navy (Retired)

During the Cold War, submarines performed three major tasks. They stood ready to attack enemy warships and merchantmen, engaged in reconnaissance and gathered information, and formed a key element of America's strategic deterrence capability. Their operations were concealed not only from potential enemies, but also from everyone not directly engaged in the work. By their nature, submarines can and do operate in waters controlled by enemy surface warships and aircraft. Between 1945 and 1968, submarines evolved from commerce raiders—a task having little application against the Soviet Union's continental strategy—to become intelligence agents, and then came to dominate the oceans as capital ships of the Navy.

In the Cold War, the Soviet navy was believed to be able to deploy large numbers of submarines against the West's sea lines of communications. The prospect of Soviet nuclear-armed submarines armed with missiles arose in American minds soon after the first Soviet nuclear detonation. These two prospects elevated antisubmarine warfare (ASW) to a mission of national importance. The development of passive acoustic sonar arrays—some on the sea bottom and some in or towed by ships or submarines—was a major effort in this battle.

In the ocean, passive acoustics is the only effective sensor because the sound from the machinery that drives submarines is the only form of energy that travels any significant distance. The submarine *Thresher* (SSN 593) combined nuclear propulsion and a streamlined hull with a large passive sonar suit and a machinery plant that radiated very little noise to create the quiet, multipurpose attack submarine. All American attack submarines thereafter followed this concept. Passive sonar arrays, starting as hull-mounted equipment and later extending into towed arrays, not only provided the first line of defense in an ASW network but made possible covert operations in close proximity to other forces.

Since early in World War II, submarines have engaged in reconnaissance missions along the coasts of actual and potential enemies. These submarine surveillance missions provided direct observation of activities ashore and afloat and garnered information from electronic emissions available in no other way. Recent revelations have disclosed that special submarines performed feats bordering on legend as the submarine's ability to maneuver undetected was coupled with ocean engineering techniques that allowed exploitation of the seabed. Disclosure of *Halibut's* (SSN 587) discovery of the sunken wreck of a Soviet missile submarine on the Pacific Ocean floor was one example. Prosecution of Soviet spies revealed missions where submarines acted as bases for monitoring undersea communications cables. But as important as these special missions and the regular reconnaissance of a potential enemy's fleet were, the routine operation of American submarines in the places where they would fight a war against forces that would be their foe presented the most likely enemy an obvious threat he could not ignore.

These deployments and missions remain clouded but the few details that have been released demonstrate their nature. *Guardfish* (SSN 612) tracked a Soviet Echo II missile submarine for twenty-six days in the South China Sea in May 1972 during North Vietnam's invasion of the Republic of Vietnam. The menace of the Echo's surface-to-surface missiles, either in fact or in argument, was neutralized by *Guardfish*. *Batfish's* (SSN 681) trail of a Soviet *Yankee*-class ballistic missile submarine has been made public. *Batfish* surreptitiously accompanied this Soviet submarine from its home waters to an operating area in the eastern Pacific Ocean, remained with it there and then followed her most of the way home. Other pictures of submarine operations show

close-up photographs and videotapes of Soviet submarines and surface ships conducting exercises—all evidence of a pervasive American submarine presence wherever a potential enemy operated.

The submarine's ability to enter waters denied to surface and air forces and to attack the Soviet navy at its source, threatening its ballistic missile strategic forces, was at the heart of the U.S. Navy's maritime strategy. Submarine presence, deployment of the very accurate long range Mark 48 torpedo, and several demonstrations of the U.S. submarine force's ability to surge quickly were instrumental in the Soviet Union's choice not to use their fleet to threaten the West's sea lines of communications, but to remain relatively close to their own coasts.

In December 1991, the Soviet Union ceased to exist, ending the Cold War that had pitted East against West for nearly half a century. It was a victory that, in many respects, was ensured by the silent service, which remains a guardian of our nation's freedom, unseen and ready to strike suddenly from the depths at those who threaten the United States.

Opposite: *With battle lights casting a red glow in the control room of a* Los Angeles-*class attack submarine, an officer scans the surface for any contacts during a 1981 deployment. The sailors in the background man controls at which they can adjust the depth of the submarine. The close-quarters and inherent dangers that characterize life on board a submarine breed a special camaraderie among the crew. (U.S. Navy)*

Above: *A Soviet* Juliett-*class guided missile submarine pictured at sea in 1988. During the Cold War, U.S. and Soviet submarines played a deadly game of cat and mouse for control of the seas. (U.S. Navy)*

Left: *Lieutenant Commander Everett Alvarez, Jr., the longest-held POW in North Vietnam, waves to the crowd gathered to welcome the arrival of two planeloads of returning POWs to Travis Air Force Base in California, 16 February 1973. (Corbis)*

Below: *Three of the first four women officers chosen to undergo flight training commence reporting-in physics exams with other students as part of their academic training at Naval Air Station Pensacola, Florida, in March 1973. Pictured from the foreground are Lieutenant (junior grade) Judith Neuffer, Lieutenant (junior grade) Barbara Allen, and Ensign Kathleen McMary. (National Museum of Naval Aviation)*

Haiphong, North Vietnam. In addition to minesweeping ships, the force employs thirty-one CH-53 Sea Stallion helicopters of HM-12, Marine Medium Helicopter Squadron (HMM) 165 and Marine Heavy Helicopter Squadron (HMH) 463 that tow minesweeping sleds and other devices. Operation End Sweep is declared complete on 18 July 1973, with the ships of Task Force 78 the last elements of the Seventh Fleet to operate in North Vietnamese territorial waters.

25 May
Eleven days after Skylab I blasts into orbit from Cape Kennedy, Florida, an all-Navy crew consisting of Captain Charles C. Conrad, Commander Joseph P. Kerwin, and Commander Paul J. Weitz take Skylab II on a twenty-eight day mission during which they execute repairs to Skylab I and conduct experiments. They splash down in the Pacific on 22 June 1973.

28 July
Skylab III, commanded by Captain Alan Bean and including Major Jack Lousma, USMC, and Doctor Owen Garriot, launches from Cape Kennedy,

Florida, spending fifty-nine days orbiting the earth before splashing down in the Pacific Ocean on 25 September 1973.

Right: *As the Royal Navy gave up some security responsibilities "East of Suez," the U.S. Navy increasingly operated in the volatile region. The U.S. Navy established the Middle East Force to protect American interests in the Persian Gulf in 1949. ("USS* Lloyd Thomas *Departing Jiddah, Saudi Arabia," Gene Klebe, National Archives)*

31 July
The first Light Airborne Multi-Purpose squadron, Light Helicopter Antisubmarine Squadron (HSL) 33, is established at Naval Air Station Imperial Beach, California.

5 October
In the first homeporting of an American aircraft carrier abroad, *Midway* arrives at Yokosuka, Japan. A forward-deployed carrier operates from the Japanese port to this day.

6 October
Egyptian forces cross the Suez Canal and attack Israeli positions in the Sinai Peninsula, the beginning of the Yom Kippur War that pits Israel against Egypt and Syria. The United States supplies Israel with military equipment and the Sixth Fleet is placed on alert status. A cease-fire is declared on 23 October.

20 December
Lieutenants Jane O. McWilliams and Victoria M. Voge become the first women designated Naval Flight Surgeons.

1974

22 February
Lieutenant (junior grade) Barbara Ann Allen becomes the first woman to complete the Navy's flight training program, receiving her wings of gold as a naval aviator on this date.

22 April
As part of Operation Nimbus Star, RH-53 Sea Stallion helicopters of HM-12 begin the process of clearing mines in the Suez Canal, which were laid during the Middle East war in 1967. The Navy's part of this international effort is completed on 3 June.

20 June
J. William Middendorf, II, a successful financier and former Under Secretary of the Navy, is named the sixty-second Secretary of the Navy.

1 July
The oldest active shipyard in the Navy, the Boston Naval Shipyard, Massachusetts, closes its gates after 174 years of service. Among the ships built in the yard were the 74-gun ships of the line *Independence*, *Vermont*, and *Virginia*, the screw sloop *Housatonic* (sunk by the Confederate submarine *Hunley* in 1864), and numerous destroyers, destroyer escorts, and tank landing ships.

Admiral James L. Holloway III, the son of an admiral and former Seventh Fleet commander, becomes the twentieth Chief of Naval Operations.

24 November
The aircraft carrier *Constellation* enters the Persian Gulf, the first time a U.S. Navy flattop has deployed to that body of water since 1948. In the ensuing three decades the Persian Gulf becomes a highly important area of operations for U.S. Navy warships.

1975

27 January
In the wake of an attack on two of her officers by a mob protesting against what it perceives as anti-Greek policies of the U.S. government, the destroyer *Richard E. Byrd* (DDG 23) departs the port of Corfu.

12 April
With the government of Cambodia facing overthrow by Communist Khmer Rouge guerillas, Seventh Fleet ships deploy to the Gulf of Siam and on this day commence Operation Eagle Pull, the evacuation of American and allied nationals from the Cambodian capital of Phnom Penh. Operating from the decks of the amphibious assault ship *Okinawa* (LPH 3) and the aircraft carrier *Hancock* (CVA *19*), Marine helicopters airlift 276 people, including U.S. Ambassador to Cambodia John Gunther Dean and Cambodian President Saukhm Khoy.

29–30 April
With invading North Vietnamese troops rapidly approaching the South Vietnamese capital of Saigon, ships of the Seventh Fleet's Task Force 76 operating in the South China Sea begin launching helicopters to execute Operation Frequent Wind. Landing in the U.S. Defense Attaché Office compound and at the U.S. Embassy, oftentimes braving enemy fire as they approached the landing zones, Marine and Air Force helicopters pull more than 7,000 Americans and Vietnamese to safety, including U.S. Ambassador to South Vietnam Graham Martin. One South Vietnamese Air Force officer loads his family into a two-seat observation plane and flies out over the South China Sea, making a landing on the flight deck of the carrier *Midway* (CVA 41). In addition, Military Sealift Command ships and Navy warships rescue Vietnamese nationals fleeing South Vietnam by sea.

2 May
The Navy selects Northrop's YF-17, a competitor in a U.S. Air Force design competition for a new fighter, for development into a new strike-fighter. This marks the birth of the F/A-18 Hornet, today the backbone of tactical aviation in the U.S. Navy.

Above: *Refugees cover every available space on the deck and superstructure of the Military Sealift Command's SS* Pioneer Contender, *en route to Phu Quoc Island. (Naval Historical Center)*

Right: *The destroyer* Spruance *(DD 963), the first major warship powered by gas turbine engines. Able to make 32.5 knots, she can carry as many as five different types of missiles. The soundness of the* Spruance-*class design is evidenced in the use of its hull and propulsion plant as the basis for the* Kidd *(DDG 993)-class guided-missile destroyer and the* Ticonderoga *(CG 47)-class guided-missile cruiser. (U.S. Naval Institute)*

7 May

In a goodwill gesture the frigate *Leahy* (DLG 16) and destroyer *Tatnall* (DDG 19) make a port call in Leningrad, U.S.S.R., while the Soviet destroyers *Boykiy* and *Zhguchiy* visit Boston, Massachusetts.

14 May

Two days after Communist Khmer Rouge forces seize the U.S. merchantman *Mayaguez* while she operates in international waters in the Gulf of Thailand, the carrier *Coral Sea* (CVA 43) launches protective air

Left: *A sailor embarked in the destroyer escort* Harold E. Holt *(DE 1074) provides cover to Marines as they storm aboard SS* Mayaguez, *an American merchantman seized in the Gulf of Thailand by Khmer Rouge guerrillas. Once the Marines secured the ship, sailors boarded her to inspect and attach a tow line to the ship. (Naval Historical Center)*

strikes against Cambodian installations ashore as Marines from Air Force helicopters land on Koh Tang Island off southern Cambodia in an effort to rescue the merchant ship's crew, and a party from the frigate *Harold E. Holt* (DE 1074) attempts to recapture *Mayaguez*. The ship is recaptured and the crew is released. Among the eighteen men killed in the operation is one Navy corpsman.

20 September
The Navy's first major warship powered by gas turbine engines, the destroyer *Spruance* (DD 963) is commissioned. She is the lead ship of a destroyer class that eventually numbers thirty ships.

22 November
The guided missile frigate *Belknap* (CG 26) collides with the carrier *John F. Kennedy* (CV 67) while the ships conduct night operations in the Mediterranean Sea. The frigate loses seven sailors killed and forty-seven injured while one of the carrier's crewmen is lost.

1976

12 February
Captain Fran McKee becomes the first female line officer nominated for promotion to flag rank.

29 May
Tarawa (LHA 1), the first of the multipurpose amphibious assault ships featuring a flight deck for

Above: *In 1976, women joined men at the United States Naval Academy for the first time. (U.S. Naval Academy)*

Below: *President Jimmy Carter talks with Commander John E. Christensen, commanding officer of the nuclear-powered attack submarine* Los Angeles *(SSN 688), following a nine-hour cruise off Cape Canaveral, Florida. The President was accompanied on the cruise by another former submariner, Admiral Hyman G. Rickover. (National Museum of Naval Aviation)*

Right: *Technicians load a Tomahawk cruise missile under the wing of a Navy A-6 Intruder during operational testing of the new missile. The Tomahawk has developed into one of the most capable offensive weapons in the Navy inventory, launched primarily from surface ships and submarines. (National Museum of Naval Aviation)*

operating helicopters and AV-8 Harrier jets as well as a floodable docking well for launching landing craft, is commissioned.

5 June

An A-6 Intruder conducts the first successful firing of a fully guided Tomahawk cruise missile over the White Sands Missile Range in New Mexico. The Tomahawk becomes the standard offensive weapon on board Navy ships, with its first operational use in the 1991 Gulf War.

30 June

The practice of naval aviation officers and chief petty officers wearing brown shoes comes to an end when they are abolished from the prescribed uniform. However, the terms "brown shoe" and "black shoe" remain Navy-wide nicknames that differentiate aviators from other naval personnel.

27 July

The amphibious transport dock *Coronado* (LPD 11), supported by the carriers *America* (CV 66) and *Nimitz* (CVN 68), evacuates 160 Americans and 148 foreign nationals from Beirut, Lebanon, as civil war threatens that nation.

28 August

While operating in the Ionian Sea, a Soviet Echo II-class guided-missile submarine collides with the frigate *Voge* (FF 1047). The submarine, with only a small section of her sail above water, strikes the frigate in the stern, injuring one sailor and damaging the propeller. The Echo II's sail suffers extensive damage.

14 September

The carrier *John F. Kennedy* and destroyer *Bordelon* (DD 881) collide during operations in the Atlantic Ocean north of Scotland. The flattop suffers only minor damage, but six of *Bordelon*'s crew are killed, and the ship is damaged to such an extent that she is decommissioned. This is the carrier's second mishap at sea in ten months.

30 September

The aircraft carrier *Oriskany* (CV 34), last active *Essex*-class carrier in front-line service and a veteran of combat in Korea and Vietnam, is decommissioned.

7 October

U.S. Navy commands in the continental United States, once divided into twelve districts, are consolidated into four naval districts with headquarters in Seattle,

Left: *Military and civilian personnel at Naval Air Station Miramar, California, get a close-up look at the YF-17 prototype for the Navy's newest strike fighter, the F/A-18 Hornet, 26 June 1977. The aircraft became a mainstay on carrier decks by the time of the first Gulf War, with versions eventually replacing the Vietnam-era A-7 Corsair II and A-6 Intruder. (National Museum of Naval Aviation)*

Below: *Robert Walker, Master Chief Petty Officer of the Navy, 1978. (Naval Historical Center)*

Washington; Great Lakes, Illinois; Philadelphia, Pennsylvania; and Washington, D.C.

13 November
Los Angeles (SSN 688), lead ship in a new class of attack submarines that will number fifty-one boats, is commissioned.

1977

16 January
Forty-nine sailors and Marines die when a landing craft operating from the amphibious transport dock *Trenton* (LPD 14) collides with the Spanish merchant ship *Urlea* in Barcelona Harbor, Spain.

18 January
The Navy conducts the first successful launch of a Trident C-4 submarine-launched ballistic missile at Cape Canaveral, Florida.

14 February
W. Graham Claytor, Jr., takes office as the sixty-third Secretary of the Navy.

7 September
In a treaty with Panama, the United States agrees to turn over control of the Panama Canal in the year

Right: *A Trident C-4 missile roars aloft during a test firing on 23 January 1979. With a range of 4,350 miles, Trident made European bases for America's ballistic missile submarine force unnecessary. The missile was designed for the* Ohio-*class submarines, which carry twenty-four of them in silos on board the boat.(U.S. Naval Institute)*

2000. A second treaty, signed by President Jimmy Carter and Panamanian President Omar Torrijos, guarantees the neutrality of the canal in time of war.

17 December
Oliver Hazard Perry (FFG 7), the lead ship in a class of frigates that eventually numbers fifty-one, is commissioned.

1978

2 February
Operating of the California coast, the submarine *Barb* (SSN 696) conducts the first successful launching of a Tomahawk cruise missile from a submerged submarine.

THE NAVY AND GUIDED MISSILES

by Dr. Norman Friedman

Since World War II, the U.S. Navy has been a prime mover in the U.S. missile program. Navy-developed missiles, Sidewinder and Sparrow, arm its fighters as well as those of the Air Force, while the armed forces' antiradar missile is the Navy-developed HARM. Polaris and its successors defined the U.S. deterrent that helped win the Cold War. Navy-developed antiaircraft missiles, namely the Standard family and NATO Sea Sparrow, arm many of the world's surface warships.

U.S. Navy interest in guided missiles can be traced to World War II, when a few Navy land-based bombers dropped Bat gliding antiship missiles on Japanese ships late in the war. In the postwar years, missiles were seen as the solution to pressing problems, particularly with respect to antiaircraft warfare. The Japanese kamikazes of 1944–1945 had demonstrated weaknesses in existing fleet air defenses, which were based on a combination of fighters and shipboard guns. It seemed that future enemies, using guided missiles, could do even better. Work on a fleet antiaircraft missile had begun in 1945, and after the war it developed into Project Bumblebee. Bumblebee envisaged a ramjet-powered radar-guided weapon.

Radar guidance was developed in parallel with the new kind of engine, and a special solid-fueled vehicle was built to test it. As the Cold War accelerated, the test vehicle was developed into a shorter-range missile, which became the Terrier. The larger ramjet version became Talos. Both missiles entered service during the 1950s. They were supplemented by a shorter-range version of Terrier, Tartar, which could be carried on board destroyers. Later a version of the air-launched Sparrow was developed to provide "close in" defense for smaller ships.

In parallel with this program, missiles were developed for fleet fighters, since guns seemed inadequate against a new generation of fast bombers. The main project was the radar-guided Sparrow, but engineers at the Navy's new weapons laboratory at China Lake, California, proposed a much simpler infrared guided weapon, initially as a course-corrected version of the standard 5-inch aircraft rocket. In final form, it became the hugely successful Sidewinder.

Ultimately, the point of defending the fleet was to leave it free to attack an enemy's territory. Thus the post-World War II Navy was interested in bombardment weapons, both surface- and air-launched. The former led to a cruise missile, Regulus, and ultimately to fleet ballistic missiles: Polaris, Poseidon, and now Trident. These missiles changed the face of deterrence, because they could threaten the Soviet Union, but could not effectively be attacked. In the past, U.S. bombers had provided an effective threat, but there had always been a risk that the Soviets could negate that threat by attacking the United States first. This deterrence did not seem very stable. Much the same could be said of land-based ballistic missiles. It could not be said of the sea-based weapons.

The air-launched land attack program produced little until much later, when the Vietnam War showed just how dangerous it could be for aircraft to venture into modern air defenses. At that time the Navy's Walleye was among the earliest "smart bombs" that could be launched from a distance. What was lacking

Opposite: *RIM-7 Sea Sparrow missiles, like this one pictured on board the carrier* John F. Kennedy *(CV 67) in 1990, provided surface ships with enhanced defensive capabilities in the event of attacks by enemy aircraft. (U.S. Navy)*

Right: *The Phoenix missile, being launched from an F-14 Tomcat in January 1985, is operated only by the F-14. The aircraft's radar intercept officer can track and engage multiple targets at extended range in the role of providing fleet air defense for carrier battle groups. (National Museum of Naval Aviation)*

through the 1960s was any missile specifically designed to attack surface ships, mainly because the Soviet surface fleet was not considered an important threat. After 1967, however, the Soviets placed a substantial surface force in the Mediterranean, and interest in such weapons expanded. This interest led to Harpoon, which could be fired by an airplane, a surface ship, or a submarine. It became the most popular of all Western antiship missiles, considerably outselling its nearest competitor, the French Exocet.

The air defense missiles all encountered severe problems, mainly because the electronics of the 1940s and 1950s were not yet very reliable. It seemed to developers that even if the early antiaircraft missiles worked as planned, they would be inadequate against the threats of the 1960s. By 1957 design work commenced on a second generation—Typhoon for surface ships and Eagle for aircraft. However, in 1964, Secretary of Defense Robert S. McNamara cancelled Typhoon on the ground and demanded a "get well" program, which ultimately produced a family of Standard missiles. Those much more reliable weapons in turn made it possible to field the sort of system conceived in 1957, but on a much more effective basis, which became the current Aegis. As for the air-to-air missiles, Eagle evolved into the Phoenix system which arms the F-14 Tomcat. It is still in service, but it is gradually giving way to the Air Force-developed Advanced Medium-Range Air to Air missile.

Another missile capitalized on advancement in electronics. By the early 1970s electronics had been miniaturized to the point where a torpedo-size cruise missile could be built. The Navy's version was authorized largely to give the United States a bargaining chip in increasingly one-sided strategic arms negotiations with the Soviets. It then took on a life of its own under the name Tomahawk. The Tomahawk began as a nuclear weapon with the great advantage being that it could be carried by any submarine, not only by a special strategic one (as with ballistic missiles such as Polaris and its successors), and also by many surface warships. These expansions of U.S. strategic platforms enormously complicated any Soviet attempt to track and engage U.S. warships.

The next stage was a Tomahawk antiship missile with a conventional warhead. Its existence inspired the Navy to develop a system to track the Soviet fleet and, indeed, all surface shipping, which was first used to support the 1990 embargo against Iraq. There was also a land-attack version with a non-nuclear warhead. It became a U.S. weapon of choice, beginning with the first war against Iraq. The Tomahawk offers a remarkable degree of precision independent of its range. Characteristic of the Navy's history of achievement in missile technology, a new Tactical Tomahawk currently under development embodies a data link, so that it can loiter near targets, then attack the one it is assigned.

Left: *Crewmen aboard the nuclear carrier* Nimitz *(CVN 68), on station in the Indian Ocean, prepare two RH-53 Sea Stallion helicopters for participation in Operation Evening Light, a rescue mission in Iran, 24 April 1980. (National Museum of Naval Aviation)*

Below: *A CH-53D Sea Stallion draws away from the frigate* Voge *(FF 1047) after lowering a netful of supplies to her helicopter deck. Vertical replenishment (VERTREP) makes the process of resupplying the fleet at sea faster and more flexible. (National Museum of Naval Aviation)*

9 February

The launching of the first satellite of the Navy Fleet Satellite Communications System provides improved command and control capabilities for the fleet.

1 July

Admiral Thomas B. Hayward, a former naval aviator, becomes the twenty-first Chief of Naval Operations.

17 August

President Jimmy Carter vetoes the Fiscal Year 1979 appropriations bill for the Department of Defense, citing the inclusion of funding for another nuclear-powered aircraft carrier. Subsequent congressional testimony by Chief of Naval Operations James L. Holloway III results in a congressional override of the presidential veto.

1 November

Nine female ensigns become the first women assigned to serve in vessels other than hospital ships and transports.

18 November

The prototype of the F-18 (later F/A-18) Hornet makes its first flight.

27 December

In response to internal turmoil in Iran, the aircraft carrier *Constellation* and her escorts deploy to the waters off Singapore.

1979

6 February

With revolution forcing the Shah of Iran to leave his country on 16 January, concern for American nationals rises. On this date the command ship *La Salle* (AGF 3); the destroyers *Blandy* (DD 943), *Decatur* (DDG 31), *Hoel* (DDG 13), and *Kinkaid* (DD 965); and the frigate *Talbot* (FFG 4) evacuate 200 Americans and 240 other foreign nationals from the port cities of Bandar Abbas and Char Bahar.

10 April

Off Cape Canaveral, Florida, the fleet ballistic missile submarine *Francis Scott Key* (SSBN 657) conducts the first submerged launch of a Trident C-4 missile. The following month she begins the first deterrent patrol carrying Trident missiles, one day before *Patrick Henry* (SSBN 449) makes the final submarine launches of the Polaris missile.

20 June

With the completion of her required traps on board the aircraft carrier *Independence* (CV 62) at the controls of a C-1 Trader, Lieutenant Donna A. Spruill becomes the first woman to carrier qualify in a fixed-wing aircraft.

19 July

President Jimmy Carter announces that he has directed the Seventh Fleet to assist refugees fleeing Vietnam by boat. Aircraft and ships support this operation in the ensuing months, assisting in the rescue of over 1,800 "boat people" during the remainder of the year.

Above: *Nuclear-powered vessels* Nimitz *(CVN 68),* California *(CGN 36), and* South Carolina *(CGN 37) at sea in 1976. The U.S. Navy's second nuclear-powered carrier,* Nimitz *is the lead ship of a class of flattops that now forms the bulk of the U.S. Navy's fleet of carriers. (Naval Historical Center)*

17 October
In response to news of a Soviet brigade conducting exercises in Cuba, the amphibious assault ship *Nassau* (LHA 4) lands 1,800 Marines at Guantanamo Bay, Cuba.

25 October
Edward Hidalgo takes office as the sixty-fourth Secretary of the Navy. A native of Mexico City, he is the first Hispanic to ever hold the post.

4 November
Spurred by the Muslim fundamentalist revolution sweeping Iran, a mob of "students" storms the gates of the U.S. embassy in Tehran, taking sixty-six Americans hostage, including three active duty Navy personnel. On 19–20 November the Iranians release thirteen hostages. The action in Iran spreads to surrounding areas, with a mob killing two American servicemen and burning the embassy in Islamabad, Pakistan, on 21 November.

3 December
A bus carrying U.S. Navy personnel to Sabana Seca Naval Communication Center near San Juan, Puerto Rico, is attacked by terrorists. Two sailors lose their lives and ten others are wounded.

12 December
The prototype of the SH-60 Seahawk, which becomes the Navy's primary rotary-wing platform, makes its first flight.

1980

10 January
Serving in the submarine tender *Dixon* (AS 37), Ensign Roberta McIntyre becomes the first female to qualify as a surface warfare officer.

14 January
The aircraft carrier *Nimitz* (CVN 68) and her escorts join the *Midway* (CV 41) and *Kitty Hawk* carrier battle groups in the Arabian Sea. *Kitty Hawk* departs for Subic Bay, Philippines, the following day.

24 April

Seventeen days after breaking diplomatic relations with Iran, the United States conducts Operation Blue Light, an attempt to rescue the Iranian hostages. The plan calls for U.S. Air Force C-130 transports flying from Egypt to rendezvous at a remote location in the Iranian desert called Desert One with eight RH-53 Sea Stallion helicopters launched from the aircraft carrier *Nimitz*. There, Special Forces troops on board the C-130s are to transfer to the helicopters and fly to the vicinity of Tehran. A sandstorm forces two Sea Stallions to land short of the objective and another makes a forced landing at Desert One due to mechanical difficulties. The loss of these vital assets prompts the cancellation of the mission. Problems continue as the force withdraws when one of the helicopters collides with a C-130, killing three Marines and five Air Force personnel.

28 May

The Class of 1980, the first to include women, graduates from the U.S. Naval Academy. Fifty-five women out of a class of 770 receive their commissions as naval officers.

8 July

Navy support of the so-called Mariel Boat Lift, which results in more than 115,500 Cuban refugees crossing the Florida Straits, ends. Eleven Navy ships and P-3 maritime patrol aircraft supported the operation.

30 September

The aircraft carrier *Saratoga* (CV 60) becomes the first flattop to participate in the Service Life Extension Program, designed to prolong the operational service lives of U.S. Navy carriers.

All naval districts, except for Naval District Washington, are disestablished.

1 October

The Office of Antisubmarine Warfare and Ocean Surveillance Programs is renamed the Office of Naval Warfare.

11 October

The guided missile cruiser *Leahy* (CG 16) is ordered to the Persian Gulf to assist U.S. Air Force E-3 Airborne Warning and Control System aircraft already deployed in providing air defense for Saudi Arabia.

18 October

The commissioning of the guided-missile cruiser *Arkansas* (CGN 41) marks the end of construction of nuclear-powered surface warships, which now number eight.

22 December

In the longest deployment of U.S. Navy warships since World War II, the carrier battle group consisting of *Dwight D. Eisenhower* (CVN 69) and the cruisers *South Carolina* (CGN 37) and *Virginia* (CGN 38) returns to Norfolk, Virginia, after 251 days abroad. During one stint in the deployment, "Ike" spent 152 consecutive days at sea.

Opposite: *A P-3C Orion of Patrol Squadron (VP) 19 conducts a maritime patrol on 18 September 1977. The long-range Orion served as a primary weapon in the Navy's antisubmarine warfare (ASW) arsenal during the height of the Cold War. (National Museum of Naval Aviation)*

Above: *Admiral Thomas B. Hayward, photographed during his tour as the twenty-first Chief of Naval Operations. His vision of a more offensive posture for the Navy in war against the Soviet Union formed the basis for the maritime strategy. (National Museum of Naval Aviation)*

SEA POWER
RESURGENT

1981-2006

SEA POWER RESURGENT

1981-2006

"The flag of the Soviet navy flies over the oceans of the world," long-serving Admiral of the Fleet of the Soviet Union S. G. Gorshkov once stated. "Sooner or later the United States will have to understand it no longer has mastery of the seas." By 1981, the United States and the Soviet Union had been engaged in a bitter Cold War for thirty-six years, and the Soviets had dramatically increased their defense expenditures, especially in their naval forces. When Ronald Reagan took the oath of office as President that year, he brought with him a determination to rid the world of what he termed the "Evil Empire." Part of this effort was recapturing maritime superiority for the United States, and with his choice of John F. Lehman, Jr., as Secretary of the Navy, Reagan set the sea service on course for a dramatic resurgence.

The new service secretary joined top Navy leaders in championing a 600-ship Navy that would carry out a maritime strategy, which called for the U.S. Navy to assume the offensive against the Soviet Union in the event of war, striking submarine bases and other vital strategic targets rather than assuming a more defensive posture. A stronger Navy would not only be capable of attacking the Soviet Union in the event of a general war, but would also serve to buttress American intervention in the Third World to thwart Soviet expansion. From a post-Vietnam War low of 521 ships, the Navy grew to encompass 594 ships manned by over 602,000 men and women by 1987. Included among the ships was a mixture of old and new in the form of the advanced *Ohio*-class ballistic missile submarines and the *Iowa*-class battleships of World War II, recalled to action to provide traditional gunboat diplomacy in the modern age. On board

ships and aircraft were advanced missile systems, including the Tomahawk, Harpoon, and the High-Speed Antiradiation Missile.

Throughout the 1980s the resurgent Navy would be on station in all of the crises that developed, supporting Marines who were serving as peacekeepers in Beirut, Lebanon; battling Libyan forces in the Gulf of Sidra; and thwarting an attempted Cuban takeover of the small Caribbean island of Grenada. When the war between Iran and Iraq threatened stability in the Middle East, the U.S. Navy intensified its presence in the Persian Gulf, escorting reflagged Kuwaiti tankers to ensure the flow of oil from the region, and even engaging in open battle with the Iranian navy in the so-called Tanker War. Events that provided a glimpse of the future appeared in the rise of terrorism against U.S. targets, most notably in the bombing of the Marine Barracks in Beirut, and the emerging power of Iraq in the Middle East. On 17 May 1987, two Exocet air-to-surface missiles struck the guided missile frigate *Stark* (FFG 31). Though this action on the part of an Iraqi warplane was deemed a case of misidentification, future combat actions between the two nations would not be accidental.

Iraq's invasion of Kuwait in August 1990 prompted the dispatch of the largest concentration of U.S. military might since the Vietnam War, and the ensuing swift campaign in January–February 1991 successfully freed Kuwait. The victory in the Gulf War launched a new era for the Navy, which though dramatically reduced in the wake of the dissolution of the Soviet Union and the end of the Cold War, found itself called to hot spots around the globe in the changing new world order. These missions involved humanitarian and peacekeeping operations, and in the

case of Operation Allied Force, combat action in support of NATO efforts to quell unrest in the former Yugoslavia. And always there was the defiance of Iraqi President Saddam Hussein, which called the Navy to action over Iraq on countless occasions.

The tragic events of 11 September 2001, when terrorist attacks struck the World Trade Center in New York City and the Pentagon in Washington, D.C., focused the attention of the nation on eradicating this frightening threat to the United States. On that day, the aircraft carrier *Enterprise* (CVN 65) was at sea just like her World War II predecessor had been at sea on the fateful morning of 7 December 1941 when an enemy launched a surprise attack. Within weeks she was launching air strikes against targets in Afghanistan as part of Operation Enduring Freedom, the war on terrorism. On 19 March 2003, Navy ships in the Arabian Gulf launched Tomahawk cruise missiles at Baghdad, Iraq, the first shots of Operation Iraqi Freedom, the successful campaign to topple the government of Saddam Hussein. It is fitting that the names of some of the ships deployed in the Arabian Gulf on that and ensuing nights bore the names of historic battles of long ago—Bunker Hill, Anzio, Cape St. George, and Mobile Bay—a reflection of the rich tradition of the U.S. Navy that continues to ensure that freedom endures.

Pages 646–647: *The guided missile destroyer* O'Kane *(DDG 77) launches an SM-2 standard missile from its forward Vertical Launch System during exercise Rim of the Pacific (RIMPAC) 2002, on the Pacific Missile Range Facility, Kauai, Hawaii, 5 July 2002. The guided missile frigate* Crommelin *(FFG 37) (right) and the* Spruance-*class destroyer* Paul F. Foster *(DD 964) (center) follow in formation. The purpose of RIMPAC is to improve tactical proficiency in a wide array of combined operations at sea, while building cooperation and fostering mutual understanding between participating nations. The 2002 exercises included Australia, Canada, Chile, Japan, Peru, the Republic of Korea, and the United States. (U.S. Navy)*

Above: *Explosive Ordnance Disposal team members attached to Explosive Ordnance Disposal Mobile Unit 8 (EODMU-8) are recovered from the Arabian Gulf by a UH-3H Sea King helicopter assigned to Helicopter Combat Support Squadron (HC) 2, 19 August 2002. EODMU-8 was deployed to Manama, Bahrain, conducting various missions in support of Operation Enduring Freedom. (U.S. Navy)*

SEA POWER RESURGENT
1981-2003

1981

20 January
On the day Ronald W. Reagan takes the oath of office as the fortieth President of the United States, Iran releases the American hostages that it has held for 444 days.

5 February
John F. Lehman, Jr., a reserve naval flight officer, takes office as the sixty-fifth Secretary of the Navy. A one-time staffer on the National Security Council, where he participated in a study that called for rebuilding the Navy force structure, Lehman espouses a maritime strategy that has as its centerpiece a 600-ship Navy. By the time Lehman leaves office in April 1987, the Navy has 594 ships and thirty under construction.

9 April
While running submerged south of Sasebo, Japan, the fleet ballistic missile submarine *George Washington* (SSBM 598) collides with the Japanese merchantman *Nissho Maru*, killing two of the Japanese boat's crew members. The sub's skipper is subsequently relieved of his command and given a letter of reprimand.

12–14 April
The Space Shuttle Columbia blasts into orbit from Cape Kennedy, Florida, in the first flight of the reusable spacecraft that returns to earth and lands like a conventional airplane. An all-Navy crew consisting of retired Captain John W. Young and Captain Robert L. Crippen makes the milestone flight.

17 June
The return of *James K. Polk* (SSBN 645) to her base at Charleston, South Carolina, marks the completion of the 2,000th deterrent patrol conducted by U.S. Navy fleet ballistic missile submarines.

27 July
The Navy commissions the guided missile destroyer *Kidd* (DDG 993). Originally destined for service in the Iranian navy, *Kidd* is the first of three ships that are variants of the *Spruance*-class destroyers, differing in the fact that they are armed with missiles.

19 August
With Libyan dictator Moammar Qaddafi proclaiming a "line of death" in the Gulf of Sidra beyond which U.S. forces should not pass, two Libyan Su-22 fighters attack a pair of F-14 Tomcats of Fighter Squadron (VF) 41 from the carrier *Nimitz* (CVN 68), which promptly splash both Su-22s.

1 October
The fleet ballistic missile submarine *Robert E. Lee* (SSBN 601) completes the last deterrent patrol of a sub carrying the Polaris missile.

11 November
Ohio (SSBN 726), lead boat of a new class of Trident ballistic missile submarines, is placed in commission

Above: *Commander Hank Kleeman of Fighter Squadron (VF) 41, the pilot of one of the two F-14 Tomcats that shot down a pair of Libyan Su-22 Fitter fighters over the Gulf of Sidra, at a news conference following the 19 August 1981 incident. (National Museum of Naval Aviation)*

Right: *President and Mrs. Ronald Reagan stand beneath the No. 1 16-inch caliber gun turret of the battleship* Iowa *(BB 61), a symbol of the resurgent Navy under his administration, 4 July 1986. (U.S. Navy)*

after much delay in her construction. She fires her first Trident missile while submerged off Cape Canaveral, Florida, on 17 January 1982. Eighteen *Ohio*-class submarines are eventually constructed, and in late 2002 *Ohio* is taken out of service for conversion to a guided-missile submarine with additional capability to transport and support special operations forces.

1982

13 February

Operating from the aircraft carrier *Nimitz* (CVN 68), VF-84 completes the first deployment of the Tactical Air Reconnaissance Photographic System. TARPS equips some F-14s to provide medium- and low-altitude reconnaissance for the fleet.

16 May

One sailor from the amphibious ship *Pensacola* (LSD 38) is killed and three are wounded during an attack by terrorists in San Juan, Puerto Rico.

20 June

While operating in the South China Sea, the guided missile cruiser *Sterett* (CG 31) and the destroyers *Lynde McCormick* (DDG 8), *Benjamin Stoddert* (DDG 22), and *Turner Joy* (DD 951) are taken under machine gun fire by an unidentified vessel. *McCormick* fires warning shots over the enemy ship.

24–25 June

In the wake of Israel's invasion of Lebanon in an effort to destroy the Palestine Liberation Organization (PLO), the amphibious ships *Nashville* (LPD 13) and *Hermitage* (LSD 34) evacuate nearly 600 Americans and foreign nationals from Juniyah near the Lebanese capital of Beirut.

1 July

Admiral James D. Watkins becomes the twenty-second Chief of Naval Operations. He is the first of three successive submariners to hold the post.

25 August

Sixth Fleet amphibious ships land 800 men of the 32nd Marine Amphibious Unit at Beirut, Lebanon where, for the following sixteen days, they serve as part of a multinational peacekeeping force. While ashore the Marines assist in evacuating some 12,000 Palestinians from Lebanon on board merchant vessels escorted by Sixth Fleet warships.

29 September

The 32nd Marine Amphibious Unit consisting of 1,200 Marines returns to Beirut from Sixth Fleet amphibious ships to serve again as part of a multinational peacekeeping force.

1 October

The ballistic missile submarine *Ohio* (SSBN 726) departs Bangor, Washington, on her first Trident missile deterrent patrol.

23 November

A 16 March announcement by Vice President George H.W. Bush that the Navy is to join in the effort to curb the influx of drugs into the United States results in E-2 Hawkeye airborne early warning aircraft and surface ships joining the Coast Guard in hunting for drug smugglers. On this date the guided missile cruiser *Mississippi* (CGN 40), with a Coast Guard boarding party embarked, becomes the first U.S. Navy ship to assist in the seizure of a drug-smuggling vessel at sea.

TOWARD A 600-SHIP NAVY: SECRETARY OF THE NAVY JOHN F. LEHMAN, JR.

by Captain Peter Swartz, U.S. Navy (Retired)

During 1981–1987, John F. Lehman, Jr., served as the nation's sixty-fifth Secretary of the Navy, one of the youngest, most energetic, and colorful personalities to ever hold that office. Brash, combative, abrasive, and savvy, Lehman proved from his first day in office to be a powerful—even ruthless—advocate for the Navy. His own personal credentials, which included a reserve commission as a naval flight officer flying the A-6E Intruder and the authorship of an important book analyzing the role of carriers, stood him in good stead as an articulate spokesman for naval aviation during much of the last decade of the Cold War. Moreover, he came to the job armed with an Ivy League Ph.D. in international relations, a dozen years of experience in a variety of key policy jobs in Washington, and many powerful and loyal friends, mentors and helpers in both the executive and legislative branches.

Lehman set for himself four major goals: to articulate clearly the need for U.S. naval power, to build a Navy of 600 ships to wield that power, to slash costs wherever possible, and to rekindle a sense of esprit and excitement on the waterfront and at sea. These goals fit comfortably within the agenda of President Ronald Reagan. "America is back!" asserted Reagan, and Lehman strove to put teeth in the administration's intentions and slogans.

Thus, the Navy of the 1980s developed and publicized its "Maritime Strategy," which increased forward presence of naval forces as a deterrent. In the event of war, the strategy's tenets were global, forward, offensive operations to bottle up, box in, and kill the Soviet fleet and its land-based air arm in time of war, while at the same time defending the North Atlantic Treaty Organization (NATO) flanks in Europe and taking pressure off U.S. and allied army and air forces battling there. Always possible as a next step were attacks on exposed but strategically vital bases of the Soviet Union itself. John Lehman was not the

Maritime Strategy's originator, but he was its highly visible spokesman and a mighty goad to uniformed Navy and Marine Corps strategists, ensuring that they stayed on message.

The fleet that Lehman inherited in 1981 numbered some 521 ships, including twelve carriers and twelve carrier air wings. President Reagan, Secretary of Defense Caspar Weinberger, and Lehman thought these numbers were far too low to protect American interests forward at sea around the globe in peacetime, deter or resolve crises, and prevail should the Maritime Strategy have to be implemented. Instead, the administration and Lehman advocated and almost achieved a 600-ship, fifteen-carrier Navy. In his first budget request to Congress, the Navy Secretary proposed immediately building two new carriers simultaneously, something not done since World War II, among other initiatives. He got what he asked for, and later again pushed for yet another twin carrier procurement in his last year in office.

Lehman also campaigned for more Navy air wings, and worked hard to keep the Navy in the deep-strike and long-range interceptor missions by improving both the venerable A-6 Intruder and the newer F-14 Tomcat fighter. Favoring proven airframes over costly new designs, he also championed the AV-8B Harrier aircraft for the Marine Corps. By 1988, a year after he left office, the force had grown to 594 ships, including fourteen carriers and fourteen active (and two reserve) air wings, and was well on the way to 600.

John Lehman believed that even with the best rationale in the world, the nation would not yield the required resources for a 600-ship Navy if it believed that its leadership would squander those resources and indulge in waste, fraud, and abuse. Consequently, his third major effort as Secretary was to contain and cut costs. He lowered the unit price of new aircraft, especially the F/A-18 Hornet, instituted firm fixed-price contracting, reduced overhaul backlogs, blocked

expense "gold-plating" of systems, increased competitive procurements, cut an entire command layer from the Navy's procurement structure, and shifted costs to private industry.

Finally, Lehman sought to boost Navy professionalism, readiness, combat capabilities, and morale, especially among naval aviators and most especially among fellow Naval Reservists. In this he lost some and he won some. His campaign against the Goldwater-Nichols Act, which subordinated Navy commanders more effectively to their joint superiors, was doomed to failure. But he successfully pushed for a needed advanced tactics school to polish the skills of the Navy's attack aviators, and gave full service support to making the movie *Top Gun*, Hollywood's paean to naval aviation. He brought back leather flight jackets and brown shoes, restructured carrier air wing command, and gave the reserves more first-line ships and aircraft. To the consternation of some senior officers, he never stopped dropping in on the fleet's

ready rooms and mess decks to find out what was really on the minds of the Navy's seamen and airmen.

John Lehman served as Secretary of the Navy for more than six years, one of the longest terms on record. During that time he changed the face of an office that with the creation of the Department of Defense shortly after World War II had diminished in power and influence. He was the spirit of the Navy as it emerged from the dark shadows of Vietnam and once again stood tall on the world stage.

Above: *A Reserve naval flight officer, Secretary of the Navy John F. Lehman, Jr., attends a preflight briefing in the ready room of Attack Squadron (VA) 65 on board the carrier* Dwight D. Eisenhower *(CVN 69) prior to launching in an A-6 Intruder, 21 August 1983. (U.S. Navy)*

Left: *A SM-2 missile is launched from the* Aegis *guided missile cruiser* Ticonderoga *(CG 47) during tests near the Atlantic Fleet Weapons Training Facility, Roosevelt Roads, Puerto Rico, 4 April 1983. (U.S. Navy)*

Below: *A view of the sign at the entrance to the headquarters compound of the United States Naval District, Beirut, Lebanon, 15 September 1983. (U.S. Navy)*

28 December

The modernized battleship *New Jersey* (BB 62), called into service for the third time since the end of World War II, is recommissioned as part of President Ronald Reagan's program to strengthen the Navy.

1983

22 January

The guided missile cruiser *Ticonderoga* (CG 47), the first ship equipped with the Aegis weapons system, is placed in commission. She is the lead ship in a class that numbers twenty-seven ships.

10 June

Lieutenant Colleen Nevius becomes the first female naval aviator to graduate from the U.S. Naval Test Pilot School at Naval Air Station Patuxent River, Maryland.

26 July–12 September

U.S. warships, which at various times include the carriers *Ranger* (CV 61) and *Coral Sea* (CV 43) and the battleship *New Jersey*, operate off the coast of Central America as a show of force against the spread of communism in the region.

1 September

U.S. Navy ships support the search for survivors and debris from Korean Air Lines Flight 007, shot down by a Soviet fighter plane after it strayed off course and overflew the Kamchatka Peninsula and Sakhalin Islands.

8 September

The frigate *Bowen* (FF 1079) conducts the first fire support mission by a Sixth Fleet warship in support of Marines operating as part of a multinational peacekeeping force in Beirut, Lebanon. The target for her 5-inch guns is a position from which Syrian-supported Druze militiamen are firing on Marine positions.

19 September

The guided missile cruiser *Virginia* (CGN 38) and the destroyer *John Rodgers* (DD 983) fire 338 5-inch rounds at the approaches to the village of Sug el Gharb, supporting its defense by the Lebanese Army.

25 September

The battleship *New Jersey* arrives in the waters off Lebanon to support operations in the war-torn nation.

Right: *The battleship New Jersey (BB 62) fires her 16-inch guns at targets in Lebanon, 1984. A cornerstone of the defense buildup under President Ronald Reagan was the recommissioning of the four* Iowa-*class battleships. (Naval Historical Center)*

1 October

The Naval Space Command is established to consolidate the sea service's space activities under one organization. Its first commanding officer is former astronaut Captain Richard Truly.

23 October

Terrorists in an explosives-laden truck crash through the barricades outsides the building housing the headquarters of the 24th Marine Amphibious Unit, which had relieved the 32nd Marine Expeditionary Unit in Beirut, Lebanon. The truck smashes into the lobby of the building, where its driver detonates his deadly cargo. The resulting explosion kills 241 Marines and injures 70 others. Shortly afterward, a second truck bomber kills 58 men of the French peacekeeping force.

25–27 October

A Communist coup on the tiny Caribbean island of Grenada threatens the safety of approximately 1,000 American citizens on the island, most of them medical students at St. George's University Medical School. Fearful that Grenada might become a base for the Soviet/Cuban military, the Organization of Eastern Caribbean States requests assistance from the United States. In response, on 25 October the U.S. launches Operation Urgent Fury. A SEAL team that infiltrates the capital of St. George's and captures Government House are the first to land. They are followed by Marines from the amphibious assault ship *Guam*

(LPH 9), who land by helicopter and secure Grenada's Pearls Airport, and Army Rangers, who drop on an unfinished airfield being constructed by Cuban troops on the island. The final U.S. forces ashore are Marines from *Guam*, who make an amphibious landing at Grand Mal Bay. U.S. forces on Grenada, which by 27 October include over 6,000 men, encounter some stiff pockets of resistance from Cuban forces and Grenadan troops, but secure the island by 27 October. Governor General Sir Paul Scoon and other government officials are evacuated by helicopter to *Guam*, while Air Force aircraft evacuate medical students. American forces find stockpiled arms on the island and plans for a Cuban garrison of nearly 7,000 troops. They also discover Soviet, North Korean, and Eastern European advisors and diplomats. Of the eighteen Americans killed and 116 wounded during Operation Urgent Fury, 5 are U.S. Navy personnel.

1 November

Fire breaks out in the engine room of the carrier *Ranger* in the Arabian Sea. Six sailors are killed and thirty-five injured in the blaze.

17 November

In the Arabian Sea, the Soviet missile frigate *Razyashchiy* collides with the destroyer *Fife* (DD 991) as she maneuvers to block the approach of the Soviet ship to the vicinity of the aircraft carrier *Ranger*. The collision results in minor damage and no injuries.

1984

3 January
Following negotiations with the Syrian government by the Reverend Jesse Jackson, Lieutenant Robert O. Goodman, taken prisoner after his plane crashed on 4 December 1983, is released.

7 February
While the Space Shuttle Challenger orbits the earth, Captain Bruce McCandless conducts the first untethered spacewalk using the spacecraft's manned maneuvering unit.

8 February
The battleship *New Jersey* (BB 62) conducts the heaviest shore bombardment thus far during American involvement in Lebanon, firing 288 16-inch shells on Syrian and Druze militia positions and killing the general commanding Syrian forces in Lebanon. The destroyers *Caron* (DD 970) and *Moosbrugger* (DD 980) together unleash 400 5-inch rounds at hostile positions ashore.

26 February
Sixth Fleet ships complete the withdrawal of the 22nd Marine Amphibious Unit from Beirut, Lebanon.

4 December
In response to attacks by Syrian antiaircraft batteries and surface-to-air missiles against U.S. aircraft the previous day, a twenty-eight plane strike group from the carriers *Independence* (CV 62) and *John F. Kennedy* (CV 67) attacks Syrian positions in the mountains east of Beirut, Lebanon. An A-6 Intruder of Attack Squadron (VA) 85 is hit by enemy fire. The pilot, Lieutenant Mark A. Lange, is mortally wounded and bombardier-navigator Lieutenant Robert O. Goodman is taken prisoner after their plane crashes. The A-7 Corsair II flown by Commander Edward K. Andrews, Commander, Carrier Air Wing Six, is also shot down. Though wounded, Andrews is rescued.

14 December
The battleship *New Jersey* conducts her first fire-support mission in Lebanon, unleashing her 16-inch guns at positions east of Beirut.

Left: *A column of Marines heads out on patrol on the island of Grenada during Operation Urgent Fury. Naval forces played a key role in the 1983 action. (National Museum of Naval Aviation)*

Right: *Secretary of the Navy John Lehman, right, promotes Captain Grace Hopper to the rank of commodore in a ceremony at the White House as President Ronald Reagan looks on. Holding a Ph.D in mathematics, Hopper first entered the Navy in 1943, and was one of the nation's foremost computer programmers. She was recalled to duty at the age of sixty-one, and did not retire until she was eighty. (U.S. Navy)*

21 March

While conducting night operations in the Sea of Japan, the aircraft carrier *Kitty Hawk* (CV 63) strikes a Soviet nuclear attack submarine that surfaces ahead of her. The flattop sustains minor damage, while the submarine is damaged to such an extent that she is towed to the Soviet naval base at Vladivostok.

2 April

The Soviet aircraft carrier *Minsk* fires eight signal flares at the frigate *Harold E. Holt* (FF 1074) as the ships operate in the South China Sea. Three flares strike the U.S. Navy warship, which passes within 300 meters of the Soviet carrier, but she suffers no casualties.

28 April

The battleship *Iowa* (BB 61) is recommissioned.

17 August

Helicopter Mine Countermeasures Squadron (HM) 14, operating from the amphibious transport dock *Shreveport* (LPD 12), commences twenty-two consecutive days of minehunting operations in the Gulf of Suez.

20 September

Terrorists bomb the U.S. Embassy Annex in East Beirut, Lebanon, killing twenty-three people. Among those killed is Petty Officer Michael R. Wagner. Two other Navy men are injured in the attack.

30 November

The aircraft carrier *Nimitz* deploys to Cuban waters in response to the Cuban government's refusal to allow the Coast Guard to tow an American ship that had lost power and drifted into Cuban territorial waters. A show of force by the carrier results in the Coast Guard being permitted to place the vessel under tow.

1985

20 May

Federal Bureau of Investigation agents arrest retired Navy Chief Warrant Officer John A. Walker, Jr., and charge him with espionage. A spy for the Soviet Union since 1967, Walker provided information on submarine and surface operations as well as keys to decipher encrypted radio transmissions.

14 June

Arab terrorists hijack Trans-World Airlines Flight 847 just after takeoff from Athens, Greece, and order it to fly to Beirut. There, they discover the presence of Steelworker Second Class Robert D. Stethem on the plane, and severely beat the sailor before murdering him and throwing him on the tarmac. The thirty-seven other American hostages are eventually removed from the plane and hidden in Beirut, the last one being released on 30 June. During the crisis the aircraft carrier *Nimitz* is ordered to the waters off Lebanon for contingency operations.

10 July

President Ronald W. Reagan nominates Admiral William J. Crowe, Jr., Commander in Chief, U.S. Pacific Command, as the eleventh Chairman of the Joint Chiefs of Staff. He assumes the post in October and serves for four years.

THE *NIMITZ*-CLASS CARRIERS

by Admiral James L. Holloway III, U.S. Navy (Retired)

In the summer of 1950, following President Harry S. Truman's approval of the construction of the first nuclear submarine, Chief of Naval Operations Admiral Forrest P. Sherman instructed Captain Hyman G. Rickover's Division of Naval Reactors to initiate plans for the first nuclear-powered aircraft carrier. The carrier, which was commissioned in 1961 as *Enterprise* (CVAN 65), was similar to the *Forrestal*-class of carrier in general size and layout, but replacing eight oil-fired boilers with eight 35,000-shaft horsepower (SHP) pressurized water nuclear reactors powering four main engines that drove four screws. This conservative approach, using moderately scaled reactors of proven design with a conventional steam plant arrangement, had substantial benefits in reducing development risk and construction time. However, the eight reactors were expensive in terms of investment, maintenance, and the manpower required to operate

them. Therefore, the Navy's concept for a follow-on carrier embodied a four-reactor propulsion plant, which at that time offered the best balance among the factors of operational flexibility, cost savings, and the technical challenge of building individual reactors with a capacity of 70,000 SHP.

However, Secretary of Defense Robert S. McNamara vetoed the Navy's proposal for the four-reactor follow-on ship on the basis of the increased cost over its conventionally powered counterpart. Thus, two more non-nuclear carriers were authorized and built in the 1961 and 1963 programs—*America* (CVA 66) and *John F. Kennedy* (CVA 67).

In the spring of 1964, McNamara visited the Bettis Atomic Laboratory, where he was shown the D1W surface ship reactor under development. This was a 60,000-SHP design intended for propulsion of a single reactor cruiser. McNamara asked Rear Admiral Rickover if two of these D1Ws could power an aircraft carrier. Rickover immediately answered "yes," but indicated that it would not be easy. To power a 90,000-ton carrier at the required speeds for flight operations and generate the steam for her four catapults would require doubling the power output of the existing D1W design. For this reason the Navy still preferred a four-reactor propulsion plant.

Under pressure from atomic energy advocates in Congress, McNamara followed up his visit to Bettis with a letter to the Navy's leadership reaffirming his objection to a four-reactor carrier plant, but expressing a favorable view of a two-reactor plant for follow-on carriers. In spite of a short timeline and unprecedented technical hurdles, Rickover's Division of Naval Reactors came through with the design for a two-reactor power plant for a large-deck carrier, which was approved for the 1967 program as CVN 68. Launched in 1972, she was commissioned *Nimitz* in 1975.

Nimitz was an unqualified success from both the operational and nuclear power plant aspects, and two more carriers of this class followed—*Dwight D. Eisenhower* (CVN 69) in the 1970 program, and *Carl Vinson* (CVN 70) in 1974. President Gerald Ford had included another *Nimitz*-class carrier in his Fiscal Year

1978 budget, but it was deleted by President Jimmy Carter. When submitted a second time by the Navy for the Fiscal Year 1979 budget, it was again cancelled by the President. In the Fiscal Year 1980 budget, the carrier was added by Congress and President Carter vetoed the entire Department of Defense appropriations bill to eliminate the carrier. In reaction, a Congress that contained staunch advocates of both nuclear power and carriers overrode the veto, and *Theodore Roosevelt* (CVN 71) was eventually commissioned. She was followed by *Abraham Lincoln* (CVN 72) and *George Washington* (CVN 73), both approved by Congress in the Fiscal Year 1983 shipbuilding program. Two more *Nimitz*-class carriers were added in 1988, *John C. Stennis* (CVN 74) and *Harry S. Truman* (CVN 75). *Ronald Reagan* (CVN 76) joins the fleet in 2003, and the tenth and final *Nimitz*-class, *George H.W. Bush* (CVN 77), is scheduled for completion in 2008.

The *Nimitz*-class carriers have proven their worth to the Navy over their more than a quarter century of service. The few modifications incorporated into the design since 1975 have been for installations to incorporate advancing aeronautical technology. The nuclear carrier continues to fulfill the role of the principal major combatant in the fleet as the centerpiece of modern carrier battle groups. By the time of Operation Iraqi Freedom, every nuclear carrier in the fleet had launched her aircraft in combat operations in such places as Vietnam, Kuwait, Serbia, Kosovo, Bosnia, Iraq, and Afghanistan.

Even as the Navy develops the prototype for the next generation of large-deck nuclear carriers, it will be upon the decks of the *Nimitz*-class that the Navy will sail into harm's way well into the twenty-first century.

Opposite: *The lower bow unit of the aircraft carrier* Ronald Reagan *(CVN 76) is lowered into place at the Northrop Grumman Newport News Shipbuilding facility in Virginia, 16 March 2000. Reagan is the first Nimitz-class carrier to feature a bulbous bow to improve buoyancy at the forward end of the flight deck. (U.S. Navy)*

Above: *The aircraft carrier* Harry S. Truman *(CVN 75), underway in the eastern Mediterranean Sea in support of Operation Iraqi Freedom in March 2003, a sovereign piece of American territory capable of going anywhere in the world. (U.S. Navy)*

7–10 October

On 7 October Palestinian terrorists hijack the Italian cruise ship *Achille Lauro* in the Mediterranean Sea, murdering a handicapped American Jewish passenger and throwing his body into the sea. Negotiations result in the terrorists being allowed to leave the ship in Egypt. On the evening of 10 October they depart on board an Egypt Air Boeing 737, an action that does not escape the eyes of American and Israeli intelligence. F-14 Tomcat fighters from the carrier *Saratoga* (CV 60) intercept the airliner, forcing it to land at an air base in Sicily, where U.S. troops and Italian police apprehend the terrorists.

8 November

The rank of commodore is changed to rear admiral (lower half).

21 November

U.S. naval intelligence analyst Jonathan Jay Pollard is arrested and charged with spying for Israel. His wife is arrested the following day and charged with unauthorized possession of classified documents.

Above: *An aerial view of the aircraft carrier* Saratoga *(CV 60) surrounded by the ships of her battle group underway in the Red Sea, 15 November 1985. Shown clockwise from bottom are:* Jack Williams *(FFG 24),* Jesse L. Brown *(FF 1089),* Scott *(DDG 995),* Monogahela *(AO 178),* Mount Baker *(AE 34),* Biddle *(CG 34), and* Capodanno *(FF 1093). (U.S. Navy)*

28 January

The Space Shuttle Challenger explodes shortly after takeoff in the space program's worst fatal accident since the Apollo I launch pad fire. Among those killed on board the spacecraft is the pilot, Commander Michael Smith. Navy ships and the nuclear-propelled submersible *NR-1* support the search for wreckage off Florida's east coast.

22 March

During a crew transfer off Midway Atoll, the ballistic missile submarine *Georgia* (SSBN 729) collides with the Navy tug *Secota* (YTM 415), causing the tug to sink with the loss of two contract crewmen.

24–25 March

On 24 March, Libyan surface-to-air missile batteries fire upon aircraft operating from the carrier *Coral Sea* (CVA 43) over the Gulf of Sidra, missing their targets. Later, in a series of actions called Operation Prairie Fire, A-6 Intruders from the carrier *America* (CV 66) fire a Harpoon missile and drop cluster bombs on a Libyan *La Combattante II*-class missile boat that approaches the carrier battle group, severely damaging her. That night carrier aircraft launch high-speed antiradiation missiles at Libyan radar sites and bomb a Libyan *Nanuchka*-class guided missile corvette, damaging her. A second

Left: *Sideboys salute Admiral William J. Crowe, Jr., (right) Chairman of the Joint Chiefs of Staff, and Marshal Sergei Akhromeyev, Chief of the General Staff of the Soviet Union's armed forces, as they arrive aboard the aircraft carrier* Theodore Roosevelt *(CVN 71) in 1988. The thawing of the Cold War brought more open relations between the two superpowers. (U.S. Navy)*

Below: *An RH-53D Sea Stallion towing a mine countermeasures hydrofoil sled during a demonstration of minesweeping techniques in the Chesapeake Bay, Maryland. The helicopter is assigned to Helicopter Mine Countermeasures Squadron (HM) 14, which conducted operations in the Suez Canal in 1984. (U.S. Navy)*

corvette is attacked and sunk the following day by A-6 Intruders firing Harpoon missiles.

29 March
The first performance of the show season by the Blue Angels includes Lieutenant Commander Donnie L. Cochran flying left wing. He is the first African-American pilot to fly with the Navy's prestigious flight demonstration squadron.

15 April
Ten days after Libyan-sponsored terrorists bomb a West Berlin discotheque, killing 2 people and injuring 229 others, including 78 Americans, U.S. Air Force and Navy aircraft execute Operation El Dorado Canyon. Naval assets committed to strikes against terrorist targets in Libya include aircraft from the carriers *America* and *Saratoga*, which hit the Jumahiriya Military Barracks and Benina Military Airfield.

6 May
For the first time in history, three nuclear-powered submarines—*Archerfish* (SSN 678), *Hawkbill* (SSN 666) and *Ray* (SSN 653)—surface at the North Pole.

10 May
The battleship *Missouri* (BB 63) is recommissioned, joining sister ships *Iowa* (BB 61) and *New Jersey*, which have previously been returned to active service.

1 July
Admiral Carlisle A.H. Trost, a former Commander in Chief, Atlantic Fleet, becomes the twenty-third Chief of Naval Operations.

20 September
Secretary of the Navy John F. Lehman reinstitutes brown shoes as part of the uniform of officers and chief petty officers assigned to aviation billets.

1 October
The signing of the Goldwater-Nichols Defense Reorganization Act results in the creation of the post of Vice Chairman of the Joint Chiefs of Staff, the placement of the Chairman of the Joint Chiefs of Staff in the official chain of command between the Secretary of Defense and the unified commanders, and strengthens the role and influence of unified commanders in the conduct of military operations.

5 November
The cruiser *Reeves* (CG 24) with the Commander in Chief, U.S. Pacific Fleet embarked, the destroyer *Oldendorf* (DD 972), and the frigate *Rentz* (FFG 46) become the first U.S. Navy warships to visit China in thirty-seven years.

31 December
H-3 Sea Kings of Composite Squadron (VC) 8 rescue seventy-five people stranded by a fire on the roof of the Dupont Plaza Hotel in San Juan, Puerto Rico.

7 March
The so-called Tanker War, in which Iranian and Iraqi forces attack tankers in the Persian Gulf as part of the war between the two nations, prompts President Ronald Reagan to announce that the United States will reflag eleven Kuwaiti tankers with the Stars and Stripes and provide them with naval protection. From the first escort on 21 July to the last in early 1988, U.S. Navy warships escort twenty-two transits of the Persian Gulf by the reflagged vessels.

10 April
James H. Webb, a 1968 Naval Academy graduate and highly decorated Marine officer during the Vietnam War, takes office as the sixty-sixth Secretary of the Navy.

21 April
While operating in foggy conditions in the waters off the Virginia coast, the frigate *Richard L. Page* (FFG 5) strikes the fishing boat *Chickadee*, sinking her.

14 May
An Iraqi Mirage F-1 fighter approaches to within ten nautical miles of the destroyer *Coontz* (DDG 40) operating in the Persian Gulf, prompting the destroyer's crew to prepare for an engagement that does not come.

Left: *A Libyan Nanuchka-class missile corvette burns after being hit by an AGM-84 Harpoon missile launched from an Attack Squadron (VA) 85 A-6 Intruder. The attack came after Libyan forces fired on U.S. aircraft in the Gulf of Sidra in the Mediterranean Sea, considered to be international waters, on 25 March 1986. The ship was later reported as sunk. (U.S. Navy)*

Left: *Bomb skids loaded with CBU-59 cluster bombs positioned on the flight deck of the aircraft carrier* Coral Sea *(CV 43) prior to being loaded aboard A-6E Intruders for an air strike on targets in Libya, 15 April 1986. The U.S. Navy engaged in a series of combat actions with Libya over the right to operate in the Gulf of Sidra. (U.S. Navy)*

17 May

During a night attack in the Persian Gulf, an Iraqi Mirage F-1 strikes the frigate *Stark* (FFG 31) with a pair of Exocet antiship missiles, killing thirty-seven and wounding five. Listing sixteen degrees, the frigate remains afloat and is towed to Bahrain. She eventually returns to the United States under her own power. The ship's defensive measures are not operational at the time of the attack despite the fact that warning of the F-1's presence was received over an hour before the first missile struck the ship. Subsequently, the frigate's commanding officer and tactical action officer are issued letters of reprimand and allowed to resign.

27 July

HM-14 deploys to the Persian Gulf for operations in the wake of the explosion of a mine that holes the tanker *Bridgeton* on 24 July. The tanker was part of the first reflagged convoy escorted by U.S. warships.

Right: *The attack submarines* Ray *(SSN 653),* Hawkbill *(SSN 666), and* Archerfish *(SSN 678) surfaced at the geographic North Pole, 6 May 1986. This marked the first time three nuclear-powered submarines simultaneously surfaced at the pole. Note the sail on the sub in the foreground is positioned vertically to shear through the ice. (U.S. Navy)*

24 August

The approach of two dhows toward a U.S.-escorted convoy in the Strait of Hormuz prompts the destroyer *Kidd* (DDG 993) to fire warning shots to drive them away.

The skipper of the frigate *Jarrett* (FFG 33) places his ship between a convoy and an approaching Iranian warship during operations in the Persian Gulf.

10 September

In the first battleship deployment of Pioneer remotely piloted vehicles, VC-6, Detachment One embarks aboard the battleship *Iowa*.

21 September

The discovery of the Iranian landing craft *Iran Ajr* laying mines off Bahrain prompts the launching of an Army MH-6 helicopter from the frigate *Jarrett*, which attacks the vessel. Subsequently, Navy SEALS board her and take her under tow the following morning. Twenty-six crewmen are captured and later released and ten contact mines are seized.

19 October

In response to a 16 October attack in which a Silkworm missile fired by Iranian forces on the Fao Peninsula damages the reflagged Kuwaiti tanker *Sea Isle City*, the guided missile destroyers *Hoel* (DDG 13) and *Kidd* and the destroyers *John Young* (DD 973) and *Leftwich* (DD 984) bombard two old Iranian oil platforms being used for military purposes. SEAL and EOD teams from the frigate *Thach* (FFG 43) complete the destruction of the two platforms the following night.

8 December

President Ronald Reagan and Soviet President Mikhail S. Gorbachev sign a treaty calling for the elimination of intermediate-range nuclear missiles by 1991.

12 December

The sinking Cypriot-flagged tanker *Pivot* is attacked by Iranian speedboats, and helicopters from the destroyer *Chandler* (DDG 996) evacuate eleven people from the sinking ship.

Above: *Her colors still flying high, the guided missile frigate* Stark *(FFG 31) lists to port after being hit by two Iraqi-fired Exocet air-to-surface missiles. The ongoing hostilities between Iran and Iraq affected other nations in the Persian Gulf region, and the U.S. Navy provided a measure of stability and protection, though not without a price. (Naval Historical Center)*

Right: *A motor whaleboat from the amphibious assault ship* Guadalcanal *(LPH 7) maneuvers to recover an Iraqi pilot downed in an air battle with Iranian forces, September 1987. The pilot was in the water for two days before being spotted by a lookout aboard the ship. (U.S. Navy)*

Below: *The guided missile frigate* Ford *(FFG 54) escorts the reflagged Kuwaiti tanker* Gas Princess *through the Persian Gulf, 31 October 1987. (U.S. Navy)*

25 December

The frigates *Elrod* (FFG 55) and HMS *Scylla* launch helicopters that rescue twenty crewmen from *Hyundai*, a South Korean-flagged tanker attacked by an Iranian frigate in the Persian Gulf.

27 December

A terrorist attack on a United Services Organization club in Barcelona, Spain, kills one sailor and injures five others.

1988

12 February

While operating in the Black Sea, the guided missile cruiser *Yorktown* (CG 48) and the destroyer *Caron* approach Soviet territorial waters exercising their right of innocent passage. They are intercepted by two Soviet patrol frigates, which after exchanging messages, close and bump the port quarters of the American ships. The incident sparks a flurry of diplomatic exchanges.

24 March

William L. Ball, a former naval officer and Assistant Secretary of State, takes office as the sixty-eighth Secretary of the Navy. Ball replaces James H. Webb, who resigned in February 1988 over Secretary of Defense Frank C. Carlucci's lack of support for the 600-ship Navy.

14 April

While operating in the Persian Gulf, the frigate *Samuel B. Roberts* (FFG 58) strikes a mine. The ensuing explosion blows a 21-foot hole in her bottom, injures ten of her crew, and causes extensive flooding.

A terrorist bombing of a United Services Organization club in Naples, Italy, kills one sailor and injures four others.

18 April
Four days after the mining of the frigate *Samuel B. Roberts*, Operation Praying Mantis against Iranian naval forces in the Persian Gulf begins. The destroyer *Merrill* (DD 976) opens the action by firing on and damaging one of two oil platforms being used as command and control centers for attacks against shipping. Marines and Navy explosive ordnance personnel then board the platform and destroy it. A second platform is destroyed by gunfire from the guided-missile cruiser *Wainwright* (CG 28), the guided missile frigate *Simpson* (FFG 56), and the frigate *Bagley* (FF 1069). In both instances, Iranian personnel on board the platforms are given the opportunity to leave before the attack begins. The destruction of the platforms prompts Iranian attacks on Navy warships and civilian vessels. During these actions A-6 Intruders from the carrier *Enterprise* (CVN 65) sink a small craft while *Wainwright* and *Simpson* sink the Iranian fast patrol boat *Joshan*. The Iranian frigate *Sahand* is also sunk by missiles from A-6 Intruders, and the guided missile destroyer *Joseph Strauss* (DDG 16) joins A-6 and A-7 Corsair II aircraft in heavily damaging the frigate *Sabalan*. The operation results in destruction or damage to about half of the Iranian navy. American casualties include the crew of a Marine AH-1T Cobra helicopter that crashes.

24 April
The diesel electric submarine *Bonefish* (SS 582) suffers a battery explosion while operating off Cape Canaveral, Florida. Three of her crew of ninety-two men are killed and the submarine is abandoned. She does not sink and is towed to Charleston, South Carolina, for decommissioning.

28 June
A car bomb planted by a leftist group kills Captain William E. Nordeen, the naval attaché to Greece, while he drives to his office in Athens.

2 July
The frigate *Elmer B. Montgomery* (FF 1082) fires a warning shot at an Iranian speedboat after it fires upon a Danish supertanker in the Persian Gulf.

3 July
With Iranian speedboats having earlier fired upon U.S. Navy helicopters operating in the Persian Gulf, the guided missile cruiser *Vincennes* (CG 49) picks up a radar contact on what her crew believes is an attacking Iranian aircraft. After making seven radio requests for the aircraft to identify itself, the ship launches two

Above: *The Iranian frigate* Sahand *burns in the Strait of Hormuz on 18 April 1988 after U.S. carrier aircraft fired Harpoon antiship missiles in retaliation for Iranian mining of the American frigate* Samuel B. Roberts *(FFG 58). (Naval Historical Center)*

surface-to-air missiles, which obliterate the contact. Tragically, the contact is an Iranian airliner and all 290 passengers and crew on board are killed. President Ronald Reagan issues a formal apology and offers to compensate the families of the deceased.

22 October

The battleship *Wisconsin* (BB 64) is recommissioned, marking the first time since 1958 that all four of the Navy's *Iowa*-class battleships are operational.

1989

4 January

The U.S. Navy once again combats the air force of Libya over the Gulf of Sidra when two F-14 Tomcat fighters of VF-32 from the carrier *John F. Kennedy* splash two Libyan MiG-23 fighters. The incident occurs over international waters after the MiGs approach the Navy fighters in a hostile manner.

19 April

While operating off Puerto Rico, the battleship *Iowa* suffers a powder explosion in her Number Two gun turret, the blast and ensuing flames killing forty-seven members of her crew. Only the quick flooding of the

Above: *Marines inspect a ZU-23 23mm automatic antiaircraft gun on the Iranian Sassan oil platform, 18 April 1988. Marines attacked, occupied, then destroyed the platform as part of Operation Praying Mantis, which was launched after the guided missile frigate* Samuel B. Roberts *(FFG 58) struck a mine in the Persian Gulf on 14 April 1988. (U.S. Marine Corps)*

Below: *A Spruance-class destroyer sails by a pair of Iranian command and control platforms set afire after being shelled by four U.S. Navy destroyers on 19 October 1987 in retaliation for an Iranian missile attack on a Kuwaiti supertanker. (U.S. Navy)*

Left: *Crew members monitor radar screens in the combat information center aboard the guided missile cruiser* Vincennes *(CG 49), 1 January 1988. (U.S. Navy)*

Below: *A photo taken from the bridge captures the explosion of the No. 2 16-inch gun turret aboard the battleship* Iowa *(BB 61). It was later determined that forty-seven sailors were killed by the blast, which occurred as* Iowa *was conducting routine gunnery exercises off Puerto Rico, 19 April 1989. (U.S. Navy)*

powder magazine below the turret saves the ship from catastrophic damage. The initial investigation of the tragedy initially points to sabotage by Gunner's Mate Second Class Clayton Hartwig, but Congress orders a review of the findings and later the Secretary of the Navy reopens the investigation.

15 May

H. Lawrence Garrett, III, a former submariner and officer in the Judge Advocate General Corps, becomes the sixty-eighth Secretary of the Navy.

14 June

While operating off Southern California, the nuclear submarine *Houston* (SSN 713) becomes entangled with a submerged tow cable from the commercial tugboat *Barcelona*. The power of the submarine pulls the tugboat underwater, resulting in the death of one of her crew.

21 July–8 August

The Soviet missile cruiser *Marshal Ustinov*, the missile destroyer *Otlichny*, and the oiler *Genrikh Gasanov* visit Norfolk, Virginia, on 21–25 July, and the guided missile cruiser *Thomas Gates* (CG 51) and the guided missile frigate *Kauffman* (FFG 59) visit Sevastopol on 4–8 August. This is the first time U.S. and Soviet warships exchange port calls since 1975.

29 October
A T-2 Buckeye crashes on the flight deck of the training aircraft carrier *Lexington* (AVT 16) during carrier qualifications in the Gulf of Mexico. The pilot and four flight deck crewmen are killed in the mishap.

30 October
While conducting bombing exercises, an F/A-18 Hornet accidentally drops a 500-pound bomb on the guided missile cruiser *Reeves* (CG 24), injuring five crewmen.

2 December
The missile cruiser *Belknap* (CG 26) provides support for a summit between President George H.W. Bush and Soviet President Mikhail Gorbachev at Malta. Though unfavorable weather prevents a meeting between the two leaders from being held on board the ship, Bush lives aboard *Belknap* during his time in Malta.

16 December
A Navy lieutenant and his wife are taken into custody by Panamanian forces at a roadblock in Panama City after witnessing an incident in which guards open fire on a car driven by four American officers in civilian clothes, mortally wounding one and injuring another. The lieutenant is beaten during the four hours before he is released.

20 December
The United States launches Operation Just Cause, the invasion of Panama in an attempt to find and arrest General Manuel Noriega, who is accused of trafficking in illegal drugs. Navy SEALS participate in the action by disabling a boat and aircraft to prevent them from being used as escape vehicles by Noriega, who surrenders after spending eleven days in the Vatican mission. Four Navy personnel are killed and nine wounded in operations in Panama through 24 December. Most are SEALS, who engage in a firefight with Panamanian Defense Force soldiers in operations at Paitilla Airport.

1990

27 February
Admiral David E. Jeremiah becomes the second Vice Chairman of the Joint Chiefs of Staff.

29 March–23 April
The ballistic missile submarine *Tennessee* (SSBN 734) completes the first deterrent patrol of a Trident D-5 missile-equipped submarine.

8 May
Off the coast of North Carolina, the guided-missile destroyer *Conyngham* (DDG 17) suffers a fire in her

Right: *F-14A Tomcats of Fighter Squadron (VF) 32 fly over the carrier* John F. Kennedy *(CV 67), 1 May 1983. Swordsmen F-14s shot down two Libyan MiG-23s over the Gulf of Sidra in 1989. Tomcats and the flattops from which they fly continue to serve as symbols of American naval might. (National Museum of Naval Aviation)*

Left: *The carrier* Dwight D. Eisenhower *(CVN 69) transits the Suez Canal on 22 August 1990, en route to the Mediterranean Sea following a deployment in support of Operation Desert Shield. (U.S. Navy)*

Opposite, top: *Vice Admiral Frank B. Kelso, Jr., Commander, U.S. Sixth Fleet, on board the flag bridge of* Saratoga *(CV 60). Admiral Kelso organized and commanded the joint Navy and Air Force bombing of Libya. He later served as Commander in Chief, U.S. Atlantic Fleet, and then Chief of Naval Operations. (U.S. Navy)*

boiler room that sweeps through several decks of the ship, killing one crewman and injuring eighteen others. The ship is decommissioned later in the year.

20 June
A fire in a storeroom on board the aircraft carrier *Midway* (CV 41) operating off Japan triggers two explosions that kill two and injure sixteen crewmen.

29 June
Admiral Frank B. Kelso, III, a former Sixth Fleet commander and Commander in Chief, U.S. Atlantic Command, becomes the twenty-fourth Chief of Naval Operations.

12 July
With the reading of her orders before members of Tactical Electronics Warfare Squadron (VAQ) 34, Commander Rosemary B. Mariner becomes the first woman to command an operational aircraft squadron.

2 August
Iraqi forces cross the border into Kuwait in the early morning hours, quickly overrunning its small southern neighbor and threatening Saudi Arabia. The action by Iraqi President Saddam Hussein prompts President George H.W. Bush to order American forces to the region. On 7 August the carrier *Dwight D. Eisenhower* (CVN 69) transits the Suez Canal into the Red Sea,

joining the carrier *Independence*, operating in the Gulf of Oman since 5 August, in theater. Their embarked air wings represent the only combat-ready aircraft in the Persian Gulf.

5 August
Operating off the coast of war-torn Liberia, an amphibious ready group consisting of the amphibious assault ship *Saipan* (LHA 2) and other ships begin Operation Sharp Edge, the evacuation of U.S citizens and foreign nationals from the capital city of Monrovia. A total of 2,609 people, including 330 Americans, are flown to safety by Marine helicopters during the operation, which ends on 3 December.

12 August
U.S. warships inaugurate a naval quarantine of Iraq to enforce a United Nations economic embargo.

18 August
In separate incidents the guided-missile frigate *Reid* (FFG 30) and the frigate *Robert G. Bradley* (FFG 49) fire warning shots without effect across the bows of two Iraqi oil tankers leaving the Persian Gulf. Also, the guided missile cruiser *England* (CG 22) and the guided missile destroyer *Scott* (DDG 995) divert freighters in the Persian Gulf and northern Red Sea, the first diversions by Navy ships.

31 August

The guided-missile cruiser *Biddle* (CG 34) intercepts and boards the Iraqi merchant vessel *Al Karamah*, the first Iraqi ship to be boarded since intercept operations began on 16 August. The tanker is empty and allowed to continue to Jordan.

5 September

The fleet tender *Acadia* (AD 42) departs San Diego, California, with a crew of 1,260, including 360 women. This is the first wartime test of a combined crew consisting of males and females.

16 September

The destroyer *O'Brien* (DD 975) intercepts the Bahamian-flagged merchant tanker *Daimon*, logging the 1,000th intercept since the multinational operations began.

27 September

The frigate *Elmer B. Montgomery* fires warning shots during a merchant interception, and then puts a boarding party on board the Iraqi tanker *Tadmur* as she proceeds south out of the Gulf of Aqaba, Jordan.

1 October

The carrier *Independence* transits the Strait of Hormuz en route to the Persian Gulf, marking the first time a flattop steams in that body of water since 1974. The carrier remains for a short period and conducts normal

operations. She departs on 4 October having demonstrated the feasibility of operating aircraft carriers in the Persian Gulf.

30 October

A major steam leak in a fire room of the amphibious assault ship *Iwo Jima* (LPH 2) operating in the Persian Gulf results in the deaths of ten crewmembers.

Right: *A civilian lifts his arms to be searched by a Marine while being processed aboard the tank landing ship* Barnstable County *(LST 1197) during Operation Sharp Edge, 6 September 1990. Civilians were brought aboard U.S. Navy ships off the coast of Liberia after being evacuated from the midst of that country's civil war. This continues an old mission of the U.S. Navy, providing a safe haven during periods of political unrest. (U.S. Navy)*

26 December
The destroyers *Fife* (DD 991) and *Oldendorf* (DD 972), amphibious transport docks *Trenton* (LPD 14) and *Shreveport* (LPD 12), guided missile frigate *Curts* (FFG 38), and two multinational craft intercept *Ibn Khaldoon* ("Peace Ship") in the Arabian Sea after the Iraqi-flagged freighter refuses repeated requests to stop. Crewmembers attempt to restrain a boarding party of Navy personnel and grab their weapons, and warning shots are fired in the air and smoke and noise grenades are set off for crowd control. The freighter is diverted to port after a search reveals prohibited cargo.

1991

2–5 January
Marine helicopters from the amphibious assault ship *Guam* and amphibious transport dock *Trenton* conduct Operation Eastern Exit, on the first day evacuating sixty-five U.S. citizens and other foreign nationals caught in civil war in Somalia. On 5 January the American and Soviet ambassadors and 193 additional foreign nationals are evacuated in four helicopter roundtrips from the U.S. Embassy in Mogadishu to ships off shore.

7 January
In a controversial decision, Secretary of Defense Richard Cheney cancels the contract for the A-12 Avenger, a proposed carrier-based stealth attack aircraft.

12 January
Congress approves joint resolutions authorizing the use of force against Iraq.

Above: *Crewmembers aboard the frigate* Elmer B. Montgomery *(FF 1082) look out from the railing upon the vessel's return to port along with four other ships of the aircraft carrier* Saratoga *(CV 60) battle group following Operation Desert Storm, 28 March 1991. Note the symbols painted on the ship noting* Montgomery's *intercepts of freighters in the Persian Gulf. (U.S. Navy)*

Left: *A diver from Detachment B, Explosive Ordnance Disposal (EOD) Mobile Unit 6, attaches an explosive charge to the side of an Iraqi mine, 1 January 1991. While operating with the U.S. Mine Countermeasures Group, the divers of Detachment B recovered or destroyed forty Iraqi mines in the Persian Gulf and Kuwait's harbors. (U.S. Navy)*

16 January

The White House announces, "The liberation of Kuwait has begun!" The offensive action against Iraq, codenamed Operation Desert Storm, is carried out under provisions of twelve UN Security Council resolutions and resolutions of both houses of Congress. On this day there are some 425,000 U.S. military personnel in theater, 60,000 of them members of the U.S. Navy.

17 January

On the first day of the Gulf War, nine Navy ships in the Arabian Gulf and Red Sea launch 122 Tomahawk cruise missiles. The guided missile cruiser *San Jacinto* (CG 56) fires the first Tomahawk from the Red Sea, while the guided missile cruiser *Bunker Hill* (CG 52) fires the first Tomahawk from the Persian Gulf. Ironically, *San Jacinto* was the name of the light aircraft carrier from which President George H.W. Bush flew while serving as a naval aviator during World War II.

Aircraft from six carriers—two in the Persian Gulf and four in the Red Sea—join other coalition aircraft in launching air strikes against Iraq. An F/A-18

Hornet from Strike Fighter Squadron (VFA) 81 from the carrier *Saratoga* is shot down over Iraq. The plane's pilot, Lieutenant Commander Michael Scott Speicher, is declared killed in action. In an unprecedented move ten years later, on 11 January 2001, the Navy changes his status to missing in action. On 11 October 2002 his status is changed to missing/captured.

18 January

In air-to-air engagements over Iraq, coalition aircraft destroy eight enemy MiG-29 and Mirage F-1 fighters. The first kills are scored by a pair of VFA-81 F/A-18s from the carrier *Saratoga* flown by Lieutenant Commander Mark I. Fox and Lieutenant Nick Mongillo, who then transition to attack mode and bomb selected targets.

Above: *During Operation Desert Shield, the fleet oiler* Andrew J. Higgins *(TAO 190) conducts an underway replenishment with the amphibious transport dock* Raleigh *(LPD 1), foreground, and the amphibious assault ship* Okinawa *(LPH 3), background, 12 October 1990. (U.S. Navy)*

JOINT OPERATIONS

by M. Hill Goodspeed

The nature of warfare as it has progressed over the course of centuries has placed fighting men in a variety of arenas, from the Roman centurion waging battle under Julius Caesar to the Viking ships sailing the frigid waters of the North Atlantic on a journey of conquest. And in the twentieth century the advent of the airplane had added another dimension to warfare. The combatants in the respective dimensions bring different perspectives to how battles are waged, use their own unique terminology, and do not place importance on the same factors on the battlefield. Bodies of water that are obstacles to foot soldiers are avenues of movement for the sailor, while the term "starboard quarter" means something to the mariner that it does not to the airman.

These inherent differences have often translated into troublesome interservice relationships between

armies, navies, and air forces, and the military history of the United States is no different. During the Civil War, Union admirals and generals struggled over command and control of amphibious landings off the eastern seaboard, while in the 1920s Brigadier General William Mitchell's bombing tests against antiquated warships sought to diminish the Navy's role in national defense in favor of air power. And on the eve of the 1942 invasion of North Africa, General George S. Patton recorded, "I'm under no illusion that the goddamn Navy will get us within a hundred miles of the beach or within a week of the date set for landing."

Yet, throughout the nation's history the services have been repeatedly called upon to support one another in joint operations, the success of a mission impossible without the cooperation of more than one branch of the armed forces. The campaign on the Western Rivers during the Civil War and amphibious landings from Fort Fisher to Normandy have staked their success on the cooperation and coordination between the Army and Navy. During the epic Battle of Midway, Army Air Forces, Marine Corps, and Navy

aircraft defended Midway Atoll, while in the skies over North Korea Navy fighters often served as escorts for Air Force B-29 bomber raids. In the modern era Navy aircraft carriers have transported Army helicopters and troops to hostile shores, and Navy EA-6B Prowlers, with their radar jamming capability, have led strikes of Air Force aircraft into battle, including the first night of Operation Iraqi Freedom.

Opposite, top: *Army First Lieutenant George Bass provides a fire control team from the cruiser* Toledo *(CA 133) with coordinates for naval gunfire in support of an advance by ground troops in Korea, April 1951. The roar of shells coming in from the sea has always been a welcome sound for grunts. (U.S. Navy)*

Opposite, bottom: *Members of a SEAL team move out after disembarking from an Air Force Special Operations MH-53J Pave Low III helicopter during a joint training exercise in the New Mexico desert, 1 March 1990. (U.S. Air Force)*

Above: *British motorized equipment, including a tank whose nickname accurately captures the fact that it has never seen combat, roll out the bow doors of a tank landing ship onto a "Rhino" floating dock in the English Channel during the early hours of the invasion of France, 6 June 1944. (U.S. Navy)*

Below: *F-14 Tomcats conduct inflight refueling from an Air National Guard KC-135 tanker over southern Turkey during Operation Provide Comfort, 28 April 1991. (U.S. Navy)*

Left: *An A-7E Corsair II from Attack Squadron (VA) 46 refuels en route to a target in Iraq, 1991. (National Museum of Naval Aviation)*

Below: *A Tomahawk cruise missile, as seen through the periscope of the attack submarine Pittsburgh (SSN 720) operating in the eastern Mediterranean, breaks the surface of the sea en route to a target in Iraq during Operation Desert Storm. Their sophisticated systems enable cruise missiles to pinpoint targets far inland. (Naval Historical Center)*

The guided missile frigate *Nicholas* (FFG 47), operating with embarked Helicopter Antisubmarine Squadron (Light) (HSL) 44 and a Kuwaiti patrol boat, engages and neutralizes Iraqi forces that are firing antiaircraft artillery and shoulder-fired surface-to-air missiles at coalition aircraft from eleven Kuwaiti oil platforms in the northern Persian Gulf. In the first combined helicopter missile and surface ship gun engagement, five Iraqis are killed and three wounded. In addition, twenty-three Iraqis become the war's first prisoners.

SEALS operating from the destroyer *Moosbrugger* board the Sudanese vessel *El Obeid*, the first boarding by a Navy ship since the commencement of hostilities.

19 January
A-6 Intruder and A-7 Corsair II aircraft from the carriers *John F. Kennedy* and *Saratoga* successfully launch Standoff Land Attack Missiles against an Iraqi target for the first time.

The nuclear-powered submarine *Louisville* (SSN 724) fires the first submarine-launched Tomahawk cruise missile in combat history while submerged in the Red Sea.

22 January
Operating over the Persian Gulf, four A-6 Intruders attack and disable an Iraqi T-43 class ship, which is capable of laying up to twenty mines. Navy warships

also attack three Iraqi patrol boats, disabling one and chasing off the others.

23 January

A-6 Intruders disable an *Al Qaddisiyah*-class Iraqi tanker that is collecting and reporting intelligence data, setting off three explosions. The attack also results in the sinking of a hovercraft being refueled by the tanker and a patrol boat.

24 January

A-6 Intruders attack and destroy an Iraqi minelayer and minesweeper, and another minesweeper hits a mine while attempting to evade fire from the aircraft. In the aftermath of the attacks in the Persian Gulf, twenty-two survivors are taken from the sea by an SH-60 Seahawk from the guided missile frigate *Curts* near Qaruh Island. The helicopter comes under attack

by Iraqi forces on the island and returns fire, killing three of the enemy. Subsequently, fifty-one enemy prisoners of war are taken into custody by SEALS landed by helicopters from the destroyer *Leftwich* and the guided missile frigate *Nicholas*. The island is reclaimed, the first liberated Kuwaiti territory.

29 January

Marines deployed from the amphibious assault ship *Okinawa* (LPH 3) capture Umm al Maradim Island, twelve miles off the coast of Kuwait. This is the second island reclaimed for the Kuwaiti government by the coalition. Navy helicopters searching Maradim Island to investigate reports of Iraqis offering to surrender are fired upon by approximately twenty Iraqi small craft. The helicopters return fire, sinking four boats and damaging twelve others.

4 February
The battleship *Missouri* fires her 16-inch guns at prefabricated concrete command and control bunkers that Iraq is moving into Kuwait, destroying them. The barrage marks the first combat firing of the "Mighty Mo's" main batteries since the Korean War, as well as the first combat use of a remotely piloted vehicle for gunfire spotting. *Missouri*'s sister ship, *Wisconsin*, joins the action three days later.

6 February
An F-14 Tomcat of VF-1 from the carrier *Ranger* downs an Iraqi MI-8 helicopter.

18 February
Within three hours and ten nautical miles, the amphibious assault ship *Tripoli* (LPH 10) and guided missile cruiser *Princeton* (CG 59) strike mines while conducting operations in the northern Persian Gulf. *Tripoli* sustains a 16-by-20-foot hole in her forward starboard side below the waterline and minor flooding to six auxiliary spaces. Four crewmembers are injured, but *Tripoli* remains fully operational. *Princeton* sustains damage that includes a crack in her superstructure, and is towed to port. Three crewmen are injured.

Above: *Dry dock repair crews inspect the hole that was ripped in the hull of the amphibious assault ship* Tripoli *(LPH 10) when the ship struck an Iraqi mine on 18 February 1991.* Tripoli *hit the mine while serving as a mine-clearing platform in the northern Persian Gulf during Operation Desert Storm. The ship was able to continue operations after damage control crews stopped the flooding caused by the explosion. (U.S. Navy)*

27 February
President George H.W. Bush addresses the nation, declaring, "Kuwait is liberated. Iraq's army is defeated." The President announces that "exactly 100 hours since ground operations commenced and six weeks since the start of Operation Desert Storm, all U.S. and coalition forces will suspend further offensive combat operations."

Left: *Crew members aboard the battleship* Wisconsin *(BB 64), deployed to the Persian Gulf, prepare a Pioneer remotely piloted vehicle for launch during Operation Desert Storm, January 1991. Pioneers provided spotting of targets for* Wisconsin's *guns, and on one occasion Iraqi troops signaled their desire to surrender to an orbiting unmanned vehicle. (U.S. Navy)*

4 March

Iraq releases its first prisoners of war. Among the ten repatriated are Navy airmen— Lieutenants Lawrence R. Slade, Robert Wetzel, and Jeffrey N. Zaun.

18 March

The combat stores ship *Sylvania* (AFS 2) arrives in Norfolk, Virginia, the first return of a ship supporting Operation Desert Storm. During her seven-month deployment, she delivers 20,500 tons of supplies and delivers spare parts and food sustaining more than 35,000 sailors aboard 150 ships. In addition, her embarked helicopters transfer 5,000 tons of supplies, 915 passengers, 31,000 pounds of mail, and perform ten emergency medical evacuations.

7 April

The United States inaugurates Operation Provide Comfort, which provides supplies to Kurdish refugees in Northern Iraq. As part of the operation, which lasts until 31 December 1996, coalition aircraft begin patrolling a no-fly zone in the region above the 36th parallel. On 1 January 1997 the patrolling of this northern no-fly zone is renamed Operation Northern Watch.

11 April

The United Nations Security Council declares a formal cease-fire ending the Persian Gulf War.

To date, Navy ships have found and destroyed 553 mines, intercepted 8,770 merchant ships, and conducted 590 boardings.

4 July

Arleigh Burke (DDG 51), lead ship of a new class of Aegis guided missile destroyers, is commissioned. Appropriately, the ship is named for the Navy's most famous destroyer skipper.

Above: *Platform guests render honors as the national anthem is played during the commissioning of the guided missile destroyer* Arleigh Burke *(DDG 51) at Norfolk, Virginia, 4 July 1991. They are, from left: Admiral David E. Jeremiah, Vice Chairman of the Joint Chiefs of Staff; Secretary of the Navy H. Lawrence Garrett III; Secretary of Defense Richard Cheney; Commander John G. Morgan, Jr., the ship's commanding officer; and retired Admiral Arleigh Burke, for whom the ship is named. (U.S. Navy)*

THE AEGIS WEAPON SYSTEM

by Vice Admiral James Doyle, U.S. Navy (Retired)

During the latter months of World War II, Japan unleashed the *kamikaze*s, a deadly form of air assault that battered the ships of the Pacific Fleet, particularly in the waters off Okinawa. The tremendous losses convinced the Navy that guided missiles would provide a far better capability than gunfire to shoot down enemy aircraft. Thus began the birth and development of the Navy's surface-to-air missile systems characterized by closed-loop fire control and beam riding, followed by semi-active homing missiles. For thirty years they provided the primary defense for the Navy's cruisers and destroyers against air attack. As aircraft and supersonic cruise missiles became a greater threat to Navy ships, Rear Admiral Frederic S. Withington conducted a landmark study to determine the best defense for the surface fleet. The final report called for a weapon system that could detect, control, and engage enemy aircraft and cruise missiles. The operational cornerstones would be firepower, reaction time, coverage, countermeasures, and availability. The result was the Aegis weapon system, developed in concert with naval laboratories and warfare centers, along with industry by Rear Admiral Wayne Meyer, the Navy Project Manager, and a team of active duty officers and civilians. At the core of the system were computers that controlled the SPY-1 multi-function phased array radar, the command and decision elements, and the evolved Standard missile with mid-course guidance.

The decision of Congress in 1977 to cancel a proposed Aegis nuclear-powered destroyer left the Navy looking for a platform for the new system. The answer turned out to be the modification of the *Spruance*-class destroyer design into guided-missile cruisers, incorporating the Aegis combat system, renamed because of the fact that the ship was engineered as a total system to fight simultaneously in all warfare areas. The project necessitated historic changes in organizations, shore based infrastructure, prototypes, testing, and manning and billet structures. New concepts of ship integration and system engineering were instituted with combat systems as the driving force. In 1982 at Ingalls Shipyard in Pascagoula, Mississippi, *Ticonderoga* (CG 47), christened by First Lady Nancy Reagan, joined the fleet as the Navy's first Aegis-equipped warship and deployed to the Mediterranean ready for war just nine months after commissioning. In addition to providing fleet air defense, *Ticonderoga* revolutionized air battle control with the SPY-1 phased array radar providing a long range, coherent air picture of fire control quality for the battle group. Combat air patrol requirements were markedly reduced and air contacts quickly sorted out. Thus, *Ticonderoga* and the next four cruisers of her class became modern day versions of the *Cleveland*-class air defense cruisers of World War II. With the development and testing of the Vertical Launching System (VLS), the Tomahawk cruise missile was integrated into the Aegis Combat System in the ensuing twenty-two Aegis cruisers, adding significantly to their offensive strike capability.

Even before *Ticonderoga* joined the fleet, the Navy completed a study that called for a new class of battle group-capable destroyers based on Aegis technology. The result was *Arleigh Burke* (DDG 51), lead ship of a new class of Aegis warships, commissioned in 1991. Armed with downsized Aegis weapon systems and VLS, the ships of the *Arleigh Burke* class are robust in strike, air defense, and antisubmarine warfare, capable of tracking over 100 targets simultaneously. They operate with aircraft carrier battle groups and amphibious ready groups, conduct maritime interception, and provide continuous forward presence. With a long-range surveillance and air defense system, they are able to protect other forces from aircraft and missile attack, and provide air battle control.

By 2003, there will be sixty-four Aegis warships at sea, including twenty-seven cruisers and thirty-seven destroyers, with seventeen additional destroyers authorized. In addition to the general surface combatant missions, the specific tasks of strike, theater air defense, force protection, and command and control are clearly defined in the two classes of warships.

Historically, cruisers have been more heavily armed and instrumented than destroyers and, in many cases, have different missions. The Aegis cruisers continue this trend with the added capability of theater-wide ballistic missile defense. This is made possible by the flexibility and growth engineered in the initial design. New capabilities have been continually inserted in both cruisers and destroyers by block upgrades to the Aegis combat system. Likewise, the Standard missile family has been upgraded to shoot down supersonic, maneuvering cruise missiles. A new missile has been developed to engage ballistic missiles in the exo-atmosphere.

For twenty years, Aegis cruisers and destroyers have been providing air defense for joint forces, firing Tomahawks at targets in Iraq, Libya, Bosnia, and Afghanistan, conducting maritime interception, and operating with allies. They have been a major forward presence in the oceans of the world. Forward-deployed Aegis missile defense ships will normally be the first on scene when a crisis is imminent, providing air and cruise missile defense to support time-critical strikes and amphibious assault and protect joint and coalition forces. When required for ballistic missile defense,

transformed Aegis cruisers and destroyers can be deployed to defend the homeland, deployed forces, and allies and friends.

Aegis has had a profound effect on thousands of naval and civilian personnel, from programmers, designers, and engineers to the men and women manning the decks and the leaders that call them to arms. The program has revolutionized shipyards, production activities, testing sites, and training facilities to fit the Aegis acquisition model. Overseas, the Aegis combat system is the core of new Japanese destroyers, and Spanish and Norwegian frigates. Its legacy is the result of strong technical and operational leadership, and an engineering philosophy of "build a little, test a little, learn a lot." Aegis cruisers and destroyers will be the backbone of the surface Navy for decades to come.

Above: *The tactical action officer on board the guided missile destroyer* John S. McCain *(DDG 56) monitors the Aegis combat system as he tracks the movement of ships in the Arabian Sea, 3 March 1998. (U.S. Navy)*

31 July

The Senate follows the House of Representatives in passing an amendment to the 1992 defense budget that allows women to fly combat missions in Navy, Marine Corps, and Air Force aircraft.

7 September

The annual convention of the Tailhook Association at Las Vegas, Nevada includes raucous parties that result in allegations by several women, including active duty officers, of sexual misconduct by male officers. The resulting investigation casts a pall over naval aviation. No officers are court-martialed, but sixty-nine receive some punishment.

11 September

The aircraft carrier *Independence* arrives at Yokosuka, Japan, to replace *Midway* as the Navy's only forward-deployed flattop.

27 September

During a televised speech, President George H.W. Bush announces that the United States will unilaterally reduce its stockpile of nuclear weapons, including the removal of all tactical nuclear weapons from ships. This includes air-launched nuclear weapons in the magazines of the Navy's carriers.

24 November

The Navy formally relinquishes the Subic Bay Naval Facility to the government of the Philippines, ending a naval presence in the islands that dates to the Spanish-American War.

8 December

The aircraft carrier *Lexington* (AVT 16), the Navy's designated training carrier since the early 1960s and the last of the World War II *Essex*-class carriers in operational service, is decommissioned at Naval Air Station Pensacola, Florida. She becomes a floating museum in Corpus Christi, Texas.

25 December

President Mikhail S. Gorbachev resigns as president after declaring that the Soviet Union no longer exists. This marks the end of the Cold War.

1992

12 February

The salvage ship *Salvor* (ARS 52) completes the deepest salvage recovery recorded to date, retrieving the forward section of a helicopter from a depth of 17,250 feet in the Pacific Ocean off Wake Atoll.

31 March

Helicopter pilot Lieutenant Commander Wendy B. Lawrence becomes the first female line officer in the Navy selected to become an astronaut.

22 July

The Chief of Naval Operations and Secretary of the Navy announce a reorganization of the OPNAV staff. The Assistant Chiefs of Naval Operations for Surface, Submarine, Air and Naval Warfare are merged into one staff under the Deputy Chief of Naval Operations for Resources, Warfare, Requirements, and Assessment (N8).

24 July

The aircraft carrier *Saratoga* begins operations in the Adriatic Sea in response to unrest in the former Yugoslavian republic of Bosnia-Herzegovina. She is the first carrier to conduct sustained operations in this body of water.

27 August

Allied aircraft begin flying as part of Operation Southern Watch, enforcing a no-fly zone that prohibits Iraqi aircraft from operating below the 32nd parallel. The first aircraft on station as part of the operation are from the carrier *Independence*.

28 September

The Secretary of the Navy, Chief of Naval Operations, and Commandant of the Marine Corps sign the document "...From the Sea," which addresses post-Cold War strategic requirements for the Navy, including war in the littorals and maneuver from the sea.

Opposite: *Rear Admiral Raynor A. K. Taylor, Commander U.S. Naval Forces Central Command, displays an Iraqi mine recovered from the Persian Gulf to officers aboard the command ship* La Salle *(AGF 3), 17 September 1992. Even after the Gulf War, U.S. naval forces remained active in the Persian Gulf, and also enforced no-fly zones over Iraq. (U.S. Navy)*

Above: *Overhead view of the carrier* Saratoga *(CV 60) underway in the Adriatic Sea, 29 July 1992. (U.S. Navy)*

Below: *During the Cold War a meeting of Soviet and American ships on the high seas produced tense moments. After the fall of the Berlin Wall, the meeting of Russian and American ships called for the rendering of honors, as the destroyer* O'Bannon *(DD 987) and this Soveremenny-class* destroyer are doing. (U.S. Navy)

1 October

During exercises in the Mediterranean Sea, the aircraft carrier *Saratoga* inadvertently launches two Sea Sparrow missiles, one of which strikes the bridge of the Turkish destroyer *Muavenet*, killing five of her crew, including the ship's commanding officer.

2 October

Sean O'Keefe becomes the sixty-ninth Secretary of the Navy. He replaces Admiral Frank B. Kelso, who has served as acting secretary following the 22 June resignation of H. Lawrence Garrett III.

9–10 December

Operation Provide Hope, one of the largest humanitarian operations in history, begins in Somalia, with SEALS and Marine reconnaissance forces the first to go ashore. Supporting the effort to provide food to the starving population of the African nation, which is racked by violence between competing warlords, are ships of the *Tripoli* amphibious ready group and the carrier *Ranger*. The ships also monitor air traffic and guide aircraft to the Somali capital of Mogadishu. During the ensuing months, Navy ships rotate service in the waters off Somalia until American forces withdraw in March 1994.

1993

13 January

Allied aircraft, including thirty-five from the aircraft carrier *Kitty Hawk*, strike Iraqi missile sites in response to a violation of the southern no-fly zone. Four days later the destroyers *Caron*, *Hewitt* (DD 966), and *Stump* (DD 978), operating in the Persian Gulf, launch forty-five Tomahawk cruise missiles against the Zaafaraniyah nuclear fabrication facility near Baghdad.

12 March

The Naval Doctrine Command is established at Norfolk, Virginia.

12 April

The North American Treaty Organization commences Operation Deny Flight, enforcing a no-fly zone over the former Yugoslavian republic of Bosnia-Herzegovina. Twelve F/A-18 Hornets from the carrier

Above: *Admiral Jerry M. Boorda, Commander in Chief, U.S. Naval Forces, Europe, and Allied Forces, Southern Europe, conducts a briefing during a press conference marking the beginning of Operation Deny Flight, the enforcement of the United Nations-sanctioned no-fly zone over Bosnia and Herzegovina. Boorda is pointing out the areas where combat air patrols will be flying during the operation. The press conference took place at the 5th Allied Tactical Air Force headquarters at Vincenza Air Base, Italy, on 8 April 1993. (U.S. Air Force)*

Opposite: *Two U.S. Navy hospital corpsmen from the Marine Expeditionary Unit, Service Support Group 15, from Camp Pendleton, California, treat the infected foot of a young Somali boy in Mogadishu, 19 January 1993. The new world order often necessitates the use of naval forces in peacekeeping and humanitarian roles. (U.S. Navy)*

Theodore Roosevelt (CVN 71) are transferred to NATO as the Navy's initial support for the operation.

28 April
Secretary of the Defense Les Aspin lifts the ban on women flying combat missions, and promises efforts to end the barriers to women serving in combat vessels. On 30 November President William J. Clinton signs legislation allowing women to serve in combat ships.

15 June
Navy surface and air assets support the North Atlantic Treaty Organization's Operation Sharp Guard, which commences on this date to enforce economic sanctions against Croatia, Serbia, and the Republic of Yugoslavia. Their missions include maritime interception, as well as airborne warning and control. The operation ends on 19 June 1996.

26 June
In response to an assassination plot on former President George H.W. Bush during a visit to Kuwait, the destroyer *Peterson* (DD 969) and the guided missile cruiser *Chancellorsville* (CG 62) launch twenty-three Tomahawk cruise missiles against the Iraqi Intelligence Service headquarters in Baghdad.

22 July
John H. Dalton, a 1964 graduate of the Naval Academy, takes office as the seventieth Secretary of the Navy.

Left: *The commanding officer of the guided missile cruiser* Normandy *(CG 60), Captain Thomas R. Fedyzyn, and his bridge crew keep an eye on the Bulgarian cargo ship* Serdetz Bourgas *as the distance between the two ships narrows.* Normandy *was in the Adriatic Sea in support of Operation Sharp Guard to insure compliance with United Nations sanctions. (U.S. Navy)*

Left: *In an example of joint operations, helicopters of the Army's 10th Air Battalion, 10th Mountain Division, sit in formation on the flight deck of the carrier* Dwight D. Eisenhower *(CVN 69) in preparation for operation Restore Democracy in Haiti, September 1994. (National Museum of Naval Aviation)*

Right: *An F-14 Tomcat of Fighter Squadron (VF) 24 undergoes service on the flight deck of the nuclear-powered aircraft carrier* Nimitz *(CVN 68) as the command ship* La Salle *(AGF 3) passes astern, 1 March 1993. Both ships were deployed to the Arabian Gulf during Operation Southern Watch, the enforcement of the no-fly zone in southern Iraq. Enforcing the no-fly zone occupied the attention of Navy aircrews for more than a decade, with the long patrols sometimes punctuated by attacks against Iraqi radar and antiaircraft sites. (U.S. Navy)*

Right: *Astronaut Robert L. Gibson, STS-71 mission commander on board the Space Shuttle Atlantis, shakes the hand of cosmonaut Vladimir N. Dezhurov, Mir-18 commander. The historic handshake on the occasion of the first Space Shuttle docking with the Russian space station took place two-and-a-half weeks prior to the twentieth anniversary of a similar in-space greeting between cosmonauts and astronauts participating in the Apollo-Soyuz Test Project. (NASA)*

11 September
The Navy decommissions its first supercarrier, *Forrestal* (CV 59), during ceremonies at the Philadelphia Naval Shipyard, Pennsylvania.

1 October
The first phase of the Joint Primary Aircraft Training Program commences with Air Force pilots reporting to Naval Air Station Whiting Field, Florida, and Navy, Marine Corps, and Coast Guard aviators reporting to Randolph Air Force Base, Texas, for training.

15 October
Secretary of the Navy John Dalton announces the consolidation of Officer Candidate School and Aviation Officer Candidate School at Naval Air Station Pensacola, Florida. The realignment means the closure of Officer Candidate School at Newport, Rhode Island.

18 October
Operation Support Democracy commences with Navy ships and Coast Guard vessels enforcing United Nations sanctions against Haiti's military regime by imposing a quarantine on the island nation.

1994

27 February
Lieutenant Shannon Workman becomes the first female combat pilot to carrier qualify, logging her traps in an EA-6B Prowler on the aircraft carrier *Dwight D. Eisenhower*.

7 March
A total of sixty-seven women receive orders to report to the carrier *Dwight D. Eisenhower*, the first Navy combat ship to have women permanently assigned to her crew.

7–18 April
The *Peleliu* (LHA 5) amphibious ready group supports Operation Distant Runner, the evacuation of American and United Nations personnel from Rwanda.

23 April
Admiral Jeremy M. Boorda becomes the twenty-fifth Chief of Naval Operations. He is the first man to rise from the rate of seaman to the highest post in the Navy.

31 July
Lieutenant Kara Hultgreen and Lieutenant (junior grade) Carey Dunai become the first women to carrier

qualify in the F-14 Tomcat during flight operations on board *Constellation* (CV 64) off the coast of California. Hultgreen is killed on 25 October in a training accident while attempting to land on board *Abraham Lincoln* (CVN 72).

19 September
Twenty-four Navy ships are involved in landings in Haiti as part of Operation Support Democracy, which begin on this date. A unique element of the operation involves the carriers *Dwight D. Eisenhower* and *America*, which deploy with an array of Army helicopters in place of their normal air wings. Diplomatic efforts help avoid the use of force in restoring a democratic government in Haiti, though American military forces remain in the island nation until 31 March 1995.

8 October
In response to Iraqi troops massing on the border of Kuwait, Navy ships rapidly deploy to the Persian Gulf region. The guided missile cruiser *Leyte Gulf* (CG 55) is the first to arrive, reaching her station in the Red Sea on this date. The *George Washington* (CVN 73) carrier battle group, *Tripoli* amphibious ready group, and other ships join her.

15 November
Commander Donnie L. Cochran becomes the first African-American to command the Navy's famed Blue Angels Flight Demonstration Squadron.

1995

2 March
Lieutenant Commander Wendy Lawrence becomes the first female naval aviator in space when she launches as part of the crew of the Space Shuttle *Endeavour*.

3 March
A multinational force that includes the *Essex* (LHD 2) amphibious ready group completes the withdrawal of the last United Nations forces from Somalia.

8 June
The amphibious assault ship *Kearsarge* (LHD 3) launches Marine aircraft for the ultimately successful rescue of Air Force Captain Scott O'Grady, an F-16 pilot shot down over Bosnia six days earlier while

Above: *U.S. Marines of the 24th Marine Expeditionary Unit (Special Operations Capable) on board the amphibious assault ship* Kearsarge *(LHD 3) in the Adriatic Sea prepare for a mission on 8 June 1995 to rescue U.S. Air Force Captain Scott O'Grady, whose plane was shot down by a Bosnian Serb missile over Bosnia. O'Grady survived alone for six days, eluding the Serb forces who were searching for him after he bailed out of his F-16C airplane, until Marines located and rescued him. (© Peter Turnley/Corbis)*

Right: *U.S. Navy aircraft maintenance personnel perform a fifty-six-day preventive maintenance inspection on an EA-6B Prowler of Tactical Electronic Warfare Squadron (VAQ) 141 on the flightline at Aviano Air Base, Italy, 12 September 1995. An airframe developed during the Vietnam War, Prowlers remain essential components of any air operation with their ability to suppress enemy air defenses. (U.S. Air Force)*

flying a mission in support of Operation Deny Flight. Four sailors are on board two CH-53E Super Stallion helicopters during the dramatic rescue.

27 June–7 July
Captain Robert Gibson commands the Space Shuttle Atlantis in the first docking with the Russian space station Mir.

17 August
Iraqi troop movements along the borders of Kuwait and Jordan prompt the dispatch of the *Abraham*

Lincoln and *Independence* battle groups and *New Orleans* (LPH 11) amphibious ready group to stations off Kuwait. The aircraft carrier *Theodore Roosevelt* is also placed on alert in the Mediterranean Sea.

30 August
Aircraft from the carrier *Theodore Roosevelt* spearhead attacks against Bosnian Serb air defense missile sites, radar sites, and communications facilities as part of the opening day of Operation Deliberate Force. Launched in response to a mortar attack against Sarajevo, the

Left: *Lieutenant Commander John Fitzgibbon, assigned to Tactical Electronic Warfare Squadron (VAQ) 139, inspects his EA-6B Prowler prior to launching from the flight deck of the carrier* Carl Vinson *(CVN 70) in support of Operation Desert Strike in response to Iraqi raids into U.N. safe zones, 3 September 1996. (U.S. Navy)*

THE CHIEF: BACKBONE OF THE NAVY

by M. Hill Goodspeed

In addressing those promoted to chief petty officer, the 1918 edition of *The Bluejacket's Manual* highlighted the many changes that came with the new rate—pay, uniforms, and quarters—before focusing on the intangible transformation that came with the title of "Chief." "Along with all these changes comes a very great change in your responsibilities. . . . The position of chief petty officer is one of special honor. . . . See to it that your entire demeanor is such as to elevate the standing of the uniform which you now wear."

The tradition of senior sailors holding positions of leadership at sea dates to the age of sail when the education of a seaman or midshipman did not occur in a classroom, but on the deck of a ship. It was from watching the weathered hands of "old salts" handle lines, sails, and guns that generation after generation of mariners learned their trade. Though the rate of chief petty officer has existed in the U.S. Navy only since 1893, the first recorded use of the term "Chief" dates to 1 June 1776, when Jacob Wasbie received a promotion to "Chief Cook" while serving in the Continental Navy ship *Alfred*. The tremendous growth of the Navy during the Civil War once again introduced chiefs into the naval hierarchy. Commanding officers who found petty officers with the same date of rank on board their ships could designate one to act as a chief in his particular rate. This was formalized in an 1864 General Order listing the ratings of Chief Boatswain's Mate, Chief Gunner's Mate, and Chief Quartermaster. However, the Navy would wait another twenty-nine years to formally create the rate of Chief Petty Officer. At that time men could hold the rate in nine specialties, ranging from boatswain to machinist to musician. In the modern era, reflecting the evolution in technology, chief ratings have included such specialties as missile technician, air controlman, and radarman.

Whatever their rate, chiefs form the backbone of the Navy. The first piece of advice given to a newly commissioned officer is to know and trust his or her chief, who represents that vital link between those in the commissioned ranks and the sailors under their command. Chiefs provide the guiding hand, oftentimes a firm one, to young sailors, instilling in them the knowledge acquired from many days on a pitching deck and the sense of honor that comes with wearing the Navy uniform.

In the years since 1893, the service of chief petty officers has upheld the finest traditions of the Navy. Thirty-nine chiefs have been awarded the nation's highest honor for heroism, the Medal of Honor, three of them posthumously. One of them was Chief Watertender Peter Tomich, who on the fateful morning of 7 December 1941 remained at his post in the engineering plant of the target ship *Utah* (AG 16) after she was hit by enemy bombs, sacrificing his own life to ensure that those in his charge could escape. Another feat of heroism on the part of a chief petty officer occurred when the German dirigible *Hindenburg* burst into flames over Naval Air Station Lakehurst, New Jersey, on 6 May 1937. Above the sounds of frightened people and the crashing airship could be heard the voice of Chief Boatswain's Mate Frederick J. Tobin booming, "Navy men, stand fast!" His efforts helped prevent the loss of additional lives in the inferno of one of aviation's greatest tragedies.

Chiefs have served in unique billets as well, reflecting their importance to the service. Beginning in 1920 the Navy began training enlisted men to fly aircraft. Designated naval aviation pilots, they served alongside commissioned officers in the air and flew all classes of naval aircraft. One squadron, Fighting Squadron (VF) 2B, was known throughout the fleet as the "Fighting Chiefs" for, aside from the squadron leadership, all of the pilots were enlisted men.

Consistently one of the best fighter squadrons in the Navy, Fighting Two operated into World War II, most notably at the Battle of the Coral Sea. Perhaps no greater recognition of the importance of the chief to the U.S. Navy has occurred than the creation in 1967 of the rate of Master Chief Petty Officer of the Navy. The Navy's senior enlisted man, he serves as an advisor to the Chief of Naval Operations and Chief of Naval Personnel on all matters pertaining to enlisted men and women.

"The tone of the ship, the tone of the service itself must come directly from the Chief Petty Officers more than from any other group in the Navy." These words, written in 1914, ring true today and capture the essence and importance of those called "Chief."

Left: *Captain Lindell G. Rutherford, Commanding Officer of the aircraft carrier* George Washington *(CVN 73), converses from the ship's navigational bridge in November 1997. The carrier* Nimitz *(CVN 68) is in the background. With both carriers and their embarked air wings, the U.S. had over 100 strike aircraft operating in the Persian Gulf in support of Operation Southern Watch. (U.S. Navy)*

operation lasts until 21 September, and includes 3,515 combat sorties by aircraft from *Theodore Roosevelt* and *America*, and thirteen Tomahawk land attack missile strikes by the guided missile cruiser *Normandy* (CG 60).

29 November
The F/A-18E Super Hornet makes its first flight at St. Louis, Missouri.

29 December
The Defense Base Realignment and Closure Commission ceases operations, having closed 243 military installations in three rounds of closures.

1996

24 February
Cuban MiG fighters shoot down two unarmed Cessna planes operated by the Miami-based Cuban exile group Brothers to the Rescue. The guided missile cruiser *Mississippi* and amphibious assault ship *Nassau* (LHA 4) join Coast Guard vessels in a futile search for survivors.

23 March
Live-fire exercises conducted by the Peoples Republic of China in the vicinity of the Taiwan Strait conclude having prompted the United States to dispatch the

Above: *The Navy's newest attack submarine,* Seawolf *(SSN 21), underway during sea trials off the coast of Groton, Connecticut, 16 September 1996. She was commissioned on 19 July 1997. (U.S. Navy)*

Right: *American citizens walk single-file through a heavily guarded perimeter to board a U.S. Marine CH-53 Super Stallion helicopter on a field inside the American Embassy housing compound in Tirana, Albania, 15 March 1997. U.S. naval forces from the* Nassau *(LHA 4) amphibious readiness group evacuated citizens from the U.S. Embassy after the Albanian government lost control of its military and dissolved into anarchy. (U.S. Navy)*

Nimitz and *Independence* battle groups, Aegis cruisers, and submarines to the region as a show of force and to monitor the exercises.

20 April
The amphibious assault ship *Guam* (LPH 9), amphibious transport dock *Trenton*, dock landing ship *Portland* (LSD 37), and guided missile destroyer *Conolly* (DDG 979) begin supporting the evacuation of American citizens and foreign nationals from Monrovia, Liberia, as civil war sweeps the country. The operation, codenamed Assured Response, began on 9 April with SEALS joining other Special Forces personnel in providing security for the arrival of Air Force aircraft. More than 1,250 people are evacuated during the operation, including 49 Americans.

13 May
President William J. Clinton nominates Vice Admiral Paul Reason to become the Navy's first African-American four-star admiral.

16 May
With reporters questioning the validity of his Vietnam-era combat awards, Chief of Naval Operations Admiral Jeremy M. Boorda commits suicide at his official home in the Washington Navy Yard, D.C.

21 May
Marine helicopters operating from the amphibious assault ship *Guam* support the withdrawal of American personnel and safeguarding of the embassy at Bangui during political unrest in the Central African Republic. When Operation Quick Response concludes on 22 June, 208 Americans and 240 foreign nationals have been evacuated from the capital by Marine C-130 transports.

4 June
While participating in exercises as part of RIMPAC '96, an A-6 Intruder from the aircraft carrier *Independence* is accidentally shot down by the Japanese destroyer *Yuugiri*, which is firing at a target towed by the aircraft. Both crewmen successfully eject from the aircraft.

Left: *Still dressed in her flight gear, Strike Fighter Squadron (VFA) 37 pilot Lieutenant Carol Watts describes her mission over Iraq to squadronmate Lieutenant Lyndsi Bates on board the carrier* Enterprise *(CVN 65) during operation Desert Fox, 17 December 1998. The lifting of restrictions prohibiting women from combat duties in 1993 paved the way for female pilots to fly combat missions. (U.S. Navy)*

Right: *The amphibious assault ship* Kearsarge *(LHD 3) operating off the West African coast near Sierra Leone, conducting non-combat evacuation orders in support of Operation Noble Obelisk. Nearly 300 U.S. citizens were evacuated after a military coup d'etat overthrew Sierra Leone's democratically elected government in May 2002. The size of World War II aircraft carriers, amphibious assault ships carry transport and attack helicopters capable of putting a sizable force of Marines ashore rapidly. (U.S. Navy)*

Right: *With its afterburner blazing, an F/A-18 Hornet from Strike Fighter Squadron (VFA) 105 launches from the deck of the carrier* Enterprise *(CVN 65) for a nighttime strike against Iraq, 17 December 1998.* Enterprise *was on station in the Persian Gulf as part of Operation Desert Fox. (U.S. Navy)*

21 June

Reflecting the era of joint operations, Commander David J. Cheslak becomes the first naval flight officer to command an Air Force squadron when he takes the helm of the 562nd Flying Training Squadron.

10 July

Rear Admiral Patricia Tracey is promoted to vice admiral. She is the first woman in any of the U.S. armed forces promoted to three-star rank.

11 July

The Naval Strike and Air Warfare Center stands up at Naval Air Station Fallon, Nevada, consolidating the Naval Strike Warfare Center, Navy Fighter Weapons School, and Carrier Airborne Early Warning Weapons School into one command.

17 July

TWA Flight 800 crashes in the Atlantic off the coast of New York shortly after taking off from John F. Kennedy International Airport. The Navy salvage ships *Grasp* (ARS 51) and *Grapple* (ARS 53) and the dock landing ship *Oak Hill* (LSD 51) support recovery efforts. Navy divers recover bodies and locate wreckage.

5 August

Admiral Jay L. Johnson, a Vietnam-era fighter pilot, takes office as the twenty-sixth Chief of Naval Operations.

8 August

Lieutenant (junior grade) Manje Malak Abd Al Muta'Ali Noe receives his commission as the Navy's first Muslim chaplain.

3–4 September

In response to the massing of Iraqi troops and tanks for an apparent attempt to seize control of Kurdish-held territory, the guided missile cruiser *Shiloh* (CG 67), the guided missile destroyers *Laboon* (DDG 58) and *Russell* (DDG 59), the destroyer *Hewitt*, and the nuclear-powered submarine *Jefferson City* (SSN 759) launch thirty-one Tomahawk cruise missiles against air defense targets in Iraq. They are joined in the effort, called Operation Desert Strike, by Air Force B-52 bombers.

1997

13 March

The three-ship *Nassau* (LHA 4) amphibious ready group begins executing Operation Silver Wake, the rescue of Americans and foreign nationals in the midst of civil war in Albania. Marines secure the embassy compound in Tirana, and over the course of five days 877 people are pulled to safety and delivered to the amphibious transport dock *Nashville*.

30 May–4 June
The *Kearsarge* amphibious ready group is rushed to the waters off the war-torn nation of Sierra Leone, where Marine Corps helicopters evacuate some 2,500 Americans and foreign nationals of over forty different nations as part of Operation Noble Obelisk.

21 July
In honor of her 200th anniversary, the venerable frigate *Constitution* sets out on a one-hour voyage from her homeport in Boston, Massachusetts. This is the first time in 116 years that she travels under sail.

6 August
Korean Air Lines Flight 801 crashes shortly after takeoff in Guam. Navy Seabees cut their way through the dense jungle to allow rescuers to reach the crash site and CH-46 helicopters pull thirty survivors from the wreckage.

1 September
The Joint Standoff Weapon (JSOW) is deployed operationally for the first time on board the aircraft carrier *Nimitz*.

1998

18 March
The Standoff Land Attack Missile-Expanded Response successfully completes its first flight after being fired from an F/A-18 Hornet over California.

19 May
Secretary of Defense William S. Cohen releases the Quadrennial Defense Review (QDR). The documents calls for the Navy to retain twelve carrier battle groups and twelve amphibious ready groups, but reduces surface combatants in the fleet from 128 to 116 and decreases the number of attack submarines from seventy-three to fifty. While the number of the Navy's planned Joint Strike Fighter purchases is increased to 480 aircraft, F/A-18E/F purchases are reduced from 1,000 to between 548 and 785. Finally, the QDR proposes a reduction in active duty personnel by 18,000 and decreases the Reserve component by 4,100 personnel.

Above: *Aviation ordnancemen attached to Strike Fighter Squadron (VFA) 15 transport AIM-7 medium-range air-to-air missiles to waiting F/A-18C Hornets on board the carrier* Theodore Roosevelt *(CVN 71) during NATO's Operation Allied Force, 5 May 1999. (U.S. Navy)*

3 April
The presence of Marines as members of ship's company on board aircraft carriers ends when *George Washington* disembarks the twenty-six leathernecks of her Marine detachment upon the completion of a six-month deployment.

June
The first women assume command of combat vessels. By January 1999, the dock landing ships *Mount Vernon* (LSD 39), *Carter Hall* (LSD 50), and *Gunston Hall* (LSD 44), the tank landing ship *La Moure County* (LST 1194), and the guided missile frigate *Jarrett* have female skippers.

18 July
Kitty Hawk replaces *Independence* as the Navy's forward-deployed aircraft carrier homeported at Yokosuka, Japan.

20 August
In retaliation for the terrorist bombings of the American embassies in Kenya and Tanzania, Navy surface ships and submarines launch seventy-five Tomahawk cruise missiles at a suspected chemical weapons facility in Sudan and at terrorist training

Right: *Equipment Operator Constructionman Dan Lasich of Naval Mobile Construction Battalion (NMCB) 4, flattens out ground at Camp Wedge, a forward operating base in Albania, 16 June 1999. NMCB 4 constructed twenty-five miles of roadwork near Kukes, Albania, in support of Operation Shining Hope, the multinational NATO and U.S. operation bringing food and shelter to thousands of Kosovo refugees. It was typical of humanitarian efforts on the part of the U.S. Navy during the 1990s. (U.S. Navy)*

camps in Afghanistan. The prime target of the attacks is terrorist leader Osama bin Laden.

4 September
The Navy deactivates its last nuclear-powered surface ship, the guided missile cruiser *South Carolina* (CGN 37).

9 September
The salvage ship *Grapple* deploys to the waters off Nova Scotia, Canada, to support recovery efforts in the aftermath of the crash of Swissair Flight 111.

16 November
Richard Danzig becomes the seventy-first Secretary of the Navy.

16–19 December
With Iraqi President Saddam Hussein obstructing weapons inspections, the United States launches Operation Desert Fox, sustained air strikes against Iraqi facilities devoted to the development of nuclear, chemical and biological weapons. Aircraft from the carrier *Enterprise*, joined by seven ships carrying Tomahawk cruise missiles, participate in the operation, the first day of which is conducted entirely by the Navy. The operation, which marks the first time women naval aviators have flown combat missions, does not force Iraq to readmit weapons inspectors.

Below: *Supplies are placed on sleds after being offloaded from an Antarctic Development Squadron (VXE) 6 LC-130 Hercules aircraft at a remote research camp during operation Deep Freeze in 1988. (U.S. Navy)*

1999

25 January

F/A-18 Hornets of Strike Fighter Squadrons (VFA) 22 and (VFA) 94 conduct the first operational launches of the AGM-154A Joint Standoff Weapon against Iraqi military targets during Operation Southern Watch.

4 February

The destroyer *Arthur W. Radford* (DD 968) collides with a Saudi Arabian cargo vessel off the coast of

Virginia near midnight. The warship suffers some $24 million in damage and her captain is relieved of command. She is back in action by December.

24 February

Three LC-130R Hercules from Antarctic Development Squadron (VXE) 6 return to Naval Air Station Point Mugu, California, after service in Operation Deep Freeze. This marks the end of VXE-6's support to the Antarctic program sponsored by the National Science Foundation.

Right: *Navy divers examine the wreck of the Japanese fishing vessel* Ehime Maru *during recovery operations in Hawaii. The ship was struck by the attack submarine* Greenville *(SSN 772) off the coast of Oahu on 9 February 2001. (U.S. Navy)*

24 March

With the collapse of diplomatic efforts to counter Serbian President Slobodan Milosevic's "cleansing" of ethnic Albanians from Kosovo, the North Atlantic Treaty Organization launches Operation Allied Force, with Navy surface ships and submarines launching Tomahawk cruise missiles and naval aircraft from bases in Italy participating in the initial attacks. During the seventy-eight-day air campaign, naval aircraft from land bases and the aircraft carrier *Theodore Roosevelt* fly electronic attack and strike missions, and also participate in humanitarian operations and the deployment of peacekeeping forces. The strikes represent the first time in history that NATO has engaged in combat operations and contributes to the forging of an agreement that results in the insertion of United Nations peacekeepers into Kosovo.

11 April

MH-53 Sea Dragons and H-46 Sea Knights from HM-14 and HM-15 embarked in the amphibious assault ship *Inchon* (LPH 12) deliver 6,000 pounds of relief supplies to refugees in Kukes, Albania, marking the beginning of the Navy's contribution to NATO's humanitarian operation, Shining Hope.

19 April

The accidental death of a civilian security guard by bombs from a Marine F/A-18 Hornet during training at the Navy's live-firing target range on Vieques Island off Puerto Rico galvanizes efforts of the local population to close the range. Training is temporarily suspended.

3 May

The nuclear-powered submarine *Hawkbill* (SSN 666) surfaces at the North Pole in the last joint Navy-National Science Foundation Science Ice Expedition.

17 May–17 November

During this period Navy strike aircraft participate in four separate retaliatory attacks against Iraqi antiaircraft positions and radar sites while patrolling the southern no-fly zone.

23 August

The *Kearsarge* amphibious ready group transits the Mediterranean Sea in response to a 7.4-magnitude earthquake that devastates Turkey on 17 August, killing over 24,000 people. Helicopters from *Kearsarge* go into action on this date, ferrying desperately needed aid to the stricken area, remaining on station through 12 September.

2 September

The keel of *Virginia* (SSN 774), the lead boat of the Navy's newest class of nuclear attack submarines, is laid. The first of thirty, she is scheduled to join the fleet in 2004.

Left: *General Henry H. Shelton, Chairman of the Joint Chiefs of Staff, presents awards to twenty-four crew members of the Navy EP-3E Aries II electronic surveillance aircraft, who were detained by Chinese military authorities on Hainan Island, Peoples Republic of China, following a mid-air collision with a Chinese F-8 fighter over international waters on 1 April 2001. The presentations were made at the 2001 Department of Defense Open House at Andrews Air Force Base, Maryland, 18 May 2001. (U.S. Air Force)*

7 October

The *Belleau Wood* (LHA 3) amphibious ready group (ARG) is on station off East Timor to support the efforts of Australian peacekeepers in the war-torn nation. The *Peleliu* (LHA 5) ARG arrives on 26 October to relieve the *Belleau Wood* group.

28 October

Cryptologic Technician First Class Daniel King is arrested and charged with passing classified data to the Russian embassy in Washington, D.C.

31 October

Egypt Air Flight 900 crashes sixty miles east of Nantucket Island, Massachusetts. MH-53 Sea Dragon helicopters from the amphibious transport dock *Austin* (LPD 4) join the salvage ship *Grapple* in the search for victims and wreckage.

3 December

The government of Puerto Rico asks the Navy to stop conducting live-fire exercises on the island of Vieques, and rejects the Navy's proposal to end the exercises in five years.

2000

31 January

Alaska Airlines Flight 261 crashes off the coast of Point Mugu, California, triggering an immediate response from Navy and Coast Guard aircraft from shore. The destroyer *Fife*, guided missile frigate *Jarrett*, and the amphibious transport dock *Cleveland* (LPD 7) assist in the recovery effort.

Puerto Rican officials approve a compromise allowing the fleet to continue to train on Vieques Island for three years, though cutting the annual training in half to ninety days and requiring that live-fire exercises be reduced to nonexplosive ammunition.

5 July

The post of Assistant Chief of Naval Operations for Missile Defense, responsible for both theater ballistic missile and cruise missile defense, is established.

13 July

The amphibious transport dock *Denver* (LPD 9) collides with the Military Sealift Command oiler *Yukon* (T-AO-202) west of Oahu, Hawaii, resulting in an estimated $7 million damage to the ships.

21 July

Destroyerman Admiral Vern E. Clark becomes the twenty-seventh Chief of Naval Operations.

27 August

The destroyer *Nicholson* (DD 982) collides with the fast combat support ship *Detroit* (AOE 4) during a nighttime underway replenishment off the coast of Virginia. This is the sixth accident in twelve months, and the Chief of Naval Operations calls for a safety standdown for all Navy ships.

12 October

While refueling in Aden, Yemen, en route to a port visit in Bahrain, the guided missile destroyer *Cole* (DDG 67) is damaged by a terrorist bomb carried by an inflatable speedboat. The blast kills seventeen sailors and wounds thirty-nine others. *Cole* suffers flooding in the engineering spaces from a forty-foot hole in her port side, but heroic damage control efforts save her. Returned to the United States on board the Norwegian commercial heavy-lift ship *Blue Marlin*, she is repaired at Ingalls Shipbuilding in Pascagoula, Mississippi, and rejoins the fleet on 19 April 2002.

2001

9 February

While operating off Hawaii with sixteen civilian visitors on board, the nuclear attack submarine *Greenville* (SSN 772) conducts an emergency blow drill, coming to the surface at a rapid rate. The sub strikes a Japanese fishing trawler carrying thirty-five crewmen and high school students, which sinks with the loss of nine people. The Navy supervises the effort to recover the bodies of the deceased, and agrees to pay Japanese families $11 million in restitution.

Below: *The launch of a Tomahawk cruise missile illuminates the cruiser* Philippine Sea *(CG 58) during a strike against al Qaeda terrorist training camps and military installations of the Taliban regime in Afghanistan, 7 October 2001. The carefully targeted actions were part of Operation Enduring Freedom and designed to disrupt the use of Afghanistan as a base for terrorist operations and to attack the military capability of the Taliban regime. (U.S. Navy)*

Greenville's skipper, Commander Scott D. Waddle, is found negligent in the performance of his duties and allowed to retire from the service.

16 February

Aircraft from *Harry S. Truman* (CVN 75), the newest *Nimitz*-class aircraft carrier, join U.S. Air Force and British aircraft in attacking twenty-five targets in Iraq, including radar sites and air-defense command centers. The attacks are in response to the firing of surface-to-air missiles at American and British aircraft patrolling the northern and southern no-fly zones.

4 March

The aircraft carrier *Ronald Reagan* (CVN 76), the first naval vessel named for a living president, is christened by Mrs. Reagan.

12 March

An F/A-18 Hornet from the aircraft carrier *Harry S. Truman*, while conducting a live fire exercise at night in Kuwait, mistakenly drops three 500-pound bombs on friendly forces, killing five American servicemen and a New Zealand Army officer. Nine American military personnel and two Kuwaitis are injured by the blast.

1 April

A People's Republic of China F-8 fighter plane intercepts a Navy EP-3E Aries II surveillance aircraft in international air space off Hainan Island. Flying dangerously close to the EP-3, the Chinese fighter collides with it, sending the Aries into an extreme bank and rapid descent. The pilot, Lieutenant Shane

Osborne, rights the EP-3, which suffers damage to its nose, a propeller, and aileron in the collision. Managing to land their aircraft on Hainan Island, the crew is taken into custody by the Chinese government and released after eleven days. The aircraft is disassembled and flown out of China on board a Russian transport on 5 July.

24 April

Stating publicly his support of Taiwan, President George W. Bush promises to sell conventional

Right: *An SH-60F Seahawk helicopter leaves the deck of the motor vessel* Kota Sejarah *after dropping off Navy SEALs and Marines, from the amphibious warfare ship* Shreveport (LPD 12), *to search for illegal contraband and al Qaeda troops on 6 December 2001.* Kota Sejarah *was released following the inspection. (U.S. Navy)*

submarines and P-3 Orion maritime patrol planes to the island nation, considered a renegade province by mainland China, for self-defense.

24 May
Gordon R. England, a former executive with General Dynamics, becomes the seventy-second Secretary of the Navy.

15 June
The Secretary of the Navy announces that the Navy will discontinue training at Vieques, Puerto Rico, by 1 May 2003. This action comes after two months of unrest during which the government of Puerto Rico files suit against the U.S. Navy and Department of Defense and protesters disrupt exercises during 27 April–1 May.

11 September
In America's second day of infamy, civilian airliners hijacked by terrorists slam into the twin towers of the World Trade Center, New York, and the Pentagon, Washington, D.C. A fourth hijacked plane crashes into a field in Pennsylvania. The Pentagon crash kills thirty-three sailors, six Department of the Navy civilian workers, and three Navy civilian contractors, and injures four sailors and two Navy civilians. In the wake of the attacks, Navy surface ships deploy to patrol the waters off the U.S. coasts and assist in the defense of American air space.

14 September
The hospital ship *Comfort* (T-AH-20) arrives at Pier 92 in New York City to provide medical services to survivors of the terrorist attacks against the World Trade Center and to emergency services personnel.

30 September
The Department of Defense issues the 2001 Quadrennial Defense Review (QDR). In assessing the future, it calls for the Secretary of the Navy to increase aircraft carrier battle group presence in the Western Pacific and look to homeport surface and submarine assets in the region. It also calls for the development of new concepts for maritime pre-positioning and amphibious warfare, shifting some of the afloat pre-positioned Marine Corps equipment to the Indian Ocean and Arabian Gulf to respond to potential crises in the Middle East.

7 October
In response to the 11 September 2001 terrorist attacks, the United States launches Operation Enduring Freedom with air strikes against Taliban and al Qaeda forces in Afghanistan. The first day of strikes includes aircraft from the carriers *Enterprise* and *Carl Vinson* (CVN 70), and fifty Tomahawk cruise missiles launched from surface ships and a submarine.

12 October
The aircraft carrier *Kitty Hawk* arrives in the Arabian Sea for service as an afloat staging base for Special Forces. A week later the first ground offensive of the war on terrorism in Afghanistan is launched from her deck.

26 October
Lockheed Martin is awarded a contract for initial development of the F-35 Joint Strike Fighter, which includes a carrier-based version for the Navy and short takeoff/vertical landing version for the Marine Corps.

Left: *Navy Lieutenant Mike Runkle, assigned to Explosive Ordnance Disposal, Mobile Unit Two, Detachment 18 (left), and U.S. Army Staff Sergeant Ben Walker (right) prepare charges to blow up stockpiled ordnance left behind by fleeing al Qaeda troops, 23 December 2001. Lieutenant. Runkle led the Joint Explosive Ordnance Disposal Detachment at a forward operating base in Kandahar, Afghanistan. (U.S. Navy)*

1 November

The Navy cancels development work begun in 1998 on the *Zumwalt*-class DD 21, a planned successor to the *Arleigh Burke*-class destroyer, and replaces it with the DDX program. The DDX features an advanced gun system that can strike targets from 100 miles away, missile capability, and low radar cross-section and quiet signature to improve survivability. "I have every reason to believe . . . the ship is going to be the definer of the next four decades of what our Navy looks like," the Chief of Naval Operations tells the Senate Armed Services Committee in April 2002. Plans call for the research and development of the DDX to form the basis for the CGX missile defense cruiser and the LCS littoral combatant ship.

18 November

Two sailors from the destroyer *Peterson*, Petty Officer First Class Vincent Parker and Petty Officer Third Class Benjamin Johnson, die while engaged in a maritime interception of a tanker suspected of smuggling oil out of Iraq when the dangerously overloaded vessel sinks in heavy seas.

25–26 November

Naval aircraft support the retaking of the Qala-e-Jhangi prison in Afghanistan after an uprising that results in the death of Central Intelligence Agency (CIA) operative Johnny Micheal Spann.

12 December

In the Indian Ocean off Diego Garcia, the guided missile destroyer *Russell* (DDG 59) rescues the crew of a U.S. Air Force B-1 bomber that malfunctioned en route to bomb targets in Afghanistan, forcing them to eject.

13 December

President George W. Bush notifies Russia that the United States will withdraw from the 1972 Anti-Ballistic Missile Treaty, thus clearing the way for the deployment of a missile defense system. This measure comes one month after an agreement between the two nations to reduce the nuclear arsenals of the respective countries by two-thirds.

27 December

The Department of Defense announces that al Qaeda and Taliban detainees taken into custody in Afghanistan will be held at the naval base at Guantanamo Bay, Cuba.

31 December

By the end of the year, Navy aircraft have flown 72 percent of the tactical and strike sorties over Afghanistan and delivered more than half of all precision-guided weapons launched during Operation Enduring Freedom. Targets have included enemy troops and vehicles and enemy strongholds at Konduz, Kandahar, and the Tora Bora cave complex in the White Mountains.

2002

29 January

Giving his State of the Union address before a joint session of Congress, President George W. Bush identifies the nations of Iraq, Iran, and North Korea as an "axis of evil," and pledges that the United States will not allow them to threaten the world with weapons of mass destruction.

4 March
Aviation Boatswain's Mate (Handling) First Class Neil C. Roberts, a Navy SEAL, is killed in action during Operation Anaconda in eastern Afghanistan.

27 March
Chief Hospital Corpsman Matthew J. Bourgeois, a Navy SEAL, is killed while conducting small-unit training at a remote site near Kandahar, Afghanistan.

1 April
The *George Washington* carrier battle group begins training on Vieques Island in Puerto Rico, sparking protests by inhabitants of the island.

19 May
The Navy's Fire Scout vertical takeoff and landing tactical unmanned aerial vehicle begins flight testing at the Naval Air Systems Command Western Test Range Complex in California.

21 May
While operating off San Diego, California, the crew of the research submarine *Dolphin* (AGSS 555) reports fire and flooding that forces them to evacuate the vessel. The guided missile frigate *Thach* (FFG 43) maneuvers into position alongside *Dolphin* to assist.

6 June
The dock landing ship *Tortuga* (LSD 46) runs aground at night while operating off North Carolina. She is refloated the next day.

Above: *The future of the Navy as his backdrop, Chief of Naval Operations Admiral Vern Clark comments on "Sea Power 21" to attendees of the 2002 Joint Undersea Warfare Technology Conference hosted by the National Defense Industrial Association at Naval Submarine Base, New London, Connecticut, 17 September 2002. (U.S. Navy)*

Left: *Aboard the carrier George Washington (CVN 73), Quartermaster Seaman Nick Coleman attempts to adjust the ship's course, while standing helm of the bridge watch during a General Quarters drill as part of integrated training exercises in the Atlantic Ocean in April 2002. Note the protective gear worn by the sailors. (U.S. Navy)*

Left: *The coastal patrol ship* Firebolt *(PC 10) sits moored in port at Camp Patriot, Kuwait, on 10 March 2003, displaying the "Don't Tread On Me" jack. This jack was authorized for all U.S. Navy ships by the Secretary of the Navy and will be displayed throughout the duration of the war on terrorism.* Firebolt *was forward-deployed conducting missions in support of Operation Enduring Freedom. (U.S. Navy)*

12 June
Chief of Naval Operations Admiral Vern Clark unveils "Sea Power 21," a strategic vision for the future, at the Naval War College. The vision revolves around three core concepts: Sea Strike, projecting offense; Sea Shield, projecting defense; and Sea Basing, projecting sovereignty. "Here's what our mission is: to take credible combat power to the far corners of the earth, to take the sovereignty of the United States of America anywhere we want," Clark says later in the year. "Our mission is to give the President options. Our mission is to be able to project combat power."

Below: *Watchtower security teams at Camp X-Ray, Guantanamo Bay, Cuba, man positions during a rehearsal for handling incoming detainees. Camp X-Ray is one of the holding facilities for Taliban and al Qaeda detainees. (U.S. Navy)*

17 June
The guided-missile cruiser *Vicksburg* (CG 69) and her embarked helicopter detachment rescue sixteen sailors from a merchant vessel that had been adrift for eleven days off Oman.

24 July
F/A-18E Super Hornets of VFA-115 begin the first operational deployment of the Navy's newest aircraft on board the aircraft carrier *Abraham Lincoln*.

26 July
Nine coal miners are trapped 240 feet below the surface following the collapse of a mineshaft in Somerset, Pennsylvania. Medical and diving experts from eight Navy commands are dispatched to the scene to render assistance, mainly in operating a portable recompression chamber.

3 September
Commander, Seventh Fleet relieves the commanding officer of the aircraft carrier *Kitty Hawk* (CV 63), citing a lack of confidence in his ability to command the Navy's only forward-deployed carrier.

4 September
Rocks hit Navy security personnel and vandals cut a section of fence during protests of Navy live-fire exercises conducted by the carrier *Harry S. Truman* on Vieques Island in Puerto Rico.

8 September
The Secretary of the Navy announces that the name of the next *San Antonio*-class amphibious transport dock will be *New York* in honor of the state, city, and people that suffered so much during the 11 September 2001

Right: *Former President George H.W. Bush (center) examines a model of CVN 77, the U.S. Navy's tenth* Nimitz-*class aircraft carrier officially named* George H.W. Bush *by Secretary of the Navy Gordon England at a ceremony held in the Pentagon, 9 December 2002. Photographed from left to right are Chief of Naval Operations Admiral Vern Clark, SECNAV England, President Bush, Senator John Warner, (R–Virginia), and General James L. Jones, Commandant of the U.S. Marine Corps. (U.S. Navy)*

terrorist attacks. In December 2002, scrap steel removed from "ground zero" at the former site of the World Trade Center is sent to New Orleans, Louisiana, to be included in the ship.

11 September
In response to a directive from the Secretary of the Navy, Navy ships commemorate the first anniversary of the terrorist attacks against the World Trade Center and the Pentagon by hoisting the First Navy Jack, a flag first employed in 1775 consisting of a rattlesnake superimposed across 13 horizontal alternating red and white stripes with the motto, "Don't Tread On Me." The directive states that the flag will be flown until the war on terrorism is concluded.

13 September
In a speech to the United Nations General Assembly, President George W. Bush calls Saddam Hussein's regime in Iraq a "grave and gathering danger" and urges the passage of a resolution readmitting weapons inspectors and mandating that Iraq disarm. He pledges that the United States will take action against the Iraqi regime if the United Nations does not act.

13 November
The nuclear attack submarine *Oklahoma City* (SSN 723) collides with a Norwegian commercial vessel in the Atlantic, suffering damage to her periscope and sail. Her commanding officer is later relieved of command.

17–18 November
Iraqi antiaircraft positions open fire on coalition aircraft patrolling the northern no-fly zone over Iraq. The aircraft respond by dropping precision-guided munitions on the emplacements. The actions come after the signing of a new United Nations Security Council resolution that authorizes strong repercussions for such aggression.

6 December
The guided-missile destroyer *Paul Hamilton* (DDG 60) collides with a vessel in the North Arabian Gulf. Though damaged, she remains operational.

8 December
Typhoon Pongsana, packing winds of over 180 miles per hour, hits Guam. During the ensuing days, Seabees of Naval Mobile Construction Battalion 74 work to restore portable water supplies to the island's inhabitants. In addition, elements of the Pacific Fleet airlift $4 million in supplies to the storm-ravaged island.

9 December
The Secretary of the Navy announces that the Navy's tenth *Nimitz*-class aircraft carrier will be named after former President George Herbert Walker Bush, who served as a naval aviator during World War II.

12 December
The F/A-18 Hornet, a mainstay in Navy strike fighter and Marine Corps fighter attack squadrons, records its 5 millionth flight hour.

2003

23 January
In the first part of the Navy's Sea Swap Initiative, in which three crews rotate through a single ship to allow for more time on station in theater, the crew of the destroyer *Fletcher* (DD 992) is relieved by the crew of the recently decommissioned *Kinkaid* (DD 965) in Fremantle, Australia.

Above: *During full military honors, the remains of NASA astronaut and U.S Navy Captain David M. Brown are carried by horse-drawn caisson to his burial site at Arlington National Cemetery, 12 March 2003. He was one of the seven crewmembers that perished during the Space Shuttle Columbia's fateful reentry into the earth's atmosphere on 1 February 2003. (U.S Navy)*

Right: *A cloud of smoke and trail of fire mark the launch of a Tomahawk missile from the guided missile cruiser* Cape St. George *(CG 71) operating in the eastern Mediterranean Sea, 23 March 2003. Tomahawks were widely employed in precision strikes against Baghdad during Operation Iraqi Freedom. (U.S Navy)*

24 January
Secretary of the Navy Gordon England steps down from his post in order to serve as Deputy Secretary of the Department of Homeland Security. Susan M. Livingstone assumes the duties of Acting Secretary of the Navy the following day and in February is replaced in this role by Hansford T. Johnson.

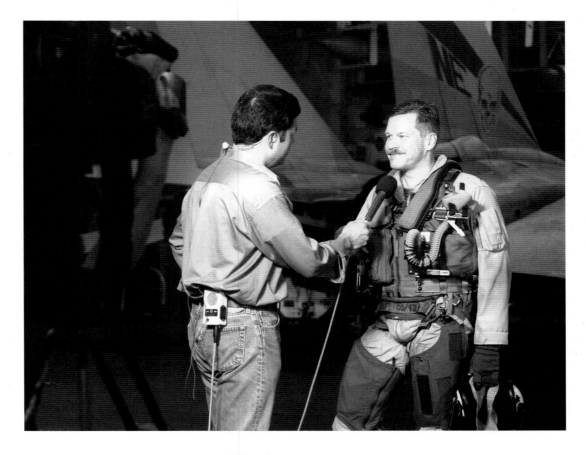

Right: *Captain Mark Fox, Commander Carrier Air Wing (CVW) 2, is interviewed by a CNN reporter in the hangar bay aboard the aircraft carrier* Constellation *(CV 64) following a mission over Iraq, 21 March 2003. Fox shot down an Iraqi MiG-21 on the opening day of Operation Desert Storm in 1991. Embedded journalists at sea and on the ground provided the American public with front-line reports from the war zone. (U.S. Navy)*

1 February

The Space Shuttle Columbia breaks up while reentering the earth's atmosphere, killing all seven astronauts on board, including three U.S. Navy officers—Captain David M. Brown, MC, Captain Laurel Clark, MC, and Commander William C. McCool. U.S. Navy salvage and dive teams participate in the recovery of wreckage from Columbia.

13 February

President George W. Bush visits Naval Station Mayport, Florida, giving a speech to sailors and their families before having lunch on board the guided missile cruiser *Philippine Sea* (CG 58).

20 February

A band's pyrotechnic display ignites a fire in a nightclub in West Warwick, Rhode Island, killing ninety-seven people, including Chief Machinist's Mate Dan Fredrickson, who is stationed at Naval Submarine Base New London, Connecticut.

10 March

To counter the threat of terrorism, North Atlantic Treaty Organization (NATO) forces, including U.S. Navy maritime patrol aircraft and the guided missile frigate *Halyburton* (FFG 40), begin escorting allied civilian shipping through the Strait of Gibraltar as an extension of the existing Operation Active Endeavor in the Mediterranean Sea.

14 March

The Center for Naval Leadership (CNL) is established at Naval Amphibious Base Little Creek, Virginia.

19 March

In a speech from the Oval Office, President George W. Bush informs the American people and the world that "On my orders, coalition forces have begun striking selected targets of military importance to undermine Saddam Hussein's ability to wage war." The first strike consists of forty-two Tomahawk missiles fired from U.S. Navy ships and submarines at a target in which Iraqi President Saddam Hussein, his two sons, and other government officials are believed to be located. The participating vessels are the guided-missile destroyers *Donald Cook* (DDG 75) and *Milius* (DDG 69); the guided missile cruisers *Cowpens* (CG 63) and *Bunker Hill* (CG 52); and the attack submarines *Cheyenne* (SSN 773) and *Montpelier* (SSN 765). In addition, Navy EA-6B Prowlers support an air strike against the target by U.S. Air Force F-117 Nighthawks.

20 March

Approximately 700 coalition aircraft participate in air strikes against military targets in Iraq, including command and control facilities, early-warning radar sites, and surface-to-surface missile systems. In addition, three U.S. Navy ships—the guided-missile destroyer *John S. McCain* (DDG 56) and the attack

submarines *Columbia* (SSN 771) and *Providence* (SSN 719)—join two British submarines in launching some fifty Tomahawk missiles at Baghdad. All told, coalition air and naval assets launch some 1,000 Tomahawk missiles and over 3,000 precision-guided munitions. In addition, U.S. Navy SEALs and Royal Marines land by helicopter to participate in a raid against the Kaabot and Mabot oil terminals in the Persian Gulf.

21 March
Aircraft from all five carriers in the region—*Abraham Lincoln* (CVN 72), *Constellation* (CV 64), *Harry S. Truman* (CVN 76), *Kitty Hawk* (CV 63), and *Theodore Roosevelt* (CVN 71)—launch into the night sky and proceed to Baghdad, Iraq, to participate in the heaviest air strikes thus far in the war, the first stage of the "Shock and Awe" campaign against the Iraqi capital. Ships in the Arabian Gulf and Red Sea launch some 320 Tomahawk missiles against Iraq.

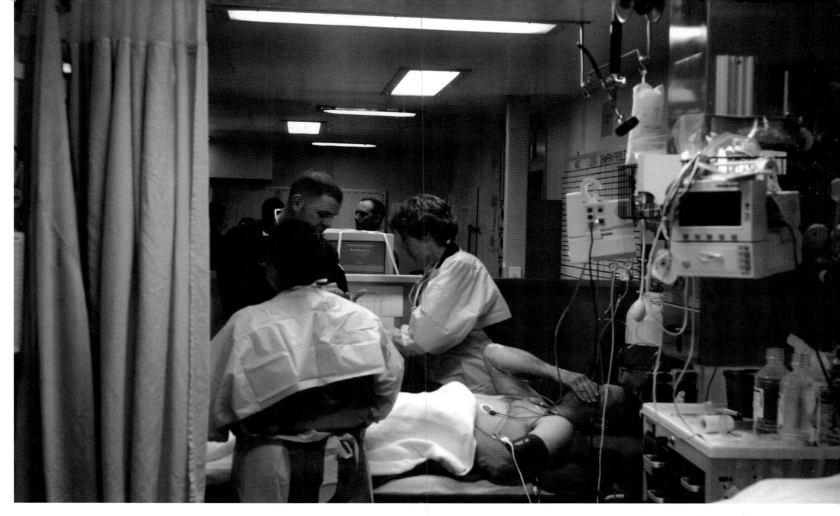

A P-3 Orion of Patrol Squadron (VP) 46 locates and tracks an Iraqi fast attack patrol boat in the Arabian Gulf, relaying the targeting information to a U.S. Air Force AC-130 Spectre gunship, which destroys it.

22 March

In his first briefing since the commencement of Operation Iraqi Freedom, U.S. Army General Tommy R. Franks, Commander, Central Command, announces "This will be a campaign unlike any other in history," one characterized "by the application of overwhelming force."

Two Royal Navy Sea King helicopters from the carrier *Ark Royal* collide over the Arabian Gulf. Among those killed is U.S. Navy Lieutenant Thomas Mullen Adams, who is on exchange duty.

23 March

The guided-missile cruisers *Cape St. George* (CG 71) and *Anzio* (CG 68) and guided missile destroyer *Winston S. Churchill* (DDG 81), operating in the eastern Mediterranean, launch Tomahawk missiles into Iraq.

24 March

Coalition forces intercept and board four Iraqi vessels in the Khor Abd Allah waterway, uncovering nearly 100 mines. A U.S. Navy explosives ordnance disposal team and security personnel join in the effort, which also includes assets from the U.S. Army and Coast Guard, Australia, and Kuwait.

25 March

Hospital Corpsman Third Class (Fleet Marine Force) Michael Vann Johnson, Jr., is killed in action in Iraq.

F/A-18 Hornets from Strike Fighter Squadron (VFA) 151 and an S-3 Viking from Sea Control Squadron (VS) 38 destroy three significant naval targets near Basra, Iraq. The strike marks the first time the Viking has conducted overland strikes in its thirty-year operational history and the first time the aircraft has fired a laser-guided missile in combat.

Opposite, bottom: *"Bunker-buster" bombs, soon to be dropped on Iraqi underground command and control centers, are staged in the hangar bay aboard the carrier* Constellation *(CV 64), 23 March 2003. The twelve years since the first Gulf War brought tremendous advances in weaponry. (U.S. Navy)*

Above: *Medical personnel work diligently on a wounded U.S. Marine inside the casualty receiving area aboard the Military Sealift Command hospital ship* Comfort *(T-AH 20) operating in the Arabian Gulf, 24 March 2003. As in previous wars, Navy medicine was on station during Operation Iraqi Freedom to care for the wounded on both sides. (U.S. Navy)*

Among the targets hit by carrier aircraft on this date is the Iraqi Presidential Yacht *Al Mansur*, which is damaged and in later attacks left a burnt-out hulk.

28 March

The British Royal Fleet Auxiliary, Landing Ship Logistic RFA *Sir Galahad* (L 3005) arrives at the port of Umm Qasr laden with tons of humanitarian aid to feed the people of Iraq. That the ship safely pulls into port is the result of successful mineclearing operations by U.S. Navy minesweeping vessels and amphibious ships, Mine Countermeasures Squadron (HM) 14 and Commander Task Unit (CTU) 55.4.3 consisting of a special clearance and explosive ordnance disposal teams and British and Australian divers.

29 March

The 24th Marine Expeditionary Unit (MEU) lands in Kuwait from ships of the *Nassau* Amphibious Ready Group (ARG), marking the first significant troop reinforcements to the coalition to occur since the war started.

Above: *K-Dog, a bottle nose dolphin belonging to Commander Task Unit (CTU) 55.4.3, leaps out of the water in front of Sergeant Andrew Garrett while training near the dock landing ship* Gunston Hall *(LSD 44) in the Arabian Gulf. Attached to the dolphin's pectoral fin is a "pinger" device that allows the handler to keep track of the mammal when out of sight. Dolphins assisted in conducting deep/shallow water mine countermeasure operations to clear shipping lanes for humanitarian relief during Operation Iraqi Freedom. (U.S Navy)*

31 March

An NP-3C Orion nicknamed "Hairy Buffalo" successfully demonstrates airborne control of an Aerolight unmanned aerial vehicle (UAV) at Webster Field in St. Inigoes, Maryland. It marks the first time that a Navy fixed-wing platform has controlled a UAV and its sensors and acted as the node for the collection of data during flight. The work is part of development in connection with the Navy's future Multimission Maritime Aircraft.

Navy strike aircraft from the carrier *Theodore Roosevelt* (CVN 71) engage in some of the most intensive operations since the beginning of Operation Iraqi Freedom, striking artillery installations, a barracks, and a surface-to-air-missile (SAM) installation in northern Iraq.

Opposite, bottom: *An AV-8 Harrier pilot gets a fuels update before taking off from the flight deck of the amphibious assault ship* Bataan *(LHD 5). One of two "Harrier carriers" participating in Operation Iraqi Freedom,* Bataan *operated twenty-four AV-8s, which provided vital close air support to advancing Marines in Iraq. (U.S. Navy)*

Above: *A boat crew made up of crewmembers assigned to inshore boat units 15 and 17 patrols the harbor at Shueiba, Kuwait, in a twenty-seven-foot patrol boat. This was a vital mission during Operation Iraqi Freedom to ensure that harbors were secure for the delivery of military material and humanitarian aid. (U.S. Navy)*

1–2 April

Navy SEALs join other Special Operations Forces, U.S. Marines, and Army Rangers in conducting a night raid on the Saddam Hospital in Al Nasiriya, rescuing Army Private Jessica Lynch, one of fifteen members of the 507th Maintenance Company taken prisoner earlier in the war. They also recover the bodies of seven of the other Americans.

2 April

While flying a night close air support mission in support of Operation Iraqi Freedom, an F/A-18 Hornet of Strike Fighter Squadron (VFA) 195 from the aircraft carrier *Kitty Hawk* (CV 63) is shot down by friendly fire. The pilot, Lieutenant Nathan White, is killed in action.

5 April

The newest version of the Navy's successful Tomahawk cruise missile, the Tactical Tomahawk, launches for the first time from an operational surface ship equipped with the Tactical Tomahawk Weapon Control System. The launch occurs from the guided missile destroyer *Stethem* (DDG 63) off the coast of California. On 8 May the first live warhead demonstration for the weapon occurs on board *Stethem*.

11 April

The amphibious dock landing ship *Portland* (LSD 37) becomes the first ship deployed in Operation Iraqi Freedom to return home, arriving at her home port at Naval Amphibious Base Little Creek, Virginia.

Left: *The aircraft carriers* Constellation *(CV 64)* and Kitty Hawk *(CV 63) steam alongside one another in the Arabian Gulf, 13 April 2003. The oldest operational carriers in the fleet—both launched strikes in Vietnam—they served alongside their nuclear-powered successors in Operation Iraqi Freedom. (U.S Navy)*

16 April
Piloted by the squadron's commanding officer, a P-3 Orion of Patrol Squadron (VP) 46 becomes the first Navy aircraft to land at Baghdad International Airport. On board is Vice Admiral Timothy Keating, Commander, U.S. Naval Forces Central Command.

17 April
In an address at the Navy League Sea-Air-Space Exposition, Chief of Naval Operations Vern Clark tells attendees, "When I look at Operation Iraqi Freedom, I think about speed. I think about agility. And I think about my new favorite word, persistence. I am so pleased with the way the Navy-Marine Corps team has responded to the challenge."

22 April
In the midst of war, the Navy's other vital missions continue as the guided missile frigate *Crommelin* (FFG 37) returns to Hawaii from a six-month deployment during which she interdicted more than six metric tons of narcotics, valued at more than $183 million, and rescued 157 Ecuadorians from a sinking fishing vessel, returning them home.

30 April
The Department of Defense formally transfers all real property on the eastern end of the island of Vieques,

Right: *Some of the more than 2,200 Marines assigned to the 24th Marine Expeditionary Unit (Special Operations Capable) begin their journey home, boarding a landing craft for transport to the amphibious assault ship* Nassau *(LHA 4), 25 April 2003. These weary leathernecks are part of the first Marine force to depart Iraq after the commencement of Operation Iraqi Freedom. (U.S Navy)*

Puerto Rico, to the administrative jurisdiction of the Department of Interior to develop the former live impact area as a wildlife refuge.

1 May
Operation Northern Watch, the mission begun on 1 January 1997 to enforce the northern no-fly zone over Iraq, stands down.

President George W. Bush, having earlier in the day trapped on board *Abraham Lincoln* (CVN 72) in an S-3 Viking as the carrier operated off California, declares an end to major combat operations in Iraq during a nationally televised speech from her flight deck.

Right: *On the flight deck of the carrier* Abraham Lincoln *(CVN 72), President George W. Bush is surrounded by some of the "redshirts" who loaded the bombs and missiles launched against Iraq. The President is still in his flight gear after a successful trap aboard the carrier in an S-3 Viking on 1 May 2003. (U.S. Navy)*

Below: *A pilot from Strike Fighter Squadron (VFA) 115 is greeted by his family upon his return to Naval Air Station Lemoore, California, with daddy receiving the kiss he has been waiting ten months to receive. (U.S. Navy)*

6 May

The aircraft carrier *Abraham Lincoln* (CVN 72) returns to her homeport of Bremerton, Washington, following a record-setting ten month cruise, the longest ever for a nuclear carrier, in which the ship and her embarked air wing participated in Operations Southern Watch, Enduring Freedom, and Iraqi Freedom and hosted the Commander in Chief.

12 July

The carrier *Ronald Reagan* (CVN 76) is placed in commission at Newport News, Virginia.

2004

2 June

In a test of the new Fleet Response Plan, the Navy announces Operation Summer Pulse, which during June–August involves the near-simultaneous deployment of seven carrier strike groups around the world, demonstrating the sea service's ability to project combat power on a global scale.

26 December

An underwater earthquake triggers a devastating tsunami that sweeps across Southeast Asia. The Navy joins other entities in dispatching relief to the beleaguered region as part of Operation Unified Assistance. Within two weeks twenty-four ships and some 15,000 personnel are on station, delivering food and medical supplies to those affected.

2005

8 January

The fast attack submarine *San Francisco* (SSN 711) collides with an underwater mountain while submerged in the Pacific Ocean. The high-speed impact kills one crew member and injures many others. The boat suffers a collapsed sonar dome and damage to her forward ballast tanks, but manages to surface and return to port.

Left: *An F-14D Tomcat traps on board* Theodore Roosevelt *(CVN 71) against the backdrop of a setting sun, the deployment marking the final front-line service of the venerable fighter that for over three decades symbolized naval aviation. (U.S. Navy)*

Below: *The heavily damaged fast attack submarine* San Francisco *(SSN 711) pictured undergoing repairs in dry dock in Guam after hitting an underground mountain during a high speed submerged run in the Pacific Ocean on 8 January 2005. (U.S. Navy)*

5 February

The Littoral Surface Craft-Experimental, also known as X-Craft, is commissioned at Nichols Brothers Boat Builders in Freeland, Whidbey Island, Washington. A high-speed catamaran, the craft is designed to test technologies planned for use in future littoral combat ships.

29 April

President George W. Bush signs a Memorandum for the Secretary of Defense that approves the redesignation of the United States Naval Reserve to the United States Navy Reserve. The continuing integration of the Navy Reserve into the day-to-day operations of the sea service also includes the 22 March 2006 renaming of Naval Reserve Centers as Navy Operational Support Centers.

2 June

The keel of *Freedom*—the Navy's first littoral combat ship, designed to operate at high speeds in shallow water environments—is laid at Marinette Marine in Wisconsin. The ship's sponsor is the widow of Sergeant Paul Ray Smith, a soldier who received a posthumous Medal of Honor for his actions in Operation Iraqi Freedom.

28 June

In one of the deadliest incidents involving the Navy's special operations forces, eight SEALs are among sixteen personnel killed when an Army MH-47D Chinook helicopter crashes in Afghanistan after being hit by enemy fire while en route to reinforce a four-man SEAL reconnaissance team under attack from Taliban forces near Asadabad. Only one member of this four-man team survives after being sheltered by Afghan villagers.

Right: *In the unfolding drama that marked search and rescue operations in the aftermath of Hurricane Katrina, a New Orleans resident clings to Aviation Warfare Systems Operator First Class Robert Webber as he is hoisted aboard an SH-60 Seahawk of Helicopter Antisubmarine Squadron (HS) 75 on 7 September 2005. (U.S. Navy)*

Below: *Chief of Naval Operations Admiral Michael Mullen, a midshipman when Vice Admiral James Stockdale was shot down over North Vietnam and captured, eulogizes the Medal of Honor recipient during services at the U.S. Naval Academy in Annapolis, Maryland, 23 July 2005. (U.S. Navy)*

22 July

During ceremonies at the U.S. Naval Academy in Annapolis, Maryland, Admiral Michael G. Mullen relieves Admiral Vern E. Clark, becoming the twenty-eighth Chief of Naval Operations. Mullen becomes the second member of the academy's Class of 1968 to hold the post, and Clark ends the longest tenure as Chief of Naval Operations since Admiral Arleigh Burke.

29 August

Hurricane Katrina makes landfall in Louisiana, devastating three states. The failure of protective levees around New Orleans results in severe flooding of areas of the city. Two days later, U.S. Northern Command establishes Joint Task Force Katrina. Navy ships dispatched to the region include the carrier *Harry S. Truman* (CVN 75); the amphibious assault ships *Bataan* (LHD 5), *Iwo Jima* (LHD 7) and *Shreveport* (LHD 12); and the hospital ships *Mercy* (T-AH 19) and *Comfort* (T-AH 20).

8 October

An earthquake measuring 7.6 on the Richter scale rocks Pakistan, prompting a multinational relief effort that eventually includes ships of Expeditionary Strike Group (ESG) 1 and MH-53E Sea Dragon helicopters to facilitate the airlifting of food and medical supplies to affected regions. In addition, on 12 October, Rear Admiral Michael A. Lefever assumes duties ashore as Coordinator, Disaster Assistance Center, Pakistan.

2006

3 January
Dr. Donald C. Winter is sworn in as the 74th Secretary of the Navy, succeeding Gordon England, who served concurrently as Secretary of the Navy and Acting Deputy Secretary of Defense.

13 January
The Navy Expeditionary Combat Command stands up during a ceremony at Naval Amphibious Base Little Creek, Virginia, consolidating the Navy's land-based operations that are increasingly on the front lines of the Global War on Terror. Eventually to include upwards of 50,000 personnel, the command includes bomb disposal, force protection, expeditionary logistics, coastal warfare, and riverine missions, the latter in the tradition of squadrons of patrol boats that operated on the Mekong Delta during the Vietnam War.

21 January
Reminiscent of one of the U.S. Navy's traditional missions dating from the age of sail, the guided-missile destroyer *Winston S. Churchill* (DDG 81) captures a suspected pirate vessel off the coast of Somalia after receiving reports of attempted acts of piracy occurring the previous day.

25 January
Harkening back to the days of the Naval Aviation Pilot program, the Navy announces plans to select an initial group of thirty sailors to receive commissions as chief warrant officers and undergo flight instruction to fill junior officer billets in the patrol, electronic attack and helicopter communities.

8 February
An F-14 Tomcat of Fighter Squadron 213 traps on board the carrier *Theodore Roosevelt* (CVN 71), marking the last combat flight by the venerable fighter after more than thirty years of service.

17 February
The amphibious assault ship *Essex* (LHD 2) and the dock landing ship *Harpers Ferry* (LSD 49) with their embarked Marines get underway from Subic Bay to support humanitarian efforts in the wake of landslides on the island of Leyte in the Philippines.

2 March
Chief of Naval Operations Admiral Michael Mullen approves a far-reaching change in uniforms worn by Navy personnel, adopting a blue, digital pattern battle dress uniform for all grades and a year-round service uniform consisting of khaki shirt and black trousers for grades E-1 through E-6.

Opposite: *With piracy an increasing threat on the high seas, gunners like these on board the guided-missile destroyer* Curtis Wilbur *(DDG 54) hone their skills in close quarters combat with one of the ship's MK-38 25mm machine guns. (U.S. Navy)*

Right: *Stars and Stripes dramatically unfurled, the guided-missile destroyer* Donald Cook *(DDG 75) returns to Naval Station Norfolk, Virginia, following a deployment in support of the Global War on Terror. (U.S. Navy)*

18 March

The guided-missile cruiser *Cape St. George* (CG 71) and the guided-missile destroyer *Gonzalez* (DDG 66) exchange fire with a suspected pirate vessel off the coast of Somalia, sinking it with the loss one crewman. The remaining twelve suspected pirates are taken into custody.

18 April

On this date 47 percent of the Navy's ships and 35 percent of its submarines are underway conducting training, supporting humanitarian missions, or carrying out operations in support of the Global War

on Terror to include maritime security, interdiction, and visit board search and seizure. In addition to 35,492 sailors on deployment, some 11,000 sailors serve in twenty-seven countries in U.S. Central Command's area of responsibility, including Afghanistan—where Navy personnel prepare to assume command of half of the Provincial Reconstruction Teams serving in theater—and Iraq, where sailors run the Fort Suse detainee camp. In the words of Chief of Naval Operations Admiral Michael Mullen, the Navy demonstrates daily its abilities as a "force for good, in addition to being able to carry out the warfighting mission."

ABOUT THE AUTHOR

M. Hill Goodspeed received his undergraduate degree from Washington and Lee University, where he was a George C. Marshall Undergraduate Scholar, and his master's degree in history from the University of West Florida. Currently, he serves as Historian and Head of Artifact Collections at the National Museum of Naval Aviation and lectures in strategy and policy for the Naval War College in the College of Distance Education. He served as Editor in Chief of the book *U.S. Naval Aviation* and is the author of articles and book reviews that have appeared in *The Journal of Military History*, *Naval History*, *Naval Aviation News*, *Wings of Fame*, *International Air Power Review*, *Foundation*, and *The Public Historian*.

ACKNOWLEDGMENTS

I write these words overlooking the historic Luce Hall at the Naval War College, within whose walls once echoed the voices of Mahan, Spruance, and Nimitz. During the course of writing this book, I have also gazed upon the waters of Mobile Bay, scene of Admiral David Farragut's great victory, and walked along the waterfront at Naval Air Station Pensacola, Florida, where pioneer naval aviators once took flight. Indeed, it has been a rewarding journey telling the story of our great Navy.

From the days of sail to the modern nuclear-powered carriers, the success of the Navy has been the sum of shipmates working together, and such is the case with this book. I thank the Naval Historical Foundation under the leadership of Vice Admiral Robert Dunn, USN (Ret.) and Hugh Levin of Hugh Lauter Levin Associates for the opportunity to participate in this project. The Foundation's executive director, Captain Todd Creekman, USN (Ret.), and Jim Muschett of Levin Associates provided guiding hands that kept the ship on course. Mr. John Reilly's unparalleled knowledge of naval history helped ensure accuracy, and the quality of the finished product is to a great degree testament to his efforts. Commander Dave Winkler, USNR, the Foundation's Director of Programs, also provided useful comments on the content. Wendy Leland brought her considerable copy editing skills to the project, earning a "Bravo Zulu" with her successful accomplishment of a truly daunting task. The photographs that appear in the book are the result of the research of photo editor Alex Macensky, whose keen eye is reflected in stunning images every time you turn a page. David Manning and Daniel Clifton also assisted in image selection. Thanks are also due to Janea Milburn and Ken Tievy for photograph processing and image reproduction, respectively.

The distinguished group of authors who wrote the sidebars represent some of the leading figures in naval history and added valuable historical perspectives to the chronology. In addition, I thank Samuel Loring Morison for his help on the Operation Iraqi Freedom section of the book. The photographs in the chronology are largely the work of Navy photographer's mates, who are a credit to the sea service in their documentation of life at sea, and thanks are due to the artists whose work appears throughout.

To my wife Maria and sons Connor and Jackson go my greatest thanks. They are my greatest inspiration and my love for them has no measure. At its core this book celebrates America's fighting men and women. Thus, I respectfully dedicate it to those members of my family who have worn the uniforms of our nation's armed forces—Lieutenant Commander Harold W. Brown, USN (Ret.), Major Jack P. Brown, USMC, Lieutenant Commander Robert F. Goodspeed, USNR, Captain Thomas G. Goodspeed, USMCR, Lieutenant John Raine, USNR, Commander John R. Ray, USNR, Captain R. C. Ray, USMC, and Captain Vince Whibbs, USAAF.

M. Hill Goodspeed